LiFE-Style Translating
A Workbook for Bible Translators
Second Edition

SIL International®
Publications in Translation and Textlinguistics 2
Second edition

Series Editors

Brian Harmelink
George Huttar

Volume Editors

Bonnie Brown
Joyce Park

Production Staff

Karoline Fisher, Compositor
Barb Alber, Graphic Design

LiFE-Style Translating

A Workbook for Bible Translators
Second Edition

Ernst R. Wendland

SIL International®
Dallas, TX

© 2006, 2011 by SIL International®

Library of Congress Catalog Card Number: 2010940070

ISSN: 1550-588X

ISBN: 978-1-55671-243-2

Printed in the United States of America

All rights reserved. No part of this publication may be reproduced, stored in a retrieval system, or transmitted in any form or by any means – electronic, mechanical, photocopy, recording, or otherwise – without the express permission of SIL International. However, short passages, generally understood to be within the limits of fair use, may be quoted without permission.

The Scripture quotations used in this publication, when not my own literal or concordant translation of the Hebrew or Greek text, are in the main taken from the following English versions: *New International Version* (NIV) © 1984 by the International Bible Society; *The Books of the Bible* © 2007 by the International Bible Society; *Revised Standard Version* (RSV) © 1973 by the Division of Christian Education of the National Council of Churches in the USA; *New Revised Standard Version* (NRSV) © 1989 by the Division of Christian Education of the National Council of Churches in the USA; *Good News Translation* (GNT; formerly *Good News Bible*), second edition © 1994 by the American Bible Society; *Contemporary English Version* (CEV) © 1995 by the American Bible Society. All these versions are used by permission, for which I am grateful.

Copies may be purchased from:
SIL International Publications
7500 West Camp Wisdom Road
Dallas, TX 75236-5699
Voice: 972-708-7404
Fax: 972-708-7363
Email: academic_books@sil.org
Internet: http://www.ethnologue.com

Dedicated to and for *The Word*

כֵּן יִהְיֶה דְבָרִי
אֲשֶׁר יֵצֵא מִפִּי
לֹא־יָשׁוּב אֵלַי רֵיקָם
כִּי אִם־עָשָׂה אֶת־אֲשֶׁר חָפַצְתִּי
וְהִצְלִיחַ אֲשֶׁר שְׁלַחְתִּיו׃

Isaiah 55:11

Ζῶν γὰρ ὁ λόγος τοῦ θεοῦ καὶ ἐνεργὴς
καὶ τομώτερος ὑπὲρ πᾶσαν μάχαιραν δίστομον
καὶ διϊκνούμενος ἄχρι μερισμοῦ ψυχῆς
καὶ πνεύματος, ἁρμῶν τε καὶ μυελῶν,
καὶ κριτικὸς ἐνθυμήσεων καὶ ἐννοιῶν καρδίας·

Hebrews 4:11

Contents

Introduction to this Revised (Second) Edition ix
Preface xi
Lesson 1: Communicating within Diverse Sociolinguistic Frames 1
   1.1 What is communication? 1
   1.2 What is sociolinguistics? 7
   1.3 What is semiotics? 10
   1.4 Communication participants and their characteristics 19
   1.5 Sociolinguistic variables that influence communication 21
   1.6 Different situational frames of communication 29
      1.6.1 Sociocultural frames 29
      1.6.2 Conversational frames 41
         1.6.2.1 Speech (text) acts 43
         1.6.2.2 Latent discourse 47
      1.6.3 Literary frames 50
      1.6.4 Organizational frames 57
Lesson 2: Does Scripture Include Literature? 61
   2.1 What is literature? 61
   2.2 What is orature and how does it differ from literature? 69
   2.3 Kinds of literary forms in the Bible 73
   2.4 What are some of the primary functions of biblical literature? 87
Lesson 3: Translating For *LiFE*: A Literary Functional-Equivalence Version ... 95
   3.1 A *relevant* functional-equivalence approach to Bible translating 95
   3.2 Defining translation more precisely 102
   3.3 Defining a *literary* functional-equivalence translation 108
   3.4 *LiFE* translation in relation to other approaches 113
      3.4.1 The translational continuum 113
      3.4.2 The Song of Songs: a case study 117
   3.5 Preparing for a poetic *LiFE* translation 122
   3.6 A ten-step exegetical methodology 126
      3.6.1 Step 1: Study the cotext 129
      3.6.2 Step 2: Specify the literary genre 130
      3.6.3 Step 3: Find the points of major disjunction 132
      3.6.4 Step 4: Plot the patterns of formal and conceptual repetition 133
      3.6.5 Step 5: Discover and evaluate the artistic and rhetorical features ... 135
      3.6.6 Step 6: Do a complete discourse analysis 136
      3.6.7 Step 7: Investigate the referential framework 142
      3.6.8 Step 8: Connect the cross-textual correspondences 144
      3.6.9 Step 9: Determine the functional and emotive dynamics 146
      3.6.10 Step 10: Coordinate form-functional matches 148
   3.7 A case study 149
   3.8 From analysis to synthesis in translation 153
Lesson 4: Text Types and Genres: Prose and Poetry in the Bible 159
   4.1 The importance of the concept of genre to Bible translators 159
   4.2 Four primary text types 162
   4.3 Some additional features of discourse types 167
   4.4 What is the difference between prose and poetry? 170
   4.5 Investigating the prose and poetry of the target language 176
Lesson 5: Analyzing and Translating Biblical Poetry 185
   5.1 The major stylistic forms of biblical poetry 185
      5.1.1 Parallel phrasing 186

  5.1.2 Sound effects. 188
  5.1.3 Figurative language 191
  5.1.4 Condensed expression. 193
  5.1.5 Emphatic devices 194
  5.1.6 Shifting patterns. 198
  5.1.7 Poetic structures 206
 5.2 The major functions of biblical poetry 220
 5.3 Genres of poetry found in the Scriptures 224
  5.3.1 Poetry of the psalmists. 227
  5.3.2 Poetry of the prophets 234
  5.3.3 Poetry of the sages 244
  5.3.4 Poetry in the New Testament 254
 5.4 Practicing a methodology for literary-poetic text analysis 260
Lesson 6: Analyzing and Translating Biblical Prose. 275
 6.1 Reviewing the four major discourse types. 275
 6.2 Identifying and analyzing Old Testament prose genres. 277
  6.2.1 Prophetic prose. 277
  6.2.2 Legislative prose. 283
  6.2.3 Sapiential prose 290
  6.2.4 Narrative prose. 294
 6.3 Identifying and analyzing New Testament prose genres. 310
  6.3.1 Narrative prose. 311
  6.3.2 The prose of direct speech (locutionary prose). 319
  6.3.3 Epistolary prose 334
  6.3.4 Poetic prose. 348
Lesson 7: Contextualizing and Testing a *LiFE* Translation 355
 7.1 Contextualizing a *LiFE* translation. 355
  7.1.1 The importance of implicit information. 362
  7.1.2 Sociological knowledge, mental spaces, and conceptual blending 367
  7.1.3 Ten types of study notes 378
  7.1.4 Suggested procedures for composing setting-sensitive notes. 383
  7.1.5 Contextualized notes for Luke 1–8 in the Chichewa study Bible. 386
  7.1.6 Examples of unhelpful and helpful notes. 394
   7.1.6.1 Unhelpful notes 394
   7.1.6.2 Helpful notes 396
  7.1.7 Other types of contextual supplementation. 398
 7.2 Testing a *LiFE* translation 406
  7.2.1 Questions, questions, and still more questions 407
  7.2.2 Aspects of acceptability. 413
  7.2.3 Testing methods for printed Scriptures. 418
  7.2.4 Testing nonprint and nonconventional Scripture products 422
Lesson 8: A Summary and Review of *LiFE* Principles. 443
References. 457

Introduction to this Revised (Second) Edition

Why the need for a revision—what's new in this second edition of *LiFE-Style Translating?*

To begin with, it gives me the opportunity of producing—with the indispensable help of SIL's Academic Editing Department—what will hopefully be a more "user-friendly" edition of this workbook. The format of the text has been loosened up to allow more "breathing space" for the eyes, and a detailed subject index has been added to help readers find their way around more easily. I express my great appreciation to Sharon Gray, Bonnie Brown, and Joyce and Jim Park in particular for their expert contribution in this regard.

There have not been many changes in the workbook's basic content, though the Preface required a rewriting. However, I have added quite a few additional exercises here and there throughout the book. These include several major additions—thanks to Robert Bascom, Anne Garber-Kompaoré, Robert Koops, Stephen Levinsohn, Robert Dooley, and Andy Warren-Rothlin—plus a number of other contributions from translation scholars working in a variety of fields that I am not very competent in. I want to express my deep appreciation to all of them, as well as to those who contributed to the first edition, for allowing me to incorporate their material, which considerably broadens the range of the issues covered and also exposes students and instructors alike to some additional perspectives.

This brings up a practical point that needs reiterating: this workbook includes many different exercises—undoubtedly *too many* for any single class or individual. I wanted to include a great variety of *LiFE*-related topics and issues for consideration so that course instructors can choose those exercises that fit their particular situations (e.g., location, time available, stage of translation)—classes (level of education, ability, etc.) needs and/or goals. Therefore, teachers should feel free to "take or leave" the material presented so as to best accomplish their pedagogical aims and objectives.

There is another issue I would like to draw attention to when introducing this revised edition: the subtitle is *A Workbook for Bible Translators*. However, this text can also be used to introduce theological instructors, students, and biblical exegetes in general to the prominent *literary* character of the Word of God. The various exercises of this workbook thus offer a practical methodology for helping readers other than translators to better comprehend as well as to communicate some of the important *poetic* and *rhetorical* aspects of the original. This vital dimension of the Scriptures is often ignored in exegetical textbooks and courses alike, so this workbook might well serve to fill a gap in the field of biblical studies.

Readers are again invited to help improve this workbook by sending in corrections, suggested material to fill in remaining gaps, plus any needed new exercises—perhaps based on your own research or teaching experience. I will gratefully receive all criticism and constructive advice at: wendland@zamnet.zm or erwendland@hotmail.com.

Ἀλλήλων τὰ βάρη βαστάζετε
καὶ οὕτως ἀναπληρώσετε τὸν νόμον τοῦ Χριστοῦ. (Gal. 6:2)

Preface

This workbook is intended to introduce translators, exegetes, Bible students, and communicators of the Scriptures to some of the main forms and functions of biblical literature, prose as well as poetry. The aim is to enable translators to better understand the original text and then convey selected texts in a correspondingly "literary"—artistic, poetic, rhetorical—manner in their mother tongue or another target language. It is assumed that the translators/students will have completed at least one to two years of comprehensive biblical studies at a recognized theological college, university, or seminary. It would also be helpful if they will have completed a basic introduction to translation theory and practice, such as that provided by Barnwell's *Bible Translation* (third ed., 1986) or the UBS Asia-Pacific *Translator Training Manual* (Pattemore 2004).

The following related goals are paramount:

1. To teach translators and other exegetes how to distinguish "more poetic" from "less poetic" passages in the Bible.

2. To introduce translators to the Scripture's principal literary types, or genres, in comparison with those of their own tradition, whether written or oral.

3. To overview and illustrate the chief characteristics and functions of biblical poetry and prose.

4. To increase translators' awareness of and sensitivity towards the esthetic beauty and rhetorical power of the various documents that make up the Scriptures as well as the literature and/or orature of their own language.

5. To suggest a practical methodology for the analysis and translation of biblical texts in a more literary manner according to the *LiFE* (Literary-Functional Equivalence) method.

6. To implement these aims by working with different poetic and prosaic texts of the Old Testament and New Testament passages.

7. To develop an awareness of the nature and importance of contextualizing a Scripture text in order to provide a more adequate frame of conceptual reference for its interpretation and application.

8. To cultivate the skills of literary evaluation and mutual constructive criticism with regard to Bible translations in a cooperative team setting.

Each of the chief topics in this workbook could first be presented by the instructor with illustrations and opportunities given for class discussion in keeping with the previously mentioned goals. Alternatively, a specific lesson portion may be assigned for study in advance and the material later reviewed and practically applied in a group session. Key to this approach is ongoing give-and-take. Intermittently, questions pertaining to the subject at hand are incorporated into the text. Their purpose is to keep the lessons interactive by encouraging a more intensive investigation and dialogue concerning the pertinent exegetical and translational issues along with their local project-related applications. These questions are merely suggestive and by no means exhaustive. They may be supplemented, modified, or replaced as needed by the course instructor or translation consultant.

Most topics of a particular lesson are treated in summary form, though a number of key issues are developed in greater detail, especially in lessons 3 and 7, with reference also to a set of recommended published works on translation that should be readily available. (These works can be supplemented according to the world region in which this manual is used.) The main points are further practiced by working through a number of text-based exercises at the end of most sections or subsections. It would be helpful if students are able to access at least an interlinear version of the Hebrew and Greek texts; if not, instructors may have to adapt or omit some of these exercises.

The suggested assignments may be done in class as time allows, or they can be given for outside additional study, with participants encouraged to work together as pairs or teams where possible. At periodic intervals, some of the homework exercises will need to be written out and handed in for closer evaluation by the instructor. The major course assignments will involve preparing written analyses and translations of several selected pericopes of prose and poetry according to the *LiFE* method. The results of these can then be presented to the class for their joint assessment and mutual correction, as necessary.

This workbook has been prepared as a practical supplement to accompany the text *Translating the Literature of Scripture* (Wendland 2004b), which expounds a literary-rhetorical approach to Bible translation. It may be termed a *literary-functional equivalence* version (*LiFE*, for short) since it combines a concern not only for the artistic, *literary* dimension of Scripture, but also for relative *functional parity* as part of a flexible translational strategy. The ideas developed here, especially in the first chapter, also arise from some of the important principles of communication discussed in *Bible Translation: Frames of Reference* (Wilt 2002a; cf. Wendland 2008, Wilt and Wendland 2008).

My reasons for adopting the term *literary functional equivalence* will be considered more fully in lesson 3, but it may be helpful at the outset to comment on some of the potential problems that may be associated with the use of the term *literary* in this setting:

- **Connotation:** By *literary* I am not referring to some esoteric high-level variety of professional writing (or translating) intended for sophisticated silent readers, but rather a manner of translating that makes full use of the artistic and rhetorical resources of the target (or host) language.

- **Implication:** While the term *literary* unfortunately may imply a written text, my aim is to encourage a translated text that can be readily articulated orally, thus one that also *sounds* natural to the ears of the primary target-language audience.

- **Usage:** My use of the term *literary* should not suggest an uncontrolled type of dynamic-equivalence version. My area of special interest is more delimited—namely, with reference to the artistic-rhetorical features that are associated with familiar target-language genres as these relate to particular biblical texts on the one hand, and specific audiences and communicative goals on the other.

As translators and their teachers/consultants work through the lessons here, they are given opportunities to put the method into practice. They can do this, first, through a review of some key aspects of its theoretical background, and then—more importantly—by means of application to a diverse range of Scripture texts and text types.

In order to develop the literary component as a special focus of the translation approach practiced in this workbook, I have adopted an eclectic, threefold theoretical model of communication that combines the following:

- a broad text-based **semiotic-code** framework, since translation involves the selective substitution of one system of verbal sign-signifiers with another within the context of their respective inventories of cultural codes that give language motivation and meaning;

- a **cognitive-relevance** approach to the interpretation process, one that promotes an inferential, "frames of reference" conceptual approach to the study of the source-language text and its re-creation in a contemporary target language;

- a contextualized **functional** methodology involving a practical set of procedures that encourages translators to apply what they are learning to specific biblical texts in their current setting of communication.[1]

My general aim in regard to the study of biblical texts may be summarized from a cognitive-poetic perspective as follows:

> [A] concern for 'literary analysis' includes the complex consideration of the connections between the particular texture of literary works, their relationship with other patterns in the literary and linguistic system, as well as effects derived in the process of literary reading....Cognitive poetics aspires to encompass emotional and motivational dimensions of reading as well as the monitoring and negotiation of propositional content. (Stockwell 2002:60, 158)

A *LiFE* strategy applies significantly to both text *analysis* (in the source language) and *synthesis* (in the target language). It favors a situation-sensitive, form-functional, *sociolinguistic* methodology with respect to all types of communication, translation in particular. There is thus an emphasis on speech *in action*—language operating in everyday life as well as in genre-shaped literary discourse—a method that will hopefully offer some new insights and possibilities when applied, in turn, to Bible translation. My main premise is that we can, with determination and practice, do more to reflect the vibrant verbal life of the excellent instances of literature that we confront in the process of *transforming* the diverse texts of Scripture. This would seem to be an appropriate thing to do, if the circumstances are right—that is, if we have the necessary perception, understanding, experience, resources, staff, and, above all, a willing receptor community of active Bible hearers and readers.

The subtitle of this workbook could well be *Translating the Bible, the Book of Forms*, since every distinct and definable pericope (a meaningful larger unit) of the Scriptures turns out to be a literary type/style/genre of one kind or another. It therefore also needs to be interpreted and transmitted as such, because the represented macro-form of a text in a given language influences the popular understanding of both its semantic content and its functional intent. In other words, for every sort of meaning-package, pragmatic purpose, and sociocultural setting of use, there is a specific literary style and genre (or some combination of such forms) that is best suited for communicating with the intended audience. This is as true for the diverse texts of the Bible as it is for any other outstanding corpus of literature.

In order to sharpen our perception of the literary component of the biblical text and to encourage at least a partial application in Bible translation, a *LiFE* method is introduced, explained, and then practiced throughout this workbook. This brings up several further considerations:

- The term *literary* implies the importance of language *form* in translation (i.e., a verbal "style," whether oral or written); this must always be evaluated according to well-defined, testable criteria, that is: *comparatively* excellent ← mediocre → poor in *quality*.

- Since oral, as well as written, texts are being considered, the term *oratorical* may be used with reference to the former, *literary* to the latter. The point is simply this: why should vibrant *phonic*

---

[1]Stephen Pattemore (with reference to the dissertation by Dave van Grootheest) has recently clarified the connection between these last two points—that is, a functional approach coupled with relevance theory: "...Gutt's [RT] approach is not really a retreat into 'literal' translation, but...in fact...requires an essentially functional-equivalent approach to the translated text, since the requirement of *'direct translation'* is not that the chosen stimulus should resemble the source stimulus in its linguistic properties, but that it should have complete interpretive resemblance; it *should produce the same cognitive effects when interpreted within the same context*. On the other hand, Gutt's 'direct translation' remains conservative about how much of the context should or can be incorporated within the text itself" (Pattemore 2007:259; italics added).

"life" not characterize the words of our vernacular translations of the dynamic Book of Life, which more often than not are *aurally* perceived and interpreted?

- Since translation entails the skillfully managed replacement of one set of linguistically—and literarily (or "oratorically")—organized forms with another, ideally translators need to be *masters* of both the source language (SL) and target language (TL) form-functional sets.

- The TL textual forms are always perceived, interpreted, evaluated, and reacted to within the general *conceptual context*—or "cognitive environment"—of the target culture, which is the ultimate frame of reference that translators must strive to fully understand and contextualize in relation to their particular audience and communication setting.

During the course of this study, most of the important literary types, or genres, found in the compilation that constitutes the Scriptures will be described, illustrated, and applied in translational exercises. This text-intensive approach is intended to sharpen the translator's eyes in order to perceive these forms in the biblical writings, analyze them for greater understanding, and then employ this knowledge in the search for an equivalent manner and mode of expression in the TL, whether wholly or partially. There are two principal concerns regarding quality control, namely, *accuracy* and *appropriateness*. As to the first of these, the basic content and communicative intentions (i.e., the "meaning") of any translation of Scripture must correspond *in sufficient similarity* to what has been determined (through analysis) to be inherent in the original text. As to the second, the final translation product must prove (on the basis of testing) to be widely acceptable to the constituency and to conform to the purpose(s) for which it was commissioned and prepared.

While a specific *LiFE* method has been adopted here as the primary point of reference with regard to translation theory and practice, it is adaptable enough to co-exist with virtually all other approaches. Indeed, an artistic and rhetorical concern can be readily incorporated into any current model of translating texts. Thus the possibility of degrees, or variable amounts, of stylistic application in any given case is emphasized throughout this workbook.

While my focus is on a literary perspective and set of procedures, I need to stress the fact that, though distinct, this often overlaps with a more linguistically-oriented, discourse-analysis technique, as presented, for example, in Levinsohn's 2000 work and in Dooley and Levinsohn's 2001 work. The latter, in particular, may well serve as a helpful complement to the present volume when analyzing and translating the literature of Scripture in all its depth and diversity. The same might be said for using the material in this workbook to supplement the *STEPS* program, an excellent electronic training tool for Bible translators and consultants that is being developed by Murray Salisbury (2002) and others. In fact, their well-stated caveat (p. 4) applies just as well to my own work to follow:

> It should be emphasised that there are often no clear boundaries between many of the categories that are taught in this resource. Figurative language, literary devices, and discourse features form something more like a continuum (like the colour spectrum) than an orderly system of distinct pigeon-holes. Like trying to identify the boundary between red and orange, some literary features could be classified in terms of more than one category. In such cases, it may not be profitable to try to decide which category is more appropriate. The important thing is to understand how a particular piece of literature works and how it achieves its purposes.

The primary reference texts used for this workbook are:

Literary Forms in the New Testament (Bailey and vander Broek 1992)

Analyzing Discourse (Dooley and Levinsohn 2001)

Relevance Theory (Gutt 1992)

The Theory and Practice of Translation (Nida and Taber 1969)

Cracking Old Testament Codes (Sandy and Giese 1995)

The Challenge of Bible Translation (Scorgie, Strauss and Voth 2003)

Cognitive Poetics (Stockwell 2002)

From One Language To Another (deWaard and Nida 1986)

Analyzing the Psalms (Wendland 2002)

Translating the Literature of Scripture (Wendland 2004b)

Bible Translating: Frames of Reference (Wilt 2002a)

Translating as a Purposeful Activity (Nord 1997)

Structure and Orality in 1 Peter: A Guide for Translators (Thomas and Thomas 2006)

Hebrew Poetry in the Bible (Zogbo and Wendland 2000)

Scripture Frames and Framing (Wilt and Wendland 2008)

Citations of these and other works will be by author and date, referring readers to the full bibliographical data at the end of the workbook. (Note: Another valuable resource is David Koudougéret's doctoral thesis in French, published as *Poétique et traduction biblique. Les récits de la Genèse dans le système littéraire sango* by the Research School of Asian, African and Amerindian Studies, University of Leiden, 2000.)

I very much appreciate the indispensable editorial assistance that I have once again received from Betty Eastman of SIL during the final production of the first edition of this workbook. Mary Ruth Wise, Freddy Boswell, and Jim Clarke have also contributed and have been a source of great encouragement. I also wish to thank all those colleagues who provided examples and quotes for this enterprise; these have added a valuable dimension to the work. Finally, all readers and users of this text are warmly invited to enter into what I see as an ongoing pedagogical process (teachers instructing one another) by corresponding with me about any corrections, additions, or other modifications that will improve the approach to Bible translation that I have tried to present here (wendland@zamnet.net).

Ernst Wendland
Evangelical Lutheran Seminary
1 Simon Mwansa Kapwepwe Rd.
PO Box 310091, Avondale 15301
Lusaka, Zambia

Centre for Bible Interpretation and Translation in Africa
Department of Ancient Studies
University of Stellenbosch
Private Bag X1 – Matieland 7602
Stellenbosch, South Africa

Lesson 1
Communicating within Diverse Sociolinguistic Frames

Aim: In this opening lesson you will survey the **process of communication** from a sociolinguistic perspective—that is, people interacting via speech in various situational settings, or "frames," of contextual influence. This introductory study is intended to lay the foundation for a literary approach to translation, which will be developed in subsequent lessons.

Goals: After working through this lesson you should be able to do the following tasks:

1. Define "**communication**," in particular, communication via human language, whether oral or written.

2. Describe some important aspects of **semiotic** and **sociolinguistic** studies that contribute to our understanding of how communication occurs (or fails to occur).

3. Begin to analyze texts in terms of their contextual, socioculturally determined *frames of reference*, which influence every act of communication, and Bible translation in particular.

4. Identify the major categories of *speech acts* and their occurrence in biblical discourse.

5. Learn about the nature and importance of several different types of latent, or implicit, information that must be taken into consideration during any communication event.

Review:
The personal background, professional experience, current occupation, present interests, and course expectations of all class participants as well as those of the instructor(s).

Read:
Chapter 1 in *Bible Translation: Frames of Reference* (Wilt 2002a).
Chapters 2–4 in *Language, Society, and Bible Translation* (Wendland 1985).
Chapters 1–5 in *Scripture Frames and Framing* (Wilt and Wendland 2008).

1.1 What is communication?

The subject of *communication* provides the broad *conceptual framework* for our study about what the task of translation entails. Communication is the generic activity of which translation is a specific subtype. We cannot properly understand what translation is without an adequate comprehension of the total process of communication. In fact, a brief definition of translation might be simply this: the communication of a message in one language that was first communicated in another language.

What do we mean by *communicate*? How would you define this action? Try to translate the following into your language: "We wish to communicate the Word of God to all the people who speak our language." What word can you use to render "communicate?" Here are some other factors to consider:

- Who are involved in the *process of communication?*

- How does one prepare to communicate a message?

- How do we know if a text-sharing activity is successful or not?

- What causes failures or only partial communication?

- How does translation differ from ordinary communication?

These are some of the issues that we will be considering in this workbook.

Webster's New World College Dictionary provides several senses of the verb "communicate":

> [from the Latin verb *communicare*: to impart, share, lit. to make common] 1. to pass along; impart; transmit (as heat, motion, or a disease) 2. to make known;…to give or exchange information, signals, or messages in any way, as by talk, gestures, or writing.

» What do you think of this definition—is it adequate? Is there anything to change or add?

» What is the central or core idea of communication?

» How does the current meaning of communicate in English relate to the original Latin concept of sharing? What is "shared" or "made common" when we communicate?

» To what extent can communication ever be complete—and how would we know this?

Basically, to communicate means to exchange or share meaningful messages with some other person or group. A *message* consists of a set of verbal and/or non-verbal *signs* that are selected, assembled, structured, and shaped in the form of an oral, written, or visual *text* in order to represent or *signify* something that a speaker/writer wishes to impart to his audience/readers.[1] The speaker has certain goals in mind as he formulates the various linguistic signs of his text—that is, in accordance with his intended audience and the situation in which they will receive his message. The message thus consists of four essential components:

1. *language form* (the text)

2. *semantic content*

3. *pragmatic intent* (the purpose for the communication)

4. *situational context* in which the communication occurs

Example: Analyze this four-word language form (utterance) in English: "The door is open."

The parts of speech of this utterance are: article + noun + predicator + adjective. Syntactically, this is a verbless Topic-Comment or simple Subject-Predicate sentence. The literal content is quite easy to perceive and understand, even in isolation. However, to analyze the intent, or purpose, of such an utterance, we need a context:

1. [A and B are sitting in a room.] A: Why is it so cold in here? B: *The door is open.*

2. [B enters a room where A is studying.] A: *The door is open!* B: Oh, I'm sorry.

3. [A and B have had a big argument.] A: *The door is open!!* B: Fine, I'm leaving!

4. [A earlier left employment with B.] A: I'd like to come back to work. B: *The door is open.*

5. [A and B are discussing mission strategy.] A: The door is open. B: *So we must act now!*

---

[1] I generally refer to nondefined singular participants in examples with masculine pronouns for convenience; no restriction in orientation or application is thereby intended.

> What is the difference in meaning of the utterance "the door is open" in the five situations above?

> Can you think of another situation and meaning for "the door is open?"

This example reveals how important the intent, or purpose, of an utterance is to its total meaning. It also illustrates the importance of *context* (the setting in which the communication occurs).

> Would there be the same pragmatic effect with the same words and settings in your language?

> Explain why or why not. If not, give a similar example to illustrate the same point.

All four of these elements—form, content, context, and intent—contribute to the overall meaning, that is, to the cognitive, emotive, and volitional significance of the message being represented by a certain medium.

> What, for example, might be some of the different goals that I have in mind as I write this workbook for you?

> What channel of communication am I using, and how does this affect the actual text of my message?

> How would a change in medium, say from a written lesson manual to an audiocassette, change the form of the text?

The author-intended meaning of a specific text is understood by a given reader/hearer with varying degrees of completeness, accuracy, and effectiveness depending on a variety of contextual factors that are essentially cognitive-emotive in nature. A reader, too, has certain goals in mind as he or she selectively perceives, interprets, and weighs its various signs and their meanings in keeping with the conceptual principle of relevance. Information that is *relevant* (appropriate, educative, corrective, useful, encouraging, etc. for the individual) is worth more effort to understand and remember. In addition, a reader's personal communicative goals and strategy of selection will be influenced by the particular physical and psychological setting and possibly also by his or her social relationship with the author.

Thus the effective exchange or sharing of communication cannot ignore the *consumer* of the message (the text processor). The consumer's purpose in reading this workbook, for example, may be different from my aim in producing it: the reader may be reading it in order to review or critique it rather than to learn about the practice of translation. This means that any act of communication may be more or less successful depending on the situation, both human (interpersonal) and circumstantial (impersonal), that apply all around when the activity takes place.

> What are some of the things that might prevent a message from being communicated with complete success in terms of accuracy and application?

> Why does a particular spoken text—such as a Sunday sermon—often fail to fully convey to a congregation all of the meaning that the preacher intended?

> What difference does it make if the sermon is read or delivered without notes?

Communication—this process of information sharing—tends to be more successful when the communicators share certain crucial features of their respective ethnic backgrounds, social settings, and personal circumstances with those of the consumers. The primary context of communication is largely psychological and includes different mental variables such as the participants' relative degrees of familiarity with each other—their current interpersonal relationships, past experiences, formal and informal education, worldviews, social class, economic status, value systems, goals in life, religious beliefs. The more of these characteristics that people have in common, the more completely they will share a mutual mind-set, and consequently, the easier it usually is for them to communicate. The more factors that are different, on the other hand, the more difficult the process becomes, and the more likely that a communication breakdown or blockage of some sort will occur. When there is a failure of this nature, whether partial or total, the hearer does not interpret the text that the speaker uttered in a way the speaker intended. The hearer may arrive at a different meaning (i.e., something added, subtracted, or changed) or fail to understand the text at all. We will be examining some of these influential cognitive *frames of reference* more closely later on in this lesson.

In the case of translation, some serious problems present themselves at the very outset of any communicative act because two different languages and cultures are involved. The greater these linguistic and conceptual differences, the more difficulties there are. Various strategies for bridging the gap and compensating for losses must then be put into effect in order to achieve even partial success in the message-sharing process. The subject of interlingual, cross-cultural communication will be considered more fully in lesson 3.

For reflection, research, and response:

1. Make a list of five words or phrases in your language (YL), including any figurative ones, that relate to the concept of communication as you understand it, and write a brief definition of each term. Write the definition first in YL and then prepare a literal back-translation into English. If there is a good dictionary available in YL, you may use its entries. Furthermore, how would you translate "frame of reference" in YL? Can you think of a better way to express this comcept in YL? Would something like "windows of knowledge/knowing/learning" work? Explain your preference.

2. The following blog-texts were posted by Wayne Leman at http://englishbibles.blogspot.com/ on Monday, February 4 and 10, 2008. This discussion directly concerns some of the major issues that will be considered in this workbook. Do you agree with the sentiments expressed by Dr. Leman below? If not, tell why. Answer the several questions posed below (in italics) with reference to English versions. Then apply these thoughts to the translation(s) in your language: Do you face similar issues regarding a "beautiful" rendition—or one that gives readers "access to the full meaning" of the original text? Explain.

   > **Is the ESV (English Standard Version) written in beautiful English?**
   > [...material omitted...]
   > Tim (Challies) ends:
   >
   > I am grateful that I have access to such a solid translation of Scripture. While I do not know Hebrew, I still have access to an accurate translation of the author's original words, complete with the phrases, words and metaphors that set one author apart from another. I have access to the full meaning, or as close as I can come without access to the original language, of what was written so long ago. I simply can't understand how anyone would be satisfied with anything less.
   >
   > I (WL) disagree. I don't believe that readers of the awkward, obsolete, and often obscure English in the ESV (or any other similarly written translation) have "access to the full meaning". Instead, they have syntactic transliterations of the original languages, but not the meaning of the wordings in those languages expressed accurately and beautifully using the natural syntax and lexical combinations of English.

   What do you think? Can a book (including any English version of the Bible) which is written with many obsolete expressions, unnatural syntax, and other literary problems sound beautiful for current speakers of English? What percentage of native speakers of English will have "access to the full meaning" of the biblical language texts in the English of the ESV?

   > UPDATE (Feb. 10): John Hobbins wrote: "I am going the way of all the earth" is a colorful biblical idiom which not by accident occurs as such in only one another passage. John, I (WL)

agree: it is a colorful biblical (Hebraic) idiom. But what does it mean? I don't know what it means, so how can it be beautiful? I guess art lovers split on this. I find beauty in realistic and impressionistic art. I do not find beauty in modern art, because I do not understand it. I totally agree with you that we should not flatten out the literary style of the Bible. But we must never forget that a translation is supposed to communicate the meaning of the biblical texts to native speakers of another language. If we translate so that only people who have specialized knowledge of biblical metaphors and idioms can understand them, then how can we call such a translation beautiful. I would far prefer to call the original biblical texts themselves beautiful. The beauty of their figures of speech is found within their original languages. Figures of speech, for the most part, are language-specific. We can learn to appreciate their beauty by education, footnotes, other Bible resources that explain the meaning of the figures.

But the purpose of translation is to enable a speaker of another language to understand the meaning of the biblical text, not to educate someone to the figures of speech uses in those texts. Literal translation of figures of speech and understanding their meaning almost never are compatible. We are trying to ask too much of general audiences if we think they can be served by essentially literal translations. Professional translators are not allowed to obscure meaning by translating figures of speech literally from one language to another. Why should we not hold Bible translators to the same standard of accuracy and excellence in translation? There is very much a place for idioms and figures of speech in a translation, and it is to use the idioms and figures of speech of the target language, when appropriate, to communicate the meaning of the biblical texts. Vivid, idiomatic, expressive literary language is beautiful and is recognized as such by literary awards such as the Pulitzer, Nobel Prize for literature.

I (WL) agree with Tim (Challies) and with you (John) that the idioms of the Bible are beautiful. I agree that there is little literary beauty in the CEV. I'm starting to use the NLT more and I'm actually finding more literary beauty in it than I expected. But I will always caution us not to take the advertising claims for translations such as the ESV too seriously when they are called "beautiful" based on having literal translations of figures of speech, if those translations do not accurately communicate their figurative meanings to the audiences for whom a translation is said to be appropriate.

3. You have no doubt seen diagrams that try to represent the **process of communication**. One of the more common representations is given below (i.e., the "conduit model," in which S = source, M = message, R = receptor[s]). What is wrong or misleading about it? What, in light of what has already been discussed in this lesson, can you suggest to make it more accurate?

   ```
   S  = = = =  M  = = = >  R
   ```

4. Now examine the two diagrams of the communication process that are found on page 40 of *Bible Translation: Frames of Reference* (Wilt 2002a). Explain how these are better representations of what is taking place, but feel free to make any corrections or modifications you think necessary.

5. What does a person (a "source") transmit to someone else when attempting to communicate? Language? Words? Grammar? A message? A text? Something else? What does the "receptor" perceive, interpret, and contribute to the process of communication? Explain your answer with reference to the use in YL of these metalingual terms (those used in talking about or describing language in general or a particular language).

6. Evaluate the following idea in relation to the task of Bible translation:

   [Frederico] Montanari suggests translating *source/target* as *source/mouth*. Perhaps *mouth* is better than *target*, which sounds too businesslike, and conveys an impossible idea of optimal scoring. But the idea of *mouth* also opens a semantic field and suggests the form either of a delta or an estuary. Perhaps there are source texts that widen out in translation, and the destination text enriches the source one, making it enter the sea of a new intertextuality; and there are delta texts that branch out in many translations, each of which impoverishes their original flow, but which all together create a new territory, a labyrinth of competing interpretations. (Eco 2003)

7. What do you think are the two most important things that two people must have in common in order to communicate effectively? Putting this another way, which two factors can cause the greatest or most problems during interpersonal communication?

8. In question 3, you considered a diagram that represents the **process of communication**. How would you have to change this, or what would you need to add, in order to better symbolize what goes on during the activity of translation?

9. A "message" consists of four principal interacting elements: context, form, goal(s), and content, defined as follows: (a) The content the author intends to communicate, (b) a language-specific form of the text used to represent the message, (c) the author's particular goal(s) for this communication event, and (d) as realized in a particular sociocultural and interpersonal context.

   The following is an example that shows how these four variables might influence each other during the activity of communication:

   > A music leader wants to compose a contemporary gospel song for his Christian youth group based on a familiar passage from Scripture; it will have to be prepared in a dynamic, poetic style or form in order to be effective; the Bible text selected will similarly have to be interesting and relevant.

   Give two other examples.

10. The context of communication, though often neglected, always has a great influence on the success of the process. Give an example of an effective *contextualization* of a Scripture portion in response to a particular sociological and religious setting. Also, give an example from your own personal experience of a communications breakdown that occurred because the *text producer* did not take into adequate consideration the wishes, needs, or limitations of the intended audience. Or give an example of a communication that was successful because the text producer *did* take these things into consideration.

11. According to relevance theory, context is essentially cognitive in nature—that is, a psychological construct composed of all our experiences, education (including the worldview and value system of our culture), social setting, and interpersonal relationships, as well as our current mental mood, feelings, and attitudes. Give an example of a communication effort that failed due to differences in the worldviews of the participants. How do such contextual factors affect the practice of Bible translation? Give an example from your own experience, if possible.

12. In this workbook, we will be speaking a great deal about the *orality* of biblical communication, both in the original setting of composition and also nowadays in the context of Bible translation. How do you respond to the following thoughts on the importance of *hearing*—or better—*listening to* the biblical text in translation?[2] Does the multiplicity of translations, even two or three, in your socio-religious setting present some "hearing" problems? If so, mention what these are, and suggest what might be done to alleviate them.

    > Of course, much of Scripture has a similar [oral-aural] origin, resonating powerfully in both oral and written traditions. The importance of memorization and oral tradition in Israelite culture played a significant role in bringing the collected works of Scripture into being. Listening to narratives, songs, and the Torah read aloud was an integral part of keeping the name of God and the history of his presence before them. Throughout the Old Testament, the people of Israel are charged with

---

[2] Jill Carratini, "Slice of Infinity" # 1691, May 30, 2008—from slice@sliceofinfinity.org.

> the command to remember: "Hear O Israel the LORD our God, the LORD is one" (Deuteronomy 6:4). Listening carefully was imperative to remembering the God among them.
>
> And it still is. In homes where we are not put to death for owning a Bible, it is easy to forget the wonder of a God who speaks. As countless translations continue to emerge and divide us, it is easy to be distracted from the authority of words that never fade, but come into new generations and changing cultures with new influence. The words of Scripture are living and active, the Spirit leading us to the person of Christ within the pages. Read aloud or studied silently, God is speaking, crying out for ears to hear and hearts to search.

13. A group's "worldview" seeks, whether explicitly (e.g., oral texts) or implicitly (e.g., traditional beliefs), to answer the basic questions about human existence: origin, reality, truth, meaning, morality, society, destiny, etc., for example: Where do we come from?—What is truth?—What happens after we die?—How do we relate to one another? Some cultures will focus on one sub-set of such fundamental questions, rather than another. How would you characterize your culture (or a specific sub-group)—if you had to pick just one of these questions as most important, which one would it be, and why? How does this fact affect the average person's view of Scripture and their understanding of what the Bible is all about? Does such a general perspective have any implications for Bible translation in YL? If so, explain what these are.

1.2 What is sociolinguistics?

In section 1.1 we noted the importance of the cultural context and social situation to any act of communication. These factors, together with the characteristics of the specific audience they encompass, will (or should) always influence how a speaker or writer composes his message in terms of form and content. Good communicators carefully study the overall context both before and during the crucial process of text production. One academic discipline that can help them to do this is *sociolinguistics*. (For an older perspective on sociolinguistics, see chapters 2 and 3 of Wendland 1985.)

Linguistics may be defined as the scientific study of language structure; it includes the following specialized subjects:

1. *phonology* (the study of the sounds of a language)

2. *grammar* (the morphology and syntax)

3. *lexicon* (the inventory of vocabulary)

4. *semantics* (the organization of meaning)

5. *discourse* (the structure of complete texts)

Now the question is, how would you define sociolinguistics? What areas of investigation need to be added to phonology, grammar, lexicon, semantics, and discourse in order to carry out a more complete, contextualized description of communication?

In practice, the different disciplines of linguistic specialization, including the study of language as it relates to human thought (cognitive linguistics) and as it is actually *used* in human society (sociolinguistics), cannot really be separated. They all mutually influence and interact with each other during the analysis of human verbal communication.

The field of sociolinguistics has two primary areas of emphasis:

1. The general study of how language is used to *communicate* in specific *communities*.

2. The analysis of specific *texts* within their local sociocultural *settings*.

Sociolinguistics thus looks at language from the standpoint of its social context – particular verbal texts as they are used by people to communicate for different purposes, in various settings, and under diverse conditions and circumstances. A typical sociolinguistic study will seek to answer questions such as the following—not in isolation, but as they interact in a given interpersonal situation:

- *Who* (speaker) says what (content) to whom (addressees)?
- *Why* (for what purpose)?
- *How* (with what sort of speech style)?
- *When* (in what social circumstances)?
- Via *which medium* (mode of communication)?
- With *what* result (outcome of the speech event)?

A sociolinguistic analysis always considers the various *functions* of speech (in addition to its forms), the *contexts* of usage (in addition to the texts uttered or written), the *connotative meaning* (in addition to referential meaning), and the current *appropriateness* of usage (in addition to the conventional rules of usage).

Some of the common topics that are investigated in sociolinguistic studies are: bilingualism and bi-dialectalism; code-switching and degree of language borrowings; the number of specialist jargons in common use (e.g., technical, liturgical, secretive); the prevalence of different social levels or styles of discourse (registers); the relative amount of pure speech within society (do people like to talk a lot or do they often communicate by such means as writing, gestures, art, music, dancing?); language assessment (e.g., use of one's mother tongue versus a *lingua franca* in various settings); the quality or density of verbalization (how redundant is a typical text in terms of the number of words used in relation to the amount of semantic content conveyed?); the effects of education (formal, Western-style) and travel on speech usage; language strategy planning; the influence of the media on public discourse, especially of newspapers, radio, television, and videos; literary genres and their settings of use; degree of functional literacy; use of special communication codes and symbolic or disguised speech; and the amount of translation and text adaptation used.

» Describe a specific difficulty that you have experienced in connection with any one of these issues during ordinary communication and tell how it was resolved.

» How do such concerns affect Bible translation? Give one example with reference to a particular passage of Scripture.

Clearly, the concerns of sociolinguistics are very important for public communicators of all types, and Bible translators in particular. Take the concept of register, for example. *Register* is a distinct, socially defined variety of language form and usage affecting one's choice of vocabulary, syntactic constructions, and patterns of intonation. Various culturally-recognized aspects of register have been identified, most of which manifest a continuum of speech styles involving such contrastive categories as non-technical versus technical, informal versus formal, urban versus rural, old-fashioned versus slang, standard versus regional, jargon versus regular, vulgar versus proper, polite versus impolite. Registers may also be described according to the typical settings, occupations, or specialties within which they are used, for example, academic, religious, medical, military, financial, fishing, hunting, marketing, and pottery-making. Each of these registers also conveys a certain set of associations that are implied when spoken or inferred when heard in public discourse.

1.2 What is sociolinguistics?

Bible translators must be aware of distinctions of register that may apply in their target language, especially when rendering quoted speech. This is to ensure that the particular verbal style they put into the mouths of the speakers matches the social context and cultural setting in which the conversation occurs (e.g., David in dialogue with others as his story moves through the Books of Samuel and he rises from a humble servant boy to the king of Israel). However, these assessments always need to be made from the perspective of the target-language environment because this scenario is what the words and utterances of the Bible text will automatically trigger in the minds of listeners.

> » Describe a certain sociolinguistic "mismatch" involving speaker, speech-style, and situation that you have noticed in the text of a Bible translation you are familiar with.

Sociolinguistic studies can be complemented by a careful consideration of the different signaling systems that people employ when they communicate (using non-verbal as well as verbal signs). This type of analysis is called *semiotics*, a subject to which we turn in section 1.3 below.

For reflection, research, and response:

1. Which of the different subject areas of sociolinguistics are important in your language and social setting? Give a concrete example of this. Have you ever participated in such sociolinguistic research and testing? If so, describe your experiences.

2. Why is a sociolinguistic study of the Scriptures necessary (in addition to a linguistic analysis of the original Hebrew or Greek text)? In what ways might the influence of the Greek language, society, and culture have affected the writings of Paul, a teacher who referred to himself as a "a Hebrew of Hebrews" (Phil. 3:5)? How do we see such influence manifested, for example, in the language and content of 1 Corinthians 2?

3. Evaluate the following suggestions by L. Johnson (2007) with respect to "using non-print Scripture as the stimulus for literacy." First, mention some of the key aspects of sociolinguistics that must normally be taken into consideration in the development of any literacy training program. How does the program outlined below compare with a literacy course that you have either participated in or know about? In particular, what are some of the distinctive features of Johnson's program that you would like to try out (or recommend to others) in your cultural setting? (Give reasons.) Which aspects, if any, might not work out so well, in your opinion? (Explain why.)

> Along with the formalized schooling approach, the literacy team began to capitalize on the interest people were giving to Scripture/song cassettes, particularly in the church. They had produced one Scripture cassette which had songs in various places in the reading. That cassette had generated a significant interest in some people to learn how to read. They used this interest in helping to develop their literacy classes....
>
> It would seem that the listening to Scripture on cassettes was a key factor in the church people which helped them see the importance of being able to read the Scriptures themselves. It was the motivating factor for many to join the literacy class and learn how to read. In other words, where people prior to this had little interest in learning to read, attending the Scripture listening meetings was the primary factor which caused them to attend literacy classes....
>
> Another positive factor that developed with these scripture cassette/scripture listening programs is that people began to buy the printed Scriptures. Whereas before this time the sale of Scripture materials was slow, the pace of sales for Scriptures dramatically increased. This in itself was a boost to the Bible Society....
>
> The increase in literacy classes and readers because of the use of these non-print forms of Scripture, I believe, may result from several factors. First these oral forms appealed to their nature. They are

an oral culture which is accustomed to oral communication methods. The oral presentation of the material drew them in and held their attention far more than someone reading or talking/preaching.

This oral presentation of Scripture meets the non-literates where they are and what they are used to. The oral presentation and the interest it created provided an environment which made it seem one step closer to their becoming literate. Once they were drawn in, their interest stimulated their hunger for learning. It motivated them towards literacy and formal education....

Initially they produced Scripture song cassettes with an accompanying booklet of these songs. Some have recently started developing Scripture drama cassettes, again with accompanying booklets. They too have started to see the same increase in interest in literacy. Both church and community have a great interest in starting classes....

A primary element which made the one literacy project successful would seem to be that they were able to raise within the community a felt need for literacy. They legitimized the schooling and capitalized on people's interest in oral Scriptures and Scripture songs.

1.3 What is semiotics?

Semiotics is the scientific study of signs—that is, with reference to their forms, meaning, use, and significance in specific sociocultural contexts. Such "signs" can be verbal or non-verbal and may originate either in human or non-human animate communication events. In this section we will focus on the human usage of signs.

A *sign* is a conventionalized form that represents or refers to a tangible object or some mental concept in accordance with the code of which it is a member. A *code* is a culture-specific system of interrelated signs used for transmitting messages, for example, language, gestures, music and song styles, dance rhythms and steps, clothing, customs of eating, and conventions of worship. Signs are conjoined and structured by the rules of the code to which they belong, thereby forming a larger unit and unity of meaning called a *text*.

During any communication event (act of signification) the signs of one code are often combined with those of another to complement or qualify the ultimate message that the sign-source wishes to convey. The clearest example of this is human speech: a person's words (code of language) are usually accompanied by the code of gestures, facial expressions, and bodily stance or movements. All of these are culture specific—a particular motion of the hand used in one society will not often mean exactly the same thing in a different cultural setting (e.g., the gesture for informing someone to come closer or to stop).

» Can you give an obvious example of a gesture, facial expression, or distinctive body movement that does not mean the same thing in Western culture as in yours?

» Can you think of some gesture you have seen in an illustration of a biblical passage that conflicted with the ordinary meaning of that gesture in your culture (e.g., John the Baptist pointing with his hand to Jesus, the Lamb of God, in John 1:29)?

Some semiotic codes are more general in nature and can be used for the same purpose in different cultures. A Bible text, for example, is always encased within the sign-system of certain publishing conventions that tend to be fairly standardized throughout the world in keeping with a particular audience, such as young or new readers versus experienced ones. These conventions have to do with style and size of print, amount and placement of white space on the page, and various degrees of indentation. The semiotic codes of notes, text references, illustrations, charts, and other figures are often very similar as well. Another semiotic code is generally activated when a verbal text is transmitted via a different medium of communication, such as an audiocassette.

1.3 What is semiotics?

> » Which semiotic factors, including the background or transitional musical style, would need to be considered for an audio performance in your sociocultural context of Christ's discourse with the Samaritan woman at Jacob's well (John 4)?

> » Is there a special problem connected with the signaling value of any aspect of the printed format of published Bibles in your language (excluding illustrations)? For example, what do section headings signify to most readers?

The following is a diagram of the "square of signification." It illustrates one older method of analysis that is useful for illustrating or thinking through certain key semiotic factors:

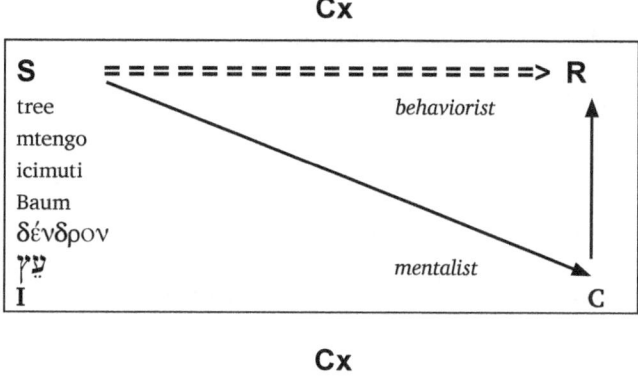

S = sign (signifier), R = referent (signified), C = concept (mental image), I = interpretant (language system/code), Cx = context (cognitive environment, mental map, conceptual world)

The following are several possible semiotic processes, represented by means of formulae, which may be derived from the preceding diagram:

1. **S => R = *reference*:** A sign (e.g., "tree" in English, *mtengo* in Chichewa, *icimuti* in Chibemba, *Baum* in German, δένδρον in NT Greek, and עֵץ in OT Hebrew) designates its referent in the real world. This is an outmoded, "behaviorist" perspective on the process of communicative signification.

2. **S => C => R = *conceptualization*:** A sign refers indirectly to its referent in the real world via a mental concept. This is a "mentalist" or "cognitive" perspective, a notion that is specific to a person's individualized conceptual network as influenced to a greater or lesser degree by his or her experience in life and particular perspective on the worldview of his or her society.

3. **[S => C => R] + I = *signification*:** An individual sign has a general, unmarked meaning when it is interpreted within the framework of a particular language system as codified in a comprehensive dictionary or encyclopedia, which serves as its general "interpretant."

4. **[{S1+S2+S3 ... Sn} => {C1+C2+C3 ... Cn} => {R1+R2+R3...Rn}] + I + Cx = *signification*:** A sign has a specific meaning, that is, to particular persons, only when it is interpreted within the framework of an actual text and a cognitive context (the latter being shaped by various social,

cultural, environmental, and personal factors).³ A text, in turn, is formed by various selections and combinations of signs that are joined by the appropriate rules of linguistic syntax according to the author/speaker's communicative intentions, guided by such basic sociolinguistic principles as relevance, appropriateness, and truthfulness.

Notice how a shift in the interpersonal setting may radically affect the significance and outcome of the same speech act in the following examples: (father to son) "I have cut down all the mango trees in back of our house"; (son to father) "I have cut down all…." The same lexical sign, too, may have different senses in different verbal and situational contexts.

» How would you interpret the word "tree" in the following sentences?

    a. The strong wind knocked down our favorite mango tree.

    b. This Bemba chief has a long and famous family tree.

    c. It is easier to polish a shoe while it is still on its tree.

    d. The hunter went out that night in order to tree and shoot a leopard.

    e. He was really up a tree, standing there in the dry river bed, surrounded by lions.

    f. "God…raised up Jesus, whom you had killed by hanging him on a tree" (Acts 5:30).

    g. "He must not…take also from the tree of life, and eat…" (Gen. 22). "On each side of the river stood the tree of life…" (Rev. 22:2).

» What is it in the cotext (the text that immediately precedes and follows) that helps to mark the intended meaning in each case?

» Which usage of "tree" in the preceding utterances would be most difficult to translate in your language and why? How could you best convey the intended sense?

The field of semiotics is traditionally divided into three areas of specialization: *syntactics, semantics,* and *pragmatics*:

1. Syntactics

Syntactics investigates the *formal* (grammatical) relationship of one sign or sign-complex to another within parts of a text and the text as a whole.

---

³Writing from a cognitive linguistic perspective, Robert Bascom (2003:1) reminds us that "words (or text-signs) do not refer directly to entities in the real world, but rather to the mental maps that cultural communities have constructed to understand that world. Since these modes of organization can differ dramatically across time and cultural space, original communication events can be and at times are in fact lost or changed almost beyond recognition.…For Bible translation, it is certainly worthwhile to reveal some of the terrain of the mental maps of the different thought-worlds, and in so doing shed light on both the ancient and modern understandings of scripture.…When mental maps diverge, are translators to explain what the text possibly meant in ancient times, or are they to try to communicate something similar (all necessary changes having been made) to a modern audience? Or are they to try to do both? And to what degree this can be done in translation? What is the role of reader's helps?" We might ask some further questions: What are some effective ways in which this cognitive terrain can be revealed to Scripture consumers in a particular situational setting? Have Bible translators (or others) paid a great deal of attention to this matter in the past? If so, what is a good example of this? If not, why not?

1.3 What is semiotics?

2. **Semantics**

    Semantics investigates the *meaning* relationship of one sign or sign-complex to another within a text, and the *meaning* relationship of one sign to its referent. There are three main types of such meaningful connection.

    a. **Syntagmatic** relations: connection by association, sequence, horizontal, diachronic ties. Examples are Noun + "of" + Noun ("love of God"); Noun <= pronoun; Verb <= adverb; main clause <= dependent clause.

    b. **Paradigmatic** relations: connection by analogy; same general/specific field of reference; vertical, synchronic links. Examples are "Abraham – Isaac – Jacob"; "love – mercy – pity – kindness"; "Passover – Feast of Tabernacles – Pentecost."

    c. **Logical** relations: spatial, temporal, cause-effect, general-specific. Examples are "one morning – later – that night"; "from Galilee down to Jerusalem"; "Christ died on a cross in order to save us."

3. **Pragmatics**

    Pragmatics investigates the relationship between signs and their interpersonal setting of use, such as degrees of formality in public address, and stylistic variations according to the speaker, the intended audience, the discourse purpose, and the dramatic situation. It is important, for example, to note who is speaking or referring to Christ with the use of the following terms (in Luke): "Jesus" (1:31, 8:24), "the Son of the Most High" (1:32), "Savior" (2:11), "my Son" (3:22), "the Son of God" (4:3, 41), "Joseph's Son" (4:22), "the Holy One of God" (4:34), "Master" (5:5, 8:24), "Lord" (5:12, 7:6), "this fellow" (5:21), "a great prophet" (7:16), "teacher" (7:40), "the Christ" (9:20).

When analyzing and interpreting any verbal text, all three aspects of semiotics need to be taken into consideration. Often the pragmatic dimension is more important than many commentators realize. An example is the term δεισιδαιμονεστέρους 'religious' in Acts 17:22, which Paul uses at the beginning of his speech at the Areopagus to characterize his eminent Athenian audience.

» Is the term to be taken as flattering, pejorative, or ironically ambiguous (a back-handed compliment)?

» Does it mean "devout," "superstitious," or seemingly the former but really the latter?

» Which interpretation do you prefer and why?

» What are the implications here for Bible translators in your language?

» Are you able to preserve semantic and connotative ambiguity when you translate it?

When specifically verbal signs are being analyzed, semiotic studies are incorporated into the field of linguistics. But where important entities or events are being designated and ordered or organized by means of non-verbal signs (or reference to them within a text), the connotative or symbolical significance that is conveyed by such semiotic systems must always be recognized. It is important, for example, to take into account the non-verbal implications associated with greetings, dressing, eating, funeral rites, marriage arrangements, taboos, and popular signs of good or bad luck. This is especially so when change of language and culture is involved, as in Bible translation.

How would the people living in your sociocultural setting interpret what is said or done in the following passages: Genesis 9:21–24; 12:11–16; 15:9–11; 16:1–5; 17:10–14; 19:30–38; 22:9–10; 24:16–20; 27:18–27; 29:21–30; 30:37–42; 31:46–50; and 37:7, 9? Where might a conceptual or connotative clash occur? Explain why.

Four types of semiotic signs may be distinguished (Wilt 2002a:36–37):

1. **Icon** (metaphoric sign): The sign resembles what it is referring to in some way; that is, the sign and its referent are linked by a prominent likeness or analogy. An example is the drawing of a man in a suit or a woman wearing a dress displayed on a restroom door to indicate whether a male or a female may enter.

2. **Index** (metonymic sign): The sign is associated with its referent in some conventional way, whether natural or figurative. Examples are the wearing of dark clothing at a funeral as an index of death and a sharp zigzag line on a poster or road sign to indicate the danger of high electrical voltage nearby.

3. **Sign** (arbitrary sign): No logical or perceptual relationship links the sign and its referent; it is a matter of cultural convention. Like most words, the following words for "God" are arbitrary signs: אֵל, θεός, *deus*, *Mulungu* (Nyanja), *Leza* (Tonga), *Njambi* (Nkoya), *Kalunga* (Luvale).

4. **Symbol** (significant sign): Any one of the preceding three types of signs may be infused with extra psychological, emotive, and social import as a result of long-time eminent usage in literature or orature or in certain culturally-central ceremonies and religious rites. An example is the cross as a sign pointing to the sacrificial death of Christ, which took place on wooden crossed posts or beams.

Translators must take particular care with verbal icons (metaphors), indices (metonyms), and especially the culturally based symbols, because of the likelihood that a literal rendering will not convey or evoke the same denotative or connotative significance in the target language. This is true also of certain sign combinations that may have an additional religious implication and/or symbolic meaning, such as "The LORD bless you and keep you" (Num. 6:24–27); "Hallelujah!" (Ps. 146:1, 10); "Our Father in heaven" (Matt. 6:9); "baptizing them in the name of the Father, and of the Son, and of the Holy Spirit" (Matt. 28:19).

» Can you cite another example of this type?

» Is there a biblical term or expression that has caused you translation difficulties due to its non-referential significance that fails to match the corresponding word(s) in your language?

» Conversely, is there an expression that has picked up additional overtones (perhaps church-influenced) that differ from the sense of that expression in the original text?

As noted earlier, all signs represent and transmit not only content, but also the intent, or communicative goal(s), of the text producer. This can happen, of course, only when communicating with one or more people who share the same system of verbal signs and the popular conventions for interpreting them. For example, in Zambia a man standing at the side of a road waving his arm up and down is doing so to indicate that he needs a ride, and is thereby requesting one from any passing motorist. A woman, on the other hand, simply has to stand there.

Verbal signs (i.e., phonological < morphological < lexical < syntactic < discourse) are combined to form a complete text, which represents an author-designated meaning, set of emotions, and one or more communicative functions or goals. The following are some of the more common discourse goals (presented from the standpoint of a speaker):

- **Expressive:** serving to reveal or verbalize the speaker's emotions, feelings, attitudes, etc.

- **Directive:** intended to influence the listener to think, speak, or act in a particular way.

- **Informative:** serving to reinforce, augment, or modify the cognitive state of the listener in specific respects.

- **Textual:** serving to organize a text through various cohesive devices (both back- and forward-referring) and by means of structural techniques that arrange, demarcate, and selectively accentuate certain aspects of the discourse.

- **Contextual:** relating a text to the surrounding speech setting (e.g., by means of various referential, deictic, spatial, and temporal forms).

- **Relational:** serving to initiate, facilitate, maintain, or (politely) terminate interpersonal relationships via the appropriate discourse forms, including ritualistic in-group language that promotes feelings of fellowship and solidarity.

- **Poetic:** promoting the artistic use of language, either for its own sake or to highlight and complement one of the other speech functions (i.e., the literary forms of the text act as "communicative clues" intended to call attention to themselves, with esthetic import, and/or to other discourse aims and objectives).

It is important to adopt a functional perspective when analyzing any act of communication for the purposes of understanding, evaluating, and, where necessary, also reproducing (as in a translation) the author's intended message. This matter will be discussed in more detail in lesson 3, but even at this point in our study, the underlying influence of communicative purpose and connotative associations needs to be kept in mind, especially when analyzing segments of direct speech.

» Can you give an example that illustrates the importance of these accompanying functional and emotive implications?

» Which ones are involved in Ezekiel 4:12–15 (shown below from the NIV)?

Check the cotext (the text that immediately precedes and follows) and context (the entire setting and situation) of this brief dialogue. What difficulties do you anticipate when rendering this passage in your language?

> 12 Eat the food as you would a barley cake; bake it in the sight of the people, using human excrement for fuel."
> 13 The Lord said, "In this way the people of Israel will eat defiled food among the nations where I will drive them."
> 14 Then I said, "Not so, Sovereign Lord! I have never defiled myself. From my youth until now I have never eaten anything found dead or torn by wild animals. No unclean meat has ever entered my mouth."
> 15 "Very well," he said, "I will let you bake your bread over cow manure instead of human excrement."

Whether or not our envisioned audience will attach the same significance to the text that its speaker/writer intended depends on many interpersonal and impersonal factors ("frames of reference"). A number of these will be considered more fully in the next sections. Accordingly, in order to better understand and appreciate a given text, one must also analyze it with respect to these same types of linguistic signs, as they are combined syntactically to achieve certain specific goals on different levels of scope and complexity, as well as with respect to the sociological setting of communication.

The following is a simple method for analyzing a literary text, especially one that includes a lot of direct speech. This set of procedures reveals the text's manner of composition in terms of a whole and its parts, unity in diversity, peaks within patterns of significance, and discourse intentions accompanied by personal feelings:

Step 1 Mark all instances of repetition (both form and content) in the text. Do you see any significant patterns?

Step 2 Note where all major breaks or shifts of form or content occur (e.g., according to topic, speaker, time, place).

Step 3 Identify areas of concentration with regard to key stylistic/rhetorical features (perhaps marking a peak or climax).

Step 4 Demarcate the major and minor boundaries of all units within the text (pericope, book).

Step 5 Analyze the connections and relationships between all structural units.

Step 6 Propose major and minor themes (thematic predications) for the various text units.

Step 7 Suggest the major and minor communicative functions or goals for all discourse units by answering the following questions:

   a. What did the writer hope to do with this text in relation to his intended readers?
   b. How has he accomplished this in terms of the stylistic devices that he used?
   c. Which sociolinguistic factors are pertinent to the interpretation of this text?
   d. How does the dialogue develop and highlight the nondialogue portions of this discourse?
   e. What purpose does character speech serve in relation to the author's larger aims?

» Can you suggest any additional steps to include in this procedure?

» Would you like to propose a different sequence of steps? If so, specify the sequence you would prefer, or even suggest a completely different method.

We will be developing this method of analysis in more detail in lesson 3. Our goal is to better understand the various semiotic dimensions of a given text, consisting of a hierarchy of interrelated subtexts in its original sociocultural context, so that we can communicate it more effectively to a particular audience that speaks a different language and lives in a distinct world setting. The analytical tools of semiotics can thus be joined to those of sociolinguistics, as we strive to explore and comprehend the total environment in which human message composition, transmission, and interpretation occurs—people interacting with other people by means of verbal, and often also non-verbal, texts. We will examine these communication participants more closely in section 1.4.

For reflection, research, and response:

1. Based on the discussion of "meaning" in this chapter, how would you define, describe, or explain it? In other words, "What does *meaning* mean?" What are the key components of this complex concept, and how do you express them in YL? (See also Wendland 2004b:23, 242.)

   One might view "meaning" as consisting of three interrelated aspects or perspectives:

   a. The aspect of the authorial source (*sense*—what the author intended to mean)

   b. The aspect of the text (*semantics*—the intended meaning formalized in a given language)

   c. The aspect of the target audience (*significance*—the meaning derived from the text through the cognitive processes of interpretation and inference)

   Each of these three aspects of meaning is embedded within and strongly shaped by a context, both *textual* (semiotic) and *extratextual* (sociocultural). What then is the meaning that we translate? Putting the question differently, which is the most important aspect of meaning that must be represented in a translation of the Scriptures? There are certain difficulties of interpretation regarding each of the three aspects of meaning. Mention some of these.

2. In this workbook, we will be exploring another dimension of meaning that is not often given much consideration; namely, that which is conveyed by the linguistic forms of the text, especially those that have a special artistic and rhetorical function. Give an example from Scripture that illustrates the assertion that form also has meaning. (The class may discuss a number of the issues raised in points 1–2 in order to highlight some of the key problems involved in the communication process of Bible translation.)

3. Discuss the importance of the semiotics of print in the preparation of Bibles in your language. What are some of the most important factors of typography and format to consider (e.g., type size and style, placement of white space on the page, foreign- versus local-origin illustrations, positioning of cross-references and verse numbers)? Why are such considerations important?

4. How well do you know the Christmas story? Carefully read Luke 2:6–22 in several versions. Then analyze this text following the seven major steps listed above (including the questions that follow step 7). Does this sort of procedural study help you to understand a familiar Scripture passage better? If so, explain how. If not, what improvements can you suggest? Next, examine the same passage from a sociolinguistic and semiotic point of view. Do these additional perspectives help you discover any other interesting features? Finally, consider whether in your own language and cultural setting there might be any potential problems that appear as you think about communicating this text to an ordinary audience. Give some examples.

5. Wilt (2002a:39) says, "The sending and perceiving of a text always involve a selection process....A person never sends a meaning…rather she sends an arrangement of signs that she intends to be under-stood in certain ways." In light of this statement, list some of the major situational variables upon which the text-sending and text-processing activities depend. Which, in your opinion, is the most important limiting or enabling factor in the communication process? Give some reasons for your opinion.

6. Robert Bascom (2003:2) notes,

> [A] serious problem for Bible translators is the mismatch between the conceptual systems of Biblical Hebrew and Modern English with regard to the terms and concepts of "heart." While prototypical meaning associations for "heart" in English are overwhelmingly sentimental (love, tender feelings, romance), the situation for ancient Hebrew is quite different. While emotions are expressed with the term, they are nearly always by metaphorical extension. Thus for example, if one is angry, one's heart is "hot." But "heart" by itself, even in the famous case of loving with one's heart, is arguably less about emotion and more about commitment.

Think of another well-known body sign or gesture from the Bible and designate its primary function(s) in the Ancient Near Eastern setting in which it was produced. Would this gesture convey the same or a similar communicative goal in your culture? If not, what would it mean? And what gesture would be equivalent in your social setting?

7. The importance of a thorough, systematic, and comparative sociolinguistic analysis of all the key terms of Scripture cannot be overemphasized. Complete the following chart (cf. Bascom 2003:3–4) to illustrate this point from the perspective of your language and culture. Note the wide range of non-literal usages of Hebrew "heart" (left column) and their basic sense in English (middle column). Check each reference given to see if you agree with the gloss given. Your main task is to fill in the column on the right for your language. What would a literal rendering of the Hebrew expression mean in YL? If the sense would not be the same in YL, give the vernacular expression that would give the intended meaning, plus a back-translation into English. The first example has been done for you as a model to follow (based on Chichewa):

Hebrew "Heart" (לב/לבב leb/lebab)	Used to convey	Your language
hard heart (Deut. 15:7)	stubborn, selfish attitude	kuuma mtima = 'stingy, miserly'; kuuma mutu = 'to be hard in the head'
heart lifted up (Deut. 8:14)	pride, self-confidence	
hot heart (Deut. 19:6)	anger, rage	
pure heart (Prov. 22:11)	single-minded, sincerity	
turn heart/cause heart to turn (Ps. 119:36)	commit to, convince people	
sustain heart (Ps. 104:15)	physical recovery (e.g., thirst)	
heart (feels) good (2 Sam. 13:28)	intoxicated	
have a full heart (Gen. 20:5-6)	have a clear conscience	
steal one's heart (Gen. 31:26)	deceive	
change heart (Exod. 14:5)	change mind	
heart goes after (2 Sam. 15:13)	be loyal to, follow a leader	
uncircumcised heart (Lev. 26:41)	be rebellious	
heart melts (Ezek. 21:12)	discouragement, fear	
depart from heart (Deut. 4:9)	forget, ignore	
be/put upon heart (Deut. 11:18)	memorize, remember	
strong, stout heart (Ps. 31:25)	bravery	
soft heart (2 Kgs. 22:19)	repentant	
steal, ravish heart (Song 4:9)	infatuation	
heart lifted up (2 Chr. 25:19)	pride, self-confidence	
be upon, write on heart (Deut. 11:18)	memorize	
heart like you (Job. 12:3)	be as wise as you	
timid, weak heart (Deut. 20:3, 8)	be timid, cowardly, fearful	
enlarge heart (Ps. 199:32)	teach, increase knowledge	
weigh heart (Prov. 24:12)	read one's mind	
slippery heart (Hos. 10:2)	deceitful, unfaithful	

10. OPTIONAL ASSIGNMENT. Examine Paul's Letter to Philemon and find an example of each of the seven steps listed above (cf. Wilt and Wendland 2008:ch.10). Write out the text segment that applies, together with its primary functional designation. Finally, render that portion in a dynamic idiomatic manner in your language, as if Paul were writing to Philemon today in your vernacular.

1.4 Communication participants and their characteristics

To discover all that is involved when we communicate with each other verbally, the complex activity of communication may be analyzed in different ways and from various sociolinguistic perspectives. In this and the following sections, we will survey some of the important considerations to be kept in mind when conducting a study of the interpersonal factors that may affect communication. Indeed, these are so numerous and disparate that one wonders how we are able to understand each other at all. But we do—and surprisingly well on most occasions. Much of the reason for this general success (over and above the redundancy that is built into human language) is due to our ability to more or less intuitively adapt to different cultural contexts and social situations and make the necessary adjustments to our discourse in order to suit the occasion. People learn how to do this as they are growing up; it is part of the general enculturation process. Some of the conventions and rules of proper speech (or writing) are learned during formal schooling, but most are acquired informally as people observe how others communicate, whether well, poorly, or not at all.

We investigate this topic as Bible translators so that we may apply what we learn to a more effective re-presentation of the Scriptures, whether in our mother tongue or some other target language. First, we need to distinguish several different kinds of communication participants (or partners), then identify some of the varied ways in which they may be related to each other as they communicate. These characteristics interact to affect the nature and outcome of any speech event, whether oral, written, or some mass medium production.

There are two main categories of participants who engage each other when communicating: the *text producers* and the *text consumers*. Different terms may be used to designate each group, depending on how the communication is taking place:

1. **Text producers:** source, author, speaker, writer, composer

    » Which term works best in YL and why?

2. **Text consumers:** receptors, text processors, target audience, hearers, readers

    » Which term works best in YL and why?

In most cases, the producer category is singular—only one person formulates and generates the message. This is especially true in direct communication such as face-to-face conversation. In the case, however, of indirect (or mediated) communication, such as a mass-media production, more than one individual (e.g., a script writer, a producer, and a director) may be involved as the corporate source of the message that is transmitted. It should also be noted that during a *dialogue* the text producers and consumers exchange roles, sometimes very rapidly, and perhaps only for short segments, especially if one person is the dominant speaker.

There can also be *secondary* producers of texts ("message mediators"), that is, persons who do not actually compose the oral or written text but who convey it to others, for example, messengers, representatives, spokespersons, reporters, and emissaries. A translator is a mediating communication participant of this kind.

» Why is this true?

» What special responsibility does this role entail?

In the case of indirect communication, we may also have *secondary consumers*, that is, persons who were not envisioned or originally intended by the source text producer as consumers of the message. With few exceptions, a translated text is always produced by and intended to reach such a secondary audience or readership. This complex process must be carried out in a manner that is acceptable to the project sponsors as well as the primary consumer group in order for it to be deemed a success and also to avoid the negative connotation that may be associated with secondary settings. This becomes a problem especially in situations where the overall process of communication is not explained or implemented very well.

These potential dangers raise issues of authority, responsibility, ethics, and control in diverse circumstances. Who, for example, bears ultimate responsibility at a news conference where a spokesperson for the national president or prime minister issues an official statement or press release? Whose authority is enforced if this communiqué involves certain directives or commands? Who, in turn, is responsible for the truthfulness of such statements—the spokesperson or the person in whose name the text is delivered? If some information of critical significance to many people must be transmitted, who normally does this—a spokesperson or the original text producer, the country's president?

» How do these concerns relate to Bible translation? List some of the key players in the setting of a long-term Bible translation project.

» Who play the primary and secondary roles here?

» How are important ethical issues that pertain to responsibility, authority, and control to be resolved?

For reflection, research, and response:

1. Describe the overall producer and consumer, and primary and secondary setting, of the introduction to Luke's Gospel (1:1–4). How does this passage relate to Acts 1:1–5 in terms of their respective communications settings and the participants involved?

2. A dialogue involving two or more speakers may be compared to a game: The speakers take their turns according to certain rules and strategies. One speech, or "move," may be more or less important than another in terms of its impact or effect on the other speaker(s). The rules and strategies of direct speech are culture specific and often differ from one society to the next with respect, for example, who may begin to speak, how much one may speak, who is allowed to interrupt another, and how the speakers address one another. Give an example of the conversational conventions of your language that will influence how you translate certain dialogue portions of the Bible.

3. Carefully read section 2.1.1 in Wilt 2002a, and then answer his questions:

   "How do the reporters' use of quotes and explanations of events compare to what the translator must do?" What are the main similarities and differences of these two communication roles and activities? "For whom is the Bible translator a spokesperson?" (ibid. :31).... Are translators able to provide "direct quotations" or "indirect quotations" of the authors and editors of the various documents found in the Scriptures—even of the speeches of God himself? Explain your answer—what would be the difference between a direct and an indirect quotation of some passage of the Bible in translation?

4. Another metaphor to describe the nature of translation besides the direct/indirect speech analogy is to make a text *foreign* to the intended audience. To *foreignize* a text would be to allow it to remain literal, thus highlighting the "strangeness" of the source text in terms of language, literary structures, concepts, cultural practices, social institutions, etc. in order to draw attention to certain aspects of the meaning in the original. To *domesticate* it would be to render it more idiomatically, thus seeking to promote naturalness in terms of the target language, literature, and social-cultural perspectives (see Wilt 2002a:41). Discuss these notions in relation to the setting of Bible translation

in your language. Which type of version is needed in your situation—one that is more foreign or more familiar? Why do you think so?

5. Summarize the participant dynamics involved in producing a Bible translation—either one that you have participated in or have some knowledge about. Consult the diagrams and discussion in Wilt 2002a:30–33. In the situation that you have in mind, who assumes the primary authority, responsibility, and control for the different aspects of the translation task as well as of the project as a whole? Have these roles and relationships been clearly defined, for example, in a document that outlines the project's purpose (termed the *Skopos*), principles, procedures, organization, and job descriptions (termed the project *Brief*)? Whom does the TL community view as being the ultimate "producer" of a Bible translation? What can be done to facilitate this highly interactive working relationship in order to improve both efficiency and effectiveness? Even if you have no specific knowledge of a project, after studying Wilt's diagrams on page 32 you should be able to offer some suggestions here.

6. Describe the participant dynamics involved in how a target group of readers/hearers processes a translation. How is a distant, removed set of participants able to interact with the text producers? Is it important that they do so? Wilt (ibid.:33) says, "In a translation project, the voices of the contemporary community must be heard as well as those of the ancient texts." Why is this so? How might an indirect dialogue process be encouraged and sustained? How does cooperation in communication benefit the project as a whole?

7. Outline a typical "chain of communication" that brings an original text of Scripture to you today in YL via a host of intermediaries and different stages of transmission. Which is the most critical stage, in your opinion—that is, where either a breakdown or serious distortion can occur? Why do you think so? What can be done through personal mediation or proactive planning to prevent such a problem or lessen its effects on the overall communication process?

1.5 Sociolinguistic variables that influence communication

There are a variety of closely interrelated factors, tangible as well as intangible, that affect how we communicate with one another on an everyday basis. They all contribute to creating a person's guiding cognitive environment by which he perceives, interprets, evaluates, and responds to others throughout life. Six such variables follow, along with some important questions associated with each one. The questions are simply suggestions to spark discussion of the relevant issues.

Consider each topic within the framework of your own society and culture and explain how it may affect the communication process in your community and work situation. Also give some thought to how these different factors may exert their influence—that is, how each sociolinguistic aspect might affect your understanding as well as your communication of a particular text. (Take your examples from Luke's Gospel when considering these issues from a biblical perspective.)

1. **Culture:** *Culture* may be defined simply as a people's worldview and way-of-life. Their *worldview* is an invisible mental model or mind-set (beliefs, norms, values, goals, attitudes, expectations, hopes). This influential cognitive grid is held more or less in common by the members of a certain social group, its many diverse facets being learned and transmitted both verbally and non-verbally from one generation to the next. A people's worldview is normally manifested in different ways and to varying degrees in a visible *lifestyle* (e.g., socio-political institutions, customs, traditions, art forms, material artifacts, and so forth).

    a. What do you feel are the three most characteristic or important components of the implicit, conceptual dimension of your people's culture, making up its worldview?

    b. Is this worldview eroding or being reinforced, changing rapidly or slowly? How, why, and in which important respects?

c. How do cultural considerations and ethnic relations affect interpersonal communication in your community, whether positively or negatively? Give some examples.

2. **Age**: The *age* of a speaker influences to whom he speaks, when, and in what manner. There are at least four age groupings in a given society that may affect public discourse: child, youth, married adult, and elder. Each of these culturally defined categories will frequently give evidence of age-related stylistic differences, for example, in the choice of vocabulary (colloquial versus archaic, limited versus unrestricted, modern versus pre-modern figurative language).

   a. Do people use honorific forms to reflect age distinctions in your social setting?

   b. How do the respective ages of message producers and processors affect the communication of important messages?

   c. Is there a difference between written and spoken discourse in this regard? If so, explain what the difference is and whether the situation is relatively fixed or in flux?

3. **Sex**: In many traditional rural societies, there is a distinct difference in male as opposed to female speech patterns, especially in intonation and word choice, but in some cases also in certain morphological and syntactic forms. These differences may arise due to the fact that women in conservative communities often do not discourse regularly with men and do not travel as widely, thus restricting their range of vocabulary (e.g., eliminating certain urban-based loanwords). In some settings women are not permitted to speak publicly before a male audience.

   a. Are there prohibitions or restrictions on overt communication that women may experience in your society? Describe them.

   b. Are these customs dying out or relatively strong?

   c. Are the same things true of written communication, or does nonliteracy itself limit this?

   d. To what extent are women meaningfully involved in your Bible translation project?

   e. What may be done to encourage a greater level of participation among the women in your society?

4. **Status**: *Status* is a feature that shows relationship to others, such as age, education, sociopolitical rank, economic level, and, of course, kinship. Status may be viewed as the product of any of these features or a combination of them. Some are more important than others in determining the status of individuals and groups in different cultures. As with age, status is likely to affect the use of honorific versus familiar forms of address, and speech styles as well. Status can also be accorded certain revered inanimate objects, for example, a crucifix, a painting of Christ, or even a particular version of the Bible.

   a. What are some of the status factors that affect communication in your society today?

   b. How many levels of honorific distinction are there?

   c. How do these concerns affect Christian communication—Bible translation in particular?

   d. Is there a "KJV (prestige) factor" operating in your denomination or wider community? Is this a good influence or detrimental? Explain.

5. **Education**: *Education* may be carried out in a formal, official way or by means of traditional, informal agencies and institutions, including the family. In most societies nowadays, a formal education, including a degree, is highly regarded and, in fact, necessary in order to establish one's credentials and gain employment. Formally educated people will normally speak and write differently from those who are not schooled. A person's level of education often determines his status in the community and, accordingly, the value or weight of his communication.

   a. Does education make a difference in your society? Explain.

   b. How has formal Western education influenced communication, especially with regard to whose communication matters most?

   c. Mention some traditional inductive methods of teaching and learning as well as oral art forms that are still highly regarded by many people. Are traditional educational methods and verbal skills being lost?

   d. How can traditional and modern educational methods be used together in the church to enhance the impact and appeal of Christian communication, including Bible translation?

6. **Religion**: The major *religions* of the world, such as Christianity, Islam, Judaism, Hinduism, and Buddhism, are generally represented in most urban communities. In addition, a local "traditional," or indigenous, religion may also flourish in many parts of the world, either in competition with or as a syncretistic supplement to one of the others. A major religion is often further divided up into denominations and sects, with a diverse range of historical and theological relationships among them. Certain religious speech patterns and customs develop within them and between them, especially in the area of confessional terminology. These groups may adhere more or less to different "holy books" as well as to certain traditions or practices peculiar to one group. The religion factor has an important influence on the religious expressions that the respective groups use, defend, and sometimes prescribe.

   a. How does religious separatism or denominationalism affect Christian communication in your society today, and Bible translation efforts in particular?

   b. Is there currently a power struggle or rivalry that certain religious bodies are engaged in? If so, why has this come about? What can be done to improve the situation?

   c. How can greater cooperation and involvement in the task of producing a new translation or revision be encouraged?

   e. Which organizations are widely viewed as being the most open, facilitating, ecumenical, and interactive agencies?

   f. Are these groups actively supporting Bible translation efforts? If not, why not?

The influence and interaction of sociological factors such as these create certain language varieties, or speech styles, and perhaps also some significant speech taboos in any community. These all need to be carefully researched and studied by anyone interested in communicating more effectively, whether in speech or in writing. This is especially true for translators of dialogue portions of the Bible.

Sociolinguists frequently group discourse varieties into two major categories, dialects and registers.

1. **Dialects** are varieties defined according to the user (speaker). These are geographical, temporal, social, standard or nonstandard, and individual varieties, which do not normally change in different social settings.

2. **Registers** (or sociolects) are varieties defined according to use. Registers may be further distinguished with regard to *field* (subject matter), *mode* (medium), and *tenor* (formality).

   a. **Fields** of discourse vary according to the major topic being presented (which usually involves different speech situations and social transactions as well). For example, a typical Christian sermon in denomination X is likely to differ from a sermon in denomination Y in discourse form and rhetorical style. It will undoubtedly differ also from a political oration. In content, the sermons may be very different, though certain texts and motifs may be held in common.

   Is there any implication here for how the epistolary sermons of Paul are represented in translation (e.g., the different sermons in Romans)?

   b. **Modes** of discourse in most communities are ordinary speaking and writing, though nowadays video and electronic communication is fast becoming popular and influential as well.

   In which ways is speech different from writing in your society? Why are there such differences? How might this factor affect a published Bible translation in your language as distinct from an audio presentation?

   c. **Tenor** has to do with the stylistically marked levels of formality, from *formal* to *regular* to *informal, casual,* or *intimate*. Speech styles also vary according to user in that they depend on who is speaking and to whom and the nature of the speakers' social interrelationship. One might compare these different varieties to the clothes that people wear depending on the formality of the occasion and setting.

   Where and when, for example, would a man wear each of the following (or the closest equivalent in your culture): a tuxedo, business suit, cardigan sweater, shirt, tee shirt? What would a woman's corresponding attire be?

Thus there are several culturally specific, interpersonal factors that are important to consider when communicating verbally:

1. Level of *formality* (What is the social situation?)

2. Degree of *politeness* (With whom are you communicating? Is an honorific needed or a familiar term of address? Are words and phrases that indicate power and/or solidarity called for?)

3. Issues of *dialect* or *sociolect* (Where are you communicating in terms of your specific setting, whether geographical, temporal [e.g., archaisms versus slang as appropriate for different ages], economic, educational, or ecclesiastical?)

4. *Mode* of communication (What means of transmission are you using? Does it involve sight, sound, hearing, touch? Is it by way of print, speech, audiocassette, radio, video, or some other medium? Is it an individual versus mass medium? Is it a single message versus multiple messages?)

The mode of message transmission is, of course, an impersonal factor, but since it is so important and often affects how the other three variables are manifested, it needs to be taken into special consideration when carrying out any analysis of a total communication event, whether oral or written.

For reflection, research, and response:

1. Read and study the dialogue portions of Luke 1–2 with sociolinguistic and cross-cultural eyes. First, do you detect any possible influences from the social situation upon the manner of anyone's speaking in this passage? Second, if you were communicating this text in your language, how would such

social factors influence the expression of the message, for example, with respect to honorific forms? Give three good examples, especially noting the following verses from Luke 1:13, 15, 18, 35, 38, 42, 44, 46, 54, 61, 66, 69, 72, 76.

2. We have seen the need for sociolinguistic studies in translating interpersonal dialogue. Such studies also help to make the biblical text sound natural and suitable with respect to the assumed author or speaker and his setting, especially in the case of the prophets or epistle writers. Furthermore, the Scriptures are very often communicated in oral form (by reading aloud or by audiocassette, radio, or video). In your community, do most people read the Bible for themselves or hear it read in some form to them? How do you know this? On what published facts, research, or personal experience have you based your answer? What effect should this continued importance of *orality* in your community have upon the Bible translation that you are preparing? (Make two concrete suggestions.)

3. In addition to distinguishing different levels of "formality" (tenor) in discourse, one may also view interpersonal communication in terms of relevance as a set of concentric circles—moving from outside to inside, from the least to the most relevant as follows: *clichés* (e.g., greetings) < *facts* (pure information) < *ideas* (convictions, decisions, evaluations, etc.) < *feelings* (including emotions and attitudes) < *core disclosures* (most intimate and personal revelations and affirmations).[4] Of course, this is a generalized perspective with much overlapping that also depends on the particular social context and speech setting involved at the time. But how might this add another sociolinguistic dimension to our analysis of the various speeches of Scripture—for example, Christ's visit with the Samaritan woman at the well (John 4): cliché (4:7), facts (4:11), ideas (4:13), feelings (4:9 versus 4:39), core disclosure (4:17, 26) (cf. Wendland 1985:ch. 5)? It may be (*we need to do the necessary research!*) that the TL into which we are translating signals these different levels of relevance in register (e.g., by means of lexical repetition or condensation, abbreviation, word order variations, the use of particles and clitics—in addition to paralinguistic modification: tone, loudness, tempo, etc.).

The question then is this: Should such distinctions be *marked* in our Bible translation, where possible and appropriate? Discuss this issue with fellow translators and come to a conclusion with regard to the passages listed for John 4 above. Then apply these pragmatic notions with respect to an actual or potential translation of the "Parable of the Great Banquet" (Luke 14:16–24)—and to Paul's discussion of apostleship in 1 Cor. 4. This exercise is simply a means of encouraging us to think more deeply about *how* and *why* we communicate with words—not just lexical items per se, but including now all the little ways in which we can meaningfully modify our words when speaking idiomatically in natural social situations.

4. In his discussion of "postcolonial aesthetics" in past and present African fictional literature, Paul Bandia makes this observation concerning "indirectness, a well-known strategy in traditional African discourse" (2008:52):

> Indirectness has been defined as the strategy of making a point or statement in a roundabout manner, through circumvention, calculated delays, pausing, etc….By using indirect language, a speaker in the traditional context can display great oratorical skills, through a display of knowledge (or wisdom) and the ability to enact such pragmatic functions as inclusion, group identity and shared meaning, as well as the ability to use such devices as textual coherence, rhetorical questions, proverbs, aphorisms, and much more.

In my 1985 study of the importance of sociolinguistic factors in Bible translation (chapters 2–3), I pointed out the need for applying indirection when rendering certain segments of direct speech in order to maintain the appropriate level of "politeness" or "respect" when relative strangers or persons of unequal social status are dialoguing. For example, in Gen. 37:15 we read that "a man found [Joseph] wandering around in the fields and asked him, 'What are you looking for?'" While a direct translation of this question is understandable in Zambian languages, to ask a stranger "what do you want" in this way turns out to be a grave insult

---
[4] I attribute this listing to Chuck Swindoll, as heard on *Insight for Living* (May 30, 2008, DSTV Radio—South Africa).

in terms of social culture. Rather, one would have to put the query in a more roundabout way, as in Chewa:[5] *Kodi bamboo, mumati n'kwabwino?*—"[Question marker] Say Mister, are you [pl.] saying that everything is well there?" Such communicative equivalence is especially important where a high level of *emotion* is also involved, as in Esau's plaintive request of his father, Isaac: "Have you but one blessing, my Father? Bless me, even me also, O my Father!" (Gen. 27:38). This is much too direct for Tonga ears in a father-son setting of blessing. An idiomatic correspondent would sound like this: "Aaaaw, pleeeease [*Acuuu, kaka!*], is there not just one more blessing, my Father?!" The initial exclamations set the tone for this more indirect, less personalized expression of the content and intent of the original text.

> » Is such polite "indirectness" in direct speech an issue in your language? Have you been able to factor this sociolinguistic feature into your Bible translation? Give three examples from the diverse dialogues of Genesis 37 (or another chapter of your choice) to illustrate how this has (or should) influence the rendering in your language and sociocultural setting.

5. In discussing "the art or oratory" in Africa, Bandia has this to say (2008:61, 63, 67):

> In Africa, as in Greco-Roman antiquity, the law case is one of the most common contexts in which public speaking ability is particularly valued. Both litigants and judges are expected to display great rhetorical skill and use various means to add to the persuasiveness of their speech....
>
> An accomplished speaker in traditional Africa is someone blessed with many qualities, amongst which is the quality of possessing profound knowledge of, and ability to transmit, notions and ideas which generally portray a man [sic] as being wise. Knowledgeability also includes the ability to manipulate language;...
>
> The importance of the art of oratory and its various forms of expression have not been lost on African writers who have woven the aesthetics of this indigenous discourse into European-language literature. ...
>
> Knowledge, or wisdom, particularly as exhibited in the use of language, is usually associated with age and professionalism. In fact, there is a popular saying in Africa that "the passing away of an old man is like a library burning to the ground." The elderly are expected to handle sayings, proverbs, euphemisms, libations, eulogies, etc. with special language skills....

- Do such observations reflect the situation in the society in which you are carrying out Bible translation?
- Are there only wise "men" in your society—or are certain women characterized in the same way?
- For those who live/work on the African continent, comment on the notion of "traditional Africa" and its "oratory."
- Where is "oratory"—the gift of effective, persuasive, powerful, etc.—speech manifested in your society?
- Is it possible/desirable to train and/or use traditional orators as Bible translators? Explain your answer.
- What happens if they are elderly—can they still be used in such specialized work? If so, in what way(s)?
- How about authors who are able to incorporate the features or oratory into their writing—could they being engaged somehow in the work of Bible translation? Why (and how) or why not?

6. Which sociolinguistic factor listed in this section do you think is the most important or influential in your society? Why do you say so? Which factor has caused you the most difficulties during your Bible translation experience? Give an example of some major communication or textual problem that you have encountered in this regard. How have you dealt with it in your vernacular text? If you have not done any direct Bible translation work, which factor would you expect to cause special difficulty, and why?

---

[5]Strictly speaking, the language of the Chewa people is referred to as Chichewa, but I sometimes use Chewa for short.

7. The several dialects (or registers) of a larger language group compete with each other in terms of prestige or status. Can you give an example of this from your speech community? What are some of the key factors that tend to rank one dialect higher or more influential than another? A language also interacts with competing ones, both regional and world languages. Give an example that you have observed in your region. Is the influence of local vernaculars retreating due to the prestige of languages of wider communication? What do such language trends imply for future Bible translation?

8. How would the communication medium affect the representation of direct discourse in Luke 1? What difference would it make if we reproduce conversations orally or in writing, for example, when the angel speaks with Zecharias, or with Mary, or when Elizabeth addresses Mary, or when the people question Zecharias?

9. Andy Warren-Rothlin makes the following observation (2003:1):

> Politeness strategies may sometimes receive a sophisticated morphological encoding, as in Japanese, but usually depend more heavily on pragmatic functions such as conversational implicatures and indirect speech acts, and their use is prescribed by features of social status, all interpreted in highly culture-specific ways....[For example,] the terms used in Grice's maxim of manner – 'obscurity', 'ambiguity', 'brevity', 'orderliness' – are seen to be highly culture-specific when a northern European tries to communicate with an African....Optatives function in HBO [Biblical Hebrew] for initial greetings, but in WALs [West African Languages] only for leave-taking and thanking. Metonymy for the 1st person is possible in HBO but not in those WALs treated here. For rhetorical questions, HBO prefers content questions, whilst WALs prefer polar questions.

Have you done a sufficient study of such "politeness strategies" in YL in order to make a comparison with the usage manifested in Biblical Hebrew? If so, how do your results compare with his comments with reference to West African languages? Do you have any additional insights to share concerning the relevance of such sociolinguistic issues to idiomatic Bible translation? How much influence should the factor of *orality* have when decisions of this nature are made?

10. Warren-Rothlin (2003:10) goes on to pose the following challenge to translators:

> Most of the functions represented by these strategies are close to equivalent, one might say, 'interchangeable'. If it is legitimate to render 'me your slave' with 'O master!' (1 Sam. 1:11 [Birifor]), might it not be equally legitimate to render the HBO default term 'lord' according to context as 'old man', 'big man' or even 'father'? Can one achieve the distinctive pragmatic force of a precative perfect or figura etymologica with an expression meaning 'please'? And can one even render blessing-greetings as normal African-style question-greetings? At what point do ancient Israelites become too African to be accurate? Most translators are not prepared to go this far. They don't want to bear responsibility for too great departures from the wording of their NRSV or BHS. But if the pragmatic functions of a wide range of linguistic forms in HBO can be more systematically described in a way which, if not really emic, can at least consider a wide range of non-western ways of classifying the world, it may be possible to suggest ways ahead for dynamic equivalence beyond semantics and into pragmatics too.

Discuss the implications of some of these important issues as they relate to your Bible translation setting, especially if the envisaged version is intended to be one that is more dynamic in nature.

11. Warren-Rothlin (2005:1) makes the following strategic proposals concerning the handling of the feature of register in Bible translation:

> When register is a feature of both the source text and the target language, we would probably all agree that it should be translated. When it is a feature of the source text but not (or less so) in the target language, we may need to look to other means to express the social differentiation involved. But if it is *not* a feature of the source text, or only debatably so (since our knowledge of such features

of Ancient Hebrew is so scarce anyway), it may nevertheless be appropriate to mark register in the target language if it allows it. Indeed the criterion of naturalness may actually *require* the marking of register in some languages, just as those with more sophisticated honorific systems force us to make decisions about social hierarchy where there is no such linguistic marking in the source text (though we know this is specially characteristic in Asia, it is often an issue in Africa too in kinship terminology, where one has to specify a sibling, for example, as younger or older).

Warren-Rothlin gives the following example (ibid.:4) from 2 Kings 7 to illustrate his point. Of course, it would have to be uttered and heard aloud for the greatest impact:

> [1] But Elisha answered, 'I hereby declare YHWH's message: "YHWH says,
> 'This time tomorrow in Samaria Gate,
> one bag of fine flour will fetch just a shekel
> and two bags of barley will be bartered so too.' " '
> [2] The Captain who was there, the king's right-hand man, retorted to the man of God,
> 'Yeah right – God's gonna send a grain storm or what?!'
> but Elisha replied,
> 'What I say you will certainly see,
> but what you see you won't live to taste.'
>
> [3] Outside the gate, there were four lepers, and they started saying to each other, 'What we doin', sittin' 'ere till we're dead? [4] If we go inside, they're all starvin' in there anyway, so we'll die. And if we stay sittin' 'ere, we're dead as well. So let's do a runner and try our luck with the Syrians – we've got nuffink to lose!'
>
> [5] So they left before it was light the next morning to go over to the Syrians. But when they got to the edge of the Syrian camp, there wasn't anyone there! [6] His Majesty had made the Syrian army hear noises – chariots, horses and a huge army – so that they thought the King of Israel had hired Hittite and Egyptian troops to attack them. [7] So they'd got up and run away before it was light, leaving all their tents, horses and donkeys – they'd left the camp just as it was and run for their lives.

12. Evaluate the preceding translation. Does it succeed as an illustration of the importance of register in Bible translation? Would you be able to use this translation as a model for a similar sort of register-sensitive rendering in YL? In what sort of a religious or social setting would such a dynamic version work out particularly well?

13. The sociolinguistic factor of "education" (noted earlier) has not always been given the attention it deserves when teaching translators how to go about their work, or indeed, when trying to instruct the community at large about the Scriptures and its interpretation. Non-Western traditional learning styles are frequently very different from those currently being practiced in Europe and America. Of course, Western-style educational methods have by and large prevailed over the world, but this does not always mean that the peoples who have adopted such methods have benefited thereby. It could well be that the introduction of certain indigenous techniques either in place of or alongside foreign ones, especially during the early stages of education or training, would bring better results in terms of efficiency and effectiveness.

Compare the following summary of "typical African ways of learning" (Adeyemo 2007), which features "story-telling" and "apprenticeship" as favored methods, with those of your culture: What are the main similarities and differences?

> Observation → Association → Imitation → Initiation → Induction → (group) Interaction

Suggest some ways in which you might introduce some of the traditional pedagogical techniques of your culture into a translator-training program. What are some of the chief difficulties that you anticipate in such an effort? What are the principal goals that you would seek to accomplish?

1.6 Different situational frames of communication

Several important *cognitive frames* (or *mental representations*) (Dooley and Levinsohn 2001:49), serve to provide a particular interpretive perspective on any text that is being communicated. It may be useful at times to differentiate these viewpoints from the popular notion of context, context being the concrete, physical setting or environment in which an act of communication takes place. A frame, on the other hand, is a cognitive construct that refers to the culturally-determined conceptual discernment and understanding of certain features of the context that influence the act of communication, both for the producer as well as the consumers of a given message, for example, with regard to relevance, impact, appeal, connotative associations, and memorability. A given frame (or window on reality) thus represents all that people generally know (or *think* they know!) about a given topic of cultural importance, whether an event, a place, a person, or some important object. These frames may strongly affect the composition as well as the perception and application of any text in its sociocultural setting.

A better understanding of such socially conditioned perspectives can assist a text producer to more effectively compose a particular message for the intended audience. It also permits the audience to more readily comprehend and respond to the organized set of verbal and non-verbal signs that make up the text. We will be considering four conceptually overlapping and mutually interacting frames of reference: *sociocultural* (section 1.6.1), *conversational* (section 1.6.2), *literary* (section 1.6.3), and *organizational* (section 1.6.4). Together they constitute the *cognitive environment* (a vital part of people's overall worldview) that both motivates and facilitates or, on the other hand, limits and distorts, the audience's comprehension of the text presented to them as part of a cooperative event of communication.

1.6.1 Sociocultural frames

Sociocultural frames may be understood as convenient mental models that function to organize mental representations and sets of associations developed for a given culture, society, community, group, or individual as a result of learning, experience, and personal reflection. They enable people to interact in an appropriate way with others in conventional kinds of social situations—that is, to perceive, interpret, organize, integrate, apply, talk about, and also remember, the information that they happen to be producing or processing at any given moment.

The customs of public worship during a worship service, for example, differ widely from one culture, community, and denomination to another. Among many non-Western peoples, an ancient, ancestor-dominated traditional religion continues to act as the most influential sociocultural framework governing a person's understanding of the Christian Scriptures. In Western societies, on the other hand, a secular, science-informed, technology-tooled humanistic perspective often replaces a biblical worldview.

> » What are some special customs relating to worship that are prominent in your society—differences that are often signaled by particular verbal or non-verbal signs and rituals, such as those in a formal order of worship or liturgy?

The subject of language in relation to culture involves a distinction that anthropologists often make between high-context and low-context communities. A *high-context* society tends to be a non-literate one, in which people prefer to communicate by talking rather than writing. Speakers depend a great deal upon the sociocultural setting and their interpersonal network as a framework for contextualizing verbal discourse. Background information therefore does not have to be explicitly verbalized during normal discourse. This may also be described as a *low-text* society. A relatively large amount of information is left implicit—it is not actually expressed. Speakers assume that people already know such information and they do not need to spell it out in words. An oral narrative, for example, when it is transcribed, tends to be lexically plain and linguistically simple in its style. This is because much of the story is depicted non-verbally—that is, by means of the performer's facial expressions, gestures, vocal intonations, and stylized body movements. A high-context culture tends to be shame-conscious: people do not like to criticize another person or group in so many words, but rather in an indirect, figurative way; conversely, they typically try to give an honored or respected person the "right answer"—the one they think is expected.

A *low-context* society, on the other hand, is one in which speakers, and especially writers, prefer to express textually all important aspects of the context, rather than leaving these features implicit or presupposed. People like to have all relevant information explicitly verbalized within the texts that they are reading or listening to. They are correspondingly also *high-text* in nature, often preferring to present a message in writing, rather than orally. Verbal texts therefore tend to be longer, more detailed, and structurally more complex in composition. People are more individualistic and direct when they speak, even when criticizing others. Americans are generally low-context (high-text) in contrast to most central African speech communities, which are high-context (low-text) in their communicative preference.

> » How would you characterize the social group that you belong to? Is it "high-context" or "low-context" or somewhere in between? Give reasons for your opinion.
>
> » Do the descriptions of these contrasting types of society seem to be accurate, or would you like to suggest some corrections or modifications in light of your experience?

Socioculturally determined, experiential, cognitive structures and verbal or non-verbal conventions are often activated and influenced by the co-occurrence of other culture-specific communicative codes, such as those involving gestures, eating habits, greetings and farewells, what clothes to wear in which situations, how to behave in public places, the way to introduce a guest, to hail a taxi, and the like. There is usually a "right" and a "wrong" way to do such things—as the cultural insider knows but the outsider at first does not. These are *learned behaviors*, a part of growing up to become a competent member of society. These mental models overlap with one another and interact (sometimes in conflict!) to influence the thinking, behavior, and discourse of an entire community (if relatively small and close-knit) or certain ethnically diverse segments within the whole.

As we will see, there are several different types of sociocultural frames that pertain specifically to a people's *speech conventions*. They may help us analyze a verbal text in terms of the various types of sub-frame that guide a speaker/writer when representing different aspects of the socially defined communication process. One must remember, however, that any oral or written text will convey only part of all the information that might be said about the event in question; the rest of the information is left implicit ("understood") since it is assumed to be known to members of the in-group.

In the case of an ancient document like the Scriptures, a large gap of time, place, language, and culture separates a modern audience from the original setting. This gap means that much of the *implicit information* that was presupposed by the original text producers is no longer available to people as part of their normal cognitive environment. It must be restored or replaced in some way so that consumers today can correctly understand, evaluate, and apply the biblical text that they read/hear. This may be done by means of a more *explicit*, communicative translation and/or, depending on the situation, a combination of supplementary helps such as *footnotes*, book introductions, section headings, glossary, cross-references, maps, diagrams, concordance, and topical index.

There are three overlapping, convention-governed sociolinguistic frames, or mental representations (called *schemas* by Dooley and Levinsohn 2001:50), that may be taken for granted as being known by a biblical writer/editor and his primary audience. These are *scripts, scenarios,* and *sketches*. Scripts pertain to typical verbal discourses, scenarios to action sequences, and sketches to character attributions. However, certain aspects of these setting-specific cognitive constructs often need to be clarified when one is translating particular texts for people who operate with a different set of conceptual representations in diverse social and cultural situations:[6]

1. **Script** can refer to one of three kinds:

    a. The first kind of script is a set pattern of frequently reiterated discourse, either a *monologue* or communal utterance, setting forth a standard argument, instruction, exposition, or expression of emotion. Examples include calling a person to repentance, testifying to the gospel, preaching a sermon, praying to God, comforting the bereaved, uttering a curse, initiating a young man or woman into new adult roles, singing a lament or a hymn, or reciting a creed.

    b. The second kind of script is a relatively fixed convention of purposeful *dialogue* that occurs in different social settings. Examples include getting and giving directions, visiting the chief, buying something at the market, testing a student, and conducting a meeting of the local council of elders.

    c. The third kind of script is a standard manner and means of telling a *narrative* sequence, such as a folktale, formal news report, biography, genealogy, history, or epic.

2. **Scenario** refers to a normal expected way of carrying out, or simply describing, a certain customary, culture-based activity. It usually involves a sequence of unspecified participants and specific actions presented or explained in a conventional way, either orally or in writing. Examples include building a house, formalizing a marriage, participating in a hunting expedition, playing a certain sport, negotiating a sale or purchase, or approaching the chief with a personal appeal.

3. **Sketch** refers to a regular form of character depiction (often stereotyped or highly predictable) associated with certain personages (real or fictional) or personifications (animate or inanimate) and social roles. Typical examples from oral narrative and written literature would be characters such as a pastor, priest, politician, mother-in-law, chief, lawyer, banker, rich man, benevolent ancestor, trickster, hero, dupe, or villain, and even the sun, moon, storm, mountain, or a great tree.

It may or may not be necessary to distinguish these three proposed mental models; perhaps it is more convenient to combine them under the cover term *cultural schema* (pl. *schemata*). In any case, from the point of view of communication in general, and Bible translation in particular, it is important to remember that "[t]he lack of the schema or schemata that are most relevant to the processing of a particular stimulus (whether linguistic or extralinguistic) can lead to failures or errors in comprehension" (Semino, in Semino and Culpeper 2002:102). For example, what schema or schemata are necessary for correctly understanding Christ's parable of the shepherd and his flock in John 10:1–13? (Consider the pertinent OT background, such as Ps 23:1; 80:1; Isa. 40:10–11; and Ezek. 34:11–16.)

---

[6] For a more detailed study of these and related terms from the perspective of "scenario theory," see Hoyle 2008:13–15. Hoyle summarizes the relevance of this type of analysis to exegesis and Bible translation as follows: "[C]ommunication relies on the communicator and audience having similar mental scenarios. These shared scenarios are the 'given' in communication, on the basis of which the communicator chooses how explicit or implicit to be, so that the audience is able to accurately guess the fuller picture of what the communicator is trying to say, by 'filling in' what is left unsaid from their existing knowledge stored in their mental scenarios. However, these scenarios are not universally the same, but are culture- and language-specific. So to understand any text, we must not rely on our own mental scenarios, but identify the mental scenarios in the mind of the original author. Thus knowledge of New Testament Greek scenarios is vital for exegesis of the New Testament texts. Similarly, to translate, we must also know the mental scenarios of the new target audience, since our message must be framed in such a way that they can accurately fill in what the author intended as implicit information, rather than make incorrect assumptions on the basis of their own cultural presuppositions....

[I]t is the mismatching of scenarios between different languages and cultures which frequently causes either concommunication, or miscommunication. This mismatch of scenarios, involving as it does the worldviews and presuppositions of differing cultures, is simply not addressed in the 'modified literal' style of translation represented by such major Bible translations as the Authorized Version, the Revised Standard Version, and the New International Version. Only a meaning-based approach to translation, seeing meaning as applying not merely at word, phrase, or clause level, but right up to discourse level, can accurately convey the message of the biblical texts to today's audience" (2008:15, cf. 16–17; 385–386).

- » How do these cultural frames compare with what would be evoked in your situational setting?

- » Do people fully understand the metaphor of Christ as the gate (or entrance) of the sheepfold?

- » What can be done in the case of serious clashes or gaps in perception and imagery?

It is important to recognize that these different conceptual models are not invariant or inflexible when they are brought to mind. On the contrary, shifts, modifications, and blends are possible, even probable, when the current conventional cognitive frame (the default) is confronted with new information or some unfamiliar textual or sociocultural setting. For example, a schema can evolve by the *addition* of new facts, by a *modification* of certain facts or relations, or by a *re-creation* of new schemata out of old ones. Take the popular literary genre of science fiction (SF), which would probably evoke varied details in the respective mental windows of different audiences:

> [F]or readers who have only a passing familiarity with science fiction, the SF schema typically has slots such as: spaceships, rayguns, robots (props); scientists, explorers, aliens (participants); extraterrestrial settings or time or space travel (entry conditions); apocalypse, or its cunning avoidance (results); and space battles or laser shoot-outs (sequence of events). As people read more SF, their schemas accrete extra features, such as the time-dilation effects of faster-than-light intergalactic travel, or 'warp' engines, or positronic brains, and so on. In the 1960s, there was a perceptible shift in science fiction from outer space to 'inner space', and a concern for psychological, biological and social science fiction, that represented a tuning of the SF schema for many readers. New sub-genres within SF later appeared, such as 'cyberpunk' or 'feminist SF'—for some critics this involved tuning their schemas further, for others it represented a thorough restructuring of the schema. (Stockwell 2002:79)

The same threefold process of addition, modification, and re-creation takes place—probably in accordance with the principle of cognitive and emotive relevance—when a contemporary audience repeatedly reads/hears an ancient document such as the Scriptures. However, Bible study is best when done in a systematic manner and enriched by various paratextual supplements. Thus, in order for people to better understand a particular biblical passage or *pericope*, their cognitive environment needs to be appropriately enriched by sociocultural and literary (genre-based) frames of information derived from the circumstantial setting of the SL text. This important process of contextualization[7] will be considered further in section 7.1; the textual representation of standardized structures involving persons, events, qualities, and relations in the form of specific TL genres will be discussed in lesson 4 and thereafter.

In section 1.3 on semiotics, we noted that a number of additional codes of signification co-occur during the verbal communication process. They may complement, reinforce, compete with, or even contradict each other. These additional meaning-bearing aspects, which are also strongly conditioned socioculturally, are grouped into two categories, *paralinguistic* and *extralinguistic*.

1. **Paralinguistic**: Examples are pitch/tone, loudness, tempo, quality of voice, intonation patterns, and varied pauses during an utterance or longer speech segment.

    a. How do such paralinguistic features of voice affect communication in your language and culture?

    b. Are there persons who speak loudly or softly, quickly or slowly, or with an English accent?

    c. What features of the print medium would correspond?

---

[7]"Fillmore (1981) uses the term CONTEXTUALIZATION to talk about the hearer's progressive attempt to develop a viable mental representation for a text" (in Dooley and Levinsohn 2001:25). It is part of the natural cognitive process of construing the meaning (a coherent mental representation) for a verbal text or any portion of one, whether spoken or written, by using the form and content of the text itself as well as the total situational setting in which the text was realized, including the speaker/writer's purpose for producing it.

d. What paralinguistic qualities of a printed page make it easier or harder to read a text (e.g., print size and style, line length, two columns of print, justification, extra white space)?

2. **Extralinguistic**: Examples are gestures, facial expressions, body stance, ritualistic movements, eye contact or lack of it, and distance between speakers.

   a. How do extralinguistic features affect communication in your society, if at all?

   b. What are the unexpressed "rules" that certain segments of society are expected to observe with regard to these non-verbal signs of communication?

   c. What happens when people do not observe the rules that accompany speech acts? In other words, what are some of the possible consequences of a non-verbal breakdown in communication?

For reflection, research, and response:

1. As a further introduction to the heuristic notion of frames during perception, conception, and communication, consider the following study contributed by Robert Bascom. Try to find in your language a similar example to the "key" / *llave, tecla, clave* (Spanish) that he gives to illustrate the point. Then use this as the basis for a class discussion on the subject.

   The Dynamic Use of Frames

   The term "frame" is essentially a static concept. It implies both external boundaries and internal structure, as is obvious when used with reference to the frame of a house or some other type of architectural construction. It is these very properties which make the metaphor so useful in communication. Frames help communicators disambiguate between competing references. Thus in Spanish *llave* can mean 'key,' 'wrench,' or 'valve/faucet' (in English), depending on the conceptual frame which is applied (locks, repairs, access to water/liquid/gas). In turn English *key* can mean key to a lock; a piano or computer key; or a key to a map, code, musical score, or problem, depending on the frame which is applied (locks, keyboards, explanatory material). To express these different frames in Spanish requires three different terms: *llave* (locks), *tecla* (piano/computer), and *clave* (map, code, musical score, problem).

   This mismatch in terminology is due to the fact that Spanish applies different frames than does English to the world of experience. All the uses of *llave* in Spanish involve a turning motion in order to access something. *Tecla*, on the other hand, refers to a pushing or tapping motion for access, and clave does not involve a physical motion at all, but access only. The other frames which distinguish one reference from another within these physical/non-physical access frames are sub-categories of this general three-part distinction or frame network. In English, *key* has to be distinguished in its various references through the frames of all the various specific uses directly, since English makes no intermediary or networked distinctions as are made in Spanish.

   Frames can be used as well as make connections between explicit signs to other internal references within an established frame (for connotative richness) as well as connections to external connections between frames (for intentional ambiguity). Thus "night" not only can refer to a time of day ("the dinner meeting was held at eight o'clock at night") but also can have other connotative and emotive associations ("that abandoned house is spooky at night," "the moon reflected on the lake is very romantic at night"), which are easily accessed radially within the frame "night" (see below further on "night").

   And word-plays (e.g., puns) are usually built on connections between different frames using the same or a similar oral or textual form. Thus a political commentator has titled her book on President

George W. Bush, "Shrub," taking the name frame and networking it with the biological frame, and placing the combined reference within the larger frame of political satire.

But the use of frames is a dynamic and negotiated process, one which the participants in communication events are making and fine-tuning dozens of decisions about which frames to apply in just a few seconds. Thus the case of *llave* outlined above can be illustrated by the diagram below. One can see the three possible source-generated frames for *llave* (locks, repair, valves), from which the receptors will have to quickly choose and adjust their frame(s) for understanding. This process is fairly straightforward in this example, as both real-world contexts and surrounding linguistic contexts will tend to quickly disambiguate the possible frames to be applied.

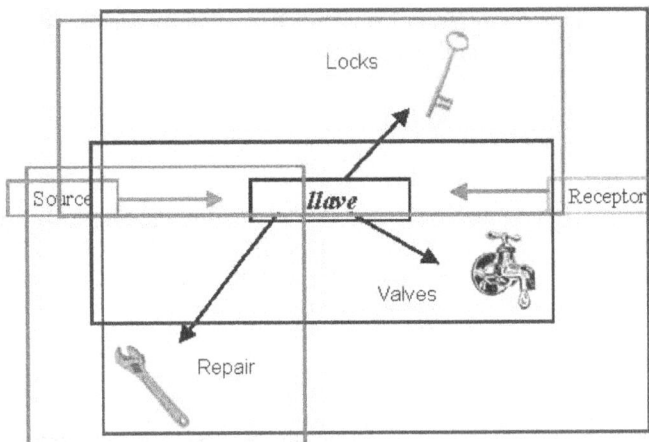

Furthermore, even though at a micro-level one can talk of the application of a single frame for disambiguation, for example, very quickly these frames stack up on one another and, of course, multiple frames are accessed simultaneously either on purpose or by accident when word-play or simple ambiguity is involved.

Multiple frames can be applied in an overlapping way to specify something which could not exist otherwise. For example, we can consider the following sentence:

> The ringing of the phone woke me up in the middle of the night. In fact, it was two o'clock in the morning!

The simultaneous use of the am/pm frame with "night" frame results in a "morning" which is still "night." This would doubtless seem as strange to someone unfamiliar with these systems as does the ancient Israelite notion that a "day" begins in the "evening" to those outside that cultural framework. Further, the entire set of usages associated with time of day would have to be seriously reworked in cultures unacquainted with timepieces.

Katan (1999:21) has described culture itself as not simply a static frame, context, or background against which linguistic expression must be understood: "Culture here is viewed as a dynamic process, constantly being negotiated by those involved." Linguists have long been used to the idea that words and their referents are matters negotiated by speakers within a given cultural frame. But students of culture are now saying the same thing about the frames themselves, and including linguistic expression itself as part of the activity of framing. This approach places culture (understood dynamically) at the center of any understanding of language and thus translation.

According to Katan (and those he cites), much of the cultural framework needed for understanding even everyday linguistic expressions is influenced by how humans tend to process sensory input. Research stemming from *Gestalt* theory indicates that frames and signs (including linguistic signs) interact

1.6 Different situational frames of communication

dynamically in the creation of communication events. Signs evoke frames ("Ladies and gentlemen" signals a formal beginning to a public event), and frames are tried out provisionally (Is it a joke? Is he serious?) to interpret emerging signs. These processes take place very rapidly in communication, with incomplete data constantly being processed on the sensory side, and provisional frames constantly being constructed, discarded, and replaced on the cognitive side: "…sensory signals are encouraged to fit preconceptions, and our general strategy is to use the information gained from the sensory system as a cue for representation, rather than as the representation itself" (ibid.:91).

In a section of his book which he titles "Shifting frames: Translation and mediation in theory and practice," Katan takes up the problem of cross-cultural translation directly, arguing that the notion of frames and framing (1999:123–125) leads not only to an understanding of translation that moves beyond the "particularly influential" model of Nida and Taber (ibid.:123) but also to an understanding of the translator as a cultural mediator:

> [A]n essential difference between a traditional translator and a mediator is the mediator's ability to understand and create frames. The mediator will be able to understand the frames of interpretation in the source culture and will be able to produce a text which would create a similar set of interpretation frames to be accessed in the target reader's mind. (ibid.:125).

Katan suggests that a translator must be a conceptual frame-mediator as well as a wordsmith—do you agree? Explain.

If you agree, how does this perception change your understanding of and approach toward Bible translation?

Try to give an example with reference to a particular translation problem in your language.

2. The influence of the sociocultural *context* on the literary *text* of Scripture is clear in the letters to the seven churches of Revelation 2–3. We can discover certain aspects of this essential background meaning by carefully studying the figurative language of these two chapters. For example, in the letter to Laodicea we read this admonition from the Lord (Rev. 3:18):

> I counsel you:
> to buy from me gold refined in the fire, so you can become rich;
> and white clothes to wear, so you can cover your shameful nakedness;
> and salve to put on your eyes, so you can see.

Certain metaphors of this passage can be understood in light of the cultural context of the wealthy city of Laodicea in ancient Asia Minor: The Laodiceans took great pride in their prosperous banking industry, which gave them much wealth; a well-developed textile industry; and a medical establishment that had developed an eye salve with a reputation for healing all sorts of diseases and ailments. How does this background information help you to better understand and apply verse 18? Find another good example like this from Revelation 2–3, where the local setting forms the backdrop for the message the Lord was giving to the people living in the respective cities (and to the members of churches today).

3. Read through Luke 1–3 and see if you can detect any examples of the three sociolinguistic frames, or schemata, described above: typical discourses (*scripts*), event sequences (*scenarios*), or character depictions (*sketches*). See, for example, Luke 1:1–4 (the literary script for an ancient historical-biographical account), 11–13, 15, 31–33, 46–55, 59–63; 2:1–2, 9–10, 17, 28–32, 43–45, 49–50; and 3:1–3, 15–16, 22, 23–37. Note three places where some important implicit information pertaining to the sociocultural setting must be made explicit in order for your target audience to correctly understand the biblical text. Summarize this necessary information and explain why it is necessary on account of the situational frame of your own cultural setting.

4. Describe the cognitive frame (sketch) that would most likely be generated in the minds of most people in your culture when they hear the word for "shepherd" in isolation? What features of this role stand out? Now compare this mental representation with what is evoked by this same word when read in your vernacular translation of Psalm 23:1. Point out any differences and suggest why they occur (see Wilt 2002a:237–239). Next, do a similar study of the word for "cherubim"—first in isolation and then in Genesis 3:24 and Psalm 80:1 (see Wilt 2002a:41).

5. In a recent article in the *Bible Translator* ("Avoiding anachronism in OT translation," pp. 59:1:14–17), Lawrenz draws attention to the need for translators "to try to keep abreast of what has traditionally and somewhat loosely called 'biblical archeology'" (ibid.:17). Lawrenz focuses his attention on "anachronisms," which he defines as all those instances where we "impose our modern or even medieval cultural knowledge on the world of the Bible" (ibid.:14). He points out the following as "anachronisms that need correction" in many translations: tambourines, sapphire, diamond, hinges (1 Kgs. 7:50), bubonic plague, and **leprosy**. With respect to the last mentioned, Lawrenz notes the following (ibid.:16):

> The Hebrew term *sâra`at* has traditionally been translated "leprosy." The term is now used for a specific medical condition known as Hansen's disease....OT references to leprosy are anachronistic. The chief diagnostic criteria of white spots on the skin and white hair given in Lev. 13.4, 10 do not match those of Hansen's disease, where neither leprous patches not hair are white; rather they are suggestive, almost diagnostic, of leucoderma. In addition, the absence in Leviticus 13-14 of any classic symptoms of Hansen's disease—loss of sensation of the skin, wasting of fingers and toes, facial nodules and blindness—further invalidates the equation.

How do you render the term rendered "leprosy" in your language? Does this rendering reflect the same error as that pointed out by Lawrenz above? If so, what solution do you propose for making a more accurate, a more functionally equivalent translation?

6. Peter Stockwell (2002:79–80) outlines several different types of *schema management*. They are summarized below and exemplified by possible instances from the book of Acts. See if you agree with the examples given (modify them if necessary) and give one more example for each category.

   a. **knowledge restructuring:** in which new schemas are created based on old templates, as in Acts 17:22–31

   b. **schema preservation:** *reinforcement – accretion:* in which new facts strengthen and confirm existing schematic knowledge, perhaps also enlarging its scope and explanatory range, as in Acts 2:14–41

   c. **schema disruption:** in which conceptual deviance occasions misunderstanding and offers a potential challenge to communication, as in Acts 14:8–18

   d. **schema refreshment:** in which an existing schema is revised and its constituent elements and relations recast (fine-tuning, defamiliarization in literature) as in Acts 19:1–7

Stockwell calls attention to the great challenge that the existence of such schemata poses for all communicators (2002:76):

> Given the vast amount of historical context that is potentially available, and the hugeness of the imagined experience of the author and the contemporary society, and given the massive encyclopedic knowledge carried around in the heads of readers, how can we decide which bits of context are used and which are not, in a principled way? That is the background of schema poetics.

This difficulty factor is multiplied where Bible translation is concerned, and we may begin to wonder how people are able to understand the original text at all, regardless of the style of translation. What

1.6 Different situational frames of communication

do you think of the great communication gap here and how to compensate for it? Mention some possibilities that come to mind. (One increasingly popular method of cognitive contextual enrichment will be considered in detail in chapter 7.)

7. The study of sociocultural frames becomes essential in dictionary-making and when seeking lexical equivalents in the translation process. Renier de Blois is currently preparing an innovative *semantic domain* dictionary for Biblical Hebrew (see de Blois 2002). He offers the following observations on this task (de Blois 2007):

> Before we can formulate the definition of a word we have to make sure that we know what it means. Since we are dealing with languages that are no longer spoken in the same form today, we have limited resources. As we can no longer consult native speakers, the only reliable source of information is the context in which each word is used. In order to obtain this information we simply need to study each occurrence of the word of which we want to determine the meaning.
>
> In cases where the context does not provide us with sufficient information we will have to resort to methods like the study of the etymology of a word, or look at data from related languages.
>
> For certain terms there are additional resources, such as archeological data, studies of ancient agriculture, geology, zoology, etc. Once we are able to match a particular Hebrew word with a concept that has been studied as part of one of these disciplines we can freely make use of this type of information. This matching process, however, can only be done reliably after a detailed study of the context of the term in focus....
>
> Before we can study each individual term we will have to determine what the frame for the definitions for these terms should look like. Four slots:
>
> - Description (symbol =)
> - Method of preparation (symbol ◀)
> - Function (symbol ▶)
> - Connotation (symbol ≈)

The following is an example of semantic domain analysis based on one of the six Hebrew words commonly rendered as "wine" in the OT *(yayin, tirosh, chemer, 'asis, shekhar,* and *chomets)*. Work through this sample entry, checking out all of the references given to see if you agree with its application to the aspect of meaning being discussed. Then evaluate this "frame of reference" approach to the analysis and representation of meaning: How helpful is this method for increasing your understanding of biblical Hebrew? Where do you encounter some difficulties? Do you have any suggestions for improvement? (Any comments in this regard would be welcomed by Dr. de Blois at r.de.blois.@solcon.nl.)

שֵׁכָר   noun, m | שכר

Objects: Liquids; Wine

[np] = יַיִן, חֹמֶץ = alcoholic liquid; ◀ made out of dates through the process of fermentation; ▶ used as beverage, though to be avoided by Nazirites, and by priests when on duty; ≈ associated with joy and well-being, but also with drunkenness and foolishness[a] - *date-wine* (LEV. 10:9; NUM. 6:3; 28:7; DEU. 14:26; 29:5; JDG. 13:4, 7, 14; 1SA. 1:15; PSA. 69:13; PRO. 20:1; 31:4, 6; ISA. 5:11, 22 ...)

Liquids

Alcohol = יין *[Contextual Gloss English]* (LEV. 10:9; NUM.6:3; JDG. 13:4, 7, 14; 1SA. 1:15; PSA. 69:13; PRO. 20:1; 31:4, 6; ISA. 5:11, 22; 28:7 ...)

Alcohol > Wisdom; Punishment; God = יַיִן *(to move in a kind of stupor caused by God and not by) date-wine* (ISA. 29:9)

Communication date-*wine (causes people to start saying things they should not say)* (PSA. 69:13; PRO. 20:1)

Food *date-wine (as a drink)* (LEV. 10:9; NUM. 6:3; DEU. 14:26; 29:5; JDG. 13:4, 7, 14; 1SA .1:15; PSA. 69:13; PRO. 20:1; 31:4, 6; ISA. 5:11, 22; 24:9 ...)

Joy = יַיִן *date-wine (gives joy to humankind; absence of wine causes grief)* (PRO. 31:6; ISA. 24:9)

King = יַיִן *(kings are advised not to drink) date-wine* (PRO. 31:4)

Law = יַיִן, חֹמֶץ *(provisions concerning) date-wine (in the law)* (LEV. 10:9; NUM. 6:3; 28:7; DEU. 14:26; 29:5)

Nazirite = יַיִן *date-wine (forbidden to Nazirites)* (NUM. 6:3; JDG. 13:4, 7, 14)

Priesthood = יַיִן *date-wine (forbidden to priests on duty)* (LEV. 10:9)

Prophecy = יַיִן *(prophets preaching about) wine (are popular)* (MIC. 2:11)

Punishment; God = יַיִן *date-wine (withheld by God, as punishment)* (ISA. 24:9)

Sacrifice; God *date-wine (sacrificed to God)* (NUM .28:7)

Well-Being = יַיִן *date-wine (in shortage or abundance)* (ISA. 24:9)

Wisdom = יַיִן *date-wine (takes away one's understanding)* (PRO. 20:1; 31:4)

Now consider how you would translate this term for "wine" (or any of the other Hebrew terms for alcoholic drinks) in your language. Should שֵׁכָר be rendered as "date wine" at every occurrence, e.g., Prov. 20:1, 31:4? Explain why or why not with reference to your translation setting. What are some of the sociocultural and lexical problems that you encounter, not only with regard to semantic *denotation*, but also the term's *connotation*? In Zambian Tonga, for example, there is no close local equivalent (e.g., "palm wine"). The English loanword *waini* suggests a bottled Western alcoholic beverage that rich folks drink at festivals and special dinners. An initial attempt at a descriptive expression, *musinza wansaana uusaside* 'the soured juice of the wild grape', turned out to be rather awkward and unacceptable to several major church groups. What term do you use and how understandable is it to most readers/hearers?

8. Imagine that you wish to compose, produce, and direct a dramatic play based on either the temptation of Christ in Luke 4:1–13 or his rejection at Nazareth in Luke 4:16–30. Give three examples of how paralinguistic or extralinguistic factors that pertain to the original text might affect this "live" production in your language and culture.

9. What type of speech society is predominant where you live? Is it a "high-context" or "low-context" society? What is your evidence for this conclusion? How does one obtain an honest answer in a face-to-face high-context community? Does this depend on who is speaking to whom? How does this preferred mode and manner of communication affect your composition of texts, as when preaching a sermon? Teaching a children's Bible study? Translating a passage of Scripture? What difference is there if the text must be prepared in writing rather than presented orally?

10. How does ancient ancestral religion (if you come from a non-Western society) or modern secular humanism (if you come from the West) influence religious communication in your society? Give two examples from some passage or book of Scripture of the pressure to distort. What can be done about this when preparing a Bible translation nowadays? Illustrate your answer with a case study that you know of.

1.6 Different situational frames of communication

11. Robert Dooley takes up some of the issues considered in the preceding exercises in much greater detail from a cognitive linguistic perspective and the Mbyá Guarani translation of Brazil. Study the following extract from Dooley 2005:3–6 (used by permission; this entire article is highly recommended) and prepare an evaluation for the purposes of group discussion: How do the ideas presented here modify your viewpoint on translation in terms of both goals and procedures? Some of these notions will be relevant later when we undertake a closer examination of a literary-functional approach to the translation task, to the degree possible in a given communication setting.

> Comprehending a text involves constructing a resultant mental representation of its meaning. This process is incremental, requiring trial and error, hypothesizing, confirmation and revision, and probabilistic conclusions. There is much that we do not know about mental representations, including the specific neurological form that they take and the best way to model them. ...
>
> **A reader's resultant mental representation of a text is not a mere copy of the text with its linguistic structures, but converts the text from a linguistic object to a conceptual object.**
>
> The word resultant [above] is important, because it seems clear that the reader initially does use the wording of the text as input to comprehension; but then, as major syntactic and textual boundaries are reached, the specific surface and semantic details are generally integrated into a more abstract form... In this way, the resultant mental representation that the reader takes away from a text is abstracted away from the linguistic form. The notion of a mental representation can be used to state a major translation goal, having to do with faithfulness to the source text.
>
> **Text-based approaches to translation generally indicate that the most important thing to be transferred is the mental representation that the author intended to convey by means of the text...**
>
> Whereas the reader's "resultant mental representation" is a product of the comprehension process, the author's "intended mental representation" is what presumably is in the author's mind as he or she approaches the task of wording. No one can see inside another's mind, but to the extent that competent exegetes agree, we can often come up with a reasonable idea of the author's communicative goals.
>
> On the other end of text comprehension, we can sometimes do testing to discern the resultant mental representation that target readers come up with. In my experience, this isn't easy; it might mean asking for a retelling of the text some time after the text was read or heard (to reduce the influence of "disposable" features) and then doing a discourse analysis on the result. Even when we can assess mental representations in the source and target situations, there is the question of what parameters should be used in comparing the two and how closely they should correspond along those parameters. For mental representations can be viewed on any level of detail, since they include different kinds and levels of meaning that readers are intended to "get from" the text.
>
> The notion of intent in translation is critically important: translations differ according to the kind and level of meaning that their "clients" want transferred, as well as whether the message should be construed in relation to its original context or to the target context. Despite these complexities, to the degree that we can compare the mental representations of author and readers, we can take [the principle stated above] as a general standard for faithfulness in translation.
>
> Given the text-based notions discussed above, and the use of natural target-language discourse features as in some sense the default choice for translation, we can use the following as a general schema for describing a given translation:
>
> **In a given translation, discourse features follow natural target-language patterns rather than source language patterns, except under the following conditions:**

(a) special condition 1
(b) special condition 2
...
(x) general constraint: all discourse features should be compatible with the author's intended mental representation.

That is, in addition to the general constraint that all discourse features be compatible with the author's intended mental representation, a translation may have one or more special conditions which constrain the use of natural target-language features. The special conditions may be of different types, having to do with such things as reader confidence in the translation, intended liturgical uses, or highly valued academic or literary qualities. For Bible translations, a common special condition has to do with the possibility of comparing the translation with a high-prestige version that exists in the same or a different language.

In the general constraint, discourse features are required to be compatible with the author's intended mental representation rather than, in stronger terms, "to be an exact expression" of it. This is because, according to [the preceding principle], not all discourse features (or functions) are essential ones. All features and functions, however, should be compatible with [the author's intended mental representation]; that is, they should never be contrary to it and they should be used to signal it when needed.

Based on this general schema, the strategy for rendering discourse features in the Guarani translation is as follows:

In Guarani, discourse features follow natural target-language patterns rather than source-language patterns, subject to the following constraints:

(a) they do not reduce reader confidence in the translation, and
(b) they are compatible with the author's intended mental representation.

Thus the translation in Mbyá Guarani has only one special condition, dealing with reader confidence in the translation.

The main point here is that, among the mother-tongue "clients" of the Guarani translation, there were two major goals with more or less equal weight: biblically unsophisticated readers need to have a reasonable chance of understanding the content, and biblically more sophisticated ones need to have confidence in the translation.

Tito Lahaye complements the preceding from a more specific oratorical-artistic perspective, also with reference to the cultural setting of the Guarani people (2003:406–407):

Most languages have great artistic richness in them, and these features must not be ignored when undertaking a Bible translation. Translations would be better understood if matching genres from the target language were used to render the source text, especially when it contains many genres equivalent to songs, prayers, and wisdom materials found in the Bible....All translations have the capacity to change, or at least to influence, indigenous cultures by bringing in "foreign" or new ideas and concepts, But where cultures have made the transition to Christianity they will find that, where materials representing special features of their language have been considered and incorporated in a Bible translation, that translation will be more acceptable and meaningful.

Can you give an example or two from your own translation setting to illustrate some of the important observations of the preceding quote?

12. The sociocultural frames of a particular ethnic group together comprise what is popularly known as their worldview (see section 1.5). It is essential for communicators to carefully investigate the

principal defining features of the worldview of the people with whom they wish to communicate. This knowledge must then be factored into any communication strategy that is designed to convey any new, different, or contra-cultural information to them. For example, how might the seven characteristics of an African worldview listed below (Adeyemo 2007) compare with key aspects of a biblical Hebrew frame of reference in a passage such as Isaiah 44:6–23? Note the main similarities and contrasts.

   a. Multiplicity of spiritual beings including ancestors.
   b. Essential connection and interaction between beings.
   c. Absence of dichotomy between the sacred and the secular.
   d. Religious interpretation of whatever happens – close to fatalism.
   e. Cosmic struggle between good and evil forces.
   f. Centrality of man in the community of the living and the dead.
   g. Belief in availability of power to manipulate and control malevolent forces.

Now suggest how this knowledge might affect one's translation of the Isaiah text referred to above. If one cannot reshape the text itself, how about expanding the paratext? Try, for example, to compose a hypothetical explanatory note that would seek to clarify what the biblical text says in Isa. 44:6–8.

How does the worldview of the people for whom you are translating, whether African or not, compare with that summarized above?

Point out any salient differences, and suggest how these might affect the understanding of average readers/hearers with respect to some specific passages of Scripture.

13. Eco (2003:82) has observed,

    [T]ranslation is always a shift, not between two languages but between two cultures—or two encyclopedias. A translator must take into account rules that are not strictly linguistic but, broadly speaking, cultural....[C]ertain texts of Shakespeare and Jane Austen are not fully comprehensible to a contemporary English reader who does not have an understanding of the vocabulary and the cultural background of their authors.

Assuming that the same thing is true for many biblical texts, what solutions to this communications gap can you propose? (Of course, this problem needs to be addressed on several different levels.)

1.6.2 Conversational frames

As has already been suggested, there are a number of distinct, but always interrelated, components that make up the *framework* or situational setting of any communication event. They all factor in to form an individual's cognitive environment (including the individual's current mental state, which governs the entire act of interpretation) from sensory reception to conceptual and emotive reaction.

It is arguable that a conversation, or dialogic discourse, is the most fundamental mode of communication in the Scriptures. There are several reasons for this:

1. Much of the Scripture was probably originally composed in oral form.

2. Most of the Scripture was composed to be received in an oral-aural manner.

3. Most people then (as now) accessed the Scriptures aurally.

Many of the various sociolinguistic elements of any conversation have already been mentioned, but in this section we will view them from a speech-act perspective. A *speech act* is defined as an utterance, or portion of one, that has a particular communicative goal, termed an *illocution*. A *speech event* is a sequence of individual speech acts.

The primary conversational constituents may be remembered by the acronym S-P-E-A-K-I-N-G (see Wilt 2002a:55–56):

Setting: the physical scene (time, place, environment, weather, and other contextual circumstances), including any actual or potential factors that might create a disturbance during the process of message transmission or a distortion in the quality of the message.

Participants: the speaker and hearer (addressee and audience, producer and processors) and their cognitive environments, noting in particular any contrastive, alien, or antithetical features in their outlook on life or value system, including their social status and psychological background in relation to each other, such as attitudes, feelings, opinions, and current level of interpersonal rapport.

Ends: the primary communication goal(s) of the participants, including conventionally expected and recognized options and outcomes as well as any implicit objectives.

Act sequence: the order and arrangement of the progression of speech acts that constitute the total speech event (text act), along with any accompanying non-verbal types of communicative action (both paralinguistic and extralinguistic).

Key: the overall tone, manner, attitude, or psychological and emotive spirit of the participants that characterizes the prevailing social atmosphere in which the communication takes place.

Instrumentality: the sensory channel (medium), communicative code, and linguistic sub-type (i.e., dialect or register/sociolect) that are activated during the speech event.

Norms: the expected or approved standards of interpersonal interaction and interpretation as determined by the preceding factors; namely, the levels of social formality, situational register, and conventional speech styles.

Genres: the specific conventional patterns of formal spoken or written discourse, including their associated structural categories and stylistic devices, along with any accompanying non-verbal features, such as stereotyped hand gestures during the public performance of a folktale, song, proverb, or riddle.

> » How would you rank these eight conversational elements in terms of their relative importance?
>
> » For example, what would you say are the top three influences when conversing in YL?
>
> » Are there any missing factors that you can suggest? Or perhaps you can provide an even better summary.
>
> » To what degree do you consider the elements of S-P-E-A-K-I-N-G when you translate the dialogue portions of the Bible? Why is it important to do so?

These different aspects of S-P-E-A-K-I-N-G must all be carefully investigated in relation to one another when attempting to delineate or specify the cognitive frame that surrounds a particular act of communication. This includes any conversation recorded in the Bible that one wishes to study exegetically—or a sequence of conversations involving a single central character, such as Joseph in Genesis 37–48. First, the passage must be examined from the sociocultural perspective that governed its *original* conception, intention, representation, and transmission. Only after fully analyzing this initial setting, to the extent possible, can one adopt a *transferred* viewpoint that represents the same text in light of a different linguistic and situational environment.

At this point, then, we may zero in upon some of the major communicative "ends." There are two complementary ways of investigating text goals, that is, in addition to a more general functional framework, which has already been introduced.

1. It is very helpful for carrying out a detailed pragmatic analysis to adopt a speech-act perspective (see section 1.6.2.1).

2. One also needs to carefully examine prominent features of what may be termed the "latent discourse" (see section 1.6.2.2)—that is, any implicit non-verbal communication.

All of these contextualizing frames that are operative during a communication event will serve to influence, or even to determine, the ultimate goal or purpose for which a given text is composed and transmitted.

1.6.2.1 Speech (text) acts

Whenever we converse with someone, we not only *say* something, we also *do* something. Our words convey a certain amount of content but, at the same time, they also perform a particular function; that is, they carry out a specific goal or goals that the speaker intended during the speech act under consideration. All too often what we say also has unintended results, for example, when unknown to us a careless comment hurts someone we are speaking to or who just happens to be on the scene. In this section, however, we will focus upon deliberate speech acts.

Speech-act analysis offers another way of analyzing the diverse goals that motivate and characterize all communication events. There is a special emphasis upon the type of action that is both expressed and effected by the performative verbs of direct speech in a discourse, whether these verbs are actually mentioned explicitly or left implicit within the text. Performative verbs indicate the special aim of a speaker when uttering a certain segment of speech ("utterance unit"). Some examples are: promise, threaten, warn, request, order, deny, complain, admit, explain, apologize, describe, urge, invite, rebuke, encourage. Can you add three more important performative verbs to this list?

There are different classes of speech act. These differ, of course, from one language to the next. Speech acts may occur individually in sequence, but they are frequently combined or overlap with each other in written or oral discourse. Notice that these speech acts normally vary according to their relative strength or intensity, especially when uttered aloud when they may be vocally modified, for example, ask < appeal < entreat, with increasing intensity of tone, volume, and/or stress. Often the textual context, content, and interpersonal dynamics of the direct discourse segment being investigated will clearly indicate the type and quality of speech act(s) being effected thereby, as in "John *said*…, 'You brood of vipers! Who warned you to flee from the coming wrath? Produce fruit in keeping with repentance' " (Luke 3:7–8, where "said" = rebuke + warning + command). In some languages, these differentiations may have to be made explicit or distinguished from one another.

The English language seems to be relatively rich in the number of explicit performative verbs available to convey different communicative goals. Other languages may have fewer, but the same functional variations can usually be expressed in other ways. For example, in the Nyanja language, they can be expressed by:

- verb conjunction (*ananka nam'dandaulira* "she proceeded and complained to him" = she protested to him)

- cognate combinations (*anam'lirira ndi kulira* "she cried for him with crying" = she grieved over him)

- verbal affixes (*anam'dzudzulitsa* "she criticized greatly him" = she castigated him)

- verb qualifiers (*anam'teteza kotheratu* "she defended him completely" = she vindicated him)

- figures of speech (*anam'phika polankhula* "she cooked him when speaking" = she censured him),

- idioms (*anam'dyetsa moto* "she made him eat fire" = she severely reprimanded him)

- ideophones (*anam'chititsa zyoli-zyoli ndi mau ake* "she caused him to look down-down," as in great shame, by means of her words).

Fairly standard terms are used by speech act theoreticians:

1. **Locution** refers to the portion of direct speech that is cited.

2. **Illocutionary force** refers to the functional purpose of that particular utterance, that is, considered from the point of view of the speaker (e.g., rebuke, warn, command with reference to Luke 3:7–8).

3. **Perlocution** indicates the desired or intended effect the speaker hopes to achieve by it, for example, to encourage listeners to repent. (In Luke 3:10–11 was John's purpose actually accomplished?)

Möller (2001:366) describes and exemplifies these distinctions as follows (citing James Austin):

> [A locution] is defined as 'the performance of an act *of* saying something', and illocution is 'the performance of an act *in* saying something' and a perlocution is 'the performance of an act *by* saying something'. Thus we can, for instance, 'distinguish the locutionary act "he *said* that…" from the illocutionary act "he *argued* that…" and the perlocutionary act "he *convinced* me that…" ' This distinction is a useful conception in that it helps us differentiate between what a prophet *said* – for instance, 'the end has come upon my people Israel; I will never again pass them by' (Amos 8:2; NRSV); what he was *doing* in making that statement (i.e., issuing a threat or declaring a verdict…); and what the *effects* of that speech act were (or might have been).

Can you cite and label another biblical example that illustrates the same three distinctions?

There are seven major speech act categories commonly represented by verbs in English. They are as follows, along with examples of each:

1. **Assertives:** advocate, affirm, claim, comment, concede, declare, describe, expound, explain, assure, inform, deny

2. **Evaluatives:** analyze, appraise, certify, characterize, estimate, figure, judge, condemn, censure, commend, praise, blame, agree

3. **Directives:** command, urge, preach, exhort, advise, warn, ask, appeal, request, beg, implore, order, caution, counsel, prohibit

4. **Expressives:** exult, apologize, regret, repent, mourn, love, hate, like, loathe

5. **Commissives:** promise, vow, pledge, commit to, dedicate, swear, undertake

6. **Transformatives:** bless, curse, baptize, commission, ordain, marry, excommunicate

7. **Interactives:** greet, bid farewell, introduce, prompt, inhibit, interrupt, conclude

Evaluate the preceding categorization in terms of its overall usefulness to you. Then propose any corrections or modifications that you feel are necessary.

» Are you able to express these different verbal actions, whether general or specific, in your language?

» Which terms are not available on a one-to-one basis in YL? In such cases, how might you express an equivalent concept, for example, through the use of a phrasal idiom or figure of speech?

The first four of these categories would appear to be the most important as far as most communication events in the Bible are concerned. However, some of the others are prominent in certain texts and settings (e.g., commissives and transformatives in Jesus' speech). There may be some disagreement regarding the classification of the specific English verbs in the list; their equivalents in YL may also be disputed. But the point of making these distinctions is not necessarily completeness or precision; it is rather to be able to recognize the great diversity of discourse actions that may occur in the form of direct speech, both in the Scriptures and in all other types of religious communication. It is also important to take note of any strongly felt emotions and attitudes that are typically expressed along with these different speech acts (e.g., condemn, implore, apologize).

For reflection, research, and response:

1. Drawing upon Luke 5–10, write down at least one good example (with its reference) of each of the seven major categories of speech act. What is the specific *illocutionary* action and *perlocutionary* aim in each case? Record any *emotion* or *attitude* that is either implicitly suggested by the words spoken or overtly mentioned in the cotext (e.g., in the "quote margin," as in Luke 2:34, 38).

2. Reconsider the examples you gave in exercise 1 from the perspective of your own cultural setting. Do you notice any potential problem areas in conveying these passages accurately and dynamically in YL—that is, with respect to the specific speech acts and communicative functions of a particular text over and above its referential content?

3. With the help of a good commentary or reliable study Bible, apply the various components of the acronym S-P-E-A-K-I-N-G to Luke 4:1–13. After thoroughly studying this passage, what can you say about its overall conversational setting with reference to the situation, the participants, speech ends, and so forth? What relevant implications for translating this text in YL become apparent through this type of analysis? Mention three concrete examples.

4. Analyze the following familiar dialogue portion from Acts 8:26–39 (RSV) according to the eight situational factors of S-P-E-A-K-I-N-G. How does such an analysis help you to understand the biblical text better and then to translate it accordingly?

> [26] But an angel of the Lord said to Philip, "Rise and go toward the south to the road that goes down from Jerusalem to Gaza." This is a desert road. [27] And he rose and went. And behold, an Ethiopian, a eunuch, a minister of the Candace, queen of the Ethiopians, in charge of all her treasure, had come to Jerusalem to worship [28] and was returning; seated in his chariot, he was reading the prophet Isaiah. [29] And the Spirit said to Philip, "Go up and join this chariot." [30] So Philip ran to him, and heard him reading Isaiah the prophet, and asked, "Do you understand what you are reading?" [31] And he said, "How can I, unless some one guides me?" And he invited Philip to come up and sit with him. [32] Now the passage of the scripture which he was reading was this:
>
>> "As a sheep led to the slaughter
>> or a lamb before its shearer is dumb,
>> so he opens not his mouth.
>> [33] In his humiliation justice was denied him.
>> Who can describe his generation?
>> For his life is taken up from the earth."

> ³⁴ And the eunuch said to Philip, "About whom, pray, does the prophet say this, about himself or about some one else?" ³⁵ Then Philip opened his mouth, and beginning with this scripture he told him the good news of Jesus. ³⁶ And as they went along the road they came to some water, and the eunuch said, "See, here is water! What is to prevent my being baptized?" ³⁷ [The RSV footnote here says, "**8.37** Other ancient authorities add all or most of verse 37, And Philip said, 'If you believe with all your heart, you may.' And he replied, 'I believe that Jesus Christ is the Son of God.'"] ³⁸ And he commanded the chariot to stop, and they both went down into the water, Philip and the eunuch, and he baptized him. ³⁹ And when they came up out of the water, the Spirit of the Lord caught up Philip; and the eunuch saw him no more, and went on his way rejoicing.

5. Compare the seven categories of speech act listed in section 1.6.2.1 with the following, proposed by Ron Ross (in Wilt 2002a:140):

   a. Acts of **asserting:** accuse, advocate, affirm, claim, comment, concede, conclude

   b. Acts of **evaluating:** analyze, appraise, certify, characterize, estimate, figure, judge

   c. Acts of **opining:** accept, acclaim, affirm, agree, acquiesce, apologize, blame, reprimand

   d. Acts of **stipulating:** abbreviate, characterize, choose, classify, describe, define, designate

   e. Acts of **requesting:** appeal, ask, beg, bid, enjoin, implore, order, request, solicit

   f. Acts of **suggesting:** admonish, advise, advocate, caution, counsel, exhort, propose

   g. Acts of **authorizing** abolish, abrogate, accept, adopt, approve, bless, condemn

   h. Acts of **committing** (accept, assume, assure, commit, dedicate, promise, undertake, swear

   What similarities and differences do you notice? Combine these two lists and compose your own list of categories, one that is more adapted to your language as well as the cultural setting and speech conventions of your people.

6. Suggest the speech acts (including the illocution plus perlocution) and accompanying emotions or attitudes manifested in Jonah 3:4 (the shortest sermon in Scripture): "Forty more days and Nineveh will be overturned!" How would you render this passage in YL in order to generate the same overall communicative force and connotative implication?

7. How would you classify the following utterance in terms of its specific *genre* and *speech act*: "As surely as the LORD lives…" (e.g., Judg. 8:19, 1 Sam. 26:10, Ru. 3:13, 1 Kgs. 2:4, Jer. 4:2)? How do you translate this expression with literary functional equivalence in YL (see Chhetri 2008)?

   Now examine the speech acts that *follow* this initial expression in each of the passages listed above. Do you observe any *functional* distinctions? Do these need to be *marked* somehow in your translation? If so, give examples for each of the passages concerned (along with back-translations into English for comparative class discussion)—for example, 1 Sam 25:27: "As surely as the LORD lives and as you live, *I wish that* your enemies and all those who want to harm you would end up like Nabal!" (cf. CEV, GNT).

8. Try to classify the different speech acts that occur in the dramatic dialogue of John 9. Which ones are the most difficult to reproduce in YL?

9. At times a speech act perspective has immediate translational implications, for example, the term παράκλητος 'paraclete' with reference to the Holy Spirit (e.g., John 15:26). Should this word be rendered with primary reference to its illocutionary intention or its perlocutionary outcome, that is, "Advocate" or "Defender" versus "Comforter" or "Encourager"? In John's semantically rich discourse, probably both are in mind. Can you think of another term like this in the Gospel of John?

1.6.2.2 Latent discourse

The term *latent discourse* refers to information that is communicated *implicitly* during a conversation—that is, unexpressed but conceptually present with the words that are overtly uttered. A great deal of

such underlying, **non-verbalized** meaning is conveyed during human speech by cognitive inference; we always understand more than we actually hear. As was noted earlier, the amount of latent discourse is especially great in a high-context (low-text) culture, where people do not feel the need to explicitly spell out many of the details regarding a certain topic of communication.

There are three main types of latent discourse: *presupposition*, *implication*, and *implicature*. All three may vary in their manifestation and implementation according to the specific cultural and sociolinguistic context at hand. They may be defined as follows (for a much more comprehensive study, see Stockwell 2002, chapter 6):

1. **Presupposition** is background ("encyclopedic") information that a speaker takes for granted as being known by the listeners or that an author assumed to be true and/or well understood when he wrote the text. Normally the writer assumes that such knowledge is held in common with the readers and, therefore, does not need to be stated explicitly because it would simply bore the readers, confuse them with too many details, or detract from the main subject under discussion.

2. **Implication** is information or an appeal for action that a speaker/author wishes to convey only indirectly, without actually spelling it out. The utterance, coupled with the situational context, or social setting, as well as the current interpersonal circumstances, is usually enough to suggest to listeners what they are expected to grasp through inference. The speaker/author may want them to *understand* something (as in the case of an informative intertextual allusion or a conventional euphemism for the sake of politeness), *feel* something (e.g., by mentioning a powerful cultural symbol), and/or *do* something—that is, be motivated to some specific action.

   In the example "Today in the town of David a Savior has been born to you; he is Christ, the Lord. This will be a sign to you" (Luke 2:11–12a), there are several important *presuppositions* behind the angel's announcement, important theological information that most Jews, even shepherds, should have known from the Scriptures: The Lord had long ago promised to send a Savior-Messiah; he would be the divine Son of God; he would originate from Bethlehem; he was coming to liberate all people, especially the poor and oppressed, from their spiritual misery and moral servitude to Satan. The *implications* for the shepherds in this setting are obvious. First, there is the fact that the prophecies about the Messiah are now in the process of being fulfilled. God's Word is credible and reliable. There is also an associated action-related motivation, which is that they are to immediately travel to Bethlehem and see whether this announcement is true or not. Then upon verification they are to go and tell the joyous good news to others (see Luke 2:20). Notice that the angel did not explicitly command them to leave their flocks and rush off to town; instead, this imperative implication is derived from his words in the context at hand.

3. **Implicature** is a more specific sort of appeal for thought, or especially action, that the author wishes to convey by seeming to break or violate one of the *cooperative principles* ("rules of verbal engagement") when communicating with someone. Thus, whenever we notice an utterance that sounds truncated, misplaced, or even inappropriate in its circumstantial context, we try—if we assume that that speaker is genuinely trying to communicate with us—to interpret the communication by going

below the surface of the text to determine what other meaning the words might have in that particular situation. The speaker desires to communicate more information than the words actually say and, for one reason or another, decides to depend on the situational context in order to do so. Therefore, knowledge derived from the extralinguistic environment or social setting of discourse is usually necessary for someone to convey meaning by means of implicatures.

The following are the four main "cooperative principles" (speech maxims) that have been found to apply quite widely in a Western society, at least in a formal discourse setting:

1. **Quantity:** Contribute as much information as is needed—not too much or too little.

2. **Quality:** Do not tell lies or provide unsubstantiated information.

3. **Manner:** Avoid ambiguity and obscurity; rather, be brief and orderly.

4. **Relevance:** Make your speech appropriate and applicable to the hearer's situation

There are, of course, many exceptions and qualifications that could be made to this set of practical guidelines, but as a rule of thumb they can help provide a rough analysis of a particular speech event.

An example of this type of latent discourse is Luke 4:22b: "All spoke well of him and were amazed at the gracious words that came from his mouth. They said, 'Is not this Joseph's son?' " Did the people not know who Jesus of Nazareth really was? Yes, they did, or so they thought. Then why did they ask such a question then? It is of course a rhetorical question, which is a question that always carries an implicature or two along with it. Thus the people on the scene were not requesting information—it was not a question of identity. Rather, they were, in this case, communicating an attitude and opinion: "Who does this fellow think he is, claiming the Spirit of God and the mission of the Messiah, as he has just done by what he has said?" (2:18–19, 21b). "He should not be bragging—he may be guilty of blasphemy!" Some who uttered the question may actually have made an added action implicature: "We ought to do something to prevent this fellow from speaking like this in the synagogue of God! Away with him!" (cf. 2:28–29).

» How does this speech act turn out when rendered literally in YL?

» How can the question be marked or transformed in order to convey its intended implicature?

Some psycholinguists claim that the most important of the cooperative maxims is relevance. They say that we process, or conceptually decode, all verbal discourse according to the principle of relevance, which is composed of the following pair of interacting, contextually determined conditions or considerations (see Gutt 1992, chapter 2):

1. **Efficiency:** what it costs mentally to interpret a particular utterance.

2. **Effectiveness:** how much is gained conceptually by that information.

There is a sort of mental balancing act of cost versus gain going on during communication. It governs how much effort we are willing or able to put into any act of interpretation versus how much we expect to get out of it in terms of cognitive, emotive, or volitional benefit. Such benefit involves a positive alteration in how much we *know*, how well we *feel*, and what we need to *do*.

The principle of relevance can serve as a handy guide during biblical interpretation. That is to say, we should choose the interpretation that best fits the immediate and the remote textual context as well as the presumed extratextual setting of communication. What sense did the original author determine would be relevant for his intended audience in order to most enrich their cognitive environment with regard to thought or behavior? What did they really need to understand here or to do in their particular situation for their ultimate spiritual good (i.e., to be in a right relationship with God)?

Interpersonal communication is a rather complicated procedure, as we all know from everyday experience. First of all, if people are serious about communicating—that is, if they are not deliberately violating ("flouting") one of the cooperative principles to convey some implicatures—then they may expect to gain from any verbal message what they must spend by way of mental effort to interpret it. Normally, this is how things work. For example, this is the way we discern and apply all the OT references, paraphrases, and allusions that are found in the poetic songs of praise uttered by Mary, Zecharias, and Simeon in Luke 1–2. Our understanding of the text is greatly enriched through our recognition of these different types of biblical text-shadowing, but only if we do not have to put too much effort into the hermeneutical process.

On the other hand, where either the textual or situational context clearly indicates that the speaker is deliberately transgressing one or more of the basic communication principles, then one must determine *why*. Is he deliberately trying to lie, hide something, or confuse me? Is he a foreigner who simply does not know the rules of speaking my language? Or is he doing this as a rhetorical (persuasive) device in order to communicate his meaning in a more forceful, but indirect manner (i.e., so that I get more benefit from his message)? Alternatively, he may be using an indirect, non-normal way of speaking in order to perform some other communicative action, such as to talk about a difficult, embarrassing, or potentially dangerous subject (i.e., as a euphemism) or, in a much different situation, to express the inexpressible; namely, something about the wondrous works or nature of God. (This option is usually made clear from the sociocultural setting of speech or the circumstances that govern the purpose of the discourse.)

For reflection, research, and response:

1. Do the four "cooperative principles"—*quantity, quality, manner,* and *relevance*—seem to apply in your cultural setting? Do you have any additions, deletions, or modifications to propose with regard to these four to make them more applicable locally? What happens when a person ignores these unwritten rules of conversation? Can you give an example of a situation in which this happened? What was the result?

2. When Mary responded to the angel standing before her (Luke 1:37–38a), her words "For nothing is impossible with God" and "I am the Lord's servant [δούλη 'female slave']" do not seem to be related at all to what he announced to her. What does this have to do with the promise of giving birth to the Messiah? In this context, by her reply Mary is simply stating her belief in and acceptance of the Lord's plan as revealed by Gabriel. "O.K.," she says in effect, "I am ready to play my part, provided that God enables me to do this" (see v. 38b). Studying the notion of the Lord's servant/slave in a number of OT texts helps to clarify what Mary meant by her reply. Does "servant" work in YL in Luke 1:38? What about "slave"? Would that be more appropriate, or less so? Explain your answer.

3. What implication or implicature do you find in Jonah's prayer in Jonah 4:3: "Now, O LORD, take away my life, for it is better for me to die than to live" (NIV)? Is a literal rendering of this text clear in YL? If not, how can you express Jonah's intended meaning more naturally?

4. Find at least one good example of each of the three types of latent discourse (presupposition, implication and implicature) in Luke 17–18. Explain any problems of interpretation in these passages and tell how you would clarify things in your language – namely, the implicit sense and significance that is necessary in order for people to understand the text.

5. Possibly another type of "latent discourse" is the kind that involves deliberate literary *ambiguity*—that is, where the author intends two (or more) senses to be understood for the same term or longer expression since both fit well in the present context. John is fond of this technique (e.g., 3:3 ἄνωθεν – "born again/from above"). Here is an example from Paul (Col. 1:7): διὰ τὸ ἔχειν με ἐν τῇ καρδίᾳ ὑμᾶς -- "because I have you in my heart" or "because you have me in your heart." Do both translations fit the context of

Col. 1:7? Does one seem to fit better than the other? Can you reproduce this ambiguity in YL? If not, how will you render this passage? What about John 3:3—how do you propose handling that ambiguity?

6. As you study Luke 5:24, 31–32, 34–35, use a *relevance* approach in order to select the most situationally appropriate interpretation. Summarize your line of reasoning in each case.

7. Study the Luke 7 references listed below in their immediate cotext and determine why these words are spoken. Is the speaker trying to communicate something to the hearer(s) over and above what the words of direct speech actually say? What does the text imply? Is there any hidden meaning involved? Is the speaker attempting to influence the listener(s) to think or do something special? Would the words sound strange or inappropriate in your language and cultural setting? If so, explain why. Then tell how you might reword the utterance to convey the intended sense.

    a. "I tell you, I have not found such great faith even in Israel." (7:9)

    b. "Don't cry." (7:13)

    c. "Go back and report to John what you have seen and heard...." (7:22)

    d. "Blessed is the man who does not fall away on account of me." (7:23)

    e. "What did you go out into the desert to see?" (7:24)

    f. "We played the flute for you, and you did not dance." (7:32)

    g. "He has a demon." (7:33)

    h. "Here is a glutton and a drunkard...." (7:34)

    i. "Do you see this woman?" (7:44)

    j. "Who is this who even forgives sins?" (7:49)

    k. "Your faith has saved you; go in peace." (7:50)

8. Study the 2003 article by Graham Ogden entitled "Literary Allusions in Isaiah," in particular pages 320–322. Observe how a complete understanding of the "Cyrus Song" of Isaiah 44:28–45:13 relates to the story of Moses in Exodus 6–8. How did the writer of this Isaiah passage use the Exodus account to create "relevance" for his readers and lead them to an understanding of the Persian King Cyrus as a "New Moses?" How would you make these same relevant connections clear for Bible readers today? What can be done to enlighten the *hearers* of this text?

1.6.3 Literary frames

There are three major literary frames, or environments, that may have some formal or semantic influence upon a particular biblical text: the frames of *genre* (text type), of *intertext* (prior text), and of *cotext* (adjacent text). These distinct literary environments need to be carefully studied in order to arrive at a more complete understanding of any pericope under investigation.

Every coherent independent or semi-independent segment of text may be classified as belonging to a particular genre (i.e., narrative, genealogy, eschatological prophecy, instruction concerning sacrifices, thanksgiving psalm, hortatory admonition). But the most basic genre distinction in literature is that of prose and poetry.

1.6 Different situational frames of communication

> » What are some of the principal stylistic features that distinguish prose and poetry, whether in English or in your language?

> » How do you designate these two macrogenres in YL?

Since this subject will be considered much more fully in lesson 4, we do not need to dwell on it here. We simply take note here of the fact that the formal characteristics manifested by a given text are determined by its genre, for example, by whether the discourse is organized according to: concerns of time and place, a *cause-and-effect argument*, major and minor topics, a particular purpose, or in some other conventionalized way. The question of genre, or text type, is one of the first and foremost issues that must be answered when carrying out any literary analysis and when deciding how to translate a text into another language. It is also important to keep in mind the fact that many biblical passages, especially narrative texts, consist of a principal discourse type that incorporates one or more secondary genres. This is particularly true where direct speech is involved.

An *intertext* is a pre-existent text, usually no longer than a sentence or two, which a subsequent document incorporates for the sake of positive or negative reflection, that is, to support the present writer's opinion or to criticize the earlier writer's position on some issue. The incorporated text may be an exact quotation, or it may take the form of a paraphrase (termed an *allusion* or *echo*, depending on the degree of paraphrase). The source (*pre-text*) of an intertext may be oral or written, religious or secular, personal or public. In this workbook, we are primarily interested in biblical intertexts: other passages of Scripture that a given text directly or indirectly refers to. The original passage that an intertext derives from must be carefully investigated in order to determine how the corresponding words were used by the initial author with regard to form, content, and purpose. The later writer may use these same words, or a paraphrase of them, with a somewhat different meaning or purpose in mind. The current author cites or alludes to the pre-text as a way of helping him to cognitively frame the reader's understanding of the discourse that he is currently presenting, thus providing a relevant background of meaning for interpretation. For example, the different Bible passages cited in the exercises of this workbook enable readers to practice or apply some exegetical or translational principle.

The *cotext* (or nearby *intra*text) of a passage refers to the adjacent texts that come either before or after the one under study. The material that precedes is of special importance because an author normally develops his story, argument, description, or prophecy in a sequential, cumulative way from the beginning of a book to its end. Especially noteworthy is the pericope that comes immediately before the text at hand. The analyst must ask, How are the two passages related in terms of form, content, and/or function? How is the ending of the prior passage marked by formal means? How is the beginning of the current text marked? And how has the author effected a transition between the two sections? Does this represent a major break in the book or only a minor one, and what is the literary evidence for such a conclusion? How do the various available versions of the Bible signal this division? Simply by a paragraph format marker, a new section with heading, a new chapter, or by some other convention? If the boundary is not clearly marked, what can be done to make it more perceptible for the reader, and especially the hearer, of the text? Such structural breaks and divisions provide an important textual frame that helps the passage under study to be understood properly; namely, as one unit of discourse being related to another and integrated within a larger compositional whole.

For reflection, research, and response:

1. Study Mark 11:1–11 with the three literary frames of genre, intertext, and cotext in mind. Note the narrative context in particular. Where in the book does this chapter occur? What has taken place in the account prior this chapter (especially 10:32–52)? What happens afterwards (e.g., in 11:12–33)? What is the significance of the quotation found in 11:9–10. What does the study of these interrelated passages contribute to our understanding of Mark 1:1–11?

2. The cotext becomes very important when interpreting certain problematic or controversial terms, phrases, or entire passages within a given book of the Bible. At times, exegetes and translators may

not even realize that there is a difficulty or a hermeneutical alternative that needs to be considered in the text. In the closing "prayer pericope" of James (5:13–18), for example, most commentators and versions construe the verbs ἀσθενέω and κάμνω in vv. 14–15 to refer to physical sickness/illness. However, this interpretation does not seem to fit either the near or far cotext within this epistle—for example, the reference to "confessing sins" in v. 16 or "wandering from the truth" in v. 19. Throughout his letter, James stresses the importance of a strong, active faith as opposed to a weak, non-responsive commitment to Christ and his fellowship. Thus, in 5:14–16, one could argue that the apostle is actually referring to spiritual (and/or moral) weakness/sickness. What does your reading of James as a whole lead you to conclude about this issue?

Does a wider contextual lexical study shed some light on these two options? Check a Greek concordance for usage of the verb ἀσθενέω and the related noun ἀσθενής *in the epistolary literature* (in the Gospels, there is a clear emphasis on physical illness). Are these terms primarily used literally or with a figurative (metaphoric) sense? How do you know?

Finally, consult the two other occurrences of κάμνω in Hebrews 12:3 and Revelation 2:3. The usage of ἰάομαι in 1 Peter 2:24 is also pertinent to this study. Of course, it is possible that James is referring to *both* physical *and* spiritual sickness/healing? What do you think? Give reasons for your hermeneutical preference here. You might also want to consider the comparative literary nature of James's writing: Does his style manifest more, or less, figurative usage as he deals with the various faith-tests of his epistle? What direction does that lead you in so far as this debatable passage is concerned?

3. Make a list of some of the important intertexts (quotations and allusions) in Hebrews 8. Give three examples of how these intertextual references serve to "frame," or specify, the author's argument in this chapter. (Also note how chapter 8 relates to chapters 7 and 9 in the author's overall argument for the preeminence of Christ.) Do readers of the Bible in YL recognize the presence of this important underlying aspect of reflected meaning? If not, what can be done to make this implicit hermeneutical framework more evident?

4. The cotext is important even in books that are divided up into very distinct units, such as the Psalms. How, for example, do Psalms 116 and 117 serve as an interpretive context, or conceptual framework, for Psalm 118? What light is shed by Psalm 118 on the narrative of Mark 11:1–11?

5. How is Ἡ ἀγάπη μακροθυμεῖ, (1 Cor. 13:4a) translated in your language (cf.. NIV: "Love is patient…")? There appears to be an intertextual issue that needs to be considered here. As one Bible translation commentator notes:[8]

> I also wanted to point out…that "long in the nostrils" is the underlying metaphor for "slow to anger" in English Bibles. This occurs in Ex. 34:6 and Ps.103:8 among other places. This expression was translated into Greek as μακροθυμεω which is found in 1 Cor. 13 as "suffers long" or "is patient." But it is the same expression. It is regrettable that there has never been enough sensitivity to the Septuagint to translate these two corresponding expressions, one from Greek and one from Hebrew, with the same English word. I have not seen this phrase cross-referenced with the Hebrew Bible either although I may have missed it. I am not mourning the loss of the literal translation for these expressions—to a certain extent both "slow to anger" and "suffers long" are literal. What is lost here is that Paul is describing love in terms of the Hebrew Bible. This passage is not in contradistinction with the Hebrew but is a reiteration of the Hebrew scriptures. So why not use "slow to anger" in 1 Cor. 13:4. "Love is slow to anger." Love is slow to anger, love does not keep track of wrongs, doesn't this remind us of Ex. 34:6 and Psalm 103? Love waits a long time before getting angry, love forgives, love hopes and love endures.

What do you think of the previous writer's argument regarding the translation of the verb μακροθυμέω in 1 Cor. 13:4a—do you want to revise your current translation? Explain why—or why

---

[8]Suzanne McCarthy on the website http://englishbibles.blogspot.com/ early in 2008.

1.6 Different situational frames of communication 53

not. Do you ever consult the Septuagint as part of your translation procedure? If so, how helpful do you find it? If not, why?

6. With respect to *inter*textuality (different texts and/or authors) and *intra*textuality (same text and author), Richard Schultz observes the following (1999:271–272):

   > Quotation is a phenomenon that is so multi-functional and semantically complex that it is difficult, if not impossible, to generalize regarding a specific author's or text's method....[I]t must be noted that every quotation will involve some change of meaning, even if the wording remains exactly the same, while some changes in wording will not necessarily affect the meaning much....On the other hand, a quotation always brings its context with it. Thus a quotation may carry with it themes, images, and associations from a first passage which are lacking in the second formulation and context.

   With respect to one set of similar passages in the book of Isaiah, Schultz concludes (ibid.:275–276):

   > In sum, the extent and degree of verbal correspondence, the existence of multiple verbal parallels, the possible use of an introductory formula, and the similarity of contexts suggest that the verbal parallels Isa. 40.10 // 62.11 involve a conscious quotation with 40.3 and 62.10 thereby being drawn into the same rhetorical dynamics.

   Examine the passages just mentioned (in the Hebrew if possible) and identify the alleged *verbal correspondences* in these passages; then answer the following questions:

   Do you agree with Schultz's conclusion, namely, that "the same rhetorical dynamics" is involved? If so, explain what this rhetorical dynamics appears to be in the respective contexts. If you do not agree, what do you think the author(s) was trying to accomplish through the use of such parallels.

   Do these verbal correspondences suggest anything about possible authorship—i.e., one or more "Isaiah"-s?

   Finally, tell what implications these parallels have (if any) for Bible translators.

7. Occasionally, a biblical writer changes the frame of reference of a source author by modifying the text that he is citing or alluding to in order to make a special point in his current message. This seems to be a prominent stylistic characteristic of the book of Joel. Compare the following passages from Joel and the OT pre-texts and point out how the former modifies the latter. Then try to suggest a rhetorical or thematic reason for this within the context of Joel's discourse:

   a. Exodus 10:1–2 _____

      Joel 1:2b–3 _____

   b. Micah 4:4 _____

      Joel 1:7 _____

   c. Deuteronomy 7:12–13 _____

      Joel 1:9b–10 _____

   d. Exodus 10:14–15 _____

      Joel 2:2b–3 _____

   e. Psalm 97:3 _____

Joel 2:3 _____

f. Isaiah 2:4 _____

Joel 3:10a _____

g. Isaiah 17:4–6 _____

Joel 3:12–14 _____

h. Zechariah 14:8 _____

Joel 3:18 _____

8. In some language settings, the literary frame established by a prominent earlier translation of the Bible produces a special sort of biblical intertextuality, one that establishes a set of expectations ("the KJV factor") that influences the translation of any subsequent version. Do you know of a situation like this? If so, describe the nature of the continued translational influence of the older version and how this has affected the new version.

9. Great care must be taken in the use of translation models, whether primary or secondary. Overdependence on any one intermediary translation will inevitably lead translators to introduce foreign lexical collocations and syntactic structures into the TL text. Even a relatively easy-to-understand model, such as the GNT (formerly, GNB) or CEV, can produce unnaturalness or unintelligibility in any translation that follows it too closely. This is because the word usage and sentence construction of the SL and TL do not match. For example, if the italicized expressions listed below from the GNT's translation of the David and Goliath narrative in 1 Samuel 17 were to be rendered literally in Chichewa, the result would be ambiguous, nonsensical, or meaningless. Would you experience any translation difficulties with the following passages in YL

   a. "What are you doing there, *lined up for battle?*" (v. 8). This question answers itself.

   b. "*I dare you* to pick someone to fight me!" (v. 10).

   c. "Jesse had eight sons, and at the time Saul was king, *he* was already an old man" (v. 12). Who was the "old man," Jesse or Saul?

   d. "David was the youngest son, and…David would go back to Bethlehem from time to time" (vv. 14–15). From where did David travel? The GNT does not make this clear. The combination of vv. 14–15 into a single sentence also makes it too long for easy comprehension.

   e. "Find out how your brothers *are getting on* and bring back something to show…" (v. 18).

   f. "David got up early…and went as Jesse had told him to" (v. 20). The two proper names in the same sentence makes it sound as if Jesse were not David's father.

   g. "…the Israelites were going out to their battle line, shouting *the war cry*" (v. 20). Men normally do not cry when they go out for battle.

   h. "*What will the man get* who…frees Israel from this disgrace?" (v. 26). This question was answered in the preceding verse, so why does David ask it?

   i. "*After all,* who is this heathen Philistine to defy…?" (v. 26). "After all" of which events?

j. "You *smart aleck, you!*" (v. 28).

k. "And if the lion or bear turns on me, I *grab it by the throat and beat it to death.*" (v. 35). A hunter does not normally kill a lion in this manner!

l. "and when he got *a good look* at David, he was filled with scorn for him because he was just a nice, *good-looking* boy" (v. 42). The two "good looks" are confusing.

m. "This very day the LORD will *put you in my power…*" (v. 46).

n. "He ran to him…and cut off his head and killed him" (v. 51). But according to the GNT text David has already killed Goliath in v. 50 – how could he kill him twice?

o. "I am the son of *your servant* Jesse from Bethlehem" (v. 58). But Jesse was not Saul's "servant," and he was not even present on the scene!

Now read through the GNT's rendering of 1 Samuel 18. What are the most important problems that a literal translation into YL would present?

The use of a foreign model can cause problems in other respects as well. The Silozi translators of Zambia, for example, closely followed the GNT format in terms of Valliton's illustrations as well as the book introductions, section headings, glossary, and cross references. This identified the vernacular translation too closely with its model, and Protestants rejected it, feeling that the Silozi version would be infected by the alleged liberalism of the model's translators. Do you know another story like this, of a translation getting "tarred with the same brush" as its model?

10. The traditional format and typography of many Bibles forms part of the "literary frame" that serves to direct the perception of readers. Often this visual framework is not as helpful as it might be—the reader being hindered, for example, by the rigid two-column, justified format with small print and little "open space" to guide the eyes. A new edition of *Today's New International Version* (TNIV), called "The Books of the Bible," is being developed to promote reading and readability. Its differences from standard Bibles are listed below:[9]

The Books of The Bible differs from the most common current formats of the Bible in several significant ways:

- chapter and verse numbers are removed from the text and a chapter-and-verse range is given at the bottom of each page;
- individual books are presented with the literary divisions that the biblical authors have indicated;
- footnotes, section headings and any other nonoriginal material have been removed from the text (translators' notes are placed at the end of each book);
- single books that later translations or tradition divided into two or more books are made whole again;
- the books of the Bible have been placed in an order that provides more help in understanding their literary genre, historical circumstance and theological tradition;
- a single-column setting is used to clearly and naturally present the books, making the text more readable and the literary form more recognizable.

Evaluate these proposals for formatting in a more "literary" manner in the light of an actual sample of the new page design (Genesis 3:11-24 given on the next page), which includes both prose and poetry. How effective do you think these procedures would be in your translation setting? Could anything else be done to improve readability? Support your suggestions with reasons.

---

[9]This citation as well as the following sample of Genesis 3:11–24 was taken from the website http://blog.thebooksofthebible.info/ on June 6, 2008.

10 | Genesis

And he said, "Who told you that you were naked? Have you eaten from the tree that I commanded you not to eat from?"

The man said, "The woman you put here with me—she gave me some fruit from the tree, and I ate it."

Then the LORD God said to the woman, "What is this you have done?"

The woman said, "The serpent deceived me, and I ate."

So the LORD God said to the serpent, "Because you have done this,

> "Cursed are you above all livestock
> and all wild animals!
> You will crawl on your belly
> and you will eat dust
> all the days of your life.
>
> And I will put enmity
> between you and the woman,
> and between your offspring˚ and hers;
> he will crush˚ your head,
> and you will strike his heel."

To the woman he said,

> "I will make your pains in childbearing very severe;
> with pain you will give birth to children.
>
> Your desire will be for your husband,
> and he will rule over you."

To Adam he said, "Because you listened to your wife and ate from the tree about which I commanded you, 'You must not eat of it,'

> "Cursed is the ground because of you;
> through painful toil you will eat of it
> all the days of your life.
>
> It will produce thorns and thistles for you,
> and you will eat the plants of the field.
>
> By the sweat of your brow
> you will eat your food
>
> until you return to the ground,
> since from it you were taken;
>
> for dust you are
> and to dust you will return."

Adam˚ named his wife Eve,˚ because she would become the mother of all the living.

The LORD God made garments of skin for Adam and his wife and clothed them. And the LORD God said, "The man has now become like one of us, knowing good and evil. He must not be allowed to reach out his hand and take also from the tree of life and eat, and live forever." So the LORD God banished him from the Garden of Eden to work the ground from which he had been taken. After he drove them out, he placed on the east

1.6.4 Organizational frames

Because a Bible translation is intended to serve the entire Christian (and non-Christian) community within a particular ethnic and social setting, many agencies are involved in its production. This is as it should be. However, this means that the organizers and administrators of the project need to take the diverse perspectives, desires, influences, and resources into consideration as they plan and carry out their work. In the past, not enough attention was paid to this crucial institutional frame of reference, with the result that many people were unhappy with the published product. In short, their opinions and preferences had not been sufficiently considered during the text-production process.

The following are some important organizations and policies that might constitute a particular framework of wider influence:

1. **Secular**: government regulations (e.g., by a "language board"); officially approved orthographies; ministry of education policies; ethnic organizations for the promotion of the indigenous languages and cultures; development agencies of the UN (e.g., UNESCO).

2. **Religious**: denominational or doctrinal statements; church "in-group" speech (a "missionary dialect"); Western sponsoring ("donor") body influence through the supply of non-local literature; policies and procedures of ecumenical organizational initiatives; the national Bible Society; ecclesiastical groupings (e.g., Evangelical Fellowship of Zambia, Zambia Christian Council, Catholic Episcopal Conference); the influence of traditional religious ideas and practices through a local healers' association.

3. **Para-religious**: organizations sponsored by larger church umbrella organizations or by Christians in general (e.g., World Vision, Geneva Global, Lutheran World Federation, Catholic Relief Service), mainly for charitable work among the disadvantaged and vulnerable in society, but which may also provide financial support (along with certain stipulations) for Bible Society projects aimed at disadvantaged groups such as widows, AIDS sufferers, street kids, and people being treated for substance abuse.

   » Which organizations are in any way involved and influential in a Bible translation project that you are aware of or participating in?

   » To what extent have they been a positive supporting and enabling force for the work?

   » Could more be done in your situation to enlist the help of such agencies for particular translation projects or for certain special audiences?

It is important that every well-organized Bible translation project have its own explicitly stated governing framework of operation. This needs to be discussed, agreed upon, and formulated by all participating churches before the translation work begins. This document, sometimes called a *Brief* (job commission), states the terms of reference for the venture. It includes the following:

- the specific type of translation desired for its primary setting of use

- the intended target audience

- the principles and procedures of the translation process

- the medium of communication for the Scripture product(s) desired

- the standing committees of the project (administration, translation, review, public relations)

- the estimated time frame of the project from start to finish

- its budget and fund-raising support programs

- its relationship with other interested organizations (ecclesiastical, governmental, cultural)

- most importantly, the project's specific goals *(Skopos)* in view of all the preceding factors

This commission sets forth all the relevant details as to how, when, why, and for whom a specific translation project is being undertaken. It constitutes the functional and procedural charter according to which the program is planned, administered, managed, and regularly evaluated during the course of its production work. (In section 3.2 we will consider this crucial organizational framework further.)

For reflection, research, and response:

1. Which organizational frames—secular or religious—are important in your translation setting? Describe three of these and how they affect the translation process. Give an example of how a certain religious organizational frame has influenced your communication or that of somebody you know, either positively or negatively. What is the danger of this sort of influence to a Bible translation project? How can unwanted pressure or unhelpful advice from outside organizations be monitored and controlled in a way that does not alienate them?

2. If you are a participant in a Bible translation project, review the two organizational diagrams on page 32 of Wilt 2002a. Then draw a sketch that represents the various interpersonal and institutional relationships that are active in your own work setting. Can you suggest additions, modifications, or improvements? Also evaluate and localize Wilt's "organizational goals" (ibid.:61).

3. Wilt (ibid.:51) discusses "gatekeeping," which refers to "the basic organizational need to control the content and quality of a product." In regard to Bible translation, various gatekeepers are assigned the responsibility of seeing to it that the project "meets professional…standards of quality and has a good chance of success with the [intended] audience" (ibid.). Who are the gatekeepers (whether individuals or committees) in a Bible translation project that you know about or participate in? Does this project have all of the categories that Wilt lists? If not, do you think that they need to be added? Why, or why not? Who manages or oversees all of these gatekeeping agencies and activities to ensure that their various responsibilities work together smoothly? What are some of the factors, organizational or otherwise, that could possibly prevent this vital quality-control function from being carried out properly, and what might be done to solve this problem?

4. Study the following case study and identify all the interested parties that are potentially involved in the contentious issue concerning the use of Arabic Script for vernacular orthographies in West Africa (Warren-Rothlin 2007). Mention some of the main conflicting interests, ideologies, and goals that appear to be engaged in this situation. If you were in a position to render any advice here, what would it be, and why? Are you currently involved in circumstances that are similar in some respects to that outlined below? If so, describe the case in terms of its opposing positions and parties, and explain from your perspective what might be done to resolve the situation in a manner that is most conducive to the concerns of Bible translation and more widespread communication of the Scriptures in the current setting.

> In our survey of the history of ABS (Arabic Script) in West Africa, we noted that some of the earliest Bible publications in West Africa were in Arabic script: Hausa, Kanuri, Fulfulde and Bambara, and several of them contained Qur'ānic and other Arabic texts. Today, at least seventeen Bible translation projects are publishing in ABS, and at least one is daring to publish Islamic material. But, in the course of the last century, ABS has changed from the standard medium of indigenous literacy, to a ubiquitous mark of globalization on the one hand (imported products), and a powerful Islamic religio-cultural symbol on the other. And it is probably fair to say that the positive spiritual value seen in the Qur'ān

by CMS scholar-missionaries at the turn of the 19th century contrasts sharply with the deep suspicion and knee-jerk tabooing of the Qur'ān by many West African Christians and churches today. What might have served as a bridge has become a wall. It is this situation which has necessitated special initiatives such as the Programme for Christian-Muslim Relations in Africa (PROCMURA), various national councils for Christian-Muslim relations, Joint Christian Ministries in West Africa (JCMWA/MICCAO), and UBS's TAZI Task Team (all, of course, initiated long before 9/11).

Stereotypically, national Bible Societies (nBSs) follow the lead of the churches and the market, whilst SIL branches and NBTOs prefer missionary-strategic projects (thereby creating churches and hence markets for Bible products). Thus nBSs which think solely in terms of meeting the needs of Christian churches will not want work on TAZI (Tawrat, Anbiya, Zabur, Injil) and ABS products, unless the churches are calling for them (which is currently not common). Those in close partnerships with missions such as SIL will probably allow their publishing policy to be influenced by their partners' agendas. And certain nBSs may have their own missionary vision beyond that of the churches. In any case, a distinctive of TAZI work as a whole is that the customers are not the consumers (Muslims), but missions and churches who require products for their own evangelistic programs.

5. Has a *Brief* been prepared for your Bible translation project? If not, why not? If one has been prepared, explain how this was done and outline its main points.

6. Which topics or exercises of this lesson have been especially difficult and, therefore, leave you in need of additional instruction, explanation, and/or practice with selected examples from the Bible? Such points of difficulty need to be noted as you interact with this workbook, and those that cannot be discussed in class should be written out and given as critical feedback at the end of the course or periodically along the way.

7. The following diagram presents the interacting set of textually based frames of reference (or "scenarios") that constitute the cognitive environment for a particular biblical pericope. Explain how they interact to influence your understanding and subsequent translation of passages like Genesis 38:9, Ruth 3:7–9, Luke 14:26, and Acts 14:11–13. Which is the most important frame in your opinion? Why do you think so? Is there a better way of illustrating this notion of contextualizing frames of reference as it relates to the practice of Bible translation? If so, make a sketch of your preferred alternative model or a modified diagram of the larger organization and process of Bible translation.

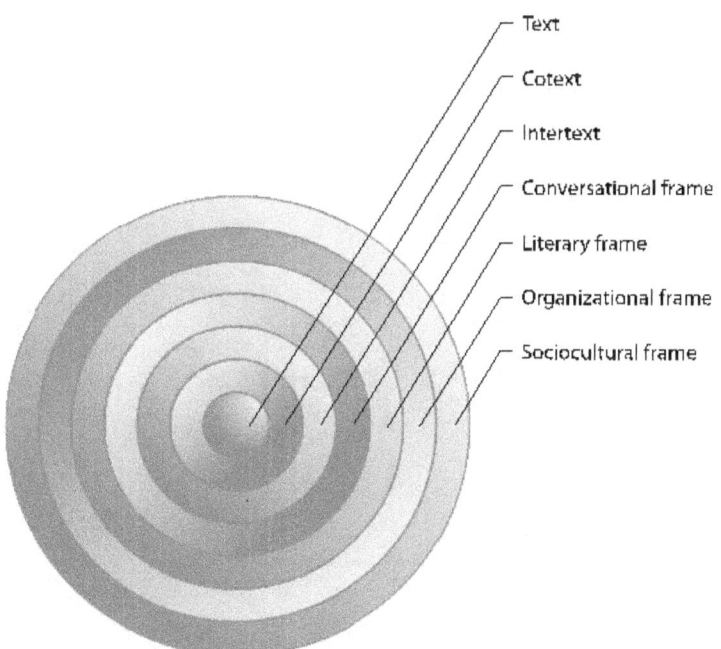

Lesson 2
Does Scripture Include Literature?

Aim: In this lesson you will learn about the nature and purpose of "literature," how to define it, and how to distinguish written verbal art from "orature." You will also learn how to recognize some of the important literary forms and functions found in the Bible and begin to develop a strategy for re-presenting these in a *LiFE* (literary functional equivalence) manner in your language.

Goals: After working through this lesson you should be able to do the following:

1. Define "literature."

2. Describe the concept of compositional style and its importance in literature.

3. Distinguish "literature" from "orature."

4. Identify some of the main characteristics and kinds of literature in the Bible.

5. Specify some of the principal functions of literature.

Review:
Lesson 1 regarding the different communication frames in which texts are translated.

Read:
Chapter 6 in *Bible Translation: Frames of Reference* (Wilt 2002a).
Chapter 2 in *Translating the Literature of Scripture* (Wendland 2004b).
Pages 175–178 of *Analyzing the Psalms* (Wendland 2002).
Chapter 4 in *Analyzing Discourse* (Dooley and Levinsohn 2001).
Pages 265–272 of *Scripture Frames and Framing* (Wilt and Wendland 2008)

2.1 What is literature?

Read passages I and II below and note the differences in their *style*, that is, their manner of writing, rather than their content, which is clearly different. Both selections have been written with reference to John 16:33: "These words have I spoken unto you, that in me ye might have peace. For in the world shall ye have tribulation: but be of good cheer, I have overcome the world."[1]

What type of writing does the first selection illustrate, and which textual markers lead you to this conclusion? Answer these same two questions in relation to the second selection.

I.

Jesus imparts to his disciples the information concerning his death and his provision for them that they might be calm and confident in the face of disillusionment and apparent disaster. "Peace" (GK *1646*) reiterates his statement in 14:27. Even in the hour of his greatest suffering he has an unshakable confidence in the victorious purpose of God. Jesus does not overlook the trial that will affect them as well as himself, for that is inevitable in a world alienated from God. He does, however, proclaim victory over it.

---

[1] The first selection is taken from the *NIV Bible Commentary*, vol. 2 (Barker and Kohlenburger 1994:355); the second from *Beyond the Sacred Page* (Cavanaugh 2003:159).

II.

> Meg looked up.
> "Who spoke those words?" the queen asked.
> "Let me see ..." Again Meg placed her hand on the page and began tracing the sentences backward. She looked up.
> "The Master," she said. "These are the words of the Master to his disciples!"
> "Read them again. Slowly."
> The queen lay her head back against her pillows. She closed her eyes. As Meg read, the queen savored every word. When Meg finished the section, the queen said, "Continue reading."

The printed format's obvious difference may be the first important clue for identifying the nature and purpose of the two passages. The alternating dialogue sequence of the second passage clearly suggests that it is some kind of narrative. The absence of identifiable characters or speakers further indicates that it is probably a piece of fiction writing. For experienced readers, the style of composition—short sentences, colloquial diction, quick exchange of speakers, evoking rather than explicating the subject ("peace")—would bring a popular novel to mind as a likely genre. The subcategory of Christian fiction is indicated by the inclusion of a Bible passage and a reference to "the Master." The style of the first passage is very different, but just as typical of a completely different form of writing; namely, that of a Bible commentary of some kind. It might have been classified as a devotional book were it not for the included reference in parentheses to some apparently technical work, GK *1646*.

Now the question is: are both of the preceding passages instances of *literature*? How would you define "literature?" Is it somehow different from "ordinary" writing (or speaking)? Consider the following definition of "literature" from the *American Heritage Dictionary* (1981:762), with its various senses numbered as follows:

1. A body of writings in prose or verse.

2. Imaginative or creative writing.

3. The art or occupation of a literary writer.

4. The body of written work produced by scholars or researchers in a given field: medical *literature*.

5. Printed material of any kind.

» Which of these five senses comes closest to your understanding of the term "literature?" Why does this particular sense seem right to you in contrast to the others?

» The first two senses are intended as the main ones. What is the difference between them? Which is more inclusive?

» Notice that the first sense does not take the criterion of quality into account—any sort of writing will do. The second sense adds "imaginative" and "creative." But what do these words mean? Can you suggest some tentative definitions?

Webster's New World College Dictionary is perhaps more helpful in dealing with the popular notion of what literature is. It is certainly more specific, defining the second sense above with additional precision:

a. All writings in prose or verse, especially those of an imaginative or critical character, without regard to their excellence: often distinguished from scientific writing, news reporting, etc.

b. All of such writings considered as having permanent value, excellence of form, great emotional effect, etc.

c. All the writings of a particular time, country, region, etc., specifically those regarded as having lasting value because of their beauty, imagination, etc.

» How does sense (a) differ from (b), and in turn from (c)?

» Notice that sense (b) includes an indirect reference to the three basic dimensions of all texts—*form* ("excellence of form"), *content* ("having permanent value"), and *function* ("great emotional effect"). Which of these three is the chief aspect of literature, and why do you think so? Is it the form of a text (how it is written)? Does the content (*what* is said) count more? Or is literature characterized more by its function, or purpose (*why* it was written)?

» Have you ever read a book that was intended to be good literature, but had a problem with one of these three characteristics? If so, what was the difficulty and how did it affect your overall assessment of the book?

Obviously, all three defining aspects are important and must be considered in relation to one another, for that is how literature is evaluated by scholars and the general public alike. A mismatch generally causes problems for most people. Perhaps the form does not suit the subject matter (e.g., a political speech composed in the form of a lyric poem), or the content is not appropriate to the purpose (e.g., a text from the Song of Songs used in a funeral address), or the function is not conveyed well by the style of the text (e.g., a prayer of thanks to God preached like a penitential sermon).

In this lesson and those to follow, we will be focusing on the two textual qualities of form and function, since they are more of a challenge to translators than is content. The content that Bible translators have to deal with in most situations is relatively fixed, other than for certain text-critical issues and matters of interpretation.[2] However, in order to establish this reservoir of content, a careful study of the original document under consideration must be carried out, whether in Hebrew, Greek, or Aramaic. Thus the translator must know how to carry out a basic *exegesis* (systematic textual analysis and interpretation) of a biblical document. It is assumed, for now, that you know how to do this and that you can determine, as accurately and fully as possible, what the author was saying to his primary audience. (This will be discussed further in section 3.6.)

» What steps do you normally follow when you study a Bible passage in order to arrive at a clear understanding of its referential content?

» Does this procedure differ when you work together as part of a team in preparation to translate that text?

It is this fixed ("given") amount of sense and significance that translators endeavor to re-state or re-present in their target language. The transfer operation must be carried out within the conceptual framework of the target cultural system—that is, their worldview, value system, way of life, social institutions, and so forth. But content is not all that there is to the message to be conveyed. In other words, the meaning (the complete import and implication that a text communicates) includes more than informative content alone. It also incorporates various functions, or communication purposes. In addition, the meaning of a given passage often includes one or more connotations, that is, all the different mental associations, whether strong or weak (sometimes termed encyclopedic meaning), as well as emotions and attitudes evoked by particular words, names, phrases, sentences, and even complete texts. Think of the associations that "freedom," "Christmas Day," "Hitler," "Our Father, who art in heaven," and *"Pilgrim's Progress"* evoke.

Information content, too, is more complex than many people realize. It is not simply a set of facts and figures to be learned; the particular form of expression can also be important, as in an *acrostic poem* or personal letter. This will become clear as we examine a number of Bible texts more carefully. Most passages actually convey several layers of content—often very closely tied to their historical and

---

[2]Ralph Hill (personal correspondence) recently reminded me that there are, in fact, special Scripture products that may require varied degrees of content modification. One example is "adaptive retelling" (see section 7.1.7).

sociocultural setting. Some of this may be stated explicitly in the text, but other important aspects of content are simply assumed, implicit in the text, alluded to, or presented in symbolic terms.

Therefore, in addition to content we need to give considerable attention to the diverse structures and shapes of literature. But we may ask why the form of an original text is important if we are going to change it when we re-express that same text in another language. This question needs to be honestly answered by translators, because the response has both practical as well as theoretical implications. We might list four main reasons that the form of the original text is important:

1. **Form** is important because it is how we first perceive a text; namely, as a sequence of interconnected signs which evoke contextually determined mental representations (or "scenarios"). These linguistic and literary forms are what we must then systematically analyze in order to correctly understand and interpret the text, whether it happens to be written in our mother tongue or in a language foreign to us.

2. **Form** is important because we must utilize the various verbal sign selections and settings of the SL, in order to recreate them as an acceptable TL text through the process of translation. In other words, we *restate* the meaning of an original document (certain aspects, at least), moving from one set of words and rules for combining them to another. Conceptually, then, we interpret the verbal signs of one text and represent them by means of some other language-culture system.

3. **Form** is important because, at times, more often than not, in excellent literature the linguistic form itself is an integral part of the meaning that the author wished to express. For example, the particular sounds of a pun or an instance of onomatopoeia are significant. So is a certain rhythm, or a chiastic arrangement of elements in which the center is highlighted, or the parallelism of Hebrew poetry in which the second line of a typical couplet comments on and complements the meaning of the first.

4. **Form** is, in sum, the artist's essential tool, no matter what the medium of communication, whether words, paint, clay, beads, dance steps, or music. In the case of a literary text, language is shaped on its various levels—sounds, sense, syntax, imagery, discourse structure—to create a product having the maximum impact ("power") and appeal ("beauty"). The author thereby aims to communicate his message in a way that is perceived to have enough relevance to reward the time and effort of interpretation. Master wordsmiths are individuals who employ their tools especially efficiently and effectively in the interest of greater communicability. If this is true of the original author, then why not also the translator?

For these reasons (and there are others) translators need to be, or become (through further education and experience), manifest experts in the discernment, interpretation, and manipulation of form, not just in one language, but in two.

» Which of these four reasons for studying the form of a biblical text seems most important to you. Why?

» Can you think of any additional reason(s)?

As the last two reasons suggest, form is a vital component of *style* (the distinctive manner or mode of doing something). In the case of literature, style refers to the way in which the text under consideration has been composed and written, and which may be critically judged as being good, bad, or mediocre according to some norm that serves as the basis for comparison. The recognition of style, its interpretation, and its evaluation always involve:

1. a *comparison*, whether formal or informal, between at least two items;

2. the *base*, that is, the norm—whether clearly defined or strongly intuitive;

2.1 What is literature?

3. one or more *correspondents* (what is/are being compared to the base).

Stylistic analysis and assessment come into play when one determines what constitutes "literature." (Recall the dictionary definition (b): "[Literature embraces] all of such writings considered as having permanent value, excellence of form, great emotional effect, etc.")

In most cases, then, it is the stylistic form of a particular oral/written text that is most prominent, that comes first to the attention of the evaluator, critic, or consumer. What degree of beauty, appeal, or excellence in this respect does the verbal form, especially when uttered aloud, give evidence of? This evaluation will, in turn, frequently impact or influence the other criteria—that is, how "valuable" or memorable the text is deemed to be in terms of content, or how "great" it is with regard to emotional effect, evocative force, rhetorical power, and/or connotative resonance. Such considerations are as crucial when one interprets the Scriptures as it is for any other type of literature. For example, the factor of style often determines why we like one translation of the Bible more than another.

> » Read John 16:33 in the (N)RSV, NIV, CEV, and GNT. Which version do you prefer in terms of style and why?

Furthermore, it is important to note that verbal form also embraces the thematic and figurative dimensions of discourse. In the Bible, this refers in particular to those key figures and images that are regularly repeated and which are so fundamental to the life and ethos of Israel that they have become essentially symbolic in nature. These are called *conceptual metaphors*, which are general mental representations "by which we understand and reason about a domain of one kind (the *target* domain) by means of knowledge drawn from a domain of a different kind (the *source* domain)" (Feyaerts 2003:87). Thus two different semantic frames or clusters are cognitively connected by a selective cross-domain mapping process that figuratively links the target (topic, tenor), which is generally more abstract, with a more concrete, experience-based source (image, vehicle). This results in the formation of a complex, but unified, cognitive whole that has greater explanatory, illustrative, and persuasive power than a simple definition, assertion, or exposition of the intended meaning. These *metaphorical mappings* occur regularly in everyday discourse, but they are especially concentrated and interconnected in literary works, often in novel ways, with new content or important aspects of theme. Some generic metaphors are specific to a work, an author, a language, or a multilingual culture (e.g., Western), while others may be more widespread in the world, for example, GOOD IS UP[3] ("She's really gone up in the world"; "those on top," which in Chichewa refers to well-off folk) or BAD IS DOWN ("he's down and out"; "his job went down," which in Chichewa means that his business failed).

The application here to biblical literature should be obvious, with respect to the major themes, motifs, figures, and images in particular, not only where exegesis is concerned but, more importantly, in translation. Thus the meaning of one conceptual metaphor is echoed and augmented through its recurrence within a text or corpus. This intertextual aspect of its sense and significance always needs to be carefully traced and factored into the activity of interpretation. For example, the image LIFE IS A JOURNEY travels the Scriptures from beginning to end: in Genesis 5:22 "Enoch *walked* with God" and in Revelation 3:4 "they shall *walk* with me in white." This image-tracking process results in another key aspect of literary form, in this case, the form of figurative or thematic content.

> » How does the core concept of a JOURNEY and TRAVEL function as a structural metaphor to delineate the development of the discourse in Luke and Acts, e.g., Luke 9:51, 13:33, 14:25, 17:11, 19:1, 19:28, 19:41, 19:45, 22:39, 23:32–33, 24:46–53, and Acts 1:8?

Such strong semantic resonance and cohesion must be preserved in translation where possible—at least those basic conceptual metaphors that distinguish and color a given book, author, genre, testament, or indeed the biblical corpus as a whole. Some core metaphors may match fairly closely between SL and

---

[3] A presumed conceptual metaphor is generally expressed in full capital letters.

TL; for example, the LIFE-JOURNEY has a match in Chichewa, as does ANGER IS HEAT (cf. Exod. 32:19 "and the anger of Moses burned hot" with Chichewa *Mose anapya mtima kwambiri* "Moses burned very much in his heart"). Others (e.g., DEATH IS A SLEEP) may be more difficult, if not impossible, to retain without meaninglessness or distortion: For 1 Samuel 1:21 "when my lord the king will sleep with his fathers," it is necessary in Chichewa to replace DEATH IS A SLEEP with DEATH IS A DEPARTURE: *inu mbuyanga mutatisiya* "when you my grandfather will have left us." The goal in such cases is to preserve the ideational-imagistic structure of the biblical text so that its intra- and intertextual unity and coherence are preserved to the extent possible and despite the need for re-expression in the vernacular rendition.

» How does the DEATH IS A SLEEP metaphor serve to organize the history of the kings of Israel and Judah in 1 and 2 Kings?

» Has this metaphor become completely dead (conventionalized), or does it retain some special semantic significance, for example, in a passage like 1 Kings 15:24? Explain your answer with reference to the different translations of this text found in the (N)RSV, NIV, CEV, and GNT.

Because the factor of formal structure and style is so important in literature—both its analysis and assessment—we will be giving the subject special consideration in lesson 3 as we learn more about preparing a *LiFE* translation of Scripture. Then, in lesson 4, we will examine some of the characteristic larger forms (i.e., text types and genres) that are found in the Bible, along with their associated stylistic features. After that, a complete lesson will be devoted to the major forms of biblical poetry (lesson 5) and of prose (lesson 6).

For reflection, research, and response:

1. Specify the "etc." in the second definition of literature that was given earlier as point (a): "All writings in prose or verse, especially those of an imaginative or critical character, without regard to their excellence: often distinguished from scientific writing, news reporting, *etc.*" Which other types of writing do most people tend to distinguish from literature? What about advertisements, wall posters, a travel flyer, telephone book, or a catechism? What makes such printed material different from *artistic* literature as defined above?

2. What kinds of literature are readily available in your national setting? Is there a great variety for sale in your mother tongue? Can people afford to buy these texts? If not, why? Who are the main publishers? Are Scripture portions published locally or out of country? Are the Scriptures (in various formats) readily available and affordable? Comment on any problems that you have experienced—and suggest how these might be resolved.

3. What can a person do to study the forms of language more thoroughly so as to become a better Bible exegete and translator—first, in relation to the text of Scripture, then with reference to his own mother tongue? Becoming such a linguistic expert is the first step for a serious translator, especially when following the *LiFE* approach, but a translator also needs to become a *literary* expert as well. How can this best be accomplished? How can the systematic study of local literature and oral art forms assist in this learning process?

4. How would you define the term "style?" Which book of the Bible do you think displays the best style of writing, in the original text or in translation? Why do you say so? What are the stylistic features of that book that are most important to you? What primary functions do these stylistic devices perform? Would this biblical book be difficult to translate into your language? Are you aware of certain literary features in your language that might match those found in this particular book—that is, in terms of function and/or form? Give three examples of such textual correspondence in Luke's Gospel.

5. The formal excellence or skill of a writer's (or speaker's) style contributes greatly to the beauty of a text. To what extent and by what means can a beautiful style be reproduced in a Bible translation?

2.1 What is literature? 67

Evaluate the following quotation (from Ryken 2005:29) and tell whether or not you agree and why. How should the examples he cites be rendered in your language—that is, in order to most effectively convey the sense as well as the impact and appeal of the original?

> *You can trust some essentially literal translations to preserve the exaltation, dignity, and beauty of the Bible.*
>
> You can expect to read, "Behold, I stand at the door and knock" (Rev. 3:20, KJV, NASB, ESV), not such things as this: "Here I am! I stand at the door and knock" (NIV, TNIV), or "Here I stand knocking at the door" (REB), or, "Listen! I am standing and knocking at your door" (CEV). In an essentially literal translation you will find the awe-inspiring lead-in, "Truly, truly, I say to you" (ESV), not a translation that has scaled the voltage down to "I tell you the truth" (NIV) or "I tell you for certain" (CEV) or "I assure you" (NLT). An essentially literal translation will fire your imagination and wonder with its evocative picture of "ivory palaces" (Ps. 45:8, KJV, NASB, ESV), not such mundane versions as "palaces adorned with ivory" (NIV) or "palaces paneled with ivory" (REB) or "palaces decorated with ivory" (GNB, NLT).

6. The notion REPENTANCE IS RETURNING (a sub-theme of the LIFE IS A JOURNEY conceptual metaphor) is very prominent in the OT literature. Check a concordance to find variations of this foundational moral theme in different contexts. Comment on their appropriateness in your language and mention any adjustments that you may have to make in order to render a given text in a more literary-sensitive manner. How does this theme serve to structure the parable found in Luke 15:11–32?

7. Identify positive and negative sub-themes of the LIFE IS A JOURNEY metaphor in Psalm 1. Find other subsidiary conceptual metaphors that are related to this crucial ethical and theological idea in the Psalms. Which of these have functional correspondents in YL? For those that do not, what is the closest formal equivalent that you can find? Some scholars have proposed certain key conceptual metaphors as being thematic within the Psalter as a whole, for example, YAHWEH IS KING or YAHWEH IS A REFUGE (shelter, dwelling, rock, shade, hiding place). Do you agree? What others would you suggest for the Psalms? Do you see any implications here for Bible translators with respect to how imagery and figurative language are handled?

8. Cite instances of the following interrelated conceptual metaphors in Ezekiel 16: COVENANT IS A WEDDING, GOD IS A BRIDEGROOM/HUSBAND, THE COVENANT PEOPLE ARE A BRIDE, IDOL WORSHIP IS ADULTERY/HARLOTRY. How do these metaphors reinforce one another to enhance and emotivize the rhetorical force of the prophet's message? How then do the different aspects of this metaphoric complex function to organize and develop the LORD's prophetic condemnation of his people in Ezekiel 16? To what extent can these metaphors be preserved in YL with essentially the same sense and significance? In cases where this is not possible, how can you creatively compensate for this loss in the text's power and persuasiveness?

9. On the basis of her preliminary research on the conceptual metaphors of "darkness" in Africa, Lynell Zogbo arrives at the following tentative conclusions (Zogbo 2007):

> African translators dealing with expressions of DARKNESS in the Bible will not have too much trouble with semantic skewing when translating. Taken in a physical sense, the reading will be determined by context, and in most cases be neutral or positive. However, expressions using DARKNESS in a figurative sense will probably automatically be processed as connoting negative notions. DARKNESS IS IGNORANCE or DARKNESS IS EVIL are common to both biblical and many African cultures. Figurative expressions such as "sitting in darkness", "walking in darkness", "coming from the darkness to light" should be readily understood, we might venture to say, whether or not the forms used are natural or not. However, there may be mismatches within the BLACK IS EVIL paradigm, as different languages attribute various kinds of unacceptable attitudes and behaviors to different parts of the body.

Interestingly, the connotations of BLACK in certain African languages may serve translators in places where the word or notion BLACK does not even occur in the source text. For example, when translating Is 1.18,

> Come now, let us reason together,
> says the LORD:
> though your sins are like scarlet,
> they shall be as white as snow;
> though they are red like crimson,
> they shall become like wool.

Samo translators (of Burkina Faso) felt uncomfortable rendering this text literally. Even substituting local equivalents for red or dark red left them unhappy. However, substituting black in place of red gave a natural and very powerful rendering: "Even though your sins are black…" Some may want to contest that this rendering robs the text of its allusions to purification, associated with blood sacrifice. But understanding this problem, translators chose to adopt a statement that made a powerful statement, rather than one that would confuse or have little meaning for the reader.

From the perspective of your cultural setting, would you tend to agree with these conclusions or not? Make a study of Isaiah 5:20, 30; 8:22; 9:2; 29:15; 42:7; 45:7; 58:10; 59:9; Luke 11:34; 12:35, 46; 22:53; John 1:5; 3:19; 8:12; Acts 26:18; Romans 13:12; 1 Corinthians 4:5; 2 Corinthians 6:12; Ephesians 4:18. How about the specific example of Isaiah 1:18—what would be the most effective literary way of expressing this in your language? Explain your preferred rendering.

10. Consider the following case study (Smalley 1995:2, 61):

    Many factors contribute to making a translation lose out, and…one of them [is]: inadequate translation theory, which often vitiates translation efforts. When the British and Foreign Bible Society began to publish what they expected would become a replacement for the Judson [Burmese] translation, missionary ideas about what translation should be like had come under the influence of the English Revised Version of 1881–85. This revision of the Authorized, or King James, Version was touted as being far more accurate in its wording than its predecessor, but part of what was called "accuracy" was a heavy literalism with none of the sensitivity to English style that characterizes many passages of the King James. The people who made the new Burmese translation adopted not only the improved textual base of the ERV but also what was considered its "modern" and "scholarly" approach to translation, so that like their model, their work sank under its own wooden literalness. A whole era of missionary translators tended to do much the same.

    » In what respects does Smalley express literary concerns here? Do you know of a situation like this in your region? If so, summarize the key facts of your particular case.

11. Landers (2001:27) says about translators of secular literature that "the majority view…has been that a translation should affect its readers in the same way that the original affected its first readers (or listeners, in the case of Homer)….[B]y the SL reader we mean the *original* source-language reader… [For example] the original readers of Quixote in no way perceived the speech of the characters as archaic or antiquated." Nor did they perceive it stylistically awkward and alien. Have you heard a similar view expressed before (e.g., see Nida and Taber 1969:1–2)? How does the assertion here by Landers relate to a literary rendering of the Scriptures? Is there a difference, or should there be? If so, in which respects? Landers also claims, "I am first and foremost a practitioner and have yet to meet a working translator who places theory above experience, flexibility, a sense of style, and an appreciation for nuance….[W]ho other than scholars would want to read prose (or poetry, for that matter) that bears the heavy imprint of foreign grammar, idiom, or syntax?" (ibid.:50–51). Discuss this opinion in relation to translating the Bible.

2.2 What is orature and how does it differ from literature?

This lesson began with an emphasis upon "literature" because the Bible is a collection of written documents. However, we know that, in ancient Bible times, most writings were produced in order to be read orally and received aurally by an audience.

- » How do you think that it would affect the process of composing a text if the author knew that it was going to be read aloud, either privately or publicly?

- » What features characterize an oral style of verbal composition?

- » Think of your own oral tradition if you have one. What, for example, are the main stylistic characteristics of an oral narrative or folktale? How about indigenous poetry?

Examine the following list of stylistic features and point out the ones that would be prominent in the oral verbal art forms of your language. Give an example of some of these, if possible.

a. Lexical repetition, often exact and overlapping ("tail-head") rather than synonymous

b. More variation from normal word order in the different types of discourse

c. Rhythmic utterances, especially in sequence

d. Parallel syntactic constructions, favoring *parataxis*

e. Shorter and looser sentence, paragraph, and other discourse units

f. More frequent speaker/author insertions and asides

g. Colloquial diction, including dialectal forms

h. Many *puns*, much *alliteration* and *assonance*

i. Formulaic discourse openers, closers, and transitions

j. Great preference for direct speech

k. *Hyperbole* and intensifiers, including *ideophones*, interjections, and exclamations

l. Many *deictic*/demonstrative words and particles

m. Vivid figurative language and local color description

n. *Ellipsis* and *anacolutha* (broken grammatical constructions)

o. Not as varied, precise, or specific in word choice

p. Accompanying non-verbal communication (gestures, facial expressions, etc.)

q. Dependence on *prosody* (intonation, pitch, pause, tempo, tone, volume, etc.)

r. Information presented at a slower pace or rate

- » Are these same features used in written forms of literature in YL?

- » Which of these stylistic traits are not used very often in writing and why?

- » Are there any other features in YL that are frequently found either in writing, or in artistic persuasive speech, but not both?

- » What can be done in writing to compensate for the loss of sound (e.g., intonation, volume, stress) when representing an oral text, like a folktale?

The larger forms of spoken discourse often differ from those of written discourse. Oral narratives in Chichewa (a Bantu language spoken in Malawi, also known as Chinyanja) tend to be more recursive and more overtly patterned in organization than narratives that are written out beforehand. The former are usually shorter and generally incorporate choral songs as well—songs that mark boundaries and move the plot forward, or express the story's theme in a figurative or symbolic way. Similarly, these thematic songs are much simpler and more repetitive in style than popular written poetry, in addition to being less explicit (more allusive) and syntactically connected. Much oral poetry can be sung as well as rhythmically recited or chanted before an audience.

- » What are some of the most important differences that you have noticed between the spoken and written art forms of YL?

- » Are such stylistic differences relatively rigid or flexible? In other words, is it more or less acceptable to use oral features in writing, or would such a hybrid not be well received or appreciated?

- » How can you find out the answers to these and related questions about oral and written composition in YL?

In many cultures, it is necessary to distinguish between written verbal art (i.e., literature) and oral verbal art (i.e., orature) because the two modes of communicating are quite different in both structure and style. This is normally true in the case of cultures that have a long history of literature. Many other cultures, on the other hand, including the majority in Africa, do not make such a clear distinction, and a great deal of mixing goes on. For example, common oral features may frequently be used in vivid writing. (The reverse is not as common, however.)

- » What is the situation in YL and cultural setting?

- » Are literature and orature distinct, or are the boundaries and norms fluid enough that a certain amount of creative experimentation is always going on among writers and oral performers?

The distinction between oral and written discourse is of considerable importance to Bible translators. In some cases, there is not much literature at all in the target language and, therefore, it is quite natural that the first translations of the Bible will be heavily patterned after oral genres and styles. In other cases, a resourceful team of translators may deliberately introduce accepted oral features into their translation, knowing that most of their target group will receive the translation in an oral-aural manner, rather than in writing. Perhaps a high percentage of people are non-literate, or perhaps an audio Scripture selection is being prepared. In addition, most translators want portions of the Bible that are direct speech, or those that are most frequently spoken aloud, to sound natural. Such a translation may be called *oratorical* since it is made with public reading or performance in mind.

On the other hand, an oral style may sometimes be deliberately avoided. If it has been predetermined that the translation is to be a very literal one, perhaps for "theological" reasons (wanting to closely reflect "the actual *Word* of God"), then the translators will stick closely to the original Hebrew and Greek text and not introduce idiomatic vernacular oral features. It may be that an earlier translation (perhaps one prepared by the first missionaries) is still very influential, honored, and widely used, and the new version is specifically aimed at being only a revision, with no major restructuring desired or even allowed.

- » Do any of these situations exist in your language area? If so, briefly explain the circumstances, both historical and current.

- » Have any difficulties of communication arisen due to past translation policy in your Christian community—or perhaps because the majority of the population adheres to a different faith with another "holy book"? If so, explain what has happened and why.

If a team wishes to develop a more *oral-aural style* of translation, rendering their text in such a way that it is more pleasing to the ears of the audience, they must recognize that it will require a high level of commitment and competency. It will be much more of a creative, perhaps even an experimental, exercise. On the other hand, the process must still manifest careful controls so that the biblical text is not distorted in terms of content, tone, or purpose. More research will be needed with respect to the oral art forms of the TL. The team will need to know which genres and styles are used for which purpose and with what intended impact, what the normal settings are for the literary genres in terms of formality, and to what extent modification can take place.

Then the team must determine which oral stylistic devices and compositional techniques can be used and where they are appropriate. Some forms may be deemed too colloquial, substandard, technical, or speaker-restricted (e.g., the jargon of youth, the argot of elders, or foreign loanwords). Their connotation may be too dubious for use in the Scriptures. Some features (e.g., ideophones or exclamations) may be acceptable in certain contexts, perhaps in dramatic direct speech, but not elsewhere, lest the biblical text sound too informal or slangy. Still others can—and must—be used freely in order for the translation to sound natural and be clearly understood (e.g., certain demonstrative particles, transitional conjunctions, word orders, tense sequence patterns, and speech registers).

- » Give examples of some high-level or low-level literary characteristics (macro- or microstylistic features) of your language that are essential, but must be used with great care when translating the Bible? Explain why.

- » Does it make a difference whether written or oral Scriptures are being prepared? Explain your answer.

The translation team must seek good oral models. In many language settings today, they may find such models of an oratorical style in popular singers, public speakers, radio broadcasters, vernacular drama groups, and skillful oral performers of ancient verbal art forms. They may also find them in Christian evangelists and revivalists who have not been influenced by Westerners. While widely recognized models of excellent oratory do exist, they must, then, be carefully collected (often by recording them for later transcription), analyzed, published, and distributed (or broadcast) in order to develop standards of popular and specialist assessment to the point where they may be effectively applied in written literature.

- » Have you (or an acquaintance) done any research into this aspect of your language's oral tradition?

- » If so, describe your investigation and summarize your findings.

Remember that the medium of print itself requires certain compositional modifications to be made during the transposition of an oral to a published text. For example, it may be necessary to modify the discourse for less repetition; a more explicit expression of content (to compensate for the lack of a human situational context); punctuation (to compensate for the lack of intonational and elocutionary features); more precise conjunctive and transitional function words; and a lower incidence of informal registers or colloquial word choices.

For reflection, research, and response:

1. What do the following passages tell you about public communication in Bible times: Ezekiel 33:30–31; Acts 8:30; 15:21; Colossians 4:16; 1 Thessalonians 5:27?

2. Study Psalm 148 and identify some of its prominent oral features, giving some specific examples. Say whether or not these are common in the oral art forms of YL. If they are not, which other devices might be used to convey a similar impact, without introducing an unwanted connotation?

3. Evaluate the following observations with regard to the importance of the phonological factor in translation. How do these thoughts about "sound" apply to a Bible translation that you are familiar with, say, with reference to 1 Corinthians 13? Give several specific suggestions in this regard.

   > Translators are potentially helped by the fact that much of the Bible was intended for oral reading and therefore has extensive oral features embedded in its text. The identification and retention of these features can enable a translation to be more accessible to listeners. The beauty of language, of course, requires the contribution of translators and their culture. (Thomas and Thomas 2006:72)

   > The beauty of any translation is best sensed in oral rendition....What the stylist of a modern translation of the Bible needs is not alone a mastery of the technicalities of prosody but a sensitive ear, kept in tune by habitually reading aloud both poetic and prose passages, giving full value to accented syllables.[4]

   > Why does excellence of rhythm matter? One answer is aesthetic: Good rhythm is beautiful, and bad rhythm is grating and ugly....Second, good rhythm is essential to any text that is uttered orally....Thirdly, good rhythm is an aid to memory as well as to oral performance....Finally, rhythm is the natural concomitant of impassioned and heightened speech.

4. Mention a Bible translation, either in your mother tongue or another language, that manifests a good *oratorical* style—that is, a text that sounds powerful, beautiful, persuasive, poetic, etc. (depending on the genre). Why do you think so—that is, on the basis of which specific linguistic features in the text?

5. The following are some practical applications with regard to the differences between oral and written discourse (Dooley and Levinsohn 2001:18). Point out the relevance to Bible translation in your setting of this advice. Describe what sort of research you (or your translation committee) have carried out in this domain:

   > [O]ne cannot set down as a criterion of good written style...merely the oral style of good speakers" (citing E. A. Nida). This has broad implications for reading material of all types, including translation (which, according to Bartsch, may need to combine features of oral as well as written texts). Nevertheless, it is becoming clear that the oral versus written dichotomy is probably an amalgam of different parameters that can be teased apart...Therefore, in field linguistics one needs to collect as many types of texts as possible and label them, not simply as oral or written, but with detailed circumstances of their production.

6. Thomas and Thomas set forth a number of important "assumptions" regarding the oral features of discourse (2006:3). Study these and point out their relevance to your particular Bible translation setting. Then give a specific example of how you can use (or already have used) such information to improve the quality of orality in your vernacular version—for example, your rendition of the Song of Songs, chapter 1.

---

[4]When composing question 3, I originally did not want to reveal the last two sources lest it influence the readers' evaluation of the opinion expressed in each case. Unfortunately, at some point in the drafting I misplaced the references and so the two sources, which are different, are now lost to me. I therefore owe an apology to their authors for this omission.

Certain oral features transcend culture and language and are universal. For example, repetition is a common features of orality, whether in ancient cultures or in contemporary usage. Rhythm, phonological resonance, and volume may likewise be components of any oral communication.

Oral features are integral to a text. Therefore, attention to the oral characteristics of a written text is always part of the translator's task.

The universal features of orality are communicable in other languages. Certain oral features may be reproduced fairly directly. Other elements of a text are amenable to the use of functional equivalents, that is, to literary devices that make an impact similar to the original although they are not identical to the components found in the original.

Every translation must utilize oral features that are particular to its own language situation. But because oral features are integral to the original text, identification of these features and their function in the original text guides the inclusion of similar or equivalent features in a translation. There is a dynamic interplay between the possibilities of the target language and the givens of the original text.

An oral translation and its presentation should be understandable to its hearers without a further explication and should attract their sustained attention. Nevertheless, oral transmission of a text is demanding. It is not for lazy listeners!

» Every translation of the Scriptures should be, in one respect or another, an oral translation—true, false, or it depends? What answer would you give and why?

» Does your vernacular translation pass the test of this final principle? If not, why? If so, how do you know for sure?

7. Read "Practical Applications" in Dooley and Levinsohn (2001:17–18) and point out the relevance to Bible translation of the advice given there.

2.3 Kinds of literary forms in the Bible

In section 2.1 we focused on the definition of literature from *Webster's New World College Dictionary*: "[Literature refers to] all of such writings considered as having permanent value, excellence of form, great emotional effect, etc." With this definition in mind, it is clear that the Scriptures are to be regarded as literature in the full sense of the term, whether the whole or in part.

» Do you agree with the preceding definition? Give some reasons for your opinion.

Now let us consider some of the "excellent forms" that are used to express the content of the Scriptures and the "great emotional effect" that we derive from them, that is, over and above the enlightening or edifying content being communicated. Perhaps this can be done best by looking at an actual passage.

The following is a reformatted version of the RSV text of Genesis 1:1–2:3 with the verse markers removed.

What are some of the *formal features* that mark this discourse as being distinct from an ordinary narrative report of a series of temporally ordered events?

In the beginning God created the heavens and the earth.
    The earth was without form and void,
        and darkness was upon the face of the deep;
            and the Spirit of God was moving over the face of the waters.

And God said,
> "Let there be light";
>> and there was light.
>>> And God saw that the light was good;
>>>> and God separated the light from the darkness.
>>>>> God called the light Day,
>>>>>> and the darkness he called *Night*.
>>>>>>> And there was evening and there was morning,
>>>>>>>> **one day.**

And God said,
> *"Let there be a firmament in the midst of the waters,*
> *and let it separate the waters from the waters."*
>> And God made the firmament and separated the waters
>>> which were under the firmament from the waters which were above the firmament.
>>>> And it was so.
>>>>> And God called the firmament *Heaven*.
>>>>>> And there was evening and there was morning,
>>>>>>> **a second day.**

And God said,
> *"Let the* waters *under the heavens be gathered together into one place,*
> *and let the* dry land *appear."*
>> And it was so.
>>> God called the dry land *Earth*,
>>>> and the waters that were gathered together he called *Seas*.
>>>>> And God saw that it was good.

And God said,
> *"Let the earth put forth vegetation,*
> *plants yielding seed,*
> *and fruit trees bearing fruit in which is their seed,*
> *each according to its kind, upon the earth."*
>> And it was so.
>>> The earth brought forth vegetation,
>>> plants yielding seed according to their own kinds,
>>> and trees bearing fruit in which is their seed,
>>> each according to its kind.
>>>> And God saw that it was good.
>>>>> And there was evening and there was morning,
>>>>>> **a third day**.

And God said
> *"Let there be lights in the firmament of the heavens to separate the day from the night*
> *and let them be for signs and for seasons and for days and years,*
> *and let them be lights in the firmament of the heavens to give light upon the earth."*
>> And it was so.
>>> And God made the two great lights,
>>> the greater light to rule the day,
>>> and the lesser light to rule the night;
>>> he made the stars also.
>>> And God set them in the firmament of the heavens to give light upon the earth,
>>> to rule over the day and over the night,
>>> and to separate the light from the darkness.
>>>> And God saw that it was good.
>>>>> And there was evening and there was morning,
>>>>>> **a fourth day**.

And God said,
> "Let the waters bring forth swarms of living creatures,
> and let birds fly above the earth across the firmament of the heavens."
>> So God created the great sea monsters and every living creature that moves,
>> with which the waters swarm, according to their kinds,
>> and every winged bird according to its kind.
>>> And God saw that it was good.
>>>> And God blessed them, saying,
>>>>> "Be fruitful and multiply and fill the waters in the seas,
>>>>> and let birds multiply on the earth."
>>>>>> And there was evening and there was morning,
>>>>>> **a fifth day**.

And God said,
> "Let the earth bring forth living creatures according to their kinds:
> cattle and creeping things and beasts of the earth according to their kinds."
>> And it was so.
>>> And God made the beasts of the earth according to their kinds
>>> and the cattle according to their kinds,
>>> and everything that creeps upon the ground according to its kind.
>>>> And God saw that it was good.

Then God said,
> "Let us make man in our image, after our likeness;
> and let them have dominion over the fish of the sea,
> and over the birds of the air,
> and over the cattle,
> and over all the earth,
> and over every creeping thing that creeps upon the earth."
>> So God created man in his own image,
>> in the image of God he created him;
>> male and female he created them.
>>> And God blessed them,
>>> and God said to them,
>>> "Be fruitful and multiply,
>>> and fill the earth and subdue it;
>>> and have dominion over the fish of the sea
>>> and over the birds of the air
>>> and over every living thing that moves upon the earth."
>>>> And God said,
>>>>> "Behold, I have given you every plant yielding seed
>>>>> which is upon the face of all the earth,
>>>>> and every tree with seed in its fruit;
>>>>> you shall have them for food
>>>>> And to every beast of the earth,
>>>>> and to every bird of the air,
>>>>> and to everything that creeps on the earth,
>>>>> everything that has the breath of life,
>>>>> I have given every green plant for food."
>>>>>> And it was so.
>>>>>>> And God saw everything that he had made,
>>>>>>> and behold, it was very good.
>>>>>>>> And there was evening and there was morning,
>>>>>>>> **a sixth day**.

Thus the heavens and the earth were finished, and all the host of them.
> And on **the seventh day** God finished his work

>   which he had done,
>   and he rested on **the seventh day** from all his work
>   which he had done.
> So God blessed **the seventh day** and hallowed it,
>   because on it God rested from all his work
>   which he had done in creation.

Notice all the repetition of form and content in this opening pericope of the Scriptures which lays the foundation for the artful manner in which this important text as a whole is structured.

- » What added meaning does this formal structure convey?

- » Is it simply "art for art's sake," or is there something more?

- » Assuming the latter, what is the communicative function of the form of this pericope?

- » Mark all the major patterns of corresponding lexical elements that are formed by this means. Does the novel print format help you to distinguish these structural arrangements?

- » Does it aid your comprehension and the legibility of the text?

- » Could this type of formatting be used in a Bible in YL (with sufficient explanation), or would it only work in a study or scholarly edition? Explain your opinion.

Ordered repetition serves at least four major functions in the Genesis 1:1–2:3 discourse:

1. **Segmentation**: to divide the text into cohesive and coherent units of different sizes;

2. **Disposition**: to organize and arrange the repeated elements into various textual patterns;

3. **Connection**: to link up one part of the text with another and unify the discourse as a whole;

4. **Projection**: to give prominence to certain formally marked portions of the text.

How are selected portions of the text marked to show that they fall outside normal, expected usage? Such discourse marking may be achieved by means of additional (exact) lexical reiteration, extra modification and detail, direct speech, the breaking up of a previously established pattern, figurative language, a rhetorical question, hyperbole, and so forth.

- » Point out examples of segmentation, disposition, connection, and projection in Genesis 1:1–2:3.

- » Why are the first three verses of chapter 2 included in this study?

- » What are some of the linguistic and stylistic features of this passage (and its cotext) that support the inclusion?

Obviously, this opening passage of Scripture is not a simple narrative. The way in which it has been stylistically marked by a variety of literary forms suggests that the text serves another purpose or two within the book of Genesis, and perhaps also within the Hebrew Bible as a complete body of literature.

- » What do you think that the purpose(s) might be?

- » What is your evidence for such a conclusion?

2.3 Kinds of literary forms in the Bible

We will be considering the matter of communicative purpose and text function more fully in section 2.4. For now, however, let us look at another passage, Ecclesiastes 3:1–8 (RSV) and try to discover how the forms serve to distinguish it as "literature" and at the same time highlight the author's message. In this case, the text has not been formatted into lines at all as in the Genesis passage above where certain parallels and correspondences were aligned by means of similar degrees of *indentation* to make them visible. Perhaps the *lineation* and indention were excessive, making the text too difficult to read (you may express your opinion concerning this matter), but what happens when it is not formatted at all?

> ¹ For everything there is a season, and a time for every matter under heaven: ² a time to be born, and a time to die; a time to plant, and a time to pluck up what is planted; ³ a time to kill, and a time to heal; a time to break down, and a time to build up; ⁴ a time to weep, and a time to laugh; a time to mourn, and a time to dance; ⁵ a time to cast away stones, and a time to gather stones together; a time to embrace, and a time to refrain from embracing; ⁶ a time to seek, and a time to lose; a time to keep, and a time to cast away; ⁷ a time to rend, and a time to sew; a time to keep silence, and a time to speak; ⁸ a time to love, and a time to hate; a time for war, and a time for peace.

» On a separate piece of paper, try to align this pericope in a manner that displays its internal structural arrangement more clearly.

» Then examine the formal features more closely in order to discover the internal patterns of lexical correspondence, whether of similarity or contrast. Notice in particular the alternation of positive and negative references.

As you do the preceding assignment, you also need to look out for instances of *chiasmus* (or chiasm, meaning a "crossed position"). *Chiasmus* is a common type of formal arrangement in the Bible (both OT and NT). It features a reversal in the order of elements, that is, **A : B :: B' : A'**. Can you detect the chiasmus, or reversed parallelism, in the poetic passage of Psalm 1:6b?

> for the LORD <u>knows</u> **the way of the righteous**,
> **but the way of the wicked** <u>will perish</u>.

Of course, the wicked do not perish of their own volition. God is the agent of their perishing, that is, of their judgment and ultimate punishment. And when the psalmist says that "the LORD knows" someone or something, this not a matter of mere cognition, acquaintance, or recognition. The contrasting elements A versus A' and B versus B' are highlighted within such a structure. A biblical chiasmus is often used for the purpose of making a thematic contrast, especially in poetry.

» Now find chiasmus in Ecclesiastes 3:1–8. Hint: there are two instances, one at the beginning and one at the end of this passage, which is in itself also a significant indicator of formal organization: an "inclusion."

There is a well-known extended chiasmus in the eight verses of Ecclesiastes 3:1–8. This is revealed as one examines the different pairing of elements in moving from one verse to the next.

Can you identify this pattern? (If you have difficulty, see Zogbo and Wendland 2000:31–32.) What function do you think that the extended chiasmus performs in the text here?

- A (3:1): _____
- B (3:2): _____
- C (3:3–4): _____
- C' (3:5–6): _____

- B' (3:7): _____

- A' (3:8): _____

You may think that perhaps some obviously "literary" passages have been chosen just to prove the point—a selective treatment of the available evidence. Would you agree that most of Scripture is similarly structured and artfully shaped? What about a doctrinal epistle—will we find the same sorts of stylistic features there? Consider Romans 12:9–13 (RSV), which is a typical Pauline *paraenetic* (hortatory) appeal:

> [9] Let love be genuine; hate what is evil, hold fast to what is good; [10] love one another with brotherly affection; outdo one another in showing honor. [11] Never flag in zeal, be aglow with the Spirit, serve the Lord. [12] Rejoice in your hope, be patient in tribulation, be constant in prayer. [13] Contribute to the needs of the saints, practice hospitality.

» Do you notice in this text any of the literary forms and effects that we have observed in previous passages?

» What stylistic device do you see in verse 11? (Literally, it reads "in zeal [be] not lazy, in spirit burning, the Lord serving.")

Now examine the Greek text of Romans 12:9–13 (below) and point out what you find. (It is hidden within the text of most translations.) The passage has been realigned on the page so as to display the various formal parallels more clearly.

If you are unable to read Greek, then look the passage up in a literal English translation such as the NRSV or ESV and write it out on a separate piece of paper so that you can see what is being illustrated here. (*This instruction applies to all subsequent exercises that refer to the original text of the Bible.*)

[9] Ἡ ἀγάπη ἀνυπόκριτος.

    ἀποστυγοῦντες τὸ πονηρόν,   A

    κολλώμενοι τῷ ἀγαθῷ,

       [10] τῇ φιλαδελφίᾳ εἰς ἀλλήλους φιλόστοργοι,   B

       τῇ τιμῇ ἀλλήλους προηγούμενοι,

       [11] τῇ σπουδῇ μὴ ὀκνηροί,

            τῷ <u>πνεύματι</u> ζέοντες,   C

           τῷ <u>κυρίῳ</u> δουλεύοντες,

       [12] τῇ ἐλπίδι χαίροντες,   B'

       τῇ θλίψει ὑπομένοντες,

       τῇ προσευχῇ προσκαρτεροῦντες,

    [13] ταῖς χρείαις τῶν ἁγίων κοινωνοῦντες,   A'

    τὴν φιλοξενίαν διώκοντες.

2.3 Kinds of literary forms in the Bible

In Greek the first line of verse 9 is a verbless predication. It acts as an introduction to the series of Christian attributes that follows: genuine love (ἀγάπη) always acts this way! In this section, consisting (after the first opening utterance) of just a single sentence in the original, a chiastic ordering is again manifested—this one based largely on *word morphology, phonology,* and *rhythm.*

> » Try to pick out some of the correspondences that help to organize the discourse.
>
> » Observe also the length of the individual lines. (This length is one reason for setting out the Greek text in this way.) What interesting pattern of reversal do you see when comparing B with B'?

Obviously, this is a carefully composed literary piece and therefore carries additional emotive impact and esthetic appeal over and above the vital ethical content that is being conveyed. But there is more to it even than that. In this case, the form of the Greek text may have some exegetical significance that leads us to prefer one translation over another. Compare, for example, the RSV rendering of lines 2–3 of verse 11 with the NIV rendering of the same lines (segment C above):

> be aglow with the Spirit, serve the Lord. (RSV)
> but keep your spiritual fervor, serving the Lord. (NIV)

> » Where do you detect a major difference between the two?
>
> » Which version would the literary structure of the Greek support and why do you say so?

Admittedly, we cannot be absolutely certain of the correct interpretation in cases of ambiguity, that is, where two (or more) interpretations of the text are possible, each supported by reliable scholars and versions. The point is that a literary feature is another important type of evidence that needs to be evaluated when making exegetical decisions.

Finally, we must call attention to the positional importance of segment C in the pattern above: Generally speaking, the central portion, as well as the ending, of a chiastically arranged passage is of special significance in terms of the author's intended message, whether on the macro- or microstructure of the book or pericope as a whole.

> » Can you see any evidence to support that twofold principle in this particular case?
>
> » As for boundaries, what is it that establishes verses 9–13 as a distinct unit (paragraph) within the larger text?
>
> » In other words, why are we justified in beginning a new paragraph at verse 9 and again at verse 14?
>
> » What formal and/or semantic markers in the original cotext would lead us to support this division?

Perhaps we might by now be inclined to include a greater number of books of the Bible within the category of *well-formed* literature, even though there are certain books and passages we may desire to exclude. Take Leviticus, for example, what could be "literary" (in the popular sense) about that book? Yet, consider the beginning and ending of chapter 11:

> [2] "Say to the people of Israel, These are the living things which <u>you may eat</u> among all the beasts that are on the earth. [3] Whatever parts the hoof and is cloven-footed and **chews the cud**, among the animals, <u>you may eat</u>. [4] Nevertheless among those that chew the cud or part the hoof, <u>you shall not eat</u> these …
>
> [44] For *I am the* Lord *your God*; consecrate yourselves therefore, and *be holy, for I am holy*. You shall not defile yourselves with any swarming thing that crawls upon the earth. [45] For *I am the* Lord who **brought**

> you **up** out of the land of Egypt, to be *your God*; you shall therefore *be holy, for I am holy.* [46] This is the law pertaining to beast and bird and every living creature that moves through the waters and every creature that swarms upon the earth, [47] to make a distinction between the unclean and the clean and between the living creature that <u>may be eaten</u> and the living creature that <u>may not be eaten</u>."

The beginning and ending of Leviticus 11 reiterate the theme of the chapter as a whole, which specifies the ritually clean and unclean animals for the people of Israel—that is, those that "may be eaten" and those that "may not be eaten." Observe the extensive repetition here, as marked in the preceding two passages. The repetition is purposefully used to verbally fix the outer borders of the pericope as a whole, a common literary device in the Bible called *inclusio*. Perhaps Leviticus is not as lackluster as we might have originally assumed!

» What else does the repetition at the close serve to emphasize?

English translations of Leviticus 11 conceal another common stylistic feature of the Hebrew: the verbs in boldface print above actually come from the same verb in the original. Anthropologist Mary Douglas (1999:49–50) has this to say about the significance of this unusual but purposeful usage here:

> The Bible is sprinkled with famous puns, and Leviticus is no exception. For example, two distinct verbs are used in the Bible to refer to God's bringing the Israelites out of Egypt: the commonest is literally 'to bring out', the rarer one, only used in Leviticus 11:45, is literally '*to bring up*'. In Hebrew the same word means 'to regurgitate'. In this one rare case the word for the Lord's saving action is the same that is used for '*bringing up the cud*', one of the criteria of a clean animal. By this literary device the whole of chapter 11 is bracketed between the opening law that says that the only animals to be used as food are ruminants which *bring up* the cud and the concluding passage: 'I am the Lord your God who *brought you up* [regurgitated you] from Egypt.' It is more than a verbal felicity, since only the clean animals and only the people of Israel are to be consecrated. This sly 'inclusio' at the opening and the ending of the chapter is typical of Leviticus, who loves to show the workings of God's mind in body-logic language.

Here we have both the forms and the functions of literature on display in a book that is not really recognized as such. The exegetical implications of these literary features are considerable.

» How is this significant literary effect going to be reproduced in another language?

» Do you have any suggestions or recommendations in this regard?

Reading the Scriptures as literature means that one approaches the text with a conscious awareness not only of its cognitively oriented information, but also of its *expressive, affective* (including the emotive and esthetic), and *directive* dimensions. Many detailed definitions of literature are, of course, available, but for now it is enough simply to point out that the *focus upon linguistic form* (the overall discourse structure as well as the many included stylistic features), which is the most important characteristic of "literature," is of double importance for translators. That is, they should be aware of the literary characteristics of the original document for their possible hermeneutical value, and they must also be prepared to do something about that value when they re-present the same text in the target language, using the oral or written artistic and rhetorical resources available.

This quality of *literariness* (recognized verbal artistry) is normally manifested on all levels of discourse organization within the Bible, from the individual word to the composition as a whole. Literary discourse thus maximizes the "how" (or style) of the text in order to highlight the "what" (i.e., content) and the "why" (i.e., intent or purpose). This is done by means of typical stylistic features such as the following:

a. underlying *structural patterning* or design

b. a *captivating theme* or central *emotive focus*

2.3 Kinds of literary forms in the Bible

    c. organic unity (including the necessary variety—theme and variation)

    d. textual *coherence* and *cohesion*

    e. verbal *balance* and *symmetry*

    f. occasional surprise and insertion of the unexpected

    g. repetition or the positioned recurrence of key linguistic forms

    h. selective *variation* and overt *contrast*

    i. a well-formed, organized progression in the text towards a *climax* and a *thematic goal*

    j. idioms, figurative language, and symbolism

    k. dramatic, intensified, emphatic diction, where appropriate

    l. citation of and allusion to well-known texts, oral or written

    m. sound patterning (puns, alliteration, assonance, rhythm, rhyme)

Not all or even a majority of these forms occur in every biblical text, of course. But they do occur often enough throughout the Scriptures to warrant an expectation of their presence rather than of their absence in a given passage.

» Which of these features are common in the literature or orature of your language?

» Which three tactics on this list are the most important in your opinion? Why?

» Can you add any other stylistic devices to this collection?

In the process of analyzing a pericope, one seeks to demonstrate how the author has used these diverse artistic forms and their associated rhetorical strategies in order to progressively (and impressively?) shape the expectations of his readers/listeners. People are thus enticed, as well as encouraged, to direct their individual interpretive activities, whether intuitively or intentionally applied, in a specific direction with reference to a certain biblical theme or pertinent life situation. Each text has a particular *plot* (structure) and *purpose* (function), and it is up to the translator to discover what these are in the SL text in order to effectively reproduce them in the TL.

Just as every art, trade, science, or technology has its standards and criteria of excellence and modes of evaluation, so, too, does the study of literature. A particular body of literature (whether the collection of an individual author, genre, or an entire people) may be viewed as having a distinct, analyzable discourse "lexicon" and "grammar." According to *poetics,* which is the scholarly study of literary forms, any verbal composition consists of four main elements:

1. **units:** the basic elements of form and meaning (e.g., themes, motifs, devices, techniques)

2. **arrangements:** preferred and predictable versus novel and unusual ways of combining the units

3. **accents:** devices for highlighting or emphasizing selected aspects of form or content

4. **rules:** the principles and conventions whereby the structured units, arrangements, and accents operate within a given text or corpus

These four elements are combined in the notion of *text type* (universal classification) or genre (language-specific classification), each variety of which manifests a particular selection, arrangement, accentuation, and distribution of stylistic features.

> » How would you express these four concepts in YL?
>
> » Do you have any difficulty with the terms units, arrangements, accents, or rules? If so, what words would work better to start?
>
> » Is it helpful to view literature in this way, or would you suggest some modifications for teaching and learning these concepts in YL?

If we aim to better understand and translate the individual passages of a foreign literature such as the Old or New Testament, which originated within the context of a time, place, and culture far removed from our own, it makes sense to learn as much as we can about the Bible's distinctive literary constitution, usage, interpretation, and situational setting. The effort to understand how a biblical narrative, for example, is told is repaid by greater insight into that story's theological, religious, and even historical significance. In other words, paying careful attention to a Scripture text's literary features, both structural and stylistic, often sheds light on its meaning, which is particularly helpful in the case of an ambiguous or problematic passage.

Thus a literary perspective, and the additional textual evidence that it reveals, may shift the balance of interpretation regarding a controversial or debatable issue from one side to the other. We saw that in the example from Romans 12:11. In such cases, the supposedly optional (but actually essential) formal embellishments of the original text are shown to be vital stylistic signals that point towards its author-intended meaning, whether this happens to be semantic or pragmatic (i.e., interpersonal) in nature.

For reflection, research, and response:

1. For many investigators, there is no doubt that "the Bible is literature, the kind of writing that attends to beauty, power, and memorability as well as to exposition" (Linton 1986:16). The case has been well put in general terms by noted author and literary critic C. S. Lewis (in Martindale and Root 1989:71): "There is a…sense in which the Bible, since it is after all literature, cannot be properly read except as literature; and the different parts of it as the different sorts of literature that they are." But what does it mean to read the Scriptures as literature? How does the recognition that the Bible is a literary text affect its reading and interpretation? What has this section taught you about the importance of a literary approach to the analysis and translation of the Bible?

2. In this workbook, we are emphasizing the meaning of literary forms in the biblical text. This is not to say, however, that other linguistic forms are meaningless and can be ignored in the translation process. With the cognitive grammarians, we are inclined to agree that all form has meaning, at least as designators or evokers of semantic, pragmatic, and emotive significance as well as indicators of the interlocking conceptual relationships within a given language and text (e.g., the subject-object distinction, case markings, tense-mode-aspect differences, foreground-background). The simple conclusion is that "meaning cannot be preserved entire in translation from one language to another" (Tuggy 2003:281). Rather, every translation leaks or draws water in this crucial regard. Decisions must therefore be made, both locally in relation to a particular passage and also globally in relation to the translation as a whole; we must ask which aspects and elements of the SL form-meaning complex we are able to preserve in our TL text. At this point in our study what general guidelines would you or your translation team establish towards this end?

3. The literary forms of literature (or the traditional oral forms of a society's *orature*) are often termed *genres*, that is, a recognized type of verbal composition that is distinguished on the basis of content, structure, style, function, and often also the sociocultural context of use (see also section 3.6.2 in

2.3 Kinds of literary forms in the Bible

conjunction with chapter 3 of Wendland 2004b). The recognition of genres, major and minor, SL- and TL-related, is a crucial aspect of effective Bible translation, especially, as we will see, when pursuing a *literary approach* (see sections 3.1–3.4). The importance of this is underscored by the observations of John Walton cited below (from 2006:22–23). Evaluate these comments and the example from Job that is given: Do you agree? If not, tell why. Then try to give another example of an important genre contrast between the Scriptures and their ancient Near Eastern setting—or, point out a biblical genre that needs to be understood in the light of its ancient Near Eastern sociocultural and religious context, so that it can be accurately and appropriately translated today.

> [T]he careful observations of similarities and differences in pieces of literature help inform the study of both the Bible and the Ancient Near East….Understanding the genre of a piece of literature is necessary if we desire to perceive the author's intentions. Since perceiving the author's intentions is an essential ingredient to the theological and literary interpretation of a text, we recognize that understanding genre contributes to legitimate interpretation. Where similarities can be observed between the biblical and ancient Near Eastern genres, they help us to understand the genre parameters and characteristics as they existed in the ancient mind…. Where there are differences it is important to understand the ancient Near Eastern genres because significant points in the biblical text may be made by means of contrast.

> For example, literature from Mesopotamia contains a couple of texts that recount the complaints of a righteous sufferer similar to what we find in the book of Job. The theology behind the book of Job, however, not only offers different explanations, but even uses the mentality of the ancient Near East (represented in the arguments of Job's three friends) as a foil. Job maintains his integrity precisely by not adopting the appeasement mentality recommended by his friends (Job 27:1-6) that was representative of the ancient Near East. The book's message is accomplished in counterpoint. If we are unaware of the contrasts, we will miss some of the nuances….

Such comparative genre study also needs to be carried out between the inventory of Scripture and that of a modern TL in terms of the principal similarities and differences. Have you (or any member of your translation team) ever conducted such research into the oral and/or written genres of your language? If so, briefly report to the class/workshop how this was done. If not, have a group discussion as to how this might be done in the various language settings represented.

4. Study the following text, Luke 1:68–79, and point out its different literary features such as artistic selection, arrangement, accentuation, and distribution. Also note the possible significance of material that seems to fall outside the parallel patterning, especially verses 75 and 79 (how are these two verses semantically related?). In anticipation of section 2.4, try to specify some reasons why the author may have chosen to use these devices when conveying the content of his message for a particular audience, noting the nature of this text and its contextual setting.

⁶⁸ "Blessed be the Lord *God* of Israel,	**A**
for he *has visited* (ἐπεσκέψατο) and redeemed his people,	
⁶⁹ and has raised up a horn of *salvation* for us	**B**
in the house of his servant David,	
⁷⁰ as he spoke by the mouth of his holy *prophets* from of old,	**C**
⁷¹that we should be saved from *our enemies*	**D**
and from the *hand* of all who hate us;	
⁷² to perform the mercy *promised to our fathers*,	**E**
and to remember his holy *covenant*,	**F**
⁷³ **the *oath***	**F'**
which he *swore to our father* Abraham,	**E'**
⁷⁴ to grant us that we, being delivered from the *hand* of *our enemies*,	**D'**
might serve him without fear,	
⁷⁵ in sincerity and righteousness before him all the days of our life.	
⁷⁶ And you, child, will be called the *prophet* of the Most High;	**C'**
for you will go before the Lord to prepare his ways,	
⁷⁷ to give knowledge of *salvation* to his people	**B'**
in the forgiveness of their sins,	
⁷⁸ through the tender mercy of our *God*,	**A'**
when the day *shall dawn* (ἐπισκέψεται) upon us from on high	
⁷⁹ to give light to those who sit in darkness and in the shadow of death,	
to guide our feet into the way of peace."	

5. Point out all the significant correspondences that you can find in the opening and closing passages of Habakkuk (from chapters 1 and 3, set out below from the RSV). What is the thematic or structural importance of these—the salient similarities, but especially the outstanding contrasts? Note the nature of the figurative language at the end. What does this signify and why should it appear here in the book? Note any special translational difficulties as you study these texts.

> ¹:¹ The oracle of God which Habakkuk the prophet saw.
>
> ² O LORD, how long shall I cry for help,
> **and thou wilt not hear?**
>
> Or cry to thee "Violence!"
> **and thou wilt not save?**
>
> ³ Why dost thou make me see wrongs
> and look upon trouble?
>
> Destruction and violence are before me;
> strife and contention arise.
>
> ⁴ So the <u>law</u> is slacked
> and <u>justice</u> never goes forth.
> For the wicked surround the <u>righteous</u>,
> so <u>justice</u> goes forth perverted.
>
> ***
>
> ³:¹⁶ **I hear**, and my body trembles,
> my lips quiver at the sound;
> rottenness enters into my bones,
> my steps totter beneath me.

> *I will quietly wait* for the day of trouble
>> to come upon people who invade us.
>
> ¹⁷ Though the fig trees do not blossom,
>> nor fruit be on the vines,
>
> the produce of the olive fail
>> and the fields yield no food,
>
> the flock be cut off from the fold
>> and there be no herd in the stalls,
>
> ¹⁸ yet I will rejoice in the LORD,
>> **I will joy in the God of my salvation.**
>
> ¹⁹ God, the LORD, is my strength;
>> he makes my feet like hinds' feet,
>> he makes me tread upon my high places.
>
> To the choirmaster: with stringed instruments.

6. The examples in exercises 4 and 5 were formatted to help you see the structural patterns and parallels. The example below from Joel 1:2–14 is not formatted. First, figure out the patterns and parallels on a separate sheet of paper. Then make a list of the main stylistic devices and their apparent purpose within the text. Finally, point out any potential translation problems and be prepared to present possible solutions in a joint class discussion.

> ² Hear this, you aged men,
>> give ear, all inhabitants of the land!
>
> Has such a thing happened in your days,
>> or in the days of your fathers?
>
> ³ Tell your children of it,
>> and let your children tell their children,
>> and their children another generation.
>
> ⁴ What the cutting locust left,
>> the swarming locust has eaten.
>
> What the swarming locust left,
>> the hopping locust has eaten,
>
> and what the hopping locust left,
>> the destroying locust has eaten.
>
> ⁵ Awake, you drunkards, and weep;
>> and wail, all you drinkers of wine,
>
> because of the sweet wine,
>> for it is cut off from your mouth.
>
> ⁶ For a nation has come up against my land,
>> powerful and without number;

> its teeth are lions' teeth,
>> and it has the fangs of a lioness.
>
> ⁷ It has laid waste my vines,
>> and splintered my fig trees;
>
> it has stripped off their bark and thrown it down;
>> their branches are made white.
>
> ⁸ Lament like a virgin girded with sackcloth
>> for the bridegroom of her youth.
>
> ⁹ The cereal offering and the drink offering are cut off
>> from the house of the LORD.
>
> The priests mourn,
>> the ministers of the LORD.
> ¹⁰ The fields are laid waste,
>> the ground mourns;
>
> because the grain is destroyed,
>> the wine fails,
>> the oil languishes.
>
> ¹¹ Be confounded, O tillers of the soil,
>> wail, O vinedressers,
> for the wheat and the barley;
>> because the harvest of the field has perished.
> ¹² The vine withers,
>> the fig tree languishes.
> Pomegranate, palm, and apple,
>> all the trees of the field are withered;
> and gladness fails
>> from the sons of men.
> ¹³ Gird on sackcloth and lament, O priests,
>> wail, O ministers of the altar.
> Go in, pass the night in sackcloth,
>> O ministers of my God!
> Because cereal offering and drink offering
>> are withheld from the house of your God.
> ¹⁴ Sanctify a fast,
>> call a solemn assembly.
> Gather the elders
>> and all the inhabitants of the land
> to the house of the LORD your God;
>> and cry to the LORD.

7. From a broader to a narrower perspective on discourse structure, we turn now to a consideration of the translation of idioms in biblical Hebrew. The following recommendations by M. van den Heever (2007) offer a point of departure for evaluating our various options in this regard. What do you think of these recommendations with reference to the examples cited?

> Given the fact that some idioms function differently in texts than their non-idiomatic synonyms do, I would suggest that the best option would be to translate such idioms with idioms or idiomatic

expressions in the target text, if at all possible. The idiom מַה־לִּי וָלָךְ in 2 Samuel 16:10 is a good example where 'What do you and I have in common?' simply does not carry the same emotional force as, for example, 'What has this got to do with you?' The Northern Sotho translation *ga se taba ya lena ye* ('this is not your matter', i.e. 'this is none of your business') seems to render the meaning and its implicatures satisfactorily in the target text.

It is, of course, often impossible to find an idiom or idiomatic expression in the target language that covers at least the primary or central semantic features of the Hebrew expression. In such cases, it may be possible to use some other form of figurative language to convey the source language expression. The idiom חָרָה אַפִּי ('my nose has become hot/burns', i.e. 'my anger burns') in Zechariah 10:3 is rendered as *ulaka lwami lubavuthela bhe* ('my anger burns fiercely at them') in one Zulu translation. Although this is, strictly speaking, not a proper idiom according to the criteria I have proposed, the metaphor ANGER IS HEAT is maintained in a way that is still idiomatic to Zulu. This translation carries more force than the generic verb *-thukuthela* ('be angry') would do (cf. Hebrew קָצַף).

When neither a suitable idiom nor another figure of speech is available in the target language, the meaning of an idiom has to be translated with a non-idiom, e.g., יִשָּׂא פָנַי ('he will lift up my face', i.e. 'he will receive me favourably/graciously') in Genesis 32:21, which was rendered in Tswana as *o tla nkamogela sentle* ('he will receive me well'). Translating an idiom literally is not advisable, unless the literal meaning of the idiom is intended in the Hebrew text. The exegete of the Southern Ndebele translation project, for example, seems convinced that the Hebrew expression וּפָרַשְׂתָּ כְנָפֶךָ עַל־אֲמָתֶךָ ('and spread your wing over your servant') in Ruth 3:9 is intended literally, i.e. that Ruth was asking Boaz to lift the corner of his coat or blanket for her to crawl under rather than pleading with him to marry her. The phrase was thus rendered as *yewungembulele amabhayi* ('please open [your] shawl to me'). How well the Tswana translation *phuthololela lelata la gago diphuka tsa gago* ('unfold to your servant your wings') communicates is not an easy question to answer without testing....

In summary: when translating an idiom that contains more implicatures than its non-idiomatic synonym(s), the following possibilities exist, in order of preference:

  a. Target language idiom
  b. Some other figure of speech in the target language
  c. Non-idiom (i.e. literal translation of the idiom's meaning)

How would you render the several idiomatic passages cited above in your language? Point out some of the difficulties that you encounter, and describe any novel solutions (equivalences) that you discover.

2.4 What are some of the primary functions of biblical literature?

As we have already seen, the various forms of biblical literature carry out different functions within the text. Indeed, we need to grasp the notion of *function* (the particular purpose or task that a given activity is designed to perform) in order to properly understand the nature of literature. During speech, for example, the different functions refer to distinctions in the speaker's communicative intentions during the utterance of a text, including rhetorical as well as pragmatic or sociological motivations (e.g., to convey a sense of power, solidarity, politeness, or deference). Moreover, marked literary forms do not exist for their own sake; rather, they invariably call attention to certain authorial aims or objectives within the text. The books of the Bible were not composed with just one purpose in mind. Yes, moral and theological education is important in the Scriptures, but that is not the only purpose for which they were written. In the case of some books, in fact, we can hardly detect any explicit teaching at all.

» Can you think of one of these books and suggest why it contains so little overt "theology?"

Let us review some of the important functions that the different texts of Scripture carry out when they are heard or read (see section 1.3). What is the primary purpose of Psalm 23, for example? Is it supposed to teach us a lesson, a certain doctrine about God? Or is the text intended rather to motivate us to do something, or not to do something? Or does the psalmist simply wish to express his fervent feelings about God, himself, his circumstances, or life in general? Or perhaps it would be correct to say that more than one function is "activated," or performed, when we read Psalm 23. If so, are these functions equal in prominence, or is one more important than the other, and how do we decide this? These are some of the issues and concerns that we will be exploring in more detail.

To begin with, I would suggest that good literature tends to be *multifunctional*. That is to say, a literary text normally manifests more than one communicative purpose as it is being conveyed, no matter the medium (e.g., a printed page, a radio broadcast, a video recording, or an electronic hypertext program on a computer).

» Is this true of the Bible too? All, most, some, or little of it?

» Select different passages of Psalm 23 that seem to express different speech functions. Specify these communicative aims and evaluate how well they are expressed in the translation of YL (or prepare an appropriate translation yourself).

The following is a list of functions that appear to be especially important in human communication, including the kind of communication that takes place whenever the Scriptures are read or heard (through the operation of God's Spirit, of course). Along with a definition of each function, a passage is given from Luke's Gospel (NIV) as an example in which that function seems to be prominent:

1. **Referential**: to convey or emphasize information (facts, the real world, truth). "Today in the town of David a Savior has been born to you; he is Christ the Lord. This will be a sign to you" (Luke 2:11).

2. **Directive**: to influence the behavior of an audience (motivate and move them). There are two subtypes.

    a. **Imperative**: to affect a person's thoughts, words, and/or actions. "No, he is to be called John....His name is John" (Luke 1:60, 63).

    b. **Emotive**: to affect one's feelings and deeper emotions. "Glory to God in the highest, and on earth peace to [people] on whom his favor rests!" (Luke 2:14).

3. **Phatic**: to initiate and maintain good interpersonal relationships during communication. There are two subtypes:

    a. **Relational**: small talk about health, sports, weather, or family; verbal formulae that initiate, continue, or conclude discourse; honorific or politeness forms. "I am Gabriel. I stand in the presence of God, and I have been sent to speak to you and to tell you this good news" (Luke 1:19); "Greetings...the Lord is with you!" (Luke 1:28); "I am the Lord's servant....May it be to me as you have said" (Luke 1:38).

    b. **Ritual**: to verbally underscore the common viewpoint and fellowship that people have or desire; to reflect corporate unity through the solidarity generated by certain key terms and familiar speech forms. "And do not begin to say to yourselves, 'We have Abraham as our father.'...'What should we do then?' " (Luke 3:8, 10).

4. **Expressive**: to manifest one's personal feelings, emotions, attitudes, and subjective opinions. " 'How can I be sure of this?!'...'The Lord has done this for me!' " (Luke 1:18, 25).

5. **Metalingual**: to define terms or speak about how language is or should be used. "How is it that they say the Christ is the Son of David? David himself declares…'The Lord said to my Lord…' David calls him 'Lord.' How then can he be his son?" (Luke 20:41b, 42a–b, 44).

6. **Contextual**: to establish links or make reference to the text and/or its situational context. There are two subtypes:

   a. **Deictic**: anaphoric or cataphoric expressions referring to the present setting of communication (e.g., this, those, here, there; now, soon, then, later). " 'This man deserves to have you do this" (Luke 7:4); "I say to my servant, " 'Do this,' "…'I have not found such great faith even in Israel' " (Luke 7:8–9).

   b. **Intertextual/extratextual**: references to what was already said either within the same text or in previous texts (e.g., quotation, paraphrase, allusion). "A voice of one calling in the desert, 'Prepare the way for the Lord, make straight paths for him" (Luke 3:4).

7. **Textual**: to establish the discourse structure of a text—its boundaries, transitions, organization, cohesion, progression, patterning, and peaks. "Blessed are you…for…men insult you…the Son of Man….Woe to you…for…men speak well of you…false prophets" (Luke 6:20–26).

8. **Poetic/artistic**: to highlight a text through formal stylistic means, often emphasizing one of the other speech functions; also to increase listeners' (to a lesser extent readers') appreciation of some specific excellent/beautiful/eloquent/powerful usage of the language. "…because of the tender mercy of our God, by which the rising sun will come to us from heaven, to shine on those living in darkness and in the shadow of death, to guide our feet in the path of peace" (Luke 1:78–79).

In addition to having more than one function active within the same text or even a short passage, exceptional literature tends to be distinguished especially by the poetic function, which serves to enhance or augment the operation of other aspects of the communication event. This will become evident as we examine some longer texts of Scripture in greater detail.

For reflection, research, and response:

1. Review the functions of communication listed above. Which ones in your opinion are the most *important* for Bible translators to try to represent in their TL texts? Why? Which functions are the most *difficult*? Why? Can you give an example based on your own experience of such problems? What was the ultimate result?

2. Try to find at least one good example from the book of Acts for each of the communicative functions listed above. Write them, along with the Bible reference, on a separate sheet of paper. Examples of some of the functions will be much more difficult to find than others, but see if you can find them all. If you pick a passage that illustrates more than one function, make sure that the particular example you seek is the dominant one. Look for two more good examples of the poetic function and explain which *other* function is being emphasized in each case. Discuss your findings in class.

3. Study Genesis 11:1–9 (RSV), presented below. At first it looks like a simple narrative. But notice the instances of lexical repetition and try to organize them into a pattern. There are actually two overlapping structures here, one being linear/sequential in nature (marked by italics), the other being concentric/chiastic (marked by underlining). Reiterated words are in bold print. Prepare a structural diagram of this pericope and point out how this particular arrangement serves to highlight the main thematic message of the passage. Then suggest a possible purpose, or rhetorical function, for this text at the point where it occurs in the book of Genesis, based on the type of discourse found on either side of it. The author is not simply telling us a story to inform us of facts; rather, he has a point to make. What is his point?

> ¹ Now **the whole earth** had *one language and the same words*. ² And as men migrated from the east, they found a plain in the land of Shinar and settled <u>there</u>. ³ And they said <u>to one another</u>, "*<u>Come, let us</u> make bricks*, and burn them thoroughly." And they had brick for stone, and bitumen for mortar. ⁴ Then they said, "Come, <u>let us *build* ourselves a city, and a tower</u> with its top in the heavens, and *let us make a name for ourselves, lest we be scattered abroad upon* **the face of the whole earth**." ⁵ And the Lord came down to see <u>the city and the tower</u>, which <u>the sons of men had built</u>. ⁶ And the Lord said, "Behold, they are *one people, and they have all one language*; and this is only the beginning of what they will do; and nothing that they propose to do will now be impossible for them. ⁷ *<u>Come, let us</u>* go down, and there <u>confuse their language</u>, that they may not understand <u>one another's speech</u>." ⁸ So the Lord scattered them abroad <u>from there</u> over **the face of all the earth**, and they left off *building* the city. ⁹ Therefore *its name was called Babel*, because there the Lord confused <u>the language **of all the earth**</u>; and from there *the Lord scattered them abroad over the face of* **all the earth**.

4. Consider Genesis 11:1–9 in terms of translation. Is there any way that the structure can be reproduced in some way in YL? What would people think of that—would they understand it? If not, what might be done to help them? What about all the repetition in the original Hebrew text (largely carried over in the RSV)—how important is it? Do you notice any places where it is not possible to reproduce this exactly in YL? If so, explain why not.

5. Any literary analysis involves a study of repetition (see section 3.6.4), that is, reiteration of phonological, lexical, syntactic, rhetorical, and larger textual forms. Such repetition—whether exact, synonymous, or contrastive—when carefully studied in the context of a larger section of discourse, usually reveals something about the original author's main communication goals for the text at hand. Examine Psalm 98 (NIV) below in terms of its repetition—whatever type you can find. Mark the repetition in the text, and then suggest how it functions in a structural and thematic way to reinforce the message of this joyous thanksgiving prayer.

> ¹ Sing to the Lord a new song,
>   for he has done marvelous things;
> his right hand and his holy arm
>   have worked salvation for him.
> ² The Lord has made his salvation known
>   and revealed his righteousness to the nations.
> ³ He has remembered his love
>   and his faithfulness to the house of Israel;
> all the ends of the earth have seen
>   the salvation of our God.
> ⁴ Shout for joy to the Lord, all the earth,
>   burst into jubilant song with music;
> ⁵ make music to the Lord with the harp,
>   with the harp and the sound of singing,
> ⁶ with trumpets and the blast of the ram's horn –
>   shout for joy before the Lord, the King.
> ⁷ Let the sea resound, and everything in it,
>   the world, and all who live in it.
> ⁸ Let the rivers clap their hands,
>   let the mountains sing together for joy;
> ⁹ let them sing before the Lord,
>   for he comes to judge the earth.
> He will judge the world in righteousness
>   and the peoples with equity.

2.4 What are some of the primary functions of biblical literature?

6. Consider Galatians 5:16–25 (below), and note the repetition of the words 'spirit' (πνεῦμα) and 'flesh' (σάρξ). See how these two key terms alternate throughout the text, a fact which serves to set it apart as a distinct unit. In which verses are they *not* found? Why not? Can you propose a possible reason? Suggest how the pattern that is created by these contrasting words serves to establish other important thematic contrasts within the larger text. What is the rhetorical function of this passage at this point in the epistle? Which other important stylistic features do you notice in the text, and what is their function? Examine the original Greek text if possible.

   > [16] But I say, walk by the **Spirit**, and do not gratify the desires of the **flesh**. [17] For the desires of the **flesh** are against the **Spirit**, and the desires of the **Spirit** are against the **flesh**; for these are opposed to each other, to prevent you from doing what you would. [18] But if you are led by the **Spirit** you are not under the law. [19] Now the works of the **flesh** are plain: fornication, impurity, licentiousness, [20] idolatry, sorcery, enmity, strife, jealousy, anger, selfishness, dissension, party spirit, [21] envy, drunkenness, carousing, and the like. I warn you, as I warned you before, that those who do such things shall not inherit the kingdom of God. [22] But the fruit of the **Spirit** is love, joy, peace, patience, kindness, goodness, faithfulness, [23] gentleness, self-control; against such there is no law. [24] And those who belong to Christ Jesus have crucified the **flesh** with its passions and desires. [25] If we live by the **Spirit**, let us also walk by the **Spirit**.

7. Find another short text in the Bible that seems to be very literary in its style. Write it out in a literal translation (including also the original text if possible), and then point out the special features that support your claim of literariness. Finally, make some suggestions with regard to how you would render these devices with similar functional effect in YL. (If you cannot think of a text, analyze a selected portion of Isa. 11.)

8. A literary approach to translation takes human emotions seriously; in fact, emotions are an essential aspect of the meaning that is communicated by all effective, influential verbal discourse. Consider the implications for Bible translation of these words of Keith Oatley (in Gavins and Steen 2003:168):

   > Emotions are centres of considerable density of meaning in texts….The effects are achieved not only because emotions are signals that some event has impinged on an important goal or aspiration, but because emotions are touchstones of our deeply held values, both those that are known to us, and those that may only be guessed at.

   What are the most important human emotions? Mention some Scripture texts that evoke them. Are these same emotions stimulated by the translations of these texts in YL? If not, why not? And what may be done to make them part of the text's meaning?

9. Gibson (1998:11) has made the following observation:

   > Israel's imaginative thinking…brings us many pictures which are attractive and helpful to us, as of God as a shepherd tending his sheep, but due to the difference in culture, not a few which we find off-putting and not at all helpful. It may simply be a matter of taste. Take these lines from the Song of Songs where the lover describes his beloved:
   >
   > > Behold, you are beautiful, my love,
   > > behold, you are beautiful!
   > > Your eyes are doves,
   > > behind your veil.
   > > Your hair is like a flock of goats,
   > > moving down the slopes of Gilead.
   > > Your teeth are like a flock of shorn ewes
   > > that have come up from the washing …

> Your neck is like the tower of David,
> built for an arsenal.
> whereon hang a thousand bucklers,
> all of them shields of warriors.
> Your two breasts are like two fawns,
> twins of a gazelle, that feed among the lilies. (Song 4:1–2, 4–5)

Discuss Gibson's comments from the perspective of your culture, and as though you are about to translate the included biblical text in YL. What are some of the challenges you would face and how do you propose resolving them? Keep in mind the genre of the passage and the specific book being dealt with here.

10. The book of Revelation is the most frequently cited example of the essentially nonliterary character of much of the New Testament. Reid (2004:931) holds such a view: "[T]he style of [John's] Gospel and letters is different from that of Revelation; the former are written in excellent Greek, but the latter is often ungrammatical and uses barbarous idioms." But contrast Reid's view with the equally categorical opposing opinion of Bauckham (1993:ix), that Revelation is "a work of immense learning, astonishingly meticulous literary artistry, remarkable creative imagination, radical political critique, and profound theology." Perhaps some scholars come to negative opinions about certain NT books simply because they investigate and evaluate the text from a surface linguistic perspective, and not from a discourse-oriented literary point of view.

In many cases, John's Revelation from the Lord certainly being one, the genre, setting, and purpose of the text can help explain the nature of its composition. The following excerpts from Green and Pasquarello (2003) point this out:

> Revelation was created for oral performance amid the Eucharistic gatherings of the early Christians. In these assemblies, the Apocalypse both described and evoked worship of the Lamb who was slain as the Lord of all creation....Although Christ is not on the stage at every moment in the unified narrative of revelation, his story is nonetheless the overarching drama within which the other layers of the narrative have their place. (p. 118)

> Revelation is also deeply conversant with the Scriptures of Israel, especially with Isaiah, Ezekiel, and Daniel, and presents the story of Christ and God's redemption of the world in terms that draw upon the narratives of God's dealings with Israel. (p. 120)

> Indeed, the discourse of Revelation cannot be captured in conceptual, propositional language, for it is meant to evoke imaginative participation – a different kind of knowledge than one gains when reading....In short, the Apocalypse is not merely an argument, but an oral performance that generates an array of experiences and reactions, thereby to transform the social space inhabited by both performer and audience. (p. 121)

> Unlike formulaic, predictable works that clearly fit a particular generic mold, Revelation 'transgresses' prior rules, offering its audience multiple generic options and interpretations from which to choose, thereby providing room for the reader to participate in the production of its meanings. (p. 123–124)

> When we approach Revelation as modern readers of texts, we are quickly tempted to look for a road map, which freezes our perspective on the performance from some supposedly objective point of view. The itinerary of the Apocalypse, with its many stops and starts, its repetitions, its shifting referents—and its inexorable journey toward the wedding of the Lamb – provides yet another indication of its character as a narrative of resistance. (p. 127)

> John is intentionally speaking an 'idiolect,' an artifice that employs grammatical transgressions as part of an attempt to alter the collective consciousness of its audience. (p. 129)

2.4 What are some of the primary functions of biblical literature?

> The effect of John's peculiar dialect, in short, is to tell the story of Jesus in the language people heard every day, but to speak this language with an alien inflection and alternative meanings. (p.131)
>
> Moreover, the compelling linguistic and cognitive effect that results from John's unique compositional style is augmented by an elaborate, interweaving structural pattern of sevens that acts as an underlying formal force for unity, stability, and forward progression throughout the book. Thus anyone who carefully studies the book of Revelation will inevitably come to the conclusion that it is a highly sophisticated literary work, one that embodies a rhetorically-powerful message for suffering people of God. (p. 148)

Reflect upon the preceding selection of quotations and try to find evidence for these claims (or contrary evidence) within the first two chapters of Revelation. Then point out some of the salient implications of studies such as this for Bible translators.

Of what relevance or practical importance is this information (assuming that it is true) as they render the mysteries of Revelation in another language and sociocultural setting?

Does such background information at least deserve a comment in an introduction to the Apocalypse? If so, what are some of the key literary facts that need to be conveyed to readers – to enable them to appreciate how the compositional style of Revelation contributes to both its theological content and rhetorical argument?

In lesson 4 we will examine the structure and function of biblical literature more systematically from the perspective of genre—that is, the different discourse types that the Bible contains. We have already begun to do this, but a literary approach requires an even closer look. Before that, however, we need to put some of the ideas of lessons 1 and 2 together as the basis for a method of translation that seeks to represent some of the outstanding stylistic qualities of the Scriptures by means of an artistic and rhetorical rendering in a given target language. Therefore, in lesson 3 we will consider some of the main principles and possibilities of a literary functional-equivalence version—a *LiFE* translation.

Lesson 3
Translating For *LiFE*:
A Literary Functional-Equivalence Version

Aim: In this lesson you will review the notion of "translation"—that is, how to define this type of communication in terms of several different form-functional options. You will also learn how to carry out a particular type of Bible translation; namely, a "literary functional-equivalence" (*LiFE*) translation.

Goals: After working through this lesson you should be able to do the following tasks:

1. Define what translation is in relation to communication.

2. Understand the method of *relevant* functional equivalence Bible translating.

3. Describe a literary functional-equivalence *(LiFE)* approach to translation.

4. Distinguish several different types or styles of translation.

5. Prepare a *LiFE* translation of a poetic biblical text.

Review:

Lesson 1, with special reference to the activity of translation as a complex act of communication, and lesson 2, especially its emphasis on the Bible's different kinds of excellent literature.

Read:

Chapter 2 in *Translating the Literature of Scripture* (Wendland 2004b).
Chapters 2 and 4 in *From One Language to Another* (deWaard and Nida 1986).
Chapters 4–5 in *Translating as a Purposeful Activity* (Nord 1997).
Pages 164–201 in *Contemporary Translation Studies and Bible Translation* (Naude and van der Merwe 2002).

3.1 A *relevant* functional-equivalence approach to Bible translating

We now turn to consider the possibility of producing a Bible version that is somewhat different from the literal or idiomatic versions that Bible translators normally think about. I have in mind a version that would make use of at least some of the literary resources of a language, where suitable—that is, in keeping with the style manifested in the original text, on the one hand, and appropriate for the intended audience, on the other. In general, *relevant* functional equivalence is the overall aim, but particularized in favor of a more (rather than less) artistically and rhetorically shaped translation. I term this "literary functional equivalence" (*LiFE*).[1] In this endeavor, the ultimate and ideal goal, where circumstances allow, is to effect a *genre-for-genre* holistic transmission of the Scriptures.

---

[1] My concept of functional equivalence is informed by three other helpful approaches to communication theory and translation: (1) **Relevance Theory**, which is a cognitive, inferential approach to text processing, communication (e.g., Gutt 1992), and translation featuring the "mini-max" notion of text processing, an essentially cognitive view of "context," and the crucial importance of "inference" in all types of communication; (2) **Skopos Theory**, which is an explicit goal-oriented, process-directed, project-based approach to translation theory and practice pioneered and developed by a German school of translation specialists (Reiss, Vermeer, Nord); and (3) **Cognitive Poetics**, which is a specific application of cognitive linguistics to the study of literary texts (poetics). This third approach stresses the perceptual notion of figure and ground; the close interconnection of experience, cognition, meaning, and language; the importance of "readerly" interpretation (how readers/hearers perceive and understand verbal texts); and the primary mental strategies that all people employ when they interpret any text, whether literary or not (Stockwell 2002). From this perspective, translation may be defined as the textual (or verbal) "mapping of different knowledge domains guided by the principle of analogy" (Feyaerts 2003:210). I might add that the principle of metonymic association (part-whole, cause-effect, base-time/place, etc.) seems to be involved along with that of metaphoric analogy, perhaps not as prominently, but essentially so nonetheless.

A functionalist method, as this is, stresses the communicative purpose that a particular translation is designed to perform for its primary target audience within a given sociocultural setting. In the "functional equivalence" proposal of de Waard and Nida (1986:36), the translators' objective is to "seek to employ a functionally equivalent set of forms which in so far as possible will match the meaning of the original source-language text." From this perspective, it is the principal communication functions of the SL text that translators must seek to discover and then reproduce in their TL text. Other theorists emphasize the particular goal of the text within the TL setting, saying that this ought to determine the manner and style of translating in accordance with the governing framework for the translation project as a whole. This is because it is necessary to have an adequate general perspective when making all the crucial decisions needed to translate a specific literary text for a particular target audience. These two functionalist positions do not necessarily conflict with one another; on the contrary, both viewpoints are needed so that the author-intended aims of the Scriptures, as well as the needs, desires, and expectations of a contemporary audience are respected and ultimately satisfied, to the degree possible, during the translation process.

The salient functions of a given Bible text may be re-presented in a target language by either a literal or a more idiomatic translation, depending on its envisaged use. The primary intentions of the original author are not ignored in this operation but, in view of the impossibility of satisfying all of them, they are evaluated for relevance in light of the TL setting and then prioritized for application in the translation itself. The main *preliminary* requirement in preparing a literary version is that its producers carefully explain beforehand what they intend to do and why. An explanatory statement of this nature could be either incorporated as part of the introduction to a translation or published as a separate, accompanying document.

> » Name a number of the key points that you feel would need to be included in an introduction to a translation that takes literary issues seriously, in the biblical text as well as the vernacular version.

Specifying the SL text's primary functions is only part of the translator's task. A greater challenge is to determine *which* of these communicative intentions, major and minor, are to be conveyed in the TL and *how* this is to be done. In other words, which stylistic devices and rhetorical strategies among those available in the TL are appropriate for use in the Scriptures according to the literary conventions that would apply to the genre and setting concerned? We recognize the impossibility of an overly ambitious, blanket goal that seeks to convey the full semantic and pragmatic value of the original text via any translation. Therefore, a choice must always be made between those aspects of the message which the translators will at least attempt to convey and those that they concede will probably be lost during the transmission process. Issues such as these will have to be thoroughly discussed and then spelled out within the project *Brief* and its *Skopos*.

It is helpful to consider these practical procedures pertaining to a functional-equivalence approach to Bible translation in light of some of the psychological insights that stem from "Relevance Theory" as adapted to translation studies by Gutt (1992). Relevance Theory (RT) offers a general way of evaluating the acceptability of a given translation. In the terminology of RT a text is deemed *optimally relevant* (or fully acceptable) if it provides "adequate contextual effects" for the audience, yet "without requiring unnecessary processing effort" (Gutt 1992:24–25). In this case, the notion of "context" is not concrete or physical in nature; rather, it refers to one's psychological state of mind, or, as it is called in RT, "cognitive environment."

Furthermore, RT highlights the extent to which we communicate with each other by *inference*, that is, by depending not only on verbal texts and their cotexts, but also on our assumed shared knowledge and crucial features of the context (the social and situational environment). Thus our aim, under most circumstances, is to communicate in a way that is able to achieve greater *efficiency* in terms of lower mental effort and *effectiveness*, or greater personal benefit for the envisaged audience. In other words, serious speakers seek to convey important matters in a manner that is easiest for their hearers to understand, yet also with an appreciable amount of rhetorical impact and esthetic appeal, resulting in a significant number of cognitive, emotive, or volitional effects within a particular setting.

- » Evaluate the inferential principle of relevance—how helpful is this for you?

- » Can you give a personal example of how it seemed to apply in a communication experience that you had recently?

- » As you study these pages with a Bible translation project in mind—whether real or hypothetical—what do you infer with regard to my intentions with this workbook?

- » How do these intentions involve you? In other words, what might my expectations be concerning the nature of your participation and application of the various issues that we are discussing?

- » On the other hand, what are some of the main expectations that you have regarding the benefit(s) that you hope to derive from your participation in this course (or from working through this manual)?

The common-sense principle of aiming for optimally relevant communication may be applied to the activity of translation in several ways. It may be applied on the general level of *policy* (e.g., formulating the goals of a Bible translation project) or more specifically with regard to translation principles and procedures (e.g., how to handle a particular metaphor in a given passage). The question always is: how can we re-present the SL text at hand in the TL so that our intended audience gets the most out of what the original has to say, yet without having to work too hard at it mentally—that is, to the point of discouragement and giving up?

During this process, when evaluating what actually needs to be communicated (or what does not), it is helpful to adopt a *functional* perspective. In other words, one first needs to identify the primary and secondary communicative aims that operate in a given source text. Next, one must compare these with the particular goals that a certain audience wants to accomplish by reading or listening to the text in their language—so that it becomes relevant for them (e.g., with respect to the informative, expressive, directive, or any other pragmatic function). Finally, one must determine how these respective priorities can best be accomplished both within the text of the translation by means of a suitable translation style and through various *paratextual* aids (e.g., *marginal notes, section introductions*, and *cross references*).

A good example of the potential benefits of a Relevance Theory approach to Bible translation may be found when dealing with the literary technique of intertextuality (see section 1.6.3). An emotionally moving, conceptually inspiring literary text often includes various references, both direct and indirect, to pre-existent texts. These intertextual citations, allusions, and echoes may sound either stronger or weaker in the ears of an audience depending on how familiar they are with the earlier texts and on how much effort they are willing to put into a study of the present text in order to discover these references or to examine their original setting to see how they were used. Most of the New Testament books are filled with instances of intertextuality, that is, direct citations of and indirect allusions to the Hebrew Bible (usually via the Greek Septuagint). The book of Revelation is an example:

> When he opened the fifth seal, I saw under the altar the souls of those who had been slain because of the word of God and the testimony they had maintained.
> They called out in a loud voice, "How long, Sovereign Lord, holy and true, until you judge the inhabitants of the earth and avenge our blood?"
> Then each of them was given a white robe, and they were told to wait a little longer, until the number of their fellow servants and brothers who were to be killed as they had been was completed.
> (Rev. 6:9–11, NIV)

In order for people today to understand the preceding passage properly, so that it gains greater relevance in their lives, their conceptual boundaries need to be expanded. In other words, their minds must be cognitively enriched by a number of OT texts, and others, including some from the Revelation itself.

These texts were undoubtedly familiar to those for whom this book was most directly intended—the first audience, who needed to access and process these prior texts in order to fully grasp the ostensible content and intent of Revelation 6:9–11. The following are several of the most pertinent pre-texts (there may well be more) that serve to create the necessary conceptual relevance that allows the process of interpretation to take its intended course. Answer the questions below by looking up the references and seeing how they create a wider context for understanding:

1. Why were the souls to be found "under the altar?" Why is that place significant, and what does this have to do with the later mention of "blood?" Read Exodus 29:10–12 and Leviticus 4:7, 18, 25, 34.

2. What is the connection between martyrdom and OT sacrifices? Read 4 Maccabees 14–17 and Philippians 2:7.

3. What does the blood of martyrs crying out for vengeance mean? Read Genesis 4:10 and Matthew 23:35.

4. How do Psalms 74 and 79 help us to understand the appeal of slain souls in verse 10, beginning with "How long...!" Also read Psalms 6:3; 13:1; 80:4.

5. Which "inhabitants of the earth" are being referred to? Read Revelation 4:10; 8:13; 11:10.

6. What is the importance of being "given a white robe," and what is the symbolical significance of this? Read Revelation 3:4–5; 3:18; 4:4; 7:9, 13–14.

7. Why are the righteous martyrs "told to wait a little longer?" Read 2 Esdras 4:35–37 and Enoch 47:4.

8. How would those who died "because of the word of God" be one day vindicated by the word of God? Read Revelation 19:1–2, 11–16.

9. How is the special relevance of the fifth seal within the set of seven manifested? In other words, how is it different from the others and how does this difference lead us to look for some greater meaning? Where do you find the report of the opening of the seventh seal and what happens after that? What then do we do with chapter 6? How does chapter 6 relate to the content of the fifth seal report? Note the introduction to the seven seals, especially 5:9–10.

10. As we have seen, the book of Revelation is full of intertextual markers of relevance. What important implications does this have for Bible translators and other Scripture text interpreters?

The preceding example from Revelation illustrates how the principle of *relevance in context* operates during biblical interpretation. An OT text that is directly quoted (probably via the LXX), clearly alluded to, or merely echoed, in a given NT passage will of course evoke its original textual context. The biblical writer depended on this for his words to have their full meaning, including a certain additional amount of impact and persuasiveness. It is therefore up to the current audience, whether those intended by the initial communicative event or all subsequent ("secondary") audiences, to determine optimal relevance with respect to the two texts and contexts involved by applying the *cost versus gain* criterion of significance within the immediate situation. In other words, which interpretation provides the greatest number of salient contextual effects (conceptual and emotive benefits) without requiring excessive processing effort in cases where there are two or more ways of understanding a given text? On the other hand, how does the inferential search for greater relevance in the case of difficult passages lead interpreters to an ever-widening circle of cotexts—those from the book at hand (*intra*textual relevance) or those from other documents of Scripture and even from extrabiblical texts (*inter*textual relevance)?

When these notions are applied to translation, we recognize that the use of a novel, creative, situationally appropriate literary device (whether a metaphor, hyperbole, irony, word-order shift, rhetorical question, or parallel construction) produces a momentary delay or pause in the conceptual processing of a text. This increase in the difficulty and length of perception in turn causes the hearer or reader to take notice, to pay closer attention in the course of interpreting the discourse at hand. Its sense and significance is highlighted at that point, and thereby made more relevant if the information being conveyed somehow stimulates or heightens the cognitive awareness and emotive experience of the interpreter(s). The aim of today's translators is to search for a particular form or set of literary forms in the TL that will stimulate a similar effect. They would thereby achieve the amount of essential functional equivalence that the original text did for its intended audience—with respect to as many artistic and rhetorical aspects of the discourse as possible.

Of course, in the case of conceptually rich, allusive passages like Revelation 6:9–11, it will often not be possible for the translated text to convey all of the information necessary for the reader/hearer to perceive and interpret the essential literal, let alone literary, meaning that the author intended. "Loss" with respect to the text's quantitative and qualitative significance, including its implicit as well as explicit content, is inevitable. Therefore, supplementary assistance is needed in the form of explanatory notes, summary introductions, section headings, and/or cross-references (see section 7.1.3).

The extent to which Bible translators are able to consider such effect-matching and context-building endeavors during their everyday work depends on their level of expertise and experience, the type of version envisioned, the competence of their target audience, and the relative size and scope of the text portion concerned. The important thing to keep in mind is that the meaning of a text involves more than its overt propositional content. Diverse feelings, attitudes, values, and connotations, along with a number of crucial socioculturally based conventional associations, are also present and must be accounted for. This is especially true when dealing with well-composed literary, especially poetic, discourse, as is characteristic of the Scriptures. This additional expressive and emotive import must be factored into the translation equation—either by means of an explicit textual or paratextual procedure or through a focused intuitive exercise of verbal creativity aimed at attaining message parity. Extratextual publications, such as those that shed light on the ancient Near Eastern setting, are also helpful in constructing for consumers a conceptual context conducive to interpreting the biblical text more completely and accurately. Such efforts, no matter how great and time-consuming, must be put forth if justice is to be done to the original author's communicative motivations, goals, and ultimate textual designs.

For reflection, research, and response:

1. In the light of the following quotation, describe in your own words how the cognitive *principle of relevance* and the heuristic method of *functional equivalence* work together in the practice of Bible translation with respect to both analyzing the SL text and then representing this in a given TL text. Would it be possible to utilize them both in the translation that you are working on, or plan to work on? Why, or why not? How then would you define "communicative clues" in the light of what you have already learned in this workbook?

    > [A] translation must retain all the communicative clues of the original….Their value lies not in their intrinsic form, but in their communicative function. Due to the structural differences between languages, it is not possible to reproduce the linguistic properties of one language in another. However, it is often possible to identify the communicative clues of the source text and formulate receptor language equivalents that serve the same communicative function. This approach is inherently similar to that of functional equivalence, which also treats the linguistic components of the source text from a functional perspective. The emphasis relevance theory places on keeping processing effort to a minimum means the reformulated communicative clues must be natural to the idiom of the receptor language. (Smith 2002:110–111)

2. Inadequate terminology is always a barrier in formulating definitions. In this lesson we understand the term "functional equivalence" in rather broad terms; perhaps *communicative correspondence* might be better. Consider this concern in light of Statham's observation (2005:42–43):

> The term 'functional equivalence'…is based on a term (function) which refers to only one – albeit absolutely fundamental—constraint (language function) among the many to which the translation of biblical texts is properly subject, such as clarity, simplicity, naturalness, idiomaticness, and faithfulness. An adequate definition of nonformal correspondence translation needs to be comprehensive of these constraints as well. Furthermore, the emphasis on functions of language and equivalence of function is too easily perceived as affirming the fundamentalist view that the role of the Bible is to evoke in contemporary audiences the same response that it was intended to evoke in ancient audiences.

Is the inferential "principle of relevance" sufficient to qualify or correct such mistaken notions about what a "functional equivalence" approach to translating is all about? If not, what proposal do you have for finding a way out of this dilemma of definition?

3. Evaluate the following suggestion by Huddleston (1988:122–123) towards an adequate definition of translation. How does it help to broaden our understanding and application of the concept of functional equivalence?

> I saw that dynamic equivalence really meant "dynamic and equivalent", i.e., dynamic in reference to the target language, and SEMANTICALLY equivalent in reference to the original meaning of the source text.…Hartmut Wiens, [in *Notes on Linguistics*, No. 3, July 1986] contends that unilingual audiences have a nativelike command of many different levels of linguistic structures. These levels are loaded with sociological implications and are used accordingly. The different forms can convey identical denotations while changing drastically the connotations. The variable factors include region, status, style, age, sex, and ethnicity. An equivalent dynamics approach should be sensitive to this sociological phenomenon. The dynamic of a text indicates that a choice is always made from among many possible levels of equally intelligible linguistic structures. The sociological implications of a translation must reflect those of the source, and the linguistic structures of the target language must be selected accordingly.

4. The twin concerns of relevance and functional equivalence come to the fore as a translation team wrestles with the problem of interpreting, and then rendering in their language, God's unique revelation of himself in Exodus 31:3–14: "I am who I am." What does the word YHWH mean here? Why does YHWH reply in this elliptical manner to Moses, who had simply asked for his name?

The redundancy is undoubtedly intentional and purposeful—an obvious signal to the exegete to call on the principle of relevance. Repetition is there for a reason. Some of its more common functions are emphasis, topicalization, foregrounding, pattern-building, cohesion, and punning. (See Isa. 5–8 for important instances of these.) Could the reiterated usage of the same verb form "I am" in Exodus 3:14 perhaps be a divine pun, intended to add a little mystery and a sense of the numinous to the Name? Surely it is an unforgettable introduction to Israel's personal Lord of the covenant (Exod. 3:6a, 15–17).

The literal translation of a literary device in Hebrew or Greek often causes considerable problems of comprehension for a TL audience: For example, the old Nyanja Bible reproduced the three Hebrew words as precisely as they could (in caps): *INE NDINE YEMWE NDIRI INE*, which turns out to be nonsense: "I I-am the-very-one I-am-(going to do something) I." The second "I am" is an inappropriate form since it is normally used only as a periphrastic linking verb, as in *ndili kupita* "I am in the process of going (somewhere)."

In contrast, the new popular-language Chichewa translation, *Buku Loyera*, tried to put this utterance in the form of a natural reply to the common question "What is your name?": *Dzina langa ndine*

NDILIPO "Name my I-am I-AM-HERE." This rendering, in which "I AM" is expressed only once and the name *YHWH* is rendered as the meaningful though somewhat mysterious *NDILIPO* "I AM HERE/PRESENT," a timeless utterance, eliminates the redundancy of the Hebrew. Thus there is a significant semantic loss but also an important pragmatic gain. It represents the translators' view of how they expect that *YHWH* would have replied to them if he were speaking Chichewa. This reading preserves a sense of the mystery of the original text: *NDILIPO* "I AM HERE—what sort of a name is that?!" At the same time the utterance is expressed meaningfully, indeed, idiomatically, so that people can focus on the possible underlying sense of the name—not puzzle over the unintelligibility of God's utterance as a whole, as is the case in the older version.

How have you handled the problems presented by this verse in YL? To what extent have you looked to a literary solution, as in the new Nyanja translation? Evaluate this version in comparison with how you feel that you must handle the matter most relevantly in your setting.

5. Read 1 Peter 1:2 and explain its meaning—especially the phrase "sprinkling of the blood of Jesus Christ." Now read Exodus 24:3–8. How does the relevance of Peter's words increase for you in light of the sacrificial ritual described in Exodus? How can this additional significance be best conveyed in a translation in YL? Suggest a possible wording that might succinctly and satisfactorily provide a key to the intended meaning.

6. Find an example from the letters to the seven churches in Revelation 2–3 in which a reference to the sociocultural setting of Asia Minor provides a vital context, or cognitive frame, that enables the process of interpretation to progress to completion. Describe how the immediate relevance of the Revelation text is dependent upon this extratextual information. Finally, compose an explanatory note that would adequately communicate this needed information to an average audience in your sociocultural setting.

7. It is important to recognize the influence of intertextuality while doing textual exegesis and translation. Study the following passages from Revelation 21–22 in relation to some probable OT pre-texts. Note any changes in the wording from the prophetic precursor, especially with reference to the concept of "the nations." What might these variations signify with regard to interpreting the author's intended meaning and then accurately translating it for a contemporary audience?

    a. Revelation 21:3 → Ezekiel 37:27; Zechariah 2:15 (cf. Isa. 19:25; 56:7; Amos 9:12)

    b. Revelation 21:24 → Isaiah 60:3, 5, 10

    c. Revelation 21:26 → Isaiah 60:11b

    d. Revelation 22:2 → Ezekiel 47:12; Zechariah 14:8 (cf. Gen. 2:10–14)

8. What paratextual or extratextual aids does your translation team depend on to enrich the cognitive-interpretive framework of people in your primary target audience? Give one or two typical examples to illustrate your procedure with reference to Revelation 22.

9. Regarding creativity in Bible translation, David Tuggy says (2003:276–277), "Translation is by its very nature a balancing act....The only hope we have of balancing well in such a situation is to interpret the source text very accurately, and to have a very thorough knowledge of, and a fertile but well-disciplined creativity in, the target language as well." What are some of the things that have to be "balanced" during the translation process? Why must creativity in Bible translation be well-disciplined? How can such creativity in the TL be increased? What methods have you employed to increase creativity?

3.2 Defining translation more precisely

Before we can actually prepare a translation, we need to be very clear about the object of this creative, yet controlled, compositional activity.

> » What is "translation"? Try defining it here at the outset of our discussion based on your own experience.

> » Why is translation a difficult process?

As you may already know from work that you have done, *meaningful* translation—as opposed to *mechanical* translation—is a very specialized, complex, and varied type of verbal communication. It involves an interpersonal, transformative *sharing* of the same text between two different systems of language, thought, and culture. In other words, translation necessitates a total *re-conceptualization* and *re-signification* of a text that comes from one linguistic and sociocultural setting so that it is intelligible in a completely different communication environment.

This multilingual, intersemiotic, cross-cultural process of textual, as well as cognitive, transformation may be defined or described and evaluated in different ways, depending on a number of important factors. Among these factors are:

1. the **model** of translation that one adopts (whether source-text oriented or target-text oriented, concordant, SMR-code, generative text-linguistic, cognitive-poetic, or relevance based);

2. the **motive**, or purpose (*Skopos*), of the translation in relation to a designated target audience in one or more preferred settings of use;

3. the **manner** in which the re-composition process is carried out (e.g., literal versus idiomatic), including one's view or opinion of the original text.

Translation may be simply defined as the practice of *intercultural* and *interlingual* communication. It is an intricate, at times artful, process of semiotic textual exchange, or verbal "transubstantiation" (transFORM-ation), involving two basic procedures:

1. The intercultural re-ideation of a given SL text, which is a meaningful and purposeful selection, arrangement, and differentiation of signs, whether oral or written, as it is conceptually transferred from one worldview domain and value system to another;

2. The semantically accurate, formally appropriate, and pragmatically acceptable interlingual re-signification of the original text in a specific TL, along with any essential paratextual or extratextual bridge and background material needed to facilitate comprehension.

The first procedure requires the cognitive processing and conversion of all the deep-level semantic and pragmatic features of the original text in terms of the target language and cultural setting, whereas the second, which follows from the first, deals with the more overt surface-level semantic, structural, and stylistic aspects of verbal composition. These procedures are both learned and intuitive in nature—that is, the product of rigorous systematic training as well as innate ability. In any case, mistakes that occur during the first step of the translation process, re-conceptualization, are always reflected in, and hence distort, the second stage, *re-composition*. Conversely, once translators can accomplish the first step in relation to a given SL text and its cognitive/emotive setting, the second, creating a linguistic re-presentation in the TL, is usually not as difficult, although determining the relevant level of *appropriateness* (accuracy, acceptability, etc.) is always a challenge.

> » What do you think of the definition of translation above?

3.2 Defining translation more precisely

- » Discuss the wording of that definition as a class exercise and propose any modifications that would produce a more suitable definition.

- » Which process do you find more difficult, re-conceptualization or re-composition? Why do you say so?

Do we translate *texts* or do we translate *meanings*? Is there a difference? Consider the following points and discuss them sequentially:

1. We translate "texts," which represent "meanings." This process considers everything: the form, content, and intent, as well as the situational and interpretive settings, of both the source text and the target text. In other words, we always translate "*texts*-in-*cotexts*-within-*contexts*."

   - » Explain the meaning of this last expression. Is it clear or should it be modified?

2. We translate the source text (and its represented meaning) *to the extent possible*—in keeping with the project's primary objectives and with the realization that any translation can be only a partial, hence imperfect, and selective representation of the full communicative value of the original text.

   - » What effect, if any, does such a perspective have on the "doctrine of verbal inspiration?"
   - » Do Bible translators even need to worry about such concerns? If so, why?
   - » How can apparent misunderstandings regarding such issues be explained?

3. The term "text" implies the importance of stylistic form, based on a phonological foundation (as pointed out by the proponents of cognitive grammar).

   - » Would you agree? Explain, and give an example to illustrate your answer.

4. A careful analysis of literary form is necessary in order to determine the author-intended content and goals of the source text (as nearly as possible based on a consensus of scholarship) within its likely, but ultimately hypothetical, contextual setting.

   - » How important is "form" in your practice of translation—with respect to the SL text?
   - » How do you demonstrate your attention to this factor?
   - » Why do translators need to be concerned about the original contextual setting at all? Is not the biblical text alone enough?
   - » Illustrate your response to this issue with reference to the books of Deuteronomy and 2 Corinthians.

5. To a greater or lesser degree, the SL form itself has meaning, that is, communicative significance, with respect to emotive expressiveness, esthetic appeal, rhetorical impact, and textual organization. Thus the Italian proverb *traduttore – traditore* "the translator [is] a traitor!" applies also to form.

   - » Explain the implications of this to the practice of Bible translation in your setting.
   - » If possible, also give an example to clarify what you mean.

6. A literary/oratorical approach pays special attention to the non-referential, connotative, and evocative features of discourse associated with the SL forms as they are uttered and heard aloud.

» How important are these formal, stylistic concerns to the composing of a translation in your language and setting? Why, or why not?

» Have such issues been thoroughly, or even partially, discussed at any stage?

7. The answer to the previous question may be: "it all depends." It depends on what the principal aims of the translation happen to be in the primary intended setting of use. If these aims include an effort to achieve naturalness in terms of textual impact and appeal, then TL literary form is vitally important and needs to be carefully researched and applied consistently and appropriately in the practice of translation.

» To what extent has this occurred in the context of your Bible translation?

» If not much has been done in this respect, particularly with respect to the oral art forms of YL, how can the situation be improved?

The complicated process of translating may be defined more precisely by breaking it down into a number of key components:

Translation is (a) the conceptually mediated re-composition of (b) one contextually framed text (c) within a different communication setting (d) in the most relevant, (e) functionally equivalent manner possible, (f) that is, stylistically marked, more or less, (g) in keeping with the designated job commission (h) agreed upon for the TL project concerned.

The sequence of these core constituents can be explained as follows (cf. Wendland 2004b:85):

a. **The conceptually mediated re-composition:** The translator acts as a "mediator," or verbal "foreign-exchange broker," who must fairly represent all his "clients," that is, the original author and his communicative intentions as well as the needs and desires of the target audience.

b. **One contextually framed text:** "Context" is the total cognitive-emotive-volitional frame of reference that influences and guides the perception, interpretation, and application of a given text.[2]

c. **Within a different communication setting:** The translator negotiates a re-formulation, that is, a verbal re-signification, of the original text in a new language, mind-set, and sociocultural environment.

d. **The most relevant:** The aim is to achieve the greatest number of beneficial conceptual, emotional, and volitional effects for readers without their expending excessive or undue processing effort.

e. **[The most] functionally equivalent manner possible:** The target text should manifest a sufficient degree of similarity to the original in terms of the meaning variables of semantic content, pragmatic intent, connotative resonance, emotive impact, artistic appeal, and/or rhetorical power in accord with its literary genre.

---

[2] I accept the principle of Relevance Theory, which views "context" as an all-encompassing cognitive construct informed by an individual's memory and current experience, including the physical, sociocultural, interpersonal, and verbal setting in which a given act of communication is taking place (see Gutt 1992:21–24). Context, according to Gutt, refers to the "cognitive environment" (CE) of a given individual—a comprehensive, all-inclusive mental construct, or conceptual-emotive framework, composed of knowledge, associations, and inferences based on that person's prior learning, both formal and informal, positive or negative; past experiences, good as well as bad; the immediate physical and social environment; the present cotextual setting of any verbal text under consideration; current assumptions (including those that pertain to the CE of other interlocutors on the scene); all other perceptible communicative stimuli (semiotic verbal or nonverbal signs, including the text that is presently being read, watched, and/or listened to); any noncommunicative stimuli, that is, any random noise that is manifested in the present setting, perhaps even hindering the current process of communication; and, finally, those particular or general emotions, attitudes, and values that happen to be associated with any of the preceding elements.

f. **Stylistically marked, more or less:** The degree of stylistic domestication (i.e., reflecting the genius of the TL) versus the degree of foreignness (reflecting the "otherness" of the SL text) must always be assessed with respect to the linguistic and literary norms, conventions, and expectations of the TL audience.

g. **In keeping with the designated job commission:** A TL text's level of accuracy and acceptability is defined with respect to the translation project's *Brief*, which includes its general terms of reference, primary communication goal(s), staff experience and training, available resources, quality-control procedures, community wishes and requirements, administrative and management procedures, and desired completion schedule.

h. **Agreed upon for the TL project concerned:** The communicative framework of the TL social and religious setting is determinative for establishing the job commission, which needs to be first carefully researched, then agreed upon by all major sponsors and supporters, and, finally, closely monitored, evaluated, and, if necessary, revised on a systematic, ongoing basis

It is important to note that translation is different from monolingual communication in that translation involves at least two different external settings and interpersonal situations, and often three (e.g., that evoked by an English translation), if the translators cannot access the original text. The formal and conceptual *distance* between these two or three contexts is variable, depending on the languages and cultures concerned. Generally speaking, the greater this distance (i.e., from the ancient Near Eastern environment), the more difficult the translation task becomes and the more active form-oriented mediation on the part of the translator is required if a meaningful, let alone a literary, version is to be prepared.

We might add the following observations to the eight components of the translating process above:

1. Translators do not, ideally, work in isolation, but rather as part of a team of mutually supportive co-translators, reviewers, technical specialists (exegetes, literary artists, keyboarders, computer technicians), and consultants, coaches, advisers, guides, and at times mentors.

2. Each communication setting incorporates interacting levels of extratextual influence that together affect all aspects of text representation—its production, transmission, and processing (factor *b*). Thus there are diverse cultural, institutional (including ecclesiastical) religious (traditional and modern), environmental, interpersonal, as well as personal (psychological and experiential) factors that affect the overall communication context either directly or indirectly. These varied and variable frames all merge to form the respective *collective cognitive framework* of the SL or TL communities—and the individual viewpoint of each individual of which the group is composed.[3]

3. The perspective and opinion of the current audience, which needs to be clearly specified at the outset, is then determinative (factor *h*) in drawing up an organizational *Brief*, which is the defining and guiding document that outlines the *Skopos*, principles, procedures, and provisions for a given Bible translation endeavor.

4. In terms of this definition, the translation of a literary version is carried out according to the general principle of psychological *relevance* (factor *d*, focus on the TL text), which governs the project-specific practice of *functional equivalence* (factor *e*, focus on the SL text), as particularized or delimited by the agreed-upon *Skopos*.

---

[3]To avoid terminological confusion, one might distinguish between the notions of "context" as a specific, external, perceivable reality and of "frame" as one individual or collective cognitive organization or mental representation. The sum total of frames of reference that are relevant to the interpretation of a given text constitutes its overall conceptual framework (see Wilt 2002a, chapter 2). However, I have not maintained such a distinction in this manual.

5. The *LiFE* method is applied with respect to the content and intent of the original text, but also in view of and guided by the genre-determined stylistic features of the TL (factors *f–g*), starting out from its significant phonological forms. Another type of translation—for example, a formal-correspondence version for liturgical purposes—may be defined in much the same way, except for specifying a different qualifier of "relevant."

6. To some degree, whether more or less, stylistic domestication (*f*) is always called for. Even a relatively literal translation needs to be stylistically marked in a discernible and appreciable manner, at least phonologically, with regard to naturalness, for this is perhaps where a translation's style is most immediately perceptible. How the text reads aloud, how it actually sounds in the vernacular, is a criterion of utmost importance for "literariness."

7. Finally, it is important to remember that every translation, no matter what kind, always involves a communicative *loss* with respect to content, intent, connotation, or some other type of significance. This fact, which is supported by the principles of cognitive grammar, argues against both the dynamic-equivalence approach (DE) and the formal-correspondence approach (FC). With regard to DE, it is not possible to change linguistic forms, even phonological forms, without altering the meaning in some way. With regard to FC, if the SL forms are not changed in the transfer process, the meaning in the TL text is inevitably altered. In other words, a literal rendering changes the intended sense and significance of the message as much as a dynamic-equivalence rendering, in fact, more so. In either case, of course, certain types of lost information may (must?) be supplied paratextually by footnotes, introductions, section headings, or a glossary. Such descriptive or explanatory information may also be supplied extratextually by means of supplementary, context-enriching publications.

For reflection, research, and response:

1. What do you think of the expanded definition of translation (with the eight components a–h) given above? Which, in your opinion, is the most important component? Why do you say so? Do you wish to simplify, clarify, supplement, or even replace it? If so, how does your proposal feature a literary approach with reference to both the SL and the TL settings of communication?

2. Evaluate the explanations that follow the expanded definition of translation. Do you have any additions or corrections to suggest? Which is the most important of these concerns from the perspective of a Bible translation in YL? Why do you say so? Try to give a concrete example.

3. Can you give an instance where the *form* of the biblical text is meaningful? Which aspects of a proverb, for example, convey some aspect of connotative, or associative, meaning? See if you can find an illustration or two from Proverbs 17 (in the original Hebrew if possible). Then evaluate the following conclusion by Unseth (2003:17) and apply the implication to your own translation setting. How does it modify your understanding of what the process of translation entails?

   > [T]he translation of proverbs requires an appreciation of the fact that proverbs have an aesthetic quality in their form in the source text and a *conscious* awareness of the aesthetic techniques used in forming proverbs in the RL. Then the translator is in a much better position to remold foreign proverbs into meaningful and aesthetic forms in the RL. This is important because for proverbial speech, part of the meaning is the form. Put another way: if passage does not have a proverbial form, it will not have (as much) proverbial meaning.

4. Discuss the meaning of the Italian proverb *traduttore – traditore* "the translator is a traitor," and apply it to your particular translation project. In what sense do translators betray the original text, and what can be done about it? How can such a "betrayal," though it cannot be eliminated, be diminished?

5. In what ways is the translator a "mediator" in the course of his or her work? What are some of the key characteristics of a mediator? How is this term rendered in YL? Can you think of any other ways in which to describe the work (and difficulties) of translation?

   Consider this: The translator is a "trader," a person who exchanges one text (in the SL) for another (in the TL), all the while striving to keep their respective communicative values approximately the same. Moisés Silva says the translator is a "transformer," someone "who, like it or not, *transforms* a text by *transferring* it from one linguistic-cultural context to another" (in Scorgie, Strauss, and Voth 2003:47).

   Umberto Eco prefers to look at the translator as a "negotiator." In his view, the process of translation is "a matter of negotiation between the translator, the reader and the original author, whose unique voice should remain in the text....Negotiation is a process by virtue of which, in order to get something, each party renounces something else, and at the end everybody feels satisfied since one cannot have everything" (Eco 2003:192, 196). Apply his comments to a *LiFE* manner of translating. Are there any aspects of the biblical text that are not negotiable? If so, which ones? Why?

6. Consider the following caveat regarding the practice of functional equivalence Bible translation (Cameron 1990:101–102):

   > Now there is sometimes in translation such a thing as the *mot juste*: sometimes there will be a word or phrase in the receptor language which precisely, or as precisely as possible, catches the meaning of the original, and in these cases no other translation will do....[I]t does seem that in many places translators are too ready to abandon formal correspondence and embark on the search for functional equivalence. Of course 'abandon formal correspondence' is an over-simplification, because it implies that formal correspondence is ready to hand, whereas it has to be uncovered: formal correspondence is not the same as literalism. The point is that there is today an implied assumption that, the aim of translation being equivalent effect, this effect is to be achieved by functional equivalence. But such an assumption is not universally valid. Indeed it may be said that functional equivalence always starts at a disadvantage in its pursuit of equivalent effect, because it invariably disrupts the rhythm of the original, and the rhythm of the original is an inseparable part of its effect. The principle should be therefore that the possibilities inherent in formal correspondence must be exhausted first, and only if they yield nothing should there be resort to functional equivalence.

   Are the translators in your team (or those in a project that you know of) capable of putting the concluding recommendation into effect? Explain why—or why not. To what extent do you take the rhythm of the biblical text seriously in translation? If you do, give an example. Also give an example of a case where literalness may be idiomatic, that is, where a formally correspondent rendering of the original text turns out to be the most functionally equivalent way of putting the concept in your language (*le mot juste!*).

7. Our definition of translation focuses strongly on the notion of context (an integrated set of cognitive frames) as a very important and influential aspect of the entire translation process. Point out several ways in which this is true. Why is it important to pay so much attention to these contextual factors?

8. In the explanation of point *a* of the above definition of "translation," the *intentions* of *the original author* are mentioned as being the key reference point in the process. However, objections can be raised against such a perspective. What do you think of Yu's (2005:236) objection:

   > [O]ften, I do not really know who wrote or edited a particular book in the Bible. This is especially true in the OT. Even in cases where I'm quite sure who the authors might be, how could I find out about their intention?...All I have are copies or translations of the texts. In practice, the appeal to authorial intention seems problematic.

Evaluate the following response to this objection. Discuss some of the problems involved with the attempt to discern (our contemporary interpretation of) *authorial intention* in ancient texts:

> Text and context do set boundaries on what meanings are plausible....A text may point to a trajectory of plausible meanings instead of 'having' only one meaning. In the case of biblical texts, we are far removed from the cultural, historical and linguistic situations surrounding these texts, and these gaps complicate matters....This is not a problem. I'm not talking about exactness, but approximations. My aim is to get at some adequate readings of the text, not the meaning of the text. (ibid.:239)

Can a literary perspective be used in conjunction with a linguistic (text) analysis to help narrow the range of hermeneutical possibility in more doubtful cases? If so, explain how this works.

9. Study Luke 10:13–14 and select the aspects of the essential contextual or background information that need to be supplied paratextually so that people of YL can properly understand the passage.

10. How do the following observations by Eco (2003:3) relate to a *LiFE* approach to translation?

> In translation *proper* there is an implicit law, that is, the ethical obligation to respect what the author has written. It has been said that translation is a disguised *indirect discourse* ("The author so and so said in his/her language so and so"). Obviously, to establish exactly *what* "the author said" is an interesting problem....

This is a problem because so often what the author said is bound up with how he said it, that is, with the formal features of the SL text. What do you think?

11. Compare our definition of translation with Wilt's definition (2002a:78, noting also his diagram on p. 79). How are the two definitions similar—or different? Do they complement each other—or not? Explain.

12. Give a definition of translation in YL that could be readily understood by a *monolingual* translator. (Do not necessarily copy the definitions of others.) Then give a back-translation into English and point out any special features of your definition and tell why you have incorporated them.

3.3 Defining a *literary* functional-equivalence translation

In section 3.1 we examined the desirability of a relevant functional-equivalence type of translation. Such a translation would be in keeping with the wider definition of translation that we have been considering. A version that manifests a good measure of literariness is the kind of translation that should have relevance for many people (i.e., benefit, utility, applicability, appropriateness), since, as we have seen, many portions of the Bible may be classified as literature. In fact, we may go so far as to argue that every translation intended for public reading/hearing should be composed, *more or less*, as a literary functional equivalent of the original. In other words, any translation, *even a literal version*, can be made to manifest some degree of recognized TL poetic and rhetorical features, depending on the version's primary purpose, setting of use, and principal audience.

How can this be done? That is the question that we will try to answer in the remainder of this lesson. Our emphasis here is a translation that is more *literary* in nature rather than less (or, we might say, more *oratorical* if we wish to emphasize orature and the oral-aural dimension of discourse). This is what we term a literary functional-equivalence (*LiFE*) translation. A well-trained and skilled translation team should be able to produce such a version, one that displays an excellent literary standard—in other words, a text that has recognized artistic qualities on all strata of linguistic structure in the TL. It is normally composed within the framework of a TL genre that is a functional equivalent of the primary SL discourse being rendered, but having its own distinctive stylistic features that operate as a formal "package" to convey the principal communicative purpose(s) of the original text.

Production is only part of the task, however. Often the job of *promotion* is just as important, including a certain amount of education concerning the translation product in mind. Thus it may be necessary to convince a project's sponsors, administrators, supporters, and at times even the public at large that a more idiomatic version of the Scriptures is not only feasible, but also highly desirable. As Landers (2001:7) observes, "One of the most difficult concepts about literary translation to convey to those who have never seriously attempted it—including practitioners in areas such as technical and commercial translation—is that *how* one says something can be as important as, sometimes more important than, what one says."

In view of this difficulty, it must be stressed that various degrees and levels of literary application are possible. The different options may be explored and finally determined on the basis of audience research in relation to the main communicative objective that the team aims to accomplish in the primary setting of intended use.

Another crucial factor necessary for success is having a translation team that is equal to the challenge. However, depending on the circumstances, a literary technique may be applied in a more limited manner. That is, it may be applied to only selected features or portions of the biblical text. Even a little bit of *LiFE* can mean a lot to any translation!

» What do you think of this notion?

» If you agree with the basic concept, try to give an example of such selectivity using a prominent stylistic feature or two from YL.

» What sort of qualifications should *LiFE* translators have in order to have a reasonable chance of doing a good job?

» What kind of supplementary training do they need?

The following are the main premises or assumptions that underlie a *LiFE* approach, each of which involves an adjustable gradient of possible perspectives, interpretations, and applications:

1. The biblical text is undeniably a book of literary forms, consisting of many different genres and their associated stylistic features. It embodies a demonstrably excellent compositional quality ("literariness") in many places, in both the Hebrew and Greek Testaments—with valid differences of opinion to be expected as to where, in which respects, and how much such artistry is manifested (e.g., cf. the books of Kings with Chronicles or 1 Peter with 2 Peter).

2. The available literary/oratorical resources of the TL are not often utilized, even partially, in most Bible translations. Nor are they, in many cases, even adequately researched to discover what is actually available in terms of stylistic features and rhetorical techniques. As a result, a whole dimension of potential cognitive enrichment is overlooked.

3. Different degrees of *LiFE* application are possible with respect to the TL text, depending on the prevailing sociocultural and ecclesiastical setting. In other words, the *functional profile* designated for re-presentation in a translation will vary in keeping with the priorities set forth in the project *Skopos* and the textual features of the biblical document at hand (e.g., its segmentation, cohesive properties, *peak points*, and *microstylistic* devices).

4. In a *LiFE* translation different features of TL form may be chosen for specific literary enhancement (e.g., marking or foregrounding), whether phonological, lexical, syntactic, or *macrotextual* (genre-related). This decision-making process is guided by the decisions made during the project-planning stage and incorporated into the project *Skopos*. *LiFE* involves the functionally oriented, selective process of *formal* text re-creation, coupled with its *semantic* preservation (insofar as possible).

5. To produce a literary translation is intellectually stimulating and emotively satisfying. It gives gifted translators the opportunity to be both individually and collectively resourceful and innovative in the use of language, whether to a greater or lesser degree. Once competent and creative communicators get used to more fully utilizing the rich artistic and rhetorical assets of the TL in order to match the communicative dynamics of the biblical text, they become captivated by the challenge and seek to engage it dynamically at every opportunity.[4]

The extent to which *LiFE* principles may be applied in a given translation project depends on a wide range of variables that interact within the total communication framework (for some ideas, see chapter 6 of Wilt 2002a). Not the least of these variables is the amount of resources allocated to the project—human, financial, and technical. As already noted, this would include the qualifications and competence of the translators as well as the level of support allocated for their ongoing training and for an ongoing assessment and possible later revision of the text.

Other important but not often considered factors are the history of translation and the influence of subsequent publications, as well as interchurch politics in the region concerned.

- » How desirable would it be, for example, for any new Bible to look (or sound) like previously published and widely used versions, whether in the same TL or a language of wider communication?

- » Will future interchurch developments have any influence one way or another on the project?

- » Have particular biblical terms, expressions, compositional styles, or published formats become identified with certain church denominations or constituencies?

The matter of *flexibility*—being willing to apply a variable degree or intensity of literary functional equivalence—is crucial to this chapter's recommendations. A *LiFE* approach does not really represent a new translation method: it can be actively applied, whether globally or selectively, at one or more linguistic levels within any translation, depending on the particular expressive genius of the TL.[5] It may embrace the text's phonology (e.g., rhythmic utterance), lexicon (e.g., ideophones), morphology (e.g., deictic affixes), syntax (e.g., strategic word-order variations), or the discourse structure as a whole (e.g., using parallel or chiastic patterning, including its formatting on the printed page).

To put it another way, *at least one prominent element of stylistic form* in the translated text needs to be artfully modified in a systematic, consistent manner and for a definite rhetorical purpose in order for it to qualify as a literary/oratorical version. Exactly how much and in which respects would have to be determined on the basis of considerable pre-translation research and formulated in an explicit *Brief*. This comprehensive statement of the project's terms of reference and job specifications, including its *Skopos*, must always be specific to the proposed target audience and the version's intended use.[6] Thus even a more formally correspondent liturgical, or "pulpit," version may be given more *LiFE* if it has been rendered artistically in certain perceptible respects in keeping with TL norms and popular expectations.

However, to produce a literary translation requires a highly skilled, creative and cooperative, experienced and biblically educated translation team. To what extent are project organizers and administrators really committed to, or even aware of, this crucial need in terms of personnel? Literary translators must first apply their knowledge and skills to a careful and thorough *analysis* of the SL document. They then *re-present* the original text and its significance in the TL, whether selectively, working from content to various aspects of form, or holistically, composing the translation as a conceptual and stylistic whole.

---

[4]This point is especially worth noting. Landers (2001:5), a secular translator and critic, observes, "[O]nly literary translation lets one consistently share in the creative process. Here alone does the translator experience the aesthetic joys of working with great literature, or recreating in a new language a work that would otherwise remain beyond reach, effectively 'in code'."

[5]The "genius" of a given language refers to the various stylistic features that distinguish the discourse of different genres as recognized and currently evaluated by sensitive lay people as well as experts in the TL and its literature/orature.

[6]For more discussion on the concept of Brief and Skopos, see Nord 1997:27-31; Wendland 2004b:292.

In the latter instance, they work more intuitively either on a complete utterance-for-utterance basis or on a paragraph-for-paragraph basis, always being guided by the style of the TL genre that is the nearest functional equivalent to that of the SL text. In cases where no TL correspondent exists, translators may have to create their own hybrid genre as they proceed, based on the appropriate speech styles that are available in the vernacular.

As already noted, text production is only part of the task. In addition to promotion, an intense process of comparative text examination, evaluation, and, when necessary, correction must also automatically follow the work of translation in order to ensure that the necessary level of overall quality has been attained. Here again, translators of the highest competence are required, and often these persons are different from those engaged in text composition. Such a translational review and critique is carried out first with reference to the exegetical and literary features of the biblical text with respect to form, content, and function—and then the vernacular draft is revised and refined accordingly.

For reflection, research, and response:

1. Try to define what a *LiFE* translation is in your own words, first in English, then in your own language. The following is what Eco, a well-known professional translator and literary scholar, had to say on the subject (2003:56):

   > [T]he aim of a translation, more than producing any literal 'equivalence', is to create the same effect in the mind of the reader (obviously according to the translator's interpretation) as the original text wanted to create. Instead of speaking of equivalence of meaning, we can speak of *functional equivalence*: a good translation must generate the same effect aimed at by the original.

   Evaluate Eco's opinion in light of the preceding discussion of a *LiFE* approach to translating the Scriptures in a dynamic manner.

2. What are some of the outstanding literary or oratorical stylistic features in YL that could well be utilized in a *LiFE* translation of the Bible? Give an example or two in relation to a specific biblical passage or a familiar vernacular saying.

3. If you do not have an immediate answer to the previous question, how might you go about finding out? In other words, how do you propose carrying out such a research project in the context of YL?

4. Can you think of a local situation where a *LiFE* version might be a possible goal to try to achieve—that is, with respect to the general ecclesiastical and social setting that you live in?

5. What would be some of the most important factors that would hinder or prevent the production of a literary translation in your community or setting of work? How might some of these potential barriers be overcome or mitigated?

6. Christiane Nord makes the following *Skopos* "suggestions for a purpose-oriented approach to literary translation" (adapted from 1997:92–93). How do these principles relate to what has already been said in this lesson about preparing a *literary* translation—now, with specific reference to the Scriptures? Record any similarities, differences, and additional ideas or implications that you discern:

   a. Interpretation: The translator interprets the source text not only with regard to the sender's intention but also with regard to its compatibility with the target situation. This means that the translator compares the target text profile (time, place, motive, addressees, medium, etc.) with the material offered by the source text, analyzing not only the sender's intention with regard to the source-culture receivers but also the possibilities that target receivers have of coordinating the source-text information with their own situation and horizon....

b. Text Function: The target text should be composed in such a way that it fulfils functions in the target situation that are compatible with the sender's intention. When analyzing the source text, the translator tries to find out which function or functions the text fulfils…in the source culture. The first question is which of these functions can be achieved in the target culture (and in what hierarchical order) by means of an instrumental [i.e., idiomatic] translation, or whether a documentary [i.e., more literal] translation would be more appropriate.

c. Cultural Distance: The text world of the translation should be selected according to the intended target-text function.…[This concerns such issues as how much local cultural adaptation to allow as opposed to the use of paratextual aids like footnotes, illustrations, a glossary, etc.]

d. Text Effect: The code elements should be selected in such a way that the target-text effect corresponds to the intended target-text functions. Like the source culture, the target culture provides linguistic means appropriate to attaining a particular text function. Using these means, the translator can be relatively sure the target receivers will recognize the intention and receive the text with the desired function.…The translator thus has to use source-text analysis to determine whether and to what extent an imitation of the source-text style could be an appropriate way of achieving the intended function and what effect this will have (such as enrichment of the target language). The result of this analysis should determine the choices made in the translation process.

With regard to this last principle, what does "enrichment of the target language" mean? Have you noted this effect in the Bible translation that you are (or were) engaged in? If so, give an example. If not, explain why. What would be the converse of "enrichment" with regard to TL style when a more literal translation approach is followed? Can you give an example of this outcome in a vernacular translation that you know of?

7. Do you agree with the following assertion by Landers (2001:8)? Discuss this in light of your own translation work or goals.

> Consider some of the capabilities that the literary translator must command: tone, style, flexibility, inventiveness, knowledge of the SL culture, the ability to glean meaning from ambiguity, an ear for sonority, and humility. Why humility? Because even our best efforts will never succeed in capturing in all its grandeur the richness of the original.

8. Is God an artist—does he really appreciate the beauty of forms? Discuss this in light of the following Scripture passages: Genesis 1:4, 10, 31; Exodus 25:9; 1 Kings 6:12–13; Ezekiel 33:32, 40–43; Psalms 19:9b–10; 45:1–2, 17; 119:54, 103; 1 Corinthians 1:17 (in comparison with 2 Cor. 5:11); Colossians 3:16; 4:6; and Revelation 21:10–27. What relevance do these passages have to *LiFE*-style translating? Mention at least one of the artistic or rhetorical features in each of these texts that needs to be addressed and accounted for, in some way, in a communicatively "honest" Bible translation. Try translating one of these texts in an overtly literary or oratorical manner in YL.

9. The interrelated factors of research and testing are always necessary in connection with Bible translation programs. However, only in rare instances is such pre- and post-project investigation actually carried out on a sustained basis—and then only by the better-funded projects. If you have ever participated in such research, summarize how it was conducted and what its main results were. What are the main reasons for testing a translation, not only while it is being prepared, but after it is published (see section 7.2)? If research and testing are not prominent aspects of your project, what can you do to stimulate community awareness concerning this need?

3.4 *LiFE* translation in relation to other approaches

3.4.1 The translational continuum

There are many ways of doing a translation. The different types are frequently classified on the basis of how closely or loosely they retain the *formal* features of the SL text in the TL text—how literal or idiomatic they are in linguistic or stylistic terms. A more literal version may be described as being *foreignized* with reference to the intended TL audience; such a text requires readers or hearers to learn many of the SL's unusual linguistic features as reflected in the translation, just as though they were learning a foreign language. In other words, translators leave the original writer more or less undisturbed and try to move today's readers towards his manner of expression. (This is an *author*-oriented focus.) Conversely, in the case of an idiomatic version, translators move the original writer and his text towards today's readers. (This is an *audience*-oriented focus.) They do this by *domesticating* the text of their translation through the use of stylistically natural linguistic forms whenever possible. This indigenous text principle always involves culture as well as language, for the two cannot be separated.

» Can you give an example of such domestication, using a term that has been borrowed into YL from the Scriptures (e.g., "bread," "wine," "prophet," "temple," "baptize")?

» What is the communicative effect if such terms are left "foreignized" in the text by means of a transliteration or the use of a loanword from another language, e.g., tempile "temple?"

An idiomatic version has the primary aim of reproducing more fully, overtly, and/or naturally the semantic content and communicative intent of the original message by employing the most expected TL forms available. From a *LiFE* perspective, we might add the qualification that the term "idiomatic" includes the various literary features that are associated with the different TL genres that would best serve as models for the translation. In any case, the point to note is that the concept of "meaning" includes the apparent major and minor communication functions and speech acts of the distinct form-content text units represented in the SL document (see section 1.3).

A form-functional approach of this kind, guided by the principle of communicative relevance, may be applied more or less comprehensively or intensively to a translation, depending on the circumstances, that is, taking into consideration the intended purpose or prospective use of the entire text within the TL community. Of course, no translation can reproduce all of the original document's elements of form, content, and function.[7] Rather, there are a number of different possibilities in terms of selection, focus, and emphasis—that is, a *gradient* ranging from versions that concentrate on the SL forms to those that seek to duplicate the principal communication functions of the base document as a whole, but using features that are effective as well as appropriate in the TL. In the diagram on the following page some of the available types are indicated, along with the English versions that are approximate examples of each. Study this diagram and then do the following exercises:

» Discuss the ratings suggested in this diagram and record any points of disagreement. (It should be emphasized that no notion of value or quality is attached to these ratings, which are approximate to begin with. The diagram is offered merely as a point of discussion concerning translation styles.)

» Give a rating to the book of Genesis as rendered in the different Bibles often used by your people, whether in their mother tongue or some language of wider communication.

---

[7]The SL message cannot be exactly reproduced or completely conveyed in a given TL—there will always be an appreciable loss, gain, or skewing of semantic and pragmatic significance that occurs in the process of interlingual representation. Translators must therefore be selective, aiming to achieve the highest possible degree of information parity. But this can be done only with respect to certain aspects of the initial communication event or smaller portions of the SL text. Thus communication via translation is invariably only partial, imperfect at best. Worse, it can also be misleading—misstating or misrepresenting the message intended by the SL author.

» Finally, compare the following diagram with the diagram on page 89 in *Translating the Literature of Scripture* (Wendland 2004b). What difference do you see?

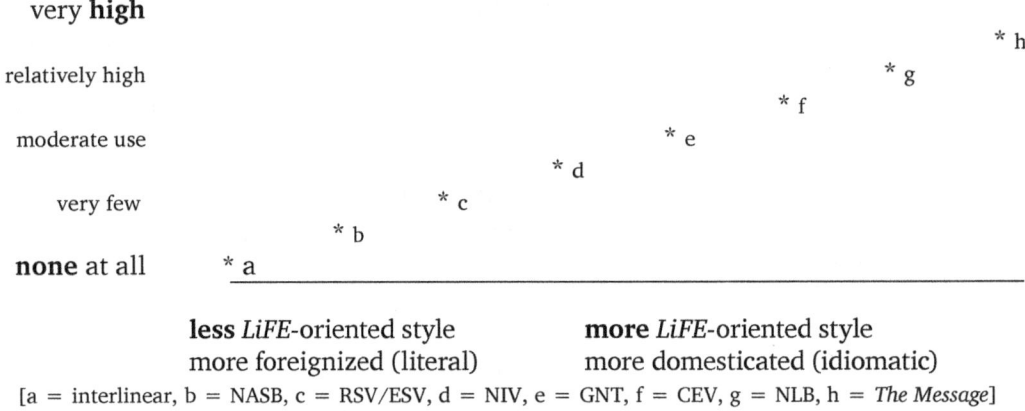

[a = interlinear, b = NASB, c = RSV/ESV, d = NIV, e = GNT, f = CEV, g = NLB, h = *The Message*]

Note that this simple diagram does not measure or evaluate the *exegetical accuracy* of the versions that have been cited. (Accuracy is, of course, a factor of great concern in Bible translation studies, and we will consider it in lesson 7.) Another point that needs to be stressed is that the more domesticated translations are not necessarily "better" than the more foreignized ones or vice versa. It all depends on the target audience and what *they* feel that they need in a contemporary translation. Their evaluation, however, may vary depending on the extent to which key persons were consulted during the translation process and how acceptable they find the translation to be once it has been completed, published, and used.

A full *LiFE* version, whatever the language, is one that generally succeeds in matching the sequence of changing minor and major communicative functions of the biblical document (from speech acts to text act) by the use of suitable TL forms, both minor ones (stylistic features) and major ones (genres), whether more or less literally in relation to the original text. In other words, while a literary version, like a literal version, stresses the importance of verbal form in translation, it is not SL form, but TL form that is primary. This is true not only in *quantitative* terms, but also from a *qualitative* perspective. Such an evaluation would need to be made on the basis of recognized stylistic criteria of excellence with respect to a wide range of phonological, lexical, syntactic, and textual features of artistry and rhetoric in the TL. Furthermore, it is clear that this critical assessment would have to be made or validated by practiced literary experts or experienced vernacular artists—not necessarily by theologians, biblical scholars, or denominational leaders, who may have a vested interest in the use of an older translation that they grew up with or based their studies on at the seminary.

» To what degree do vernacular experts or stylists who are not trained in theology participate in your translation project? Summarize the nature of this involvement.

» Alternatively, summarize the reasons why such resource persons have not yet (or not fully) been utilized.

» What steps could be taken to get such essential participants involved in the work of Bible translation?

As to the preceding diagram's vertical axis, which represents the relative frequency with which recognized literary forms occur in the translations, there are various options open to the creative translator. The *sound structure* of the text would need to be modified as a first step in a literary direction. In other words, a literary version should feature a discourse that is aurally enhanced with respect to one or more *phonic* devices such as parallel lineation, rhythm, rhyme, alliteration, assonance, and/or various kinds of word play (*paronomasia*). In order to produce this sort of *euphony* and rhythmic symmetry in utterance progression, certain preferred types of balanced syntactic construction, interclausal linkage, and lexical selection or collocation are often required. A literary rendering, even a limited one, would also seek to retain most of the evoked *visual* component of the biblical text—that is, its major images, core cultural symbols, and metaphoric language. This goal would be modified only as needed to incorporate certain lexical cues, for example, to guide the reader/hearer's interpretation in the case of the more difficult or foreign figures of speech.

The most comprehensive and inclusive way of satisfying this form-functional criterion, if the goal is a more literary translation, is by means of a globally applied, *genre-for-genre* rendition of a complete book, text, or pericope. In other words, the translators move from a specific biblical text type (e.g., a lament psalm) into the nearest functionally equivalent vernacular genre. According to such a strategy, the stylistic and rhetorical quality of the SL literary text is analyzed, assimilated, and then transformed *as a whole* in keeping with the stylistic characteristics that have been previously established for the most closely corresponding TL genre, whether oral, written, or a hybrid of the two.

Such a holistic, more intuitively implemented approach aims to attain *communicative correspondence* (or at least sufficient similarity) at a much higher discourse level during composition than simply matching form-functional features on a one-to-one basis with regard to individual sentences. Competent translators would thus endeavor to immerse themselves conceptually in the original message by thoroughly studying the SL text and its context. They would then with like intensity search out, or more likely, intuit, the communicative resources available in the target language and cultural setting. The final step would be that spontaneous act of creative *synthesis* whereby the biblical message is transformed in translation—reformulated in the most relevant way for a particular contemporary audience (cf. the "interpretive approach" to translation; Wendland 2004b:66–71).

But if a local translation commission or job description calls for a version that is not so dynamic or idiomatic in nature, a greater degree of formal correspondence will be required with respect to the structural and stylistic features of the biblical text such as its metaphoric imagery, sentence construction, lexical combinations, instances of repetition, and consistency in key-term usage. Nevertheless, it would still be possible to render certain other aspects of the text in a pleasing literary manner, especially on the phonological level. Thus *every* translation of Scripture can—and probably should—reflect a discernable measure of the artistic style that can be recognized in the TL as appropriate for the genre being conveyed. In this case, the translation continuum in the preceding diagram would manifest a specific literary component at every stage along the way, with the differences among the respective versions being only a matter of quantity, not completely different types of translation. That is the expanded vision of a literary version that could, ideally, be realized in virtually all Bible translation work.

The question, then, would not be *if* a particular version is to be literary—only *to what extent*, in *which respects*, and *where in the text*. How much TL literary style or rhetoric is it possible to reflect in a given translation, and what crucial determining factors are present in the local setting? What then are the main practical, teamwork-related implications of this decision? These are important issues for any project to consider *before* translation work begins and even before the translators are selected.

Even if the *Skopos* is to achieve a significant amount of functional parity in the translation, the answers to such questions could vary, depending on the particular SL documents to be rendered: The more persuasive and vigorous the rhetoric and/or artistry displayed in the original text (i.e., with special emphasis on the expressive, affective, and poetic functions of communication), the more marked the printed translation ought to be, stylistically, in terms of TL verbal conventions, and the more evocative it ought to sound in turn to the ears of its intended audience.

» List one OT and one NT book that you feel would fall into the preceding category.

» Name an OT and a NT book that you consider to be manifestly less "literary" (artistic-rhetorical) in nature. Give reasons. Discuss your choices in class.

For reflection, research, and response:

1. The following saying is attributed to Rabbi Judah in *The Babylonian Talmud*: "If someone translates a verse [of Scripture] literally, he is a liar; if he adds thereto, he is a blasphemer and a libeler." What does this mean, and to what extent is it actually true or an exaggeration? Is there scope for a compromise in this respect? Explain your position on the matter.

2. Literal translations are often said to follow the principle of formal correspondence, but how far does such formality or correspondence go with respect to literary features of the SL text such as alliteration, paronomasia (word play), rhythm, euphony, frontal displacement for emphasis, or—to cite one of the most challenging—the acrostic pattern in poetry? Why are such features generally ignored? What is lost in terms of meaning when they are neglected?

3. Evaluate the following definition of the "translation process" (Munday 2009:235), with special reference to the underlined expressions. Discuss the difficult portions of this definition in class and suggest clarifications, simplifications, explanations, etc. as necessary.

    A <u>mental activity</u> performed by a translator/interpreter allowing him/her to render an ST [source text] (oral, written, audiovisual, etc.) formulated in an SL [source language], into a TT [target text] using the <u>resources of a TL</u> [target language]. It is a complex cognitive process which has an interactive and <u>non-linear nature</u>, encompassing controlled and <u>uncontrolled processes</u>, and requiring processes of <u>problem solving</u> and decision making, and the <u>use of strategies</u>. Its specific characteristics vary according to the type of translation (written, oral, audiovisual, etc.).

4. Moisés Silva, a prominent NT scholar, makes the following observation (in Scorgie, Strauss, and Voth 2003:39, 43):

    All successful translations of literature…sound *natural*, as though they had originally been written in [the TL] (while also preserving a feel for the original cultural setting). Therefore, they are more easily read and understood than if they reflected the foreign syntax and word usage. (Incidentally, since the message communicates more clearly, one can argue that they are more accurate than literal renderings would be.)…The point here is that a nonliteral translation, precisely because it may give expression to the genius of the target language…, can do greater justice to that of the source language (Greek).

    What do you think of this opinion, especially as it applies to the translation that you are working on or to the version that you like the most in your mother tongue?

5. Another well-known NT scholar, D. A. Carson, calls attention to the following crucial distinction (in Scorgie, Strauss, and Voth 2003:68–69):

    But the question that must always be asked is whether the original text sounded "foreign" to the first readers and hearers. In other words, is the "otherness" of God and thus that "foreignness" of the Bible's message concretized in the foreignness of the language itself?…In fact, the more direct [i.e., literal] form of translation may draw attention to the foreignness of the original language to the modern reader (though it was not foreign to the first readers) and thus actually distract the reader from the far more important "otherness" of God.

    Explain this in your own words, in particular, its implicit warning to Bible translators.

6. The following chart shows four different renderings of part of Clément Marot's poem "A une Damoyselle malade" (cited by Moisés Silva in Scorgie, Strauss, and Voth 2003:45 and slightly modified here). Which

3.4 LiFE translation in relation to other approaches

version do you prefer? Why? Describe the differences in translation technique (and outcome, including impact) for the four versions. Which type of audience might each version best suit? (This exercise is good preparation for the next section, where we will consider a biblical love poem.)

SL	T1	T2	T3	T4
Ma mignonne	My cute one	My darling	My sweet maid	Lover mine,
Je vous donne	I give thee	I bid thee	You I wish	Here's a sign
Le bon jour;	The good day;	Good day;	A good day;	Of my love,
Le séjour	The stay	Thy stay in bed	Your sickbed	Turtledove.
C'est prison.	It's prison.	Is like prison.	Is a jail.	You're not well,
Guérison	Healing	Thy health	Total health	I can tell.
Recouvrez,	Recover,	Recover,	Please regain,	All cooped up,
Puis ouvrez	Then open	Then open	Then unlatch	Buttercup?
Votre porte	Thy door	Thy door	Your room's door	How about
Et qu'on sorte	And that one leaves	And go out	And go out	Going out?
Vitement,	Quickly,	Quickly,	With full speed,	Hit the town!
Car Clément	For Clément	For Clément	For Clement	Lose that frown—
Le vous mande	Informs it to thee.	Orders thee	Does insist	Clem's command!

3.4.2 The Song of Songs: a case study

The love lyric found in Song of Songs 8:5b–7 begs for a literary exegesis and translation. The Hebrew text of this artistically beautiful and rhetorically powerful passage reads as follows:

תַּחַת הַתַּפּ֙וּחַ֙ עֽוֹרַרְתִּ֔יךָ
שָׁ֚מָּה חִבְּלַ֣תְךָ אִמֶּ֔ךָ
שָׁ֖מָּה חִבְּלָ֥ה יְלָדַֽתְךָ׃
שִׂימֵ֨נִי כַחוֹתָ֜ם עַל־לִבֶּ֗ךָ
כַּֽחוֹתָם֙ עַל־זְרוֹעֶ֔ךָ
כִּֽי־עַזָּ֤ה כַמָּ֙וֶת֙ אַהֲבָ֔ה
קָשָׁ֥ה כִשְׁא֖וֹל קִנְאָ֑ה
רְשָׁפֶ֕יהָ רִשְׁפֵּ֕י אֵ֖שׁ שַׁלְהֶ֥בֶתְיָֽה׃
מַ֣יִם רַבִּ֗ים לֹ֤א יֽוּכְלוּ֙ לְכַבּ֣וֹת אֶת־הָֽאַהֲבָ֔ה
וּנְהָר֖וֹת לֹ֣א יִשְׁטְפ֑וּהָ אִם־יִתֵּ֨ן אִ֜ישׁ
אֶת־כָּל־ה֤וֹן בֵּיתוֹ֙ בָּאַהֲבָ֔ה
בּ֖וֹז יָב֥וּזוּ לֽוֹ׃ ס

To examine this passage more closely, first read the text in a literal English version such as the RSV and pick out the poetic features that stand out.

» Why did these particular items seem especially noteworthy?

> » Now read this passage in a more dynamic translation such as the GNT or The Message. How do you like this version in comparison with the first one? Explain why and give examples to support your preference.
>
> » Which translation sounds more poetic to you?
>
> » Do you have any literary improvements to propose concerning either translation? Try to give several specific instances.

It may be soundly argued on literary as well as structural grounds that the thematic peak of the Song of Songs is reached in the colorful, highly emotive strophe of 8:5b–7. Its onset is delineated first by the formulaic *closure* of 8:3–4 (RSV):

> 3 O that his left hand were under my head,
> and that his right hand embraced me!
> 4 I adjure you, O daughters of Jerusalem,
> that you stir not up nor awaken love
> until it please.

This prominent structural border is followed by an equally strong marker of *aperture* in 8:5a; namely, the rhetorical question that duplicates the corresponding strophe-initial query in 3:6a. (This is a compositional device termed *anaphora*; see also 6:10a and section 5.1.7).

> 5 Who is that [fem.] coming up from the wilderness,
> leaning upon her beloved?

This question serves to fix our attention on the participant next referred to, in this case the female speaker. She begins, in 8:5b, with a figurative, allusive, and rather enigmatic description of her intimate relationship with her lover:

> *Under the apple tree* I awakened [or aroused] you.
> *There* your mother was in travail with you,
> *there* she who bore you was in travail.

(Note the intratextuality here, for example, the wake-up call that reverses the choral prohibition of 2:7 and 3:5.)

In the ancient Near East, the topics of love and sexuality were often expressed figuratively using the imagery of fruit and fruit trees (cf. 2:3). Here, in 8:5b, the female speaker picturesquely compares the birth and growth of love that she produced in her man to his mother's giving birth to him. Assonance in the vowel-sound /a/ reinforces the point that it is the woman who is the main actor in this event (i.e., the reiterated object, *-cha* 'you', is masculine singular).

The words of 8:5b lead to a highly personal appeal for intimate proximity in verse 6—not only physically, but socially as well, as the imagery suggests, that is, in their communally and religiously "sealed" marriage vows (a development of the metaphor of 1:13). The seal ('cylinder-seal' or 'signet-ring') symbolized personal identity and ownership along with connotations of preciousness and authority. The closeness of this amorous relationship is further reinforced by the heart and arm (or wrist) figures, since seals would always be closely attached to them.

> 6 Set me as a seal upon your heart,
> as a seal upon your arm;
> **for** love is strong as death,
> jealousy is cruel as the grave.

3.4 LiFE translation in relation to other approaches

> Its flashes are flashes of fire,
> > a most vehement flame.

The consequential 'for' (*kiy*) in the middle of verse 6 announces what sounds like a clear shift in the speaking voice—from the woman to the implied author/poet as he expresses the point of the Song, which in Hebrew goes like this (as shown by a very literal English translation):

For strong	like (the) death	[is]	love,
unyielding	like Sheol	[is]	passion---
its blazes the blazes of fire	[like]	[are]	the flame of **Yah**[weh]!

A host of Hebrew literary devices converge here to mark this as a high point in the book (possibly the ultimate peak). It is also distinguished by a shift in genre, for the overtones of Wisdom literature are obvious here. Observe the poetic features: strict parallelism (the first two lines); syntactic placement (the utterance-final key terms 'love' and 'passion'); imagery (simile and metaphor); symbolism (death and fire); paradox (the compelling power of death [destructive] versus love [creative]); condensation (especially the final line); an ascending rhythmic pattern (3+3+4) with variation (the last word, or is it a half-line?); more assonance in the vowel sound /a/ (to tie the text to v. 5b); alliteration (the repeated *sh* of lines 2–3) with possible onomatopoeia (imaging the hissing of a fire); and finally, a possible cryptic mention of the divine name (*-yah*) in ultimate, climactic position (שַׁלְהֶבֶתְיָה).

In verse 6, then, we have the fullest, most sustained attempt to describe (or better, evoke) the supreme subject of the Song; namely, paired male-female love (note the definite article of abstraction in verse 7). It is indeed a most irrepressible, irresistible, unquenchable force. Furthermore, the clipped and suffixed reference to Yahweh, while it could be a mere idiomatic substitute for the superlative (i.e., the "hottest/brightest" flame), in this structural position (cf. the equally unique "your name" in balance as a possible *inclusio* at 1:3) and in conjunction with so much stylistic embellishment, definitely seems to signify something more. Thus the final term *shalhebet-yah* 'the flame of Yah(weh)' could well stand as the apex of the credo and of the Song. God is the Source not only of love in all its power and passion, but of the marriage relationship, in which affection is most completely and intimately experienced. Yahweh would surely seem to be present in this context (see NJB, GW, and ASV), for fire is employed as a symbol of God's purifying presence throughout the Bible—here too then as the inexhaustible spark of a shared life of total devotion.

Also here towards the end of the Song, the subdued presence of Yahweh in the single theophanic flash of a flame contrasts in implicit intertextuality with the contemporary love poetry of other cultures (e.g., *mowt* 'death' and *reshep* 'flames' in Ugaritic cultic texts). Pagan poems made frequent mention of the deity, often in conjunction with immoral, allegedly worshipful sexual activities. The divergence in the case of the Song would thus seem to indicate a radically different nature, purpose, and message.

There's still more of course; the poet does not finish in 8:6 but goes on in grand panegyric fashion to figuratively suggest the significance of "[this] love" (*ha'ahaba* with still more accentuating assonance) in verse 7:

> ⁷ Many waters cannot quench love,
> > neither can floods drown it.
> If a man offered for love
> > all the wealth of his house,
> it would be utterly scorned.

From a mighty fire to a cosmic flood, a divinely motivated affection cannot be quenched. The allusions here need not be primarily mythological, for the psalmists had already dealt polemically with that issue through *defamiliarization* (citing the supposedly sacred only to deny it)[8] when proclaiming the almighty Lordship and mercy of Yahweh in caring for his people (e.g., Ps. 18:6–16; 32:6; 93; cf. Exod. 15:1–10). The image of water is especially relevant here due to the preceding references to the fiery passion of love. The extra long cola of 7a and 7c mimic both the amplitude of the content and the rhythmic movement of the language, each concluding with the key word "love."

This magnificent depiction is rounded out in a more conventional fashion by means of a contrastive, probably ironic, reference to the proverbial fool who misunderstands and hence by implication also misuses love. No price can purchase love. Such a misguided consumer deserves only "utter scorn" (an intensified *bôz yâbûzû lô*) from society at large for polluting a godly gift (as does the adulterer, who is severely punished for his desecration of love). The strophe-final pronoun *loh* 'to him' is *homophonous* (same-sounding) with the preceding double occurrence of the negative *lo'* 'not/no'. *No* self-seeking idiot can either buy or bar love!

The problem for translators is how to give a contemporary audience some idea of the significance of the many diverse, but related figures of the Song without overly explicating it, hence destroying its essential poetic nature. A certain amount of literary and cultural contextualization in terms of an appropriate indigenous lyric genre expressing affection will undoubtedly be necessary in order to preserve the dynamic impact and esthetic dimension of the original. But one cannot go too far in this regard so that the biblical situational context is contradicted or important intertextual resonances are lost (e.g., vines and vineyards, cedars, sheep and goats, Lebanon, Mount Carmel—even the pejorative allusion to a fool). A possible solution in such cases, in addition to the essential use of explanatory notes, is the exploitation of indigenous conventional figures that have lost their immediate semantic reference and which convey an idealized impression of ardor and affection in the target language.

We may see how this might be done in Chichewa with regard to the crucial passage of 8:6b by comparing the translation of 8:6b in three different versions: (1) the 1923 missionary version (first selection below); (2) the 1996 popular language version (second selection below); and (3) in a poetic *ndakatulo* lyric (a poetic genre that is popular in published, spoken, or sung form). Relatively literal English back-translations are given after each of the renditions that follow:

1.
Pakuti cikondi cilimba ngati imfa;
Njiru imangouma ngati manda:
Kung'anima kwace ndi kung'anima kwa moto,
Ngati mphenzi ya Yehova.

> Because love is strong like death;
> Envy becomes hard like a grave:
> Its flashing is the flashing of fire,
> Like lightning of Jehovah.

2.
Paja chikondi nchamphamvu ngati imfa,
nsanje njaliwuma ngati manda.
Chikondi chimachita kuti lawilawi ngati malawi a moto,
ndipo nchotentha koopsa.

> As you know, love is powerful like death,
> jealousy is stubborn like a grave.
> Love often goes flash-flash! Like flames of fire,
> and it is terribly hot.

---

[8] "'[D]efamiliarisation' proposed by Russian Formalists [is] a device by which an artist succeeds in persuading his readers to perceive the described object under a different light and [so] to understand it better than before" (Eco 2003:90).

3.

Kunena inetu, chikondi sichitha mpaka imfa;
chayaka psi! monga moto uwala wa Chauta!
Changu changa n'chouma gwa! ngati manda.

Well as for me, [my] love does not end until death;
it's on fire, ashes! like the shining flame of Creator God!
My zeal is rock-hard! just like the graveyard.

For reflection, research, and response:

1. How many different translations of the Bible do you have in your language? How would you classify each of these based on the diagram of translation possibilities given in section 3.4.1? Or how would you rate the translation that you are currently working on? Why was its particular style chosen? Is there any need for a *LiFE*-style version in your wider translation setting? Would it be opposed by influential local church bodies? Explain with reference to your own TL situation.

2. Compare the RSV (or NIV) translation of Song of Songs 8:5–7 with that of the GNT (or CEV). Where do some major differences occur? List three places where you see significantly different renderings for the same Hebrew words. Which version do you consider to be the most literary in nature in each case?

3. Evaluate the three Chichewa translations of Song of Songs 8:6 above. Does any seem to distort the sense of the Hebrew text? List five major differences among them. Pick out three instances where the Chichewa poetic version tries to reproduce the rhetorical power of the original. Which type of translation would work best in your language for a modern situation and a youthful audience?

4. Prepare a dynamic literary translation of Song of Songs 8:5b–7 in your language. Do you have a genre of love poetry or wisdom poetry in YL that would be suitable for this task? Explain. Give a back-translation into English and point out three special stylistic devices that you have used to reproduce the beauty or power of the Hebrew text. Compare your draft with the Nyanja *ndakatulo* rendition that follows. What are the major similarities and differences that you observe? Be prepared to describe (and possibly defend) your version in class.

Ine ndidakuyatsa mtima patsinde pa mango –	I aroused your heart at the base of that mango [tree],
uja mtengo adachirirapo amai pakubala iwe.	the very tree where your mother labored delivering you.
Umatirire mtima ndi chosindikiza chosalekeza	Fasten your heart with a seal that does not let go
kuti musalowedi winanso, koma ine ndekha.	lest any other enter there at all, except me alone.
Kunena inetu, chikondi sichitha mpaka imfa,	**Well, as for me, [my] love does not end until death,**
Chayaka psi! monga moto uwala wa Chauta!	**It's on fire, ashes! like the shining flame of Creator God!**
Changu changa n'chouma gwa! ngati manda.	**My zeal is rock-hard! just like the graveyard.**
Chikondi chimenechi palibe madzi a chigumula	A love like this, there are no flood waters
angathe kuchizimitsa kapena kuchikokolola, ai!	able to put it out or sweep it away, not at all!
Ngakhale munthu atapereka chuma chonse,	Even if a person were to give all [his] wealth,
kufunitsitsa kugula chikondi choterechi,	trying his best to purchase a love of this sort,
iyeyu adzangonyozeka nazo zyolizyoli!	he would be fully embarrassed in the effort – shame!

The following poetic features are found in the preceding sample:

a. balanced lineation

b. internal rhythm and rhyme

c. emphatic syntactic displacement

   d. graphic imagery and vivid idioms

   e. condensation

   f. deictic and emphatic affixes

   g. assonance, alliteration, and punning

   h. topical reversal (illustrated by the following couplet, v. 6e–f)

   i. dramatic ideophones: Chayaka **psi**! monga moto uwala wa Chauta!

   Changu changa n'chouma **gwa**! ngati manda.

5. Consider the first two lines in the Chichewa version of Song of Songs 8 that appears in exercise 4. Are there any cross-cultural conceptual problems with respect to the specific kind of tree mentioned and giving birth under it (apparently publicly)? Explain. What may be done to resolve any difficulties here—or anywhere else in the poem as a whole?

6. Where is there an instance of *enjambment* (a run-over thought, a concept that carries on to the next line) in the Chichewa version? What seems to be its likely poetic function? Does the poetry of YL make use of this device? If so, can it be used for the same discourse purpose?

7. Tito Lahaye (2003:407) makes this important observation:

   Along with a growing awareness of a distinct local identity…there needs to emerge a willingness and desire to explore one's own cultural richness and wherever possible to incorporate that into Bible translation by drawing on the full range of genres present in the target language.…[W]here cultures have made the transition to Christianity they will find that, where materials representing special features of their language have been considered and incorporated in a Bible translation, that translation will be more acceptable and meaningful.

   In class discuss the implications of this and give some actual examples that arise from your own setting of Bible translation.

8. Leland Ryken (2002:9–10) expresses his view of literary translation as follows:

   The Bible is a written document that obeys the rules of literary discourse at every turn. A narrowly focused linguistic approach to translation has often lost sight of larger **literary** principles.…[O]nly an essentially **literal** translation of the Bible can achieve sufficiently high standards in terms of literary criteria and fidelity to the original text. (bolding added)

   Do you agree with Ryken? With his whole statement, with parts of it, or nothing at all? Give your reasons. (For a cogent critique of Ryken's position, see Simon Crisp 2004:43–51 and Mark Strauss 2005.)

3.5 Preparing for a poetic *LiFE* translation

A *LiFE* translation must always be based upon a thorough artistic and rhetorical study of the original SL document. Such an analysis would alert translators to the specific literary character of the biblical text under consideration (which is an integral part of its total meaning package).

The sort of text study envisaged includes two distinct general operations over and above the usual word-by-word, verse-by-verse exegetical-hermeneutical analysis. These operations help us more completely and accurately determine the non-referential dimensions of meaning presented by any independent biblical pericope (i.e., a self-standing unit of discourse at the paragraph level of structural organization and above).

The two areas of emphasis (though they do converge and overlap in many places) are:

1. **Artistic text analysis**. An *artistic* text analysis highlights the formal, esthetic, and iconic facets (beautiful, euphonious, memorable, sensually appealing) of verbal discourse, whether oral or written. The focus is upon the poetic and expressive functions of communication.[9]

2. **Rhetorical text analysis**: A *rhetorical* text analysis highlights the functional, dynamic element (powerful, persuasive, influential, purposefully effective) of verbal discourse. The focus is upon the affective and imperative functions of communication.

A literary, form-oriented approach thus extends in two directions: to stimulate emotive *solidarity* and communicative *power* within the audience. At the same time, there is a special concern for:

1. The **appeal** of the text, both the original and its translated version.

   The analyst asks what makes the text *esthetically* attractive—capturing the eyes and ears of the audience and facilitating the other communicative aims that the author sought to achieve in and through his text.

2. The **potency** of the text—the power and persuasiveness of both the SL and TL texts.

   The analyst asks what it is that compels listeners to feel *experientially* the Bible's impact, emotions, attitudes, moods, exhortations, and admonitions (under the operation of the Holy Spirit).

The artistry and rhetoricity of the Scriptures operate in tandem to enhance the overall *credibility, authority,* and *authenticity* of the various writings. Each constituent document features an artful, at times unique, manner of expression that is most fitting for subject matter of lasting significance. A literary method of analysis is needed to fully investigate the compositional aspects of biblical discourse since such an approach pays special attention to a text's macro- and microstructure, its stylistic distinctives, its functional dimension, as well as the emotive and connotative aspects of the discourse. By this means, then, the necessary foundation is also laid for effecting a corresponding communication of the literature of Scripture in another language, literary tradition, and cultural setting.

---

[9]In an earlier development of the *LiFE* approach, I used the term "poetic" instead of "artistic" to describe this interest in and concern for the formal dimension of literature. However, poetic seems too specific (being so closely identified with pure poetry), while artistic may be too broad. In any case, I understand artistic rather generally as describing the product of "a person who does anything very well, with imagination and a feeling for form, effect, etc." *(Webster's New World College Dictionary)*.

What makes an artistic translation? You be the judge. Consider Psalm 23:4 in several versions:

גַּם כִּי־אֵלֵךְ בְּגֵיא צַלְמָוֶת	'Even though I walk through the valley of the shadow of death'
לֹא־אִירָא רָע כִּי־אַתָּה עִמָּדִי	'I fear no evil; for thou art with me'
שִׁבְטְךָ וּמִשְׁעַנְתֶּךָ הֵמָּה יְנַחֲמֻנִי׃...	'thy rod and thy staff, they comfort me' (MT/RSV)

Yea, though I walk in death's dark vale,
yet will I fear none [sic] ill:
For thou art with me; and thy rod
and staff me comfort still. (**Church of Scotland**)

Even when the way goes through
    Death Valley,
I'm not afraid
    when you walk at my side.
Your trusty shepherd's crook makes me feel secure. (**Peterson**)

He guides them with his staff, keeps them in line, on the right path, however dark the shadows...
    (**Wilt**)

I may walk through valleys
    as dark as death,
but I won't be afraid.
You are with me,
    and your shepherd's rod
    makes me feel safe. (**CEV**)

M'chigwa cha mdima bii! n'kayendamo,   If in a deep dark valley BLACK! I happen to walk,
Mantha onse balala! poti Chauta alipodi.   All [my] fear GONE! since Chauta is right there.
Inu Abusa, muli pafupi n'zida zotetezera,   O Herdsman, you are close by with weapons for defense,
Ine mtima pansi phee! nthawi zonsezo.   As for my heart, it's completely QUIET! at all times
    (a **Nyanja** *ndakatulo* **lyric translation**)

» Which version do you think is more poetic and why? According to which criteria?

» How would you translate this verse poetically in your language?

» In what setting could such a poetic rendition be used?

» Would an oral-aural medium be more appropriate? Explain.

Together—and they must always be considered in a close conjunctive relation with each other—the two facets, the artistic and rhetorical, comprise the creative essence of any eloquent, excellent, influential, inspiring instance of written or oral communication. It is this semiotic import and pragmatic implication that constitute the heart of the meaning of any literary discourse. It is not limited to the referential dimension of significance; rather it includes all of the different functional aspects noted above. Unfortunately, the diverse passages of Scripture—both the well-known and the unfamiliar—are not often thought of, let alone analyzed or translated, along such lines.

A literary-sensitive exegesis of the biblical text prepares the way for a corresponding literary functional-equivalence (*LiFE*) translation into any target language. As the SL literary features are analyzed in terms of form and function, proactive translators already begin to anticipate how they might render them accordingly—at least to the extent determined by the project *Skopos*. A *LiFE* style of translation is not a "one-way-only (mine!)" method; rather, it offers a broad continuum of possibilities, as schematized below:

A translational *LiFE*-style continuum

less ←==========*literariness* ==========→ **MORE**

features applied: *phonological* + *morphological* + *lexical* + *syntactic* + *textual* **(genre-based)**

In other words, there are different options that can be selected to render the graded *functional profile* derived from an analysis of the SL text. They range from a more to a less freely applied set of artistic choices in the TL. The functional profile is a prioritized list ranging from the more general communicative goals (pragmatic intentions) of discourse (informative, expressive, imperative, etc.) to the specific speech acts (e.g., warn, praise, appeal) that are manifested in the sequence of utterances that make up a given text. It is an inventory of aims that may well vary from one section to the next. The stylistic choices in the vernacular are also determined in accordance with the designated *purpose* of the version at hand, the particular *genre* chosen to be its receptacle in the TL, and the *Brief* that governs its overall manner of production.

Bottom Line: Any biblical text—large or small, poetry or prose—*can* be translated artistically in selected, relevant respects, that is, with an ear keenly attuned to the TL's rich phonic beauty (euphony) and full rhetorical potential (*verbal energy*). There is no translation that does not need at least a little *LiFE*. It is an inherent part of an overall communication methodology that aims to accent the stylistic resources and compositional techniques of the vernacular in service of an original text that surely deserves such attention in terms of its message form, content, and ultimate goals.

For reflection, research, and response:

1. The literary dimension of discourse may be factored into two aspects—the artistic and the rhetorical. What is the difference between the two, as you understand them from the preceding discussion? How would you express these distinctions by way of explanation in YL? What difficulty would you encounter when trying to communicate these concepts, and how could you get around that?

2. How does a literary perspective stimulate a sense of communicative *power* (rhetorical impact) and *solidarity* (esthetic appeal) within a given biblical text? Answer this with reference to Isaiah 6:8–10 (the RSV text is displayed below in a reformatted form). After you have studied this text, answer the question: how do artistic features and rhetorical concerns converge to enhance and empower Yahweh's message of judgment to his people?

> [8] And I heard the voice of the Lord saying,
>   "Whom shall I *send*,
>   and *who* will **go** for us?"
> Then I said,
>   "Here am *I*!
>   *Send* me."

> [9] And he said,
>> "**Go**, and say to this people:
>
>> 'Hear and hear,
>>> *but do not* understand;
>> see and see,
>>> *but do not* perceive.'
>> [10] Make the **heart** of this people fat,
>>> and their **ears** heavy,
>>>> and shut their **eyes**;
>>>> lest they see with their **eyes**,
>>> and hear with their **ears**,
>> and understand with their **hearts**,
>> and turn and be healed."

3. How do oral-aural concerns affect the translation process, for example, with respect to the preceding text from Isaiah? How would you render this passage in YL in order to make the appropriate auditory impression, one that complements the divine message of prophetic judgment?

4. Evaluate Peterson's rendering of Isaiah 6:9b–10 from the point of view of literary as well as exegetical considerations:

> "'Listen hard, but you aren't going to get it;
>> look hard, but you won't catch on.'
> Make these people blockheads,
>> with fingers in their ears and blindfolds on their eyes,
> So they won't see a thing,
>> won't hear a word,
> So they won't have a clue about what's going on
>> and, yes, so they won't turn around and be made whole."

5. What do you think of the continuum of translational possibilities shown in the diagram above? Have you ever thought about Bible translation in these terms? Is it helpful to do so? Explain. Try to give an example of the application of each of these features—phonological, morphological, lexical, syntactic, and textual—from your own literary rendition of Isaiah 6:8–10? Would you be inclined to use all of these features in translating this passage, or use them in a more limited manner? Explain. Why does a TL community need to be educated as to the nature and purpose of these different options *before* a new translation project is undertaken? How can this educative process be best carried out in your communication setting?

6. Do you agree with the proposal that *every* Bible translation, even a more literal, liturgical version, could benefit from applying *LiFE* principles to one degree or another, whether less or more? If so, give reasons for your conclusion; if not, explain your doubts and problems concerning this approach—that is, in the framework of your specific church setting and translation situation.

3.6 A ten-step exegetical methodology

We will now consider one possible methodology that lends itself to a *LiFE* approach. It is offered merely as a general suggestion as to how a text analysis might be carried out in ten steps. It will be applied to Matthew 25:31–46, a passage that is basically narrative in nature, but exhibits a number of literary, even poetic, characteristics. Obviously, various modifications could be made to the ten steps in terms of composition and order of arrangement, and perhaps several steps could be combined into one. (For a somewhat different presentation of these steps applied to the book of Obadiah, see Wendland 2004b,

3.6 A ten-step exegetical methodology

chapter 7; cf. Wilt and Wendland 2008: chapters 8–10). Even so, all of the critical factors mentioned would somehow need to be included within any comprehensive exegetical study.

This set of procedures is designed to prepare the ground for a subsequent *LiFE*-style translation, which would already have been anticipated as the analysis is being carried out. As we have already seen, a *LiFE*-style translation is one that aims to extract more of the vital artistic essence from a given biblical document and then articulate this "soul" of the text within a specific TL version, whether intuitively in response to one's creative gift or in accordance with some specific compositional guidelines. One should be ready to apply what is learned during the exegetical stage to the preparation of an artistic-rhetorical translation, whether to a greater or lesser extent, in accordance with the principle of relevance and the *Brief*, in particular, its primary TL-oriented *Skopos*.

The following exercise will be carried out as a cooperative and interactive, question-driven venture. After an initial explanation of each step, the process of analysis is started according to a recommended procedure or through a series of questions for investigation. The student is required to complete a study of the discourse for that particular step, either according to the outlined procedure, or using another method that is more familiar. The object of the exercise is not simply to mechanically follow a given technique of discourse analysis but to experiment, whenever possible, with different procedures during the process of discovering a practical methodology that one is confident about applying on a regular basis. The ultimate goal is to derive from a close exegetical study the information and insights that will prove useful for translating the text at hand more accurately, appropriately, and acceptably in another language.

Now let us examine Matthew 25:31–46 in a literal English translation (RSV) and in the original language. The RSV will be given first, in an unformatted form, and the formatted Greek text next. Read the passage through several times in order to familiarize yourself with its content. Make a mental note of any aspect of discourse form or content that strikes a special chord. At least one of your readings should be *aloud*—of the Greek text in particular. Why is an *oral* articulation of this passage helpful, even necessary, for understanding it (consider its textual setting)? Which structural features are thereby highlighted?

> [31] When the Son of man comes in his glory, and all the angels with him, then he will sit on his glorious throne. [32] Before him will be gathered all the nations, and he will separate them one from another as a shepherd separates the sheep from the goats, [33] and he will place the sheep at his right hand, but the goats at the left. [34] Then the King will say to those at his right hand, 'Come, O blessed of my Father, inherit the kingdom prepared for you from the foundation of the world; [35] for I was hungry and you gave me food, I was thirsty and you gave me drink, I was a stranger and you welcomed me, [36] I was naked and you clothed me, I was sick and you visited me, I was in prison and you came to me.' [37] Then the righteous will answer him, 'Lord, when did we see thee hungry and feed thee, or thirsty and give thee drink? [38] And when did we see thee a stranger and welcome thee, or naked and clothe thee? [39] And when did we see thee sick or in prison and visit thee?' [40] And the King will answer them, 'Truly, I say to you, as you did it to one of the least of these my brethren, you did it to me.' [41] Then he will say to those at his left hand, 'Depart from me, you cursed, into the eternal fire prepared for the devil and his angels; [42] for I was hungry and you gave me no food, I was thirsty and you gave me no drink, [43] I was a stranger and you did not welcome me, naked and you did not clothe me, sick and in prison and you did not visit me.' [44] Then they also will answer, 'Lord, when did we see thee hungry or thirsty or a stranger or naked or sick or in prison, and did not minister to thee?' [45] Then he will answer them, 'Truly, I say to you, as you did it not to one of the least of these, you did it not to me.' [46] And they will go away into eternal punishment, but the righteous into eternal life.

I

31 Ὅταν δὲ ἔλθῃ ὁ υἱὸς τοῦ ἀνθρώπου	A
ἐν τῇ δόξῃ αὐτοῦ καὶ πάντες οἱ ἄγγελοι μετ' αὐτοῦ,	
τότε καθίσει ἐπὶ θρόνου δόξης αὐτοῦ·	
32 καὶ συναχθήσονται ἔμπροσθεν αὐτοῦ πάντα τὰ ἔθνη,	
καὶ ἀφορίσει αὐτοὺς ἀπ' ἀλλήλων,	
ὥσπερ ὁ ποιμὴν ἀφορίζει τὰ πρόβατα ἀπὸ τῶν ἐρίφων,	
33 καὶ στήσει τὰ μὲν <u>πρόβατα</u> ἐκ δεξιῶν αὐτοῦ,	
τὰ δὲ <u>ἐρίφια</u> ἐξ εὐωνύμων.	

34 τότε ἐρεῖ <u>ὁ βασιλεὺς</u> τοῖς ἐκ δεξιῶν αὐτοῦ,	B
Δεῦτε οἱ εὐλογημένοι τοῦ πατρός μου,	
κληρονομήσατε τὴν ἡτοιμασμένην ὑμῖν βασιλείαν	
ἀπὸ καταβολῆς κόσμου.	

35 ἐπείνασα γὰρ καὶ ἐδώκατέ μοι φαγεῖν,	Ca
ἐδίψησα καὶ ἐποτίσατέ με,	b
ξένος ἤμην καὶ συνηγάγετέ με,	c
36 γυμνὸς καὶ περιεβάλετέ με,	d
ἠσθένησα καὶ ἐπεσκέψασθέ με,	e
ἐν φυλακῇ ἤμην καὶ ἤλθατε πρός με.	f

37 τότε ἀποκριθήσονται αὐτῷ <u>οἱ δίκαιοι</u> λέγοντες,	D
Κύριε, πότε σε εἴδομεν πεινῶντα καὶ ἐθρέψαμεν,	a
ἢ διψῶντα καὶ ἐποτίσαμεν;	b
38 πότε δέ σε εἴδομεν ξένον καὶ συνηγάγομεν,	c
ἢ γυμνὸν καὶ περιεβάλομεν;	d
39 πότε δέ σε εἴδομεν ἀσθενοῦντα	e
ἢ ἐν φυλακῇ καὶ ἤλθομεν πρός σε;	f

40 καὶ ἀποκριθεὶς ὁ βασιλεὺς ἐρεῖ αὐτοῖς,	E
Ἀμὴν λέγω ὑμῖν,	
ἐφ' ὅσον ἐποιήσατε ἑνὶ τούτων	
τῶν ἀδελφῶν μου τῶν ἐλαχίστων,	
ἐμοὶ ἐποιήσατε.	

II.

41 Τότε ἐρεῖ καὶ τοῖς ἐξ εὐωνύμων,	B'
Πορεύεσθε ἀπ' ἐμοῦ [οἱ] κατηραμένοι εἰς τὸ πῦρ τὸ αἰώνιον	
τὸ ἡτοιμασμένον τῷ διαβόλῳ καὶ τοῖς ἀγγέλοις αὐτοῦ.	

42 ἐπείνασα γὰρ καὶ οὐκ ἐδώκατέ μοι φαγεῖν,	C'a'
ἐδίψησα καὶ οὐκ ἐποτίσατέ με,	b'
43 ξένος ἤμην καὶ οὐ συνηγάγετέ με,	c'
γυμνὸς καὶ οὐ περιεβάλετέ με,	d'
ἀσθενὴς	e'
καὶ ἐν φυλακῇ καὶ οὐκ ἐπεσκέψασθέ με.	f'

44 τότε ἀποκριθήσονται καὶ αὐτοὶ λέγοντες,	D'
Κύριε, πότε σε εἴδομεν πεινῶντα	a'
ἢ διψῶντα	b'

```
                    ἢ ξένον                                              c'
                    ἢ γυμνὸν                                             d'
                    ἢ ἀσθενῆ                                             e'
                    ἢ ἐν φυλακῇ καὶ οὐ διηκονήσαμέν σοι;                  f'

     45             τότε ἀποκριθήσεται αὐτοῖς λέγων,                      E'
                         Ἀμὴν λέγω ὑμῖν,
                         ἐφ' ὅσον οὐκ ἐποιήσατε ἑνὶ τούτων
                         τῶν ἐλαχίστων, οὐδὲ ἐμοὶ ἐποιήσατε.

46 καὶ ἀπελεύσονται οὗτοι εἰς κόλασιν αἰώνιον,                           A'
     οἱ δὲ δίκαιοι εἰς ζωὴν αἰώνιον.
```

3.6.1 Step 1: Study the cotext

Step 1 is to investigate the wider linguistic setting of the passage to be analyzed and note any points of continuation, correspondence, and/or contrast.

Before beginning a detailed study of the focal text itself, one must scrutinize its surrounding discourse cotext, both immediate and remote, in order to determine any close lexical or conceptual connections with the passage under consideration. It is also necessary to confirm the structural integrity and unity of the passage, in particular, the features that demarcate it as a discrete and self-standing compositional unit. Especially important in this respect is the cotext that occurs prior to the text under examination, since certain aspects of it are likely to have some influence upon the overall development of the author's current discourse.

» Do you think Matthew 25:31–46 is an independent pericope and thus worthy of a section heading, or not? Cite some textual evidence in support of your conclusion.

» What links this passage with the preceding pericope and what separates the two?

A discourse analysis of the major section of Matthew's Gospel covering chapters 24–25 reveals the following: First of all, we observe that the 25:31–46 pericope appears to form the final section of a tripartite, seven-sectioned **A-B-A'** ring composition. After an initial narrative opening, or *aperture* (in 24:1–3; see 26:1 for the next major aperture), Christ begins his paraenetic instruction concerning the end of the age by describing some of the salient signs of "those days." His words unfold a subtle blend of key events that will occur during the prophetic times of both the messianic and also the eschatological ages (24:4–31//unit **A**).

This semi-narrative prediction suddenly breaks off at 24:32 ("So from the fig tree learn this parable"), and the discourse shifts into a parabolic mode with a series of five dramatic object lessons. One hortatory passage reinforces another in stressing the need for people to get ready for a day of decision (segments 24:32–35, 36–44, 45–51; 25:1–13, 14–30 of unit **B**).

An apparently resumptive section **A'** (25:31–46) then appears, the seventh portion of the larger discourse begun in chapter 24. This vividly climactic unit appears to continue the eschatological account where **A** left off; namely, with the Son of Man's coming from heaven in glory, accompanied by his angels and in the presence of all humanity (24:30–31; cf. 25:31–32). The contrastive judgment dialogue scene ends with the consignment of the wicked to "eternal punishment," a theme that marks the ending of several of the preceding parables (e.g., 24:51, 25:30), a case of structural closure (*epiphora*). Thus the ambiguity of genre (i.e., is it history and/or parable?—see section 3.6.2) may be a deliberate rhetorical device intended to focus not so much on the individual details of the eschatological event but on the certainty of its occurrence and the need to prepare in advance. The text has clearly been constructed to produce a structural and rhetorical peak in this third and final section, especially with its summary conclusion regarding the great separation between "the righteous" and the rest (25:46). Such a perspective is supported by the similar passage at the end of the first major discourse of Christ in Matthew's Gospel, in 7:24–27 (the parable of the wise and foolish builders), which also manifests a binary structure and is ethically toned as well as thematically contrastive.

- » What do you think of this proposed A-B-A' structural arrangement of the larger discourse of which Matthew 25:31–46 is a part? Do you have any revisions to suggest?

- » Is the middle, parabolic section (B) clearly distinct?

- » What are the implications of this sort of literary segmentation of the biblical text for translation?

- » If such a textual arrangement is valid and helpful for understanding Christ's teaching here, how can its relevance be expressed or made apparent in a contemporary Bible translation?

Major text-critical issues should also be studied as part of the cotext at this initial stage of the analysis. In such an investigation one considers the principal variants or alternative readings which may apply at different points in the passage. Any special problem areas must be identified and tentative resolutions arrived at *before* the text itself is examined in detail as an integral unit of discourse. Preliminary decisions in this regard may be reviewed and revised later in light of the text-analysis procedures that follow.

With respect to the original Greek text of Matthew 25:31–46 there do not seem to be any outstanding difficulties. Metzger's *Textual Commentary* (1994) and Omanson's *A Textual Guide* (2006) do not list a single point of contention here. Carlton's *Translator's Reference Translation* (2001) notes two minor variants, but neither one has much manuscript support or is supported by the various versions.

According to Carlton (ibid.), a number of manuscripts have the adjective "holy" in 25:31 used as a modifier of "angels."

- » How important is this addition?

- » How might a copyist have introduced the word "holy" here (see Luke 9:26)?

- » Why, in light of Matthew 16:27, is the reading without "holy" probably the correct one—that is, over and above the external manuscript evidence?

Regarding 25:41, Carlton (ibid.) says that a few manuscripts specify "the Father" as having prepared the fire of punishment for the devil and his angels.

- » What might have caused this addition (see v. 34)?

- » If "the Father" is left out of your translation, is it clear to most readers who prepared the fire?

- » Many might conclude that the speaker, Christ, is the agent. This ambiguity thus turns out to be a major translational issue rather than a minor textual one. How would you deal with it in YL?

3.6.2 Step 2: Specify the literary genre

Step 2 is to identify the principal text type and subtypes along with their associated stylistic features and functional implications.

A prior read-through of the pericope or book designated for analysis should give one an indication of the text's primary genre (discourse type), plus any minor genres incorporated within it. This involves specifying the major communicative purpose for which the text was prepared in light of a given sociocultural setting or interpersonal situation. It also involves identifying any typical literary features that mark this kind of composition. The text type may be the same as, similar to, or different from what precedes or follows it in the surrounding discourse.

The genre may be compound or mixed—that is, composed either sequentially or simultaneously of two or more distinct literary categories, some of which may be clearly secondary in importance. Each distinct (sub)genre will normally manifest a distinctive style and function, with the primary genre often modifying the communicative aim of any secondary ones included within it.

We see an example of this sort of combination at the beginning of Paul's letter to the Galatians.

» What is the function of Paul's personal narrative testimony in Galatians 1:11–2:14?

» Does this section end at 2:14 or is there another possible terminus? Explain your conclusion.

This step in the analysis includes an identification of all the individual compositional features and stylistic devices that serve both to constitute and also to distinguish, or mark, the primary genre and its subtypes. Any credible analysis of the structure and rhetoric of a given literary work must begin with the notion of genre, for the conventions of a given genre are normally reflected both in the macro- and microstylistic features of the text, whether oral or written. The genre of Matthew as a whole may be specified most generally as a *biographical narrative*.

» How would you define the term "narrative?" Compare your definition with one from a dictionary or handbook on literature.

» What are the primary characteristics of a narrative discourse?

» In the case of Matthew, why is it necessary to qualify the designation of narrative with biographical? What does this suggest about the story that is being told?

» Why is it important to keep this qualification in mind as we read this (or any) of the Gospels?

Matthew's narrative is also dramatic in nature—that is, it features an internal plot that guides the selection and presentation of characters and events. A plot normally moves gradually toward some major peak in the depiction of the life of the chief character(s), followed by a much shorter resolution.

» Where does the major peak of Matthew's narrative occur? Why do you say so?

» How does this compare with the plots of the other Gospels?

Many analysts prefer to specify the discourse type of a work like Matthew even more precisely in an effort to better account for its structure, content selection, and style. For example, some would say that Matthew also exhibits the characteristics of an *apology*, that is, a formal defense of the person of Christ and/or the Christian religion. Evaluate this opinion with an argument either for or against it.

Several questions confront us as we attempt to further specify the nature of the Matthew 25:31–46 pericope. Is it presented as a historical or a parable text? Some scholars classify the discourse as *prophetic history*—that is, as nonfiction that incorporates certain apocalyptic features within an eschatological temporal setting (cf. Dan. 7:13–14). Others point to the prominent comparative element that is introduced with the metaphor of the sheep and goats in verse 32, the imagery of which then implicitly colors the remainder of the text. These scholars view this pericope as a parable that appears to function as a climax—the significant seventh occurrence!—in the sequence of Christ's "parables of separation," all of which (7:24–27; 13:24–30 [explained in 36–43]; 13:47–50; 24:45–51; 25:1–13; 25:14–30; 25:31–46) are oriented towards the final judgment.

> » How would you label the Matthew 25:31–46 passage—as factual prophetic history or as an illustrative parable?
>
> » Would your classification make any difference in how you eventually translate this text in YL?
>
> » For example, does a parable in your oral or written tradition present any formal markers (e.g., introductory or concluding formulae, special tense-aspect markers, or distinctive particles of participant reference) to indicate that it is a non-historical discourse?
>
> » What difference does it make to one's understanding of this pericope whether it is construed as historical or fictional?
>
> » If the text is not marked with regard to genre in your translation, how will the audience be likely to interpret it?
>
> » Is an explanatory note needed to clarify this issue? If so, how would you word it?

3.6.3 Step 3: Find the points of major disjunction

Step 3 is to note all "break points" in the text, that is, places where one or more prominent shifts in form or content occur.

> Breaks, or points of disjunction (major) and transition (minor), are created within a literary text whenever there is a notable change or content modification with respect to time, place, topic, personal participants, central participant, speaker, addressee, text type (genre), and/or sequence of events. Where several of these indicators of shifting co-occur, such as a variation in place and time or speaker and subject, the break is more prominent, hence better substantiated. Normally, a new paragraph begins at that point—or a new section, if the disjunction is greater in terms of the number of breaks manifested. Thus an adjacent pair of disjunctions create between them a "chunk" of text, that is, a conceptual or thematic unit consisting of a variable number of sentences that manifest a perceptible, memorable coherence based on time, place, topic, discourse type, and/or communicative purpose. Other supporting signals of disjunction within a literary text are the formal markers of a new topic or a digression (e.g., NP-fronting, nominalization, use of an independent pronoun), characteristic discourse formulae and transitional expressions (e.g., conjunctions or phrases of aperture like "And it came to pass," "In that day," "Thus says the LORD," and "After this," or of closure like "oracle of Yahweh," "Selah," and "Amen"),[10] and concluding summary statements that typically signal the end of a complete unit of discourse (e.g., "Then they will know that I am the LORD" and "And [X] his son succeeded him as king" and "To him be the glory forever!").
>
> » Where would you posit break points (new paragraph units) in connection with the Matthew 25:31–46 pericope?

Finding the breaks is not very difficult to figure out for this text, but the exercise will help you practice this aspect of discourse analysis in preparation for more difficult passages.

List the verses at which you would begin a new paragraph as well as the shift(s) that occur at that point, along with any supporting text-break markers. Write your choices in the blank spaces of the diagram that follows. (More lines are provided than you will need.) The first and last segments, which are the outer boundaries of this pericope, have been done for you.

---

[10] These are not completely predictable markers. For example, note the position of "amen" in Rev. 7:12 and what the twofold mention of "amen" serves to mark.

Verse number	Type of shift(s) that occur as the preceding verse moves to this one
25:31	new central participant explicitly identified: "the Son of Man"; shift from parable to prophecy; a different setting and dramatic situation is established.
26:1	shift from direct speech to narrative report; introductory transitional margin ("When Jesus had finished"); a change in the topic to be developed in subsequent verses.

3.6.4 Step 4: Plot the patterns of formal and conceptual repetition

Step 4 is to record and posit the significance of any obvious patterns of linguistic reiteration within the discourse: phonological, lexical, syntactic, and textual.

Repetition may be exact *(replication)* or synonymous to varying degrees *(recursion)*. The device occurs in oral as well as written discourse and may be of many different formal and semantic types, extending for textual spans that may be long or relatively short within a given composition. Recursion includes contrasts as well as similarities and may be manifested in parallel expressions as well as by intertwined and overlapping instances. Repetition is normally the most prominent, hence obvious, characteristic of any literary discourse. The more repetition that occurs and the more exact it is in nature, the more poetic a text is regarded.

> » Why is exact repetition especially important for those who are aurally apprehending a text, and what are the implications of this for Bible translation at large and translation technique in particular?

The individual instances of repetition will often create larger, sometimes overlapping patterns of formal structure and thematic significance within a passage. These may link up with the surrounding cotext on either side of the pericope under study. Such replication or recursion thus physically organizes and demarcates a text, both externally, on the boundaries of structural units, as well as internally by creating varied patterns of formal cohesion, including variable spans of participant reference. All this contributes to the text's distinct thematic meaning and communicative purpose, certain areas or aspects of which may also be foregrounded by reiteration as a marker of *prominence*.[11] By coordinating the key repetition patterns of a text with its major shifts in form and/or

---

[11] Anne Garber Kompaoré points out that in directive discourse "the most thematic referent will have the highest frequency of pronominal references. The least thematic referent is the least likely to have any pronominal references" (2005:8; see also Kompaoré 2004). On the importance to Bible translators of analyzing the patterns of participant reference in Hebrew discourse, see de Regt, 1999. Such a more detailed linguistic study could be profitably carried out during step 6 of our set of analysis procedures.

content (step 3), the analyst is able to make a preliminary proposal of the principal paragraph-level or strophe-level breaks within the discourse at large.

The main contours of the recursive patterns of the Matthew 25:31–46 pericope are shown in the diagram of the Greek text that was displayed at the beginning of section 3.6. There are two larger "panels" of constituent structure, I and II, each of which consists of five sub-units (A, B, C, D, and E). As it turns out, each of the internal elements of II (B'–E') contrasts with and serves as an effective counterfoil to those of the initial and corresponding unit I (B–E).

> » Can you discern this arrangement of the text in the SL text?
>
> » If not, refer to an interlinear version and make a copy of this display, including the letters that indicate the text's structural organization, using an English translation.

The parallelism of panels I and II serves to reinforce both the dual and also the polar nature of the heavenly trial scene: Only two clearly defined groups are in the dock, and these are strongly antithetical in terms of character and hence also of the judgment that each group receives. (Notice that the only negatives of this passage, eight of them, occur in panel II.) One group, the one "on the right," is publicly vindicated and lauded by the Lord; the other "on the left" is just as incisively repudiated and condemned.

> » Is this great division, or contrast, clear to you in the structure of the text?
>
> » Does the special format reveal this more clearly?
>
> » Would such an arrangement be too difficult or complicated for your typical TL audience to interpret? If so, can you propose any modifications that would simplify the format, but still highlight the text's contrastive nature?

The repeated subsections of this larger structure (a–f and a'–f') may have further suggested to the original audience the absolute certainty of the Lord's judicial process as well as the legal precision whereby it is conducted. In addition, this carefully organized structure possibly may have been composed as an *isomorphic*, aural reflection that depicts the perfectly measured justice of the verdict and the corresponding righteousness of the Judge, as well as the great moral divide that now distinguishes, and will ultimately separate forever, two fundamentally antithetical ways of life (see Psalm 1).

> » Will the associations listed above be apparent to people of your cultural and literary setting when they read this passage? Explain why, or why not.

In a tightly constructed pattern of similarities such as we see in Matthew 25:31–46, one must also consider any prominent variations or differences in terms of their possible rhetorical implications.

Consider and comment on the following disparities and their possible semantic implications:

1. Note the obvious condensation that appears in the response to the king from the defendants on his left (compare panels D' and D above). It is tempting to view this as a verbal reflection of the very lack of concern for the disadvantaged and needy that such people had just been found guilty of.

2. The Son of Man is referred to as speaking to "the righteous" in his judicial capacity as "king" in verses 34 and 40 (i.e., an inclusio within panel I), whereas he is not referred to in this way in the corresponding verses 41 and 45. This suggests that the unrighteous did not recognize or respect the Son's royal authority and thus treated the lesser of his subjects accordingly.

3. The Lord, on the other hand, honors the righteous by calling them "my brothers" (v. 40); significantly the unrighteous are not so addressed in the parallel passage (v. 45). The notion of brotherhood certainly distinguishes the ethical attitude and actions of those mentioned in panel I, in sharp contrast to their counterparts in II, who could not even perceive a brother, let alone respond to the obvious needs of one (cf. Matt. 7:12).

4. It is obvious that segment A' of panel II is located out of its expected place. What might be the reason for this shift of position in terms of the larger narrative structure?

» Which of the preceding observations do you think is the most significant for understanding this text?

» Would it be helpful to point out any of these interpretive possibilities in marginal notes for this passage? Explain why or why not in relation to your own current or proposed Bible translation setting.

3.6.5 Step 5: Discover and evaluate the artistic and rhetorical features

Step 5 is to identify the chief artistic devices and rhetorical techniques within the whole text, especially at points of special concentration, and then to determine their local or global textual significance.

As steps 3–4 demonstrated, the internal break points and major recursive patterns reveal formal linguistic structures of different sizes in a literary text. Any biblical pericope will also manifest various kinds of poetic or prosaic stylistic technique. This compositional feature makes an added contribution to the pericope's wider esthetic appeal and rhetorical impact, both on the local and global level of functional significance. A great diversity of Hebrew and Greek literary devices may be included here: figures of speech (*tropes*), comparative or contrastive elements of imagery, ellipsis and other types of condensation, word plays (paronomasia), alliteration and assonance, rhythm and rhyme, artful redundancy and conceptual expansion, syntactic relocation front or back, rhetorical and deliberative questions, irony and sarcasm, humor, paradox, enigma, and a balanced or patterned strophic/paragraph structure.

Such stylistic techniques are generally introduced for the purpose of polishing and persuasion, that is, with respect to a text's form (artistry) and function (rhetoric). Therefore, these features need to be examined in relation to the salient patterns of repetition and the shifts in content previously noted as a way of indicating more overtly where structural boundaries and areas of focal, or foregrounded, meaning appear within the discourse (e.g., the emotive *climax*, thematic *peak*, *end-stress*, or *closure*). One's initial conclusions in this regard are often supported or confirmed at places where these devices appear to be especially concentrated through *reiteration, juxtaposition*, or *incorporation*.

Comment on the special meaning and function (including any possible positional significance) of each of the following literary features that occur in Matthew 25:31–46. Refer to the UBS *Translator's Handbook for Matthew* and/or some other reliable exegetical commentary or study Bible for additional assistance. For each literary feature, also identify a possible equivalent in YL. The first one has been done for you as an example of what to do here. Feel free to comment on any other rhetorical feature that you happen to notice in this text as you carry out the analysis.

Literary feature + verse no.	Identification of the feature	Function within the discourse
"in his glory," "throne of his glory" (v. 31)	repetition of the key term "glory" together with the reference to "his"	highlights the magnificent nature of this judgment scene and of its central character—the Son of Man—at the very beginning of the pericope
"as the shepherd separates the sheep from the goats" (v. 32)		
"on his right...on (the) left" (v. 33)		
"inherit...(the) kingdom" (v. 34)		
"from (the) foundation of (the) world" (v. 34)		
"naked" (v. 36)		
"you came to me" (v. 36)		
"the righteous" (v. 37)		
"when...and when...and when" (vv. 37–39)		
"truly I tell you" (v. 40)		
"one of my brothers, the (very) least" (v. 40)		
"from me" (v. 41)		
"the cursed (ones)" (v. 41)		
"also they" (v. 44)		
"neither to/for me you did (it)" (v. 45)		
"into eternal punishment...into eternal life" (v. 46)		

3.6.6 Step 6: Do a complete discourse analysis

Step 6 is to prepare a detailed linguistic study of all verses within the pericope and propose an inclusive *topical-thematic summary*.

The preceding investigations of genre, textual demarcation, recursion, and the artistic and rhetorical features prepare the ground for a more systematic analysis of the chief linguistic properties of the passage at hand. Step 6 usually reveals some additional aspects of the passage's literary character as well. Such a study of the discourse as a whole may be carried out in different degrees of detail, ranging from a simple overview of the main clause constituents (S, V, O, etc.) as they occur in sequential combination to a full syntactic structural breakdown (kernel, colon) of the entire text.

The aim of such an analysis is to determine the specific *grammatical constructions* (morphological and syntactic) chosen by the author to convey his content contribute to the expression of the text's overall meaning and function. The analyst considers, for example, the order of syntactic constituents within a clause, tracing the sequential reference to key participants in the text, the relationship of dependent clauses to each other and to independent clauses within sentence units (foreground-background),

3.6 A ten-step exegetical methodology

complexes of possessive constructions, sequences of prepositional phrases, juxtapositions of event nouns, and use of the passive voice, of non-finite verbal forms (participles, infinitives), and of tense-sequence patterns. The analyst also seeks to discern what is distinctive (*marked* or non-normal usage) within the microstructure of any passage and what is the implied literary significance of this, for example, with respect to topic or focus..

Two methods of analysis will be illustrated in the rest of this section. The first involves a simple literal charting of clause units as they occur in the progression of the discourse. In order to do such an analysis you will need to refer to the Greek text or an interlinear version, which often reveals patterns and parallels that are not apparent in any translation, whether literal or idiomatic. The following, for example, is a display of the lexical constituents of Matthew 25:31–34. (Note that English words used to render one Greek word are connected by hyphens.) Complete the chart for verses 35–40. When finished, compare your chart with those of other members of the class as a joint discussion exercise.

Ref.	LINK	Pre-Verb 1 (2)	VERBAL	Post-verb 1 (3)	Post-verb 2 (4)*
31a	Now when		he-comes	the Son of Man and all the angels	in the glory his with him,
31b	then		he-will sit	on (the)-throne	of-glory his;
32a	and		they-will-be-assembled	before him	all the nations,
32b	and		he-will-separate	them	from-one another
32c	just-as	the shepherd	he-separates	the sheep	from the goats,
33a	and		he-will-set	the sheep	on (the)-right-his,
33b	but		---------------	the goats	on (the)-left.
34a	Then		he-will-say	the king on (the)-right-his:	to the-(ones)
34b			"Come	the blessed-ones	of Father my,
34c			inherit	the prepared for-you From (the)-foundation	kingdom Of-(the)-world."
35a					
35b					
35c					
35d					
35e					
35f					
36a					
36b					
36c					

36d

36e

36f

37a

37b

37c

37d

37e

38a

38b

38c

38d

39a

39b

40a

40b

40c

40d

* The numbers in parentheses simply indicate additional syntactic constituents that may be filled sequentially in either "pre-verb" or "post-verb" position. Obviously, the more distinct fillers there are, the more marked the clause is at that point. The term "verbal" includes finite verbs as well as predicative non-finite forms, such as participles, infinitives, and gerunds used verbally within a clause.

What can such a linguistic charting tell us about the text before us? Any noun, full pronoun, or noun phrase that occurs before the main verb (or an object/comment before a subject/topic in a non-finite or verbless clause) is potentially significant and normally marks something of interest or importance within the discourse (see also step 5).

» Does that hold true on the chart above, for example at verse 32c? Discuss any other examples of this nature that you find.

» Who are the chief participants of this discourse? Do you notice anything special about how any one of them is referred to in the text?

» Does a single participant stand out as the main character of the account? If so, how is this person and discourse role marked linguistically?

Anything unusual—that is, anything falling outside a normal (*unmarked*) NT Greek pattern—should be examined for its possibly special semantic significance within the text, e.g., ellipsis, expansion of information within a phrase, or repetition. (The same heuristic principle applies when a Hebrew text is being charted.)

» Do you notice any instances of these marked phenomena in your chart?

» Consider the various transitional expressions that appear, including any non-default conjunctions: What can these tell you about the construction of the discourse? (An example is τότε 'then' at v. 34a.)

A chart like the one above can also be used to more systematically reveal the repetition of key words and semantic fields that form the basis for the theme or sub-theme that synopsizes the semantic essence of a particular paragraph (or larger) unit within the discourse. The salient elements in any thematic statement derived from such a study may also be highlighted by the various marked linguistic structures and literary devices that have already been mentioned (e.g., fronting of subject or object). These thematic summaries, which may be condensed further as section headings within the biblical text, are usually generated intuitively after a careful analysis of the discourse, but scholars are currently developing more explicit principles and procedures for elucidating the nature of "theme" (and "rheme") as well as theme-shifting in literary texts.[12]

» Which prominent notions appear already in the small text portion charted above? Study the entire pericope of Matthew 25:31–46 and identify the three or four most important thematic ideas, based on conceptual recursion and stylistic marking.

» Next, compose a thematic summary for this portion of the book.

» Then condense your summary into an appropriate set of section headings for the unit. (You may decide that only one section heading is needed.)

» Compare your proposal to those of other Bibles and record any major differences.

If you have time, complete a constituent charting of the remainder of the pericope (through verse 46) and comment on any item in your chart that is noteworthy. (This type of systematic study provides a framework within which to integrate the results of steps 1–5.)

---

[12]See, for example, Floor 2004, which may be accessed in a pdf file on the website of the Centre for Bible Interpretation and Translation in Africa (http://academic.sun.ac.za/as/cbta/). Floor (2004:v) defines the notion of theme as the "developing and coherent core or thread of a discourse in the mind of the speaker-author and hearer-reader, functioning as the prominent macrostructure of the discourse. The information structure, with its topics and focus structures and its strategies, can be used as a tool to identify and analyse themes. These categories and strategies together are called theme traces when they occur in marked syntactic constructions or in other prominence configurations like relexicalisation, end-weight, and repetition of macrowords. Theme traces are defined with the following wording: A theme trace is a clue in the surface form of a discourse, viewed from the perspective of information structure, that points to the cognitive macrostructure or theme of a text. This clue is in the form of (1) a marked syntactical configuration, be it marked word-order or marked in the sense of explicit and seemingly 'redundant', all signaling some thematic sequencing strategy, or (2) some recurring concept(s) signaling some prominence and coherence."

For another important collection of literary-oriented cognitive linguistic studies of theme see Louwerse and van Peer 2002.

The second method of discourse analysis is a more detailed type of *syntactic-semantic* study. It is illustrated below with reference to Matthew 25:33–35b. This kind of analysis is useful in certain cases, as when dealing with a particularly difficult passage (which the following is not).[13]

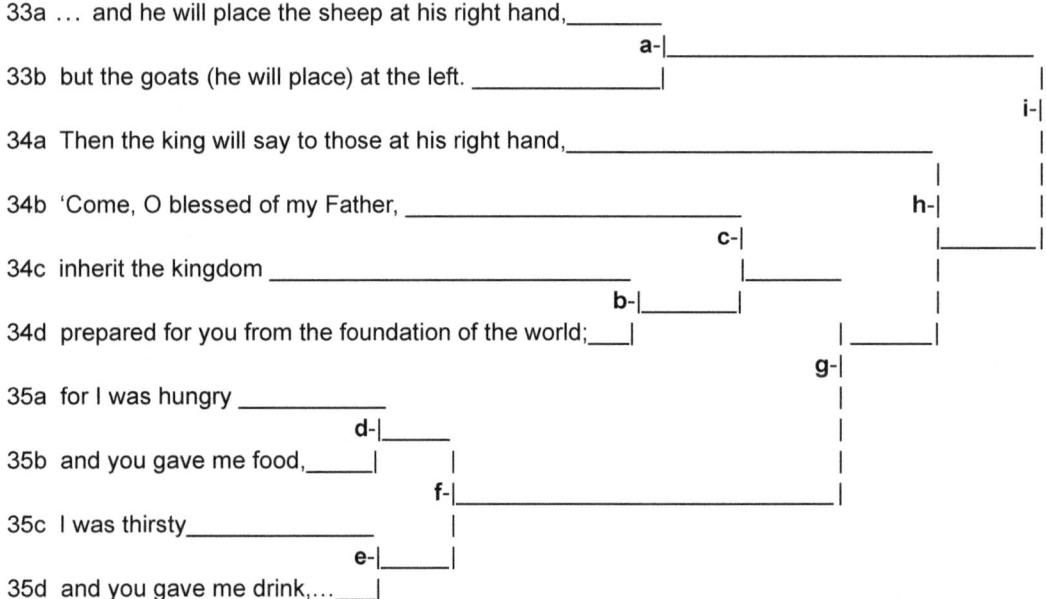

The various semantic relationships between clause units may be specified as follows (the *base* is the clause that occurs first in a symmetrical pairing, or is the principal clause of an asymmetrical pair; 33a is of course connected to the last clause of v. 32, and 35d to the next clause in v. 35):

a = base-contrast	**b** = base-attribution	**c** = base-addition
d = circumstance-base	**e** = circumstance-base	**f** = base-addition
g = command-reason	**h** = base-content	**i** = base-sequential time

This diagramming technique in effect forces the analyst to examine the text more carefully in terms of its sequence of meaningful relationships. In all probability, there will be differences of opinion as to how to classify the various paired relationships; for example, are *d* and *e* better viewed as "circumstance-base" or as "base-sequential time?" There will also be differences of opinion as to how to link them up in a hierarchical structure that incorporates the entire passage under consideration. The aim is not to seek the single "correct" answer in each case, but simply to become more aware of the possibilities for interpreting the text and the different types of evidence that supports one option over against another. It is especially important to observe the higher-level (rightmost) connections since these provide overall sense and coherence to the section as a whole and consequently need to be clearly reflected in any translation (e.g., at *g* where two major text constituents are joined by the relation of command-reason).

---

[13]For further explanation of this method, see Wendland 2002, sections 3.3–3.4. Levinsohn (2006b) recommends a more pragmatic approach to the interpretation of Greek (presumably also Hebrew) conjunctions. Thus the connective γάρ at the beginning of v. 35 serves "to signal that what follows strengthens a preceding assertion" and does not necessarily indicate the semantic relations of explanation, grounds, or reason. If no marking of such a relationship of reinforcement is included in a translation (e.g., by omitting any conjunction as in the CEV), the original inferential connection between the discourse constituents (in this case, v. 34 and vv. 35ff.) is weakened or even lost. Similarly, the conjunction δὲ signals "that what follows marks progression (development)" in the discourse; καί signals "that what follows is to be associated with what precedes, without specifying how"; and οὖν signals "that what follows is a resumption (in most instances) and advancement of the same theme line as before" (Levinsohn 2006b:18). Clearly, further research is needed in this area so that the primary implications inherent in these conjunctions can be reproduced in translation, whether by corresponding conjunctions (if available) or some other device, e.g., tail-head repetition, word-order variations, deictic particles, etc.

» Evaluate the semantic relationships shown above and suggest any modifications or corrections that you feel are needed.

» How would you mark the structural relationship indicated at point g so that it is clearly evident in YL?

» Why is this transition of special importance in the discourse?

» Now try to make your own diagram of the logical links between constituent clauses in verses 44–46. Discuss your individual results in class.

An even more detailed *semantic structure display* can be prepared after or in place of the preceding text analysis. This sort of display is similar to the syntactic-semantic diagram illustrated above but goes further in that it attempts to make all implicit information explicit, including the hierarchically arranged logical connections that relate individual *propositions* on different levels of compositional organization.[14] But for most purposes in the normal translation setting, such precision will not be necessary: a simple topical outline will suffice. This should be formulated in any case after the linguistic analysis of step 6 in order to prepare any section headings that will be needed. Consider, for example, the following outline for the pericope of Matthew 25:31–46:

Drama of the Last Judgment

a. Introduction: The Son of Man enacts his judgment: "the sheep" are separated from "the goats" (31–33)

b. The king invites and commends "those on his right" (34–36)

c. 'The righteous' query their commendation and the king responds (37–40)

d. The king condemns and accuses "those on his left" (41–43)

e. The left query their condemnation and the king responds (44–45)

f. Conclusion: the king's judgment is carried out (46)

» How well does the above outline express what you feel are the essential theme and sub-themes of Matthew 25:31–46?

» Based on your own linguistic and literary analysis of the text, do you wish to propose any changes to this outline, whether to remove a certain heading, re-word one, or add another?

» What do you begin to notice about the larger organization of Matthew 25:31–46? Point out any salient correspondences or contrasts of thematic significance.

» Compare this outline with the section heading(s) that you proposed earlier. Do any modifications seem necessary in light of the additional discourse analysis that you have carried out? If so, explain where and why.

---

[14] SIL International has published a number of helpful New Testament analyses of this nature, a recent example being *A Semantic and Structural Analysis of James* by George and Helen Hart (2001).

3.6.7 Step 7: Investigate the referential framework

Step 7 is to study all key concepts, technical terms, images, and symbols along with their interrelationships in light of the text's ancient Near Eastern sociocultural and religious setting.

Having examined the basic lexical, syntactic, and semantic shape of the discourse during the previous steps, in this seventh step we focus upon the distinctive content of the pericope and its main individual constituents, that is, the principal lexical clusters, key thematic and associated concepts (whether literally or figuratively expressed), any cultural symbols, plus all prominent semantic fields, or *mental spaces*, that the text evokes or alludes to (see Stockwell 2002, chapter 7). In short, the analyst must carefully think through the entire passage and all that it either presupposes or implies, especially in light of its ancient Near Eastern background.

We may distinguish here between *key concepts* and *technical terms*. Key concepts (e.g., "law," "righteousness," "grace," "evil") tend to be more abstract and thus may allow for a variable translation in keeping with the context and lexical collocation. Technical terms (e.g., "sacrifice," "tabernacle," "angel," "synagogue," "centurion," "wine") are more specific or concrete and are normally rendered the same way throughout the Bible. Most of the important items of vocabulary in Matthew 25:31–46 are technical terms, but two key concepts appear in the first and last verses of this pericope: 'glory' (δόξῃ) in verse 31 and 'eternal' (αἰώνιον) in verse 46.

» How would you translate 'glory' and 'eternal' in the Matthew 25 passage?

» Can you think of other contexts in which you would use different terms (e.g., in 2 Cor. 3:7 where 'glory' has reference to the face of Moses and in Rom. 16:26 where 'eternal' has reference to God rather than to eternal life and eternal punishment as it does in Matt. 25:41)?

But before one can come to grips with the wider referential world of the discourse, it is necessary to do an adequate background study of its situational context. This refers to the entire nonverbal *extralinguistic* setting in which the biblical document as a whole was authored, transmitted, received, and responded to (i.e., the political, economic, educational, artistic, sociocultural, philosophical, religious, and ecological milieu). How might their contemporary communication environment have influenced what was written (or not written), and how might it have affected the manner of writing?

At times it is possible to posit a particular setting of communication for a distinct pericope within a given book. Is that true for Matthew 25:31–46? Explain why or why not. The hypothetical situational context for this passage will be considered as we do our analysis of its crucial terms and concepts.

There is one important theological expression at the very beginning of this pericope.

» What is this expression? To whom does this title refer?

» What special significance is attached to this title in the Old and New Testaments?

» Do a word study of this expression, using your study Bible, Translator's Handbook, Bible dictionary, and/or lexicon. Determine how it is to be understood here in Matthew 25:31.

» Compare it to the following passages: Ezekiel 2:1; Daniel 7:13, 8:17; Mark 8:29–31; Revelation 1:13.

By linking "the Son of Man" with "all the angels," "sitting on the throne of his glory," and "all the nations" (vv. 31–32a), Matthew evokes a certain *scenario* in the minds of the original audience. He has set a great stage (in literary narrative terms) for the twofold action that follows: first the "gathering," then the "separating." Who is doing the judging here (cf. Isa. 4:2)—what would have been the normal Jewish expectation? In this case, the royal Judge is earlier identified as the one who is speaking these words. And who is that?

- » Is the same judgment scene conceptually apparent to the consumers of your translation today?

- » Does it make any difference? If so, what can be done either within the text or alongside the text to help people to visualize, understand, and appreciate the momentous event that is taking place here, as recorded by Matthew?

The magnificent royal throne-room scene shifts for a moment to a rural pastoral setting with the reference in verse 32 to a shepherd separating the sheep from the goats.

- » In literal terms with reference to an ancient Palestinian setting, what practice is being carried out here?

- » How does this apply figuratively to the future situation that the Son refers to?

- » What symbolic associations were connected with sheep and goats by people living in the time of Christ? What connotations do these animals have in your social setting and oral or literary tradition?

- » What is the significance of "the right" and "the left" sides in ancient Near-Eastern culture? How does this compare with the meaning of "the right" and "the left" in your culture?

At verse 34 a seemingly new participant enters the text; namely, the king. To whom does this refer and how do you know?

- » What does kingly imagery evoke in the minds of people who live in your sociocultural setting?

- » How can you make this reference to the antecedent "Son of Man" clear for your readers and hearers? What would a literal rendering of this messianic title mean to average non-Christians?[15]

- » Where does the conceptual metaphor RULING IS SHEPHERDING (see section 2.1) originate in the Bible? Cite several key passages in this regard.

In the New Testament, Christ shifts the notion of RULING IS SHEPHERDING to LEADING (or CARING FOR) IS SHEPHERDING.

- » What's the difference? Cite several key passages to this effect.

- » Do such concepts transfer well to your language and culture? If not, do you need to qualify them within the translated text or paratextually? Explain.

- » What would the collocation of the three phrases "blessed of my father," "inherit…the kingdom," and "from the creation of the world" suggest to Christ's original audience?

- » Is this different from what it suggests to people who hear this promise today in YL? In other words, which people, at the time of Christ, considered themselves to be the "blessed?"

- » Why would perhaps even the disciples be shocked by Christ's announcement? (Recall who are gathered there before the throne in v. 32a.)

---

[15]In Chichewa the literal expression "Son of Man" (*mwana wa munthu*) refers either to the child of an African or, idiomatically, to some extraordinary fellow, a man who has just performed a strange or extraordinary feat (cf. *mwana wa mkazi* "child of a woman").

Note the sorts of activities and individuals mentioned in verses 35–36.

- » How are corresponding persons and deeds viewed within the context of your culture?
- » To whom does Christ refer when he says "one of the least of these brothers of mine?" Why are such people singled out?
- » With whom are they being contrasted in general ancient Near-Eastern society?
- » Who then are "the righteous" of verse 37? What characteristics are associated with righteous people in your society?
- » Who are the "cursed" of verse 41?
- » What image does Christ conjure up for his audience when he says "eternal fire?"
- » Who "curses" people in your culture? Is it some evil person, such as a hateful individual or even a sorcerer?
- » Does a curse normally result in death or injury (according to popular belief)? In other words, could this passage be misunderstood in YL? If so, what kind of an explanatory footnote would clarify the intended meaning?
- » What would Christ's listeners think about the devil and his angels? Would they tend to fear them or not, and why?
- » How would their feelings and attitudes compare with those of people today in your religious setting?
- » What contrasting images did the phrases "eternal punishment" and "eternal life" in verse 46 evoke for the members of Christ's audience or readers of Matthew's Gospel?
- » How might this differ for the readers of your translation?
- » Do non-Christians know or use such expressions? If so, what do they mean by them?

3.6.8 Step 8: Connect the cross-textual correspondences

Step 8 is to look for prominent intra- and intertextual references and allusions that are embedded within the discourse, whether explicit or implicit.

From a literary as well as a thematic perspective, it is important to record all significant, topically related concepts and propositions that derive from either previously mentioned material within the same composition (*intra*textual) or from other texts (*inter*textual) that were likely to have been known to the original audience. The apparent purpose for such citations, paraphrases, allusions, and echoes (moving down from the most to the least noticeable within the text) then needs to be ascertained. That is, were they used for reinforcement, validation, foregrounding, contrast, or further *logical-rhetorical development*? The same goes for any important cultural or religious symbols that may be discerned within the text, whether explicitly mentioned or only alluded to (cf. step 7).

Assuming that these different types of culturally based meanings were recognized by the original readers and hearers of the text at hand, the question arises, How can such semantic relevance be made apparent to our target audience today?

3.6 A ten-step exegetical methodology

» Are standard cross-references effective for most people?

» Would there be a more helpful way of pointing out significant intra- and intertextual references? Explain.

Look up the Scripture passages listed below and make a note of what sort of information has been alluded to "behind" the text of Matthew 25:31–46. Suggest what might be the rhetorical function of this rather heavy intra- or intertextual conceptual linkage. In other words, what special aspect of denotation or connotation is being appealed to and applied within the cognitive framework of Matthew's judgment scene in this passage? The first two references have been complete as examples of how to proceed in digging beneath the surface of the discourse for elements of additional implicit meaning.

Verse	Cross-reference	Corresponding element(s)	Their significance within Matthew 25:31–46
31	Daniel 7:13–14; Zechariah 14:5	"Son of Man"	Matthew's text (including v. 32) clearly alludes to Daniel's Messianic vision, thus forging a crucial identity of reference involving "the Christ" – past and present.
31	Matthew 19:28	"on his (my) glorious throne"	Matthew 19:28 says that Christ's followers (those who have left all for him) will also participate with him in judging the nations.
31	Matthew 13:37–43; 16:27; 24:31	"the (his) angels"	
32	Ezekiel 34:17; Micah 4:3; Malachi 3:18	???	
34	Matthew 18:23; 22:2; 27:11, 29, 37	"the king"	
34	Matthew 5:3–11; 23:38; 24:46	"blessed"	
34	Matthew 19:29	"inherit"	
34	Matthew 13:35	"the creation of the world"	
35–36	Isaiah 58:7	???	
40	Matthew 12:48–50; 23:8	"brothers"	
41	Isaiah 66:24; Matthew 5:22, 18:8	???	
46	Matthew 1:19; 5:6, 10, 20; 6:1; 13:43; 23:28	"the righteous"	
46	Matthew 7:14; 18:8; 19:16; Daniel 12:2	"eternal life" + ???	

Note that some of these expressions are exactly the same in two or more passages:

- » What is the standard translation procedure that applies if the sense is the same in these places?
- » What if the sense is significantly different (e.g., "blessed" in Matt. 21:9 and 23:39)?
- » What can we do with those allusions that are clearly recognizable (by a biblically literate reader), but where the wording is not exactly the same?

3.6.9 Step 9: Determine the functional and emotive dynamics

Step 9 is to ascertain the main communicative functions and primary speech acts of the text, along with their associated emotive and connotative elements.

This is another way of examining the biblical text as a whole: It zeroes in on its individual and conjoined pragmatic (interpersonal) properties, again with the possibility of applying different degrees of specificity and shading. It builds upon the genre study of step 2 as well as our investigation of the text's rhetorical devices in step 5 and also benefits from the knowledge gained when carrying out the manifold discourse analysis of step 6. First, in step 9, the main communicative functions of the discourse are determined (e.g., informative, expressive, imperative, relational, esthetic, and ritual), and then the more specific *speech acts* as they occur in sequence, either in a monologue sequence or a dialogue exchange (e.g., speech acts that encourage, comfort, rebuke, condemn, appeal, certify, authorize, and inform). In addition, any strong connotative elements (i.e., emotional and attitudinal overtones) that are expressed during the act of "speaking" need to be noted, for these non-semantic elements also need to be represented, if possible, in a *LiFE*-like translation.

Study the verses from Matthew listed below and identify the principal speech act that is represented in each, as well as any strongly felt emotions or attitudes which the speakers seem to be expressing along with their words. Certainly, in any oral presentation of this pericope (and any other one composed primarily of direct discourse) vocal qualities would have to be represented as an integral part of the text. In some languages certain non-semantic lexical features must also be included in order to properly reproduce these personal, attitudinal aspects of human speech (e.g., exclamations or interjections, honorific or pejorative terms, and deictic particles), without which the text would sound very flat and unnatural. The first example has been completed as an illustration of the analytic method desired.

Verse	Primary speech act	Accompanying attitude(s) and emotion(s)
25:34	invitation	sincerity, delight, enthusiasm
25:35		
25:37		
25:40		
25:41		
25:43		
25:44		
25:45		

No matter how the text of Matthew 25:31–46 is classified in terms of genre, it is clear that the point of the end times discourse is not primarily *informative*—to reveal and explain the earth-shaking events that will transpire at the end of time. Rather, it is *imperative*—intended through Christ's visionary account to motivate here-and-now ethical behavior. Thus what we have is not simply a descriptive narrative intended to instruct the audience; instead, it is a vivid pastoral appeal calculated to encourage attitudes and actions that befit "the righteous" who enter into eternal life (25:46). This identification of the central communicative purpose leads us to a consideration of certain prominent rhetorical features that help set the scene and animate the Lord's graphic portrayal of his post-*parousia* judgment activity.

By virtue of the naturally prominent narrative device of end stress, the burden of this private instruction to his disciples would seem to be Christ's dramatic exhortation to put their professed faith into practice as a life-long habit of acts of loving assistance on behalf of "the least" of the Lord's brothers (25:40, 45; cf. 22:34–40). This is where real "kingdom of heaven" work begins (25:1, 14), and this is the evidence which Christ the king will testify for—or against—in the judgment. Thus "salvation" for the righteous is initiated in this earthly life, being manifested by selfless deeds of "service" (25:44). This implicit encouragement (or warning, as the case may be), though set within a particular historical setting, is timeless in its persuasive relevance and potential application to any individual or audience in attendance.

> » Would you agree that this pericope builds up to a *peak of intensity* at the very end in terms of both form and content?
>
> » How do verse 40, 45, and 46 relate thematically to each other?
>
> » What are some of the key emotive elements that contribute to this progression of intensification?
>
> » Is this development apparent in your translation? If not, what can be done, whether textually or paratextually, to call attention to it?

It is interesting to observe that this deceptively simple account reflects aspects of all three of the so-called "species" of classical Greco-Roman rhetoric: The surface of the text reveals certain *judicial* as well as *epideictic* concerns; that is, it seeks to influence the audience with regard to a right versus wrong legal standard as well as an honorable versus dishonorable value system. However, the message's real import is *deliberative* in nature: it is intended to convince listeners concerning the expediency of specified beneficial behavior in contrast to detrimental actions in view of a future day of public reckoning.

Give an example of a passage or expression within this pericope that conveys each of these rhetorical motivations.

a. **Judicial**—a precise judgment of right or wrong: _____

b. **Epideictic**—an appeal to what is praiseworthy or shameful: _____

c. **Deliberative**—a concern for the beneficial as opposed to what is harmful: _____

The artfully composed discourse structure of this challenging pericope is obviously being used as a persuasive (rhetorical) device. The literary style is thus enhanced as a means of shaping and sharpening the intended message so that it will have the greatest possible impact, upon *listeners* in particular. It may thus be viewed as a macrotextual equivalent of the "A, and what's more, B; not only A, but B" type of parallel patterning that characterizes biblical poetry (with discourse panel I of the Greek text displayed at the beginning of section 3.6 corresponding to "A" and panel II to "B"). As our examination of the original text would indicate, this passage could be classified as an instance of *oratorical prose*, being marked by stylistic features such as rhythmic utterances, alliteration, balanced syntactic patterns, figurative language, conclusion-focused interrogatives, and incorporated direct speech.

The question now is, To what extent can this prominent artistic and rhetorical dimension be reproduced in a contemporary translation? This leads to the final step in preparing the ground for a *LiFE*-style translation.

3.6.10 Step 10: Coordinate form-functional matches

Step 10 is to collect, categorize, and prioritize all potential correspondences between the SL and TL and then prepare a provisional translation of the pericope or complete book.

This final stage involves a selective listing of all *form-functional matches*—whether confirmed, pending, or just possible—that have been identified during the preceding steps. This would be based on a prior survey of all distinctive and frequently used artistic and rhetorical features of the TL that are available for rendering those of the biblical document. If *both* textual form and function can be matched across languages, so much the better; often, however, the function of a particular SL device will have to be reproduced by a different TL form. The aim is to keep the divergence in such cases as small as possible, even though at times only a complete re*form*ulation will do. The compositional inventory might well include suggested biblical texts and representative samples to which the designated TL literary/oratorical genres and their related stylistic features could apply.

These different devices then need to be classified and catalogued for future reference. An electronic "dictionary file," database, or some other categorized retrieval system should be created and continually updated with new and revised artistic and rhetorical data entries as the project continues. Even as the exegetical procedures are being conducted with reference to the biblical text, translators can begin to consider their possible translational implications. Important questions and issues that pertain to form (style, structure), content, and function should be thought of in terms of how they might be handled in the TL, especially from a *LiFE* perspective.

Step 10 is probably the hardest of all the steps to carry out because it requires that translators begin to think in the TL even as they are analyzing SL language forms. It is perhaps best to carry it out in two separate stages: one with an emphasis upon inventorying the chief SL literary forms and their assumed communicative functions, and the other with a corresponding emphasis on discovering close literary/oratorical equivalents in the TL, in keeping with the particular genre of literature in focus.

Following the analysis of a biblical text according to the set of procedures considered up to this point, the initial translation of it may be done in several ways. A relatively literal rendition would be the easiest to get the compositional process moving. This literal draft can later be enlivened by appropriate literary devices in a relevant, functionally equivalent manner. The opposite approach would be to have a literary artist compose a complete genre transformation at the outset, that is, prepared intuitively according to the closest functional model text type in the TL oral or written tradition. This draft could then be sharpened exegetically with reference to the SL text at a later time. Many variations of these two approaches might be applied, depending on what is most efficient and effective for the translation team. In most cases, however, the first draft should be prepared by a single experienced translator, rather than by a team trying to patch concepts and texts together as a committee.

> » What operational procedures does your translation team or committee follow to carry out its work, from researching the target language and literature/orature through the initial draft stage and on to polishing the final pre-publication document?
>
> » Do you have any practical revisions or modifications to suggest with respect to the preceding ten steps of analysis?
>
> » What can be done to stimulate and encourage the vernacular creativity and resourcefulness of translators when rendering the biblical text?

This is often a rather difficult thing to do, even in the case of gifted verbal artists. Could it be that they are intimidated by the critical eyes of biblical scholars or pastors on the review committee who may be prejudiced in favor of some other, more foreignized translation? If so, what can be done to resolve the situation?

3.7 A case study

The following is a case study pertaining to the development of several Chichewa Bible translations (Malawi). As you read through it and the *LiFE* example at the end, compare it with the situation in your language and translation setting, either past or present. Be prepared to discuss any noteworthy similarities or differences that become apparent.

The magnificent structure, artistry, and rhetoric of many biblical texts often turn out to sound quite the opposite in a translation, whether ancient or modern. This is true of the 1923 Chichewa version, *Buku Lopatulika*. In terms of verbal style, expression of content, and typographical format, this translation speaks with a very heavy "foreign accent." In places it is almost unintelligible to ordinary listeners. The 1998 idiomatic "popular-language" version (*Buku Loyera*), which was prepared by trained mother-tongue translators, is a great improvement. But even though its language is natural and very understandable overall, in a number of places, including the passage under consideration, this modern version still fails to reproduce the dynamic style and full persuasive force of the original.

More recently, some experimental efforts have been undertaken to produce a text that more adequately represents the oft-missing literary dimension in Chichewa. While a *LiFE* translation is not to be thought of as *the* ideal, it is just one viable option among the others available with reference to a specific audiences and religious settings. The downside to a *LiFE* translation is that in trying to duplicate the vital artistry and rhetoric of the original text, certain of its microstructural features will certainly be lost, for example, strict lexical repetition. However, the benefit in terms of greater communicability and acceptability for a particular target group is a significant factor that may well make it worth the extra effort necessary to produce such a translation.

> » In YL, what would some of the most important of these losses be in terms of the Matthew pericope, and why are such deficits probably unavoidable during the translation process?

> » How might these losses be compensated for by certain gains through the use of literary forms that more closely duplicate the biblical text's communicative functions, including its prominent rhetorical effects?

One of the first things to consider in preparing a *LiFE* version is the issue of *genre equivalence*. Is there a TL genre available that can serve as a close, if not exact, functional equivalent for Christ's last judgment discourse—a dramatic narrative parable that manifests a prominent oratorical style? As it so happens, there *is* such a flexible literary form in Chichewa; namely, the *ndakatulo* genre of lyric poetry, which functions well to translate highly emotive, rhetorically toned passages of the Scriptures. In fact, all of the stylistic features that were listed earlier as being noteworthy with respect to Matthew's Greek text are very prominent also in the *ndakatulo* mode of dramatic composition.

In addition, the narrative macrostructure itself is quite common in the Chichewa oral tradition. A common form of story telling involves the use of what may be termed *parallel image sets* in which human attributes are objectified, with traditional narrative characters being used to portray certain important positive and negative values. First, one model of behavior is presented, then the other by way of contrast—quality for quality. There is a similar parallel image set in our Matthew 25:31–46 judgment passage: the first positive, leading to a blessed outcome, and the second negative, resulting in disaster. Each of these is reflected off the other to heighten the thematic and moral point of the passage as a whole. This wedding of a dynamic rhetorical style with a familiar narrative structure has the potential for creating a great impression on any Chewa listening audience.

The medium of *hearing* must be stressed. It is highly probable that this pericope in Greek was initially composed with an oral-aural manner of communication in mind. The entire text is eminently recitable (or chantable) due to its verbal recursion, parallel patterning, rhythmic sequences, euphony, and an incremental climactic development. As a result, this passage is most memorable, hence transmittable as well. Bible translators need to seriously consider this aspect of the discourse as they re-present the text in the TL in order that it be as easily and effectively conveyed to hearers as the original was.

This necessitates, in turn, a *reader-friendly display* of the discourse on the printed page. The text must be formatted as a sequence of meaningful *utterance units* combined within clearly delineated narrative "paragraphs." One possibility would be to follow the Greek text as set out at the beginning of section 3.6, using a balanced and terraced sequence of corresponding segments in the vernacular (either with or without the accompanying letters along the right margin). If that technique is felt to be too sophisticated or complicated, however, some simplification could be introduced. The goal of such an integrated procedure (sound connected closely with sight) is to enhance the general readability, hearability, and intelligibility of the whole passage, including its interconnected parts.

A sample translation of Matthew 25:34–36, composed in the *ndakatulo* lyric style and manifesting a more natural printed format, is set out below, together with a relatively literal back-translation into English. This particular version has been stylistically reduced in its verbal dynamism, however, that is, limited in terms of its vividness of expression and rendered more prosaic in nature. This was done to prevent the form of the text from overshadowing or detracting somewhat in any way from the solemn content that is being communicated. Nevertheless, several graphic ideophones (shown in boldface) that appeal to the drama of the original setting have been included (used only in the first, connotatively positive panel. This experimental rendition represents the ultimate in terms of functional equivalence. It is intended to satisfy a specific need for a clearly defined contemporary audience, for example, to provide a version to be used by a youth drama group in a public performance. How effective would a translation like this be in such a situation? That can be determined only after a thorough program of audience-testing has been carried out and the results carefully evaluated.

Tsono Iyeyo ngati Mfumu	So this one, just like a king,
adauza akudzanja lamanja:	told those at his right hand:
Bwerani kunotu inu	Come right here you
odalitsidwa ndi Atate anga.	people blessed by my Father.
Lowani mu ufumuwu	Enter into this kingdom
umene adakukonzerani Iyedi,	which He actually prepared for you,
chilengedwere dziko lapansili.	since the creation of this very world.
Paja Ine ndidaali ndi njala,	You know, I was hungry,
inu nkundipatsa chakudya.	right away you gave me some food.
Ndidaali kumva ludzu,	I was feeling thirsty,
inu nkundipatsa chikho **pha**.	right away you gave me a cup, **full up**.
Ndadaali mlendo, **balamanthu**,	I was a stranger, **arriving all of a sudden**,
inu nkundilandira kwanuko.	right away you received me into your home.
Ndidaali wamaliseche Ine,	I was naked, I was,
inu nkundibveka bwino.	right away you dressed me up well.
Ndinkadwala mpaka kumanda **tswii**,	I was so sick I could have gone to the grave **straight**,
inu nkumandizonda ndithu.	indeed, you kept coming to see how I was.
Ndidaali **mange** *mu ndende,*	I was **bound up** in prison,
inu nkumadzandichezetsa.	You would keep on visiting me.

No matter how dynamic or idiomatic a translation is, however, it can never reproduce in the TL the full communicative value of an excellently composed literary source text—not if the closest possible content equivalence also remains a matter of priority (cf. section 7.2.2). A poetic re-creation can perhaps handle most aspects of the textual or stylistic richness, but like any rendering, it too often fails with regard to the implicit level of communication and the great amount of contextual information that is normally presupposed by the original.

What can be done to redress this regrettable loss of significance? Of course, various *supplementary helps* can be pressed into service: illustrations, cross-references, footnotes or marginal notes, section headings, a key-term glossary, concordance, and so forth. But even these will ultimately fall short to a greater or lesser degree due to a lack of adequate background knowledge on the part of most receptors, a situation that is usually exacerbated as a result of intercultural differences and even outright contradictions.

Explanatory footnotes (or sound-marked asides in an audio version) offer perhaps the best means of supplying such information, including the major extralinguistic implications and applications that arise from the passage at hand (see section 7.1.3). A footnote would be needed, for example, with regard to the concept of a post-death divine judgment, which is alien to African religious beliefs. (The African view is that a person is judged progressively, based on traditional social norms and contemporary mores; the result of this indigenous public verdict is manifested in the afterlife only in terms of how one is ultimately regarded and revered as an ancestral spirit.) A footnote would also be needed to explain why sheep were so highly regarded in the ancient Near East, including their religious symbolism, as distinct from goats. Sheep are little known in south-central Africa, except on large, foreign-owned commercial farms. Goats, on the other hand, are very common and have a largely negative connotation similar to that of Bible times, but with rather different contextual associations. In the Scriptures, goats are connected with sin in general; in Bantu societies, with illicit sexual relations in particular.

Finally, what is the pragmatic relevance of rhetoric in relation to discourse structure as far as Bible translation is concerned? The answer depends on the type of translation that is being produced and how crucial the values of appropriateness and acceptability are to it. When the goal is greater contemporary communicative value, then the dimension of *effectiveness* will be somewhat more important to achieve than *efficiency*. In other words, the conceptual "cost" in terms of the relative ease of text processing will be less important than a potential "gain" with regard to cognitive and emotive contextual effects such as relative impact, appeal, artistry, aurality, and memorability. To be sure, Bible translators always want to be "on the right side" as they re-signify the biblical text within the framework of another language and culture, but such a critical decision can be determined only in relation to a particular audience or constituency who need to hear the Word proclaimed to them in a manner that closely resembles that of the original setting of communication. This includes, to the extent possible, the dramatic content as well as the dynamic style and structure of the Scriptures as they were first written, proclaimed, and have subsequently been transmitted to us by the extant textual witnesses.

For reflection, research, and response:

1. What do you think of the Chichewa poetic-prose version given above? Compare it with Peterson's contemporary English rendition of Matthew 25:34–36, presented below as originally formatted. Does either version seem to go too far in certain respects, whether exegetically or stylistically? Pick out some of the chief literary features that appear in these dynamic translations and give a brief evaluation, keeping the respective audiences in mind.

> Then the King will say to those on his right, "Enter you who are blessed by my Father! Take what's coming to you in this kingdom. It's been ready for you since the world's foundation. And here's why:
>
>> I was hungry and you fed me,
>> I was thirsty and you gave me a drink,
>> I was homeless and you gave me a room,
>> I was shivering and you gave me clothes,
>> I was sick and you stopped to visit,
>> I was in prison and you came to me."

> Then those "sheep" are going to say, "Master, what are you talking about? When did we ever see you hungry and feed you, thirsty and give you a drink? And when did we ever see you sick or in prison and come to you?" Then the King will say, "I'm telling you the solemn truth: Whenever you did one of these things to someone overlooked or ignored, that was me – you did it to me."

2. Now, reconsider Peterson's version, The Message, in light of what its aims are, as expressed in the following excerpt from his preface. What do you think about his assessment of the biblical text in view of these aims?

> In the Greek-speaking world of that day, there were two levels of language: formal and informal. Formal language was used to write philosophy and history, government decrees and epic poetry....But if the writing was routine—shopping lists, family letters, bills, and receipts—it was written in the common informal idiom of everyday speech, street language....In order to understand the Message right, the language must be right—not a refined language that appeals to our aspirations after the best but a rough and earthy language that reveals God's presence and action where we least expect it....The goal is not to render a word-for-word conversion of Greek into English, but rather to convert the tone, the rhythm, the events, the ideas, into the way we actually think and speak. (Peterson 2003:8)

In what sense could the writings of the New Testament be considered "routine?" To what extent could the discourse of Christ and his apostles be regarded as "street language?" Base your answer on the text studies that we have already carried out. Can an argument be made for a third level of language in the NT—somewhere between formal and informal? Which body of writings greatly influenced the Greek structure and style of the NT? How great was this OT (LXX) influence? Discuss these issues in class. In particular, consider how our conclusions concerning these matters would affect our approach to and philosophy of Bible translation.

3. Prepare your own *LiFE* translation of Matthew 25:34–36. First of all, specify your target audience and the purpose for which you are preparing your translation. Then, with these criteria in mind, create a literary rendering, to the degree that is appropriate. Next, give a fairly literal English back-translation of your vernacular text. List the specific artistic and rhetorical devices that you used and tell why you used them. Finally, in class, present orally the several versions that have been produced; then critique them so that the class members can learn from one another about the different communicative possibilities that exist for a version of this nature.

4. Compare the method of charting the sequential clause-constituent order of a biblical text given in section 3.6.6 with the more detailed plan proposed by Dooley and Levinsohn (2001:43–48). What are the major similarities and differences? What can you learn from the method outlined by Dooley and Levinsohn that can make your discourse charting procedure a more informative and/or accurate exercise? Note: Dooley and Levinsohn also outline "A methodology for analyzing [participant] reference patterns" in (2001:127–134). If time and interest allow, this approach may also be studied to see how it can help us better understand the organization of a text, especially with reference to the important communicative aspects of structure and function that need to be reproduced in a translation. A good text to further practice these discourse analysis procedures on is Matthew 25:14–30, "the parable of the talents."

5. In *deictic shift theory* a number of the hermeneutical concerns addressed in our analytic framework are combined. This theory posits "a speaking, writing or thinking 'voice' [that] represents a *deictic center*, which a reader can mentally project by adopting the *cognitive stance* that best accounts for the sense of coherence across a text" (Stockwell, in Semino and Culpeper 2002:78–79; see also Stockwell 2002:53–55). Changes in perspective are stimulated by *deictic shift devices* that may be perceptual (personal), spatial, temporal, relational (social), textual (medium-based), or compositional (structural) in nature. Areas of interest and importance within a text generally coincide with those points at which "the deictic centre has to be moved within the readerly projection." These are marked in a printed text by paragraph breaks and other typographical devices.

Where does the major deictic shift occur in the Matthew 25:31–46 passage? What is your evidence for this? (Recall the earlier structural and stylistic analysis.) Do a greater number of these shifts occur at the onset of chapter 26 (in vv. 1–5), which is the start of a new principal unit of the Matthew narrative of Christ? Identify them. How can you assist the reader/hearer to keep track of these perceptual movements in your translation? (These may occur on several discourse levels, such as implied author – implied audience, Christ – disciples, and Son of Man – those on the right/left.)

6. In her basic typology of literature in translation, Katharina Reiss (2000:31–33) posits the *form-focused text*, which she describes as follows:

> In these texts the author makes use of formal elements, whether consciously or unconsciously, for a specific esthetic effect….Therefore, the expressive function of language, which is primary in form-focused texts, must find an *analogous* form in the translation to create a corresponding impression, so that the translation can become a true equivalent….This can be done by creating equivalents through new forms. Thus in a form-focused text the translator will not mimic slavishly (adopt) the forms of the source language, but rather appreciate the form of the source language and be inspired by it to discover an analogous form in the target language, one which will elicit a similar response in the reader.

Discuss the preceding quotation in light of what you have learned about a *LiFE* approach: What are the main similarities and differences?

Do you think that a given biblical text is *form-focused* to the exclusion of other emphases, that is, *content focus* or *appeal focus*? (These are the other principal categories Reiss posits, ibid.:26.) Explain.

To what extent is there a special focus on the structural and stylistic forms of the Matthew 26 pericope—and what is the implication of this for your vernacular translation of this text?

3.8 From analysis to synthesis in translation

There is obviously a considerable amount of overlapping and interconnection in the ten operations proposed as steps in section 3.6, in both the analytical tools applied and their respective areas of application. In other words, top-down (general => specific) and bottom-up (specific => general) text-processing procedures take place, either *together* or in *close alternation* (see Dooley and Levinsohn 2001:51–52). As Qvale (2003:249) points out,

> In mental processing…the various stages are not chronologically separate; introspection reveals that we move back and forth between the operations that constitute the translation process, shuttle-like, according to Lomheim [who says,] "…[I]t is therefore closer to reality to view the entire translation process as a continuous activity in which the various stages are interwoven and govern one another.…"

For example, genre identification (step 2) must be carried out with reference to the microstylistic features (step 7) that characterize or distinguish one genre in relation to another, either in the SL or the TL. On the other hand, as was suggested earlier, the syntactic-semantic discourse analyses (step 6) may be carried out in a more detailed manner, by diagramming all the logical relationships between propositions (semantic clause units in which all implicit information is explicitly stated).

Each of the ten steps (guidelines) reflects at least some difference with regard to focus, scope, or emphasis when applied in relation to a given biblical pericope. However, the individual steps must always be carried out in conjunction with and in light of one another (usually in a back-and-forth progression) in order to produce a holistic, systematic, audience-oriented, and context-sensitive study of the original text. And this must be done *before* to the attempt to communicate it in a very different, contemporary language-culture setting and religious milieu.

The goal of the methodology proposed above is to apply the knowledge gained during exegesis to an actual translation, one that reproduces at least partially (feature-selectively) a literary-equivalent rendition for a designated audience within the contextualized frame of reference specified by a given project *Skopos*. Of course, even a more formal-correspondence version may be rendered in an esthetically motivated *LiFE*-like manner, normally through some sort of phonological enhancement, utilizing, for example, a simple metrical pattern, rhythmic diction, and/or strategically placed rhymes, puns, or alliteration. Thus if so desired, *any* Bible translation—from the most literal to one that is largely idiomatic—can, in practice as well as theory, be expressed in one or more relevant literary respect(s).[16] This may be done by capitalizing on one or more of the distinctive stylistic features that best manifest the genius of the TL in the most appropriate manner for the intended audience.

Our ten text-processing procedures, which apply in particular to an initial analysis of a selected biblical pericope (or, less likely, an entire book) are personal suggestions only. They may easily be rearranged, supplemented, or modified as necessary. When it comes to a specific translation project, they need to be restated in more specific TL terms. It would be a good idea to put the agreed system into operation during the course of a team's day-to-day work schedule so that translators are continually practicing their procedures (revising them as the need arises). After some trial and testing, they may become recommended guidelines, included in the project *Brief*. Not that they need to be slavishly followed—they are merely a framework within which to conceptualize the transfer operation and the process of textual synthesis.

I will conclude with another, this time a somewhat more dynamic, example of a *LiFE* rendition in the Chichewa poetic translation of the third and concluding stanza of Job 28. Job 28:23–28 is an especially suitable passage for a distinctive, skillful manner of composition to be manifested. It would act as a means of drawing verbal attention to the significance of the text at this crucial, culminating point in the poem and also serve to distinguish it stylistically from its cotext. The challenge to translators is simply this: How can they verbally convey the most significant dimensions of the lyric meditative instruction of Job 28 with the impact, attraction, and connotation of pious reverence that pervades the original Hebrew text?

This pericope was formulated in Chichewa with a specifically oratorical presentation in mind, so that it can be orally declaimed or even sung to the accompaniment of a musically complementary melody. The printed text was also formatted on the page in measured flowing lines so as to facilitate a rhythmic recitation or reading aloud and hopefully a better understanding. The Chichewa version appears below in parallel with a back-translation into English, one that is relatively literal so as to draw attention to some of its outstanding stylistic features.[17]

Mulungu ndiye yekha amadziwa,	God is the one who knows,
kudziwa njira yopitira kumeneko,	knows the way of going there,
kumene kumapezeka nzeru imene.	to where wisdom itself may be found.
Paja amayang'ana soo! mpakana	In fact he looks long and hard, SOO! right up
[#] kumathero a dziko lonse lapansi,	[#] to the ends of the whole land down here,
kuona zonse zakunsi kwa thambo.	to see everything that is below the sky.
Iyetu [^] popatsa mphepo mphamvu	Surely he [^] in giving power to the wind
ndi kuyesa kuchuluka kwa mvula,	and in measuring out the amount of rain,
poika lamulo loti madziwo agwe	in setting a command for those waters to fall down
ndikukonza njira yoyenda mphezi,	and in preparing a path for the lightning to travel,

---

[16]Such a technique is clearly stated in the introduction to Wilt's *LiFE* translation, *Prayer, Praise, and Protest* (2002b): "I have often restructured texts in the attempt to represent in contemporary English style their genre, thematic accents and coherence of images as well as information content....I have tried to reflect the Hebrew's use of devices such as wordplay, assonance (repetition of the same sound) and thematically linked ambiguity (a certain word or line can be understood in more than one way, both according with themes of the text), though with less frequency than they occur in the Hebrew texts."

[17]The symbols such as the pound sign and caret in the display below are explained in the paragraph that follows the display.

pamenepo ndiye adapeza nzeruyo *ndi kufufuzafufuza wake [@] mtengo,* *inde*, n' kuvomereza phindu lake.*	then is when he found that wisdom and carefully investigated of it [@] the worth, yes*, and to assert its value.
Tsono Mulungu anthu onse awauza, *'Kuopa Chauta [$] ndiyo nzeru ndithu,* *kuchotsa zoipa m'moyo, apo ndipo!' [%]*	So now God all people he tells them, "Fearing Chauta [$] the Creator is really wisdom, removing evils from life, that's where it's at!%"

The main artistic attributes of *ndakatulo* lyric-expressive poetry are clearly evident from this selection, for example, use of the vivid ideophone *sooo!* 'looking intently' to duplicate the intensity of the utterance that is introduced at the beginning of Job 28:24 by the combination of the conclusive-consequential conjunction כִּי 'for, surely, that is to say' followed by the fronted separable pronoun הוּא 'he', referring to God. Other features include balanced lineation; inclusion of interlineal transitional devices (e.g., at marker *); divergences from a prosaic syntactic word order (at marker @); enjambment (at marker #); additional emphasizers and intensifiers (^); introduction of a distinctive divine name ($); alliteration/assonance (%); reiteration; and contemporary idiomatic language (including the final rhythmic verbal capstone *apo ndipo!*). As already noted, the poetic manner of composition is complemented by the text format, which highlights the lined progression and calls visual attention to the first and last utterances (foregrounded also in the Hebrew text of Job 28).

An effort was made in this translation exercise to ensure that the literary style does not overpower or detract from the biblical message. To do so would disturb the text's overall reflective tone and solemn content, in which case the verbal form would be unworthy of its subject, making it unsuitable for use in public worship. A poetic mode of oratorical expression is not foreign to a didactic communicative purpose, for research has indicated that it would sound appropriate if employed in a traditional Bantu setting of Christian religious initiation and catechetical instruction. Such a dynamically rendered version may not be suitable for all audiences or fit for every occasion. But if composed, for example, with an active, community-involved youth group, drama troupe, or gospel choir in mind, a rhetorically heightened text would certainly help the intense debates of the original Hebrew to become *audibly* and *emotively* alive in the Chichewa vernacular for a contemporary generation of wisdom-seekers.

For reflection, research, and response:

1. What do you think of the Chichewa lyric rendition above? Give your general assessment of it (based on the English back-translation) and indicate some possible points of caution. Do you recognize in this text any stylistic devices that are common in the poetry of YL? Specify what these are.

2. Prepare a *LiFE* translation of Job 28:23–28 in YL along with a literal back-translation into English. Then summarize some of the main literary features that you have included in your version.

3. Discuss the differences between *LiFE* as a translation *philosophy* and a translation *procedure*. Which, if any, of these would fit into your setting of translation—and why?

4. Discuss the following quotation from Martin Luther (1960:213–214) in relation to a *LiFE* approach to translating:

   > What is the point of needlessly adhering so scrupulously to words which one cannot understand anyway? Whoever would speak German must not use Hebrew style. Rather he must see to it—once he understands the Hebrew author—that he concentrates on the sense of the text, asking himself, "Pray tell, what do the Germans say in such a situation?" Once he has the German words to serve the purpose, let him drop the Hebrew words and express the meaning freely in the best German he knows.

5. Read the introduction to Wilt's English translation in *Prayer, Praise, And Protest* (2002b) and identify the main goals of his literary version. Then read his translation of "Pigeon" (Jonah) and pick out three good examples that illustrate his recommended translation procedures.

6. Study Wilt's literary rendition of Psalm 23, presented below (II, from Wilt 2002b:30). Carefully compare this to Peterson's Psalm 23 in *The Message* (I, also below). If possible, also compare them to the original Hebrew text or an interlinear version. Then carry out the exercises that follow with reference to YL:

I

A good shepherd looks after his flock's every need: fresh grass, clean, calm streams, and safety. He guides them with his staff, keeps them in line, on the right path, however difficult the way, however dark the shadows. He gains a good reputation because of his care for his sheep.

This is how it is with Yahweh's care for me. I fear no harm. I'm completely at ease and healthy, because he shepherds me.

A loving host makes sure that her guests are refreshed before eating, gives her best drinks, then invites them to a fine meal.

This is how it is with Yahweh's care for me.
Goodness and Commitment will always come looking for Me, so that I may stay in Yahweh's house for many days.

II
A DAVID PSALM

GOD, my shepherd!
    I don't need a thing.
You have bedded me down in lush meadows,
    you find me quiet pools to drink from.
True to your word,
    you let me catch my breath
    and send me in the right direction.

Even when the way goes through
    Death Valley,
I'm not afraid
    when you walk by my side.
Your trusty shepherd's crook
    makes me feel secure.

You serve me a six-course dinner
    right in front of my enemies.
You revive my drooping head;
    my cup brims with blessing.

Your beauty and love chase after me
    every day of my life.
I'm back home in the house of God
    for the rest of my life.

3.8 From analysis to synthesis in translation

    a. Pick out and evaluate a clear example of Wilt's having applied a literary translation technique.

    b. Find three places where Wilt's translation of Psalm 23 clearly differs from Peterson's. Then try to explain and evaluate the differences. What appears to be the literary motivation in each case? Which rendering do you prefer? Give reasons.

    c. Would there be any expressions in the following translations that would cause difficulties if rendered literally in your language? How could you say it in YL in an alternative but still *LiFE*-like way?

    d. Do you have any revisions to suggest with regard to the English text of either of these two translations?

7. Prepare a *LiFE* version of Psalm 23 in your mother tongue. Also give a fairly literal back-translation of it into English. The class may then compare their respective renditions of Psalm 23.

8. Summarize in YL the ten steps of sections 3.6.1–3.6.10. Which of them are especially difficult to understand and express? How might you paraphrase them so that they are more clearly stated? Are there any steps that you would like to modify, or any that you wish to add to the list? Would you prefer to perform the steps in a different order when working in YL? Explain.

9. Which topics or exercises in lesson 3 were especially difficult and therefore in need of additional instruction, explanation, and/or practice with selected examples from the Bible? Has any subject of interest to you been left out? Has any exercise been presented in a way that you were unable to understand and apply in the field? Do you feel comfortable now about applying a *LiFE* method of translation to a biblical pericope in YL, at least to a limited extent? If so, which text would you like to try it on? If not, which aspects of this approach remain problematic for you, and why?

10. Daniel Shaw (2004:9–10) says that "the hermeneutical process is a progression of four movements," which may be summarized as follows:

    a. Read the text: Understand what God actually said.

    b. Experience the context: Why was this text communicated in the first place? Understand the interaction between the divine and human authors, the rationale for that time and place, and appreciate the particulars and intricacies of the context that in large measure precipitate the content and structure of the message.

    c. Relate this understanding to comparable structures in the communicator's world or horizon.

    d. Use this understanding to pass the message along: Information gained from the first three movements can then be used to transform the message into symbols and manifestations that enable new audiences to appreciate the intent of the source and apply it to their own circumstances.

How do these four hermeneutical procedures relate to the ten steps of sections 3.6.1–3.6.10? Note the emphasis on an adequate contextual understanding of the text of Scripture in its original as well as its contemporary setting. This is absolutely essential if accurate and acceptable communication is going to occur via any type of translation. What can you do to encourage people to desire and work to gain such an understanding—to increase their level of biblical literacy?

11. Evaluate the following set of procedures for preparing a "creative translation" in comparison with the "ten steps" of the *LiFE* methodology presented earlier.[18] What are the main similarities and differences between these two approaches? Do you have any suggestions for revising (changing, adding to, or deleting) the five guidelines listed below? Explain the final sentence in your own words and give an example from your own translation experience, if possible.

    "In making a translation, a translator (often, probably even usually)

    (i) creates semantic resemblance out of linguistic variance;

    (ii) selects target-language-norm-conforming forms that are as close as possible to the source text formalities;

    (iii) decides how to deal with cultural and contextual variance; and

    (iv) considers the purpose of and audience for the translation, all against the background of

    (v) his or her understanding of the source text.

    This task presents translators with numerous types of choice and opportunities for creativity…

---

[18]This selection is taken from an email communication (from James.St-andre@manchester.ac.uk) citing an Abstract for the paper "Translating a very short story" which was presented by Kirsten Malmkjaer at the Monday Seminar Series of the Centre for Translation and Intercultural Studies of the University of Manchester on Monday 24 November, 2008.

Lesson 4
Text Types and Genres: Prose and Poetry in the Bible

Aim: In this lesson you will investigate some of the different text types and genres of literature that are found in the Bible. You will also learn how to define and distinguish the two principal literary text types, prose and poetry.

Goals: After working through this lesson you should be able to do the following tasks:

1. Describe what a text type is as distinct from a genre.

2. Define the four major literary text types found in the Scriptures and tell why it is important for Bible translators to recognize them.

3. Identify the main markers of poetry in the Bible.

4. Identify the main markers of prose in the Bible.

5. Distinguish prose from poetry in a given biblical text with respect to both form and function.

6. Describe some of the chief textual markers of prose and poetry in the oral and written literature of your language.

7. Identify the major communication functions of prose and poetry in your language.

8. Evaluate a number of Bible passages in terms of how they might best be rendered in your language—whether as prose, poetry, or a hybrid—in order to be acceptable to different audience groups.

Review:
Lesson 2 on the forms and functions of literature in the Bible, and the difference between literature and orature.

Read:
Chapter 3 in *Translating the Literature of Scripture* (Wendland 2004b).
Chapter 2 in *Analyzing Discourse* (Dooley and Levinsohn 2001).
Chapter 2 in *Hebrew Poetry in the Bible* (Zogbo and Wendland 2000).
"Introduction" of *Literary Forms in the New Testament* (Bailey and vander Broek 1992).
Chapters 1–2 of *Cracking Old Testament Codes* (Sandy and Giese 1995).

4.1 The importance of the concept of genre to Bible translators

The term *genre* means a distinct class, category, kind, or type of discourse as used in specific sociocultural settings. It has particular reference to verbal art forms, oral as well as written. The folktale, for example, belongs to a different genre than a proverb, a riddle, or a legend. A hymn is similar to, but not the same as, a psalm, and both of these are very different from a lullaby. Such genres provide listeners or readers with different frameworks and strategies (sets of social and verbal conventions) that they can use to identify and interpret a particular text. One genre differs from another in terms of its discourse structure, stylistic form, content, social function, and/or cultural setting of use. The more differences there are, especially with respect to form, the easier it is to tell genres apart and use them correctly in speech and writing.

Every culture and language has its own inventory of genres and subgenres (cognitive text models) differing from the inventories of other languages and cultures. The proper use of these discourse types, or text models, and the expectations associated with them also differ from language to language to a greater or lesser extent. We will be using the concept of genre in order to distinguish and analyze the various kinds of literature found in the Bible. This perspective enables us to better understand the diverse texts of Scripture and then communicate them more effectively in the language into which we translate.

> » Is the story in Luke 16:19–31 of Lazarus and the rich man a parable or a historical account of events that really happened? What are some of the textual and contextual cues that lead you to favor one interpretation or the other?
>
> » Why would Luke 16:19–31 *not* be construed as a factual narrative used by Christ for the purposes of exemplification?
>
> » Does the cotext lend support to one or the other of the two options (e.g., Christ's emphasis in 16:13–18 on a correct interpretation of the Mosaic law)?
>
> » Would it make a difference in your language? In other words, does a parable have certain stylistic and structural markers that distinguish it from history in your oral or literary tradition?
>
> » If you were to render Luke 16:19 with no introductory or transitional expression, would most people then understand what follows as some type of historical narrative?

As questions such as these suggest, the matter of genre is very important to Bible interpreters and translators alike. If the specific genre of a given biblical text is ignored or misconstrued, the passage will probably not be correctly communicated via translation. That is, it would not be perceived, understood, contextualized, and re-composed in another language in a relevant manner that is appropriate for its intended audience.

It must also be remembered that literary and oral genres are not isolated from each other. Rather, they are all related, though some are closer to one than to others while some are more remote, just as your relatives are to you and to one another. And just as there are certain key features that distinguish the members of your family from you (e.g., sex, age, and origin on your mother's or father's side), so there are assorted characteristics that distinguish one literary genre from another. These characteristics provide readers/listeners with certain expectations about a text and also a strategy for its interpretation when they recognize that it belongs to a particular genre.

For example, a sermon normally includes quite a bit of exhortation in the form of prohibitions, commands, encouragements, and warnings based on specific texts of Scripture. A prayer, on the other hand, does not usually manifest such features; rather, it consists of requests and appeals made directly to God, along with certain utterances of praise, penitence, profession, and/or thanksgiving, depending on the occasion. People might become confused or even upset if their pastor began to pray for the sick when they expected him to preach a sermon or, alternatively, following his sermon, if he started preaching again after saying, "Let us pray." It would be just as disconcerting and non-communicative if the pastor preached his formal public sermon to a Sunday-school class of children.

It is important, therefore, to use the appropriate genre at the right time and place and for a suitable audience. The same is true when we translate the various genres of the Bible. There are four general procedures to keep in mind here—two that focus on the SL text and two others that focus on the TL text:

1. We must learn to accurately recognize and interpret the different types and subtypes of discourse to be found in the Scriptures, the Old as well as the New Testament.

2. We should be able to identify the various stylistic and rhetorical features that tend to be associated with any particular literary genre in the Bible.

4.1 The importance of the concept of genre to Bible translators

3. We must be able to represent the SL genres and subgenres naturally, in terms of literary/oratorical form and also in a functionally equivalent way in the target language.

4. Finally, we must use a particular genre in a suitable TL cultural context; namely, the one suggested by the textual setting of the biblical passage that features the genre in question.

Genre relationships may be likened to the hierarchical classification of the words of a language (its vocabulary as listed in a dictionary or lexicon). Some words have a more general, inclusive meaning; others are more specific and referentially narrow in scope. The general category of "living creatures" can be divided into two subclasses: plants and animals. There are different kinds of animals too: mammals, birds, fish, reptiles, and amphibians. Then in the class of mammals are many individual species: cattle, elephants, goats, lions, dogs, and so forth. There are different kinds of dogs: Doberman, Alsatian, Rottweiler, poodle, collie, and many more.

» Which types of dogs (or other common domestic animal in your culture) are distinguished by specific names in your language?

» On what basis, if any, is this categorization made?

» Which features differentiate one dog from another?

It is important to distinguish a general category from a specific one if one is to use a language correctly. Other languages and cultures may classify these entities and their relationships differently.

» Does the bat, for example, belong to the category of birds or of mice in your language? What is the apparent reason for this?

» What about a tomato—is it a fruit, a vegetable, or some other type of food? Would it be classified differently from an apple or an onion? Explain.

» How about a psalm—how would you classify that—as a song or a prayer or something else, and why? Would your classification change if you think of a psalm in terms of your own language categories? Explain. What are the implications here for Bible translators?

For reflection, research, and response:

1. How can you best translate the term "genre" in your language? Give a typical sentence in YL that uses this particular term (along with a back-translation into English).

2. Does the closest correspondent of genre in YL differ in meaning from the English word? Explain any variations in sense or usage.

3. How does a proverb in English differ from a riddle in terms of its form, content, and function? Do the same differences apply in YL for the most closely corresponding terms?

4. What are the most important oral and/or written genres in the social and cultural life of your people? Explain why, with examples.

5. How can a better understanding of genres help you to be a more effective Bible translator? Give a practical example to illustrate the point.

6. Discuss in class some issues raised by the Lazarus parable (Luke 16:19–31). Do these issues apply only to this particular parable or to others as well? Explain the importance of these issues for the practice of hermeneutics and Bible translation in YL.

7. Name several specific features that distinguish a dog from a goat in English and in YL. What are some of the characteristics that differentiate a sheep from a goat? Why is it harder to distinguish this second pair of mammals? Are there any special positive or negative connotations that are associated with any of these animals in your cultural setting? Which one is more important or well liked and why? Carry out the same sort of comparative evaluation for a horse and a cow.

8. Give a good example of how some important animate or inanimate thing is classified differently and/or evaluated differently in your language and culture than it is in Western culture.

9. How would you translate the word "literature" in YL? Do you have a generic word for it or only terms for specific types of literature such as *history, folktale,* or *royal praise poetry*? Give a classification of some of the main kinds of verbal art in YL.

10. Do the vernacular terms that you just mentioned apply *only* to written works or *only* to oral works or to *both* oral and written works with no difference? Do you know any local experts in literary matters who can answer questions such as these? Have you tried to find out what sort of local experts with regard to vernacular verbal arts are available to your translation project? If not, how might you go about locating such essential resource persons and involving them in your work?

11. Have you ever witnessed a situation where someone used a certain genre of literature or orature at the wrong time, place, or occasion? Or perhaps employed the wrong mode or medium of communication? For example, the person may have spoken the text instead of singing it. Describe what happened and what effect it had on the readers/hearers.

4.2 Four primary text types

Analysts often posit four major text types that are very general in nature.[1] They are described below in terms of the principal discourse features that distinguish each from the other. These text types provide a broad framework that helps us recognize and interpret the various major categories of literature in the Bible, whether they happen to be poetic or prosaic. This fourfold classification is based upon the work of Robert Longacre in the field of discourse analysis (see Dooley and Levinsohn 2001:8–9). It is a general, universal method of classification, that is, an *etic* system which can be applied more or less to any language by offering analysts a set of basic text types to look for and work from. (This is different from an *emic* classification of categories to be found in a particular language.) An etic classification helps us get started in the analysis of a given literature or literary type; it can be revised and refined later as more and more vernacular texts and genres are studied in terms of their content, form, and communicative function in specific sociocultural situations.

Longacre's four main types of discourse—narrative, expository, hortatory, and procedural—may be defined by the presence (+) or absence (–) of two principal diagnostic features: (1) whether or not the text manifests a definite *time sequence* of events and (2) whether or not there is a particular *agent focus*, that is, a person or group of persons who are essentially or especially involved in the events being described. The four etic text types may be diagrammed as follows (from Dooley and Levinsohn 2001:8):

---

[1] Although the terms *genre* and *text type* are often used interchangeably (also in this workbook), at times it is useful to differentiate them: *Genre* refers to the various literary types that one finds in a particular language (e.g., *mizmor, shir, mashal* in Hebrew, or *parabolee* in Greek, or *ndakatulo* in Chewa); in other words, genre is an *emic* (language-specific) term. *Text type*, on the other hand, refers to a literary category that one can expect to find in *any* of the world literatures (e.g., prose, poetry, proverb, narrative); thus it is a more general, or *etic,* term.

4.2 Four primary text types

diagnostic features		Agent Focus	
		+	**−**
Time Sequence	+	NARRATIVE	PROCEDURAL
	−	HORTATORY	EXPOSITORY

In a *narrative* text such as the story of David and Goliath in 1 Samuel 17, we find a chronological sequence of primary events. This *event line* is normally marked for past or present time. The events, whether historical or fictitious, are usually told from a first or a third person perspective (point of view), and they feature one or more *agents* (the main characters or participants) and *scenes* (places where the reported events take place). When dialogue (direct speech) is incorporated into the account, a second person perspective (singular or plural) is added. A narrative text answers such questions as what happened, who said what to whom, and how, when, where, and why the main events occurred.

In an *expository* text, the primary features of a narrative are reversed. An example of an expository text is Paul's *didactic* depiction of the sinful state of humanity in Romans 1:18–32, where there is no special concern about time—how one event is related chronologically to another—and no particular agent in focus. Such a text tends to be more impersonal and is used for explanation, description, or instruction, with a particular emphasis upon its principal subject matter. It features *logical* relationships between its constituent clauses, sentence units, and paragraphs, such as cause-effect, reason-result, condition-consequence, and means-purpose.

The next two text types, *procedural* and *hortatory,* have mixed features. In a *procedural* text there is an emphasis upon a time-based sequence of events, stages, or progressive steps; however, no particular person or agent is in focus. The discourse is goal- or result-oriented and often its chief purpose is to tell how something is done or made. Other procedural texts indicate what should take place in the accomplishment of a particular objective, or in the carrying out of some legal obligation, or in the correct observance of a ceremony (e.g., the sacred rituals on the Day of Atonement in Lev. 16). Most procedural texts are *prescriptive* since the series of individual actions or steps must occur or be carried out in a certain way for the desired results to occur.

As for the *hortatory* text type, it is strongly person-centered and intended to influence the thinking, speech, emotions, and/or behavior of those to whom it is addressed. For example, a behavioral appeal may be made to reinforce, to forbid, modify, or to encourage some activity relating to morality. However, there is no special emphasis upon establishing or following a temporal sequence of events. The speaker or writer seeks to persuade the readers/hearers to adopt some belief, opinion, point of view, set of values, or course of action which may reflect the perspective of a larger group or indeed the society as a whole (e.g., Eph. 5:21–6:9). Hortatory discourse, also called *normative* discourse, tends to include many explicit (variously mitigated) or implicit commands in the form of *prescriptions* ("do!") or *proscriptions* ("don't do!").

Another way of describing the four primary discourse types is to use the parameters of time (+/−chronological framework) and the amount of direction, or prescription, that is manifested in the text.

» Briefly define each discourse type according to the framework shown in the figure below and explain how one type differs from another (adapted from Salisbury 2002:88).

	nonprescriptive	prescriptive
chronological framework	Narrative	Procedural
no chronological framework	Expository	Hortatory

Of course, there is always a certain degree of inconsistency or overlapping when attempting to apply this sort of an etic system to the literary discourse of a given language. For example, Ephesians 6:10–17, the Christian Armor text, may be analyzed in different ways and from several perspectives. It is primarily a hortatory appeal ("Put on …!"), but it incorporates a certain amount of exposition in the description of the pieces of armor. Some commentators even feel that a rough set of unfolding spiritual procedures is also involved. Thus in many cases a biblical pericope may be classified as mixed, consisting of two or more discourse types in varied proportions—not *this-or-that*, but *both-and*. The preceding classification serves simply as a point of reference from which to begin the analysis, which must then be refined and specified as more study is applied to the text in question.

For reflection, research, and response:

1. Try to define in your own words the four general text types described above, making whatever adjustments or additions are needed in order to communicate these concepts effectively in YL.

2. Which discourse type is the most difficult to define or describe in YL? Why is this? Which type is the most common in YL, whether oral or written? Which is the least common?

3. Study the following passages: Ezekiel 12:3–6; 12:7; 12:11–15; 48:30–35; Daniel 3:4–6; 3:7; 3:14–15; Galatians 2:1–14; Titus 2:1–10; 3:3–8; and Revelation 13:11–17; 22:17–19. In your opinion, which of the four discourse types (narrative, procedural, expository, or hortatory) does each of them best exemplify. To answer, use the three parameters of chronological sequence, agent focus, and +/− prescription (direction).

4. The hortatory category can be divided into several subtypes. (Some analysts may prefer to see them as independent groupings.) Following Kompaoré (2004:17), for example, we might distinguish according to the "orientation of the *volitive* focus—either on the speaker or on another person." In the case of the former, termed *commissives*, the speaker makes an explicit commitment to do something, as when making a promise or taking an oath. In the case of *directives*, on the other hand, the speaker conveys his or her desire that the addressee (or some third party) think or do something, as in prayers, instructions, requests, commands, and precepts. Cite a biblical text that you feel is either primarily commissive or directive. What stylistic and rhetorical features distinguish such texts in YL? Can they be used in Bible translation? Explain, giving a typical example or two.

5. The following steps may be used as a guide for analyzing a hortatory text (adapted from Levinsohn 2006a):

    a. Identify any sentences of the text that provide the external *message framework* (i.e., its introduction or conclusion).

    b. Identify any exhortations that only function as *attention getters* (e.g., "behold," "you see," "indeed").

    c. Classify each remaining sentence as *hortatory* (directive: e.g., command, appeal, encouragement, warning, rebuke) or as *supportive* material (e.g., topic-introducer, establishment of author's authority/credibility, situational/background information, explanatory, consequential, or in some other way persuasive and motivational discourse).

    d. If an expository paragraph is used to present supportive information, identify its thesis and how that thesis is supported.

    e. When a hortatory or expository thesis is supported by motivational material other than consequences, is the style typically *inductive* (with the supportive material preceding the thesis), *deductive* (with the supportive material following the thesis) or a combination of the two (e.g., an inclusio with theses both preceding and following the supportive material)?

f. Outline or diagram the entire text with regard to the various distinctions (mentioned above) that you identified within it. For example, it is often helpful to distinguish the predicted consequences from other types of support material.

g. Think through how the different aspects of the exhortation will need to be expressed in YL, noting those functional elements in particular that must be marked in some way in translation.

These procedures may be illustrated and applied as follows (Levinsohn 2006a:4):

When the LORD gives commands to the people of Israel through Moses, he typically uses deductive style.

For example, Exodus 20:5:

5a HORT. THESIS: You shall not bow down to them or worship them;
5b supportive: for (kîy) I, the LORD your God, am a jealous God.

Similarly, when David appeals to God in Psalm 54, he uses deductive style:

1-2 HORT. THESIS: Save me, O God, by your name and vindicate me by your might. Hear my prayer, O God; listen to the words of my mouth.
3 supportive: for (kîy) strangers attack me and ruthless men seek my life; they give no thought to God. Selah.

When the daughters of Zelophehad present a request to Moses, in contrast, they use inductive style (Num. 27:3–4):

3-4a supportive: Our father died in the desert. He was not among Korah's followers, who banded together against the LORD, but he died for his own sin and left no sons. Why should our father's name disappear from his clan because he had no son?
4b HORT. THESIS: Give us property among our father's relatives.

Similarly, when the LORD speaks to Moses in Exodus 3:7–10, he uses inductive style:

7-9 supportive: I have indeed seen the misery of my people in Egypt. I have heard them crying out because of their slave drivers, and I am concerned about their suffering. I have come down to rescue them from the hand of the Egyptians and to bring them up out of that land into a good and spacious land... Now the cry of the Israelites has reached me, and I have seen the way the Egyptians are oppressing them.
10 HORT. THESIS: And now, go. I am sending you to Pharaoh to bring my people the Israelites out of Egypt.

Now analyze accordingly David's instructions to Solomon (1 Chr. 22:7–13, NIV):

⁷ David said to Solomon: "My son, I had it in my heart to build a house for the Name of the Lord my God. ⁸ But this word of the Lord came to me: 'You have shed much blood and have fought many wars. You are not to build a house for my Name, because you have shed much blood on the earth in my sight. ⁹ But you will have a son who will be a man of peace and rest, and I will give him rest from all his enemies on every side. His name will be Solomon, ᶻ and I will grant Israel peace and quiet during his reign. ¹⁰ He is the one who will build a house for my Name. He will be my son, and I will be his father. And I

> will establish the throne of his kingdom over Israel forever.' ¹¹ Now, my son, the <u>Lord</u> be with you, and may you have success and build the house of the <u>Lord</u> your God, as he said you would. ¹² May the <u>Lord</u> give you discretion and understanding when he puts you in command over Israel, so that you may keep the law of the <u>Lord</u> your God. ¹³ Then you will have success if you are careful to observe the decrees and laws that the <u>Lord</u> gave Moses for Israel. Be strong and courageous. Do not be afraid or discouraged."

Finally, prepare an idiomatic rendering of this exhortation in YL: How would a king/chief traditionally instruct his son like this in your cultural setting? Can the text format be used to more clearly delineate the hortatory theses from the supporting material? Explain how you would do this.

6. Which discourse types are exhibited in the book of Jonah and which stylistic markers lead you to this conclusion? Notice that one type may be included within another. Give a good example of this in Jonah. How does your classification of the discourse affect your interpretation of the text—its primary communicative purpose in particular?

7. Find your own examples of the four principal discourse types in the Bible—at least one of each kind. Make notes on some of the difficulties you encounter when trying to apply this system of classification. Do you have any suggestions for overcoming these difficulties?

8. How would you define "description" in relation to the four types? Does descriptive discourse need to be added as a separate type, or can it be included as a subgenre of one of the others (e.g., expository)? What are the pros and cons of each alternative? How would you define description in terms of the threefold grid of +/− agent focus, +/− time sequence, +/− prescription?

9. The following systematization of four generic text types comes from Gavins and Steen (2003:79), with a few minor modifications. How does it compare with the one proposed above? Which perspective do you prefer and why? Or can you forge some sort of combined, hybrid classification that is more appropriate for the literature/orature of YL?

    a. Narratives exhibit a marked use of semantically (content-based) causal relations.

    b. Arguments exhibit a marked use of pragmatically (setting-based) causal relations.

    c. Descriptions exhibit a marked use of semantically additive relations.

    d. Expositions exhibit a marked use of pragmatically additive relations.

    Gavins and Steen define these text types as follows (ibid.:81):

    > In *narrative*, there is a causal chain of specific events in reality, which is presented by the producer of the message as relatively independent of that producer. In *argumentation*, there is an assumption of a causal connection between situations or events in a logical premise, and it is understood that this is not an objective connection between two specific events that have already taken place….In *description*, the additions to the previous utterances in a message are relatively independent of the sender: they are about specific properties of the topics and based on the semantics of the connections between sentences. In *exposition*, by contrast, the additions consist of utterances that are more dependent on the sender: they may involve the background knowledge a sender has about that topic which needs to be made explicit for the addressee, so that the addressee can understand previous utterances better.

10. The Scripture passages that we have considered here in section 4.2 are all prose texts. But the four general text types may also be found in poetic form in the Bible. What sort of poetic text type is Psalm 1? What are your reasons for saying so? How would you classify Psalm 23? 106? 119?

4.3 Some additional features of discourse types

As you may have discovered by now, certain text types are often embedded within other types. This is particularly true in the case of narrative discourse, especially the kind that contains a lot of direct speech, whether monologue or dialogue. Thus a narrative account may contain significant portions of description, admonition, or instruction. Similarly, letters, such as we find in the New Testament Epistles, often consist of several different discourse types combined to form the whole.

Embedding may cause some uncertainty as to how to classify the larger text. For example, is a parable a special kind of narrative with a hortatory bit added on at the end, or is it a hortatory discourse containing a large embedded narrative? And what about a parable such as the weeds in a wheat field (Matt. 13:24–30), in which the teaching, imperative, or application is not given explicitly but is only implied? Some analysts might classify it according to its form (as a narrative), while others would classify it by its function (as a hortatory text)—in the latter case the embedded narrative comprises nearly all of it! Of course, each language is different from another, and translators will undoubtedly have to take both form and function into consideration as they search for the closest natural correspondent of a biblical text in the TL. The most crucial consideration for them is not classification but communication, and how to represent a particular passage most effectively for the specific audience in mind.

It is usually possible to determine the primary text type of a longer discourse by examining the main linguistic and literary characteristics that it exhibits overall. But it is more important to distinguish the different individual text types that are combined *within* the larger pericope: where one begins and the other ends, where there is structural and/or thematic overlapping, how they all relate to one another, as well as the purpose for each one's inclusion within the composition as a whole. The text's major and minor communicative functions must then be reproduced along with its semantic content during the process of Bible translation.

Other variable features that help us to distinguish one text type from another include *linkage, central person,* and *orientation*. Linkage refers to the semantic connections (whether chronological or logical) that prevail between the main segments of a discourse. Central person is a grammatical category that designates the main actor or speaker of the text, whether represented in the first, second, or third person. Orientation indicates the primary personal focus of the text, whether the doer of the action (agent), the receiver of the action (patient), the hearer of the discourse (audience), or no special individual or group at all. In this last case the content or theme of the text is of utmost importance.

Longacre (cited in Dooley and Levinsohn 2001:9) calls attention to two additional features that pertain to his four general text types. The first is *projection,* which helps to distinguish texts that refer to a set of actions or circumstances that have already happened (– projection) from texts that deal with a situation that has not yet occurred (+). In the latter case, the temporal reference tends to focus upon something that is contemplated, anticipated, predicted, or enjoined (i.e., what people are called upon to do in the future). Projection, or forward orientation, is a prominent feature of predictive discourse, often found in the prophetic literature, whether a complete text or only a portion of one.

The second additional feature is *tension,* which refers to a discourse that includes some sort of conflict, trial, dispute, enigma, or uncertainty that needs to be resolved. A writer or speaker often uses tension as a means of holding the attention and interest of the audience. This is most obvious in dramatic narratives that are built around a plot. Here, the main character faces an opponent, test, challenge, or some other obstacle. Such discourse evokes tension that usually reaches a high point (an eventive peak or emotive climax) during the account, after which the tension is lessened or removed in some way. Other types of text can also incorporate a certain amount of tension. In the case of procedural discourse, the instructions may build up in an explicit way towards the intended result or a final outcome; in hortatory discourse the argument or appeal may be constructed so as to rise to a peak of intensity or impact.

The five features of linkage, central person, orientation, temporal projection, and tension are summarized in the following diagram:

Prose text type features	NARRATIVE	PROCEDURAL	EXPOSITORY	HORTATORY
Linkage	chronological	chronological	logical	logical
Central person	first or third	indefinite or third	non-specific	second
Orientation	agent/patient	patient	theme/content	addressee
Temporal projection	accomplished or current	current or projected	non-specific	projected
Tension	normally + climax	+ result – tension	+ argumentation – tension	+ argumentation +/– tension

While these different stylistic characteristics apply to most prose texts of the Bible, certain exceptions and variations do occur at times, depending on the specific nature of the discourse and the purpose for which it was written. For example, when a predictive prophecy includes an element of narration, more verbs will of course occur in the future tense (sometimes also in the dramatic present), rather than in the past. An example of this is Yahweh's predictions concerning the battle of Gog in Ezekiel 38–39. On the other hand, an expository text normally includes some features of argumentation, as in Romans 1, where Paul appears to build up to a little climax in his conclusion at verses 24–25.

If an exposition consists of pure description, however, there will not usually be any sort of an argument or peak, as is the case in Ezekiel's serene vision of the divine temple in Ezekiel 40–48. Note, however, that this closing section of Ezekiel does include one chapter that is not primarily descriptive.

» Which one is that, and how does it serve as a concluding climax for the book as a whole?

» How does your understanding of 43:10–12 affect your evaluation of the function of the descriptive discourse that prevails in these chapters?

In lesson 3 we studied the principal *functions* of communication, including informative, expressive, affective, relational, and esthetic. These have to do with the general reasons for which a text may be composed and the effect the author intends to have on the primary readership (or audience), as nearly as this can be posited on the basis of available textual and contextual evidence. Such communicative goals, or intentions, may also be applied to the four major text types that we have been discussing here, but only when they are considered in relation to a particular passage of Scripture and its context of use. A narrative, for example, may be classified as being primarily *informative* in one case (Acts 26:9–18), *affective* in another (Gal. 1:13–23), and *relational* in yet another (1 Cor. 11:23–25).

In order to be more precise in our investigation of a particular discourse of the Bible, we may apply the methods *of speech-act analysis* (see section 1.6.2.1). This is a pragmatic approach (i.e., studying verbal discourse in relation to its interpersonal context and social setting) that focuses on what an author intends to *do* with a text during communication—that is, what goal he hopes to achieve in the original context of writing his text. A given directive discourse, for example, that seeks to influence the attitudes and/or behavior of people may be described as the writer's aiming to instruct, advise, encourage, strengthen, console, warn, rebuke, or condemn his hearers or readers. Thus a wide range of attitudes and emotions may also be conveyed: compare Paul's forceful reproof in Galatians 1:6–10 with the warm affection that he expresses in Philippians 1:3–11.

These major and minor text types will generally correspond or differ in various degrees with respect to their primary function as we move from one language, culture, and set of indigenous genres to another.

4.3 Some additional features of discourse types

For example, no traditional Chewa song was ever used as a *personal* confession of one's sins such as we have in Psalm 51; a *corporate* lament, however, was often used in this way; namely, as part of a public ceremony pleading to the ancestors for rain in a time of drought (cf. Ps. 106). Similarly, in a Chewa sociocultural setting the letter format would not be employed in order to preach a sermon or present a theological essay, such as the one presented in the Epistle to the Hebrews.

A Chewa proverb (*mwambi*) is normally employed either to instruct the young about proper behavior or to make a point as elders are engaged in some serious public debate or argument. A biblical proverb, on the other hand, may be used for the former purpose (as in the book of Proverbs, e.g., 26:11) but not usually for the latter—that is, in an argumentative discourse (though there are exceptions, e.g., 2 Pet. 2:22). Another difference is that texts called proverbs are conceived of and classified differently in the biblical literature. In Hebrew, for example, the literary category of *mâshâl* includes not only the graphic and condensed, typically two-part saying called a "proverb" in English or Chichewa, but also a much more extensive didactic passage, such as Ezekiel 17:2–10. In Greek, on the other hand, the term *parabolê* is normally used to designate the figurative story termed a parable, but it may also refer to a very short wise saying such as Luke 4:23.

For reflection, research, and response:

1. Where would you fit the subcategory of description in the chart shown in section 4.3? How then would you classify the passage found in Daniel 7:1–14? Where would that fit on the chart? Does a text like this require a special type of discourse in YL? Explain.

2. Under which of the four basic text types would you classify *legislative passages* such as those in the Pentateuch (e.g., Exod. 20–23)? Why do you say so? What about *wisdom directives* in the book of Proverbs? Again, give a reason for your answer. Do you have texts like these in YL? If so, describe the different kinds that are common in the oral or written tradition of your people.

3. Which of the four text types are embedded in Luke 20? Give the verses that apply to each type that you specify.

4. List the aspects of textual projection and tension that you find in Luke 19.

5. Find another text from the Gospels in which you detect some emotive tension that leads to a definite high point in the account. Specify the verses where this climax in tension occurs and mention any special linguistic or literary markers that would be needed in YL in order to distinguish such a passage.

6. Pick what you feel is the primary text type of the following pericopes, and then tell what appears to be the main communicative function or intention of each one: Revelation 4; Philemon; Hebrews 11; Jude; Matthew 5:3–12; 14:1–12; 18:15–20; 24:15–28; 25:31–46; Luke 1:1–4; 3:23–38; 10:2–12; 20:34–38.

7. Go back to the passages that you considered in question 6 and specify the verses where you detect a peak in the action and/or climax in the emotive tension of some kind. Perhaps you will not find a high point at all, or it may be that more than one peak or climax is present. Give reasons why you have specified these particular places in the text.

8. How would you define a proverb in YL—what are the stylistic features that characterize this genre? Where, when, and why is this genre used? Give an example to illustrate what you mean.

9. Consider the following formulae or discourse-specific utterances (quoted from the NRSV). These formulae are of the kind that often helps us recognize a particular literary genre. Specify the genre in each case. Then choose its Scripture reference from the passages listed below the bulleted list.

- ___These are the descendants of Esau…
- ___To what should I compare the kingdom of God?
- ___The word of the Lord came to me:
- ___To the exiles of the Dispersion in Pontus, Galatia…
- ___How lonely sits the city that once was full of people!
- ___Happy is everyone who fears the Lord
- ___Then I saw another beast that rose out of the earth
- ___The wise woman builds her house, but the foolish tears it down
- ___The churches of Asia send greetings
- ___[T]he people of Aram shall go into exile to Kir, says the Lord. Thus says the Lord:
- ___And now, O priests, this command is for you.
- ___On that day the branch of the Lord shall be beautiful and glorious
- ___Very truly, I tell you, I am the gate for the sheep.
- ___…son of Enos, son of Seth, son of Adam, son of God.
- ___In the first book, Theophilus, I wrote about all that Jesus did
- ___You are beautiful as Tirzah, my love, comely as Jerusalem
- ___Slaves, obey your earthly masters with fear and trembling
- ___This shall be the ritual for the leprous person at the time of his cleansing:
- ___In a certain city there was a judge who neither feared God nor had respect for people.
- ___Let the day perish in which I was born
- ___Grace to you and peace from God our Father
- ___Rehoboam slept with his ancestors and was buried in the city of David
- ___What shall I do with you, O Ephraim?
- ___Now a bishop must be above reproach, married only once
- ___Woe to you, Chorazin! Woe to you, Bethsaida!
- ___The Israelites again did what was evil in the sight of the Lord

a. 1 Timothy 3:1	b. Leviticus 14:2	c. Genesis 36:1	d. Isaiah 4:2
e. 1 Corinthians 16:21	f. Job 3:3	g. Luke 18:2	h. Ezekiel 35:1
i. Acts 1:1	j. Song of Songs 6:4	k. 1 Peter 1:1	l. Psalm 128:1
m. Philemon 3	n. 2 Chronicles 12:16	o. Judges 10:6	p. Ephesians 6:5
q. Luke 13:20	r. Malachi 2:1	s. Lamentations 1:1	t. John 10:7
u. Revelation 13:11	v. Proverbs 14:1	w. Matthew 11:21	x. Hosea 6:4
y. Luke 3:38	z. Amos 1:5–6		

4.4 What is the difference between prose and poetry?

In some literary or oral traditions, the difference between prose and poetry is relatively clear-cut and easily specified.[2] This is normally the case where the various kinds of poetry are strictly defined in terms of fixed linguistic or literary categories, such as meter, rhyme, regular line length (syllable count), and verses (several lines grouped together). Certain types of poems may be designated by particular technical terms (e.g., *sonnet, choric ode, epic, hymn*). However, in the case of other world literatures, perhaps most of them, including Biblical Hebrew, the distinction between prose and poetry is quite a bit more flexible and depends more on a particular concentration or combination of what may be termed *poetic*, as opposed to *prosaic* stylistic features.

Carefully read texts I and II below. Notice the stylistic differences between them.

---

[2]Stockwell (2002:34) says, "In genre studies, a hierarchy has been suggested as follows:
- *mode*   prose, poetry, drama, conversation, song…
- *genre*   comedy, tragedy, gothic, surrealism…
- *subgenre*   mock-epic, comic opera, airport fiction, war novel, political memoir…
- *type*   sonnet, ballad, email, one-act play, short story…
- *register*   reporting language, letter-writing, narrative, lyricism…."

4.4 What is the difference between prose and poetry?

» What are the most obvious features that immediately catch your attention?

» Which passage is written as prose and which as poetry?

» Why do you think so in each case? (Give some reasons or the linguistic signals that you look for when distinguishing prose from poetic texts.)

I

But Sisera fled away on foot to the tent of Jael,
the wife of Heber the Kenite;
for there was peace
between Jabin the king of Hazor
and the house of Heber the Kenite.

And Jael came out to meet Sisera, and said to him,
"Turn aside, my lord, turn aside to me; have no fear."
So he turned aside to her into the tent,
and she covered him with a rug.
And he said to her, "Pray, give me
a little water to drink; for I am thirsty."

So she opened a skin of milk
and gave him a drink and covered him.
And he said to her,
"Stand at the door of the tent,
and if any man comes and asks you,
'Is any one here?' say, No."

But Jael the wife of Heber took a tent peg,
and took a hammer in her hand,
and went softly to him
and drove the peg into his temple,
till it went down into the ground,
as he was lying fast asleep from weariness.
So he died.

And behold, as Barak pursued Sisera,
Jael went out to meet him, and said to him,
"Come, and I will show you the man
whom you are seeking."
So he went in to her tent;
and there lay Sisera dead,
with the tent peg in his temple.

So on that day God subdued Jabin
the king of Canaan before the people of Israel.
And the hand of the people of Israel
bore harder and harder on Jabin the king of Canaan,
until they destroyed Jabin king of Canaan.

II

Most blessed of women be Jael, the wife of Heber the Kenite, of tent-dwelling women most blessed.
He asked water and she gave him milk, she brought him curds in a lordly bowl. She put her hand to the

tent peg and her right hand to the workmen's mallet; she struck Sisera a blow, she crushed his head, she shattered and pierced his temple. He sank, he fell, he lay still at her feet; at her feet he sank, he fell; where he sank, there he fell dead. Out of the window she peered, the mother of Sisera gazed through the lattice: "Why is his chariot so long in coming? Why tarry the hoofbeats of his chariots?" Her wisest ladies make answer, nay, she gives answer to herself, "Are they not finding and dividing the spoil?—A maiden or two for every man; spoil of dyed stuffs for Sisera, spoil of dyed stuffs embroidered, two pieces of dyed work embroidered for my neck as spoil?" So perish all thine enemies, O Lord! But thy friends be like the sun as he rises in his might. And the land had rest for forty years.

One of the texts above is the RSV translation of Judges 4:17–24, the other of Judges 5:24–31.

» Which is I and which is II? Can you tell without looking it up in your Bible?

» Which text is the prose passage and what are three features that indicate this to you?

» Which is the poetry passage and what three stylistic devices are the evidence of this?

» Try to identify a climax (emotive or action peak) in each of the two texts. Give reasons for your choice (i.e., mention specific stylistic markers).

Poetry characteristically emphasizes the *oral-aural* sound qualities of a text and the sight of one's inner eyes, that is, the *visual* dimension, through figurative, evocative, and imaginative devices. In Biblical Hebrew (and in many other literatures), poetic discourse manifests many of the following devices:

- **parallelism** (i.e., short, balanced A and B lines forming a sequence of parallel pairs)
- **condensation** (e.g., ellipsis of elements in the B parallel line or omission of conjunctions)
- **rhythmic cadence** of word accents and/or syllable counts (a kind of meter)
- **concentrations of figures of speech** (especially simile and metaphor)
- **word order variations** (e.g., divergence from prosaic V-S-O, more chiastic constructions)
- **word plays** (puns) and **sound plays** (alliteration, assonance)
- **lexical repetition** (both exact and synonymous, random and structured)
- **intensified language**, occasionally exclamatory
- **rhetorical questions** and **deliberative questions**
- **specialized vocabulary** including technical liturgical or archaic words and poetic word pairs
- **direct speech** as the preferred mode of text presentation
- **allusion** and **symbolism** (especially characteristic of religious discourse)

We will be looking at these poetic devices more closely in another lesson. For now, describe the ones that you may have learned about during your previous biblical or language studies. The first three features are probably the most diagnostic of Hebrew poetry. Would you agree? If not, which three features would you propose, and why?

4.4 What is the difference between prose and poetry?

In addition to a greater frequency, density, and intensity of usage with respect to the preceding stylistic characteristics, Hebrew poetry is also distinguished by a significant reduction in the incidence of two narrative features: (1) the *narrative construction* (*waw-* consecutive or *wayyiktol* sequential structure); and (2) the *prose particles*; namely, the sign of the direct object *('eth)*, the definite article (h-), the relative clause marker *('asher),* and the inseparable prepositions *(m-, l-, k-, b-).* In contrast, Hebrew prose discourse features a higher concentration of these narrative characteristics along with a reduction in the number and variety of the poetic devices.

For reflection, research, and response:

1. Study the II text above with reference to the Hebrew text or an interlinear version. If this is not possible, look it up in a literal English version such as the NASB or the RSV. Then answer this and the following questions. First of all, reformat the passage (Judg. 5:24–31) as poetry. That is, on a separate piece of paper set out the poetic lines in parallel fashion down the page.

2. What stylistic or structural criteria indicate beginning of a new poetic unit (strophe) at Judges 5:24?

3. How is Jael distinguished as the heroine of text II? How does this compare with her treatment in the prose text (I)? Who is the anti-heroine of the poetic version? Note the significance of where she appears within the discourse. Where is she mentioned in the prose text? What is the rhetorical and historical implication of this omission?

4. How are the parallel lines of Judges 5:24 related to each other? In what ways does the second line augment, intensify, specify, or heighten the first line? Can you find a chiasmus in this verse, that is, A – B :: B' – A'? How does this passage compare with 4:19? What are the differences?

5. Point out the *word order shifts* that create parallel expressions in 5:25. Point out the *asyndeton* (lack of conjunctions) that gives this verse its compact, condensed quality.

6. Evaluate the reformatted text of 5:24–27 below (RSV). (Compare it with the original Hebrew if possible.) Does it help display the poetic dynamics of this passage more precisely? Give reasons for your judgment and make any suggestions for improvement that come to mind.

>Most blessed of women be Jael,
>the wife of Heber the Kenite,
>of tent-dwelling women most blessed!
>
>He asked water and she gave him milk,
>she brought him curds in a lordly bowl.
>She put her hand to the tent peg
>and her right hand to the workmen's mallet;
>>she struck Sisera a blow,
>>she crushed his head,
>>she shattered and pierced his temple.
>>>He sank,
>>>he fell,
>>>he lay still at her feet;
>>>at her feet he sank,
>>>he fell;
>>>where he sank,
>>>there he fell
>>>**dead**!

7. In the vivid poetic description of Judges 5:26 you can see the shocking events take place before the eyes of your imagination. How does this differ from the prose account of 4:21? For example, observe the synonyms that are used. If you can read the Hebrew text, note which lexical concept is repeated; then refer to 5:22 where this same word appears. In what connection? How is the meaning of verse 26 intensified if listeners recall what was said in verse 22? Such intratextual connections are common in biblical poetry.

8. What prominent poetic device is manifested in Judges 5:27? What is the function of this device in this context? Compare the prose account of this incident (4:21). What difference in the facts of the account do you observe? What is the poet trying to do by giving his impression of this climactic scene? Does the *tempo* of the poetic discourse in verses 26–27 seem fast or slow? What is it that evokes this impression, and what purpose does it serve here?

9. Consider the scene that is told so poetically in Judges 5:28–30. Where is the corresponding account in the prose text of chapter 4? How do you explain this in terms of the two types of discourse that we have here? For example, what is the overall communicative purpose of each of these two texts?

10. What type of questions do we find in verses 28 and 30? How do they heighten the dramatic irony of the scene that the poet is painting for us? What sort of emotions does the text evoke here?

11. What is the meaning of Judges 5:29? Consult several different versions, including the original Hebrew text if you can. What common poetic characteristic is illustrated in this passage? What do you think of the CEV's rendering, "She and her wisest women gave the same answer?"

12. Notice all the repetition in Judges 5:30. What appears to be its special poetic function at this point?

13. What potential problem do you see in Judges 5:31a–b as far as pronominal usage is concerned? Such shifting back and forth between persons (*enallage*) is another common feature of Hebrew poetry. Can you use pronouns this way in YL? Explain.

14. Notice the position of the divine name YHWH in this verse. Can you suggest any special reason for this utterance-final placement of the vocative?

15. If you can read the Hebrew, point out the play on words (pun) in the first line of Judges 5:31. Also fill out the ellipsis of line 2 (see the CEV).

16. How does the NRSV translate the original "the ones loving him" in the second line of Judges 5:31? Evaluate this rendering in terms of its accuracy and poetic effectiveness.

17. What prominent simile is present in verse 31? What is its point of similarity?

18. Is the final line of verse 31 written in prose or poetry? What are the linguistic or literary indicators that show this? Note the contrastive style that is evident in the text. What is the structural significance of such a shift at this point? That is, who speaks these final words of the chapter?

19. Observe how the prose narrative account ends in Judges 4:23–24. Notice all the repetition that is found here too (even a chiasmus). But what are the features that make this passage sound prosaic, not poetic as in 5:31a–b? What is the special function of this repetition in the narrative at large?

20. Evaluate the style of the RSV in the I and II passages reproduced in section 4.4. Propose two revisions of a literary nature to the translation of each text, based on the preceding study.

21. Can you render the style of Judges 5 effectively as poetry in YL? Will a poetic text in YL convey a similar dramatic effect (with rhetorical impact and esthetic appeal)? Explain, with reasons. If not,

4.4 What is the difference between prose and poetry?

how will you distinguish the different nature and purpose of these two chapters, Judges 4 and 5? Keep in mind what Nida (2003:81) said about this passage of Scripture: "[Judges 5] is highly sophisticated dramatic poetry, as fine as Homer produced."

22. Adele Berlin (cited in Doyle 2003:168) summarizes the essence of biblical poetry as follows: "[T]he combination of likeness and difference is the essence of the relationship between parallel lines in biblical poetry." To this Brian Doyle adds (ibid.): "One can agree with her that parallelism of one form or another lies at the core of biblical poetic composition. It is equally fair to say, however, that virtually every stylistic technique in biblical poetry boils down to some sort of parallel repetition based on one or other degree of similarity and difference." Do you agree with these sentiments? If not, explain why not. If you do agree, give a good example of similarity combined with difference in Judges 5.

23. Does a "close" linguistic-literary analysis like the one carried out above help or hinder the serious Bible translator? Give some reasons for your opinion.

As we have seen in Judges 4–5, a given biblical text may be classified or interpreted as being more or less poetic (or prosaic) on the basis of the relative amounts of the structural and stylistic features present as well as their distribution in the discourse. But some uncertainty and indeterminacy—hence also scholarly controversy—occurs in some other texts, for example, in a number of prophetic and wisdom texts.

> » On what basis is poetry distinguished from prose in Jeremiah 47–50 and Ecclesiastes 1 by the NRSV text layout?

> » How would you classify these two passages? Explain why in each case.

Problems of classification also arise in connection with certain epistolary passages (e.g., 1 Cor. 13, Phil. 2:6–11, Col. 1:1–20), including those that quote poetry from the Septuagint. For example, how poetic is Hebrews 1:5–13 in Greek? What purpose could poetry serve in such quotations? Even in texts that are predominantly narrative in nature, distinctive poetic inserts occur for the purpose of highlighting, as in many of the crucial speeches of Genesis (e.g., 1:26; 2:23; 3:14–19; 4:23; 8:22; 9:6, 25–26; 12:2–3). In such cases it is not so much the form or classification that is important for interpreters, but rather the function, especially where the poetically heightened style of discourse is being used to achieve greater emotive expression or to foreground or emphasize a particular portion of the text. What might the function be in the several Genesis passages cited earlier?

The chart below is a summary of the principal types of literature found in the Old Testament. The middle of the chart indicates the overlapping that is manifested by text types that may be either more poetic or more prosaic in style. But even here there may be some significant variations, as in the case of *didactic wisdom* passages. Discuss the chart's different terms in class, especially the unfamiliar ones. Then *try to prepare a set of corresponding terms in your language*—as close as you can come for now. You will have a chance to revise your list as you proceed through this workbook.

PROSE Report (sequential recording [+/– description] of events, persons, places
  Ezek. 40–48; also *letters* and *decrees,* e.g., Ezra 6–7; minimum
  form = *genealogy,* e.g., Gen. 36, or a *census,* e.g., 1 Chr. 23–27)
 | **Law** (formal commands, ritual or architectural instructions, covenantal language)
 | **Exposition** (explanation of meaning, e.g., Gen. 41; Esth. 9:26–28)
 | **Exhortation**
 | **Blessing, encouragement** (if you act righteously, the LORD will prosper you)
 | **Cursing, admonition** (if you act badly, the LORD will punish you, Deut. 28)
 | **Argument** +/– **appeals** (the prophetic indictments of Malachi)
 | **Prayer** (a more formalized exhortation, coupled with appeals to Deity, 1 Kgs. 8;
   includes the category of *confession* as in Neh. 9)
 | **Narrative** (historical, dramatic [+plot], parable, prose visionary report)

Prosaic Prophecy
Poetry **Apocalyptic visions** (decorative and distant salvation oracles; special diction;
| symbolic and visionary; text requiring a hermeneutical key)
| *In terms of its poetic qualities, didactic wisdom verse fits here.*
| **Salvation oracles** (divine promises of blessing, restoration, fruitfulness)
| **Judgment decrees** (divine predictions of punishment for sin/impenitence)
| **Wisdom Verse** (Proverbs, Ecclesiastes)
| **Proverbial** (minimal length; concise and concentrated mnemonic microform)
| **Didactic** (longer length; parabolic, sapiential, instructional, enigmatic poetry)
| **Lyric Verse** (Psalms, Song of Songs)
| **Lament** (appeal for protection, rescue, healing, and other kinds of help)
| **Eulogy** (praise for the attributes and actions of a person or God)
| **Thanksgiving** (grateful acknowledgment of blessings or help received)
POETRY

» Do you have any modifications to suggest for the preceding chart? There is a problem involving the relative generality of some of these categories and their relationship to the prose ↔ poetry continuum. For example, prophetic oracles of salvation or judgment normally include passages of exposition and/or exhortation. The chart here is merely an example and the stimulus for a more precise consideration and class discussion of some of the main classificatory issues involved

» How does the preceding classification compare with the different literary genres found in the New Testament? (Remember that NT genres tend to be more prosaic than poetic in nature.)

» Which terms or categories do you need to modify in order to describe the writings of Christ's apostles? Are there any you need to add?

» In anticipation of the next section, mention the types of literature or orature in your language that are the closest functional equivalents to those listed in the above chart.

4.5 Investigating the prose and poetry of the target language

Learning to recognize and interpret the different text types and genres of the Bible and being able to distinguish poetic from prosaic passages is just half of what skilled translators need to know. The second half is just as important, though it is often neglected. The aim in this section is to suggest a way to discover and describe the TL's diverse literary resources so that they may be pressed into service when one is rendering the text of Scripture, especially for a more stylistically dynamic and functionally corresponding version. The TL was already investigated to a certain degree in the course of answering the questions of some of the previous lessons, but now we will consider genres and styles with the aim of finding some formal and functional equivalents—or at least close translational matches—for those present in the original text (see Zogbo and Wendland 2000, chapter 3).

To carry out such a study in the literature of a vernacular, it is necessary to collect a considerable number of diverse texts. A broad selection of representative examples must also be transcribed and printed out for group consideration. All sorts of texts should be gathered—oral and written, religious and secular, in various styles by different authors and/or orators, and in the major dialect that has been agreed upon for use in the translation. Be sure to also investigate the compositional technique of skilled radio performers—narrators, debaters, teachers, preachers, and poets. Why would the radio be a good source of models for translators (cf. Wendland 2004a, 2005)? Simply because these rhetors and artists often write out their performances, at least in outline form, for oral presentation ("broadcasting") to a vast, invisible, diverse audience. Even if they do nothing in writing, they must still prepare their discourse in their minds ahead of time. For this reason an accomplished and popular broadcasting style often combines effective features from both the oral and written modes of communication, which is what Bible translators must also endeavor to do. Why is that so?

The following questions should be asked by the translation team or their research assistants with regard to collected texts as they begin their investigation.

   a. What is the social *occasion* and physical, temporal, and spatial *setting* where this text was or will be spoken, written, recited, or sung? Will it be in public or private, inside or out of doors, at a certain time of year or day, in a particular type of publication, on a secular or religious occasion, in sad or happy or neutral circumstances (funeral, wedding, childbirth, year-end, harvest-time, new moon festival, etc.)?

   b. What is the text's *communicative purpose*? Is it intended to teach, warn, encourage, entertain, predict the future, initiate the youth, give some history, or simply help pass the time? Is it to give comfort, express the speaker's deepest feelings, attitudes, or opinions in an implicit way, celebrate a royal occasion or communal festival, or some combination of these?

   c. Does any sort of *formula* begin or end the text? For example, a formula characteristic of Chichewa oral narrative is *Padangotere, dziko likadali ndi mphonje* "It just happened that way, when the earth was still very young" (lit., "it still had a fringe" like a garment); another is *Aphike chidzungu gwa! Chimwala wisu! Chathera pomwepo!* "Cook a big pumpkin—it comes out rock hard! A big stone—soft as mush! It [my tale] has ended right here!"

   d. What is the text's *speaker and addressee orientation*? Are the speaker and addressee referred to as first, second, or third person, impersonal, singular or plural, active or passive? For example, in Nyanja a "how-to" text or a proverb is normally encoded with a third singular impersonal speaker and a second person singular addressee, while a folk narrative or a historical text would be a third singular personal speaker and second person plural addressees.

   e. What is the text's *discourse organization* and *verb usage*? For example, a text may be primarily situated in the past, present, future, or some other time setting (e.g., perfect), and the events recorded in chronological or a-chronological order (as in a description or a royal praise poem). Special tenses and verb forms may be used (e.g., the *narrative sequential tense* in Chichewa historical reports or in other types of oral narrative). Other special linguistic markers may occur to help distinguish a certain genre (e.g., conjunctions; verbal affixes; particles that indicate modality such as "can," "must," "should," "may"; conditionality words; interjections signifying truth; emphasis words; and ideophones to inject drama and humor into the account).

   f. In the case of oral texts, what are some important *non-verbal features* (facial expressions, hand gestures, body movements, etc.) that add meaning to the discourse, a narrative for example, which is not represented verbally in the text itself? On the other hand, are there certain aspects of the biblical text that would need to be accompanied by such non-verbal devices if the passage were being read aloud or performed in public? Do any examples come to mind when you consider Hosea chapter 2?

The preceding are merely some suggested general questions given for the purpose of illustration. They need to be made more specific, revised where necessary, and expanded to suit the local setting of communication. (There are more investigative queries below.) All variations due to differences in dialect, place, age group, and sex must also be noted, including the specific production frame of reference that has been agreed upon for a particular Bible translation project. After a number of potentially useable vernacular genres have been identified, the process of comparison may begin; namely, searching for form-functional equivalents and trying them out (perhaps in modified form) on actual TL audiences in order to determine their suitability for use in the Scriptures.

Remember: a *LiFE* approach always begins with the source text and the essential form-content-functional significance found there, but it must end with the target language and a search for the closest, most relevant communicative correspondents with respect to the primary audience. Just as much time and effort needs to be devoted to the literary genres and associated stylistic features of the TL as is given to a study of the SL in relation to the biblical text to be translated.

For reflection, research, and response:

1. Review the main features that characterize a narrative text type. List the different kinds of narrative discourse that are in your language, both oral and written. Give the vernacular names that designate these TL-specific genres. Give their equivalent in English or French, if you can.

2. Describe each of the narrative genres you just listed in terms of form (its main stylistic features), content (the main topics that this genre deals with), function (what the communicative purposes of this genre primarily are), and setting (where and when it is used).

3. Give examples of some specific biblical narratives that could be translated by means of these TL genres.

4. How close is the match between the SL narrative types and your TL genres with respect to the primary mode of transmission and reception that is envisioned for your translation of the Bible, whether written or oral? Do certain adjustments need to be made? If so, what are the most important of these? It may be necessary to conduct further research and testing in the TL in order to fully answer this question.

5. If time allows, repeat the steps outlined in exercises 1–4 for the other three discourse types in YL: procedural, expository, and hortatory (+/– description). They could be investigated on some other occasion, if necessary. The main thing is to master the procedure first with respect to narrative discourse, which is the most familiar. Then it can be applied at a future time to the other types on the basis of what has been learned in class about narrative.

6. Return now to the two selections from Judges 4 and 5 that were considered earlier. Translate Judges 4:17–24 idiomatically in YL in keeping with the narrative genre that seems most suitable, including the normal stylistic features that would be used in a historical discourse of this type.

7. Earlier you were asked whether Judges 5 could be rendered as poetry in YL. Let us assume that this can be done. Pick an appropriate vernacular genre and try it out on Judges 5:24–31 as a test case. What are some of the specific stylistic features that make it possible for people to recognize this passage as being poetry in YL? Are there certain poetic devices that would not be appropriate to use in the Scriptures? List which ones (if any) and why. What are the main problems that you encountered in this translation exercise? Are these problems mainly SL or TL related? Explain.

8. Describe the following passages in terms of each one's social occasion and physical setting, purpose or goal, the occurrence of formulae, speaker and addressee orientation, discourse organization and verb usage (see the earlier bulleted list): Exodus 1:9–10; 3:7–10; 5:7–9; 6:20–23; 12:1–5; 13:14–15; 15:21; 22:1; 23:14–15; 25:31–32; 32:31–32; 33:12–13; 34:6–7, 11–14. (The course instructor may select some of these to be done or assign specific passages to different members of the class.)

9. Now examine the following passages from Genesis and consider how they might best be rendered in YL—whether as prose, poetry, or a mixture of the two—in order to be acceptable to different audience groups: Genesis 1:1–2:3; 2:10–14, 23; 3:14–19; 4:23–24; 5:6–32; 9:1–17; 10:21–31; 11:1–9; 14:1–16; 17:9–14; 20:1–18; 25:7–11. 23; 27:27b–29, 39–40; 37:1–36; 41:17–36; 46:8–27; 49:2–27. In each case give a reason for your decision. If you are able to specify a particular genre or style in YL, do so and then indicate which formal and/or functional features of the original text call for that

genre as its closest literary equivalent. Also point out several features of the TL genre or style that would be close functional matches for the corresponding devices of the SL text.

10. If time allows, members of the class may translate several of the preceding Genesis passages, either completely or only in part, keeping a particular audience and type of translation in mind. These drafts may then be discussed and critically evaluated by the group as a whole.

11. Carry out a study of Exodus 14 and 15:1–18 like the one you did of Judges 4–5 in section 4.4. (You may consult Zogbo and Wendland 2000:3–6 for assistance.) Follow these steps: List five major structural and/or stylistic differences between the two chapters, citing specific examples. Describe the two chapters' different communication goals and how they relate to each other in the book of Exodus. Cite three examples that demonstrate that Exodus 14 is needed as a frame of reference in order to correctly understand chapter 15. Explain how Exodus 15:13–18 relates to the rest of the song of Moses. Suggest how 15:19 and 15:20–21 relate to chapter 14 and 15:1–18 in terms of discourse function (e.g., compare 15:1 and 15:21).

12. Have you ever done any research on the style of radio performers who are poets or orators? Do you know of any such broadcasters whose programs you can easily listen to? Do you think that it would be worth the effort to investigate this possibility as a means of finding an appropriate writing style for your translation? Explain.

13. The American poet Robert Frost once said, "Poetry is that which is lost in translation." What did he mean by that? Is it true? Does this necessarily apply to every translation? What might translators do to falsify this assertion? The theory of cognitive poetics claims that "poetry exploits, for esthetic purposes, cognitive (including linguistic) processes that were initially evolved for non-esthetic purposes....Quite a few (but by no means all) central poetic effects are the result of some drastic interference with, or at least delay of, the regular course of cognitive processes, and the exploitation of its effects for esthetic purposes." (Reuven Tsur, in Semino and Culpeper 2002:281). To what extent do you agree with this theoretical perspective? If you do agree, give an illustration of it from Judges 5. If you disagree, tell why.

14. Read Isaiah 11 carefully. What might "get lost in translation" when working with this passage? Note the potential text-critical benefit of a literary approach. When you have finished reading through the text, suggest some ways in which you might lessen the loss in artistry and rhetoric as you translate it into YL. Graham Ogden points out some artistic features in the less familiar second half of this chapter, Isaiah 11:11–16 (n.d. cited with permission):

> Isaiah 11.11–16 is a clear and discrete unit of text. It is marked by some quite special features and it is these I want to highlight. It treats the matter of Yahweh bringing the remnant back from dispersion to Jerusalem. "The opening line begins: "In that day the Lord will extend his hand a second time…" Although some commentators suggest that שֵׁנִית (second time) be omitted in light of the opening verb יוֹסִיף (to repeat an action), there is evidence from Qumran indicating that MT is the correct text. Reference to a "second time" points to a future action based upon or parallel to a former act, a "first time." That former act, the first time, is described in the final line of the section: "…as happened…in the day of his coming up from the land of Egypt." Thus the final line answers the question, what was the first time God acted? It indicates that the second Exodus (v. 11), the return of the Diaspora, is a repeat performance of the first Exodus (v. 16). In this way, the final line actually completes the first. As an inclusio, verses 11 and 16 provide an example of a highly sophisticated sectional marker.
>
> However, the inclusio is even more finely crafted, and it is this feature that I wish to draw to your attention. The crafting becomes clear when we look at the second and the second last lines of the unit. Here the Hebrew text of both lines reads literally, "…the remnant which is left of his people, from Assyria…" Added to the repeated form of the two lines is yet another feature which may well

be unique in the book. It is the elaborate play on the three root letters א, שׁ, and ר....The line reads שְׁאָר עַמּוֹ אֲשֶׁר יִשָּׁאֵר מֵאַשּׁוּר (sh'ar 'ammo 'asher yishsha'er me'ashshur). The alliteration produced by these repeated sounds is a very powerful one, adding yet another feature to the inclusio. These structural and rhetorical features serve to draw greater attention to the content, the fact that a remnant does have a future. Proof that there will be a second Exodus lies in the past, in the first Exodus. What God has done in the past he will repeat.

The clever development of a phrase built around those three consonants is witness to the poetic skills of Isaiah. Obviously it will be more than a challenge for translators to reach the same level of sophistication in their literary presentation. *Although modern translators would probably never be able to match the sophistication of the inclusio in this section, it might help them to strive for a higher degree of artistry if they appreciate what Isaiah managed to achieve* [emphasis added]. Even if a small measure of semantic value has to be sacrificed, it might well be possible to achieve some kind of sound resemblance and in so doing to achieve the kind of highlighting that the original text intends.

Ogden adds the following caveat with regard to the goal of preparing practical textual aids for Bible translators: "A Handbook for Translators is only doing part of its job if it deals merely with the text yet fails to *excite* the translator. Pointing to the poetic genius of an author or editor should help translators appreciate more of the beauty of the language of the text and challenge them to do a much better job in their own rendering of it."

Do you agree with this sentiment? If so, can you think of another Scripture passage that really "excited" you as you analyzed it so that you tried to re-create the intended impact and appeal of the original text—over and above its propositional content? Note the local and global significance of the sonic structure of Isaiah 24:16b. How would you reproduce this impressive sound effect in YL?

15. In the Psalms, is the addressing of God a case of poetics, pragmatics, or both? With reference to this issue, Andy Warren-Rothlin (2003:7) asks,

> If HBO [Biblical Hebrew] culture does lay significant stress on greeting (more than EUR [European] culture; less than WALs [West African Languages]), and if HBO greetings are prototypically optatives and blessings, what are we to make of the four בָּרֵךְ -phrases which divide the Psalter into five books, and what of the many Psalm introits in הַלְלוּ 'Praise!', הוֹדוּ 'Acknowledge!', שִׁירוּ 'Sing!', and בָּרְכוּ 'Bless!'? Does the Psalmist in fact "greet" God? And if so, in any form at all, should this not be reflected in translations intended for a culture as "greeting-oriented" as WA?...[T]he very high occurrence of most of these modal forms in the Psalter should lead us to expect to find the interjection "please" used frequently in English translations. In fact, we find that, among the better-known modern versions, only CEV uses "please," and that only eight times! Even if, as in some WALs, the only equivalents available are rather "heavy" expressions, should we not find ways to incorporate the tone of entreaty, lest the desperate cries of the Psalmist, like those of a blind beggar screaming to Jesus to help him, get sanitised into the lilting cadences of a "Kyrie eleison"?

How would you answer the explicit and implicit questions that Warren-Rothlin raises here in relation to a translation of the Psalter in YL? Do you have any additional insights to offer on this, or any other pragmatic-poetic, translational issue? How does this example call attention to the importance of a thorough, systematic study of the TL language and literature/orature *prior to* Bible translation?

16. Evaluate the following proposals (from Kompaoré 2008) for helping translators deal with similar text-types, genres and biblical themes in their work. Would this method work in your situation? Do you have any additions or modifications to suggest to this text-specific translation approach?

> Thematic and text type classification of Biblical texts can also be effectively used to facilitate both more accurate and more rapid translation work. It is already a common practice to have translators work on narrative texts together, on Biblical law, on prophetic literature, and on wisdom literature.

In each genre, one finds similar discourse structure, similar expressions and themes. A translator can rely on his memory and his experience in the translation of each book within the genre.

However, I believe we can do better in helping the translator deal with repetitive themes and text types, especially those text types that do not form large blocks of material but which are scattered throughout the Bible. For instance, recently, I was helping a translator deal with oath and vow texts. It seemed to me a good idea for us to look at a number of oath and vow texts, examine their structure and context in order to develop a good and consistent translation. However, the only way to do this was to look for Bible dictionary entries, do a concordance search on key words, or find and read through monographs on the topic. This requires a fair amount of time for research, and access to good Biblical studies libraries, which is the not possible for the ordinary hardworking translator who feels compelled to produce a certain number of verses each day.

The ideal strategy would be to have a few people collect data and do the research necessary and then to develop software based on this research that would allow the translator to examine all oath and vow texts consecutively, and to either do a first draft translation of each text in sequence, or at later stage, to check the consistency of the translation. A person using such a tool would be able to check not only the same expressions, but also similar expressions, similar discourse structure, and similar themes in light of the context of each oath. Not only will it facilitate accuracy in translation, it will speed up the process of translation of oaths and vows; the translator would not be obligated to rethink how to translate an oath, trying to remember what passage it was where he had last translated an oath. Everyone also knows how time-consuming it is to go over the entire Bible and correct inconsistencies in a translation.

Other text type categorizations that would be useful for more accurate, consistent, and speedy translations are:

- types of volitive speech such as laws, counsel, requests and prayers, and exhortation

- types of prophetic passages, both salvational and judgmental

- poetic inserts in narrative material

- types of genealogical notices

…In addition to text type classifications, thematic categorization within the Biblical text would also prove quite useful. Translators can already use cross references in a Bible, which alert the reader of passages of similar themes, but what I am thinking of would simplify the research and even allow for consecutive translation of passages of the same theme.

…Translating the book of Psalms is a long and arduous affair. However, it need not be if translation proceeded according to text type and theme. Many commentaries take pains to identify the genre of each Psalm, and most Psalms could be thus classified rather easily and quickly. However, as a translator works through the Psalms, again he is most likely to start with Psalm 1 and continue through to the end. He is not likely to take the time to group together Psalms of the same genre and theme and then translate them out of order. But if he were able to do so, he would translate together the psalms mostly likely to have the same and similar expressions, and probably move ahead much more quickly.

…For instance, I went through the entire Psalms and codified each psalm according to text type using the criterion of major communication function…:

- Didactic (Instruction),

- Judgment (Retribution, this includes both the act of deliberating judgment as well as the events that take place as a result of the judgment—destruction of enemies, etc.)

- Confidence (Trust)

- Request (Petition)

- Lament

- Thanksgiving

- Praise

- Promise

- Wish

All of these categories can also be found as sub categories within a number of psalms. In fact several are more frequent as subcategories than as major text types, such as:

- Lament—referring to a complaint to God about certain painful circumstances

- Confidence

- Promise—including oaths, prophetic prediction,

- Wish - these include jussive (or subjunctive) types of structures.

…There are also other secondary categorizations which can be useful for the translator such as:

- Pardon (repentance and forgiveness)

- Blessing (i.e. God's blessing humans)

- Temple (including any reference to being in God's presence, as well as different terms used for God's abode)

- Bad behaviour (could be further subcategorized, such as Arrogance, Idolatry, Enemy)

- Good behaviour (a useful subcategory is Innocence)

- Good attributes (This label is used to group together terms such as loyalty, compassion, justice, etc. most often used to describe God's character)

- Acts of God (grouping together any display of God's power, in particular in natural circumstances)

- Fragility (referring to the fragility of human existence)

- Direction (including requests for or statements of God's guidance in our lives. A subcategory could be labelled Law)

- Historical Recall

- Election (including the act of choosing a king or a people)
- Royalty
- Help (or Salvation, with subcategories of Protection and Restoration)
- Distress (grouping together passages describing one's personal distress depression, and suffering.
- Vows and Oaths
- Figurative reference to animals and plants.

This is not an exhaustive list, and it certainly is still under construction, but it needs to be constrained to the primary categories that can group together more than passages, keeping in mind the goal to facilitate translation.

17. Which topics or exercises of this lesson were especially difficult and therefore in need of additional instruction, explanation, and/or practice with selected examples from the Bible? Your suggestions for improvement and critical comments are welcome in this regard; these may also be used as the basis for a group discussion on the subject of genre-based Scripture translation.

Lesson 5
Analyzing and Translating Biblical Poetry

Aim: In this lesson you will further explore the nature and purpose of biblical poetry—in particular, that which is found in the Old Testament, but also in some important passages of the New Testament. You will learn to recognize the main genres of Hebrew poetry and how to apply this knowledge when preparing a *LiFE* translation in your language.

Goals: After working through this lesson you should be able to do the following tasks:

1. Specify the major forms and functions of biblical poetry.

2. Describe five different genres of psalms.

3. Identify several important kinds of biblical prophecy as well as wisdom verse.

4. Examine some examples of poetry in the New Testament.

5. Discover poetic features (or genres) in your language which match those of the Bible.

6. Analyze and translate several longer passages of Scripture by the *LiFE* method.

7. Make a comparison of your version with others and prepare a revised common text.

Review:
Lesson 4 and the notion of "text types," or "genres," and the difference between prose and poetry in the Bible as well as in your own literary/oral tradition.

Read:
Sections 3.1.2.1 and 7.1–7.12 in *Translating the Literature of Scripture* (Wendland 2004b)
Chapters 1–4 in *Hebrew Poetry in the Bible* (Zogbo and Wendland 2000)
Chapters 7–12 in *Cracking Old Testament Codes* (Sandy and Giese 1995)
Chapters 2–5 in *Analyzing the Psalms* (Wendland 2002)
Prayer, Praise, and Protest (Wilt 2002b; perhaps obtainable through your consultant)
Chapter 9 in *Scripture Frames and Framing* (Wilt and Wendland 2008)

5.1 The major stylistic forms of biblical poetry

In section 4.4 we briefly surveyed some compositional devices that characterize the poetry of the Scriptures. We will now examine these features in greater detail so that we are better able to distinguish poetic from prosaic texts in the Bible. Many of these stylistic techniques may be found in prose passages, but either they are used differently there or they do not occur with the same frequency. We also need to determine *why* poetic texts are used, that is, what some of the principal functions of poetry in biblical discourse are. The functions of poetry will be discussed in section 5.2.

The main stylistic characteristics of Hebrew poetry are described in sections 5.1.1–5.1.7, where they are organized into seven general categories. Since they are defined and illustrated here only briefly, students are referred to the books given in this lesson's reading list for a fuller description. (We will spend a bit more time with the less familiar features.) In some cases, the Hebrew text must be consulted, especially for the devices based on sound. The challenge to *LiFE* translators in such cases is to see whether they can, perhaps through the use of a different phonological device, somehow duplicate their textual purpose, beauty, and impact in the TL.

Another general point to note is that the poetry of Scripture is almost always represented in the form of *direct speech*. It is either God, the biblical author, or some narrative character such as Jacob, Moses, or David who speaks the poetic text in question. Alternatively, the passage has been composed to be uttered aloud (recited, chanted, perhaps even sung), as is the case for the Psalms. When translating such passages, then, they must always be tested as they are being *spoken aloud* in the TL—for naturalness, effectiveness, and phonic appeal.

5.1.1 Parallel phrasing

Parallelism is probably the most prominent and important characteristic of Hebrew poetry. Fortunately, it is a feature that can often be reproduced, with similar poetic effect to a large extent, when translating into another language. This technique involves composing a text in the form of paired, comparatively short, rhythmic lines called cola. (The plural form is *cola,* the singular is *colon,* the two together are referred to as a *bicolon.*) These lines, here designated as A or B (plus C or D in the case of a less common third or fourth line), are closely related to each other semantically, and often with regard to certain formal aspects as well (e.g., similar length, vocabulary, sounds, word forms or word order, and grammatical constructions). At times, especially in the Psalms, two common religious or poetic terms are put together—one in the A line, the other in the B line—to form a word pair, for example, "heavens" and "earth" in Psalm 96:11, "sun" and "moon" in Psalm 121:6, "Zion" and "Jerusalem" in Amos 1:2, "Judah" and "Israel" in Psalm 76:1.

The main hermeneutical implication of such parallel phrasing is that the pair of lines must always be interpreted together as a single unit of meaning within the text, not as isolated segments. Most obvious are the coupled poetic lines that occur adjacent to each other, one after the other—A + B. However, other sets of corresponding lines may be separated from one another, normally serving to mark discourse boundaries in lyric texts as in Psalm 8:1 and 8, and 98:4a and 6b (see section 5.1.7).

In addition to having formal linguistic parallels, the poetic lines of a bicolon are usually related to each other in one of four main ways: That is, line B functions to complement line A by means of a relationship of (1) similarity, (2) contrast, (3) cause-effect, or (4) addition. Examples of each of these types are given below (using, except where noted, the NIV, which is a relatively literal version). Another feature to watch out for in these parallel lines is *heightening*, in which the B line is often found to be more specific, intensive, graphic, rhetorically marked, or semantically significant than A (see section 5.1.5).

1. Similarity

An example of *similarity* is in Psalm 61:1 (NIV; compare the GNT rendering):

> A: Hear O-God my-cry; [3 words in Hebrew]
> B: heed my-prayer! [2 words]

The 3 + 2 word (accentual) pattern that we see here is the *second* most common kind of pairing found in the Psalms; it is often associated with laments. A balanced 3 + 3 bicolon is the most common, but there are many variations within a range of from one (long) to six words. (Hebrew word counts and syntactic word orders may be roughly discerned by consulting an interlinear Bible based on the Masoretic text.) In Psalm 61:1, syntactic parallelism accompanies and reinforces the semantic similarity: Line A is composed of Verb + Vocative + Object, and line B of Verb + Object (with the Vocative left implicit). Such synonymous parallelism often manifests a certain heightening of meaning in the B line; in Psalm 61:1, we note that line B is somewhat more specific in its appeal than A ("cry" => "prayer").

> » Try to find another example of parallel similarity in which line B gives evidence of one or more elements that are more intensive or vivid than their correspondents in line A.

5.1 The major stylistic forms of biblical poetry

> » Refer to an exegetical commentary in order to determine the nature and possible purpose of this heightening.

2. Contrast

A clear example of *contrast* is in Psalm 145:20 (NIV; compare the GNT rendering):

> A: The Lord watches over all who love him,
> B: But all the wicked he will destroy.

A paired contrast is sometimes arranged in the form of a chiasmus, as here, perhaps as a way of emphasizing the opposing (antithetical) elements. Line A of Psalm 145:20 is composed of Verb + Subject + Object, and line B of Object + Subject-Verb:

> A: Watching Yahweh DO-all-those-loving-him [3 words; DO = direct object marker]
> B: and-DO all-the-wicked-ones he-will-destroy [3 words]

> » What are the two contrasts present in this verse? (Normally, there are at least two per bicolon.)

> » Find and analyze another good example of contrastive parallelism in the Psalms.

3. Cause-effect

Examples of *cause-effect* are seen in Psalm 116:2 and 119:11. Several different types of cause-effect relations can link a line A and line B, but two common types are illustrated by these verses:

> Because he turned his ear to me,
> I will call on him as long as I live. (Ps. 116:2)

> I have hidden your word in my heart
> that I might not sin against you. (Ps. 119:11)

> » Try to specify the logical connection between the two lines after comparing the NIV rendering with the original Hebrew.

> » Which bicolon do you think is means-purpose and which reason-result? Perhaps, based on the Hebrew text, you wish to propose a different relationship between the A and B lines. If so, explain your interpretation.

At times, distinct causal relationships occur *within* a poetic line because two or more verb (predicative) ideas are involved, as is the case in the B line below:

> For the sake of your name, O Lord,
> forgive my iniquity,
> though it is great. (Ps. 25:11; i.e., *reason + appeal + concession*)

Furthermore, two (or more) complete bicola may be closely connected with each other, for example:

> Test me, O Lord, and try me,
> examine my heart and my mind; (Ps. 26:2, *similarity*)
> for your love is ever before me,
> and I walk continually in your truth. (Ps. 26:3, *addition*)

Here verse 3 (as a whole) is linked to verse 2 by the relationship of *appeal + reason,* which is a very common pairing in the Psalter. The sequence of such bicola forms a hierarchy of interdependent semantic relationships throughout a given psalm (see Wendland 2002:98–107; see also section 3.6.3 in this workbook). A careful analysis of the relationships that link bicola enables the reader/analyst/translator to more fully explore the Psalter's depths of meaning, including not only its referential content but also the connotations of personal attitudes, emotions, and motivations.

- » Examine the colon connections of Psalm 139:23–24. What similarities and differences do you find?

- » Find another pairing of cause-effect lines in the Psalms, but one with a linkage that differs from the types illustrated above.

4. Addition

An example of *addition,* the fourth type of relationship that can join a line B (the complement) to a line A (the base) is in Psalm 14:1a:

> The fool says in his heart,
> "There is no God."

There are several different types of paired addition relations.

- » How does Psalm 1:1 (below) differ from Psalm 14:1a in the way its complementing line B relates to line A? Which bicolon is base-alternative and which is base-content?

  > Blessed is the man who does not walk in the counsel of the wicked
  >   or stand in the way of sinners
  >   or sit in the seat of mockers. (Ps. 1:1)

Observe that Psalm 1:1 is an instance of three lines in parallel, a *tricolon* (A + B + C). When such a combination appears—or, alternatively, just a single unpaired line (a *monocolon*)—it may serve as a point of emphasis within the psalm.

- » What might be the reason for the tricolon in this case?

- » Do you notice any special heightening in the C line, that is, in comparison with lines A and B? (You may need to consult a commentary or the UBS Handbook on Psalms.)

- » Find another good example of additive parallelism in the Psalms and explain how the poetic lines are cumulatively related to each other—that is, how line B (+/– C) complements A to make the sum of overall significance (A + B) greater than the meanings of the individual lines.

5.1.2 Sound effects

Poetry is composed with the intention that it be recited aloud and usually in public. Therefore it features various sound techniques in order to enhance the oral-aural articulation of the text in the ears of its audience and thereby also increase its memorability. Qvale (2003:173) describes the poetic construction process and its product as follows:

> [E]ach individual line has its rhythmic character, and…this is not only determined by the metrical pattern, but also by phonetic nuances, by [aural] associations and alliterations, by the length of words and rhythmic quality, by logical and emotive emphasis, by intonation, dramatic tempo, metrical and syntactic pauses, by repetition, parallels or contrasts in relation to the surrounding lines—by all this all at the same time.

5.1 The major stylistic forms of biblical poetry

These sound effects are created as part of the esthetic dimension of the text, but the skilled poet also uses them to highlight certain aspects of meaning within a given poem. Often this is done by means of some prominent phonological similarity or contrast between the A and B lines of a bicolon. These too are concrete instances of parallelism, even though they involve phonic form rather than content.

Three kinds of special audio effects are illustrated below (with reference to the Hebrew text, for which a literal rendering is provided):

1. rhythm
2. assonance/alliteration
3. puns

1. Rhythm

Rhythm is manifested by the regular recurrence of some perceptible, often predictable pattern of sound, though the pattern may be modified at any time to create some added impact. This can be a rather complicated subject in scholarly discussions, but here we will consider only the very basic technique of counting the major Hebrew words within the poetic line.

The rhythm of Hebrew poetry follows a system of free (i.e., roughly regular, but not fixed or predictable) *meter* composed of variable word-accent (word-stress) patterns. These patterns tend to be fairly uniform within a given poem so that any variations from the norm tend to be significant. Each *poetic word*, which may be extended by a Hebrew hyphen (*maqqeph*, represented by the [=] sign), is considered to have one major beat (accent). The most common poetic line, as mentioned before, has three such accents. Four-beat or two-beat lines also occur relatively frequently, but other types do not, so when they appear within a poem they may serve to emphasize the text at that point.

The following is a sequential listing of the line-accents in Psalm 1:

[v. 1] **2+5+4+4**, [v. 2] **4+4**, [v. 3] **5+4+3+3**, [v. 4] **2+2+2**, [v. 5] **4+3**, [v. 6] **4+3**.

» What is the most common poetic line length for the psalm as a whole?

» Where does an obvious shift in the prevailing rhythm occur?

» Can you see any significance for this—in other words, do the shorter (two beat) lines in verse 4 appear to serve as some sort of a marker? If so, what is it?

In the following literal rendition of Psalm 1:4, the short lines may represent a vocal reflection of the wind that suddenly and completely blows the wicked away:

not=so the-wicked,
for rather=like-the-chaff,
which=it-blows-away wind

In Judges 16:23, we observe a syllabic rhythm that slightly increases in length for climactic effect. This is coupled with an internal rhyming pattern that highlights the key terms (set in bold):

[He]-delivered **our-God** ['elohêynu] (2 words, 5 syllables)
into-**our-hand** [beyadênu] D.O.=**our-enemy** ['oyebênu], (2 words, 6 syllables)
and-D.O.=the-one-ravaging **our-land** ['artsênu], (2 words, 6 syllables)
and-who [he]-multiplied D.O.=**our-slain-ones** [chalalêynu]! (3 words, 7 syllables)

» What is poetry doing in a narrative book of the Bible like Judges?

» Note that GNT uses the verb "sang" to introduce the direct quotation here: "They sang, 'Our god has given us victory over our enemy Samson!'" Is "sang" (for the Hebrew "saying") appropriate as a translation here? Explain.

» Check the context and explain why this passage is poetic in the original. Moffat translates the verse in this way:

> Our God has now put
> the foe into our hands,
> who wasted our lands
> and slew us in bands!

» What do you think of this poetic rendition? Does it convey the same connotation, impact, and appeal for you as the original?

» Render this verse in a *LiFE*-like manner in your language. Provide a literal back-translation into English for the purposes of class comparison and discussion.

2. Assonance and alliteration

Assonance is the close reiteration of vowel sounds; *alliteration* is the reiteration of consonants. These devices are quite common in Hebrew poetry. They may be used either separately or together to mark certain key lines within a book, poem, or section.

» Which of these devices occurs in the two lines below? Underline the repeated sounds.

» Look these passages up and suggest what these "sound effects" may be intended to distinguish, highlight, or emotively color in each case.

> shiyr hashiyriym 'asher lishlômôḥ (Song. 1:1)
>
> qâdôsh, qâdôsh, qâdôsh, yâhwêh tsebâ'ôth melô kol hâ-ârets kebôdô (Isa. 6:3)
>
> rediy uwshebiy 'al-'aphâr betulat bat-bâbel (Isa. 47:1a)

When assonance and alliteration are combined within a verse or section (as in the preceding verse from Isaiah), they may function to focus upon certain concepts, actions, or characters that are being depicted. We hear this, for example, in Psalm 137:3, in the song *(shir)* that is used to insult "us" (*-u-* sound, with reference to the people of Israel in Babylon). Also observe the minor climax that occurs at this point in Psalm 137 to conclude the first strophe:

> kiy sham she'êlunuw shôbêynuw
> dibrêy-shiyr wetôlâlêynuw simchâh
> shiyruw lanuw mishiyr tsiyyôn.

Notice, too, how the chiastic arrangement of key vowels and consonants in the following line of Ecclesiastes 2:25 serves to heighten the rhetorical question and the internal disjunctive notion that it embodies. What can be done in YL to duplicate this poetic effect?

> kiy miy yôkal[1]
> *uwmiy* yâ**chuwsh chuwts** *mimmeniy.*

---

[1] The appearance of a word that does not fit the iterative sound pattern of this verse, yôkal 'the eater', may be explained as a repetition that ties this verse to the preceding one, v. 24.

3. Puns

Puns (a form of word play) involve two words with similar sounds but different meanings. The words are played off each other for mutual reinforcement, or for contrastive effect (perhaps with a connotative touch of irony, criticism, or even humor). Listen, for example, to the word of judgment upon the apostates in Israel in Amos 5:5c: *hagilgâl gâlôh yigleh* "[the]-Gilgal going-into-exile he-will-go-into-exile."

In Isaiah 5:7 there is a highly dramatic double word play:

> And he looked for justice [mishpât], but he saw bloodshed [mispâh];
> for righteousness [tsedâqâh], but heard cries of distress [tse'âqâh].

» Look up the context of Isaiah 5:7b. What does this special sound correspondence achieve?

» Who is doing the looking in this case, whom is he looking at, and why?

» Notice where in the poem this pun occurs—what is the significance of this textual location?

Now consider Esau's pathetic complaint in Genesis 27:36, when he discovers his brother's deception:

> "Is his name not rightly called <u>Jacob</u> [ya'aqôb]?
> For <u>he has deceived me</u> [wayya'qêbeniy] these two times!
> <u>My birthright</u> [bekôrâtiy] he took [lâqach],
> and look now he has taken [lâqach] <u>my blessing</u> [birkâtiy]!"

» What effect does the chiastic arrangement of key words achieve in these last two lines?

Most versions indicate that this passage is pure prose, but if it is, it certainly incorporates a number of poetic effects as a way of indicating the relative importance of these words within the dialogue as a whole. This is typical of biblical poetry—not simply "art for art's sake," but "art that plays a part," that is, in highlighting, memorializing, or intensifying the intended meaning of the discourse.

» Try to find another good example of such purposeful sound effects in the Psalter.

» Read and discuss the following observation (from Scorgie, Strauss, and Voth 2003:203) about some well-known Bible translators of the past who gave serious attention to the sound structure of the text. Does this apply to the translation that you are preparing? If not, why not?

> An interesting and important detail about Luther's translation is that he wanted his Bible to be in *spoken* rather than in *bookish* or *written* German. Before any word or phrase could be put on paper, it had to pass the test of Luther's ear. It had to sound right. It is not surprising, as we will see, that the translators of the KJV had the same concern.

5.1.3 Figurative language

Skilled poets like to use vivid imagery and colorful language, especially when they are describing certain new or noteworthy objects, events, and personages in their poems. Figures of speech enable them to appeal to the imagination for a specific communicative purpose. Often figures and idioms are repeated or combined in the same passage of Scripture, or in adjacent passages, in order to heighten the descriptive outcome, usually with particular reference to some crucial theological or ethical subject. Any such figure adds another cognitive frame of reference (mental space) to interact conceptually with that of the religious topic being talked about.

Three common pairs of figures in Hebrew poetry are presented below (paired because of the similarity between them).

1. **Metaphor and simile**

    Though your sins are like scarlet, they shall be as white as snow;
    though they are red like crimson, they shall be like wool. (Isa. 1:18b–c)

    See how the faithful city has become a harlot!...
    Your silver has become dross, your choice wine is diluted with water! (Isa. 1:21a, 22)

2. **Metonym and synecdoche**

    Your incense is detestable to me! (Isa. 1:13b)

    Your hands are full of blood! (Isa. 1:15d)

3. **Personification and anthropomorphism**

    They have become a burden to me; I am weary of bearing them! (Isa. 1:14b–c)

    The Daughter of Zion is left like a shelter in a vineyard. (Isa. 1:8a)

These are figures that should already be familiar to you.

» Explain how each is different from the other member of the pair, giving a brief definition of each figure. (To refresh your memory, see Zogbo and Wendland 2000:41–46 and Wendland 2002:139–153.)

» Explain what each figure contributes to the poetic passage in each example in terms of its content, impact, feeling, and esthetic appeal.

» Suggest how such vivid imagery might be effectively reproduced in YL.

All of the preceding examples come from the opening chapter of Isaiah. Most of them are exclamatory utterances. Note who is speaking: Yahweh is not pleased with his people, and his poetic language clearly and dramatically reveals his strong feelings throughout this oracle. God is a powerful, effective preacher as well as a poet, and his words ought to sound that way in translation. As Ryken (2002:247) says, "Poets speak the language of images because they want readers to experience the content of their utterance *as image and concretion,* not simply as an idea. The meaning that literature conveys is affective, imaginative, and experiential as well as ideational." Have you seriously thought of the poetry of Scripture in this way—and more, have you represented it as such in your translation? How important is this aspect of meaning in the Bible? Explain.

Figures of speech often occur in combinations as well as with other types of non-literal usage.

» Find the metonyms amidst the metaphors of Isaiah 1:21–22.

» Which of the figures of speech in the preceding examples might present a problem for translation into your language? Why?

» Find another challenging set of images from the especially picturesque book of Isaiah and explain how you can reproduce them in a dynamic, *LiFE*-like manner in your language.

5.1.4 Condensed expression

Poets do not waste words when writing poetry; every word is purposeful and made to count. Often certain expected words or concepts are deliberately left out. That is, they are not explicitly expressed in the biblical text but are left implicit so that the reader or hearer must figure them out from the cotext. Usually this is not difficult, but it does require the listener's mind to be fully engaged with the text's meaning. Such a condensed, compact manner of expression is what gives poetry its typical rhythmic form and evocative content.

Therefore, it is necessary to dig more out of a poetic text than the words themselves actually say. The listener must work a little harder in order to derive the author's intended sense and significance. This includes the additional beauty, feelings, connotations, and cognitive associations that are connected with the subject at hand and render the text "rich," or "pregnant" with meaning—hence memorable as well. At times the poet must use a more condensed form of speech in order to maintain a certain rhythm or flow of discourse that is pleasing to the ear.

It was pointed out earlier that a normal poetic line of the Psalms and other lyric and sapiential discourse averages three "words" (lexical units), each of which manifests a single major accent. The lines of Hebrew *prophetic* poetry, however, tend to be somewhat longer, depending on the genre. Another feature of prophetic poetry is the insertion periodically of a contrastive prosaic passage to provide some historical or descriptive background or a detailed *visionary prediction* (see Isa. 6; Jer. 1:11–19; Ezek. 37; and Dan. 7).

Scholars often use the presence of not only parallelism, but also condensation (see section 4.4) as a diagnostic clue to determine whether a particular prophetic passage is more or less poetic in nature (and less or more prosaic). They look for the relative absence of the prose particles in a text of poetry, which in their consonantal and transcribed form are as follows: the sign of the direct object *('eth)*, the definite article *(h-)*, the relative clause marker *('asher)*, the inseparable prepositions *(m-, b-, k-, l-)*, and the conjunction waw before the B line of a bicolon (cf. 4.4). The more of these particles that are manifested in a passage, the more prosaic it is likely to be. However, this criterion must always be employed together with the other main characteristics of poetry in order to come to a reliable conclusion on the matter. (And even then, scholars do not always agree in certain ambiguous cases.)

There are three common, but quite different, kinds of condensation to be found in Hebrew poetry (although they are not the only ones). The first two, *verb gapping* and *pronominal reference,* are more formal in nature, while the third, *allusion,* involves a semantic contraction. Of course, it is often necessary to consult the Hebrew text itself or a good interlinear version in order to clearly discern such features in the biblical text.

1. **Verb gapping**

   > Do not take away my soul along with sinners,
   > my life with bloodthirsty men. (Ps. 26:9)

   > Your men will fall by the sword,
   > your warriors in battle. (Isa. 3:25)

   » Which verb is missing in the B lines of the above passages?

   » Are they needed in YL? Explain why.

2. **Pronominal reference**

   > They cry out and Yahweh hears,
   > and from all their troubles he delivers them. (Ps. 34:17)

» Check Psalm 34:16 to see what the referent of "they" in verse 17 is. Now look at verse 17 in the NIV and explain why the NIV translators felt it necessary to clarify this condensed reference.

> It will not take place,
> it will not happen. (Isa. 7:7b)

» In Isaiah 7:7b what is the referent of the pronoun "it" in each line?

» How do you know?

3. **Allusion**

> Sons of man, until when my glory to shame,
> you will love a delusion, you will seek a lie. (Ps. 4:2)

» Psalm 4:2 makes no sense because of both allusion and ellipsis. Consult several modern translations to see how they have clarified such poetic condensation in the Hebrew text. Which wording would work best in YL?

> Cleanse me with hyssop, and I will be clean. (Ps. 51:7)

» Check a commentary or study Bible to find out the condensed meaning that lies behind the figurative allusions of Psalm 51:7. How can you best express the meaning in YL?

» Do you have a close form-functional equivalent to "hyssop?"

» What about the notion of being "clean?" Explain.

» Perhaps these words cannot be used due to their cognitive and emotive association with pagan traditional religious beliefs and practices. Is this true in your cultural setting? If so, what alternatives do you propose?

5.1.5 Emphatic devices

All literature is distinguished by a number of devices that signal and emphasize points of special prominence in the text, whether these have to do with form (discourse structure) or content (theme). They are common to both poetic and prosaic composition wherever there is direct speech or a text specifically written to be uttered aloud. Emphatic forms are therefore not in and of themselves diagnostic of poetry, but they serve to augment the rhetorical effect of the other more characteristically poetic features, such as parallelism. In this respect, then, they also help to mark boundaries and thematic peaks in the discourse arrangement of both poetry and poetic prose.

We have already called attention to a common characteristic of parallel expression; namely, the tendency for the B line to be stylistically heightened in some way (e.g., extra focus, intensity, specificity, immediacy, descriptive color, direct speech): "A, and what's more B" or "not only A, but also B" or "not A, and not even B." (This does not always happen, but the feature occurs often enough for one to be on the watch for it.) Point out the different ways in which the indented B lines emphasize the thought of line A in the following examples from Psalm 3:

> O LORD, how many are my foes!
>   How many rise up against me!...
> But you are a shield around me, O LORD,
>   my Glorious One, who lifts up my head....
> Arise, O LORD!

5.1 The major stylistic forms of biblical poetry

> Deliver me, O my God!
> For you have struck all my enemies on the jaw;
>   you have broken the teeth of the wicked. (Ps. 3:1, 3, 7)

Listed below are several other techniques that provide special emphasis in Hebrew discourse: *intensifiers, exclamations, rhetorical questions, hyperbole, irony,* and *sarcasm*. These are seen especially in the prophetic literature and frequently in conjunction with imperative commands. Because they are quite obvious in their character and operation, they will just be noted and illustrated here. Some of these emphatic features are often very difficult to translate with similar impact in another language. This is true of hyperbole and irony in particular. As you study these examples, consider how you would render them with corresponding power and appeal in YL.

1. Intensifiers

Intensifiers, unlike exclamations (see below), are normally single words in Hebrew:

> Surely *(kiy)* the joy of mankind is withered away! (Joel 1:12d)

> Alas *('ahâh)* for that day! For the day of the Lord is near... (Joel 1:15a)

> See *(hinniy)*, I am going to rouse them out of the places to which you sold them... (Joel 3:7a)

> Blessed *('ashrêy)* is he whose transgressions are forgiven... (Ps. 32:1a)

> Praise be *(bâruwk)* to the Lord, for he showed his wonderful love to me... (Ps. 31:21a)

> Praise the Lord! *(halluw-yâh)*...Praise the Lord! (Ps. 146:1a, 10c)

We might also include in this category a number of familiar conventional formulae that function as semantic units, emphatically opening or closing a prophetic utterance. They also help establish the borders of poetic structures (see section 5.1.7). A good selection of these occurs in the prophecy of Amos:

> "This is what the Lord says" (1:3)

> "says the Lord" (1:5)

> "declares the Lord" (2:11)

> "Hear this word the Lord has spoken" (3:1)

> "Therefore this is what the Sovereign Lord says" (3:11)

> "Woe to you who" (5:18)

> "The Sovereign Lord has sworn by himself—the Lord Almighty declares" (6:8)

> "says the Lord your God" (9:15)

2. Exclamations

Exclamations are short, intensified utterances that serve to emotively heighten a certain aspect of the prophet's message, usually one of rebuke or condemnation:

> Wake up you drunkards and weep! (Joel 1:5a)
>
> Go to Bethel and sin! (Amos 4:4)
>
> Fallen is Virgin Israel, never to rise again... (Amos 5:2)
>
> Seek me and live! (Amos 5:4)
>
> Away with the noise of your songs! (Amos 5:23)

- » What are some of the poetic devices included within these exclamations?
- » Would a literal translation cause any misunderstanding?
- » If so, how would you resolve the problem while preserving the intensity of the original text?

3. Rhetorical questions

Rhetorical questions (RQs) are question forms that do not expect an answer. They are a forceful expression of the speaker's attitude, opinion, and emotions with regard to a particular issue. At times they are simply a vigorous way to emphasize the known answer, often with added pragmatic (behavioral) implications. For example, the speaker may want to persuade the addressees to change their manner of thinking or acting. Thus RQs may serve as an indirect form of encouragement or, more likely, of criticism, reprimand, or the like. The more RQs that occur in a sequence, one after another, the more powerfully and insistently the speaker's psychological state and feelings are communicated.

The following are examples of sequential RQs in Jeremiah 8:4–5:

> When men fall down, do they not get up?
> When a man turns away, does he not return?
> Why then have these people turned away?
> Why does Jerusalem always turn away?
> They cling to deceit; they refuse to return.

- » What did Yahweh desire to convey to his people by this sequence of RQs?
- » Can RQs be used in YL for this same purpose? If not, how would you convey the divine speaker's intentions with the same degree of force and emotion?
- » Observe that Jeremiah 8:4–22 (of which the above passage is a part) closes with another set of RQs, forming a literary-structural inclusio. But what difference in connotation and implication do you notice in verse 22, which is the concluding set of RQs?

Now look at the RQ in Jeremiah 8:12:

> Are they ashamed of their own loathsome conduct?
> No, they have no shame at all

- » How does this RQ differ from the ones above?

The utterance in Jeremiah 8:12 is called a *leading question* because it leads up to an explicit answer in the text. A leading question often serves to open or close a major discourse unit and announce its main theme.

5.1 The major stylistic forms of biblical poetry

> » Point out how this device operates in Psalms 15 and 121 and in Song of Songs 5:9–16.

> » Are you able to use questions in an introductory or preparatory way like this in your language? If not, what equivalent device might you substitute?

4. Hyperbole

Hyperbole is an obvious exaggeration that serves to emphasize and highlight a particular perspective or strong opinion. It is quite a common feature of biblical poetry, especially in the prophets. Hyperbole is not intended to be taken literally; rather, it foregrounds the topic that is being spoken about, usually with a certain amount of strong feeling and a particular attitude as well. The following are examples of hyperbole in the Psalter:

> All night long I flood my bed with weeping and drench my couch with tears. (Ps. 6:6b)
>
> Though an army encamp against me, my heart shall not fear. (Ps. 27:3)
>
> Though you test me, you will find nothing; I have resolved that my mouth will not sin. (Ps. 17:3)
>
> May they be blotted out of the book of life and not be listed with the righteous! (Ps. 69:28)

> » What is the meaning of each of these hyperboles in its context?

> » What sort of emotion or attitude is associated with each one?

> » Can they be translated literally in YL? If not, how must you render such expressions in order to preserve their connotative implications? Illustrate, using the passages cited above.

Note the special literary qualities of the following passage from 1 Samuel 18:7:

> Saul has slain his thousands,
> and David his ten thousands!

> » What is the deeper meaning of this lyric hyperbole?

> » What problem did this implicit but obviously emphatic meaning cause for David?

Such poetic insertions in a narrative always foreground the content of what is being said. The hyperbolic nature of the utterance serves to heighten its level of emotive expression and the effect upon an audience.

> » Explain how this is manifested in Genesis 4:23–24.

> » Is hyperbole a common feature in your literary tradition? If so, is it found primarily in prose, poetry, or both?

> » Does hyperbole need to be overtly marked in a special way? If so, explain how, and illustrate this using one or more of the passages considered above.

5. Irony and sarcasm

Irony and the similar device of *sarcasm* are perhaps the most difficult devices to recognize and then translate with equivalent effect in another language. Irony is frequently used to convey an indirect complaint or criticism, but this is only implied by the words that are actually uttered. The speaker says one thing but means something else; the underlying intent of the words does not match their overt content in the setting of use. There is usually some manner of contra-expectation involved: something happens or is spoken that seems out of place. Thus the listener(s) must search for relevance elsewhere in the speech situation.

Sarcasm is a more intense and forceful type of irony. The speaker clearly desires to ridicule, reprove, rebuke, warn, condemn, or verbally injure the addressee. In the tense debate between Job and his friends, irony and even sarcasm often appear, as in the following examples:

> Doubtless you are the people, and wisdom will die with you! (Job 12:1)
>
> If only you would be altogether silent—for you, that would be wisdom! (Job 13:5)
>
> Will your long-winded speeches never end? What ails you that you keep on arguing? (Job 16:3)
>
> How you have helped the powerless! How you have saved the arm that is feeble! (Job 26:2)

Here Job is criticizing the faint "comfort" of his friends. Notice that the rhetorical questions, which abound in this debate, may have an ironic tone as well, as in the following example:

> Where were you when I laid the earth's foundations? Tell me if you understand.
> Who marked off its dimensions? Surely you know! (Job 38:4–5a)

Thus Yahweh himself employs irony to help Job recognize his problem—that he is God and Job is a mere mortal. The aim is to correct Job's point of view and to provide him with a glimpse of things from a divine perspective, which often differs radically from a human point of view.

» How do you express the chiding tone of Yahweh's questions in YL?

5.1.6 Shifting patterns

The category of *shifting patterns* includes a miscellaneous collection of linguistic forms that may be manipulated for particular rhetorical impact. Such a pointed shift is manifested in a poetic text whenever the poet utilizes a deliberate departure from the norms of discourse in order to foreground a specific aspect of content or create some special artistic or emotive effect, perhaps also to help mark a new unit within the larger text (as discussed in section 5.1.7).

There are four types of shift that are exemplified below: *pronouns, word order, insertion,* and *style.* Once again it will be necessary to inspect the Hebrew text or an interlinear version, if possible, to see what is going on in each case.

1. Pronouns

Observe where a prominent pronominal shift (*enallage*) occurs here in Psalm 46; the pronouns change, but the personal referent remains the same:

> ⁸ Come and see the works of the LORD,
>   the desolations he has brought on the earth.
> ⁹ He makes wars cease to the ends of the earth;
>   he breaks the bow and shatters the spear,
>   he burns the shields with fire.
> ¹⁰ Be still, and know that I am God;
>   I will be exalted among the nations,
>   I will be exalted in the earth.

> ¹¹ The LORD Almighty is with us;
>> the God of Jacob is our fortress.

» What discourse function does such a variation serve in this case?

» Does a literal rendering work in your language? If not, do you have a functional equivalent that would serve the same purpose?

Observe the pronoun shift in the following passage from Joel 3:

> ¹⁶ The LORD will roar from Zion
>> and thunder from Jerusalem;
>> the earth and the sky will tremble.
> But the LORD will be a refuge for his people,
>> a stronghold for the people of Israel.
> ¹⁷ Then you will know that I, the LORD your God,
>> dwell in Zion, my holy hill.
> Jerusalem will be holy;
>> never again will foreigners invade her.

» What purpose does this pronoun shift carry out in this case?

» Is there any additional marking that you must use in YL to make this discourse boundary clear?

2. Word order

The normal *word order* for finite verb clauses in Hebrew prose is Verb + Subject + Object. For non-finite verb clauses it is Subject + Verb + Object. For verbless clauses it is Topic + Comment. Word order, along with other devices such as pronominalization, syntactic dependency relations, additional qualifying attribution, and varied transitional expressions, is used to establish as well as to modify the information structure of a discourse.

Where the default syntactic pattern is not observed, and the subject or object (or some other nominal constituent) is *fronted* to the beginning of a clause and before the main verb, or in some other way dislocated,[2] one of two things is signaled: either a new topic is introduced (or reintroduced) into the discourse (*topicalization*) or some information in the text is marked as being in focus (*focalization*), meaning that the information is somehow novel, more important, or topically contrastive in relation to the cotext.[3] The current topic is "given" and engages a listener's attention throughout a sequence of utterances, while an element in focus manifests a higher level of cognitive salience, but usually for

---

[2] At times, an element may be foregrounded (focused) by placing it at the end of the clause outside its expected position (termed back-shifting). In a recent insightful article, Stephen Levinsohn (2006b:14) has clarified what is going on in such cases: According to the "Principle of natural information flow" (Jan Firbas) non-verbal constituents that convey old, established information are placed before those that convey new, non-established information, with the most important piece of non-established information coming last in the sentence/clause. An example is found in 1 Cor. 2:7b: ἣν προώρισεν ὁ θεὸς πρὸ τῶν αἰώνων εἰς δόξαν ἡμῶν·, literally, 'which he ordained God before the ages for the glory of us'. The amazing fact that sinful mortals—those indwelt by God's Spirit—will one day be glorified thus occurs last in the clause.

[3] This is admittedly an inadequate, oversimplified treatment of a rather complex, though very important, subject in the linguistic (and literary) analysis of biblical discourse. For more detailed studies, see Floor 2004, Lunn 2006, and Levinsohn 2006b. Over 30 years ago, K. Callow pointed out a threefold distinction in types of "prominence," which refers "to any device whatever which gives certain events, participants, or objects more significance than others in the same context" (1974:50). We thus have topic, " 'This is what I'm talking about'...[which] contributes to the progression of the narrative or argument," focus, " 'This is important, listen"...[which] picks out items of thematic material as being of particular interest or significance," and emphasis, "which says to the hearer either, 'You didn't expect that, did you?', or 'Now, I feel strongly about this.' In other words, emphasis has two different functions: it highlights an item of information which the narrator [author/speaker] considers will be surprising to the hearer, or else it warns the hearer that the emotions of the speaker are quite strongly involved" (1974:52). In cases where **two** syntactic constituents occur before the main verb, the **first** will be a new (or resumed) **topic**, while the **second** constitutes the information having some special contrastive or emphatic **focus** (Levinsohn 2006b:13).

only a single sentence. The term *emphasis* may then be used in a specific sense to indicate the particular semantic stress or emotive intensity that is placed (e.g., through repetition) upon a given word or phrase within a clause unit. The wider context and perhaps also some special linguistic marking such as a distinctive intonational pattern or discourse particles, usually indicate what is in focus versus what is emphasized (see Dooley and Levinsohn 2001, chapter 11).

These rules for prose may or may not apply to poetry, however; there are other reasons for moving certain syntactic elements around within the short poetic clause (colon). Such reasons would be (1) for the sake of *euphony* (a pleasing sound), (2) for the sake of a flowing *rhythm,* or (3) to create *topical focus* by means of an *antithetical* chiasmus (especially in Proverbs). It requires a rather close and careful analysis to determine which function is being effected by the word order shift—a study that translators may have to leave to the commentators to sort out. But if translators can consult the Hebrew text, it is worthwhile to note any prominent departures from the syntactic norm (by means of a discourse chart, as described in section 3.6.6). Any such modification may prove to be supplementary evidence to support their interpretation of a point of special emphasis, a change in subject, a reinforcement of the basic theme of a passage, or a structural boundary (normally a new beginning).

Note the word order in Psalm 12:5a–b. What sort of syntactic constituent begins this verse?

> "Because of the oppression of the weak and the groaning of the needy,
> I will now arise," says the LORD...

Check out the cotext of this verse and suggest what this front-shifting helps to mark in terms of the overall structure and/or the main theme or argument of Psalm 12.

» Is word order used similarly to indicate focus in YL? If not, which devices are used instead? Illustrate with reference to Psalm 12:5a–b.

The following are literal renderings of Nahum 1:7a, 8a, 9a, and 11a:

> Good (is) Yahweh, for a refuge in a day of trouble...
>
> And with an overwhelming flood, an end (of Nineveh) he will make her place...
>
> Whatever you (pl.) plot against Yahweh, an end (to it) he is bringing...
>
> From you (Nineveh) he came forth, the one plotting against Yahweh evil...

Observe the front-shifted syntactic constituents within the wider cotext of each of the above passages from Nahum 1 and then consult different translations and perhaps the *Translator's Handbook on Nahum* (Clark and Hatton 1989).

» Can you suggest why these particular features are positioned at the head of their respective clauses? Is it to heighten a contrast, to spotlight a participant, to mark a strophic boundary, to emphasize an aspect of Nahum's primary theme, or to effect some combination of these?

» How would you signal the distinct rhetorical functions that you find here in YL?

3. Insertion

Insertion (hyperbaton) is a poetic device that involves a very specific shift in Hebrew word order. It is patterned according to the formula $A - X - B$, where A–B is a standard grammatical construction that has an unexpected, seemingly misplaced or added element, X, inserted within it for special effect (especially for focus or emphasis). The included text may be a single word, a phrase, or an entire clause (colon). The following is an example (rendered literally):

> For not you delight in sacrifice,
>   and (or) I would bring (it);
> burnt offering not you take pleasure in. (Ps. 51:16 [v. 18 in the Hebrew text])

The added verb in the middle (וְאֶתֵּנָה) falls outside the regular accent pattern of the surrounding A and B cola, but semantically it could apply to either line, which thus emphasizes its content. It also anticipates the climactic meaning of the next verse, verse 17 (v. 19 in the Hebrew text), which concludes the strophe.

In the next example the first and third lines are grammatically very similar, while the inserted middle line manifests some noticeable differences, including the shift from a third person to a second person singular pronoun (enallage). In this case, the absolute medial utterance reinforces the descriptive praises on either side of it.

> There is no Holy One like YHWH,
>   indeed, there is no (One) besides you (sg.);
> and there is no Rock like our God! (1 Sam. 2:2)

» How could you reproduce this heightening effect in YL?

» Can you retain the word order of the biblical text, or not? Explain your answer.

In Psalm 24:6, below, there is a double insertion, A – X + X' – B: The initial construct clause "This is (these are) the generation(s) of Jacob" is interrupted by two descriptive expressions that characterize the sort of persons who are being referred to. The verse may therefore be expressed prosaically as "The true descendants of Jacob are people who seek after God and long to come into his presence."

> This [is the] generation of
>   the ones who pursue him [God],
>   the seekers of your [God's] face,
> Jacob. Selah. (Ps. 24:6)

» Notice how this verse is rendered in the standard English versions. Does any one of them get it right?

» The NEB has: "Such purity characterizes the people who seek his favor, Jacob's descendants, who pray to him." Suggest any improvements to this rendition that come to mind.

» How will this affect its translation into YL?

4. Style

The category of *style* covers a variety of distinctive cases—features that are difficult to classify anywhere else. The Hebrew poet or prophet may creatively employ his literary skills, his personal style, to inject some formal and/or semantic surprise into the text. Usually, he does this through a pronounced modification in the current referential content, an ordinary linguistic construction, the prevailing connotative tone, or the general communicative purpose. Style is not a gratuitous flourish, however, or simply an attempt to display one's artistic technique; rather, it is applied to serve the poet's message. Therefore, an analyst must always study the text from several different literary perspectives in order to determine a form's most likely communicative function.

Compare the two passages below and note the variations between them:

> Therefore because-of-you they-have-withheld the-heavens their-dew
> and-the-earth it-has-withheld its-crops. (Hag. 1:10)

> ...and-the-ground it-will-produce its-crop
> and-the-heavens they-will-drop their-dew. (Zech. 8:12)

» Did you notice the chiasmus in the Haggai text? Could there be any special significance to this?

» If Zechariah is quoting Haggai (as seems likely), what effect do his changes have on the specific meaning and rhetorical impact of these words?

In this case, the different situational settings and communication goals of the two prophets probably provide the explanation for this contrastive type of intertextuality.

» Can you suggest any reason for these differences, based on changed religious and rhetorical circumstances (cf. the general order reflected in Deut. 28:11–12; see also Hag. 2:19)?

There is an unexpected utterance and a decided stylistic shift in the following text (Amos 9:1b–4):

> Strike the tops of the pillars
>   so that the thresholds shake.
> Bring them down on the heads of all the people;
>   those who are left I will kill with the sword.
> Not one will get away,
>   none will escape.
> Though they dig down to the depths of the grave,
>   from there my hand will take them.
> Though they climb up to the heavens,
>   from there I will bring them down.
> Though they hide themselves on the top of Carmel,
>   there I will hunt them down and seize them.
> Though they hide from me at the bottom of the sea,
>   there I will command the serpent to bite them.
> Though they are driven into exile by their enemies,
>   there I will command the sword to slay them.
> I will fix my eyes upon them
>   for evil and not for good.

» Where do the unexpected change in content and the stylistic shift occur?

» What is their apparent purpose?

» Would a literal rendering in YL convey this effect? If not, what would do this in a subtle, but perceptible way?

Notice that the rhythmic pattern established by the prolonged sequence of concessive clauses is broken at the end of Amos 9:1b–4 with a summary statement featuring a strong anthropomorphism that reverses the usual application and connotation of this figure (cf. Ps. 33:18 and 34:15). Notice too that the closing mention of a sword of judgment echoes a similar utterance at the beginning, thereby marking a partial inclusio for this strophe. Amos is full of these suddenly introduced, shocking pronouncements of judgment upon a people who were proud and complacent in their pious godlessness. Often a pointed *reversal in expectation* is expressed within the context, like the concluding refrain "yet you have not returned

5.1 The major stylistic forms of biblical poetry

to me" in chapter 4. The prophet thus suggests that people who continually refuse to heed God's call to repentance will one day, perhaps all too soon, hear his summons for punishment.

For reflection, research, and response:

1. Find another good example for each of the four categories of parallelism in the Psalms; namely, similarity, contrast, cause-effect, and addition. In any of your examples, does the B line seem to heighten the intended meaning in any way? Describe any instances of this that you find and suggest how you might duplicate the effect in translation.

2. How do the four lines (two bicola) of Psalm 121:1–2 relate in meaning to each other? What central idea is emphasized in the passage as a whole?

    > I lift up my eyes to the hills –
    >> where does my help come from?
    >
    > My help comes from the Lord,
    >> the Maker of heaven and earth. (Ps. 121:1–2)

3. Study the following strophe (Isa. 51:7–8) and indicate the sequential *semantic relations* between the poetic A and B lines. Then indicate the relations of the four bicola to each other. Make explicit (in parentheses) any instances of ellipsis that you find.

    > Hear me, you who know what is right,
    >> you people who have my law in your hearts:
    >
    > Do not fear the reproach of men
    >> or be terrified by their insults.
    >
    > For the moth will eat them up like a garment;
    >> the worm will devour them like wool.
    >
    > But my righteousness will last forever,
    >> my salvation through all generations.

4. Examine some of the many puns found in Micah 1:10–16 (see Zogbo and Wendland 2000:40–41). Pick out the one you consider to be the most significant for the meaning of the oracle as a whole. Tell why and propose a translation of this in YL.

5. Psalm 6:10b reads like this: "may-they-turn (יָשֻׁבוּ) may-they-feel-shame (יֵבֹשׁוּ) suddenly!" What meaning does this word play emphasize? Notice where it occurs in Psalm 6. Can you preserve the pun in YL? If so, describe how you have done this.

6. Eco (2003:137) claims that "in translating poetry one should render as much as possible the effect produced by the sounds of the original text, even though in the change of language a lot of variations are unavoidable….[T]ry at least to preserve, let us say, rhythm and rhyme." Assuming that this suggestion is valid with respect to good literary poetry, have you ever considered such a strategy when translating the poetry of the Bible? If not, why not? (The answer to this question may be quite simple or very complex.) If so, describe what you or your team have done to take this vital phonological factor into consideration, giving an example or two. How would you answer Eco's question: "What does esthetically equivalent mean?" (ibid.)?

    Compare Eco's short list of sound effects with the longer list suggested by another experienced European literary translator, Per Qvale (2003:225): "Poetic qualities and paralinguistic and prosodic elements: the emotional qualities of the words and sounds, rhythm, tempo (reasonably detectable from the syntax, word length, punctuation); sounds, acoustic effects (assonance, alliteration, rhyme)."

7. Read through Isaiah 1 and find one more example of each of the six figures of speech listed in section 5.1.3. (These should be different from the examples cited earlier.) Isaiah 1 is one of the most colorful, forceful, and passionate passages of Scripture. How difficult would it be to express these figures with the same intensity in your language? Point out any problems that you anticipate.

8. Read about "lexical features designed for special effects" in *The Theory and Practice of Translation* (Nida and Taber 1969:150). Point out those features that are important in the poetic discourse of YL. Give an actual example or two.

9. Identify the instances of ellipsis in Psalms 57:2, 103:9, 119:56, and 137:5. Then consult the NIV, NRSV, GNT, and CEV to see how each version filled in the gaps. Which do you think is correct in each case, and why? Did you discover any significant allusions in these passages? If so, describe the most important one, also indicating how you would deal with it in your translation.

10. Try to find examples in Obadiah of the various emphatic devices listed in section 5.1.5. Write out each of the utterances in which they occur and underline the emphatic expressions.

11. Explain the meaning and function of the emphatic device found in Amos 2:6. How would you translate this with rhetorical equivalence in YL?

12. What is the general idea that is accented by the series of rhetorical questions in Psalm 77:7–9? How do these verses relate in structure and content to the following strophe, 77:10–12?

13. How does repetition serve both an ironic and structural function in the book of Esther? Carefully compare 3:1–4:3 and 8:1–17. What do you find? Can you suggest a way of calling attention to this important literary feature in your translation other than by a note or cross-reference?

14. Find three examples of irony or sarcasm that Job's friends use against him in their debate. Explain the criticism that underlies these remarks and suggest how they might be rendered with similar biting effect in YL.

15. Notice the patterns of pronominal reference to God in Psalm 23. There is a shift from third person to second and back again to third. These variations help to demarcate the psalm into three sections. Give verse numbers of these sections. How would you handle these shifts in YL?

16. Describe the prominent stylistic shift found in Amos 6:9–10. What is the rhetorical significance of this passage within chapter 6?

17. The poetic lament of 2 Samuel 2:33b–34 could be taken as an illustration of insertion, which as such forms a chiastic construction: A – B = B – A. How does a recognition of this literary device help one to interpret the passage? Why does this snatch of poetry occur here within a narrative account? Does 2 Samuel 2:33b–34 pose any translational difficulty in YL? If so, how do you propose solving it?

18. Carefully read Isaiah 4:2–6 (quoted from the RSV below), then pick out and describe the different poetic features that you discover. Can you propose any thematic reason why all this poetic marking is employed here? Now consult other major English versions to see how this text has been formatted on the page. Comment on what you find with particular reference to the question of whether this text is more poetic or more prosaic in nature. Finally, translate this entire passage in a *LiFE*-like manner in YL.

> In that day the branch of the Lord
> > shall be beautiful and glorious,
> and the fruit of the land
> > shall be the pride and glory of the survivors of Israel.
> And he who is left in Zion
> > and remains in Jerusalem
> > will be called holy,
> every one who has been recorded
> > for life in Jerusalem,
> when the Lord shall have washed away the filth
> > of the daughters of Zion
> and cleansed the bloodstains
> > of Jerusalem from its midst
> > by a spirit of judgment
> > and by a spirit of burning.
> Then the Lord will create
> > over the whole site of Mount Zion
> > and over her assemblies
> > > a cloud by day,
> > > and smoke and the shining
> > > of a flaming fire by night;
> > for over all the glory
> > > there will be a canopy and a pavilion.
> It will be for a shade by day from the heat,
> and for a refuge and a shelter from the storm and rain.

19. At the end of his revealing study of word-order variations in Hebrew poetry, Lunn comes to the following conclusions (among others, 2006:275–276). Discuss these as a group, first with reference to what they mean for the *analysis* of biblical poetry, second in terms of their implications for Bible translation. Then apply these principles to the analysis and translation of Psalm 1 (to the extent possible), which has been reproduced below (in non-Masoretic lineation). Finally, evaluate your results and later compare these with Lunn's own analysis of this psalm (ibid.:195–200).

    a. It is primarily within the B-line of synonymous parallelisms that word-order variation as purely stylistic or rhetorical device, i.e., *poetic defamiliarisation*, is admissible.

    b. Such variation is an optional not obligatory feature, and chiefly occurs where the A-line of the parallelism is *canonical*, that is, unmarked.

    c. Where the A-line of a parallelism is marked, the B-line is equally marked. Only a small number of classifiable exceptions exist to this rule.

    d. Gapping of clause constituents mostly occurs in the B-line of synonymous parallelisms.

    e. Where the A-line is marked, gapping does not generally occur of the corresponding fronted constituent(s).

    f. Any departure from the norms described above is a deliberate literary device which serves to set apart that particular unit as performing some higher-level text function, i.e., aperture, closure, or climax.

5.1.7 Poetic structures

Just as sentences of prose are combined to form larger units having a single major topic and/or a unified structure called *paragraphs*, so also the lines (cola) and couplets (bicola) of Hebrew poetry connect with one another to form units at a higher level of textual organization. These segments may be termed *stanzas* if they are similar in size and structure, or *strophes* if they are not. Strophes, which are more variable in shape as they follow one another within a longer poem, are more common in the Hebrew corpus of lyrical, elegiac, and prophetic books than stanzas.

There are various ways of demarcating such structures in Hebrew poetry, and biblical scholars themselves often do not agree as to how a given poetic text ought to be divided into its constituent units. This subject can get rather technical, so in most cases one may simply consult the relevant *Translator's Handbook* (UBS) or *Exegetical Guide* (SIL) and/or some other reliable commentary that deals with these issues in relation to a particular book of the Bible. The disagreement of scholars is reflected in the different divisions that one often finds for a poetic passage in one of the standard translations. Nevertheless, translators must come to a decision on this matter, and in order to do so they may refer to several of these versions in search of the majority opinion on a particular division. The most helpful English Bibles in this regard are the NIV and GNT. The NRSV, NJB, and CEV may also lend evidence that favors one solution or arrangement of the text over another.

A translation team would certainly be wise to seek considerable external support—normally based on the general conventions of vernacular poetry or on the characteristics of specific TL genres—before deciding to compose poetic paragraphs that differ from the standard versions in English, French, or Spanish. However, there are some basic literary criteria that will help when evaluating and resolving differences of opinion, which will be summarized below.

But first the question needs to be asked, Why worry about this matter at all? Why not simply choose one recognized translation and mechanically follow it throughout—making paragraphs and larger divisions wherever that selected version does? Well, for one thing, as already noted, such an automatic policy may produce units that conflict somehow with natural poetic conventions in the TL. For example, the relatively small size of "normal" Hebrew strophes for a particular type of poetry such as a thanksgiving, lament, judgment speech, or divine oracle may differ from the length of corresponding paragraph units in TL poetry.

Second, one must recognize that the standard versions are by no means perfect in this regard—far from it. This is especially true of those translations (e.g., CEV) that tend to collapse, or fuse, certain poetic lines of the original text, perhaps in the interest of avoiding redundancy for content-oriented Western readers. However, the feature of repetition may be a familiar and very desirable attribute in the case of vernacular poetry, and if it is, it should be retained.

Finally, we recall our basic literary premise that *form has meaning*, the larger text structures in particular. Therefore, this aspect of discourse must also be carefully investigated so that its significance may be re-presented in the TL text whenever and wherever possible.

The main principle to keep in mind when seeking to discover the structures of Hebrew poetry (and prose as well) is that there are definite linguistic and literary *markers* that help us to posit where a larger unit begins and ends (especially where it begins). This leads to the following heuristic: The more of these markers that converge in a particular passage, the more sure the analyst can be that they are signalling an opening or closing boundary. Many of these indicators also serve to mark peaks within a section, especially in the middle or at its ending; this possibility needs to be investigated as well.[4] I have grouped these different stylistic signs into several larger categories below.

1. **Markers of aperture (a new beginning)**

    a. **Repetition** is by far the most important marker of discourse divisions in biblical literature, prose as well as poetry, in both the Old Testament and the New Testament. Exact lexical recursion (repetition) is the most diagnostic, but close similarity (or strong contrast) also counts, and to a lesser degree so do corresponding structures and common themes or motifs. In many cases, these types of recursion may be regarded as instances of "separated" (non-adjacent) parallelism (see section 5.1.1).

    There are five main kinds of boundary-marking recursion, though not all of them mark the beginning of a new unit (aperture). It is important that they be carefully distinguished from one another. (In the diagram below, a/a' = the reiterated material; X = the same discourse unit; Y = a different discourse unit; and Z = a third discourse unit.)

    i. **Inclusio** [a – X – a']: The significant recursions occur at the beginning and ending of the same structural unit.

    ii. **Exclusio** [X – a, Z, a' – Y]: The significant recursions occur at the ending and the beginning of different units, with a distinct bounded section in the middle of these two.

    iii. **Anaphora** [a – X, a' – Y]: The significant recursions occur at the respective beginnings of different structural units, whether adjacent or separated in textual space.

    iv. **Epiphora** [X – a, Y – a']: The significant recursions occur at the respective endings of different structural units, whether adjacent or separated in textual space.

    v. **Anadiplosis** [X – a, a' – Y]: The significant recursions occur at the ending of one unit and the very beginning of the next, that is, at the border between the two units.

    » Now read Hosea 11, which follows. Identify its principal boundary-marking devices based on repetition plus any other important discourse markers that you observe in the text. Some of the key reiterated expressions that serve as markers are highlighted in the passage for easier recognition, and the recommended strophic breaks have already been made.

    » While you are doing this assignment, notice the difference in the RSV and NRSV wordings for verse 7. Which of the two would the overall structure tend to support? Why do you come to this conclusion?

---

[4]For further background with regard to this type of poetic discourse analysis, see chapter 2 of Wendland 1995.

» In what way(s) does the poetic structure support a major break after verse 11, not after verse 12, as the English versions have it?

» After completing the first part of this assignment, consult several other translations (e.g., GNT, CEV, NJB, NIV) to see how they have demarcated this chapter. What differences do you notice? Which version best supports the arrangement below?

» What boundary markers are available in YL to help distinguish these poetic units of structure?

¹ When **Israel** was a child, I <u>loved</u> him,
  and out of Egypt *I called my son*.
² The more I called them,
  the more they went from me;
they kept sacrificing to the Baals,
  and burning incense to idols.
³ Yet it was I who taught **Ephraim** to walk,
  I took them up in my arms;
  but they did not know that I healed them.
⁴ I led them with cords of compassion,
  with the bands of <u>love</u>,
and I became to them as one
  who eases the yoke on their jaws,
  and I bent down to them and fed them.

⁵ They shall <u>return</u> to the land of *Egypt*,
  and *Assyria* shall be their king,
  because they have refused to <u>return</u> to me.
⁶ The sword shall rage against their cities,
  consume the bars of their gates,
  and devour them in their fortresses.
⁷ My people are bent on <u>turning</u> away from me;
  so they are appointed to the yoke,   (To the Most High *they call*,
  and **none** shall remove it.   but he does **not** raise them up at all.—NRSV)

⁸ How can I give you up, O **Ephraim**!
  How can I hand you over, O **Israel**!
How can I make you like Admah!
  How can I treat you like Zeboiim!
My heart recoils within me,
  my compassion grows warm and tender.
⁹ I will not execute my fierce anger,
  I will not again destroy Ephraim;
for I am God and not man,
  the Holy One in your midst,
  and I will **not** come to destroy.

¹⁰ They shall go after <u>the Lord</u>,
  he will roar like a lion;
yea, he will roar,
  and his sons shall come trembling from the west;
¹¹ they shall come trembling like birds from *Egypt*,
  and like doves from the land of *Assyria*;
  and I will return them to their homes, says <u>the Lord</u>.

¹² [12:1 in Hebrew] **Ephraim** has encompassed me with lies,
    and the house of **Israel** with deceit;
but Judah is still known by God,
    and is faithful to the Holy One.

b. **Formulae** (conventional literary expressions) are especially common in the Hebrew prophets. They announce a message from Yahweh and can be used for emphasis ("intensifiers") in poetic discourse (see section 5.1.5). They function most clearly to open a unit (i.e., they are markers of aperture). The longer the formula, the more important it is as a textual marker. This is the case at the beginning of the book of Hosea: "The word of the LORD that came to Hosea son of Beeri during the reigns of Uzziah,..." The book of Amos includes the largest concentration of such formulae in relation to its size, marking units both large and small within the book (e.g., 3:1, 11, 12, 13). In this category are included certain common temporal (actually messianic or eschatological) formulae (e.g., "In that day," as in Hos. 2:16, 21) and logical markers (e.g., לָכֵן 'therefore' to introduce a judgment or promissory speech, as in Hos. 2:6, 9, 14).

c. **Shifts** in textual form, content, or function are a good indication that a new unit of poetry (or prose) is beginning. The various kinds of shifts include an overtly marked change in the speaker, addressee(s), setting (time, place), dramatic circumstances, interpersonal relationships, tone or atmosphere, point of view or perspective, topic under discussion, literary genre, main event sequence, or principal character. *The more shifts that occur at a particular point in the discourse, the more significant the boundary that occurs there.*

d. **Intensifiers**, while not diagnostic in and of themselves, often occur at the beginning of a new poetic unit, thus strengthening one of the other three markers that may be already present. In this diverse category we find literary forms such as vocatives (especially divine names and praise epithets), imperatives, rhetorical or leading questions, exclamations, graphic figurative language, contrastive imagery, asyndeton (i.e., the absence of any conjunction or transitional expression), and utterances that express irony or hyperbole.

2. Markers of closure (a point of conclusion)

The literary indicators of closure are not as obvious as those that mark aperture. But they still need to be considered, because together the two make a more convincing case for a poetic division within the text. In other words, where the markers of aperture are not very strong or prominent, then one would look to the preceding verse in the text to see if any forceful signs of a closure are present. If they are, then one can be more confident about positing a structural boundary between the two verses.

Three prominent signals of closure, especially when occurring together, are repetition, formulae, and intensifiers.

a. **Repetition** – An ending of a unit may be indicated by the closing segment of a structural pattern of *epiphora, inclusio, exclusio,* or *anadiplosis.* (Note the types of repetition previously listed under "Markers of Aperture.") They must be used in conjunction with each other in order to determine discourse boundaries since in many cases the textual evidence is debatable. The following summary may be helpful:

    APERTURE is marked by *anaphora,* **CLOSURE** by *epiphora,* and **BOTH APERTURE AND CLOSURE** by *inclusio, exclusio,* and *anadiplosis.*

b. **Formulae** that mark closure (sometimes of only a minor strophe-internal unit of structure) include prophetic speech expressions such as נְאֻם־יְהוָה "oracle of Yahweh" (Hos. 11:11) and the similar discourse margin אָמַר יְהוָה "says Yahweh" (Am. 5:17). Can you think of any others?

c. **Intensifiers** normally take the form of some kind of emphatic utterance that either summarizes, underscores, or in some other obvious way concludes the topic or argument that has been developed in the preceding text. Examples include a snatch of direct speech (Hos. 10:8); an exclamation (Hos. 4:6); a prediction (Hos. 9:17); a monocolon or condensed utterance (Hos. 11:9), especially one preceded by asyndeton (Hos. 7:7); graphic imagery (Hos. 13:8); and a key thematic or theological assertion (Hos. 5:15).

3. **Markers of cohesion (bonds of connection)**

The outer boundaries of a poetic text as indicated by markers of aperture and closure should always be supported by various connections that link together the inner parts of a segment, whether a strophe or larger unit. Such cohesion is both semantic and structural; that is, there will be ties of content and ties of form throughout the same unit. The formal features include similarities of sound (rhythm, rhyme, alliteration); analogous, closely associated, or antithetical lexical items; corresponding syntactic constructions; elements of interconnected parallelism (intertwined bicola); and perhaps even larger patterns of text organization, either linear (e.g., a terraced progression) or concentric (e.g., an extended chiasmus).

> » Go back to Hosea 11 above and point out several of the markers of cohesion that bind together each of the four constituent strophes internally.

The linguistic terms *cohesion* and *coherence* are closely related and often confused. *Cohesion*, as just described, involves the formal connections (phonological, syntactic, structural) that bind a text into a unified whole. *Coherence,* on the other hand, refers to the *semantic* quality of a text by which it "hangs together" conceptually and makes sense as it is read or listened to. The reader/listener progressively develops a unified *mental representation* (scenario) of the content of a particular text as he or she interprets it on the basis of the different linguistic and literary forms that the author/speaker has used to compose that text. Such text-based conceptualization must always be coupled with a sufficient amount of situational, background information pertaining to the historical, environmental, and sociocultural setting of the passage under consideration. The diverse linguistic and literary devices of cohesion and coherence allow the process of contextualization and interpretation to take place, and direct it towards the author/speaker's implied communicative goals for the text (see section 7.1). Therefore, it is important that suitable TL devices be found to retain the original discourse function in a translation. While the Hebrew forms will work well at times in another language, often additional vernacular literary techniques are needed in order to preserve the full connective effect.

The cohesion-producing devices of Hebrew poetry are literary markers, to be distinguished from purely linguistic markers.[5] The more important ones are *refrain, overlap, chiasmus,* and *acrostic.*

a. **Refrain** (a repeated colon/bicolon)

An example of a refrain is in Psalm 46:7 and 11. It functions to divide Psalm 46 into two parts and also to highlight its conclusion. This is an instance of *end stress,* which is a common literary feature throughout the world. Is such a feature found also in the literary/oral tradition of YL?

> The Lord Almighty is with us;
> The God of Jacob is our fortress. (vv. 7, 11)

---

[5]Linguistic markers include extended descriptive expressions, simple repetition and synonymous recursion, pronouns, deictic forms, lexical and conjunctive interrelationships (e.g., general-specific, part-whole, cause-effect), collocational expectations based on common semantic domains, inflectional usage (e.g., tense, concordial-agreement sequences, case relations), and of course patterns of intonation in the case of actual speech (e.g., rising > falling sequence, pause breaks) (see Dooley and Levinsohn 2001, chapters 5–6).

5.1 The major stylistic forms of biblical poetry

» Find another bicolon in Psalm 46 that is similar to Psalm 46:7 and 11, though not exactly the same. What is the significance of its location, that is, in relation to the verses of the refrain?

» Where do you find the short refrain "His love endures forever" in Psalm 136? What does its frequency suggest about the use of such a refrain during public worship?

» There is another refrain in this psalm—not exactly the same in wording, but similar. Where is this refrain found, and what is the significance of its location within the psalm as a whole?

» Find another psalm with a refrain. Point out where the refrain occurs and how it serves to demarcate the text into strophic segments.

b. **Overlap**

An example of conceptual overlapping is in Psalm 77 (quoted below from the RSV). There are various types of overlapping depending on their form and/or content as one colon leads to the next throughout a given unit, ranging from a single verse to a complete poem. One such structure is the "terrace" pattern of parallelism, which is manifested in an interestingly varied manner throughout Psalm 77. Its overlapping lexical items are highlighted here and also reformatted to better show the intended strophic structure:

¹ I cry <u>aloud to God,</u>
   <u>aloud to God</u>, that he may hear me.
² In the day of my trouble *I seek the Lord*;
   in the night *my hand is stretched out* without wearying;
   my soul refuses to be comforted.
³ <u>I think of God</u>, and *I moan*;
   <u>I meditate</u>, and *my spirit faints.*

                                        Selah

⁴ Thou dost *hold my eyelids from closing;*
   I am so troubled that I cannot speak.
⁵ *I consider* the days of old,
   I remember the years long ago.
⁶ *I commune* with <u>my heart</u> in the night;
   I meditate and search <u>my spirit</u>:

⁷ "Will the Lord *spurn for ever,*
   and *never again be favorable?*
⁸ Has <u>his steadfast love for ever ceased</u>?
   Are his <u>promises at an end for all time</u>?
⁹ Has God *forgotten to be gracious?*
   Has he in anger *shut up his compassion?*"

                                        Selah

¹⁰ And I say, "It is my grief   [Then I thought, "To this I will appeal: the
   that the right hand of the Most High has changed."   years of the right hand of the Most High."]
¹¹ *I will call to mind* <u>the deeds of the</u> Lord;
   yea, *I will remember* <u>thy wonders</u> of old.
¹² *I will meditate* on <u>all thy work</u>,
   and *muse* on thy mighty deeds.

> ¹³ Thy way, O God, is holy.
>> What god is great like our God?
> ¹⁴ Thou art the God who *workest wonders*,
>> who hast *manifested thy might* among <u>the peoples</u>.
> ¹⁵ Thou didst *with thy arm* redeem <u>thy people</u>,
>> the <u>sons of Jacob and Joseph</u>.
>
>   Selah
>
> ¹⁶ When *the waters saw thee*, O God,
>> when *the waters saw thee*, <u>they were afraid</u>,
>> yea, *the deep* <u>trembled</u>.
> ¹⁷ *The clouds* poured out **water**;
>> *the skies* gave forth **thunder**;
>> thy **arrows** flashed on every side.
> ¹⁸ The crash of thy **thunder** was in the whirlwind;
>> thy **lightnings** lighted up the world;
>> the earth trembled and shook.
> ¹⁹ <u>Thy way</u> was *through the sea*,
>> <u>thy path</u> *through the great waters*;
>> yet <u>thy footprints</u> were unseen.
> ²⁰ Thou didst lead thy people like a flock
>> by the hand of Moses and Aaron.

» Give some reasons to support (or revise) the strophic structure of Psalm 77 as proposed by the RSV, that is, five strophes of three verses each and a final strophe of six verses.

There are three verses that do not seem to fit into the strongly cohesive overlapping lexical pattern: verses 10, 13, and 20. (Note the alternative NIV rendering of v. 10 above to the right.). It may be no accident that these passages express the great theological truths of this psalm.

» Verse 20 would fit nicely in terms of content after verse 15. What might be a structural reason for the displacement of verse 20 to the end of the psalm?

Observe the double length of the final, climactic strophe, verses 16–20, which begins with a powerful theophany (God's mighty manifestation mirrored in nature) and ends in a quiet, comforting conclusion to the entire prayer.

» What needs to be done in your translation to reproduce these different structural and stylistic effects?

c. **Chiasmus**

The structure of a chiasmus was given earlier as A – B = B' – A'. This pattern may be extended, however, to form what is sometimes termed a "palistrophe," "introversion," or "reverse parallel structure," which may be represented as **A – B – C … X … C' – B' – A'**, where *X* stands for additional, optional structural elements. (Usually, there are no more than seven in either direction.) This sort of a structure provides *cohesion* to the entire unit that it forms, both as a forward linear progression and also as a concentric arrangement with special emphasis at its center and often at the end as well. The core of a chiasmus often presents information of special thematic importance and/or pragmatic import (e.g., in the form of an imperative of exhortation or prohibition). But a chiastic structure of this nature, remember, needs to be supported in some formal way so as to ensure its credibility or reliability, for example, by means of a significant recursion of lexical and/or grammatical features. The following is such an example, embracing the whole of Psalm 67 (NIV), a joyous song of thanksgiving:

> **A** May God be gracious to us and bless us
> **A** and make his face shine upon us,
>   **a** that your ways may be known on earth,
>   **a** your salvation among all nations.
>
>   **B** *May the peoples praise you, O God;*
>   *may all the peoples praise you.*
>
>   **C** May the nations be glad and sing for joy,
>
>   **C'** for you rule the peoples justly
>   and guide the nations of the earth.
>
>   **B'** *May the peoples praise you, O God;*
>   *may all the peoples praise you.*
>
>   **a'** Then the land *will yield* its harvest,
> **A'** and God, our God, will bless us.
> **A'** God *will bless* us,
>   **a'** and all the ends of the earth will fear him.

This chiastic structure is established by the refrain in B and B'.

» What significant aspect of meaning is introduced in the center (C'), and also at the end (a')? How can this be marked in YL?

Due to the flexibility of the Hebrew tense/aspect system in poetry, the verbs at the end may be interpreted as referring to either completed or incomplete action/time. There is a point of variation in the GNT and NRSV (cf. also the NIV above).

The land *has produced* its harvest;	The earth *has yielded* its increase;
God, our God, *has blessed* us.	God, our God, *has blessed* us.
God *has blessed* us;	*May* God *continue to bless* us;
may all people everywhere honor him.	let all the ends of the earth revere him.
(GNT)	(NRSV)

» A choice must be made here when re-presenting this verse in YL. How will you make that choice with regard to each line?

» Which interpretation seems to fit the context and potential purpose of this thanksgiving song better—a past or a future reference, a statement of fact or a wish/prayer? Explain your decision. Accordingly, how you will handle this matter in YL?

d. **Acrostic**

An *acrostic* is a highly formalized type of poetry in which a composition's individual cola or short strophes/stanzas follow the order of the twenty-two letters of the Hebrew alphabet. There must have been a reason for the use of such an elaborate literary structure. There are several possibilities.

    i. An acrostic may serve as an aid to the memory and/or to assist in the poem's composition and memorization.

ii. An acrostic may serve as a pedagogical tool in the instruction of the young about biblical wisdom.

iii. An acrostic may serve to reinforce the idea of perfection and completion that is a blessing to all the righteous who follow the will of Yahweh.

iv. An acrostic may serve to convey the notion of an underlying divine order and coherence in a seemingly chaotic and disorganized world.

The last two suggestions apply to an acrostic poem's interpretation, and therefore both will probably not apply to the same example.

» Which suggestion would better harmonize with the nature and purpose of the book of Lamentations, which features the acrostic form throughout?

» Would such a formal device be effective in your translation? Explain why or why not (see Wilt 1993). If you have a different way of marking the acrostic form, describe what this is.

Psalm 34 is another good example of an acrostic wisdom poem. In most translations the reader is not informed that the text is structured in this manner. An exception is the NJB. Consult the NJB to see how it indicates the acrostic form.

» If you know Hebrew, determine which letter of the alphabet has been left out of the sequence. Can you suggest a possible reason for this omission?

» Verse 22 falls outside the acrostic framework, which might be of some special significance. Can you propose any reason for the omission in this case?

The center of an acrostic pattern also may express something noteworthy. In Psalm 34 that would be verse 11 and/or 12.

» Do you notice anything important about either of these two verses?

» How does "the fear of the Lord" (11) relate to the psalm's theme as a whole and, indeed, to the entire wisdom tradition of Israel's biblical sages?

» How does this notion relate in turn to "long life" (v. 12)?

The question now is, *why* should Bible translators pay so much attention to these poetic structures and the various literary markers of aperture, closure, and cohesion as they carry out their work? Why not simply adopt one recommended English version (or French or Spanish) with regard to these difficult passages of poetry? Or perhaps we might examine two or three versions and selectively choose from among them which features to imitate. But then how do we decide in places where they do not agree among themselves as to how to demarcate the text into paragraphs and larger units? Should the translator just follow the majority opinion?

To be sure, some translation teams will not be able to do any better than this. But those translators with the necessary competence and training may desire to be more independent and creative in their work, especially if they are preparing a *LiFE* rendering. A version of this nature demands excellence in all respects—especially with regard to the form of the text as well as its content. For such translators, the question becomes: What more can we do to improve and perfect the literary and rhetorical as well as the semantic quality of our text?

5.1 The major stylistic forms of biblical poetry

This goal does not stem from a desire to augment or embellish the original, but to more adequately represent what is already there in the biblical text. Or stated negatively, the goal is to prevent further literary loss with respect to esthetic appeal and rhetorical impact.

The structure of the Hebrew prophetic books in particular presents a rather serious problem to those who would simply allow their decisions to be guided completely by other translations, no matter how highly recommended they might be. This is because the standard versions in English only rarely agree in their segmentation throughout a given pericope. Commentaries, too, tend to differ from one another when proposing a textual arrangement for a given passage. Let us look at just one extended example: The NIV text below is a reformatted version of Hosea 5:1–7 (plus 5:8, which begins the next unit); notice that certain poetic features are highlighted and explanatory notes given on the right.

¹ "Hear this, you priests!	The parallel imperatives and vocatives signal an *aperture*.
Pay attention, you **Israelites**!	"Israel" is mentioned at the start of each strophe—*anaphora*.
Listen, O royal house!	
This judgment is *against you*:	A Judgment announced (by God) against Israel (you).
You have been a snare at Mizpah,	B Reason (indictment) specified figuratively
a net spread out on Tabor.	
² The rebels are deep in slaughter.	B' Reason (sin) specified generally
[And] *I [myself]* will discipline all of them.	A' Judgment announced by God (I) against Israel (them)
³ I [myself] *know* all about **Ephraim**;	A (Yahweh) *knows* Israel's sin [NB—*asyndeton*].
Israel is not hidden from me.	[In A–B–C Israel is referred to in 2d person.]
Ephraim, you have now turned to *prostitution*;	B The sin is ritual and spiritual *prostitution*.
Israel is corrupt.	C Israel is corrupt—general result.
⁴ "Their deeds do not permit them	C' Israel is corrupt—specific result.
to return to their God.	[In C'-B'-A' Israel is referred to in 3d person.]
A spirit of *prostitution* is in their heart;	B' The sin is ritual and spiritual *prostitution*.
they do not acknowledge [*know*] the LORD.	A' Israel does not *know* Yahweh [NB—*pun*].
⁵ **Israel's** arrogance testifies against them;	The place names signal *anaphora*,
the **Israelites**, even **Ephraim**, stumble in their sin;	but "Judah" is new.
Judah also stumbles with them.	
⁶ When they go with their flocks and herds	The indictment against the people is now specified
to seek the LORD,	in graphic, figurative sacrificial terms, tinged
they will not find him;	with *irony*.
he has withdrawn himself from them	IRONY: the people seek God in worship but he is gone!
⁷ They are unfaithful to the LORD;	IRONY: infidelity produces illegitimacy.
they give birth to illegitimate children.	
Now their New Moon festivals	IRONY: God will not "eat" (accept) their sacrifices;
will devour them and their fields.	they and all their produce will be "eaten" (destroyed).
⁸ "Sound the trumpet in Gibeah,	The imperatives and series of place names, coupled with a
the horn in Ramah.	different vocative at the end and no mention of "Israel"
Raise the battle cry in Beth Aven;	clearly mark the onset of a new oracle in vv 8–15.
lead on, O Benjamin.	

Now, consult the various other translations that you have at hand and note the differences of opinion regarding the poetic discourse structure of this passage. Then come to your own conclusion as to how to segment the text into strophic units. Also note any special translation problems that appear and suggest how you might handle them in your language.

Once the main principles of Hebrew poetic structure and rhetorical highlighting are learned, dealing with a passage like this becomes less difficult. As the discourse organization becomes clearer, so does one's perception of the operation of individual literary devices, all of which tend to work together to communicate the poet-prophet's message in a convincing and compelling manner—as they should, ideally, also work together in a translation.

The key strategy is to utilize these criteria *all together* as a means of identifying the structure, looking for patterns of *correspondence* and *convergence*, of *conjunction* and *disjunction*, of *correspondence* and *contrast*, which operate in textual interaction to point the analyst in a particular direction of interpretation that seems faithful to the original author's communicative intentions as well as credible in terms of both the textual cotext and also the external situational context.

Finally, it may be possible—at least in some publications designed for special audiences—to re-present some of the more important of these larger poetic structures in print. De Waard and Nida (1986:118) put the case clearly:

> To do justice to the intricate structure [that may be presented by the biblical text], a translator is well advised to attempt by the formal arrangement to highlight these relationships and thus reproduce by [the printed] format an isomorphic equivalent of the formal and thematic structure.

As an example, the dramatic introduction to a new divine oracle in Amos 5:4b–6a (below) might be formatted as an *isomorphic equivalent* to better reveal its structural parallels and initial point of emphasis (to be coupled, of course, with a dynamic *LiFE* rendering of these words).

> Seek me and live!
> Do not worship at Bethel –
>   do not travel to Gilgal –
>   do not pilgrimage to Beersheba!
>   For sure, Gilgal will go into exile –
> Bethel will be blown away!
> Yes, seek the Lord and live!

» As you study Amos 5:4b–6a, ask yourself where the main point of the text occurs. Why do you think so?

» What is the special meaning that is brought out by this structural device?

» Would such formatting signal a similar thing in YL? If not, what would do so?

For reflection, research, and response:

1. Point out the refrain of Psalm 8 and explain its primary structural and thematic significance.

2. Two refrains—one major, the other minor—link Psalms 42 and 43 into a cohesive unit. (This suggests that in some early Hebrew prayer books or liturgical traditions the two formed a single psalm.) Write the words of these refrains and the verses in which they are found. How do these two refrains relate in content to the central core of both psalms found in 42:8?

3. Study the elaborate overlapping pattern found in Micah 1:10–16. What is it that ties these verses together into a larger poetic unit? Explain the significance of three of the puns on place names that occur in this section. Point out the *epiphoric* (unit-ending) refrain that divides the first portion into two strophes: verses 8–9 and 10–12. The sudden reappearance of another first person singular pronoun divides the final portion into another two strophes: verses 13–14 and 15–16. To whom do the two "I" pronouns in this poem refer (at the beginning, and at the end)? Notice the shocking revelation that is given in the poem's final line, which is a good example of end stress.

4. Job may be classified as a well-formed poetic book despite its narrative beginning and end (which forms a structural inclusio around the whole contentious debate about righteousness and evil, blessing and judgment). It is interesting to observe the extended chiasmus that relates these two prose portions to one another and at the same time creates a strong cohesive element within each section. Look up the passages listed below for each constituent of the chiasmus and summarize the main similarities or contrasts that you can find in each corresponding lettered element, for example, passage A' in comparison with A, B' in comparison with B, and so forth.

   A (1:1) _____
     B (1:2) _____
       C (1:3) _____
         D (1:4–5) _____
           E (1:6–2:10) _____
             F (2:11) _____
               G (2:12–13) _____

               G' (42:7–8) _____
             F' (42:9) _____
            E' (42:10) _____
         D' (42:11) _____
       C' (42:12) _____
     B' (42:13–15) _____
   A' (42:16–17) _____

   Notice that at the core of this extended chiasmus, G' presents an important speech by Yahweh to Job's friends. Its significance is underscored by the fact that it is itself chiastically arranged as shown below. Explain how this divine utterance relates to the overall theme of Job. We observe in this example how poetic features also occur in the important prose dialogues of Scripture. How will you re-present this formal aspect of meaning in your translation? Explain why.

     A My wrath is kindled against you and against your two friends;
         for you have not spoken of me what is right, as my servant Job has.

       B Now therefore take seven bulls and seven rams, and go to my servant Job,
         and offer up for yourselves a burnt offering; and *my servant Job shall pray for you*,

       B' for *I will accept his prayer* not to deal with you according to your folly;

     A' for you have not spoken of me what is right, as my servant Job has. (RSV)

5. Study the translation of Psalm 34 by Wilt (2002b:44–45). A small sample follows:

   Always, I will praise Yahweh.
     I will proclaim his greatness,

> **B**ragging of Yahweh,
> > Urging others to join me.
>
> **C**ome and join with me,
> > You who have been oppressed…

How has Wilt handled the acrostic form in English? Evaluate the effectiveness of this creative literary re-presentation. Would something like this work in YL? Explain why or why not and give an explanation of any alternative form that you can suggest to reproduce at least part of the significance of the acrostic form in the original text. *This Hebrew poetic form (structure) is too important to simply be ignored!*

Now compare Wilt's manner of handling acrostic poems with that of Boerger (1997), who makes use of end rhyme, alliteration, synonymy, word plays, word order, making implicit information explicit, and other literary devices in an effort to "extend naturalness" while maintaining the accuracy of her poetic renditions. The following is an excerpt from Boerger's translation of Psalm 111 (ibid.:40):

> 1. Allelujah! Praise Yahweh, the almighty King!
>   Bless him ! I thank him with all of my being,
>   Commune with my righteous companions and sing.
> 2. Dynamic his deeds in every detail,
>   Eagerly studied in all they entail,
>   For delight can be found in them all without fear.
> 3. God's glory glows from his every endeavor,
>   His heavenly holiness enduring forever.
> 4. Incomparable marvels make us recall,
>   Just, gentle, good Yahweh is Lord over all.

In his recent study of Hebrew alphabetic acrostics and their translation, Van der Spuy concludes that "an alphabetic acrostic translation is possible and that it preserves the essence of what the original poet strived to present. It contributes towards the cognitive, mnemonic, visual (even more when the letters are written as headings to each stanza) and aural (especially when the letters are mentioned as the poem is read) effectiveness, and it evokes a sense that it is one fully complete unit" (2008:531).

Evaluate this from the perspective of your translation program as well as in light of the following sample of Van der Spuy's rendering of Psalm 145 "following the Latin alphabet, with the exception of less used letters," i.e., C, X, Q and Z in Afrikaans (ibid.:529):

> 1. **A**ltyd wil ek u loof, my God en Koning, ek wil U verhoog sonder einde!
>   *Forever I will praise your name, o King, I will exalt thee without end!*
> 2. **B**esing die lof van die Here, Ek (sic) wil U loof, vir tyd en ewigheid!
>   *Sing the Lord's praises, I will praise thee, I will always praise your name.*
> 3. **D**ie Here is groot, Hy moet sonder perke geprys word,
>   oor sy grootheid is daar geen twyfel nie.
>   *The Lord is great, He has to be praised without end, his greatness is unquestionable.*
> 4. **E**en geslag prys u werde by die ander, hulle vertel van u magtige dade.
>   *One generation praises your deeds in front of the other, they proclaim your mighty deeds.*
>   …

6. Keeping in mind the different poetic structural devices of aperture, closure, and cohesion, prepare a discourse analysis of Isaiah 5. Do the following:

   a. Divide Isaiah 5 into constituent strophes and larger units of structure and point out the main markers of these divisions.

5.1 The major stylistic forms of biblical poetry

    b. Comment on how your analysis of the structure of this chapter helps you to better understand its content and purpose as a prophetic word from God to his people.

    c. If there is a way you can reflect the textual organization of this passage in writing, try preparing a printed isomorphic equivalent of the Hebrew structure.

    d. Finally, compare Isaiah 5:1–7 with Isaiah 27:2–6, which is another "song of Yahweh." Note the similarities and differences. What is their significance? Should this literary (and theological) connection be noted in a paratextual note on Isaiah 27:2–6? If you think that this would be helpful, what would you say?

7. As we have already seen, poetic structures are also found in the New Testament and not only in passages where OT poetry is quoted or recomposed (as in Luke 1–2). For example, Paul's paean to Christian love in 1 Corinthians 13 is clearly very lyrical in its style. Examine the formatted version of the first three verses below (from the NRSV) and pick out some of the more obvious poetic features. (The Greek text is included for those who are able to discern the literary devices that are not expressed in the English translation.)

> If I speak in the tongues of mortals and of angels,
>   **but do not have love,**
>   I am a *noisy gong*
>   or a *clanging cymbal*.
> And if I have prophetic powers,
>   and understand all mysteries
>   and all knowledge,
>   and if I have all faith,
>   so as to remove mountains,
>   **but do not have love,**
>   I am *nothing*.
> If I give away all my possessions,
>   and if I hand over my body
>   to be burned,
>   **but do not have love,**
>   I gain *nothing*.

> Ἐὰν ταῖς γλώσσαις τῶν ἀνθρώπων λαλῶ
>   καὶ τῶν ἀγγέλων,
>   **ἀγάπην δὲ μὴ ἔχω,**
>   γέγονα χαλκὸς ἠχῶν
>   ἢ κύμβαλον ἀλαλάζον.
> καὶ ἐὰν ἔχω προφητείαν
>   καὶ εἰδῶ τὰ μυστήρια πάντα
>   καὶ πᾶσαν τὴν γνῶσιν
>   καὶ ἐὰν ἔχω πᾶσαν τὴν πίστιν
>   ὥστε ὄρη μεθιστάναι,
>   **ἀγάπην δὲ μὴ ἔχω,**
>   οὐθέν εἰμι.
> κἂν ψωμίσω πάντα τὰ ὑπάρχοντά μου
>   καὶ ἐὰν παραδῶ τὸ σῶμά μου
>   ἵνα καυχήσωμαι,
>   **ἀγάπην δὲ μὴ ἔχω,**
>   οὐδὲν ὠφελοῦμαι.

8. Consider 1 Corinthians 12:14–20 (the RSV and Greek are below) in terms of its poetic features. Then format the text according to its patterned repetitions. Call attention to any other devices that you notice. What is their apparent purpose (both in specific respects and as a whole) in highlighting or embellishing the content of this section? Would these devices cause any translational difficulties in YL? Explain. How would you represent this text in YL—as more poetic or more prosaic? Why? Finally, translate the passage in a *LiFE* manner and give a close English back-translation.

> [14] For the body does not consist of one member but of many. [15] If the foot should say, "Because I am not a hand, I do not belong to the body," that would not make it any less a part of the body. [16] And if the ear should say, "Because I am not an eye, I do not belong to the body," that would not make it any less a part of the body. [17] If the whole body were an eye, where would be the hearing? If the whole body were an ear, where would be the sense of smell? [18] But as it is, God arranged the organs in the body, each one of them, as he chose. [19] If all were a single organ, where would the body be? [20] As it is, there are many parts, yet one body.

> [14] καὶ γὰρ τὸ σῶμα οὐκ ἔστιν ἓν μέλος ἀλλὰ πολλά. [15] ἐὰν εἴπῃ ὁ πούς, Ὅτι οὐκ εἰμὶ χείρ, οὐκ εἰμὶ ἐκ τοῦ σώματος, οὐ παρὰ τοῦτο οὐκ ἔστιν ἐκ τοῦ σώματος; [16] καὶ ἐὰν εἴπῃ τὸ οὖς, Ὅτι οὐκ εἰμὶ ὀφθαλμός, οὐκ εἰμὶ ἐκ τοῦ σώματος, οὐ παρὰ τοῦτο οὐκ ἔστιν ἐκ τοῦ σώματος· [17] εἰ ὅλον τὸ σῶμα ὀφθαλμός, ποῦ ἡ ἀκοή; εἰ ὅλον ἀκοή, ποῦ ἡ ὄσφρησις; [18] νυνὶ δὲ ὁ θεὸς ἔθετο τὰ μέλη, ἓν ἕκαστον αὐτῶν ἐν τῷ σώματι καθὼς ἠθέλησεν. [19] εἰ δὲ ἦν τὰ πάντα ἓν μέλος, ποῦ τὸ σῶμα; [20] νῦν δὲ πολλὰ μὲν μέλη, ἓν δὲ σῶμα.

9. De Waard and Nida (1986, chapter 6) discuss six *rhetorical processes*: repetition, compactness, connectives, rhythm, shifts in expectancies, and the exploitation of similarities and contrasts in the selection and arrangement of the elements of a discourse (p. 86). How does this list of literary features relate to those that have been discussed here in section 5.1?

10. Read about "formal features designed for special effects" in *The Theory and Practice of Translation* (Nida and Taber 1969:147–148). Point out those features that are important also in the poetic discourse structures of YL. If possible, give an actual example of some of these devices as applied to some Bible passages of your choice.

5.2 The major functions of biblical poetry

Earlier we discussed some of the main general goals that individually or in combination initiate and also guide the interpretation process during a communication event, with special reference to verbal acts of literary or oral creation (section 1.3).

> » Can you recall a working definition for each of the following functions: referential, imperative, emotive, relational, ritual, expressive, metalingual, deictic, intertextual, textual, and poetic?

Our emphasis has been on the *poetic* function in which selected literary forms are used to create a special effect of some kind for the purpose of highlighting or enhancing the performance of one of the other primary aims of communication. The following is a more specific list of *operations* performed by various stylistic devices and rhetorical techniques during the formal composition or the conceptual processing of a literary text, the Bible in particular:

1. To broadly organize and arrange (i.e., give definition and coherence to the thematic structure of) a given poetic text

2. To spotlight within the text a set of selected theological truths, religious instructions, and moral imperatives that the author wishes to emphasize in particular

3. To forcefully impress upon listeners, by means of the very style of language that is used, the dignity and authority, the conceptual importance as well as ethical significance of the entire message being transmitted

4. To express with greater or lesser degrees of intensification the author/speaker's emotions, moods, and attitudes, and to *evoke* corresponding feelings within the audience

5. To render the translation more memorable, hence also more memorizable and transmittable

6. To engage God's people psychologically and spiritually more fully in a meaningful worship experience, especially via the familiar phatic (ritual) forms of liturgical language

» What additional important discourse function does the expert use of stylistic forms carry out, whether in the original biblical text or in our modern translations? Can you think of any others?

It is a vital part of the translation task to attempt (at least) to reproduce in the TL a similar level of specific as well as general communicative significance as found in the SL text—including its connotative as well as denotative aspects. This is accomplished by selecting from the total inventory of vernacular linguistic and literary resources those that most closely match the biblical genre being translated in keeping with the designated method of translation (in our case, a *LiFE* rendition, more or less). As part of this exercise of determining functional correspondents in the TL, it is often necessary to differentiate several types of poetry, especially if these happen to be associated with disparate communication settings and purposes in the receptor culture. These diverse discourse types are designed to carry out different goals during the communication process (see section 5.3).

De Waard and Nida (1986:79–80) call attention to a number of *rhetorical functions* that are performed by "the effective exploitation of selection and arrangement of formal features...designed to produce impact and appeal." These rhetorical functions are paraphrased below in a somewhat modified arrangement (ibid.:80–85):

1. **wholeness** with regard to the dimensions of completeness and unity of the subject being presented in the text under consideration

2. **impact** that is created through the use of novelty and appropriateness in relation to the linguistic cotext as well as the extralinguistic context

3. **coherence** involving a suitable conceptual fit with the prevailing worldview, both ancient (biblical) and contemporary (considering also a local traditional religious perspective); with the current communicative setting; and with any other relevant oral or written texts, either from the Scriptures themselves or from some modern work (intertextuality)

4. **cohesion** marked not only by the internal connection of the constituent parts of a text, but also by their manifest progression towards a tangible goal

5. **focus** whereby new information is distinguished from old information in the text, topic is differentiated from comment, and foregrounded material is set off from that of the background

6. **emphasis** whereby some selected aspect or feature of the discourse is given special prominence within its particular context of occurrence

7. **appeal** deriving from the discourse's esthetic dimension, that is, the beauty of linguistic forms as they are chosen and combined to form pleasing rhythms, syntactic patterns, phonic groupings, lexical collocations, and so forth

In section 2.3 we examined the four principal macrofunctions of the diverse artistic and rhetorical features found in literary discourse. These were:

1. **segmentation**: dividing the text up into structural units of different sizes

2. **disposition**: organizing and arranging the repeated elements into various textual patterns

3. **connection**: linking one part of the text with another and unifying the discourse as a whole

4. **projection**: giving prominence to selected marked portions of the complete text

» How do these four macrofunctions relate to de Waard and Nida's set of "rhetorical functions?"

» Speech act analysis is yet another, more detailed way to explore the communicative purpose of a particular passage, or even a portion of one as we saw in section 1.6.2.1. Mention five common illocutions (discourse intentions) that are important in poetic discourse, and cite a Bible verse that illustrates each one.

For reflection, research, and response:

1. What significant repeated elements do you see when you compare Genesis 1:1 and 2:1–3? What is the structural function of this repetition? How can this function be highlighted in your translation?

2. Study Psalm 23 (reproduced below from the RSV, including several footnotes, which also need to be evaluated). Consult several other English versions and the original Hebrew text or an interlinear version, if possible. Then try to identify a specific poetic device that carries out each of the rhetorical functions of wholeness, impact, coherence, cohesion, focus, emphasis, and appeal. (You may need to choose a single device to represent several functions.)

> ¹ The LORD is my shepherd,
>   I shall not want;
> ² he makes me lie down in green pastures.
>   He leads me beside still waters;
> ³ he restores my soul.ᵃ
>   He leads me in paths of righteousnessᵇ for his name's sake.
> ⁴ Even though I walk through the valley of the shadow of death,ᶜ
>   I fear no evil;
> for thou art with me;
>   thy rod and thy staff, they comfort me.
> ⁵ Thou preparest a table before me
>   in the presence of my enemies;
> thou anointest my head with oil,
>   my cup overflows.
> ⁶ Surelyᵈ goodness and mercyᵉ shall follow me all the days of my life;
>   and I shall dwell in the house of the LORD for ever.ᶠ
>
>> a. 23:3 Or *life*
>> b. 23:3 Or *right paths*
>> c. 23:4 Or *the valley of deep darkness*
>> d. 23:6 Or *Only*
>> e. 23:6 Or *kindness*
>> f. 23:6 Or *as long as I live*

3. Now do a more detailed study of Isaiah 5:1–7 (RSV), presented below without any instructive formatting. Dividing it into strophes is your job. Analyze the structure and style of the passage, following the ten steps outlined in section 3.6. Step 7 is especially important because of its focus on the poetic devices. Then, try to specify some of the possible rhetorical functions for the main artistic features you identified.

> ¹ Let me sing for my beloved
>   a love song concerning his vineyard:
> My beloved had a vineyard
>   on a very fertile hill.
> ² He digged it and cleared it of stones,
>   and planted it with choice vines;
> he built a watchtower in the midst of it,
>   and hewed out a wine vat in it;
> and he looked for it to yield grapes,
>   but it yielded wild grapes.
> ³ And now, O inhabitants of Jerusalem
>   and men of Judah,
> judge, I pray you, between me
>   and my vineyard.
> ⁴ What more was there to do for my vineyard,
>   that I have not done in it?
> When I looked for it to yield grapes,
>   why did it yield wild grapes?
> ⁵ And now I will tell you
>   what I will do to my vineyard.
> I will remove its hedge,
>   and it shall be devoured;
> I will break down its wall,
>   and it shall be trampled down.
> ⁶ I will make it a waste;
>   it shall not be pruned or hoed,
>   and briers and thorns shall grow up;
> I will also command the clouds
>   that they rain no rain upon it.
> ⁷ For the vineyard of the LORD of hosts
>   is the house of Israel,
> and the men of Judah
>   are his pleasant planting;
> and he looked for justice,
>   but behold, bloodshed;
> for righteousness, but behold, a cry!

4. Read the case study entitled "Translating Poetry for Oral Presentation" by E. R. Hope in *Hebrew Poetry in the Bible* (cited in Zogbo and Wendland 2000:179–184) in which some of the outstanding features of Hebrew and African poetry are compared. The African devices noted are rhythm and meter, repetition, refrain for audience response, metaphors, juxtaposition of ideas, and condensed style. Now answer the following questions:

   a. How does the African list compare with the features commonly found in the oral genre *love poetry* in YL? Do you need to add some features (e.g., ideophones) to compensate for those that are not present or common in your own poetic tradition?

b. After reading E. R. Hope's case study, evaluate the text of the English poem at the end. How do you like it? Can you suggest any possible improvements?

c. Try translating this poem in YL in a *LiFE*-like manner so as to make an effective oral (or sung) presentation. Then give a literal back-translation of it into English. Point out some of the key poetic devices that you have employed and their rhetorical purpose in the text.

5. Study and then meaningfully reformat the passage below (1 Cor. 15:51–57 from the RSV, followed by the Greek text). Then suggest why this passage has been structured by Paul in such a clearly poetic fashion. What can you do in your translation to give people an indication of how (and why) the text is organized poetically in this fashion? How does the last verse, 15:58, relate to this poetic section?

> 51 Lo! I tell you a mystery. We shall not all sleep, but we shall all be changed, 52 in a moment, in the twinkling of an eye, at the last trumpet. For the trumpet will sound, and the dead will be raised imperishable, and we shall be changed. 53 For this perishable nature must put on the imperishable, and this mortal nature must put on immortality. 54 When the perishable puts on the imperishable, and the mortal puts on immortality, then shall come to pass the saying that is written: "Death is swallowed up in victory." 55 "O death, where is thy victory? O death, where is thy sting?" 56 The sting of death is sin, and the power of sin is the law. 57 But thanks be to God, who gives us the victory through our Lord Jesus Christ.

> 51 ἰδοὺ μυστήριον ὑμῖν λέγω·
>   πάντες οὐ κοιμηθησόμεθα,
>   πάντες δὲ ἀλλαγησόμεθα,
> 52 ἐν ἀτόμῳ,
>   ἐν ῥιπῇ ὀφθαλμοῦ,
>   ἐν τῇ ἐσχάτῃ σάλπιγγι·
>   σαλπίσει γὰρ
>   καὶ οἱ νεκροὶ ἐγερθήσονται ἄφθαρτοι
>   καὶ ἡμεῖς ἀλλαγησόμεθα.
> 53 δεῖ γὰρ τὸ φθαρτὸν τοῦτο ἐνδύσασθαι ἀφθαρσίαν
>   καὶ τὸ θνητὸν τοῦτο ἐνδύσασθαι ἀθανασίαν.
> 54 ὅταν δὲ τὸ φθαρτὸν τοῦτο ἐνδύσηται ἀφθαρσίαν
>   καὶ τὸ θνητὸν τοῦτο ἐνδύσηται ἀθανασίαν,
>   τότε γενήσεται ὁ λόγος ὁ γεγραμμένος,
>   Κατεπόθη ὁ θάνατος εἰς νῖκος.
> 55   ποῦ σου, θάνατε, τὸ νῖκος;
>   ποῦ σου, θάνατε, τὸ κέντρον;
> 56   τὸ δὲ κέντρον τοῦ θανάτου ἡ ἁμαρτία,
>   ἡ δὲ δύναμις τῆς ἁμαρτίας ὁ νόμος·
> 57 τῷ δὲ θεῷ χάρις
>   τῷ διδόντι ἡμῖν τὸ νῖκος
>   διὰ τοῦ κυρίου ἡμῶν Ἰησοῦ Χριστοῦ.

5.3 Genres of poetry found in the Scriptures

Lesson 4 introduced the subject of genres, or conventional types, of literature, which are characterized by sets of different linguistic and literary features, by distinct communication goals, by diverse social settings of use, and consequently also by differing expectations which readers/hearers have about them. It was also noted there that the Bible, as literature, contains a variety of genres and that translators need to recognize them in order to accurately analyze the original text and re-present it with equivalent literary quality, impact, and appeal in the TL.

5.3 Genres of poetry found in the Scriptures

The different genres of literature may be investigated from one of two perspectives: either from an insider's *emic* perspective (language-specific) or from an outsider's *etic* perspective (language in general). Where enough comparative language and sociocultural data exists, the local emic viewpoint is preferable, for that is more specific and precise in terms of characterizing the various genres and subgenres. However, where insider information is lacking, we are forced to adopt the external, more generalized viewpoint and work from there, dependent on the textual context to help us categorize the distinct text types we encounter. This is the situation that we face in the case of the Hebrew Scriptures, and to a much lesser degree also in Greek. The NT literature is problematic not because of a lack of comparative data in Greek, but simply because the biblical writers did not slavishly follow Greek literary forms, but often adopted a mixed, or eclectic, writing style, combining certain Hellenistic features with those of their Semitic roots.

Here in lesson 5 we are concentrating on the different genres of poetry and will be dealing mainly with the Hebrew text. The following is a list of some of the designated emic poetic varieties. Look up each of the Scripture references cited (often psalm titles) and see if you can propose a definition of the specific genre that it illustrates, based on the form and content of the text itself, coupled with information derived from the surrounding cotext (the textual context):

- *shiyr* (Isa. 5:1; Ps. 30:1) _____
- *mizmôwr* (Ps. 23:1; 82:1) _____
- *maskiyl* (Ps. 32:1; 42:1) _____
- *miktâm* (Ps. 16:1; 60:1) _____
- *shiggâyôwn* (Ps. 7:1) _____
- *qiynâh* (Jer. 9:9; Ezek. 32:2) _____
- *massa'* (Nah. 1:1; Hab. 1:1) _____
- *ne'um* (Hos. 2:13; Amos 3:15) _____
- *chiydâh* (Judg. 14:14; Num. 12:8) _____
- *birâkâh* (Gen. 49:28; Exod. 32:29) _____
- *qilâlâh* (Deut. 23:5; Judg. 9:57) _____
- *mi'êrâh* (Prov. 3:33; Mal. 3:9) _____
- *muwsâr* (Ps. 50:17; Prov. 1:3) _____

Bible scholars today face considerable difficulties in the attempt to classify these Hebrew genres when they encounter texts such as Psalm 85:1 and Psalm 86:1 (the two psalm titles) or Jeremiah 9:19b, Micah 2:4, or Ezekiel 17:2.

» What problem do you notice in these passages with reference to the genre designations that are used?

» A similar problem appears in the heading of Psalm 88. What is the difficulty there?

Now take the example of mâshâl: What kind of literary form does this genre designation refer to in the following passages?

   a. 1 Samuel 10:12 _____

   b. Psalm 69:11 _____

   c. Numbers 23:7–10 _____

   d. Isaiah 14:4–21 _____

   e. Ezekiel 17:2–10 _____

   f. Numbers 21:27–30 _____

   g. Psalm 78:2 _____

   h. Proverbs 10:1 _____

The Greek *parabolê* corresponds partially to the Hebrew *mâshâl*: Examples of the genre designation parabolê appear in Mark 4:30; Luke 6:39, 13:6; and Hebrews 9:9, 11:19.

» What sort of diversity do you notice among these passages, even though the term *parabolê* is used in all them?

As you worked through the examples of the Hebrew genres given above, you perhaps came to the conclusion that it is not very satisfactory to use the Hebrew terms in the search for translation equivalents in the TL. This is not the fault of the original writers; it is a simple fact resulting from our relative ignorance of the initial communicative setting. The diversity of terminology does indicate that the Jewish people took their literature/orature seriously and were very creative in this respect. However, we are too far removed today from the original language and settings in which these terms were used to be able to understand them very well. For that reason we must depend on some sort of external, general system of classification in order to analyze the many potentially different poetic (and prose) genres that we find in the Scriptures, from beginning to end.

Four principal etic types (macrogenres) of biblical poetry may be proposed, although these often appear in mixed form or closely combined within a given text. They are as follows (compare this with the diagram given at the end of section 4.4):

   1. **Lyric** – for panegyric, liturgical, expressive, and evocative proclamation (e.g., Psalms).

   2. **Didactic** – for conveying moral instruction and religious information (e.g., Proverbs).

   3. **Hortatory** – for pastoral reproof, criticism, consolation, and encouragement (e.g., Amos).

   4. **Predictive** – for dramatic visions or oracles revealing future events +/– explicit warning for the wicked or comfort for the faithful (e.g., Ezek. 38–39).

   » Examine the following passages from Hosea. Which of the four etic types does each one most closely resemble? Then find another passage of the same type and give its reference:

   a. 7:1–10 = _____   _____

   b. 11:8–9 = _____   _____

c. 14:4–7 = _____   _____

   d. 14:8–9 = _____   _____

> » Is it possible to convey these four poetic text types—along with some of their associated stylistic features and essential functional and contextual implications—by means of similar genres in the language of your translation?
>
> » If so, describe some of the categories that you would use. If not, how great would the loss be in terms of meaning equivalence, and how might this deficit of overall message significance be at least partially replaced or compensated for?
>
> » Do you have any literary forms that perform a similar communicative and rhetorical function in analogous social or religious settings even though they are different?

Literary analysts normally subdivide the preceding four general classes of poetry according to form and/or function. One subcategory, for example, is *epic*, in which segments of narrative are included; another is *drama*, in which segments of dialogue are included. We do not have to be concerned about all the details of classification at this stage; however, it would be helpful to be able to discern some of the basic structural categories and stylistic devices that are found in the three major types of OT poetry: lyric, hortatory, and didactic. These three kinds of poetic composition may be distinguished on the basis of content (especially characteristic vocabulary, e.g., liturgical, judicial, and sapiential) and also on the basis of purpose. The chart below presents nine purpose-oriented subtypes:

Examples:	Psalms Song of Songs	Job Joel Nahum Hosea Habakkuk Isaiah Ezekiel	Proverbs Ecclesiastes
	LYRIC ←================	**HORTATORY** ================→	**DIDACTIC**
Functions:	lament	warning	instruction
	appeal	reproof	admonition
	praise	blessing	encouragement

It is rather difficult at times to differentiate lyric, hortatory, and didactic on a strictly structural or stylistic basis, except to note that lyric verse tends to manifest regular parallelism and associated poetic features the most consistently, whereas hortatory and didactic verse periodically introduce sections of a more prosaic, even (semi-)narrative, nature (e.g., a personal account within a text that manifests a higher percentage of the prose particles and looser kinds of parallel construction, as in Ecclesiastes). There are of course exceptions to these general observations; Proverbs, for example, manifests a very tight type of binary parallelism, but the coupled bicola are not often linked together as clearly into larger strophic units.

We will examine each of the categories of lyric, hortatory, and didactic more closely in sections 5.3.1–5.3.3.

For reflection, research, and response:

1. Find a verse or passage that exemplifies each of the poetic functions in the preceding chart. Write out each of the nine examples that you have selected. Discuss these examples in class.

2. Translate the nine passages that you chose in the previous exercise into YL using the *LiFE* method. Then point out the most prominent TL artistic or rhetorical feature that you incorporated into your rendering of each text.

5.3.1 Poetry of the psalmists

In the Psalms we may distinguish five etic classes of lyric poetry based on their predominant function and manner of expression, including characteristic topically related vocabulary: *petition, thanksgiving, praise, instruction,* and *profession*. These functional types are often combined in various ways within a single text, which may be further differentiated into *individual* ("I") and *communal* ("we") psalms. Descriptions and examples of the five classes follow (quotations are from the NRSV):

1. **Petition** (lament) – appealing to God for help in a time of danger, testing, or need

   > Rescue me, O my God, from the hand of the wicked,
   > from the grasp of the unjust and cruel. (Ps. 71:4; see also Ps. 70)

2. **Thanksgiving** (eulogy) – thanking God for assistance or deliverance received during some past situation of deprivation, illness, trial, or threat.

   > He delivered me from my strong enemy,
   > and from those who hated me;
   > for they were too mighty for me. (Ps. 18:17; see also Ps. 30)

3. **Praise** (hymn) – praising the person, character, and behavior of God in terms of his greatness, goodness, and glory.

   > Praise the LORD!
   > How good it is to sing praises to our God;
   > for he is gracious… (Ps. 147:1; see also Ps. 100)

4. **Instruction** (homily) – teaching how to live a "God-fearing" life pleasing to the Lord in thought, word, and deed, often in contrast to the wicked.

   > Fools say in their hearts, "There is no God."
   > They are corrupt, they commit abominable acts;
   > there is no one who does good. (Ps. 53:1; see also Ps. 1)

5. **Profession** (creed) – expressing the psalmist's complete trust in and dependence upon God as the unfailing provider and protector of his life and entire being.

   > God is our refuge and strength,
   > a very present help in trouble.
   > Therefore we will not fear… (Ps. 46:1–2a; see also Psalm 23)

We see in the text of Psalm 54 below how these different goals of religious communication may be combined to form a coherent and unified lyric poem:

> ¹ Save me, O God, by thy name,... PETITION
>   and vindicate me by thy might.
> ² Hear my prayer, O God;
>   give ear to the words of my mouth.
>
> ³ For insolent men have risen against me,..[PROBLEM]
>   ruthless men seek my life;
>   they do not set God before them.
> ⁴ Behold, God is my helper;..PROFESSION
>   the Lord is the upholder of my life.
>
> ⁵ He will requite my enemies with evil;
>   in thy faithfulness put an end to them.

5.3 Genres of poetry found in the Scriptures

> ⁶ With a freewill offering I will sacrifice to thee; ....THANKSGIVING
>   I will give thanks to thy name, O Lord, for it is good.
>
> ⁷ For thou hast delivered me from every trouble,......................................PRAISE
>   and my eye has looked in triumph on my enemies.

Notice that an element designated the "problem" ("complaint") simply states the basis for the petition (the cause for thanksgiving in cases where the psalmist's appeal has been answered). Psalm 54 may be classified somewhat differently depending on whether the final word of praise for deliverance is viewed as being past, already accomplished (in which case it would be a psalm of thanksgiving), or whether it is being anticipated or hoped for (in which case it would be a psalm of petition).

The aim of a literary approach is not to discover the single "right answer" in terms of a formal classification of the text at hand. Rather, it is to encourage translators to think more precisely in terms of form and function, both as they analyze the biblical text and also while they are rendering the passage in their languages. The psalms are certainly not nearly as similar in nature as many people think. There are many shades of compositional diversity, some hues obviously disparate and others less so. These differences in style and content may well have been associated with corresponding differences in the original interpersonal context, psychological mood, and communicative purpose. We cannot of course determine for sure what these situational influences may have been; our job is simply to re-create the text in a dynamic, yet appropriate manner so that it may serve in analogous religious settings and personal circumstances today. This means that both the semantic as well as the pragmatic significance of the psalm needs to be conveyed effectively in the TL, whether via an available genre of poetry or some other form of poetically heightened discourse. The goal is to ensure that the translated text carries a level of impact and appeal, of rhetorical power and verbal beauty, which matches its emotively charged religious message.

Having recognized the five broad communicative classes of psalms, translators may consider several subcategories. For example, there are individual passages as well as larger strophes that may be labeled as exhibiting the subsidiary topical-functional notions of *repentance* (penitential), *remembrance* (historical), *retribution* (imprecatory), *royal* (panegyric), and *liturgy* (ritual). The following verses (quoted from the NRSV) illustrate these five subtypes. See if you can distinguish one from the other.

> Our ancestors, when they were in Egypt,
>   did not consider your wonderful works;
>   they did not remember the abundance of your steadfast love,
>   but rebelled against the Most High at the Red Sea. (Ps. 106:7)

> Let them be put to shame and dismayed forever;
>   let them perish in disgrace. (Ps. 83:17)

> It is he who remembered us in our low estate,
>   for his steadfast love endures forever;
>   and rescued us from our foes,
>   for his steadfast love endures forever;
>   who gives food to all flesh,
>   for his steadfast love endures forever. (Ps. 136:23–25)

> Against you, you alone, have I sinned, and done evil in your sight,
>   so that you are justified in your sentence and blameless when you pass judgment. (Ps. 51:4)

> Then he will speak to them in his wrath,
>   and terrify them in his fury, saying,
>   "I have set my king on Zion, my holy hill." (Ps. 2:5–6)

The five examples above illustrate the subtypes of remembrance, retribution, liturgical, repentance, and royal, in that order.

> » If you do not agree, present your own classification and rationale in a class discussion.

Surely it is possible, if translators have the necessary poetic competence and personal commitment, to convey the varied moods, emotions, attitudes, and overtones associated with these lyrical psalms in languages other than Hebrew. But those commissioned with this challenging literary and theological assignment first need to recognize what is actually present in the SL text in terms of overall semantic and pragmatic significance. They must also be aware of the full store of poetic resources available to them in their mother tongue. For example, are there any TL genres that match the Hebrew in terms of general communicative function? Are there specific literary/oratorical devices available in the TL to distinguish vernacular texts that are commemorative (historical), retributive, liturgical, penitential, or royal in nature and purpose? Clearly, a great deal of research may be necessary in order to uncover such artistic features, if present, or to discover suitable literary functional equivalents. (For more on the subject of TL research, see section 7.2 and also section 4.5.)

Now we will look at another poetic praise text in the Old Testament. This one, the Song of Songs, is quite different in style, topic, and tone from the Psalter. The interpretation of this book can be rather complicated, depending on the levels of symbolism that one sees in the text, but there is no controversy over the nature of its poetry—composed as it is, almost completely of pure love lyrics.[6] While it is usually not too difficult to find an equivalent genre in most target languages, the imagery may be quite a challenge to re-present, for the Song of Songs is a text which, in addition to its alternating speakers throughout, is characterized by vivid, rapidly changing images and diverse figures of speech, especially similes.

The Song of Songs also features a great deal of lexical recursion, which gives considerable cohesion and unity to the whole and serves as a structural device as well, most notably through the repeated refrains, including several formulaic expressions that function as sectional boundary markers.

> » There are seven demarcating refrains in the Song of Songs. See if you can specify what these are by comparing the two references given at the beginning of each blank line below. Which topics or key words do the two cited passages have in common?

(2:6, 8:3) _____

(2:9, 8:14) _____

(3:5, 8:4) _____

(1:5, 3:5) _____

(2:16, 6:3) _____

(4:16, 6:2) _____

(3:6, 8:5) _____

> » Now examine 2:6–9 and write down all the refrains identified above that you find in this passage:

---

[6]Some scholars and commentators see an underlying analogy here that likens the loving, faithful, completely-devoted relationship between a God-fearing husband and wife to the relationship between the Lord and his reverent people. Be that as it may, the point is to render the powerful language, imagery, and feelings of the Song of Songs in a manner that adequately reflects the lyric diversity and emotive intensity of the original surface text.

5.3 Genres of poetry found in the Scriptures

» The convergence of these refrains indicates a strong boundary somewhere in this section. Between which two verses does this break occur? Why do you think so?

There is a great deal of descriptive imagery in the Song of Songs. Two representative passages are presented below, 5:10–16 and 6:4–9 (NIV).

> ^{5:10} My lover is radiant and ruddy,
>   outstanding among ten thousand.
> ¹¹ His head is purest gold;
>   his hair is wavy and black as a **raven**.
> ¹² His eyes are like **doves**
>   by the water streams,
> washed in **milk**,
>   mounted like jewels.
> ¹³ His cheeks are like beds of **spice**
>   yielding perfume.
> His lips are like **lilies**
>   dripping with **myrrh**.
> ¹⁴ His arms are rods of gold
>   set with chrysolite.
> His body is like polished **ivory**
>   decorated with **sapphires**.
> ¹⁵ His legs are pillars of **marble**
>   set on bases of pure gold.
> His appearance is like Lebanon,
>   choice as its **cedars**.
> ¹⁶ His mouth is sweetness itself;
>   he is altogether lovely. (Song 5:10-16)
>
> ^{6:4} You are beautiful, my darling, as **Tirzah**,
>   lovely as Jerusalem,
>   majestic as **troops** with banners.
> ⁵ Turn your eyes from me;
>   they overwhelm me.
> Your hair is like a **flock of goats**
>   descending from Gilead.
> ⁶ Your teeth are like a **flock of sheep**
>   coming up from the washing.
> Each has its twin,
>   not one of them is alone.
> ⁷ Your temples behind your veil
>   are like the halves of a **pomegranate**.
> ⁸ Sixty queens there may be,
>   and eighty concubines,
>   and virgins beyond number;
> ⁹ but my dove, my perfect one, is unique,
>   the only daughter of her mother,
>   the **favorite** of the one who bore her.

> The maidens saw her and called her blessed;
>> the queens and concubines praised her. (Song 6:4-9)

- » Would such imagery designating adult males and females convey the same overall effect if rendered literally in your language?

- » If not, what sort of adjustments would need to be made in order to recreate the same impact and appeal? (Consider the boldfaced similes and metaphors in particular.)

- » Note the type of parallelism manifested in these passages. Of what kind is it (see section 5.1.1)?

- » Compare chapters 5–6 of the Song of Songs in the NIV, NRSV, GNT, REB, and NJB. Do they identify the different speakers in the text? What differences do you observe? Can you posit a reason for these differences?

- » Do "speaker titles" help to reveal the discourse structure and interpersonal dynamics of each text, or not? Explain your answer.

- » Do you have a song genre that uses alternating singers in your tradition of verbal art forms? Could this genre be used to translate the Song of Songs with greater formal and functional equivalence? Explain. If this would be possible, give an example from chapters 5–6.

- » Do you use the device of identifying different speakers in the book of Job? If not, give your reasons.

There are also some brief semi-narrative snatches in the Song of Songs such as 3:1–4 (NIV), which is reformatted here to read like a personal stream-of-consciousness account:

> All night long on my bed I looked for the one my heart loves. I looked for him but did not find him. I will get up now and go about the city, through its streets and squares. I will search for the one my heart loves. So I looked for him but did not find him.
>
> The watchmen found me as they made their rounds in the city.
>
> "Have you seen the one my heart loves?"
>
> Scarcely had I passed them when I found the one my heart loves. I held him and would not let him go till I had brought him to my mother's house, to the room of the one who conceived me.

- » Is this text prose or poetry? On what do you base your answer? What poetic features are in these verses?

- » Notice how the passage has been formatted in the NIV (and most other English translations). Do you agree with the NIV's arrangement of the text, or do you think that it would be more accurate to format it like a narrative? Explain your answer.

The Song of Songs is found in the Wisdom literature section of the Old Testament in our modern Bibles, and indeed it is regarded as such by many scholars. This is based on correspondences that seem to exist between its descriptive and semi-narrative passages and similar texts in the book of Proverbs (e.g., 5:15–20, 6:24–29, and 7:6–23). Also important is the wisdom text that appears as the book's climax in 8:6–7. Some would say that the book as a whole seeks to present a biblical perspective on sexual morality. Other scholars would class the Song of Songs along with the Psalms despite their clear differences.

- » What do the Song of Songs and Psalms have in common?

5.3 Genres of poetry found in the Scriptures

» How would you classify Song of Songs according to the literary standards and conventions of YL?

» Does that classification affect the way in which you must translate this book? Explain.

It may be noted at this point that the Hebrew Bible is traditionally divided into three categories:

1. **Torah**: Genesis, Exodus, Leviticus, Numbers, Deuteronomy

2. **Prophets**:

    The Former Prophets: Joshua, Judges, Samuel, Kings

    The Latter Prophets: Isaiah, Jeremiah, Ezekiel; Hosea, Joel, Amos, Obadiah, Jonah, Micah, Nahum, Habakkuk, Zephaniah, Haggai, Zechariah, Malachi

3. **Writings**: Psalms, Proverbs, Job, Song of Songs, Ruth, Lamentations, Ecclesiastes, Esther, Daniel, Ezra-Nehemiah, Chronicles

» Is there any reason for the books of your OT translation to be ordered according to the sequence of the Jewish Bible? What would be the best reason for not doing this?

» In what sense are the books of Joshua, Judges, Samuel, and Kings "prophetic" in nature?

» How does this Hebrew sequence help explain the deeper significance of Christ's words in Luke 24:44 (which is a metonym)?

» Into which major groupings are the OT books of your translation arranged? What is the basis for this division?

» Does your translation include an introduction explaining the major sections? If not, explain why this is not necessary or, alternatively, why it would be helpful for many readers.

For reflection, research, and response:

1. Find an additional example from the Psalms to illustrate each of the five main functions of petition, thanksgiving, praise, confession, and instruction. Write down the references along with the function exemplified by each.

2. Now find one passage from the Psalms to illustrate each of the five minor functional subcategories: repentance, remembrance, retribution, royal, and liturgical poetry.

3. Identify the functional category of each verse of Psalm 3 (quoted below from the NIV) using the major and/or minor functions mentioned in exercises 1 and 2. If you have difficulty classifying any verses or individual lines, write a suggestion on the blank line as to how you would classify it in functional terms.

> ¹ O Lord, how many are my foes!
> How many rise up against me!   _____
> ² Many are saying of me,
> "God will not deliver him."   _____
> ³ But you are a shield around me, O Lord;
> you bestow glory on me and lift up my head   _____
> ⁴ To the Lord I cry aloud,
> and he answers me from his holy hill   _____

⁵ I lie down and sleep;
I wake again, because the Lord sustains me
⁶ I will not fear the tens of thousands
drawn up against me on every side
⁷ Arise, O Lord!
Deliver me, O my God!
Strike all my enemies on the jaw;
break the teeth of the wicked
⁸ From the Lord comes deliverance.
May your blessing be on your people

5.3.2 Poetry of the prophets

The poetry of the prophets differs from the lyric poetry of the Psalms with respect to stylistic form, semantic content, and communicative function. The passage given below is a good example of these differences.

» Point out some of the ways in which the style of this text differs from Psalm 78:64–72.

» Can you guess the biblical book from which the following text is taken?

¹³ When Ephraim saw his sickness,
    and Judah his sores,
then Ephraim turned to Assyria,
    and sent to the great king for help.
But he is not able to cure you,
    not able to heal your sores.
¹⁴ For I will be like a lion to Ephraim,
    like a great lion to Judah.
I will tear them to pieces and go away;
    I will carry them off, with no one to rescue them.
¹⁵ Then I will go back to my place
    until they admit their guilt.
And they will seek my face;
    in their misery they will earnestly seek me.

The preceding text is Hosea 5:13–15 (NIV).

» What are some of the stylistic markers that distinguish it as a separate unit of poetic discourse (a strophe) within chapter 5?

» Study this passage in light of its textual cotext. Review the ten steps of discourse analysis in section 3.6 and point out the clear signals of aperture and closure that demarcate this as a distinct unit.

Hebrew poetic features such as lined parallelism, figurative language, and graphic imagery can be seen in Hosea 5:13–15 as we hear Yahweh through the mouth of the prophet Hosea reflect upon the sinfulness of his people Israel (*indictment*), then threaten, indeed forcefully promise, to punish them for their persistent wickedness (*judgment*). But in conclusion we learn of an unexpected reversal: the sinners repent and God relents ("goes back to his place"). This is a functional discourse pattern that is repeated throughout the prophetic literature, both within the scope of a single chapter and also as part of the compositional plan of an entire book (see Hosea 14). Note that v. 15 above functions as the *hortatory thesis* of this strophe as well as the whole of chapter 5, while all the rest is supportive material, consisting of various rebukes, warnings, and condemnation for the people's wickedness (see section 4.2, exercise 5).

5.3 Genres of poetry found in the Scriptures

We notice some other stylistic variations as well. One major difference is that, as primarily divine proclamation (God to people), prophetic discourse tends to be more aggressively imperative or prescriptive and less petitionary or penitential (people to God), which is characteristic of the psalmic genres. In the prophetic books, YHWH speaks with very strong feelings and desires both to and about his people. There are exceptions, of course: In the passage that follows Hosea 5:13–15 (6:1–3), Israel's hypocritical (cf. 6:4ff.) prayer of repentance is recorded as part of the prophetic message. But while the prophets may be just as expressive or affective in places as the psalmists, the emotions and attitudes involved are somewhat different. They reflect their respective roles and the general subject matter of their discourses—the prophets, as covenant-mediators, being more judicial and hortatory, the psalmists more liturgical and supplicatory in nature. Hosea certainly provides us with an intimate anthropomorphic glimpse of the inner "feelings" of God (as in chapter 11).

As can be seen in the short text above from Hosea 5:13–15, the prophetic preachers are greatly concerned with individual as well as corporate issues of sin and judgment, or repentance and forgiveness, along with their inevitable contrasting outcomes, whether denunciation or deliverance. The message of the various prophets is normally highly contextualized; in other words, God's communication is very closely tied to the history and immediate life-setting of his chosen people, Israel—past, present, and future. The psalms, on the other hand, are more often timeless in reference, though they do of course reflect a certain historical, cultural, religious, and often even a highly personal setting. Furthermore, in the predictive passages of prophecy, there is usually a definite (albeit indeterminate) future referential aspect (whether national, messianic, or eschatological), which is not often found in the poetry of prayer, praise, and worship.

Prophetic poetry is also distinguished by its stylistic forms from the lyric poetry of the Psalms. Its distinctive features include the following: less strict parallelisms; longer and less regular poetic lines (cola); occasional prosaic insertions; a predominance of cause-effect relations; scatological and other types of shocking imagery; and the prevalence of criticism, rebuke, accusation, and warning.

Another notable feature of prophetic poetry is its explicit and emphatic marking of words spoken directly by God (see section 5.1.5). An *oracular formula* typically announces the onset of a new speech or thematic/pragmatic segment; less frequently a conventional prophetic phrase announces the close of such a unit. Even a medial passage of special importance may be similarly distinguished. Among these signals are familiar expressions such as "Hear the word of the Lord" (Isa. 10:1); "Go and say to…" (Isa. 7:3–4); "Thus says the Lord" (Isa. 44:6); "The word of the Lord that came to…" (Mic. 1:1); "This is what the Lord God showed me" (Amos 7:1); "On that day" (Hos. 2:16); " then you/they will know that…" (Ezek. 33:33); and "says the Lord God" (Amos 4:8). Such so-called *messenger speech* was a constant reminder to the audience that the prophets were spokesmen for God, not independent creators of the words of their oracles. Appropriate formulaic, discourse-marking equivalents in the TL must be discovered, or carefully created, and then appropriately placed in the translated text at positions that signal the beginning, ending, or peak point of a prophetic discourse segment, whether major or minor in its scope or prominence.

The various levels, or degrees, of *quotative embedding* that often occur with prophetic formulae also need to be formally marked in an appropriate, unambiguous manner. An example of a passage where such marking is needed is at the beginning of the book of Zechariah in 1:1–6 (NRSV), which is reformatted below to show the various levels of discourse embedding:

> ¹ In the eighth month, in the second year of Darius, the word of the Lord came to the prophet Zechariah son of Berechiah son of Iddo, saying:
>
>> ² The Lord was very angry with your ancestors. ³ Therefore say to them,
>>> Thus says the Lord of hosts: Return to me, says the Lord of hosts, and I will return to you, says the Lord of hosts. 4 Do not be like your ancestors, to whom the former prophets proclaimed,
>>>> "Thus says the Lord of hosts, Return from your evil ways and from your evil deeds."

> But they did not hear or heed me, says the Lord. ⁵ Your ancestors, where are they? And the prophets, do they live forever? ⁶ But my words and my statutes, which I commanded my servants the prophets, did they not overtake your ancestors? So they repented and said, "The Lord of hosts has dealt with us according to our ways and deeds, just as he planned to do."

» How many levels of speech embedding do you see in the preceding text? Compare this with the same selection from the GNT:

> ¹ In the eighth month of the second year that Darius was emperor of Persia, the Lord gave this message to the prophet Zechariah, the son of Berechiah and grandson of Iddo. ² The Lord Almighty told Zechariah to say to the people,
>> "I, the Lord, was very angry with your ancestors, ³ but now I say to you,
>>> 'Return to me, and I will return to you. ⁴ Do not be like your ancestors. Long ago the prophets gave them my message, telling them not to live evil, sinful lives any longer. But they would not listen to me or obey me. ⁵ Your ancestors and those prophets are no longer alive. ⁶ Through my servants the prophets I gave your ancestors commands and warnings, but they disregarded them and suffered the consequences. Then they repented and acknowledged that I, the Lord Almighty, had punished them as they deserved and as I had determined to do.'"

» How many levels of embedding are shown here? What has the GNT done to reduce the number? Which text is easier to read and understand? Is there some loss of emphasis in the GNT text? If so, where does this occur?

» Which format would work most effectively in YL? Or do you have another option? If so, what would it be, and why?

» Does the use of indentation help to show the levels of quotation?

» How about the use of quotation marks—single or double? Do most people perceive and understand the significance of these?

» Is there anything else that might be done to make passages like this more readable and/or hearable in YL?

Another major diagnostic of prophetic discourse is the divine *pronouncement speech*. It should be carefully distinguished in any translation. Typically, it falls into a two-part pattern. (The order of the two parts may fluctuate, as we will see.) First, there is a *declaration* from Yahweh, one that threatens a just punishment upon his people or the pagan "nations" for their wickedness or else promises deliverance and blessing for those who remain true to his covenantal principles (good deeds are usually not specified). Second, a corresponding *reason*, or set of reasons, normally supports this divine declaration. The wicked are condemned for their evil actions against God and man. The righteous, on the other hand, may be commended for their loyalty or encouraged to remain faithful to Yahweh, although they are more often simply promised blessings on the basis of their relationship with a merciful God.

The order of these two discourse functions, divine *decree* and judicial *rationale,* may vary from one text to another. Either one may appear first, and they also may alternate back and forth contrastively within the same oracle. An example of this is in Isaiah 30:12–22 (quoted below from the NIV, except for the format), which combines declarations of judgment with promises of deliverance:

¹² Therefore, this is what the Holy One of Israel says:	[FORMULA]
"Because you have rejected this message,	[REASON]
relied on oppression and depended on deceit,	
¹³ this sin will become for you	[PREDICTION OF JUDGMENT]
like a high wall, cracked and bulging,	
that collapses suddenly, in an instant.	
¹⁴ It will break in pieces like pottery, shattered so mercilessly	
that among its pieces not a fragment will be found	
for taking coals from a hearth or scooping water out of a cistern."	
¹⁵ This is what the Sovereign Lord, the Holy One of Israel, says:	[FORMULA]
"In repentance and rest is your salvation,	[CONTRAST]
in quietness and trust is your strength,	
but you would have none of it.	
¹⁶ You said, 'No, we will flee on horses.'	[REASON]
Therefore you will flee!	
You said, 'We will ride off on swift horses.'	
Therefore your pursuers will be swift!	[PREDICTION OF JUDGMENT]
¹⁷ A thousand will flee at the threat of one;	
at the threat of five you will all flee away,	
till you are left like a flagstaff on a mountaintop,	
like a banner on a hill."	
¹⁸ Yet the Lord longs to be gracious to you;	[CONTRAST]
he rises to show you compassion.	[DIVINE ATTRIBUTION]
For the Lord is a God of justice.	[REASON]
Blessed are all who wait for him!	
¹⁹ O people of Zion, who live in Jerusalem,	[PROMISE OF BLESSING]
you will weep no more.	
How gracious he will be when you cry for help!	[DIVINE CHARACTER]]
As soon as he hears, he will answer you.	
²⁰ Although the Lord gives you the bread of adversity	[CONTRAST]
and the water of affliction,	
your teachers will be hidden no more;	[PROMISE OF BLESSING]
with your own eyes you will see them.	
²¹ Whether you turn to the right or to the left,	
your ears will hear a voice behind you, saying,	
"This is the way; walk in it."	
²² Then you will defile your idols overlaid with silver	[PROMISE OF REGENERATION]
and your images covered with gold;	
you will throw them away like a menstrual cloth	
and say to them, "Away with you!"	

Note that in verses 15, 18, and 19 Yahweh, speaking through his prophet, inserts a significant point of *contrast* that constitutes an implicit call to repentance, such as is stated explicitly in Isa. 55:6-7 ("Seek the LORD....Let the wicked forsake his way..."). This then constitutes the text's *hortatory thesis* (i.e., "Repent, return to the LORD!"), while the rest of the discourse is *supportive material*, both warnings (e.g., v. 14) and predictions (e.g., v. 22). Note too that verses 19–22, which are formatted as prose in the NIV, are reformatted above as poetry.

» Read through these lines carefully again and see if you agree that this is poetry. Give reasons for your opinion.

A more elaborate type of prophetic discourse is the *lawsuit pattern*, in which God accuses his people of various violations of the Mosaic Covenant and predicts that stipulated punishments will befall them. Hope of a reprieve may or may not be extended should they turn and repent. This formal sort of speech reflects both judicial proceedings and international treaty agreements. Most of the following five elements are included at some point or another in a divine lawsuit. After each component below, write the verse numbers of a passage from Isaiah 1 that illustrates it:

1. **Introduction**, in which Yahweh calls the audience to pay attention and also calls "heaven and earth" to act as witnesses to the truth of his indictment.   Isaiah 1:_____

2. **Indictment**, presenting in detail God's case against his people (with or without a specification of a particular group and the evidence against them).   Isaiah 1:_____

3. **Elaboration**, contrastively showing that the people have acted unfaithfully despite God's many attested acts of provision, protection, and deliverance on their behalf.   Isaiah 1:_____

4. **Rebuke**, disparaging idolatry and highlighting the futility of worshiping false gods and/or the total inability of these "gods" to help the people.   Isaiah 1:_____

5. **Warning** of punishment due to violations of the Sinaitic Covenant, at times including an explicit summons to repent and be forgiven (and prevent the disaster to come).   Isaiah 1:_____

This warning of punishment may in fact specify various problems and difficulties that the people were already experiencing. The divine "plagues" normally pattern after the "covenantal curses" specified by Yahweh for persistent acts of disobedience on the part of his people. A good example of this is in Haggai 1.

» Note the various chastisements that the people were suffering and list cross-references to the verses where these have been predicted in Leviticus and Deuteronomy.

» What provoked God to levy such afflictions?

» What could the people do to stop them?

» What happened when they did obey the words of Yahweh through his prophet Haggai?

You should now be able to outline the literary structure of Haggai 1. Note the different types of prophetic discourse that this passage incorporates. Point out the chapter's key verse (peak) and explain how it is distinguished in the text. Also, explain how you would highlight this same verse in a poetic manner in YL.

Sometimes the divine decree, especially a promise of salvation, arises from Yahweh's desire to defend his honor and glory, either in the eyes of his chosen people or of the Gentile "nations" in general. This is illustrated in Isaiah 41:17–21 (quoted below from the NIV), which seems to stem from an implicit lament on the part of the downtrodden in society:

¹⁷ "The poor and needy search for water,
    but there is none;
    their tongues are parched with thirst.
	[LAMENT]

But I the Lord will answer them; I, the God of Israel, will not forsake them.	[REASSURANCE]

> ¹⁸ I will make rivers flow on barren heights,   [PROMISE OF FUTURE
>   and springs within the valleys.   TRANSFORMATION]
>   I will turn the desert into pools of water,
>   and the parched ground into springs.
> ¹⁹ I will put in the desert
>   the cedar and the acacia, the myrtle and the olive.
>   I will set pines in the wasteland,
>   the fir and the cypress together,
> ²⁰ so that people may see and know,   [REASON]
>   may consider and understand,
>   that the hand of the Lord has done this, [CLIMAX]
>   that the Holy One of Israel has created it.

» Do you agree that there is a climax right at the end of this poetic structure?

» Study the passage in its cotext and propose some literary reasons for your opinion, whether for or against this interpretation.

» Wherever you feel the climax belongs, what stylistic devices will you use to mark it in YL?

Another prophetic discourse type that occurs from time to time is the *disputation*. A disputation generally consists of the three basic elements shown below, the first two of which may alternate back and forth to set up the third.

T. **Thesis** – the theological position or moral principle that a prophet, speaking for Yahweh, advocates or defends.

A. **Antithesis** – an overt or implicit expression of a counter-thesis or a reference to contrary ethical behavior manifested by the people.

J. **Judgment** – an extended argument for Yahweh's perspective, which may be coupled with the appropriate motivation; namely, promises of blessing for obedience or bane for continued disobedience.

The book of Malachi manifests a recurrent cycle of this sort of tripartite judicial structure. An example is in 1:2–5:

² "I have loved you," says the Lord.	T	
"But you ask, 'How have you loved us?'	A	
"Was not Esau Jacob's brother?" the Lord says	J	a contrastive case study
"Yet I have loved Jacob, ³ but Esau I have hated,		
and I have turned his mountains into a wasteland		prophetic assertion (1)
and left his inheritance to the desert jackals."		
⁴ Edom may say, "Though we have been crushed,		analogy (a defiant attitude)
we will rebuild the ruins."		
But this is what the Lord Almighty says:		prophetic formula
"They may build, but I will demolish.		divine judgment (prediction)
They will be called the Wicked Land,		an implicit warning to the impious
a people always under the wrath of the Lord.		
⁵ You will see it with your own eyes and say,		prophetic prediction (2)
'Great is the Lord—		contrastive appeal to faith
even beyond the borders of Israel!'"		potential blessing

Compare the printed format above with the format found in the NIV, which displays this passage as well as the rest of Malachi as pure prose.

> » Is the NIV format acceptable, or is there some advantage to setting the text out as poetic prose? Give reasons for your opinion.

> » Evaluate the view that this passage is more poetic than prosaic, as suggested by the format above. Would a poetic manner of speaking be used to express such an argument in YL? If not, what would be a suitable style of discourse to use?

Whatever your conclusion in this particular case, it is essential that translators pay special attention to the SL text types so that both the rhetorical impact and the pragmatic (life-related) implications of the message may be clearly and naturally reproduced in any TL translation. If this is not attended to, at least some measure of skewing will result for many readers, and through a less than accurate enunciation of the biblical text, even more hearers will be adversely affected as well.

Still another important type of prophetic discourse is *apocalyptic speech*. In Daniel 8:3–12a we find a typical example (below). See if you can find here all eight of the features of apocalyptic poetry that are listed below the following text (quoted from the NIV, but reformatted as poetry):

> [3] I raised my eyes and saw, and behold,
> a ram standing on the bank of the river.
> It had two horns; and both horns were high,
> but one was higher than the other,
> and the higher one came up last.
> [4] I saw the ram charging westward and northward and southward;
> no beast could stand before him,
> and there was no one who could rescue from his power;
> he did as he pleased and magnified himself.
>
> [5] As I was considering, behold,
> a he-goat came from the west
> across the face of the whole earth,
> without touching the ground;
> and the goat had a conspicuous horn between his eyes.
> [6] He came to the ram with the two horns,
> which I had seen standing on the bank of the river,
> and he ran at him in his mighty wrath.
> [7] I saw him come close to the ram,
> and he was enraged against him
> and struck the ram and broke his two horns;
> and the ram had no power to stand before him,
> but he cast him down to the ground
> and trampled upon him;
> and there was no one who could rescue the ram from his power.
>
> [8] Then the he-goat magnified himself exceedingly;
> but when he was strong, the great horn was broken,
> and instead of it there came up four conspicuous horns
> toward the four winds of heaven.
> [9] Out of one of them came forth a little horn,
> which grew exceedingly great toward the south,
> toward the east, and toward the glorious land.
> [10] It grew great, even to the host of heaven;

5.3 Genres of poetry found in the Scriptures   241

    and some of the host of the stars it cast down to the ground,
    and trampled upon them.
    ¹¹ It magnified itself, even up to the Prince of the host;
    and the continual burnt offering was taken away from him,
    and the place of his sanctuary was overthrown.
    ¹² And the host was given over to it
    together with the continual burnt offering through transgression;
    and truth was cast down to the ground,
    and the horn acted and prospered.

Eight common features of apocalyptic writing are exemplified in Daniel 8.

> » Below, on the line beside each one write the number of the verse in which that particular feature is used.
>
> » Which of these would be the most difficult to translate in YL, and why?

Visionary revelation: _____

Future orientation: _____

Repeated elements: _____

Graphic imagery: _____

Elaborate symbolism: _____

Strong emotions: _____

Cosmic disruption: _____

Fierce warfare: _____

> » What are the characteristics of poetry and prose that you find mixed together in Daniel 8?
>
> » Do you agree with how the text as formatted above has been divided into three sections? If so, what are the structural markers that support this division? If not, what division would you propose and what is the evidence for your division?
>
> » In what sense is an apocalyptic text "prophetic?" What was the primary work of God's prophets and how does that task relate to Daniel 8? What is the function of apocalyptic discourse in relation to the people of God? (Note the interpretation of this vision that is given in Dan. 8:19–26.)
>
> » Should a text of this type be translated in YL as prose or poetry or some combination? Is there any literary genre in YL for apocalyptic topics like this? If so, describe it. (Note that apocalyptic prose will be considered again in the next chapter, section 6.2.1.)

For reflection, research, and response:

1. Identify some of the major characteristics of three different types of *prophetic oracle* listed below by listing the pertinent verses within the texts specified as references:

a. *Covenant lawsuit* in Isaiah 3:13–26:

   summons ____, indictment (charges) ____, judgment (sentence) ____

b. *"Woe" oracle* in Habakkuk 2:6–8:

   announcement of woe ____, prediction of punishment ____,
   reason for this divine punishment ____

c. *Salvation oracle* in Amos 9:11–15:

   future time setting ____, a radical change ____, covenantal blessings ____

Can any of these different types of discourse be marked in a special way to distinguish them in YL? If so, give an example or two.

2. Search for a good example of a *judgment oracle* and of a *salvation oracle* from the same prophetic book (your choice of book). Then write out each text and label its functional components in the same manner as shown in section 5.3.2 for the passages from Isaiah. Try to identify the *hortatory thesis* (theses) for each passage, as well as in the texts considered in exercise 3 below. Do you need to mark such *directive* discourse in a special way in YL in order to make it stand out more strongly or explicitly? If so, tell how you will do this and give an example or two to illustrate the point.

3. What special type of prophetic *judgment speech* occurs in Isaiah 10:1–10? Do you have any genre similar to this in your literary or oral tradition? What is a dynamic functional equivalent of the term *Woe!* in YL? Note that a judgment oracle may be applied to an entire nation. Which nations are included under the divine indictment in Isaiah 13–23? Compare this with the judgment oracles found in Jeremiah 46–51 and Ezekiel 25–32. In which ways does the formal style of these "oracles against pagan nations" differ in Amos 1–2? What big surprises are found in Amos's list of guilty nations? Is there any way to call attention to this special negative significance in your translation?

4. The first passage examined in the present section (5.3.2) was Hosea 5:13–15. How would you describe this text in terms of its *communicative function*? Now have a closer look at the passage with reference to its wider cotext: Walton proposes that "Israelite prophecy tended to come in four oracular categories that diverge from those found in Ancient Near Eastern prophecy: indictment, judgment, instruction, and aftermath" (2006:250). First of all, do you regard these four categories as separate oracles—or as components of the same kind of judgment oracle? Explain your answer.

   Point out the verses that pertain to indictment, judgment, and instruction in Hosea 5. Do you see any passage that expresses an aftermath or outcome of the Lord's judgment? How about 6:1–3, does that seem to fit as an aftermath? Explain. But read 6:1–3 now in the light of 6:4-11. Do you need to revise your last answer? Why or why not?

   Of what importance are such functional distinctions to the translator? For example, would an indictment need to be marked in some way to distinguish from a passage of judgment or of instruction? If so, how would this be done? What about a text dealing with the aftermath of God's punitive activities—would that type of discourse need to be marked or transitioned to in a special way in your language? If so, how?

5. Study Ezekiel 6:1–4 and note the *levels of speech embedding* there. Compare this passage in the NRSV and GNT. Then write this text in YL as you would like to see it turn out. Use indentation and quotation marks in order to clarify the text for the readers. (An additional text for you to unravel in the same way and for the same purpose is Zech. 1:1–4.)

5.3 Genres of poetry found in the Scriptures

6. Find a passage from the book of Revelation that displays many typical features of the *apocalyptic* genre (similar to the sample from Daniel in section 5.3.2). Give the reference and note which apocalyptic characteristics occur. Is this passage composed of more prose or more poetry? What is the basis for your conclusion?

7. Look up the words "apocalyptic" (or "apocalypse") and "eschatological" (or "eschatology") in a theological dictionary: What difference in meaning (if any) do you detect? Look up the prophecies found in Ezek. 28:25–26 and 38:19–22 and identify which one is apocalyptic and which eschatological? Are these passages more poetic or prosaic in nature, and what are the stylistic features that lead you to this conclusion in each case? Which passage is easier to translate in YL, and why is this the case?

8. In an interesting study of orality and "writtenness" in ancient Near Eastern prophetic texts, Stephen Voth identifies three major characteristics of an oral style, namely: "the repetition of certain key terms…strong imagery and language…[and] action-oriented language" (2005:123). He then suggests that "most prophetic texts in the Hebrew Bible are 'orally derived' texts" (ibid.:124). Thus:

   > [E]ven though these texts are highly stylized written texts, they betray an oral context. The oral culture continued to have a large influence on the work of scribes at all times…. [M]any of these texts were originally performed orally, and thus were conceived orally. At some point in time—which shall remain I think forever a mystery—that performance was dictated to a scribe. Or, maybe a scribe was present at the oral performance and through some kind of ancient shorthand was able to write down the essence of the oral performance. … (ibid.: loc.cit.)

   If these assumptions are true, what implications to you see for both the analysis as well as the translation of these prophetic texts? Is there any special relevance to such findings for translating the Scriptures in your cultural setting? If so, specify what these are.

   In a search for relevant communication techniques for the Scriptures, Voth then reverses the process of oral to written text transformation:

   > For many years I have considered that a key way to communicate the message of the Bible to young people in many parts of the world is through the medium of rap music. As best I can understand rap, it is a medium that uses semi-spoken rhymes that make use of a rhythmical musical background. (ibid.:127)

   The following is a paraphrase of Isaiah 5:8–14 (CEV) composed in English rap style (ibid.:128):

   You're In For Trouble!

   You're in for trouble!
   You take over house after house after house
   Until there ain't no room left for us
   In the hood, in our lives
   I'll make this promise come true
   Someone more powerful than you
   Will make you pay for what you do Will make you pay for what you do

   You're in for trouble!
   You keep the party on
   You keep the drinkin' on and on
   Until your mind gets slow
   And you don't care no more
   You have played deaf and blind
   For too long and too much

>   Now time has come to pay back
>   And you will do it in blood And you will do it in blood

How does this rap rendition strike you (from an English-speaking perspective)? Do have any possible revisions to suggest—perhaps for a different dialect of English? Is it appropriate to "rap" the Scriptures for any particular audience in your cultural setting? Why or why not? Do you have a different oral genre to recommend for making the prophetic message come alive for youthful listeners? If so, briefly describe its main stylistic characteristics—and then compose Isaiah 5:8–14 in that genre in YL and provide an English back-translation.

5.3.3 Poetry of the sages

Wisdom literature is a category that covers a very wide range of themes, styles, and communicative purposes in the Hebrew Bible, including some obvious prose as well as poetry. This striking diversity is highlighted by the juxtaposition in our present Bibles of the book of Ecclesiastes (prolix, pessimistic, and largely prosaic) and the book of Proverbs (succinct, optimistic, and mostly poetic). Couple these two books with Job's ancient imagery, disputational techniques, and bombastic rhetorical flourishes and it is quite a mixed literary pot indeed.

- » What are we to make of this disparity? More importantly, how are we to deal with it in a vernacular translation?

- » Is there a traditional category of wisdom literature/orature extant in the culture of your TL community? If so, what are its specifically religious functions?

- » What sort of style characterizes the wise sayings, written or oral, of your society? Give an example.

While we cannot undertake a complete analysis of Ecclesiastes, Proverbs, and Job here, we will at least sample some representative passages of these three books in order to give translators a taste of the type of discourse that has come from the tongues and pens of Israel's wise men. To discover why this kind of discourse is called Wisdom literature, we will first examine the following representative texts to see what their subject matter and communication goal(s) have in common.

JOB

>   then he looked at **wisdom** and appraised it;
>   he confirmed it and tested it.
>   And he said to man,
>   "The **fear of the Lord** – that is **wisdom**,
>   and to shun evil is **understanding**." (28:27–28)

>   "You asked, 'Who is this that obscures my counsel **without knowledge**?'
>   Surely I spoke of things **I did not understand**,
>   things too wonderful for me to know."....
>   "My servant Job will pray for you,
>   and I will accept his prayer and not deal with you according to **your folly**.
>   You have not spoken of me **what is right**,
>   as my servant Job has." (42:3, 8b)

5.3 Genres of poetry found in the Scriptures

PSALMS

Blessed is the man
    who does not walk in the counsel of the wicked
    or stand in the way of sinners
    or sit in the seat of mockers.
But his delight is in **the law of the Lord**,
and on his **law** he meditates day and night. (1:1–2)

The **fear of the Lord** is the beginning of **wisdom**;
    all who follow **his precepts** have good **understanding**.
        To him belongs eternal praise.
        Praise the Lord!
Blessed is the man who **fears the Lord**,
    who finds great delight in **his commands**. (111:10, 112:1)

Your hands made me and formed me;
    give me understanding to learn your commands.
May those **who fear you** rejoice when they see me,
    for I have put my hope in **your word**. (119:73–74)

PROVERBS

The proverbs of Solomon son of David, king of Israel:

<u>for</u> attaining **wisdom** and **discipline**;
    <u>for</u> **understanding** words of insight;
        <u>for</u> acquiring a disciplined and prudent life,
            [<u>for</u>] **doing what is right** and just and fair;
            <u>for</u> giving prudence to the simple,
                knowledge and discretion to the young –
let the wise listen and add to their learning,
and let the discerning get guidance –
                <u>for</u> **understanding** proverbs and parables,
                      the sayings and riddles of the wise.

The fear of the Lord is the beginning of **knowledge**,
    but **fools** despise wisdom and **discipline**. (1:1–7)

Charm is deceitful, and beauty is vain,
    but a woman who **fears the Lord** is to be praised.
Give her a share in the fruit of her hands,
    and let **her works** praise her in the city gates. (31:30–31)

ECCLESIASTES

For with much **wisdom** comes much sorrow;
the more **knowledge**, the more grief. (1:18)

Wisdom, like an inheritance, is a good thing
    and benefits those who see the sun.

> **Wisdom** is a shelter
>> as money is a shelter,
> but the advantage of knowledge is this:
>> that **wisdom** preserves the life of its possessor. (7:11–12)

> The end of the matter; all has been heard.
> **Fear God**, and **keep his commandments**;
>> for that is the whole **duty** of everyone.
> For God will bring every deed into **judgment**,
>> including every secret thing,
>>> whether good or evil. (12:13–14)

Why, it might be asked, are these passages considered to be representative, and in what way are they textual pointers to the ancient sapiential tradition of Israel's wise men? It is due to their explicit theological instruction and straightforward moral content as well as their important structural positions in the respective books, for example, at the close of the centrally placed "wisdom poem" in Job (28:27–28, quoted above), at the beginning of the Psalter (Ps. 1:1–2), at the beginning and ending of Proverbs (1:1–7 and 31:30–31), and in several places in the book of Ecclesiastes including its distinctive conclusion (12:13–14).

» Check these texts again and see if you agree with the preceding assessment.

» What do you think of the following definition of wisdom (adapted from Salisbury 2002:451), which is a summary of how this central concept is manifested in the book of Proverbs?

In the Book of Proverbs "wisdom" is:

choice:	making *God-pleasing* decisions concerninging the *way* we think, speak and behave.
knowledge:	knowing *what* is best to do or say
skill:	recognizing *how* best to do or say it
propriety:	appreciating *when* and *where* to do or say it (in the right circumstances).
an art:	succeeding in the art of living well (with peace).
a way of life:	building *God-fearing* character as its ultimate goal.

» How does a definition like this relate to the message of the book of Ecclesiastes?

» What is the difference in perspective in Ecclesiastes that makes it sound so different from Proverbs (cf. Prov. 1:2)? Can this difference in outlook be formally marked in YL? Explain.

It is clear that, despite some important formal and semantic elements which the wisdom books have in common, the literary style of these books differs considerably from one to the other and even within the same book. These variations in composition and tone—along with their associated communicative functions—need to be replicated in translation to the extent possible given the circumstances of production. Thus "wisdom" is also manifested in skillful ways of *verbal expression* such as we find in many passages of Scripture where the literary form complements and enhances the theological and moral content.
It is this assumption that motivates a *LiFE* approach to Bible exegesis and translation. In the words of someone who ought to know: "The Teacher searched to find just the right words, and he wrote what was upright and true" (Eccl. 12:10).

» Notice the blank lines (lettered A–H) following each of the eight passages below. On each line list some of the stylistic and topical characteristics of Wisdom literature that you observe in the respective texts.

5.3 Genres of poetry found in the Scriptures

» First try to guess which book the passage comes from. (The references are given following the eighth one.) Indicate the principal communicative purpose of the text at hand and also suggest some of the salient speech acts that are included.

» Next, state how the content and purpose of each passage pertain in some way to the macrosubject of covenantal wisdom from the perspective of Biblical Hebrew.

» Finally, point out any special difficulties that you expect to encounter when translating these texts into YL. Write your answers on a separate sheet of paper if more space is needed:

> I am the most ignorant of men;
> > I do not have a man's understanding.
> I have not learned wisdom,
> > nor have I knowledge of the Holy One.
> Who has gone up to heaven and come down?
> > Who has gathered up the wind in the hollow of his hands?
> Who has wrapped up the waters in his cloak?
> > Who has established all the ends of the earth?
> What is his name, and the name of his son?
> > Tell me if you know!

A: _____

> Woe to you, O land whose king was a servant
> > and whose princes feast in the morning.
> Blessed are you, O land whose king is of noble birth
> > and whose princes eat at a proper time –
> for strength and not for drunkenness.
> > If a man is lazy, the rafters sag;
> if his hands are idle, the house leaks.

B: _____

> Naked a man comes from his mother's womb,
> > and as he comes, so he departs.
> He takes nothing from his labor
> > that he can carry in his hand.
> This too is a grievous evil:
> > As a man comes, so he departs,
> > and what does he gain, since he toils for the wind?
> All his days he eats in darkness,
> > with great frustration, affliction and anger.

C: _____

> Why is life given to a man
> > whose way is hidden,
> > whom God has hedged in?
> For sighing comes to me instead of food;
> > my groans pour out like water.
> What I feared has come upon me;
> > what I dreaded has happened to me.
> I have no peace, no quietness;
> > I have no rest, but only turmoil.

D: _____

Though the arrogant have smeared me with lies,
    I keep your precepts with all my heart.
Their hearts are callous and unfeeling,
    but I delight in your law.
It was good for me to be afflicted
    so that I might learn your decrees.
The law from your mouth is more precious to me
    than thousands of pieces of silver and gold.

E: _____

Blessed is the man who finds wisdom,
    the man who gains understanding,
for she [wisdom] is more profitable than silver
    and yields better returns than gold.
She is more precious than rubies;
    nothing you desire can compare with her.
Long life is in her right hand;
    in her left hand are riches and honor.
Her ways are pleasant ways,
    and all her paths are peace.
She is a tree of life to those who embrace her;
    those who lay hold of her will be blessed.

F: _____

Remember your Creator
    in the days of your youth,
before the days of trouble come
    and the years approach when you will say,
    "I find no pleasure in them" –
before the sun and the light
    and the moon and the stars grow dark,
    and the clouds return after the rain;
when the keepers of the house tremble,
    and the strong men stoop,
when the grinders cease because they are few,
    and those looking through the windows grow dim.

G: _____

Man born of woman
    is of few days and full of trouble.
He springs up like a flower and withers away;
    like a fleeting shadow, he does not endure.
Do you fix your eye on such a one?
    Will you bring him before you for judgment?
Who can bring what is pure from the impure?
    No one!

H: _____

A = Proverbs 30:2–4	B = Ecclesiastes 10:15–18	C = Ecclesiastes 5:15–17	D = Job 3:23–26
E = Psalm 119:69–72	F = Proverbs 3:13–18	G = Ecclesiastes 12:1–3	H = Job 14:1–4

Perhaps the best-known genre in Wisdom literature/orature in all cultures is the *proverb,* though it is not necessarily the most important, especially in the biblical corpus. A good definition of *proverb* (patched together from a number of sources) is the following:

5.3 Genres of poetry found in the Scriptures

A proverb is a short, widely known sentence of folk wisdom which contains the teachings, truth, morals, and traditional views of society in a metaphorical, fixed, and memorizable form and which is handed down from generation to generation. This literary form is characterized by shortness, sense, salt, and a bit of mystery (enigma). The Biblical Hebrew literary proverb is usually a self-contained, often elliptical sentence in the form of a bicolon, comprising at least one topic and one comment, which together express some kind of similarity, contrast, or consequence. It is pedagogically and rhetorically motivated, casting vivid imagery within a striking and memorable saying. This is achieved by the complex interplay between its several poetic features, such as sound patterns, rhythm, parallelism, repetition, figurative language, and paronomasia.

» What are the five most important stylistic features of proverbs according to the lengthy definition above? Try to summarize.

» How does this definition match the proverbs of your language? Are they different in some respects? Be specific.

» Can the proverbial forms of YL be used to render those in the book of Proverbs? Try to give a good example of close correspondence with respect to both form and content.

Often translators find that even if the specific content of biblical proverbs does not match their own very closely, they can still use certain of their stylistic features when translating the biblical proverbs. Try to render any three passages of your choice from Proverbs 20:1–9 (quoted below from the NIV) so that they sound "proverbial" in YL:

> [1] Wine is a mocker and beer a brawler;
> whoever is led astray by them is not wise.
>
> [2] A king's wrath is like the roar of a lion;
> he who angers him forfeits his life.
>
> [3] It is to a man's honor to avoid strife,
> but every fool is quick to quarrel.
>
> [4] A sluggard does not plow in season;
> so at harvest time he looks but finds nothing.
>
> [5] The purposes of a man's heart are deep waters,
> but a man of understanding draws them out.
>
> [6] Many a man claims to have unfailing love,
> but a faithful man who can find?
>
> [7] The righteous man leads a blameless life;
> blessed are his children after him.
>
> [8] When a king sits on his throne to judge,
> he winnows out all evil with his eyes.
>
> [9] Who can say, "I have kept my heart pure;
> I am clean and without sin"?

» Read through the following pericope from Proverbs 3:1–7, which has been rendered in rhyming couplets.[7] What do you think of this translation? Does the English style seem to fit the original genre? Can you suggest any improvements to it? Perhaps before making any critical remarks, you might like to try your own pen in a similar exercise using this same text.

> [1] My child, don't forget my instructions.
> Always keep in mind my commandments.
> [2] They'll help you live for many years
> And bring to you prosperity.
> [3] Keep showing loyalty and dependability.
> Keep them adorning your neck with beauty.
> Engrave them in stone in your memory.
> [4] Then God and all people will love you,
> And they will think highly of you.
> [5] Completely trust the Lord inside.
> Don't rely on your own insight.
> [6] Let Him guide you in all you do,
> And He will make your paths smooth.
> [7] Don't think you're wise enough to get along.
> Honor the Lord and refuse to do wrong.

Still another type of wisdom discourse that we should consider is *disputation* (discussed in section 5.3.2), because it is so common in the book of Job. A dispute always takes the form of *direct speech,* generally as part of an argument intended to persuade an addressee or audience to adopt a certain cognitive stance with regard to some issue or controversy, often concerning justice or injustice, righteousness or wickedness. A disputation speech usually includes certain aspects of the opponent's position and then contrasts this with the counter-argument of the speaker, as in the following passages from Job.

» Analyze the changing argument as you progress from one speaker to the other, and note the special literary and rhetorical techniques that are used to persuade the addressee.

JOB (chap. 7)

[17]"What is man that you make so much of him, that you give him so much attention, [18] that you examine him every morning and test him every moment? [19] Will you never look away from me, or let me alone even for an instant? [20] If I have sinned, what have I done to you, O watcher of men? Why have you made me your target? Have I become a burden to you? [21] Why do you not pardon my offenses and forgive my sins? For I will soon lie down in the dust; you will search for me, but I will be no more.	Job's words here are an instance of **apostrophe**, a figure in which a speaker addresses an imaginary absent, or personified opponent. Even though no addressee is mentioned, to whom is Job speaking? Does this style of discourse cause any problems for translation into YL? If so, explain the difficulty. What is Job's point here? What is his complaint?

BILDAD (chap. 8)

[2] "How long will you say such things? Your words are a blustering wind. [3] Does God pervert justice?	Summarize Bildad's accusation against Job. What is the purpose of his rhetorical **questions**?

---
[7]Contributed by Dan Vail, dvail@pactec.net; see also Vail 2005.

5.3 Genres of poetry found in the Scriptures

      Does the Almighty pervert what is right?
⁴ When your children sinned against him,
      he gave them over to the penalty of their sin.
⁵ But if you will look to God
      and plead with the Almighty,
⁶ if you are pure and upright,
      even now he will rouse himself on your behalf
      and restore you to your rightful place.

What does he urge Job to do?
Does his appeal to Job come out clearly in a literal translation in YL?
If not, what must be done to clarify it?

JOB (chap. 9)

² "Indeed, I know that this is true.
      But how can a mortal be righteous before God?
³ Though one wished to dispute with him,
      he could not answer him one time out of a thousand.
⁴ His wisdom is profound, his power is vast.
      Who has resisted him and come out unscathed?
⁵ He moves mountains without their knowing it
      and overturns them in his anger....
²¹ "Although I am blameless,
      I have no concern for myself;
      I despise my own life.
²² It is all the same; that is why I say,
      'He destroys both the blameless and the wicked.'

Job makes two **concessions** in this passage.
What are they and how do you convey such "negative conditionals" in YL?
Do debaters **quote themselves** when arguing in YL, as Job does in the last line?
Does this assertion need to be marked more clearly in YL?

ZOPHAR (chap. 11)

² "Are all these words to go unanswered?
      Is this talker to be vindicated?
³ Will your idle talk reduce men to silence?
      Will no one rebuke you when you mock?
⁴ You say to God, 'My beliefs are flawless
      and I am pure in your sight.'
⁵ Oh, how I wish that God would speak,
      that he would open his lips against you
⁶ and disclose to you the secrets of wisdom,
      for true wisdom has two sides.
Know this: God has even forgotten some of your sin.

Zophar asks more **rhetorical questions** (a mainstay of Hebrew argumentative discourse and debating technique).
How does this correspond to your oral tradition?
Next, Zophar quotes Job in order to use Job's own words against him.
Is this a practice in your society?
If not, what would be the equivalent?

» Is it difficult to translate this sort of argumentation in YL? Do you have a special genre that is used for such public disputations or debates? If so, describe the form that it takes. Is it poetic or prosaic discourse?

» Identify any expressions that sound similar to how people debate in your culture.

» Point out three passages from the selections above that are especially problematic when translating into YL; explain the difficulty and suggest what you can do to express the content and intent of the speech more accurately as well as precisely.

There are several other types of Wisdom literature, but they will not be treated in this section because they are better classified as prose, not poetry (see sect. 6.2.3). However, we should consider one more wisdom genre here, though minor and relatively rare, known as the *riddle*. At his wedding feast, Samson gave a well-known biblical example:

> Out of the eater—something to eat;
> Out of the strong—something sweet. (Judg. 14:14, NIV; for the answer, see Judg. 14:18)

A riddle is a short enigmatic saying that sometimes takes the form of a question that the audience has to answer. The point is to teach and/or test the listeners who have to think about their response. In the Bible there are only fragments of full riddles, which appear either as allusions or partial citations, and mainly in the book of Proverbs. The following is an example:

> Death [*Sheol*] and Destruction [*Abaddon*] are never satisfied,
> and neither are the eyes of man. (Prov. 27:20)

In this case, the original riddle might have been something like "What is it that eats and eats but is never satisfied?"—Answer: "*Sheol*" (or "*Abaddon*"), referring to death. In Proverbs 27:20 it is expressed in the form of a simple comparison, though the underlying concepts and implications are rather more complex in nature.

» How would you bring out the force of Proverbs 27:20 in a pithy manner in YL?

For reflection, research, and response:

1. Pick out a strophe from the Song of Songs that seems to you to be one of the most beautiful instances of vivid poetic description in the entire book. Why do you think so? Would you have any difficulty translating this text in your language and cultural setting? Give it a try and make note of the SL problems that you encounter as well as some specific TL solutions that you discover.

2. What is the meaning of "fear of the LORD?" Do a collocational text study based on the wisdom passages given in section 5.3.3 (after further study in a Bible commentary or dictionary). How will you render this expression in YL? Can you use the same rendering in every cotext in which it occurs? Explain why or why not. Is there any literary relevance to this question? Compare with "Fear God…" in Eccl. 12:13.

3. Examine the following passages from the book of Proverbs and give a brief definition or description of the type of "wise saying" that you find. Mark with an asterisk (*) the ones for which a similar kind is found in YL. Give an example of each, if possible.

4:1	_____
4:23	_____
8:1	_____
14:21	_____
15:8	_____
16:16	_____
25:15b	_____
26:4–5	_____
30:18–19	_____
30:33	_____
31:10–31	_____

4. Practitioners of a *LiFE*-style approach would affirm the following pair of recent recommendations with regard to translating the book of Proverbs:

> If the goal in translating the book of Proverbs into African languages is academic or purely informational, then translators need not consider whether the shapes that biblical proverbs take within African languages sound like proverbs within that culture. But if the goal of translating Proverbs is that the biblical proverbs should be meaningful, powerful, compelling observations about life, which will transform those who hear them, then the translated proverbs must have a proverbial shape. In African cultures, which are permeated with proverbial sayings, a translation of proverbs will be successful to the extent that the biblical proverbs are assimilated into the language and become part of the cultural fabric of the society. (Miller 2005:144; cf. also Miller 2006)

> [T]he translation of proverbs requires an appreciation of the fact that proverbs have an aesthetic quality in their form in the source text and a conscious awareness of the aesthetic techniques used in forming proverbs in the RL. Then the translator is in a much better position to remold foreign proverbs into meaningful and aesthetic forms in the RL. This is important because for proverbial speech, part of the meaning is in the form. Put another way: if a passage does not have a proverbial form, it will not have (as much) proverbial meaning. All this is not to take the place of careful exegesis of proverbs, but to provide the most attractive container for serving the fruits of exegesis. As translators consciously study RL proverb patterns, they will be better able to translate proverbs in a way that more closely matches RL proverb patterns, eliciting more appreciation from readers. (Unseth 2006b:169-170; cf. also Unseth 2006a)

Now put the preceding advice into practice by preparing a corresponding translation of each of the passages listed in exercise 3 above. Point out any special TL devices that you used when carrying out this goal.

5. What translational difficulties does the following passage from Ecclesiastes 1 present in relation to both style and content? Try to render this text in YL in a *LiFE* manner, while at the same time conveying a similar attitude and connotation. (You will have to give special attention to the key word "meaningless"—*che̱bel*; consult a good Bible dictionary or commentary on Ecclesiastes.) When you finish, give a literal back-translation into English and point out some of the literary-poetic features that you have used. Would you make any strophic divisions in this passage? If so, where, and why? If not, why not? What kind of parallelism appears predominantly in this text? Is there a reason for this?

> [2] "Meaningless! Meaningless!"
> says the Teacher.
> "Utterly meaningless!
> Everything is meaningless."
> [3] What does man gain from all his labor
> at which he toils under the sun?
> [4] Generations come and generations go,
> but the earth remains forever.
> [5] The sun rises and the sun sets,
> and hurries back to where it rises.
> [6] The wind blows to the south
> and turns to the north;
> round and round it goes,
> ever returning on its course.
> [7] All streams flow into the sea,
> yet the sea is never full.
> To the place the streams come from,
> there they return again.
> [8] All things are wearisome,
> more than one can say.

> The eye never has enough of seeing,
> nor the ear its fill of hearing.
> ⁹ What has been will be again,
> what has been done will be done again;
> there is nothing new under the sun.
> ¹⁰ Is there anything of which one can say,
> "Look! This is something new"?
> It was here already, long ago;
> it was here before our time.
> ¹¹ There is no remembrance of men of old,
> and even those who are yet to come
> will not be remembered by those who follow.

6. Analyze the stylistic features and meaning of the paired proverbial passage below (Prov. 26:4–5, NIV, with italics added), doing so in the context of its wider discourse structure. Is there a contradiction here? Explain, basing your answer on some helpful literary criteria. Then translate this text with a "sapiential" style in YL.

> *Do not answer a fool* according to his folly,
> or you will be like him yourself.
> *Answer a fool* according to his folly,
> or he will be wise in his own eyes.

7. Consider the following principle (quoted from Salisbury 2002:462) in relation to your translation of the proverbs of the Bible. How does your rendering measure up to this?

> If we fail to present the proverb in a *proverbial form* in the TL,
> it will lose some of its *power!* In other words:
> It will have *less impact;*
> it will have *less verbal appeal* (beauty);
> it will be *less memorable;* and therefore,
> it will be less likely to be used.
> What's more, if we paraphrase too much,
> it will have a smaller range of applications.

8. Re-examine the eight wisdom texts in section 5.3.3 (A through H). Which one would be the most difficult to conceive of and translate into YL. Which one would be the easiest? Explain why. Is it a matter of content only or of stylistic form as well? Be specific. Now prepare a LiFE rendering of each of the two passages that you have selected—the hardest as well as the easiest.

5.3.4 Poetry in the New Testament

The text of Phil. 2:5–11, which is a distinctive epistolary passage presenting Paul's apostolic instruction on the person and work of Christ, is formatted in the RSV as prose:

> ⁵ Have this mind among yourselves, which is yours in Christ Jesus, ⁶ who, though he was in the form of God, did not count equality with God a thing to be grasped, ⁷ but emptied himself, taking the form of a servant, being born in the likeness of men. ⁸ And being found in human form he humbled himself and became obedient unto death, even death on a cross. ⁹ Therefore God has highly exalted him and bestowed on him the name which is above every name, ¹⁰ that at the name of Jesus every knee should bow, in heaven and on earth and under the earth, ¹¹ and every tongue confess that Jesus Christ is Lord, to the glory of God the Father.

» Do you think the preceding text is prose or poetry? Give reasons for your conclusion.

5.3 Genres of poetry found in the Scriptures

Now consider this same passage formatted differently (as adapted from several versions):

> Let the same mind be in you
> >that was in Christ Jesus:
>
> He had the very nature of God,
> >but did not regard such equality
> >as a reality to be thus exploited.
>
> Rather, he emptied himself,
> >assuming the nature of a slave,
> >becoming as human beings are.
>
> Having taken on true human form,
> >he humbled himself more,
> >to the point of accepting death –
> >even death on a cross.
>
> For this God also greatly exalted him,
> >and gave him the Name
> >that is above every name.
>
> So then, at the name of Jesus
> >all beings should bend the knee
> >in heaven above and on earth,
> >even in the underworld below.
>
> And every tongue should proclaim –
> >"Jesus the Christ, he is Lord!" –
> >all to the glory of God the Father.

» Is this a poetic text or a prose text that only looks like poetry because of the format? Which stylistic features of poetry can you find here?

Now consider the overall structure of this same passage from a different perspective. In the display below, the arrangement is based on some key instances of repetition within the text, including contrasts as well as close correspondences. (The instances of conceptual recursion are underlined.)

```
Have this mind among yourselves, which is yours in
A Christ Jesus, who, though he was in the form of God,
|   did not count equality with God a thing to be grasped,
|     B but emptied himself, taking the form of a servant,
|     |   C being born in the likeness of men.
|     |     |   D And being found in human form
|     |     |     |   E he humbled himself and became obedient
|     |     |     |     |   F unto death,
|     |     |     |     |   F' even death on a cross.
|     |     |     |     E' Therefore God has highly exalted him
|     |     |   D' and bestowed on him the name which is above every name,
|     |   C' that at the name of Jesus every knee should bow,
|     |       (those) in heaven and on earth and under the earth,
|     B' and every tongue confess that Lord
A' is Jesus Christ, to the glory of God the Father.
```

By means of its inverted compositional arrangement, this lyrical pericope focuses in paradoxical, contrastive fashion on both the *deity* of Christ (A/A') and his supreme act of *human* self-humiliation; namely, his vicarious sacrifice on the cross (F/F'). It is "this mind" that Christians too are exhorted to have (v. 5), especially in their relations with one another. The text structure, as displayed above, serves to highlight the focal thematic points being conveyed. Notice too the intensification that occurs as the text moves from the first to the second (reversed) set of parallel components, for example, from "the form [nature] of God" in A to "the glory of God the Father" in A'; from "death" in F to "death on a cross" in F'. This is an example of discourse-level heightening (see the discussion of parallelism and heightening in the microstructure in section 5.1.1). We also observe that the boundary-marking parallel correspondences feature parallels that are the same or synonymous in meaning, while the internal units are contrastive in nature (antithetical: B–E/E'–B').

It cannot be denied that the Philippians 2 passage, if not actually composed in a Greek poetic meter, is about as close as prose can come to purely expressive lyric. In other words, it is a mixed, or hybrid, genre—"poetic prose." The rhetorical effect is naturally more prominent in the original language and also when the text is expressively read, recited, or chanted aloud. The euphonious, balanced, and rhythmic literary form clearly contributes to the ultimate transmission of meaning here, not only in terms of this panegyric piece itself, but also with respect to the epistle as a whole. In fact, a good case could be made for viewing this segment as the thematic and stylistic epitome of the entire letter in that it represents the *ideal model* according to which all Christian behavior (as discussed elsewhere in the text) needs to be modeled and measured.

» How does this crucial section of Philippians 2 as expressed in your local translation compare stylistically to the renditions above—as well as to the original text?

» How close or comparable is the overall esthetic effect of the text as rendered in the vernacular version that you are translating or presently using?

» What would a format like the one we just considered contribute to the overall meaning of this passage in your language? Suggest any needed modifications that come to mind.

To be sure, even the best human efforts will be found wanting from a literary or rhetorical point of view when weighed against such an excellent original. However, that does not absolve translators of the obligation to at least consider an attempt to reproduce certain aspects of the obvious poetic dimension in Philippians 2:5–11.

The next example is from one of the didactic discourses of Christ: Matthew 6:19–21. I have used the Greek text here for the benefit of those who can read it; others will have to consult a literal version in English (or some other language) and write out the text in order to visualize the key verbal correspondences and poetic parallels.

Μὴ θησαυρίζετε ὑμῖν	θησαυροὺς	ἐπὶ τῆς γῆς,
ὅπου σὴς	καὶ βρῶσις	ἀφανίζει
καὶ ὅπου κλέπται	διορύσσουσιν	καὶ κλέπτουσιν·
θησαυρίζετε δὲ ὑμῖν	θησαυροὺς	ἐν οὐρανῷ,
ὅπου οὔτε σὴς	οὔτε βρῶσις	ἀφανίζει
καὶ ὅπου κλέπται	οὐ διορύσσουσιν	οὐδὲ κλέπτουσιν·
ὅπου γάρ ἐστιν	ὁ θησαυρός σου,	
ἐκεῖ ἔσται	καὶ ἡ καρδία σου.	

Do <u>not</u> store up for yourselves	*treasures*	on earth,
where moth	and rust	destroy,
and where thieves	break in	and steal.
But store up for yourselves	*treasures*	in heaven,
where moth	and rust	do <u>not</u> destroy,
and where thieves	do <u>not</u> break in	and steal.
For where is	your *treasure*,	
there will be	**also your heart**.	

5.3 Genres of poetry found in the Scriptures

As you study the above passage, select instances of the following ten literary features. Suggest how you might render them in a functionally equivalent manner in YL.

1. rhythm
2. rhyme
3. sound play
4. parallelism
5. metaphor
6. contrast/antithesis
7. allusion
8. end stress
9. deictic emphasis
10. break-up of a syntactic pattern

The following example, too, is so artfully patterned that it could well be regarded as an instance of Greek *poetic prose*.

» Examine this passage, known as "the Beatitudes" (Matt. 5:3–10), and see whether you agree as to its lyrical qualities from the perspective of your language and literary tradition. If you cannot read the original text, consult an interlinear English version and then set out the passage on a separate sheet in the format you see below.

» After studying it, list five different poetic features that you notice, listing them in their order of importance as you see it. Suggest how you might render these in an equally artistic and rhetorical manner in YL.

» A Chichewa poetic translation of this passage is provided as an example of a *LiFE* version of this passage. Critically evaluate this rendering, based on the English back-translation.

I

Μακάριοι οἱ πτωχοὶ τῷ πνεύματι,	[3]
ὅτι αὐτῶν ἐστιν ἡ βασιλεία τῶν οὐρανῶν.	
μακάριοι οἱ πενθοῦντες,	[4]
ὅτι αὐτοὶ παρακληθήσονται.	
μακάριοι οἱ πραεῖς,	[5]
ὅτι αὐτοὶ κληρονομήσουσιν τὴν γῆν.	
μακάριοι οἱ πεινῶντες καὶ διψῶντες τὴν δικαιοσύνην,	[6]
ὅτι αὐτοὶ χορτασθήσονται.	

II

μακάριοι οἱ ἐλεήμονες,	[7]
ὅτι αὐτοὶ ἐλεηθήσονται.	
μακάριοι οἱ καθαροὶ τῇ καρδίᾳ,	[8]
ὅτι αὐτοὶ τὸν θεὸν ὄψονται.	
μακάριοι οἱ εἰρηνοποιοί,	[9]

ὅτι αὐτοὶ υἱοὶ θεοῦ κληθήσονται.
μακάριοι οἱ δεδιωγμένοι ἕνεκεν δικαιοσύνης, [10]
ὅτι αὐτῶν ἐστιν ἡ βασιλεία τῶν οὐρανῶν.

Ngodalatu anthuwo	Surely how blessed are those people
odzichepetsa mu mtima,	[who are] humble at heart,
popeza Ufumu wakumwamba,	since the kingdom of heaven,
indedi, aloweratu iwo kale.	yes indeed, they've already entered in.
Ngodalatu anthuwo	Surely how blessed are those people
omvera chisoni m'mtima,	[who] feel sorrow in [their] heart[s],
popeza Mulungu mwini,	since God himself,
inde, adzawasangalatsadi.	yes, he will certainly give them joy.
Ngodalatu anthuwo	Surely how blessed are those people
ofatsa mtima kwambiri,	[who are] most meek at heart,
popeza adzapatsidwa dziko,	since they will be given the land,
indedi, kuti likhale lawolawo.	yes indeed, so it becomes their very own.
Ngodalatu anthuwo	Surely how blessed are those people
omva ludzu la chilungamo,	[who] feel a thirst for righteousness,
popeza Mulungu adzawamwetsa,	since God will give them to drink,
indedi, zofuna zao adzazithetsa.	yes indeed, their wants he'll put to an end.
Ngodalatu anthuwo	Surely how blessed are those people
ochitira anzao chifundo,	[who] treat their fellows mercifully,
popeza Mulungu nawonso	since God for his part too
chake chifundo adzawamvera.	his mercy he'll grant them.
Ngodalatu anthuwo	Surely how blessed are those people
oyera mtima koti mbee!	[who are] pure in heart so bright (ideophone)!
popeza onse oterewa, zoona,	since all those of this type, truly,
Mulungu mwini adzamuona.	God himself they will see.
Ngodalatu anthuwo	Surely how blessed are those people
obweretsa mtendere m'dziko,	[who] bring peace in the land,
popeza kuti Mulungu nayenso	since in fact God he also,
indedi, ana ake eni adza'acha.	yes indeed, his own children he'll call them.
Ngodalatu anthuwo	Surely how blessed are those people
amene amawazunza pansipo	who are persecuted down here below
kamba ka chilungamo chaocho,	on account of that righteousness of theirs,
popeza Ufumu wakumwamba,	since the kingdom of heaven,
indedi, ndi wao kwamuyayaya!	yes indeed, it's theirs forever (ideophone)!

» How does the artistic and rhetorical patterning of this passage help to convey the content and purpose of Christ's message?

» What can we do about such structures (and their effects) when translating the biblical text? Is there any alternative formatting technique or stylistic device that we might use?

» What about doing nothing at all—is that a valid option? If so, what are the consequences as far as communication are concerned? How much LiFE will we have removed from the original text if we simply render this passage in a literal manner?

» Now translate the second half of this pericope (vv. 7–10) so that it sounds like literature (orature) in YL.

In summary, we can say that a dynamic, more "mediated" manner of translating is generally needed to successfully communicate a literary, stylistically marked SL document in another language and culture. This is necessary not only to promote a fuller understanding and appreciation of the structure and significance of the original text, but also to prevent a misunderstanding of the author's rhetorical objective. Communication problems may occur either if translators simply render the biblical text literally (the proverbial path of least resistance), or if they paraphrase it too loosely. Content and intent (including purposeful artistic forms) are equally important in any translation of the Scriptures.

These are serious issues indeed—and they have considerable implications as far as the full "meaning potential" of an artfully composed pericope is concerned. The point is that translators can never let their guard down, so to speak, no matter how lackluster or unimportant a passage might look at first glance. Just about any text of Scripture can carry implicit structural and stylistic meaning hidden beneath a very familiar surface wording. The very purpose of this workbook, in fact, is to encourage us to probe below the surface and systematically analyze such texts from a diverse, coordinated literary perspective: The first step is to carefully examine the original document in order to more accurately determine what it actually says in terms of form, content, and communicative aim. We then endeavor to faithfully represent in our target language both the essential biblical content and as much as possible of its accompanying artistic and/or rhetorical significance. The goal is to translate in a creative, but also controlled manner so that more of the literary life of the author's intended message is reflected in the vernacular text. Even a pale reflection of this lively non-referential dimension of meaning is better than none at all.

For reflection, research, and response:

1. The Lord's Prayer (Matt. 6:9–13) manifests a number of artistic features. It may be divided into two strophes, based on the content and nature of the petitions and also the phonological patterning evident in each strophe. Point out as many of the poetic qualities as you can find in the Greek text below, or consult an interlinear version.

    Πάτερ ἡμῶν ὁ <u>ἐν τοῖς οὐρανοῖς</u>,
      ἁγιασθήτω τὸ ὄνομά **σου**·
      ἐλθέτω ἡ βασιλεία **σου**·
      γενηθήτω τὸ θέλημά **σου**,
    ὡς <u>ἐν οὐρανῷ</u> καὶ ἐπὶ γῆς·

    Τὸν ἄρτον ἡμῶν τὸν ἐπιούσι<u>ον</u>
      δὸς ἡμῖν σήμερ<u>ον</u>·
    καὶ ἄφες ἡμῖν τὰ ὀφειλήματα <u>ἡμῶν</u>,
      ὡς καὶ ἡμεῖς ἀφήκαμεν τοῖς ὀφειλέταις <u>ἡμῶν</u>·
    καὶ μὴ εἰσενέγκῃς <u>ἡμᾶς</u> εἰς πειρασμόν,
      ἀλλὰ ῥῦσαι <u>ἡμᾶς</u> ἀπὸ τοῦ πονηροῦ.

    The following Chichewa "poetic" (*ndakatulo*) version of this passage is intended to be a contemporary *LiFE* rendering:

Inu 'Tate wakumwamba,	O Dad in heaven,
Dzina lanu lilemekezeke.	may your name be honored.
Wanu Ufumu ukhazikike.	Your kingdom may it be established.
Kufuna kwanu kuchitike,	May your will be done,
pano pansi ndi kumwambako.	down here and there in heaven.

Choonde tipatseni lero, 'Tate,	Please, give us today, Dad,
kudya kokwanira moyo wathu.	food sufficient for our life.
Machimo onse mutikhululukire,	Forgive all our sins,
nafe tichite chimodzimodzinso.	and we, let us do the same.
M'zotiyesetsa tisagwemo ayi.	Let us not fall at all into the things that test us.
Kwa Woipa uja, Mdani wathu,	From that Evil One, our Enemy,
mutipulumutse nthawi zonsetu.	deliver us at all times.
Ndithudi, ufumu ndi mphamvu,	To be sure, kingship and power,
ulemunso n'zanu kwamuyaya!	honor too is yours forever![8]

Point out some of the stylistic characteristics of the above rendering and then evaluate it. Finally, prepare your own *LiFE* version of Matthew 6:9–13.

2. Study the entire text of 1 Corinthians 13. As a whole, is it more poetic or prosaic in nature? Which artistic features do you find here? Why do you think that this pericope is structured in such an expressive, lyrical manner? (Consider also the content and intent of chapters 12 and 14.) On a separate paper, write out 1 Corinthians 13 in a poetic format, making any adjustments that you feel are necessary to give the text a more rhythmic sound when uttered aloud.

3. Find another poetic text in the NT—one not discussed above—and point out its various literary features, both *structural* (larger text arrangements) and *stylistic* (individual poetic devices). Why, in view of the surrounding cotext, has this passage been composed in this manner; in other words, what is its primary communicative function? Lastly, prepare a *LiFE* translation of this text in YL.

5.4 Practicing a methodology for literary-poetic text analysis

The twelve steps that follow are based on chapter 7 of *Translating the Literature of Scripture* (Wendland 2004b), which outlines a general methodology for examining non-narrative, especially poetic, texts. These steps are to be applied to complete textual units, whether an entire biblical book or a clearly defined portion of one, sometimes called a pericope. (Some guidelines for studying and translating *narrative* texts will be given in lesson 6; cf. Wilt and Wendland 2008:chapter 8.)

» Compare these twelve steps with the ten procedures given in section 3.6. Note any apparent differences and evaluate them in terms of your own preference.

» Then summarize (or explain) each step in your own words in the spaces provided below; it may prove helpful for you do this also in your own language.

Step 1: Study the complete textual, intertextual, and extratextual context.

---

[8]Despite the absence of the traditional concluding doxology from the better-attested Greek manuscripts, it is included in the Chichewa text due to popular demand.

5.4 Practicing a methodology for literary-poetic text analysis

Step 2: Read the entire text aloud and determine its genre and subgenres.

Step 3: Plot all occurrences of exact and synonymous repetition.

Step 4: Find all instances of disjunction ("breaks") occasioned by formulae and content shifting.

Step 5: Isolate and record the obvious areas of special stylistic concentration.

Step 6: Identify the major points of discourse demarcation (boundaries) and projection (peaks).

Step 7: Outline the structural-thematic organization of the entire pericope.

Step 8: Prepare a complete semantic (word/symbol/motif) analysis, especially of the key concepts.

Step 9: Identify any outstanding linguistic and literary features that remain.

5.4 Practicing a methodology for literary-poetic text analysis

Step 10: Note the major speech functions and speech acts and their interaction in the discourse.

Step 11: Search for all possible form-functional matches between the SL and TL.

Step 12: Prepare a well-formatted, trial *LiFE* translation and test it against other versions.

These twelve steps are only one suggested set of procedures for accomplishing the task of text exegesis in preparation for a *LiFE* translation. The exegete might prefer to rearrange the order of some of the steps and, for example, begin with step 2. Other steps could no doubt be added; for example, examining the most significant literary features could be set as a distinct exercise. The important thing is that the approach be precise, systematic, and comprehensive: Bible translation involves a careful *analytical* and *comparative* text-based process. It requires the close parallel examination of a number of different versions, literal and idiomatic, especially versions in related languages to see how others have understood and expressed the aspects of meaning presented by the same pericope. The different printed formats, too, need to be tested for accuracy and legibility.

It is particularly important to pay special attention to the formal and functional *differences* that appear among the several versions consulted. (Hopefully, there will *not* be major *semantic* disparities!) Translators must be able to specify not only what these differences are in terms of linguistic form but also what the stylistic or functional effect is on the respective texts. In many cases, the variation is simply a reflection of the languages involved or of different methods of translating, that is, whether more "foreignizing" or "domesticating" in nature. But at times the differences might be more serious. They may represent a partial (or even a complete) failure to convey the author-intended meaning (content + intent), which is always closely connected with textual form. At other times, less serious errors may be noted, such as a slight unintended addition, modification, or detraction with respect to the sense and significance of the biblical text. But even these, when repeated, can quickly build up to a rather large problem and so must be avoided.

Finally, it is important to extend this comparative method of text checking to the TL constituency, using various formal and informal testing methods (see section 7.2). In many local settings, this will require the development of *oral-aural assessment procedures* in addition to the written ones. How do people best perceive and understand the vernacular text? Is it when hearing it or reading it? The purpose of testing is to gain enough feedback—both corrective and also creative—from a variety of listeners and readers so that when the translation is finally published, whether as portions or in its entirety, it will be met with the widest possible acceptance.

A rigorous comparative examination of texts, together with the response that is generated when testing early drafts with members of the target audience in various settings of use, will always reveal certain problems. But such information is an essential part of perfecting the text; without it, the necessary improvements will probably not be made. Perhaps during the testing process, some individuals will catch the *LiFE* vision and be inspired to try their hand (or tongue) at "domesticating" the Scriptures in their own language and literary/oratorical tradition.

For reflection, research, and response:

1. "The first step in Bible translation is the determination of the text" (Scorgie, Strauss, and Voth 2003:31). How does this apply to your translation methodology and where does it fit in our twelve steps? How does your team deal with text-critical issues, especially where the textual footnotes of the major translations give different opinions? How would you go about establishing the original text of Job 19:23–29? Now translate this passage into YL in a way that matches the dramatic expression and emotive intensity of the original text.

2. How does a translation team prepare for translating a *LiFE* version? Evaluate and discuss the following procedures (adapted from Wendland 2004b, chap. 8) based on your own experience or as part of a strategy for translating a future *LiFE* version in your language.

    a. **Collection** – gather as much TL data as possible in various genres, oral and written, secular and religious, standard and dialectal.

    b. **Classification** – analyze and categorize the available material with respect to form, content, function, setting of use, and primary users.

    c. **Comparison** – compare the TL stylistic resources with the inventory of literary and rhetorical features of the SL text, noting the major similarities and differences.

    d. **Compensation** – devise innovative *LiFE* strategies for dealing with mismatches of form or function, especially the latter, in the effort to achieve communicative parity.

    e. **Creation** – verbally reconstitute the essential message at the points of mismatch through informed intuition and insight, using the appropriate TL-based compensation strategies.

    f. **Criticism** – evaluate the translation, especially where some creative work has been done, by means of an explicit comparison with the corresponding features of the original text.

3. Qvale (2003:62) emphasizes the importance of a translator's ability to empathize with the original:

> The translator ought to be receptive to all the qualities of the source text, and, through spiritual affinity with the author and a process of internalization, be able to access the author's intention and grandeur and be armed for the hunt for a corresponding poetic expression....[T]he main thing is to have the translator's most important hallmark: Empathy. Empathy is the key.

How does empathy pertain to *compensation* in exercise 2? How can a Bible translator today generate empathy with the original authors of Scripture? Make a suggestion or two.

4. Working in pairs (or teams), apply the twelve steps in section 5.4 to a complete analysis and translation of Habakkuk 3. (A possible model of discourse analysis is found in Wendland 2004b, section 7.3.) To help you complete this exercise, a variety of literary-structural notes on Habakkuk 3 are given below, but other reference material may also be used. Prepare a brief written report of your exegetical study and be ready to hand it in to your instructor along with your *LiFE*-style translation. Some of the reports may be selected for class presentation, if time allows.

A PLEA TO YAHWEH FOR DELIVERANCE[9]

Title. A prayer of the prophet Habakkuk: with a tune as for dirges

Prayer

Yahweh, I have heard of your renown;	2
your work, Yahweh, inspires me with dread.	
Make it live again in our day,	
make it known in our time;	
in wrath remember mercy.	

Theophany: Yahweh's approach

Eloah comes from Teman,	3
the Holy One from Mount Paran.	[Pause]
His majesty covers the heavens,	
and his glory fills the earth.	
His brightness is like the day,	4
and rays flash from his hands,	
that is where his power lies hidden.	

Pestilence goes before him,	5
and Plague follows close behind.	
When he stands up, he shakes the earth,	6
with his glance he makes the nations quake.	
And the eternal mountains are dislodged,	
the everlasting hills sink down –	
his pathways from of old.	
I saw the tents of Cushan in trouble,	7
the tent-curtains of Midian shuddering.	

Yahweh's battle

Yahweh, are you enraged with the rivers,	8
are you angry with the sea,	
that you should mount your chargers,	
your rescuing chariots?	

---
[9]The text of Habakkuk 3 that appears here is from the NJB, but somewhat altered and reformatted.

You uncover your bow,	9
and give the string its fill of arrows,	[Pause]
You trench the earth with torrents.	
The mountains see you and tremble,	10
great floods sweep by,	
the abyss roars aloud,	
lifting high its waves.	
Sun and moon stay inside their dwellings,	11
they flee at the light of your arrows,	
at the flash of your lightning-spear.	

In rage you stride across the land,	12
in anger you trample the nations.	

YOU MARCHED OUT TO SAVE YOUR PEOPLE,	13
TO SAVE YOUR ANOINTED ONE!	

You wounded the head of the house of the wicked,	
you laid bare his foundation to the very rock.	[Pause]
With your shafts you pierced the leader of his warriors	14
who stormed out with shouts of joy to scatter us,	
as if they meant to devour some poor wretch in their lair.	
With your chargers you trampled through the sea,	15
through the surging abyss!	

Conclusion: human fear and faith in God

When I heard, I trembled to the core,	16
my lips quivered at the sound;	
my bones became disjointed,	
and my legs gave way beneath me.	
Yet calmly I await the day of anguish,	
which is dawning on the people now attacking us.	

For the fig tree is not to blossom,	17
nor will the vines bear fruit;	
the olive crop will disappoint,	
and the fields will yield no food;	
the sheep will vanish from the fold,	
no cattle in the stalls.	
But I shall rejoice in Yahweh,	18
I shall exult in God my Savior!	
Yahweh the Lord is my strength,	19
he will lighten my feet like a doe's	
and set my steps on the heights.	

For the choirmaster; played on stringed instruments.

A schematic look at Habakkuk as a two-part whole, divided into seven major sections:

(Note the principal *structural markers* on the borders and the *cohesive ties* within each section.)

    I. A. **Superscription:** Introduction of the prophet and his message (1:1)

B. Habakkuk's first **complaint**: Why does injustice in Judah go unpunished by Yahweh? (1:2-4)

   C. God's **response**: The fearsome Babylonians will punish Judah
      along with the rest of the nations of the world (1:5-11)

D. Habakkuk's second **complaint**: Why pick the wicked Babylonians
   to execute judgment upon Judah? (1:12-17)

   E. Habakkuk rests his case (**transition**):
      How will God respond to me and I to him? (2:1)

II.   F. God's **response**: I will provide a vision pronouncing a verdict
      of condemnation upon proud, unrighteous Babylon (2:2-5)

G. A satiric **taunt** against Babylon: Five judicial "woes"
   declared against this unjust nation (2:6-20)

H. The **prayer** of Habakkuk: A poem in praise of Yahweh's mighty deliverance of his people in
   the past, concluded by Habakkuk's calm, faith-filled acquiescence to the divine will (3:1-19)

The general structure of Habakkuk's prayer:

```
A performance margin (1):
|
|   B lament introduction      petition
|   |              fear – "I heard" (2a) + anticipatory faith (2b)
|   |
|   |   C theophany – Yahweh marches to battle
|   |   |        revelation:  Yahweh displays his glory (3-4)
|   |   |        result:  fear on the part of the ungodly (5-7)
|   |   |
|   |   C' theophany – Yahweh engages in battle
|   |            revelation: violent imagery of water/warfare (8-12)
|   |               => purpose = peak:  SALVATION! (13a)
|   |            result: violent imagery of water/warfare (13b-15)
|   |
|   B' lament conclusion profession
|              fear – "I heard" (16) + confirmatory faith (17-19b)
|
A' performance margin (19c)
```

The central divine-prophetic "argument" of Habakkuk:

Prophetic hortatory discourse (rhetoric) often assumes a three-part progression: *problem* => *appeal* => *motivation*. In Habakkuk, these rhetorical constituents are expressed in dual form as follows:

a. problem = i the prevalence and predominance of evil
                 in a world created and controlled by "God" (3:3);
              ii the wicked continue to persecute the "righteous" followers
                 of "the Sovereign LORD" (3:19).

b. appeal = i initial – to the ultimate justice of "the Holy One" (3:3), i.e.,
                 "Do something about it!"

ii final – to the "faith-fulness" of his righteous ones (2:4b), i.e.,
"Put your complete trust in the just judgment of Yahweh!"

c. motivation = i who our God is – the "Rock," the "almighty LORD"
(1:12b, 2:13, i.e., his theological credibility);
ii what he has done for his people as their eternal "Savior"
(1:12a, 3:18, i.e., his historical reliability).

From conflict to resolution in Habakkuk, encoding a judicial theme:

Habakkuk's initial situation		*his final situation*
he has no apparent answer (1:2a)	→	he has been answered (3:2, 16)
salvation is lost (1:2b)	→	salvation is assured (3:13, 18)
injustice goes unpunished (1:3a)	→	wickedness is defeated (3:8–12)
conflict is everywhere (1:3b)	→	he is at peace (3:16b)
no hope of justice (1:4)	→	restoration will come (3:2, 17–18)

INJUSTICE (man)	versus	**JUSTICE** (God)
Chapter I: 2, 3, 4, 6, 7, 9, 10, 11, 13b, 17		2*, 3*, 12, 13a, 13b*
Chapter II: 4a, 4b*, 5, 6, 7, 8, 9, 10, 11, 12, 15, 17		7, 8, 10, 13, 16, 17
Chapter III: 13b, 14		12, 13, 14, 15, 16, 19

*The asterisk marks a conceptual reversal, i.e., human *justice*, divine *injustice* (so perceived).

Conceptual recursion within Habakkuk 3 and connections with chapters 1–2:

III: verse(s) strophe	recursive concepts	other, strophe-external references inside => CHAPTER 3 <= outside	
2	Yahweh…Yahweh	8,* 18,* 19*	1:2*, 12*; 2:2*, 13, 14*,16, 20*
	I heard your hearing	16*	1:2*
	your deed		1:5*
	in midst of years…in midst of years		
	make him/it live		2:4
	make him/it know		2:14
	in trembling	7*, 16*	
3–4	God…even the Holy One	18*	1:11, 12*
	he came		2:3
	his glory…and splendor		2:14
	it filled the earth		2:14
5–7	before him…before his steps		

5.4 Practicing a methodology for literary-poetic text analysis

	he saw…I saw	10*	1:3, 5, 13, 2:1*
	plague…pestilence		
	earth…mountains…hills…land 17, 20*	3, 9, 10, 12	1:6; 2:8, 14*,
	long ago…eternity…eternity		
8–10	rivers…rivers…sea…rivers…torrent of waters…the deep…waves (hands)	15*	1:14; 2:14*
	you rode…your riding things (chariots) he raged…your anger…your wrath 12		
	salvation uncovered it is uncovered	13*, 18*	
11–13	sun…moon…light…flash…lightning		
	your arrows…your spear	9, 14	
	to save…to save	8, 18*	
	nations…your people	6, 7, 16	1:5, 6, 7, 17*, 2:5*, 8*, 10, 13, 16*
12–15	head…thigh…neck…head		
	your horses	8*	1:8
	the sea…the waters	8*	1:14; 2:14*
16	it trembled…I trembled	7*	
17–18	my belly…my lips…my bones not…there is no…not…there is no		
	fig tree…fruit on the vines…crop of olives…fields…food…sheep…cattle		1:16
	I will rejoice…I will be glad		1:15
19	Yahweh my Lord	2*, 3*, 18*	
	he makes me walk upon	15*	

*The asterisks mark those terms with special structural or stylistic significance where they occur.

Significant patterned parallelism at the close of the book (end-stress)—3:17–18:

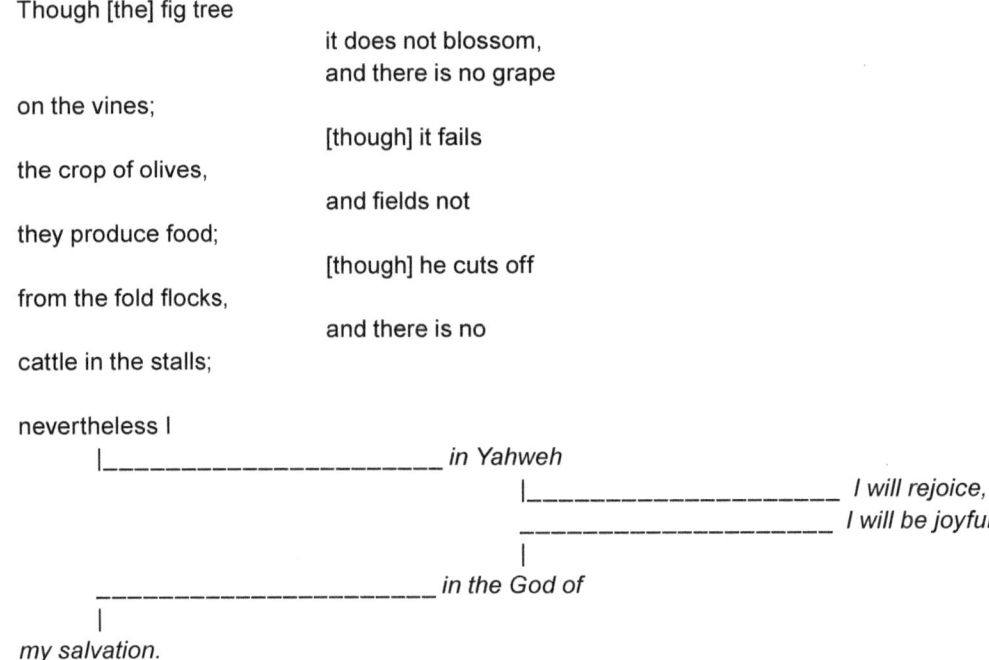

```
Though [the] fig tree
                          it does not blossom,
                          and there is no grape
on the vines;
                          [though] it fails
the crop of olives,
                          and fields not
they produce food;
                          [though] he cuts off
from the fold flocks,
                          and there is no
cattle in the stalls;

nevertheless I
    |_____ in Yahweh
                              |_____ I will rejoice,
        _____ I will be joyful
                              |
    _____ in the God of
    |
my salvation.
```

Intertextuality in Habakkuk 3:

verses	topic-narrative motif	cross-references
2	**prologue:** to the poetic-narrative revelation of the "deeds" of Yahweh, righteous in "anger" but great in mercy	Psalms 68:28; 77:5–12
3–4	Yahweh appears on the scene from the desert south/Sinai in all his splendor and might	Exodus 19:16–19; Judges 5:4a; Deuteronomy 33:2; Psalm 68:7–8
5–7	**rising action:** the effects of Yahweh's advance are felt in the shocking/shaking of nations and nature	Exodus 15:13–16; 19:18; Judges 5:4–5; Psalm 18:7, 12; Psalms 77:18; 78:43–51
8–10	Yahweh vents his anger against the seas (= superiority over all pagan deities) as he rides to war on a chariot of clouds	Exodus 15:8; Psalm 18:9–12, 15; Psalms 68:4; 77:16–19; 89:9–10; Psalm 104:3–4
11–13	**climax:** Yahweh, armed with the weapons of nature, battles and completely routs the enemy to deliver his people and anointed one	Psalms 18:14; 68:7, 11–14, Psalms 68: 17–18; 74:13–14; Psalms 77:14–15, 17–18; Deuteronomy 32:23, 40–42
14–15	**denouement:** with a flashback to the prior time of oppression; all enemies, both natural and supernatural, are impressively defeated	Exodus 15:2–5, 9–10; Deuteronomy 32:43; Psalms 68:21; 77:19; 144:6–7

16–19	***conclusion:*** a personal, meditative response to the narrative; patient and joyful hope for future deliverance and vindication	Deuteronomy 26:17–18; 32:13, Deuteronomy 32–33, 41–43; Deuteronomy 33:29; Joel 1:7–12; 2:23–24; Psalms 4:7; 18:32–33; 28:6; Psalms 31:7–8; 32:11; 35:9–10

The structural-thematic organization of Habakkuk's psalm:

The semantic and logical relationships between the paired propositional utterances below from paired passages of Habakkuk are designated by *letters* that are explained in the box below the display (cf. Wendland 2002:ch.3). The twofold relations given in *italics* in the box are especially important for the psalm's thematic development. Feel free to disagree with any of these interpretations and to propose alternatives that you feel fit the text and context better. Some variation in perspective is to be expected since poetry typically allows a certain range or flexibility in the expression of meaning. The aim of this exercise in structural analysis is to explore this range with a bit more precision *before* preparing to translate Habakkuk 3 in a *LiFE*-like manner in YL.

```
2:1         O-Yahweh I-heard your-report ----a
   2        I-revere O-Yahweh your-work    |--------------------
   3        in-midst-of years renew-him ----------------b       d --------------------------------------
   4        in-midst-of years you-make-[him]-know  |-----c   |
   5        in-trembling mercy you-remember_____|

3:1         God from-Teman he-comes ---------------------e
   2        even-the-Holy-One from-Mount=Paran (S)   |----------------p
   3        it-covered heavens his-glory ------------ f             |____                       |--j"
   4        and-his-praise it-filled the-earth    |------------------ n__|
4:1         and-brightness like-the-light it-is --------------- g_____|
   2        horns from-his-hand [are] to-him --------- h__|
   3        and-there [is] a-covering of-his-power ___|
- - - - - - - - - - - - - - - - - - - - - - - - - - - - - - - -              |---r
5:1         before-him it-goes a-plague ------------------i           |
   2        and-it-followed a-pestilence to-his-steps__|-----o        |
6:1         he-stood and-he-measured [the]-earth ------j  __|------------- |  |--s
   2        he-looked and-he-startled [the]-nations___|                                                      |--k"
   3        and-they-crumbled the-mountains-of=long-ago----k     |--- q__|
   4        they-sank the-hills-of eternity _____|----l__|
   5        the-ways-of eternity [are] to-him _____|
7:1         under iniquity I-saw the-tents-of Cushan -------------m _____|
   2        they-tremble the-curtains-of the-land-of Midian ___|

8:1         at-rivers did-he-rage Yahweh?---------------t                          |--i"
   2        or against-the-streams [was] your-anger__|----u
   3        or=against-the-sea [was] your-wrath_____|---w
   4        when you-ride upon=your-horses----v_____|-----z
   5        your-chariots-of deliverance?_____|            |
9:1         uncovered it-is-uncovered your-bow---x   |__
   2        oaths-of shafts [are] spoken (S) _____|----y_____| d'
   3        [with]-rivers you-split=[the]-earth_____|           |__
10:1        they-saw-you they-writhe [the]-mountains---a'         |--j'
   2        a-torrent-of waters it-overflowed_____|----c'____|
   3        it-gave [the]-deep its-voice---------------b'____|
   4        [on]-high his-hands it-lifted_____|
- - - - - - - - - - - - - - - - - - - - - - - - - - - - - -
11:1        sun moon it-stood [in-the]-high-abode---------f'         |__
   2        to-the-light-of your-arrows they-went ---e'__|----i'    |--k'
   3        to-the-shine-of the-flash-of your-spear___|       |_____|
12:1        in-wrath you-march=[the]-earth-----------g'_____|
   2        in-anger you-thresh [the]-nations_____|
13:1        you-came-out for-the-deliverance-of your-people---h'_____|       |--i"    |--k"
   2        for-the-deliverance-of your-anointed-one_____|
- - - - - - - - - - - - - - - - - - - - - - - - - - - -
   3        you-crushed the-head from-the-house-of evil ---l'              r'--|       j"-|
   4        uncovered [from]-thigh unto-[the]-neck (S)____|----------o'
14:1        you-pierced with-his-shafts [his]-head -------------n'  |
   2        his-warrior[s] they-storm-out to-scatter-me---m'  |__|   |--q'
   3        their-exultation as-[if]=to-devour [the]-poor   |____|       |
            in-the-secret-place _____|              |
15:1        you-trampled on-the-sea [with]-your-horses---p'_____|
   2        the-surging-of waters abundant_____|
```

5.4 Practicing a methodology for literary-poetic text analysis

```
16:1    I-heard and-it-trembled my-belly-------s'                      |      |
   2    at-[the]-sound they-quivered my-lips_|-----u'                  |      |
   3    it-comes rot into-my-bones -------------t'__|-----------w'     |      |
   4    and-beneath-me I-trembled_____|            |_____|      |
   5    which I-will-wait for-the-day-of distress---------v'_|                |
   6    to-come-over on-[the]-people they-invade-us__|                        |
- - - - - - - - - - - - - - - - - - - - - - - - - - - - - - - - - - - - - -  |
17:1    though=[the]-fig-tree not=it-blossoms------------x'                   |
   2    and-there-is-no fruit on-the-vines_____|-----a"                 |
   3    [though]-it-fails [the]-produce-of=olive[s]-------y'__|--b"           |
   4    and-fields not=it-produces food_____|      |                     |
   5    [though]-it-is-cut-off from -[the]-fold flock----z'_____|---d'        |
   6    and-there-is-no cattle in-the-stalls _____  |_                    |
18 1    yet-I in-Yahweh I-will-rejoice--------------------c"_____  | g"       |
   2    I-will-exalt in-the-God-of my-deliverance____|             |_____|
19:1    Yahweh my-Lord [is] my-strength------------------f"'_____|
   2    and-he-set my-feet like-the-deer's-------------e"_|
   3    and-upon my-high-places he-makes-me-tread__|
```

a = *reason-result*u	u = base-restatement	o' = *generic-specific*	
b = base-restatement	v = base-amplification	p' = *means-result*	
c = base-addition	w = base-circumstance	q' = base-amplification	
d = *grounds-request*	x = base-sequential	r' = *means-result*	
e = base-restatement	y = *means-result*	s' = base-restatement	
f = base-amplification	z = base-sequential	t' = base-restatement	
g = general-specific	a' = base-addition	u' = base-addition	
h = base-location	b' = base-addition	v' = *result-reason* (?)	
i = base-restatement	c' = base-addition	w' = *concession-contraexpectation*	
j = base-amplification	d' = *reason-result*	x' = base-amplification	
k = base-restatement	e' = base-restatement	y' = base-amplification	
l = base-description	f' = *result-reason*	z' = base-amplification	
m = base-restatement	g' = base-restatement	a" = base-addition	
n = base-addition	h' = base-restatement	b" = base-addition	
o = base-sequential	i' = base-addition	c" = base-amplification	
p = base-circumstance	j' = base-sequential	d" = *concession-contraexpectation*	
q = reason-result	k' = *means-purpose*	e" = base-restatement	
r = base-addition	l' = base-addition	f" = *means-result*	
s = *reason-result*	m' = base-circumstance	g" = base-addition	
t = base-restatement	n' = base-addition	h" = *means-result*	
i" = base-addition	j" = *request-grounds*	k" = *grounds-conclusion*	

Lesson 6
Analyzing and Translating Biblical Prose

Aim: In this lesson you will further explore the nature and purpose of biblical prose—in particular, New Testament prose, but also some important prose passages of the Old Testament. Our main emphasis will be on learning and applying a methodology for recognizing and analyzing different types of prose passages in both the Bible and your language. The point is to search for TL models that will be the closest possible literary functional equivalents to the various prose genres and styles found in the Scriptures.

Goals: After working through this lesson you should be able to do the following tasks:

1. Describe the four major prose discourse types of the Bible.

2. Identify and analyze some of the main prose genres of the Old Testament.

3. Identify and analyze some of the main prose genres of the New Testament.

4. Learn and apply a methodology for investigating different types of prose discourse.

5. Identify prose genres and features in your language which match those of the Bible.

6. Analyze and translate selected prose passages of Scripture by the *LiFE* method.

7. Evaluate your version in comparison with others and prepare a revised common text.

Review:
Lesson 4 and the differences that we commonly find between prose and poetry texts, both in the Bible and in the target language of a given translation project.

Read:
Chapters 6–7 in *Translating the Literature of Scripture* (Wendland 2004b)
Pages 23–37, 91–113 in *Literary Forms in the New Testament* (Bailey and vander Broek 1992)
Chapters 4–6 in *Cracking Old Testament Codes* (Sandy and Giese 1995)
Chapters 7–8 and 18 in *Analyzing Discourse* (Dooley and Levinsohn 2001)
Chapters 1–2 and 8–9 in *Discourse Features of New Testament Greek* (Levinsohn 2000)
Chapter 10 in *Scripture Frames and Framing* (Wilt and Wendland 2008)

6.1 Reviewing the four major discourse types

The four principal discourse types found in the Scriptures (see section 4.2) are summarized in the following chart. They are found in both prose and poetry, though some are more common than others depending on the particular book that is being considered.

Universal (etic) categories of text type

diagnostic features		Agent Focus	
		+	−
Time	+	NARRATIVE	PROCEDURAL
Sequence	−	HOTATORY	EXPOSITORY

» In our earlier discussion of these four types of discourse, it was noted that another feature that is helpful for distinguishing one from the other is the presence (+) or absence (−) of "direction," or "prescription," within the text.

» How did we classify the four discourse types in this respect? Write either + or − as appropriate for the following types: Narrative ___, Procedural ___, Hortatory ___, Expository ___.

» Four selections from Deuteronomy follow. Study them and on the line below each one write the name of the text type it exemplifies. Give reasons for your choices. Do you have similar prose types in YL? If so, give their vernacular names.

¹ Next we turned and went up along the road toward Bashan, and Og king of Bashan with his whole army marched out to meet us in battle at Edrei. ² The Lord said to me, "Do not be afraid of him, for I have handed him over to you with his whole army and his land. Do to him what you did to Sihon king of the Amorites, who reigned in Heshbon." ³ So the Lord our God also gave into our hands Og king of Bashan and all his army. We struck them down, leaving no survivors. ⁴ At that time we took all his cities. There was not one of the sixty cities that we did not take from them—the whole region of Argob, Og's kingdom in Bashan. ⁵ All these cities were fortified with high walls and with gates and bars, and there were also a great many unwalled villages. ⁶ We completely destroyed them, as we had done with Sihon king of Heshbon, destroying every city—men, women and children. ⁷ But all the livestock and the plunder from their cities we carried off for ourselves. (Deut. 3:1–6, NIV)

Discourse type = _____

⁸ So at that time we took from these two kings of the Amorites the territory east of the Jordan, from the Arnon Gorge as far as Mount Hermon. ⁹ (Hermon is called Sirion by the Sidonians; the Amorites call it Senir.) ¹⁰ We took all the towns on the plateau, and all Gilead, and all Bashan as far as Salecah and Edrei, towns of Og's kingdom in Bashan. ¹¹ (Only Og king of Bashan was left of the remnant of the Rephaites. His bed was made of iron and was more than thirteen feet long and six feet wide. It is still in Rabbah of the Ammonites.) ¹² Of the land that we took over at that time, I gave the Reubenites and the Gadites the territory north of Aroer by the Arnon Gorge, including half the hill country of Gilead, together with its towns. ¹³ The rest of Gilead and also all of Bashan, the kingdom of Og, I gave to the half tribe of Manasseh. (The whole region of Argob in Bashan used to be known as a land of the Rephaites. ¹⁴ Jair, a descendant of Manasseh, took the whole region of Argob as far as the border of the Geshurites and the Maacathites; it was named after him, so that to this day Bashan is called Havvoth Jair.) (Deut. 3:8–14, NIV)

Discourse type = _____

³ You saw with your own eyes what the Lord did at Baal Peor. The Lord your God destroyed from among you everyone who followed the Baal of Peor, ⁴ but all of you who held fast to the Lord your God are still alive today. ⁵ See, I have taught you decrees and laws as the Lord my God commanded me, so that you may follow them in the land you are entering to take possession of it. ⁶ Observe them carefully, for this will show your wisdom and understanding to the nations, who will hear about all these decrees and say, "Surely this great nation is a wise and understanding people." ⁷ What other nation is so great as to have their gods near them the way the Lord our God is near us whenever we pray to him? ⁸ And what other nation is so great as to have such righteous decrees and laws as this body of laws I am setting before you today? ⁹ Only be careful,

and watch yourselves closely so that you do not forget the things your eyes have seen or let them slip from your heart as long as you live. Teach them to your children and to their children after them. (Deut. 4:3–9, NIV)

Discourse type = _____

² You shall offer the passover sacrifice for the Lord your God, from the flock and the herd, at the place that the Lord will choose as a dwelling for his name. ³ You must not eat with it anything leavened. For seven days you shall eat unleavened bread with it—the bread of affliction—because you came out of the land of Egypt in great haste, so that all the days of your life you may remember the day of your departure from the land of Egypt. ⁴ No leaven shall be seen with you in all your territory for seven days; and none of the meat of what you slaughter on the evening of the first day shall remain until morning. ⁵ You are not permitted to offer the passover sacrifice within any of your towns that the Lord your God is giving you. ⁶ But at the place that the Lord your God will choose as a dwelling for his name, only there shall you offer the passover sacrifice, in the evening at sunset, the time of day when you departed from Egypt. ⁷ You shall cook it and eat it at the place that the Lord your God will choose; the next morning you may go back to your tents. ⁸ For six days you shall continue to eat unleavened bread, and on the seventh day there shall be a solemn assembly for the Lord your God, when you shall do no work. (Deut. 16:2–8, NRSV)

Discourse type = _____

Now we will take a little closer look at some of the more specific prose genres to be found in the Scriptures—first of all, some from the Old Testament and then some from the New. During this review, continually compare what we find in the Bible with the corresponding prose discourse types in YL. Note especially where there may be a lack of functionally equivalent forms in the language of your translation. These will have to be investigated in detail later on.

6.2 Identifying and analyzing Old Testament prose genres

To accommodate the four general text types more closely to literature as it actually appears in the Hebrew Scriptures, we will combine the procedural, hortatory, and expository categories into three major mixed groupings: *prophetic*, *legislative*, and *sapiential* writing. They are called "mixed" because the prose texts found in a given category—prophetic, for example—often feature literary composition that includes procedural, hortatory, and/or expository discourse. The narrative category likewise is not really distinct because all the dialogue that it normally incorporates may contain any of the other three types of discourse. Despite all this convergence and coalescence, it is still helpful to use the broad categories as one way to analyze and classify biblical prose passages. This is a "top-down" approach, moving from larger text structures to included subtypes and down to the various stylistic features that tend to characterize different kinds of discourse. Accordingly, in sections 6.2.1–6.2.4 the major genre distinctions of the Old Testament will be briefly defined and illustrated (including some practical exercises) with reference to prophetic, legislative, sapiential, and narrative literature.

6.2.1 Prophetic prose

Ordinary hortatory (technically termed "paraenetic") prophecy stresses how God's people are to respond to him in the here and now—that is, with sincere repentance and loyal obedience. Faith must have its effect on one's life.

Apocalyptic prophecy, on the other hand, is always future oriented, focusing on the mighty acts that Yahweh is going to perform at some unspecified time in order to deliver his people from their powerful enemies. Prophecy of this nature was usually written in times of great national distress and physical persecution. As noted in chapter five, apocalyptic prophecy may be poetic or prosaic in style—or somewhere between.

» What type of literature would you consider the text of Ezekiel 38–39 to be? Why do you say so?

In the spaces below, list examples from Ezekiel 38–39 to illustrate the eight features of apocalyptic poetry (see section 5.3.2):

Visionary revelation: _____

Future orientation: _____

Repeated elements: _____

Graphic imagery: _____

Elaborate symbolism: _____

Strong emotions: _____

Cosmic disruption: _____

Fierce warfare: _____

In contrast to the passage from Daniel 8 that we examined in section 5.3.2, Ezekiel 38–39 (after its initial prophetic introduction in 38:1-2) reads more like a narrative—that is, a story with a *plot* composed of events related by cause and effect with a climax and a final outcome at the end of the discourse. In fact, this Ezekiel pericope may be read like a drama having seven major "scenes," each of which begins with the prophetic formula "This is what the Sovereign LORD says" (כֹּה אָמַר אֲדֹנָי יְהוָה). Write in the spaces below the verse numbers that cover each of these seven scenes. Give a short summary of each scene. (The first one has been done for you.)

38:3–9: <u>The LORD God predicts that he is going to forcibly use the wicked armies of Gog in order to attack his defenseless people in Israel</u>

_____: _____

_____: _____

_____: _____

_____: _____

_____: _____

_____: _____

The final scene in this prophetic drama is climactic—representing the high point of the entire discourse. This peak is marked as such at the very beginning by means of a small addition to the opening formula in Ezekiel 39:25. This passage is shown below as rendered in the NRSV, but in a poetic format.

> ²⁵ Therefore thus *says the Lord God*:
> Now I will restore the fortunes of Jacob,
> and have mercy on the whole house of Israel;
> and I will be jealous for my holy name.
> ²⁶ They shall forget their shame,
> and all the treachery they have practiced against me,
> when they live securely in their land
> with no one to make them afraid,
> ²⁷ when I have brought them back from the peoples
> and gathered them from their enemies' lands,
> and through them have displayed my holiness
> in the sight of many nations.
> ²⁸ Then they shall know that I am the Lord their God
> because I sent them into exile among the nations,
> and then gathered them into their own land.
> I will leave none of them behind;
> ²⁹ and I will never again hide my face from them,
> when I pour out my spirit upon the house of Israel,
> says the Lord God.

» What is the addition to verse 25 and what is its significance here (i.e., the initial לָכֵן)?

» What would be the best way of representing the text in YL—as prose, poetry, or a mixture of both? Explain why you think so.

» Translate the portion accordingly, giving also a back-translation into English. Try to make sure that your version expresses the same sort of verbal vigor and emotive impact as the original text.

Hebrew prophetic writing may contain a variety of other literary types or genres. Sometimes one genre is embedded within a larger, more inclusive style of composition.

» Examine the following passages from Jeremiah (be sure to look up the respective cotexts) and tell what kind of writing each seems to most closely represent.

» Describe the text type as best you can in your own words. For each of these passages, tell whether it seems more poetic or prosaic (comparing the printed format in several major versions).

» Then discuss each passage from the perspective of your own cultural setting and how you would translate the text in a *LiFE*-like manner, whether as prose, poetry, or some combination of the two.

» What are some of the specific stylistic or rhetorical features that these instances of prophetic discourse would need to exhibit so that people can correctly identify their distinctive communicative functions in your language? You may have to use a separate piece of paper in order to comment fully on these passages.

Jeremiah 1

⁴ The word of the Lord came to me, saying, ⁵ "Before I formed you in the womb I knew you, before you were born I set you apart; I appointed you as a prophet to the nations." ⁶ "Ah, Sovereign Lord," I said, "I do not know how to speak; I am only a child." ⁷ But the Lord said to me, "Do not say, 'I am only a child.' You must go

to everyone I send you to and say whatever I command you. ⁸ Do not be afraid of them, for I am with you and will rescue you," declares the Lord. ⁹ Then the Lord reached out his hand and touched my mouth and said to me, "Now, I have put my words in your mouth. ¹⁰ See, today I appoint you over nations and kingdoms to uproot and tear down, to destroy and overthrow, to build and to plant."

Your comments: _____

_____

_____

_____

Compare the format of the NIV with that of the NRSV and other translations, with respect to Jeremiah 1 above.

Jeremiah 3

⁶ During the reign of King Josiah, the Lord said to me, "Have you seen what faithless Israel has done? She has gone up on every high hill and under every spreading tree and has committed adultery there. ⁷ I thought that after she had done all this she would return to me but she did not, and her unfaithful sister Judah saw it. ⁸ I gave faithless Israel her certificate of divorce and sent her away because of all her adulteries. Yet I saw that her unfaithful sister Judah had no fear; she also went out and committed adultery. ⁹ Because Israel's immorality mattered so little to her, she defiled the land and committed adultery with stone and wood. ¹⁰ In spite of all this, her unfaithful sister Judah did not return to me with all her heart, but only in pretense," declares the Lord. ¹¹ The Lord said to me, "Faithless Israel is more righteous than unfaithful Judah.

Your comments: _____

_____

_____

_____

Jeremiah 8

¹ " 'At that time, declares the Lord, the bones of the kings and officials of Judah, the bones of the priests and prophets, and the bones of the people of Jerusalem will be removed from their graves. ² They will be exposed to the sun and the moon and all the stars of the heavens, which they have loved and served and which they have followed and consulted and worshiped. They will not be gathered up or buried, but will be like refuse lying on the ground. ³ Wherever I banish them, all the survivors of this evil nation will prefer death to life, declares the Lord Almighty.'

Your comments: _____

_____

_____

_____

Jeremiah 13

¹ This is what the Lord said to me: "Go and buy a linen belt and put it around your waist, but do not let it touch water." ² So I bought a belt, as the Lord directed, and put it around my waist. ³ Then the word of the Lord came to me a second time: ⁴ "Take the belt you bought and are wearing around your waist, and go now to Perath and hide it there in a crevice in the rocks." ⁵ So I went and hid it at Perath, as the Lord told me. ⁶ Many days later the Lord said to me, "Go now to Perath and get the belt I told you to hide there." ⁷ So I went to Perath and dug up the belt and took it from the place where I had hidden it, but now it was ruined and completely useless.

Your comments: _____

_____

_____

_____

Jeremiah 17

²⁴ But if you are careful to obey me, declares the Lord, and bring no load through the gates of this city on the Sabbath, but keep the Sabbath day holy by not doing any work on it, ²⁵ then kings who sit on David's throne will come through the gates of this city with their officials. They and their officials will come riding in chariots and on horses, accompanied by the men of Judah and those living in Jerusalem, and this city will be inhabited forever. ²⁶ People will come from the towns of Judah and the villages around Jerusalem, from the territory of Benjamin and the western foothills, from the hill country and the Negev, bringing burnt offerings and sacrifices, grain offerings, incense and thank offerings to the house of the Lord. ²⁷ But if you do not obey me to keep the Sabbath day holy by not carrying any load as you come through the gates of Jerusalem on the Sabbath day, then I will kindle an unquenchable fire in the gates of Jerusalem that will consume her fortresses.' "

Your comments: _____

_____

_____

_____

Jeremiah 23

³⁷ This is what you keep saying to a prophet: 'What is the Lord's answer to you?' or 'What has the Lord spoken?' ³⁸ Although you claim, 'This is the oracle of the Lord,' this is what the Lord says: You used the words, 'This is the oracle of the Lord,' even though I told you that you must not claim, 'This is the oracle of the Lord.' ³⁹ Therefore, I will surely forget you and cast you out of my presence along with the city I gave to you and your fathers. ⁴⁰ I will bring upon you everlasting disgrace—everlasting shame that will not be forgotten.

Your comments: _____

_____

_____

_____

Jeremiah 24

³ Then the Lord asked me, "What do you see, Jeremiah?" "Figs," I answered. "The good ones are very good, but the poor ones are so bad they cannot be eaten." ⁴ Then the word of the Lord came to me: ⁵ "This is what the Lord, the God of Israel, says: 'Like these good figs, I regard as good the exiles from Judah, whom I sent away from this place to the land of the Babylonians. ⁶ My eyes will watch over them for their good, and I will bring them back to this land. I will build them up and not tear them down; I will plant them and not uproot them. ⁷ I will give them a heart to know me, that I am the Lord. They will be my people, and I will be their God, for they will return to me with all their heart.

Your comments: _____

_____

_____

_____

Jeremiah 25

¹⁵ This is what the Lord, the God of Israel, said to me: "Take from my hand this cup filled with the wine of my wrath and make all the nations to whom I send you drink it. ¹⁶ When they drink it, they will stagger and go mad because of the sword I will send among them." ¹⁷ So I took the cup from the Lord's hand and made all the nations to whom he sent me drink it: ¹⁸ Jerusalem and the towns of Judah, its kings and officials, to make them a ruin and an object of horror and scorn and cursing, as they are today; ¹⁹ Pharaoh king of Egypt, his attendants, his officials and all his people, ²⁰ and all the foreign people there; all the kings of Uz; all the kings of the Philistines (those of Ashkelon, Gaza, Ekron, and the people left at Ashdod); ²¹ Edom, Moab and Ammon; ²² all the kings of Tyre and Sidon; the kings of the coastlands across the sea; ²³ Dedan, Tema, Buz and all who are in distant places; ²⁴ all the kings of Arabia and all the kings of the foreign people who live in the desert; ²⁵ all the kings of Zimri, Elam and Media; ²⁶ and all the kings of the north, near and far, one after the other—all the kingdoms on the face of the earth. And after all of them, the king of Sheshach will drink it too.

Your comments: _____

_____

_____

_____

Jeremiah 29

⁴ This is what the Lord Almighty, the God of Israel, says to all those I carried into exile from Jerusalem to Babylon: ⁵ "Build houses and settle down; plant gardens and eat what they produce. ⁶ Marry and have sons and daughters; find wives for your sons and give your daughters in marriage, so that they too may have sons and daughters. Increase in number there; do not decrease. ⁷ Also, seek the peace and prosperity of the city to which I have carried you into exile. Pray to the Lord for it, because if it prospers, you too will prosper."
⁸ Yes, this is what the Lord Almighty, the God of Israel, says: "Do not let the prophets and diviners among you deceive you. Do not listen to the dreams you encourage them to have. ⁹ They are prophesying lies to you in my name. I have not sent them," declares the Lord.

Your comments: _____

_____

_____

_____

> » Note how the genre of the preceding passage is classified in Jeremiah 29:1. Does the discourse style match this particular genre? Explain.
>
> » What is the primary communicative function of this "letter" from the LORD?

All preceding texts from Jeremiah have been printed as block prose text, not even distinguishing the different speakers that may be found in a given section. This is not a helpful format because it greatly decreases the readability as well as intelligibility of the text.

> » Point out three good examples of such confusion in the preceding selections.
>
> » Do any of these passages sound more lyrical in nature?
>
> » If so, do you think a poetic, balanced-line arrangement would be easier to follow? Explain.

For reflection, research, and response

1. Find examples of five different types of prophetic prose in the book of Ezekiel. List their references and describe each style of writing, as you did above for the passages from Jeremiah. Then tell how you would translate each passage so that it presents the same purpose, impact, and appeal in YL.

2. Study the passage found in Jer. 33:14–18. What type of prophetic writing is this? Describe this text as best you can in terms of its poetic or prosaic characteristics. List three features of this passage that you will have to give special attention to when translating it into YL. Verses 15–16 are found in another place in Jeremiah. Where is that and what is the significance of this repetition?

3. What distinct features make a particular passage sound less like prose and more like poetry to you? Would you render any of the above passages from Jeremiah as poetry in YL? If so, demonstrate how this would be done, giving a back-translation also in English.

6.2.2 Legislative prose

Three closely interrelated "C"-words describe the legislative, or juridical, literature of the Old Testament: *covenant* + *cult* + *commandment*.[1] As part of the framework of Yahweh's formal covenant with the people of Israel, the Levitical priesthood was designated to administer the legal code of the cultic community, which was set apart through their observance of a host of commands pertaining to national governance, regular worship practices, and interpersonal religious relationships with both God and man (the so-called civil, ceremonial, and moral laws). Most of this legislative discourse is found in the Pentateuch, but it is often referred to elsewhere as "the law" *(tôrâh),* especially in the prophetic literature.

It is important for translators to remember that the key term *tôrâh* does not refer only to "laws" or "commandments" per se.

---

[1] The material presented in STEPS (Salisbury 2002) is especially helpful with the category of "Legal Texts" (see section 12 on the STEPS CD). A more detailed categorization of such "directive" discourse along with a methodology for analysis is found in Kompaoré 2004, chap. 2.

- » What other types of discourse are included under this broad category according to the following passages from Genesis: 1:1–31; 3:14–19; 10:1–32; 12:2–3; 18:23–32; 31:49–50; 35:23–26; 41:17–32, and 49:1–28?

- » What word is used to render *tôrâh* in YL?

- » In view of the preceding text study, can you propose a more inclusive literary term, e.g., "instructions?" Explain.

These different law-oriented writings of the Hebrew Scriptures cannot be properly understood apart from an understanding of the Ancient Near Eastern concept of *covenant*. A covenant in such a context may be defined as a formal (usually public), binding, and mutually agreed-upon means of establishing a significant, long-term personal relationship between two parties, one that involves important reciprocal obligations or responsibilities as well as stipulated, oath-reinforced sanctions for "breaking" it (Foster 2005:16). In the Bible the central covenantal agreement is made between God and his chosen people ("Israel") upon the initiation of the former, Yahweh, who is also the sole determiner of whether or not the human parties, whether individually or collectively, have kept their part of the agreement, the sacred relational bond with their God. There are also several examples of purely human (man ⇔ man) covenants in the Old Testament.

- » How do you best express the concept of *covenant* in your language?

- » Is there any corresponding institution in your culture? Which is the one that comes the closest?

- » Describe its major similarities and contrasts with the biblical practice of covenant.

The ritual of actually agreeing upon (in Hebrew, "cutting") a covenant normally followed these four steps or stages:

	Yahweh – Israel	Jacob – Laban
1. **Proposal** to enter into a covenant relationship	Exod. 19:3–6	Gen. 31:43–44
2. **Acceptance** of the covenant proposal	Exod. 19:7–8	Gen. 31:45–46
3. **Stipulations** (commands) of the covenant	Exod. 20:1–23:33	Gen. 31:49–52
4. **Formalization** of mutual commitment	Exod. 24:3–8 **oath** Exod. 24:9–10 **meal**	Gen. 31:53 Gen. 31:46, 54

Another, somewhat more formal, model of covenant agreement follows the ancient Near Eastern pattern for making a *treaty*. This seems to be the literary genre that was adopted to set forth Yahweh's reiteration of his covenant with Israel as recorded in Deuteronomy. The following is a list of the key components of such a treaty and key examples of their realization in Deuteronomy:

1. **Preamble** (introductory information)   Deut. 1:1–5

2. **Historical prologue** (involving both parties)   Deut. 1:6–3:29

3. **Relationship** specified and encouraged   Deut. 4–11

4. **Stipulations** of the covenant   Deut. 12–26

5. **Witnesses** specified Deut. 27:1–10; 30:19; 31:19, 21, 26, 28; 31:30; 32:1, 46

6. **Curses** for breaking the covenant Deut. 27:11–16; 28:15–68

7. **Blessings** for keeping the covenant Deut. 28:1–14

Covenant was thus the image that God used in relating himself personally to the people of Israel. Various sacrifices and offerings were also involved—those of commitment, thanksgiving, fellowship, or repentance—thus symbolizing this interpersonal religious bond in a concrete way (see, e.g., Deut. 27:5–7). It is especially when the sinfulness of the people or their violation of the laws of the covenant had to be dealt with that a blood sacrifice was required. It symbolized the *substitutionary death* needed for the expiation of guilt and the restoration of a right relationship with Yahweh. These offerings, multiplied on a daily basis, became a regular part of the ritual life of the Jews. It is important to understand their underlying motivating purpose: Yahweh in mercy desired to preserve an intimate relationship with his people and demonstrate this loving desire for fellowship. The many diverse laws of the OT were simply a detailed, but necessary means for stimulating and encouraging the close covenantal connection.

There are many different terms to express the general concept of *law* in Hebrew. At times, several of these terms are used together to emphasize the importance of the law in the religious life of God's people. Genesis 26:5 is an example:

עֵ֕קֶב אֲשֶׁר־שָׁמַ֥ע אַבְרָהָ֖ם בְּקֹלִ֑י וַיִּשְׁמֹר֙ מִשְׁמַרְתִּ֔י מִצְוֺתַ֖י חֻקּוֹתַ֥י וְתוֹרֹתָֽי׃

because Abraham obeyed me and kept my requirements, my commands, my decrees and my laws

» What words do you use in YL to express these four Hebrew legal terms: requirements, commands, decrees, laws? See also Psalm 19:7–9.

There are two basic kinds of laws, or commands, in the OT legislative literature. Examples of these two types follow. Try to define the difference between them.

Do not make any gods to be alongside me; do not make for yourselves gods of silver or gods of gold. (Exod. 20:23)

If you make an altar of stones for me, do not build it with dressed stones, for you will defile it if you use a tool on it. (Exod. 20:25)

The first type, illustrated by Exodus 20:23, is termed a *categorical* (or *apodictic*) command. It is a positive or negative general (unconditional) rule and thus applies to every situation within its scope. No particular exceptions or punishments are mentioned. The idea is, "*Do* it!" or "*Do not* do it!" The prescription or prohibition, sometimes reinforced by a curse (Deut. 27:16), is simply to be obeyed at all times as behavior that publicly affirms the people's loyalty to the covenantal relationship that they have with their God. The law in question might pertain to their belief system, religious practice, public morality, or civic responsibility, but in any case it also carried a significant theological component since all of the laws were given by divine decree. This premise is emphasized in Leviticus, with its repeated reminders like Leviticus 19:32: "Rise in the presence of the aged, show respect for the elderly and revere your God. I am the LORD."

» What is the reason for adding "I am the Lord?" Were the people in danger of forgetting this fact?

» How can you bring out the significance of this personal expression of affirmation in your translation?

As was mentioned in exercise 4 of section 4.2, categorical commands in the OT are generally presented in a *deductive* manner, that is, first the hortatory thesis and then the supportive material (in *italics*), e.g.,

> Honor your father and your mother,
> *as the LORD your God has commanded you, so that you may live long...* (Deut. 5:16)
>
> Walk in all the way that the LORD your God has commanded you,
> *so that you may live and prosper and prolong yours days...* (Deut. 5:32; cf. 10:12–13)

There are occasional exceptions to this order, e.g.,

> *I am the LORD your God, who brought you out of Egypt, out of the land of slavery.*
> You shall have no other Gods before me. (Deut. 5:6–7)

» Is there a possible special discourse function that could explain the reversal of normal order in the preceding example?

» What is the normal way of giving commands or instructions in YL: hortatory thesis (command) first, then supportive material (deductive), or vice-versa (inductive), or does it not make a difference?

» If YL prefers the inductive order, do you need to restructure these types of commands for the sake of naturalness, e.g., "Since the LORD will not hold anyone guiltless who misuses his name, you must not misuse the name of the LORD your God" (Deut. 5:11)? Explain your translation procedure in such cases.

Often we find categorical laws that relate to a certain general subject that includes a number of specific instances.

What, for example, is the broad prohibition that unites the commands of Leviticus 18? Note the significance of the theological saying in 18:2b which prefaces these commands and is also found at their ending in verse 30 as well as several times in between.

The second type of law, of which Exod. 20:25 (above) is an example, is termed a *conditional* (or *casuistic*) command. It usually takes the form "If..., [then]..." and applies only to a specific situation. Examples of the two main kinds of conditional commandment follow:

> If you buy a Hebrew servant, he is to serve you for six years. But in the seventh year, he shall go free, without paying anything. (Exod. 21:2)
>
> If a man beats his male or female slave with a rod and the slave dies as a direct result, he must be punished... (Exod. 21:20)

The first of the above examples is a *relational* command: The *if* clause specifies a particular relationship (with or without its attendant circumstances), while the *then* clause, here rendered "but" (lit., "and"), stipulates the conditions of the relationship.

The second example is an instance of a *remedial* commandment: The *if* clause describes some sort of violation, improper behavior, or impure condition; the *then* clause prescribes the appropriate compensation or retaliation that needs to be applied.

» How must these different "laws" be rendered in your language?

The conditional idea needs special attention, because the corresponding word for "if" in the TL may be either more limited or considerably broader in semantic scope or logical usage than the corresponding biblical term. Is this true in your language?

As we noted in the case of prophetic poetry, the persistent violation of Yahweh's sacred covenant with Israel, especially where gross apostasy was involved, regularly resulted in a "lawsuit indictment." In such instances, one prophet or another would act as Yahweh's spokesman to summon the whole nation, as it were, into God's universal court of justice to answer charges (which they could not) and to receive the pronouncement of due punishment (which they either had already received or would face in the near future).

This type of legal discourse is very common in the prophets. We would do well to remind ourselves of the five principal elements of such a covenantal lawsuit (see section 5.3.2).

» List some examples below from Jeremiah 2, citing the verses that fit into each category:

1. **Introduction:** _____
2. **Indictment:** _____
3. **Elaboration:** _____
4. **Rebuke:** _____
5. **Warning:** _____

Many of the laws and instructions found in legislative prose have to do with the rules and regulations of worship in ancient Israel, for example, concerning the sacrifices, holy days, purification and cleansing rituals, and the instruments and accompaniments of worship, as well as commands governing the lives of priests and Levites. Usually, the various laws are collected into groups that cover the same general category, for example, concerning sacrifices in Leviticus 1:1–7:38, clean versus unclean items and practices in Leviticus 11:1–15:33, the crucial Day of Atonement ritual in Leviticus 16, and priestly regulations in Leviticus 21:1–22:16. But the discourse ordering and patterning often goes much further than that, as Mary Douglas has shown in her detailed studies of Leviticus (1999) and Numbers (1993). For example, with regard to Leviticus she writes as follows (1999:46, 50, 52, italics added):

> Once Leviticus' delight in craftsmanship and design is recognized, the interpretation is transformed. The priestly writing would have used the rhetorical forms that were most highly esteemed in the region.... *As in the rest of the Bible, Leviticus' favorite literary form is parallelism.*...In Leviticus and Numbers *the ring form dominates the whole composition* [A-B-A', i.e., the conclusion matches the beginning in form and/or content, with a significant turning point somewhere in the middle], every couple of chapters, or four or five chapters, form a clearly defined ring, and each book is a maxi-ring containing all the constituent rings....One of the technical problems of any writer is how to conclude. Clear signals of closure are necessary when literary conventions require numerous digressive analogies to build up the theme [as in the legislative literature]....Awareness of structure throughout gives the antique composer many other techniques for signaling that the end of a ring or the end of the whole narrative or treatise is imminent.

One of the common markers of closure in Leviticus is the formula "I am the LORD" (e.g., Lev. 22:2, 3, 8) plus or minus some further attribution such as "who makes them holy" (Lev. 22:9, 16). There may also be extra marking at the close of a major discourse unit, as in Leviticus 22:31–33.

An instance of a lower-level, paralleled ring structure is in Leviticus 22:10–13 (RSV), which features a series of alternating prohibitions and permissions regarding the key concept "holy thing(s)":

A ¹⁰ "An outsider <u>shall not eat</u> *of a holy thing.*
    A sojourner of the priest's or a hired servant <u>shall not eat</u> *of a holy thing;*
B ¹¹ but if a priest buys a slave as his property for money, the slave <u>may eat</u> *of it;*
    and those that are born in his house <u>may eat</u> *of his food.*
C ¹² If a priest's daughter is married to an outsider
    she <u>shall not eat</u> *of the offering of the holy things.*
B' ¹³ But if a priest's daughter is a widow or divorced, and has no child,
    and returns to her father's house, as in her youth,
    she <u>may eat</u> *of her father's food;*
A' yet <u>no</u> outsider <u>shall eat</u> *of it.*

Such encircling mini-structures are common in legislative prose, serving to demarcate the discourse as well as to highlight certain key concepts within these bounded units, for example, the exceptional case involving "a priest's daughter" in verse 12 above (C).

In Numbers 35:33–34 (below, RSV) we see a "terrace structure." This is a pattern of parallelism that is somewhat different from a ring structure, but it performs a similar function in that it marks one major concluding portion of the book of Numbers, in this instance, by means of the common device of end stress (C'):

A ³³ You shall not thus pollute the land
B   in which you live;
C   for blood pollutes the land,
            and no expiation can be made for the land,
            for the blood that is shed in it,
                except by the blood of him who shed it.
A' ³⁴ You shall not defile the land
B'   in which you live,
C'   *in the midst of which* <u>I dwell</u>;
            for <u>I the L</u>ᴏʀᴅ <u>dwell</u> in the midst of the people of Israel."

Certainly, this is not poetry, but such literary patterns are nevertheless poetic in nature and hence also represent an important stylistic and functional aspect of the original text. Translators will probably not be able to do anything about these original artful constructions in their vernacular rendition, but they should at least recognize their presence so that any special semantic or structural significance that appears may be reproduced in the TL by means of an equivalent device and/or explanatory note.

The preceding text from Numbers also provides an extended example of metaphor, a prominent literary feature that translators will have to confront in legislative discourse, as well as in more poetic passages. As Bartholomew (Bartholomew, Greene, and Möller 2001:xxix) observes: "In the priestly literature there *are* central metaphors, such as clean/unclean, and holy/unholy, that structure the entire discourse....It must also be borne in mind that a text like Leviticus is more than a legal text; it is also educative material. And it can be argued that, in educative material, metaphors play a crucial role." The problem is that figurative usage (e.g., blood polluting the land in Num. 35:33) is often so familiar that interpreters (and translators) forget its essentially non-literal nature, which then creates communicative pitfalls.

The following passage from Leviticus 12 (RSV) illustrates another type of problem that frequently arises in connection with ritual texts:

¹ The <u>Lord</u> said to Moses, ² "Say to the people of Israel, If a woman conceives, and bears a male child, then she shall be unclean seven days; as at the time of her menstruation, she shall be unclean. ³ And on the eighth day the flesh of his foreskin shall be circumcised. ⁴ Then she shall continue for thirty-three days in the blood of her purifying; she shall not touch any hallowed thing, nor come into the sanctuary, until the days of her purifying are

completed. ⁵ But if she bears a female child, then she shall be unclean two weeks, as in her menstruation; and she shall continue in the blood of her purifying for sixty-six days.

> » What is the special problem that confronts translators in the preceding text? Give an example.

> » Which words or phrases in this passage would need to be expressed by a euphemism in YL?

Speaking of figurative language, McConville (in Bartholomew, Greene, and Möller 2001:332–333) notes that "Deuteronomy uses a number of important metaphors and symbols in individual ways when compared with their use in other parts of the Old Testament…." There are other notable topics in Deuteronomic theology that might be considered in relation to this issue, such as kingship, treaty, land, the divine name, the brotherhood of Israelites, and circumcision. Deuteronomy 11:16–20 (RSV) is a good illustration of this:

> ¹⁶ Take heed lest your heart be deceived, and you turn aside and serve other gods and worship them, ¹⁷ and the anger of the Lord be kindled against you, and he shut up the heavens, so that there be no rain, and the land yield no fruit, and you perish quickly off the good land which the Lord gives you.
>
> ¹⁸ "You shall therefore lay up these words of mine in your heart and in your soul; and you shall bind them as a sign upon your hand, and they shall be as frontlets between your eyes. ¹⁹ And you shall teach them to your children, talking of them when you are sitting in your house, and when you are walking by the way, and when you lie down, and when you rise. ²⁰ And you shall write them upon the doorposts of your house and upon your gates, ²¹ that your days and the days of your children may be multiplied in the land which the Lord swore to your fathers to give them, as long as the heavens are above the earth.

For reflection, research, and response

1. Pick out all the figures of speech in Deuteronomy 11:16–20 and tell whether you are able to translate them literally in YL. If not, how must these concepts be expressed so as to reproduce the vigorous legislative prose in an appropriate manner.

2. Write a hypothetical "study Bible note" in which you explain the biblical notion of *covenant* for the people of your language and cultural setting. If you compose this note in YL, give also a back-translation into English.

3. Find clear examples of a *categorical* command as well as a *conditional* command in Exodus. Look for passages that present a cultural problem for you in translation; then explain what this is and tell how you would have to resolve it in YL.

4. In Exodus 25:17 we read: "Make an atonement cover of pure gold—two and half cubits long…." What type of command is this—a "categorical" or a "conditional" one? Or is this some other type of discourse (literary genre)? Check the cotext to make sure. Explain your answer.

5. Study Leviticus 17 (in the Hebrew text or an interlinear translation if possible) and use some of the literary-rhetorical criteria that we have practiced in this workbook to identify its thematic center. Give reasons for choosing this passage as the discourse peak, making use of a structural diagram if necessary to clarify your argument. How would you distinguish this focal point in your translation?

6. How would you translate the legislative refrain "I am the Lord" in Leviticus 19:12: "Do not swear falsely by my name and so profane the name of your God. I am the Lord" (NIV). What is the function of this refrain in Leviticus? How can you give it the same impact in YL?

7. How would you classify Deuteronomy 8:1–20 and Joshua 23:2b–16? What is the principal discourse type that each of these texts manifests? What other genres of discourse are included in each passage? List them and note how they serve to divide the text into smaller segments. Tell where you would put paragraph breaks in each one and give reasons for your breaks. Use features such as reiteration, patterns of participant or topical reference, structural parallelism, marked syntactic movements, the embedding of direct speech, unusual vocabulary, concentrations of figurative language, and distinctive verb sequences in conjunction with each other in order to demarcate the internal discourse units and indicate points of special prominence within the text.

6.2.3 Sapiential prose

In section 5.3.3 we examined a number of examples of sapiential, or wisdom, poetry. Now we will consider several compositions that are clearly more prosaic in form. These are not so common in the Old Testament (except in the book of Ecclesiastes), but they do serve to illustrate the great variety of literary genres found in the Scriptures as a whole. The prose types listed below fall into two pairs of closely related genres that an author uses for rhetorical purposes as part of an argument. One pair—parable-allegory and fable—is comparative in nature and highly figurative, while the other—reflection and autobiography—is more personal and meditative in style.

1. Parable

The *parable* is a genre that employs a figurative comparison to make a pragmatic point, teach a lesson, or influence the audience regarding a particular issue. Most OT parables are relatively short. Analogy is the essence of the Hebrew generic term *mâshâl* (מָשָׁל), and in the case of a parable the comparison is usually based on a fictional little story or some familiar experience or situation in life that has clear beginning and end points. The contextual setting is crucial to the understanding of a parable, for it provides listeners with the clues for both interpreting and then applying its key character(s) and event(s).

In 2 Samuel 12:1b–4 (RSV) we can see the emotive tension that a longer parable can generate:

> ¹ᵇ There were two men in a certain city, the one rich and the other poor. ² The rich man had very many flocks and herds; ³ but the poor man had nothing but one little ewe lamb, which he had bought. And he brought it up, and it grew up with him and with his children; it used to eat of his morsel, and drink from his cup, and lie in his bosom, and it was like a daughter to him. ⁴ Now there came a traveler to the rich man, and he was unwilling to take one of his own flock or herd to prepare for the wayfarer who had come to him, but he took the poor man's lamb, and prepared it for the man who had come to him.

It is rather hard to differentiate a parable from the related genre known as an *allegory*. In fact, the Hebrew language itself makes no distinction, nor does the Greek term *parabolê* (παραβολή). One way to explain the difference (in English) is to note that an allegory tends to involve more of a direct, point-for-point comparison between the "image" (usually a closely related set of them) and its intended meaning, the "topic," whereas a parable presents a less overt, comparative lesson based on analogy.

» Is the following passage a parable or an allegory? Why do you think so? Does this literary distinction matter when translating these passages in YL? Why or why not?

> ¹ Remember also your Creator in the days of your youth, before the evil days come, and the years draw nigh, when you will say, "I have no pleasure in them"; ² before the sun and the light and the moon and the stars are darkened and the clouds return after the rain; ³ in the day when the keepers of the house tremble, and the strong men are bent, and the grinders cease because they are few, and those that look through the windows are dimmed, ⁴ and the doors on the street are shut; when the sound of the grinding is low, and one rises up at the voice of a bird, and all the

> daughters of song are brought low; ⁵ they are afraid also of what is high, and terrors are in the way; the almond tree blossoms, the grasshopper drags itself along and desire fails; because man goes to his eternal home, and the mourners go about the streets; ⁶ before the silver cord is snapped, or the golden bowl is broken, or the pitcher is broken at the fountain, or the wheel broken at the cistern, ⁷ and the dust returns to the earth as it was, and the spirit returns to God who gave it. (Eccl. 12:1–7, RSV)

» Explain the meaning of this passage.

» Some major translations format this text as poetry and others as prose. What type of discourse do you think it is and why?

» Would you render it as prose or poetry in YL (or something in-between)?

» If you feel that poetry is more appropriate, draw vertical strokes to mark the places in this text where you would propose starting a new poetic line.

2. Fable

A *fable* is a minor genre that is similar in many ways to a parable or allegory, except that it typically is set in the world of nature and uses animals or plants as its chief characters. A fable is normally used to teach a lesson warning against or reproving bad behavior and encouraging or commending the good.

A rare example of a fable in the Old Testament is in Judges 9:8–15 (RSV):

> ⁸ The trees once went forth to anoint a king over them; and they said to the olive tree, 'Reign over us.' ⁹ But the olive tree said to them, 'Shall I leave my fatness, by which gods and men are honored, and go to sway over the trees?' ¹⁰ And the trees said to the fig tree, 'Come you, and reign over us.' ¹¹ But the fig tree said to them, 'Shall I leave my sweetness and my good fruit, and go to sway over the trees?' ¹² And the trees said to the vine, 'Come you, and reign over us.' ¹³ But the vine said to them, 'Shall I leave my wine which cheers gods and men, and go to sway over the trees?' ¹⁴ Then all the trees said to the bramble, 'Come you, and reign over us.' ¹⁵ And the bramble said to the trees, 'If in good faith you are anointing me king over you, then come and take refuge in my shade; but if not, let fire come out of the bramble and devour the cedars of Lebanon.'

» What is the intended contextual meaning of this fable?

» Do you have such fables in your cultural setting?

» Would this type of text be classified differently from a parable in YL? Explain why or why not.

» Does this passage present any kind of translation challenge for you? If so, specify what this is and how you propose handling it.

3. Reflection

A *reflection* is a *proposition* or *hypothesis* put forward by the speaker/author, who then reflects upon it from various perspectives in order to bring the audience to a certain conclusion. It is a type of discourse that characterizes the book of Ecclesiastes.

A typical example is the Teacher's reflection found in Ecclesiastes 6:1–9 (RSV):

> ¹ There is an evil which I have seen under the sun, and it lies heavy upon men: ² a man to whom God gives wealth, possessions, and honor, so that he lacks nothing of all that he desires, yet God does not give him power to enjoy them, but a stranger enjoys them; this is vanity; it is a sore affliction. ³ If a man begets a hundred children, and lives many years, so that the days of his years are many, but he does not enjoy life's good things, and also has no burial, I say that an untimely birth is better off than he. ⁴ For it comes into vanity and goes into darkness, and in darkness its name is covered; ⁵ moreover it has not seen the sun or known anything; yet it finds rest rather than he. ⁶ Even though he should live a thousand years twice told, yet enjoy no good—do not all go to the one place? ⁷ All the toil of man is for his mouth, yet his appetite is not satisfied. ⁸ For what advantage has the wise man over the fool? And what does the poor man have who knows how to conduct himself before the living? ⁹ Better is the sight of the eyes than the wandering of desire; this also is vanity and a striving after wind.

The Teacher usually propounds what may be termed "counter-wisdom" (or "anti-wisdom"), discussing the common sapiential themes of Israel's religious sages from a skeptical, antithetical, or pessimistic perspective. The aim is to challenge dead orthodoxy and a mechanical *do ut des* religious practice—that is, simply follow the standard rules of morality and God will be good to you.

» What is the author's conclusion here?

» Do you have examples of such critical, pessimistic discourse in your cultural setting?

» If not, are people going to have difficulties in understanding a book like Ecclesiastes?

» What might be done to clarify the nature and purpose of this insightful didactic and reflective genre?

4. Autobiography

A subtype of "reflection" (see above), an *autobiography* is told as if it were an actual personal experience of the speaker/writer. The account, told in the first person, may even be true to a greater or lesser extent, but the point is not its historicity so much as the fact that it is an ethical or theological lesson that the writer is trying to get across, whether directly and positively as in Proverbs, or indirectly and negatively as in the Teacher's discourse.

An example of autobiography is that expressed by the Teacher in Ecclesiastes 1:12–18 (NIV):

> ¹² I, the Teacher, was king over Israel in Jerusalem. ¹³ I devoted myself to study and to explore by wisdom all that is done under heaven. What a heavy burden God has laid on men! ¹⁴ I have seen all the things that are done under the sun; all of them are meaningless, a chasing after the wind. ¹⁵ What is twisted cannot be straightened; what is lacking cannot be counted. ¹⁶ I thought to myself, "Look, I have grown and increased in wisdom more than anyone who has ruled over Jerusalem before me; I have experienced much of wisdom and knowledge." ¹⁷ Then I applied myself to the understanding of wisdom, and also of madness and folly, but I learned that this, too, is a chasing after the wind. ¹⁸ For with much wisdom comes much sorrow; the more knowledge, the more grief.

» The conclusion of this autobiographical account is the same as in the literary reflection above—what is it?

» Included within this text are two passages that might be interpreted as poetic sayings or aphorisms. Where are they located?

» Do they need to be marked in a special way in YL?

- » What harm or loss is there if these two aphorisms are not distinguished at all?

- » Do you find the book of Ecclesiastes relatively easy or hard to translate? Why does this seem to be the case?

For reflection, research, and response:

1. Summarize the long *allegory* in Ezekiel 17 in terms of its imagery and intended meaning (which is explicitly given in the same chapter). Would there be a need to mark this type of discourse in YL, and if so, how could this best be done? There is actually a second and related allegory at the end of Ezekiel 17, but in this case no interpretation is given—it takes the form of a prophecy. Would readers have a hard time determining the meaning of this prophetic allegory? If so, what can be done about it?

2. The issue of *euphemism* comes to the fore in Ezekiel 23:1–10 (quoted below from the RSV). What kind of a literary text is this? How does recognizing its genre affect your interpretation of it? Do you have an equivalent genre or discourse style in your oral or written tradition of verbal art? If so, briefly describe it. Mention some of the difficulties that you face when translating this text in YL.

   > [1] The word of the Lord came to me: [2] "Son of man, there were two women, the daughters of one mother; [3] they played the harlot in Egypt; they played the harlot in their youth; there their breasts were pressed and their virgin bosoms handled. [4] Oholah was the name of the elder and Oholibah the name of her sister. They became mine, and they bore sons and daughters. As for their names, Oholah is Samaria, and Oholibah is Jerusalem.
   >
   > [5] "Oholah played the harlot while she was mine; and she doted on her lovers the Assyrians, [6] warriors clothed in purple, governors and commanders, all of them desirable young men, horsemen riding on horses. [7] She bestowed her harlotries upon them, the choicest men of Assyria all of them; and she defiled herself with all the idols of every one on whom she doted. [8] She did not give up her harlotry which she had practiced since her days in Egypt; for in her youth men had lain with her and handled her virgin bosom and poured out their lust upon her. [9] Therefore I delivered her into the hands of her lovers, into the hands of the Assyrians, upon whom she doted. [10] These uncovered her nakedness; they seized her sons and her daughters; and her they slew with the sword; and she became a byword among women, when judgment had been executed upon her.

3. Identify the *fable* and its interpretation in 2 Kings 14:9–10. Is there a danger that people might misunderstand this piece of advice, if you translate it literally? If so, how might you mark it as non-literal and didactic in YL?

4. What sort of discourse do we find in Jeremiah 29:4–23? You may wish to classify this text in more than one way, but give reasons based on the text's formal features and function why it may be viewed as a distinctive instance of literary communication. Would this passage present any problems if you translated it meaningfully in YL? Explain why or why not.

5. What is the meaning of the sapiential *reflection* in the following text, Ecclesiastes 4:13–16 (RSV):

   > [13] Better is a poor and wise youth than an old and foolish king, who will no longer take advice, [14] even though he had gone from prison to the throne or in his own kingdom had been born poor. [15] I saw all the living who move about under the sun, as well as that youth, who was to stand in his place; [16] there was no end of all the people; he was over all of them. Yet those who come later will not rejoice in him. Surely this also is vanity and a striving after wind.

Compare the preceding translation with that of the GNT for the same passage:

> ^{13–14} Someone may rise from poverty to become king of his country, or go from prison to the throne, but if in his old age he is too foolish to take advice, he is not as well off as a young man who is poor but intelligent. ¹⁵ I thought about all the people who live in this world, and I realized that somewhere among them there is a young man who will take the king's place. ¹⁶ There may be no limit to the number of people a king rules; when he is gone, no one will be grateful for what he has done. It is useless. It is like chasing the wind.

Why is the order of verse 13 and verse 14 reversed in the GNT? Which version is easier to understand? Cite several examples to support your answer. Then tell how you might prepare a *LiFE*-like translation of this passage in YL—that is, a rendering that is not only understandable and stylistically natural, but also pragmatically compelling, as in the original.

Would you consider Ecclesiastes 12:9-14 to be a "reflection?" What is the special importance of this pericope within the book as a whole? Is there any way to stylistically "mark" this conclusion? Explain.

6.2.4 Narrative prose

In the Old Testament, narrative prose is the most familiar and perhaps also the easiest genre to translate, although degrees of literary excellence are certainly possible. The simplest sort of narrative is a *genealogy*, which is a record or table of the descent of an individual, family, or larger kinship group from a notable ancestor or line of ancestors. The OT genealogies are all patrilineal (with descent traced through the male line). They may be either *linear*, as in Genesis 11:10–26, or *segmented* (i.e., branched in nature, listing two or more lines of descent from the founding personage), as in Genesis 36:20–28. Biblical genealogies were not only summary historical records, but they also functioned to distinguish the people of Israel from their most closely related neighbors in Palestine. In addition, they reaffirmed the people's covenantal status in relation to Yahweh; in the turbulent post-exilic times they served also to formally document the purity of the nation, the priestly lineage in particular.

In a succinct genealogical record, any special elaboration, qualification, or variation from the standard manner of reporting is noteworthy. Observe for example the importance of what is said by means of such novelty in Genesis 5:18–31:

> ¹⁸ When Jared had lived a hundred and sixty-two years he became the father of Enoch.
> > ¹⁹ Jared lived after the birth of Enoch eight hundred years, and had other sons and daughters.
> > > ²⁰ Thus all the days of Jared were nine hundred and sixty-two years; **and he died**.
>
> ²¹ When Enoch had lived sixty-five years, he became the father of Methuselah.
> > ²² Enoch walked with God after the birth of Methuselah three hundred years, and had other sons and daughters.
> > > ²³ Thus all the days of Enoch were three hundred and sixty-five years.
> > > > ²⁴ *Enoch walked with God; and he was not, for God took him.*
>
> ²⁵ When Methuselah had lived a hundred and eighty-seven years, he became the father of Lamech.
> > 26 Methuselah lived after the birth of Lamech seven hundred and eighty-two years, and had other sons and daughters.
> > > ²⁷ Thus all the days of Methuselah were nine hundred and sixty-nine years; **and he died**.
>
> ²⁸ When Lamech had lived a hundred and eighty-two years, he became the father of a son,
> ²⁹ and called his name Noah, saying,
> "Out of the ground which the Lord has cursed this one shall bring us relief from our work and from the toil of our hands."
> > ³⁰ Lamech lived after the birth of Noah five hundred and ninety-five years, and had other sons and daughters.
> > > ³¹ Thus all the days of Lamech were seven hundred and seventy-seven years; **and he died**.

The special text formatting above helps distinguish the exceptional material in these passages, especially when translating for a more literarily sophisticated readership. There might also be ways to do this in an oral-aural manner if a certain language happens to have a rich genealogical tradition and a distinctive mode of preserving ancestral names for posterity, for example, through the use of royal "praise poetry."

» What is the situation in your culture and language? Are genealogies very highly valued in your oral narrative or ancient musical tradition? Explain.

» Is there any need to stylistically mark Genesis 5:24 in your translation to draw attention to its special significance? If so, how could this be done?

» How does the preceding genealogy differ from the list of names reproduced below from 1 Kings 4:2–6 (NIV, reformatted)? What are the main differences?

> ² And these were his *chief officials*:
> Azariah son of Zadok—*the priest*;
> ³ Elihoreph and Ahijah, sons of Shisha—*secretaries*;
> Jehoshaphat son of Ahilud—*recorder*;
> ⁴ Benaiah son of Jehoiada—*commander in chief*;
> Zadok and Abiathar—*priests*;
> ⁵ Azariah son of Nathan—*in charge of the district officers*;
> Zabud son of Nathan—*a priest and personal adviser to the king*;
> ⁶ Ahishar—*in charge of the palace*;
> Adoniram son of Abda—*in charge of forced labor.*

» How would you classify 1 Kings 4:2–6 in terms of the four major types of prose discourse?

» Which type is it the closest to. Why do you say so?

» Now look at 1 Kings 7:2–8 and 48–50 (quoted below from the NIV). Where does each fit into our system of classification in terms of both form and function? Give reasons for your conclusions in this case.

> **A.** ² He built the Palace of the Forest of Lebanon a hundred cubits long, fifty wide and thirty high, with four rows of cedar columns supporting trimmed cedar beams. ³ It was roofed with cedar above the beams that rested on the columns—forty-five beams, fifteen to a row. ⁴ Its windows were placed high in sets of three, facing each other. ⁵ All the doorways had rectangular frames; they were in the front part in sets of three, facing each other. ⁶ He made a colonnade fifty cubits long and thirty wide. In front of it was a portico, and in front of that were pillars and an overhanging roof. ⁷ He built the throne hall, the Hall of Justice, where he was to judge, and he covered it with cedar from floor to ceiling. ⁸ And the palace in which he was to live, set farther back, was similar in design. Solomon also made a palace like this hall for Pharaoh's daughter, whom he had married (1 Kgs. 7:2–8)

> **B.** ⁴⁸ Solomon also made all the furnishings that were in the LORD's temple:
> the golden altar;
> the golden table on which was the bread of the Presence;
> ⁴⁹ the lampstands of pure gold (five on the right and five on the left, in front of the inner sanctuary);
> the gold floral work and lamps and tongs;
> ⁵⁰ the pure gold basins, wick trimmers, sprinkling bowls, dishes and censers;
> and the gold sockets for the doors of the innermost room, the Most Holy Place, and also for the doors of the main hall of the temple. (1 Kgs. 7:48–50)

> List the formal and functional differences between text A and text B above.

> Does either of these discourse types cause problems when you translate them in YL? If so, explain why and how they may be handled by way of a LiFE method.

Old Testament *narratives* are more developed than genealogies in that they present a sequence of "events" that are related by cause-and-effect. *Events* are significant actions, activities, or happenings that involve a perceptible change of state or situation. Narratives may be studied from a narrower or wider perspective—that is, from standpoint of a story or a history. We will briefly consider each of these approaches in turn.

A "story" is a dynamic narrative typically consisting of an interaction of seven essential components: *structure, setting, plot, point of view, characterization, dialogue,* and *rhetoric*. The analyst needs to carefully examine these components, first individually and then in relation to each other in the complete text. We will now analyze the major story components of the Joseph story of Genesis 37 (see also Wendland 2004b, section 4.3). The sample questions here are suggestive of the things that should be asked when carrying out a detailed narrative study. (They may be supplemented by the additional questions in section 7.2.4 of Wendland 2004b.)

1. Structure

First we are interested in how a story is "demarcated," both externally and internally. The initial and final boundaries of a story are normally established by major shifts in any of the other six features of narrative, but primarily by a change in the setting and/or cast of characters. A story's internal organization involves some sort of segmentation into smaller *episodes* consisting of one or more *scenes*, which in turn consist of one or more *paragraphs*. These internal units may be similarly delineated, except that the shifts involved are not as prominent. All of the episodes and scenes of a given plot-based story are normally quite closely related to one another, usually by featuring one or two main characters who are engaged in a unified and coherent sequence of actions interconnected by cause-and-effect relations.

> What are some structural reasons for beginning a new chapter at Genesis 37 and at 38?

> At which point may Genesis 37 be divided into two "episodes?"

> What are the literary features that support such a division of the text?

Episode 1 consists of three scenes. Write out the verse numbers of each one and give some textual evidence to support your proposed organization of the discourse.

> The scenes of episode 2 are not so easy to distinguish. How many do you find and where?

> Is it helpful to begin a new paragraph unit in YL at every new set of actions or speeches?

> Why is it important to do a structural study at the start of every narrative analysis?

> What are some of the most important literary (or oral) structural indicators in YL, whether of aperture or closure?

2. Setting

The features of time, place, and background circumstances are important because they serve to orient the audience so that they can better perceive and interpret the events recorded. These contextual variables may change during the course of the account, thus breaking it up into "episodes" and perhaps also smaller "scenes," as noted above. The more aspects of the setting that change at any given point, the more important the structural boundary that may be posited there. If these major shifts are accompanied by a significant change in the cast of characters, then a new "story" may be said to begin. Several distinct stories that pertain to a certain important character constitute that person's "history" (e.g., the history of Joseph as recorded in Genesis 37; 39–45; 47–48; 50). Usually, some important information about the setting is given at the beginning of a story, but other details may be added later on as "background" (e.g., to provide some qualification, an explanation, a preview of future events, or a review of past events).

- » Notice how the setting of the Joseph story is given in 37:1. But what is the deeper, thematic meaning here (see 35:27)?

- » Notice the instance of "exclusion" by which chapter 36 is set apart, while the main narrative line continues from 35:29 to 37:1. What is the particular significance of the setting specified in these passages?

- » Of what special importance is the formulaic opener "This is the account of Jacob" in 37:2a?

- » Why is "Jacob" mentioned here, not "Joseph?"

- » What crucial aspects of this story's circumstances are included as part of the setting in 37:2b?

- » Verses 3–4 move us from the story's background setting to the "initial situation," from which point the "plot" begins to develop.

- » What kind of verb tenses (or other linguistic markers) do you need in YL to describe the actions and states that are represented here?

- » Is verse 5 a setting statement or part of the narrative proper? Explain your answer.

- » How does the overall psychological mood of the story's setting change as we move through this chapter? What is it that contributes to this shift? (It could be such things as a parenthetical narrator comment, a highly emotive character speech, and/or a subtle shift in the main sequence of events.)

- » Are the characters' spatial movements noteworthy for any special reason? For example, are they fast or slow or directed up or down, in or out, to or from some prominent place or goal?

- » What contextual information pertaining to the temporal, spatial, or sociocultural setting appears to have been left implicit in the original text of chapter 37 because the author assumes it to be known by his intended audience?

- » Which aspects of this implicit material need to be made explicit so that people today can correctly understand the biblical message?

- » How can these relevant facts best be conveyed—within the text of the translation (e.g., a noun classifier) or in supplementary helps (e.g., an explanatory note)?

Of special importance (since it is often overlooked or ignored) is information concerning ancient social and political institutions, class structures, economic systems, religious rituals, culturally distinct customs, and conventions of politeness.

3. Plot

As noted earlier, this concerns the narrative plan of a given story's events. This dynamic plan moves along an obvious trajectory from one point of interpersonal equilibrium ("steady state") to another that may be similar to (e.g., the story of Job), or as is usually the case, different from the original state (e.g., Jonah). A plot presents a crucial problem, conflict, crisis, test, or task along with its ultimate resolution (whether a success, failure, or somewhere in between). During the course of a plot's consequential *cause-to-effect* development, there may be a high point in the action (a "peak") where a decisive step is taken in determining the eventual outcome. The high point is normally somewhere near the close of the story and is sometimes referred to as the *turning point* of a plot. Often there is some type of additional stylistic marking when the peak is reached, such as a "crowded stage," the introduction of a new character, rapid and dramatic action (or, conversely, slow and drawn-out activities), a "flashback," personal expression of great emotion, or a decisive explanation or important revelation. In some stories an emotive high point, or "climax," may also be present, usually represented in intensified direct speech. The movement, or "pace," of a plot's unfolding action may be relatively fast or slow and with more or less detail (in accordance with TL norms), depending on such devices as sentence length, lexical repetition, the amount of qualifying attribution included, the use of ellipsis, and the inclusion of direct discourse and/or a comment (aside, parenthesis) by the narrator.

» How is the plot of Genesis 37 presented? Try to give a summary outline.

» What is the central "problem," or motivating cause that generates the plot action of Genesis 37? In what way is this problem reinforced or highlighted by repetition or some other literary device?

» How is this plot "complicated"—that is, what happens to make the problem worse, or more difficult to resolve than before?

» Does any flashback or some other deflection from the main event sequence occur in this chapter? If so, at which verse(s)? What is the function of this temporal displacement?

» Where do events of the plot seem to move the slowest? Where the fastest? Why does this happen in each case?

» Where does the action peak of the plot occur? How is it marked in the text?

» Do you notice any emotive climax in this chapter? If so, how is it highlighted?

» Are there special devices in YL that can be used to foreground the peak or the climax of stories? If so, explain what these are and how they might apply in a Bible translation.

» What is the final outcome or interpersonal situation of this story? Why is this important for the larger history of Jacob and Joseph's lives?

4. Point of view

Every story has either a third person point of view (as when a narrator or author tells the story) or a first person point of view (as when one of the characters or participants tells what was witnessed, told, or personally experienced). The use of dialogue, of course, shifts the perspective to that of the speakers. When telling a certain story, the biblical narrator often, but not always, gives us the point of view of the main character, which may include even a revelation of that person's thoughts and feelings. At times, a narrator may directly intervene in a story to make an explanatory comment or offer his own perspective on the events that he is recounting. Such "asides," or parenthetical remarks, are frequently marked by transitional words or phrases at the beginning and/or ending of the digression (e.g., "that is" in Gen. 35:6, 19b).

» What is the primary point of view from which Genesis 37 is told, or is there no single dominant perspective? On what basis do you come to this conclusion?

» Where do major shifts in the point of view occur, and what is their rhetorical effect?

» Whose point of view is adopted at the chapter's climax? What might be the reason for this?

» Whose point of view is represented in verse 36? What effect does this have on our perception of the story?

» Should Genesis 37:36 be regarded as an aside? Why or why not? What difference does it make?

» How does the point of view shift at the onset of chapter 38? Which other narrative elements change at this point?

5. **Characterization**

We need to carefully examine the manner in which the narrator introduces and portrays the persons in his account. Usually, there is only one or at most two major characters in a given episode or scene, though there may be a number of minor ones. Often two or more of the characters will be set in *contrast* to one another. In Hebrew narrative, descriptions of characters tend to be rather brief. Normally, only the most essential details are given, and readers are left to depend on the characters' words and actions for a fuller picture of who they really are. Some analysts distinguish further between "round" and "flat" characters, the former being more complex and fully developed, though less predictable. Flat characters, on the other hand, have very little personality and usually manifest only a single noteworthy trait. Other distinctions that may be included in more detailed stories include "agents" (e.g., servants), who simply perform some necessary action at the moment, and "props," which are important inanimate objects within a certain account (e.g., Noah's ark, the ark of the covenant, Judah's seal, cord, and staff of chap. 38).

» Name the major character(s) of Genesis 37. Why do you consider him (them) to be the most important?

» How do we learn the most about these characters—from their words, actions, or the narrator's description of them? Give an example.

» Who are the minor characters? What makes them less important?

» How would you classify the characters in this story: to be "round" or "flat" (or somewhere in between)? Explain, with examples.

» Which character expresses the most intense feelings and attitudes? Give examples.

» Which pair or pairs of characters contrast most strongly with each other? What is the significance of this?

» Are there any "agents" or important "props" in this chapter? Name them.

» In the narratives of your oral or written tradition, are major characters marked in any special manner? If so, tell how.

» How are characters introduced in narratives of YL as compared with Hebrew or Greek? Do any special linguistic devices mark their appearance (e.g., front-shifting to the head of a clause, use of much descriptive attribution)?

» What is the preferred way in YL of referring to characters once they have been introduced (i.e., "participant reference")? Is it with pronouns, demonstrative forms, indefinite mention? Is there any difference in this respect between major and minor characters?

» Is any character in the Genesis 37 account portrayed in a very positive or a very negative light? If so, name the person and tell what is it that depicts him the most strongly.

6. **Dialogue**

The direct speech of the characters is really the key to understanding and interpreting biblical narrative. Often a story consists mostly of direct discourse, while pure narration is present only for the introduction, conclusion, and internal transitions that move the plot development forward from one speaker and speech to another. The conflict or problem, as well as the thematic peak and resolution of the plot, may be manifested entirely in direct discourse. The speech of a particular character in the vicinity of the peak may include an especially high degree, or "climax," of personal feelings and emotions. When analyzing a dialogue-rich story, it is important to note who does most of the speaking and what he (it usually will be a male character) says in contrast to other speakers on the scene (e.g., any repetition, alterations, elaborations, rejoinders, objections, rebukes, and reprimands). How does what speakers say relate to the main action that they are engaged in, or the central topic that they are conversing about. It is also important to note how dialogue moves the plot forward and brings it to a final resolution. A more detailed analysis will, in addition, investigate the major "speech acts" of the discourse and how they function in interrelation with each other.

» Who speaks the most in Genesis 37? Which other characters speak, and for what purpose?

» Which characters do not speak in this chapter? Is there any reason for this?

» Who utters the most important speech in the entire chapter? Where does this occur, and how is this speech marked in a distinctive way?

» Which are the most important speech acts of the story? Do you anticipate any difficulty in expressing these clearly in YL? Explain.

» Give several specific examples of how direct speech helps reveal the character of the speaker.

» Notice where the narration occurs in this chapter in relation to the dialogues. What does this tell you about the discourse structure and its purpose?

» What is the point of the little dialogue in 37:15–17?

» What does Jacob's utterance in verse 35 suggest about him?

7. **Rhetoric**

Finally, we also need to look for the special stylistic features that the narrator employs to foreground key aspects of the narration or dialogue. We must identify the diverse devices that add greater impact, appeal, and persuasiveness to the account. That is what rhetoric is all about—using language effectively to achieve particular communication goals in and through a given text, oral or written. Several literary forms common in Hebrew narrative discourse are found in poetry as well (see section 5.1), but in prose they are used somewhat differently and for different purposes. The most important one is formal and semantic *recursion* of various kinds (from reiterated key words to repeated type-scenes), which serves to emphasize an author's main theme, develop character, and help demarcate, order, and arrange his text. Other common techniques are figurative language, ellipsis, allusion and enigma, parallelism (e.g., inclusio, chiasm), syntactic displacements, irony and sarcasm, hyperbole, and euphemism. The point where many rhetorical features come together in a story is normally an emotive climax or a thematic peak.

» Try to give one good example each of five distinctive stylistic devices found in Genesis 37.

» Find a point in this story where several literary features converge? What do you think their rhetorical purpose is at this place in the account?

» Notice where the chief instances of repetition occur in this chapter. What is their apparent function in each case?

» Point out the significant instances of recursion—exact, synonymous, and equivalent—that are found in 37:31–33 and 38:17–18, 25–26. These two stories are not quite as different as they may seem on the surface.

» Identify three rhetorical questions in Genesis 37, each with a different communicative goal. How would you express these in YL?

» The word *blood* is repeated in the Genesis 37 story but used in a different sense at least four times. What are the different senses? (You may have to consult an interlinear version to find all the instances.)

» Joseph's account of his dream in verse 7 might be a good place for several ideophones in Bantu languages. Would these be effective stylistic devices to use in YL? If not, what narrative technique would you use to heighten the impact of this "dream report?"

» In the Hebrew text of chapter 37, several instances of poetic phrasing appear (e.g., in the direct speech of verse 7). If you can access the Hebrew text or an interlinear version, point out where this occurs and its rhetorical impact.

» Jacob's cry of anguish in verse 33 sounds like this in Hebrew: *târôp tôrâp yôsêp* ("Joseph has surely been torn to pieces!"). How could you express this poetically in YL, that is, with the same measure of oral-aural forcefulness and feeling?

» What is the primary rhetorical purpose of Genesis 37 within the larger Joseph narrative?

Since the rhetoric of *dialogue* is such a prominent and functional part of OT stories, it may be helpful to examine its crucial operation in another example: 2 Sam 16:15–17:14 (NIV).

> [15] Meanwhile, Absalom and all the men of Israel came to Jerusalem, and Ahithophel was with him. [16] Then Hushai the Arkite, David's friend, went to Absalom and said to him, "Long live the king! Long live the king!"
>
> [17] Absalom asked Hushai, "Is this the love you show your friend? Why didn't you go with your friend?"
>
> [18] Hushai said to Absalom, "No, the one chosen by the LORD, by these people, and by all the men of Israel—his I will be, and I will remain with him. [19] Furthermore, whom should I serve? Should I not serve the son? Just as I served your father, so I will serve you."
>
> [20] Absalom said to Ahithophel, "Give us your advice. What should we do?"

²¹ Ahithophel answered, "Lie with your father's concubines whom he left to take care of the palace. Then all Israel will hear that you have made yourself a stench in your father's nostrils, and the hands of everyone with you will be strengthened." ²² So they pitched a tent for Absalom on the roof, and he lay with his father's concubines in the sight of all Israel.

²³ Now in those days the advice Ahithophel gave was like that of one who inquires of God. That was how both David and Absalom regarded all of Ahithophel's advice.

¹⁷¹ Ahithophel said to Absalom, "I would choose twelve thousand men and set out tonight in pursuit of David. ² I would attack him while he is weary and weak. I would strike him with terror, and then all the people with him will flee. I would strike down only the king ³ and bring all the people back to you. The death of the man you seek will mean the return of all; all the people will be unharmed." ⁴ This plan seemed good to Absalom and to all the elders of Israel.

⁵ But Absalom said, "Summon also Hushai the Arkite, so we can hear what he has to say." ⁶ When Hushai came to him, Absalom said, "Ahithophel has given this advice. Should we do what he says? If not, give us your opinion."
⁷ Hushai replied to Absalom, "The advice Ahithophel has given is not good this time. ⁸ You know your father and his men; they are fighters, and as fierce as a wild bear robbed of her cubs. Besides, your father is an experienced fighter; he will not spend the night with the troops. ⁹ Even now, he is hidden in a cave or some other place. If he should attack your troops first, whoever hears about it will say, 'There has been a slaughter among the troops who follow Absalom.' ¹⁰ Then even the bravest soldier, whose heart is like the heart of a lion, will melt with fear, for all Israel knows that your father is a fighter and that those with him are brave.

¹¹ "So I advise you: Let all Israel, from Dan to Beersheba—as numerous as the sand on the seashore—be gathered to you, with you yourself leading them into battle. ¹² Then we will attack him wherever he may be found, and we will fall on him as dew settles on the ground. Neither he nor any of his men will be left alive. ¹³ If he withdraws into a city, then all Israel will bring ropes to that city, and we will drag it down to the valley until not even a piece of it can be found."

¹⁴ Absalom and all the men of Israel said, "The advice of Hushai the Arkite is better than that of Ahithophel." For the Lord had determined to frustrate the good advice of Ahithophel in order to bring disaster on Absalom.

Compare the speeches of Hushai and Ahitophel in the preceding passage.

» Do you see differences between the two in terms of argument structure, stylistic form, and rhetorical function?

» Which one of the two debaters was verbally more effective in your opinion (regardless of who actually won)? Explain why you think so.

It will help you to answer if you understand the background, which you can read in 2 Samuel 15:13–16:14.

» Point out three aspects of the rhetoric of dialogue in 2 Samuel 16:15–17:14 that would be difficult to translate in YL and explain why.

» Suggest some functionally equivalent stylistic features that might overcome the problems and keep the same level of impact and appeal in YL.

History is a broader type of narrative discourse than *story*. A history may include a number of distinct but interrelated (to varying degrees) "stories" as well as other literary genres, and it may cover the span of many years, for example, the "David history" of the Books of Samuel. The guiding hand of a history's author is more evident in the text as he weaves different genres together to create a unified account with an ideological (yet still essentially theological) plan and purpose. As history, the Books of Samuel tell how the Davidic monarchy was established by Yahweh in Israel. A major goal is to show how it was God who brought David to power and sustained him despite his serious character flaws, errors of judgment, and outright sinfulness. Similarly, the book of Genesis is history; in fact, it is composed of ten "histories" (*tôle<u>d</u>ôwt*), each (except the first) recounting the important events in the life of one of the great men of God, as the "beginnings" of the human record and God's monumental interventions on behalf of a chosen family and nation are unfolded from one era to the next.

Below is a list of fifteen different genres and subgenres that may be incorporated within a narrative text, along with a reference to a passage that exemplifies it. Following that a series of unidentified passages is listed. Choose a letter from the options in the box to identify each passage, using each letter just once. If any of the terms are unfamiliar, look them up in a Bible dictionary.

- a. dirge (2 Sam. 1:26–27)
- b. battle taunt (1 Sam. 17:43–44)
- c. indictment decree (1 Sam. 15:22)
- d. oath (1 Sam. 15:44–45)
- e. judicial parable (2 Sam. 14:5–7)
- f. battle report (2 Sam. 10:15–19)
- g. eulogy (1 Sam. 29:5)
- h. divine dedication (1 Sam. 1:28)
- i. judgment decree (1 Sam. 15:33)
- j. prophecy (1 Sam. 10:6–7)
- k. royal listing (2 Sam. 23:24–28)
- l. thanksgiving psalm (2 Sam. 22:2–4)
- m. petition (2 Sam. 7:25–26)
- n. sacred vow (2 Sam. 15:8)
- o. blessing (1 Sam. 25:32–33)

____Asahel the brother of Joab was one of the thirty; Elhanan the son of Dodo of Bethlehem, Shammah of Harod, Elika of Harod, Helez the Paltite, Ira the son of Ikkesh of Tekoa, Abiezer of Anathoth, Mebunnai the Hushathite, Zalmon the Ahohite, Maharai of Netophah....

____The Lord is my rock, and my fortress, and my deliverer, my God, my rock, in whom I take refuge, my shield and the horn of my salvation, my stronghold and my refuge, my savior; thou savest me from violence. I call upon the Lord, who is worthy to be praised, and I am saved from my enemies.

____I am distressed for you, my brother Jonathan; very pleasant have you been to me; your love to me was wonderful, passing the love of women. How are the mighty fallen, and the weapons of war perished!

____Saul has slain his thousands, and David his ten thousands!

____Am I a dog, that you come to me with sticks?...Come to me, and I will give your flesh to the birds of the air and to the beasts of the field.

____Has the Lord as great delight in burnt offerings and sacrifices, as in obeying the voice of the Lord? Behold, to obey is better than sacrifice, and to hearken than the fat of rams. For rebellion is as the sin of divination, and stubbornness is as iniquity and idolatry. Because you have rejected the word of the Lord, he has also rejected you from being king.

____And now, O Lord God, confirm for ever the word which thou hast spoken concerning thy servant and concerning his house, and do as thou hast spoken; and thy name will be magnified for ever, saying, 'The Lord of hosts is God over Israel,' and the house of thy servant David will be established before thee.

____Blessed be the Lord, the God of Israel, who sent you this day to meet me! Blessed be your discretion, and blessed be you, who have kept me this day from bloodguilt and from avenging myself with my own hand!

____God do so to me and more also; you shall surely die, Jonathan....Shall Jonathan die, who has wrought this great victory in Israel? Far from it! As the Lord lives, there shall not one hair of his head fall to the ground; for he has wrought with God this day.

____As your sword has made women childless, so shall your mother be childless among women.

____Alas, I am a widow; my husband is dead. And your handmaid had two sons, and they quarreled with one another in the field; there was no one to part them, and one struck the other and killed him. And now the whole family has risen against your handmaid, and they say, 'Give up the man who struck his brother, that we may kill him for the life of his brother whom he slew'; and so they would destroy the heir also. Thus they would quench my coal which is left, and leave to my husband neither name nor remnant upon the face of the earth.

____For this child I prayed; and the LORD has granted me my petition which I made to him. Therefore I have lent him to the LORD; as long as he lives, he is lent to the LORD.

____Then the spirit of the LORD will come mightily upon you, and you shall prophesy with them and be turned into another man. Now when these signs meet you, do whatever your hand finds to do, for God is with you.
____But when the Syrians saw that they had been defeated by Israel, they gathered themselves together. And Hadadezer sent, and brought out the Syrians who were beyond the Euphrates; and they came to Helam, with Shobach the commander of the army of Hadadezer at their head. And when it was told David, he gathered all Israel together, and crossed the Jordan, and came to Helam. And the Syrians arrayed themselves against David, and fought with him. And the Syrians fled before Israel; and David slew of the Syrians the men of seven hundred chariots, and forty thousand horsemen, and wounded Shobach the commander of their army, so that he died there. And when all the kings who were servants of Hadadezer saw that they had been defeated by Israel, they made peace with Israel, and became subject to them. So the Syrians feared to help the Ammonites any more.

____If the LORD will indeed bring me back to Jerusalem, then I will offer worship to the LORD.

Autobiography may be classified as a subtype of narrative (as well as "sapiential prose," as shown in section 6.2.3). Why would an autobiography be classified as a "narrative" text? Read the following autobiographical account, which is from Nehemiah 2 (RSV), and list what you find to be its distinctive feature(s):

> [1] In the month of Nisan, in the twentieth year of King Artaxerxes, when wine was before him, I took up the wine and gave it to the king. Now I had not been sad in his presence. [2] And the king said to me, "Why is your face sad, seeing you are not sick? This is nothing else but sadness of the heart." Then I was very much afraid. [3] I said to the king, "Let the king live for ever! Why should not my face be sad, when the city, the place of my fathers' sepulchers, lies waste, and its gates have been destroyed by fire?" [4] Then the king said to me, "For what do you make request?" So I prayed to the God of heaven. [5] And I said to the king, "If it pleases the king, and if your servant has found favor in your sight, that you send me to Judah, to the city of my fathers' sepulchers, that I may rebuild it." [6] And the king said to me (the queen sitting beside him), "How long will you be gone, and when will you return?" So it pleased the king to send me; and I set him a time. [7] And I said to the king, "If it pleases the king, let letters be given me to the governors of the province Beyond the River, that they may let me pass through until I come to Judah; [8] and a letter to Asaph, the keeper of the king's forest, that he may give me timber to make beams for the gates of the fortress of the temple, and for the wall of the city, and for the house which I shall occupy." And the king granted me what I asked, for the good hand of my God was upon me.

» Are autobiographical accounts common in your oral or literary narrative tradition?

» If so, do they manifest any special stylistic characteristic other than the first-person perspective to differentiate them from stories, for example? If possible, describe these features and give examples.

» Point out three special translation problems that you noted in the preceding text, whether major or minor, and tell how you would deal with them in YL.

6.2 Identifying and analyzing Old Testament prose genres

A more detailed way of analyzing the Bible's narrative discourse (as well as other types of discourse) is to prepare a "sequential discourse segmentation chart" (see section 3.6.6 for an NT Greek-based illustration of this procedure). To do this, one needs a very literal, preferably interlinear, translation of the Hebrew or Greek text; for those who know the biblical languages, of course, no translation is needed. In the example below, the Hebrew text is not reproduced, but a hyphenated translation gloss for the words comprising each "lexical unit" has been written down in designated columns with reference to every main "verb" (including the substantive verb 'be', whether expressed or unexpressed) of the passage under consideration. These are set out line by line as indicated by verse numbers and letters along the right-hand margin. This is illustrated below using Genesis 37:1–7 (DO designates the sign of the direct object *'eth*, the = sign designates the Hebrew "hyphen" [maqqeph], and all implicit information is indicated in brackets):

post-verb3	post-verb2	post-verb1	VERB	pre-verb2	pre-verb1	ref.
in-land-of Canaan	in-land-of journeys of his-father	Jacob	and-he-dwelled			1a
		generations-of Jacob	[are]		these	2a
	to-the-flock	with=his-brothers	he-was tending	son-of=seventeen year(s)	Joseph	b
wives-of his-father	with=sons-of Bilhah and-with=sons-of Zilpah	a-young-man	[was]		and-he	c
unto=their-father	their-report bad	Joseph	and-he-brought			d
	more-than=his-brothers	DO-Joseph	he-loved		and-Israel	3a
		to-him	[was]	he	for=son-of=old-ages	b
	a-robe-of decorations	for-him	and-he-made			c
			and-they-saw			4a
	more-than=his-brothers	their-father	he-loved	that-DO-him	their-father	b
			and-they-hated			c
	for-peace	to-speak-to-him	they-were-able		and-not	d
		a-dream	Joseph	and-he-dreamed		5a
		to-his-brothers	and-he-told (it)			b

post-verb3	post-verb2	post-verb1	VERB	pre-verb2	pre-verb1	ref.
	DO-him	to-hate more	and-they-increased			c
		unto-them	and-he-said			6a
		the-this the-dream	hear=now			b
			I-dreamed		which	c
	in-the-middle-of the-field	sheaves	ones-binding [were]	we	and-look!	7a
		my-sheaf	it-rose-up		and-look!	b
			it-stood-upright		and-even=	c
		your-sheaves	they-gathered-around		and-look!	d
		to-my-sheaf	and-they-bowed-down			e

A sequential discourse segmentation chart of this type may be analyzed for various kinds of information and to several degrees of detail, depending on one's knowledge of Hebrew. (Note that it would be better if the chart could be laid out on the long side of the paper so that the vertical columns could be made to line up more evenly.) At a basic level, the items to look out for are these five: (1) syntactic constituents that are shifted out of the normal, default prose order (V-S-O); (2) full noun phrases in pre-verb position; (3) any expanded syntactic "slot," whether Subject, Verb, Object, or Adjunct; (4) non-verbal predications; and (5) all explicit conjunctions or transitional expressions.

With regard to word-order shifts in Hebrew, there are several important distinctions to be noted. A particular syntactic constituent, usually a subject, less often an object or adjunct, may be advanced either to the head (pre-verb) of its clausal unit or, less frequently, reversed to the very end. Constituent advancement, or "front-shifting" (see section 5.1.6 and also Floor 2004, Levinsohn 2006b, and Lunn 2006: chap. 3), has two principal discourse functions: topicalization and focalization.

1. **Topicalization** = introducing (or reintroducing) a new major or minor "topic" into the discourse, usually as a full noun or noun phrase within the main clause of a sentence. The relative strength of a given topic is greater if it is an *agent* (vs. a patient), *human* (vs. inanimate), and/or *definite* (vs. non-specific).

2. **Focalization** = linguistically marking certain information, other than the topic, as being "in focus," that is, having a special salience or holding the greatest attention within a particular clause or sentence. This process normally involves some sort of contrast, disjunction, restriction, expansion, replacement, specification, or shift of emphasis within the prevailing flow of information. In cases where both topicalization and focalization are present in the same predication, the constituent in focus normally occurs after the topic.

Both of these functions need to be distinguished from *intensification,* which refers to a very localized heightening of the qualitative nature of a specific concept or proposition within a clause. Intensification may be produced by exact repetition, the addition of intensifying affixes, use of a graphic figure of speech, an exclamation, ideophone, or any close combination of such literary forms.

As to the salient "markers" in the short sample text of Genesis 37:1–7 that was displayed in the sequential discourse segmentation chart above, we may make some preliminary observations as an example of what to look for and how to interpret what is found. The summary that follows is of course subject to revision as the rest of the pericope is similarly charted ("spatialized") and examined with a sharp linguistic and literary eye.

1. **Markers of Topicalization:**

   - "these" (2a) – marks the onset of the tenth and final "generations" section in Genesis.
   - "Joseph" (2b) – indicates that Joseph is a chief character in the account that follows.

2. **Markers of Focalization:**

   - "and he" (2c) – begins the crucial contrast between Joseph and his brothers in this initial stage-setting section of the narrative.
   - "and Israel" (3a) – introduces a significant element of conflict into the Joseph story.
   - "son of his old age" (3b) – highlights the special reason for Jacob's great love for Joseph.
   - "their father" (4b) – Jacob provoked the family crisis because of his favoritism, at least from *their* perspective ("and they saw…").
   - "which I dreamed" (6c) – use of the cognate object in this redundant relative clause is another way of turning the spotlight on a key aspect of the narrative; namely, Joseph's dreams.

3. **Markers of Intensification:**

   - "with [the] sons of" (2c) – expansive description heightens the element of contrast.
   - "and they hated him all the more" (5c) – an intensification of 4c–d in this narrative preview that summarizes and sets the stage for the detailed account to follow.
   - "and look!" (7a, b, d) – progressively underscores the excitement in Joseph's voice as he naively recounts his dreams to his unwilling audience (hence perhaps also ironic here).
   - "and even" (7c) – creates a mini-climax in Joseph's description of his provocative dream.
   - "sheaf/sheaves" (7a, b, d, e) – repetition accents the respective metaphorical referents, Joseph versus all the other family members.

   » Do you agree with the preceding analysis? Discuss this in class and make any revisions that the group feels is necessary.

The same sort of chart as the one given for Genesis 37:1–7 can be prepared to analyze narrative discourse in the Greek New Testament (see Dooley and Levinsohn 2001, chaps. 8, 11, 18) and also texts of other genres. Such syntactic displays are particularly helpful for studying OT *prophetic* and NT epistolary types of literature.

Of course, analysis is only the first part of the translator's task; the second part is just as important; namely, to render the text at hand not only accurately, but also as dynamically and beautifully as in the biblical text. Salisbury (2002:273) says of this goal with reference to narrative discourse, "If a hearer or reader of your translation cannot visualize the story scene by scene, then some of the impact is lost. Your translation should capture and hold the attention of its readers in the same way that the original story did to its original hearers."

For reflection, research, and response:

1. What is the rhetorical purpose of the genealogies in 1 Chronicles 1–9? Skim through these texts and locate three passages where some additional information is included. Suggest why this material is important to the Chronicler, and tell how it is distinguished in the original text (if it is so marked). Is there any way of calling attention to this information in YL so that the reader does not simply jump over it?

2. Write out a summary analysis of the 1 Samuel 17 narrative of David and Goliath according to its seven principal story constituents: (1) structural organization, external and internal; (2) plot progression; (3) setting/scene; (4) point of view; (5) characterization; (6) dialogue development; and (7) stylistic and rhetorical features. Be prepared to present aspects of your analysis in class and hand in the written assignment for evaluation.

3. Look again at the list of fifteen passages from 1 and 2 Samuel that were cited earlier in this section. Try to identify the *poetic* passages. Point out several distinctly poetic features in each one that lead you to this conclusion, and suggest how you might render them in translation.

4. In a fascinating study of "reading the lines" of the Hebrew Bible (as well as "between" them, i.e., via inter- and intra-textual analysis), Pamela Tamarkin "Reis challenges many commonly held assumptions of scholars by reading biblical texts as integrated, intelligible literary masterworks. She does not find warrant in these stories for the too-easily accepted conclusion that they are patchworks from multiple authors and sources. Her analyses are patently literary, though she is well informed by modern scholarship and traditional (medieval rabbinic) interpretation" (from the dust cover of Reis 2002). The following is a summary concluding her careful literary analysis of 1 Samuel 28 (ibid.:166) [my additional comments are in brackets].

   » Check out her conclusions for yourself and, if you agree, explain where and how these might affect your translation, e.g., with respect to lexical usage (or the text's accompanying paratext).

   I have presented arguments that expose the witch's motivation and King Saul's defection from monotheism. The charge against Saul is grave, but the text demands it. His record of yielding to entreaty, his proclivity for magic, and his fear-numbed stupor constitute the background for his penultimate act of desperation. Among the evidence in the foreground is the pointed use of the root בֶּגֶד [in 28:8, i.e., "clothing" or "treachery," used with the verb "put" on" לבשׁ; cf. the verb in v. 7: בקשׁ "seek out" *contra* Lev. 19:31!] tying Saul to treachery, to the eating of blood by his army, and to *teraphim*. The phrase אֶל־הַמִּטָּה (on the bed) used in the [Hebrew] Bible only of Saul and of *teraphim*, again links Saul to ancestor worship. The witch's use of distinctly covenantal terminology—the technical term, כרת [though in a different, perhaps ironic verbal context in v. 9], plus her equation in the form of: as I did x, now you do y—delineates the heretical bargain. The absence of detail in the meat preparation (made noticeable by juxtaposition of fuller detail in the preparation of the bread) becomes substantive evidence of the bloody rite when coupled with the word זבח [v. 24] (sacrifice, rather than a verb meaning, simply, slaughter) and the needlessly explicit mention of the unleavened, and thus sacrificial character of the bread [מַצָּה, v. 24; cf. Lev. 2:4, 11]. That the witch's meal is a blasphemous ritual is further indicated by the surprising use of the allusive word נגשׁ (offer, approach) [v. 25] where we are led by double precedent to expect שׂים (set) [vv. 21-22]. Saul's end, his final terror [v. 20]—not of death but of life—shows the playing out of an inexorable justice. It is the unforetold penalty for his treacherous blood worship of false gods.

5. Identify some of the different literary genres that are incorporated within the *history* of 1 and 2 Kings. Beside each passage listed below, write the name of the genre that it illustrates.

1 Kings	2 Kings
8:25–30 _____	19:21–28 _____
1:29–30 _____	7:1 _____
2:2–4 _____	7:2b _____
20:39–40 _____	10:34–35 _____
19:11b–13a _____	15:13–14 _____
11:31–36 _____	22:19–20 _____
19:19–21 _____	19:29–31 _____

6. Note the *repetition* in Daniel 3:2–3. How "artistic" is that repetition? Some modern translations (e.g., GNT) go so far as to eliminate it. But the principle of relevance (as well as common sense) tells us that the exact repetition must be there for a reason. Note other instances of repetition in Daniel 3, of the lists in particular, which are characteristic of the style of Daniel. What rhetorical intention could repetition serve in this case—especially when the text is read aloud? Is *satire* a possibility? Would such repetition serve the same purpose in YL? If not, how could the same effect be created in your translation of Daniel?

7. The narrative accounts of Ezra and Nehemiah contain a number of examples of the following type of discourse (from Ezra 7, RSV). What would you call this particular genre? Tell why in terms of both form and function?

> [12] "Artaxerxes, king of kings, to Ezra the priest, the scribe of the law of the God of heaven. And now [13] I make a decree that any one of the people of Israel or their priests or Levites in my kingdom, who freely offers to go to Jerusalem, may go with you. [14] For you are sent by the king and his seven counselors to make inquiries about Judah and Jerusalem according to the law of your God, which is in your hand, [15] and also to convey the silver and gold which the king and his counselors have freely offered to the God of Israel, whose dwelling is in Jerusalem, [16] with all the silver and gold which you shall find in the whole province of Babylonia, and with the freewill offerings of the people and the priests, vowed willingly for the house of their God which is in Jerusalem. [17] With this money, then, you shall with all diligence buy bulls, rams, and lambs, with their cereal offerings and their drink offerings, and you shall offer them upon the altar of the house of your God which is in Jerusalem. [18] Whatever seems good to you and your brethren to do with the rest of the silver and gold, you may do, according to the will of your God. [19] The vessels that have been given you for the service of the house of your God, you shall deliver before the God of Jerusalem. [20] And whatever else is required for the house of your God, which you have occasion to provide, you may provide it out of the king's treasury. [21] "And I, Artaxerxes the king, make a decree to all the treasurers in the province Beyond the River: Whatever Ezra the priest, the scribe of the law of the God of heaven, requires of you, be it done with all diligence, [22] up to a hundred talents of silver, a hundred cors of wheat, a hundred baths of wine, a hundred baths of oil, and salt without prescribing how much. [23] Whatever is commanded by the God of heaven, let it be done in full for the house of the God of heaven, lest his wrath be against the realm of the king and his sons. [24] We also notify you that it shall not be lawful to impose tribute, custom, or toll upon any one of the priests, the Levites, the singers, the doorkeepers, the temple servants, or other servants of this house of God. [25] "And you, Ezra, according to the wisdom of your God which is in your hand, appoint magistrates and judges who may judge all the people in the province Beyond the River, all such as know the laws of your God; and those who do not know them, you shall teach. [26] Whoever will not obey the law of your God and the law of the king, let judgment be strictly executed upon him, whether for death or for banishment or for confiscation of his goods or for imprisonment." [27] Blessed be the Lord, the God of our fathers, who put such a thing as this into the heart of the king, to beautify the house of the Lord which is in Jerusalem, [28] and who extended to me his steadfast love before the king and his counselors, and before all

the king's mighty officers. I took courage, for the hand of the LORD my God was upon me, and I gathered leading men from Israel to go up with me.

The preceding passage has not been formatted to show paragraph units. What effect does this have on your reading and understanding of this text? Give an example. Where would you put paragraph breaks if you were translating the passage in YL? Tell why. In other words, which markers indicate to you that a new unit should begin at such-and-such a verse?

Note that Artaxerxes' "letter" actually includes two distinct types of discourse with respect to communicative function. Designate and describe these two. Then list the formal markers within the text that help you to recognize them as such.

8. Where is a significant chunk of *narrative* text in the book of Isaiah? What is the function of this large medial section of divergent discourse? What part does it play in the organization of Isaiah as a whole? Observe the combined evidence of structural, stylistic, and thematic unity demonstrating that Isaiah was conceived of and composed as a single book, not several "books" simply patched together. Does the issue of compositional history of a given book have any relevance for Bible translators? If so, what is it?

9. List the chapter and verse references of the sections covered by each of the ten "histories" of Genesis. The first section is different in several respects from the nine that follow. How does it differ? Mention several of its main distinguishing features. How and why do the histories of Esau and Jacob differ from one another?

10. *Irony* plays a crucial role in the story of Jonah. Look it up in a dictionary and note the different senses listed there (cf. 5.1.5). One type of irony is a rhetorical device in which words are used to convey some contrast to their literal meaning. The writer presents something that sounds out of place, absurd, inappropriate, inconsistent, contradictory, or the opposite of what might be expected. In the Scriptures the ironic element is often manifested in the words or actions of a major character. Mention three instances of verbal or situational irony that you notice in the book of Jonah.

11. (This exercise is only for students who can use a Hebrew interlinear text.) Prepare a sequential discourse segmentation chart for Genesis 37:17–25. What does the chart tell you, especially with regard to any instances of focalization or intensification that you find? In other words, how can such a study help give you a better picture of the rhetorical dynamics of this stage of the Joseph story? Finally, point out how such a detailed text study can also help you to become a better translator.

6.3 Identifying and analyzing New Testament prose genres

Only a selection of the main New Testament genres and subgenres of prose will be considered in this section. They are grouped into four main categories: *narrative*, *epistolary*, *locutionary*, and *poetic* discourse. The first two of these are primary macrogenres, while the second two refer to specific styles of composition; namely, a representation of direct speech (*locutionary*) and a text that manifests a lyrical overlay (*poetic*). In these two latter cases, we are dealing with texts that certainly were originally meant to be read and heard aloud. Therefore, the analytical concerns of aural esthetics and persuasive rhetoric must be taken into consideration during the analytical process.

It will be helpful here to review of a set of possible analysis procedures. The following twelve steps (see sections 3.6 and 5.4) may be applied to all four categories of prose discourse:

1. Read the entire text aloud (several times) and determine its main genre and subgenres.

2. Study the complete textual, intertextual, and extratextual context as carefully as possible.

3. Plot all occurrences of exact and synonymous repetition in the pericope.

4. Find all instances of disjunction and content shifting (e.g., topic, setting) within the discourse.

5. Isolate and describe the obvious areas of special stylistic concentration within the text.

6. Identify the major areas of discourse demarcation and the points of projection (peak, climax).

7. Analyze the larger compositional (syntactic-semantic) structure of the entire pericope.

8. Prepare a complete thematic (word/symbol/motif) study, especially the key concepts and clusters.

9. Explain any outstanding linguistic and literary features that remain unaccounted for.

10. Note the major speech functions (speech acts) and their interaction in the discourse overall.

11. Do an explicit stylistic and structural comparison of the features of the SL text with TL features for possible form-functional matches.

12. Prepare a well-formatted *LiFE* translation as a trial, testing it comparatively against other versions.

We will not be able to carry out all of these steps for the various prose text types considered here, but students are encouraged to at least keep them in mind when reading through sections 6.3.1–6.3.3. Of course, it must always be remembered that there is more than one way by which a set of text analysis procedures can be formulated and performed, as a comparison of the lists of steps in sections 3.6 and 5.4 reveal.

The class should discuss the various options and come up with a sequence of steps that seems to work the best for the group. The course instructor may assign certain selected procedures to be performed with respect to one or more of the sample passages in the following sections.

6.3.1 Narrative prose

Each of the four Gospels and the book of Acts manifests a mixed macrogenre. That is, the text exhibits a variable combination of significant aspects of ancient biography and history (both of which are types of narrative prose), with the Gospels favoring the former and Acts the latter. Moreover, depending on the particular book and passage, the Greek text appears to be influenced by a Semitic style derived either directly from the Hebrew Old Testament or indirectly via the relatively literal Septuagint translation. According to Bailey and vander Broek (1992:91–92), Greco-Roman *history* focused on the great deeds (*praxeis*) of significant personages as viewed from a larger social, cultural, political, and/or military perspective, while *biography* emphasized the character (*ethos*) of such individuals and how their words (*logos*) and deeds served to reveal that character, whether good or evil, as a model to be emulated or avoided.

An ancient biography might be composed to fill an apologetic or ideological function in relation to its central character. For this reason it is important to carefully examine any synoptic parallels (with respect to Matthew, Mark, and Luke), noting any differences of treatment or perspective that might indicate a different authorial purpose or audience (e.g., the parallel passages of Matt. 9:18–26, Mark 5:21–43, and Luke 8:41–56). Biblical history-biography was of course written from the wider viewpoint of God's comprehensive "salvation-history" as centered in the person and works of the promised Messiah. For that reason, certain pertinent OT citations are often included to demonstrate the intertextual and theological connection between the two testaments.

Scholars have identified a number of different subgenres in any given Gospel narrative (including *genealogy*, considered in section 6.2.4. The four most prominent subgenres are:

1. Miracle story

A *miracle story*, as the name suggests, is a narrative text that recounts how Christ (or in Acts, an apostle) performed some miraculous action in demonstration of God's power over the limitations and afflictions of human life or the forces of nature. Such a conquest might involve an *exorcism* (with typical motifs such as confrontation, expulsion, and reaction, as in Mark 5:1–20); a *healing* (petition, challenge, expression of faith, therapeutic action, and outcome, as in John 2:1–11); a *controversy* (challenge, key counter-question, debate, and final saying supported by miraculous action, as in Luke 13:10–17; a *rescue* (crisis, appeal, and act of deliverance, as in Mark 4:35–41 and Acts 12:1–17); and an *epiphany* (as in Matt. 14:22–33). The striking interplay between Christ's (or an apostle's) speech and actions is especially prominent in such stories. This dynamic progression or movement should be reflected in a literary translation, using narrative devices of the TL oral or written tradition. Other features of importance in this subgenre are: the reactions of other characters on the scene; the peak point of the central crisis; the role played by Christ's miraculous intervention; and any subsequent discourse that the miracle provides an occasion for.

Analyze Mark 3:1–6 (RSV) in terms of the relevant distinctions noted in the preceding paragraph:

> [1] Again he entered the synagogue, and a man was there who had a withered hand. [2] And they watched him, to see whether he would heal him on the sabbath, so that they might accuse him. [3] And he said to the man who had the withered hand, "Come here." [4] And he said to them, "Is it lawful on the sabbath to do good or to do harm, to save life or to kill?" But they were silent. [5] And he looked around at them with anger, grieved at their hardness of heart, and said to the man, "*Stretch out your hand.*" He stretched it out, and his hand was restored. [6] The Pharisees went out, and immediately held counsel with the Herodians against him, how to destroy him.

» Where does the peak of this miracle story occur, and what is your evidence for this conclusion?

» Why is Christ's command "stretch out your hand" quoted exactly?

» Why is this statement so important in the context?

» How would you format this text on the printed page to better reveal the narrative development?

» Give some specific examples and reasons for your suggestions.

2. Commissioning story

A *commissioning story* is a narrative type with the following basic sequence of plot elements: (a) *introduction,* (b) *confrontation,* (c) *reaction,* (d) *objection,* (e) *reassurance,* (f) *commission,* and (g) *conclusion.* The sequence may vary according to the cotext, however, with the elements sometimes occurring in a different order or some omitted or repeated. A commissioning story features the calling of a man or woman of God to perform a special service for the Lord. An example is Christ's calling of Saul on the Damascus road (Bailey and vander Broek 1992:145): (a) Acts 9:1–3a, (b) 3b, (c) 4a, (b) 4b, (c) 5a, (f) 5b–6, (c) 7, and (g) 8–9.

Commissioning stories are most frequently found in Luke. The same pattern occurs also in a number of OT narratives.

» Why would the "objection" and "reassurance" elements not be necessary in the Acts 9 story?

» Find another example of a commissioning account in the NT and analyze it into the narrative stages listed in the preceding paragraph.

3. **Didactic story**

A *didactic story* is a kind of narrative that usually begins with a brief narrative section (sometimes a simple "bridge" text) that leads up to a dialogue involving Christ and some other person or group. There are several overlapping subtypes, depending on the perspective. If the story is told from the perspective of Christ, subtypes include *correction* (e.g., Mark 9:33–37), *exhortation* (e.g., Mark 11:20–25), and *commendation* (Mark 9:33–37). If the story is told from the perspective of the character(s) whom Christ addresses, subtypes include *quest* (e.g., Mark 12:28–34), *objection* (Mark 2:15–17), and *inquiry* (Mark 7:17–23). When analyzing a discourse of this type, one must pay attention to how the biblical writer employs the narrative segments of the text to build up to a rhetorical climax in a memorable saying (aphorism) of Christ, which often ends the section/scene. Such a didactic account is sometimes termed a "pronouncement" story.)

Read the following passage from Mark 12:13–17 (NIV) and answer the questions that follow:

> [13] Later they sent some of the Pharisees and Herodians to Jesus to catch him in his words. [14] They came to him and said, "Teacher, we know you are a man of integrity. You aren't swayed by men, because you pay no attention to who they are; but you teach the way of God in accordance with the truth. Is it right to pay taxes to Caesar or not? [15] Should we pay or shouldn't we?" But Jesus knew their hypocrisy. "Why are you trying to trap me?" he asked. "Bring me a denarius and let me look at it." [16] They brought the coin, and he asked them, "Whose portrait is this? And whose inscription?" "Caesar's," they replied. [17] Then Jesus said to them, "Give to Caesar what is Caesar's and to God what is God's." And they were amazed at him.

» What device does Christ use to help teach his point? Explain the meaning of his concluding line.

» Does this need to be clarified in your translation so that readers will not miss the intended lesson?

» Where in Mark 12:13–17 are paragraph breaks needed so that the reader can more easily follow the dialogue's development and recognize its peak point?

» How would you express Christ's final aphoristic saying most fittingly in YL?

4. **Parable**

Parables are the best-known subgenre within the narrative accounts of the Gospels. They usually present a vivid extended simile in which some common experience from nature or everyday experience is likened to the kingdom of God as in Matthew 13:33 and Luke 13:20–21. In the Septuagint the word *parabolê* (παραβολή) 'parable' is used to translate the Hebrew *mâshâl* (מָשָׁל), which refers to a didactic saying or proverb. Literally, παραβολή means a saying that is placed alongside another, implying some sort of comparison or analogy between them. Normally, the main point, or ground, of this comparison is obvious from the context; however, at other times some research will be necessary in order to discern it. In any case, it always pays to check this out in a reliable commentary or translator's handbook.

The longer parables of Christ present a condensed fictional story that often incorporates direct discourse. They feature one or more personages, whether royal or lowly, religious or secular, who are realistically engaged in some sort of daily activity. Typically, there is something unusual, surprising, ambiguous, enigmatic, or unexpected about the events, and this element provokes or leads up to the main point of the parable. This is normally not stated explicitly; rather, the hearers on the scene (as well as those today) must make their own interpretation or come to their own conclusion. The implicit "lesson" always has something to do with God's rule and purpose in the world, which frequently involves his chosen Messiah. In addition to their realism, vividness, conciseness, and open-endedness, Christ's parables may be characterized by certain literary features such as a single narrative perspective; a duality in which only two characters or groups interact at one time; patterned repetition in sets of three (triads); a predominant end stress, lots of embedded direct speech; and a provocative issue that stimulates a new vision or an altered conception of reality—God's manner of doing things in contrast to the world's way.

The first challenge confronting translators is to correctly interpret the parable, that is, to identify the implicit lesson that Christ sought to teach by this popular method and then to convey it with a corresponding degree of literary artistry, rhetorical force, verbal fluency, narrative focus, didactic impact, and perhaps even subtle ambiguity as manifested in the Greek text. Parables cannot be taken for granted simply because they seem so familiar. They need to be repeatedly worked over and polished stylistically so that they can stand in the translation as worthy representatives of the vividly told original stories. A perfect match is of course impossible in compositional terms, but an informed, practiced, and creative procedure does tend to train translators to be ever more excellent in their efforts as they endeavor to emulate these well-known discourses. Often such repeated text shaping will serve to identify the team member who has the gift of storytelling, whether orally or in writing, and from there he or she can take over in producing that essential first draft which may then be revised where necessary and improved where possible.

Study the following parable, Luke 15:11–24 (RSV), and be prepared to comment on the skill of the Master Storyteller:

[11] And he said,   **A**
"There was a man who had two sons;
[12] and the younger of them said to his father,
'Father, give me the share of property that falls to me.'
And he divided his living between them.

    [13] Not many days later,   **B**
    the younger son gathered all he had
    and took his journey into a far country,
    and there he squandered his property in loose living.
    [14] And when he had spent everything,
    a great famine arose in that country,
    and he began to be in want.

        [15] So he went and joined himself to one of the citizens of that country,   **C**
        who sent him into his fields to feed swine.
        [16] And he would gladly have fed on the pods that the swine ate;
        and no one gave him anything.

            [17] But when he came to himself he said,   **D**
            'How many of my father's hired servants have bread enough and to spare,
            but I perish here with hunger!

            [18] I will arise and go to my father,   **D'**
            and I will say to him,
            "Father, I have sinned against heaven and before you;
            [19] I am no longer worthy to be called your son;
            treat me as one of your hired servants."'

> ^{20} And he arose and came to his father.
> But while he was yet at a distance,
> his father saw him and had compassion,
> and ran and embraced him and kissed him.
> ^{21} And the son said to him,
> 'Father, I have sinned against heaven and before you;
> I am no longer worthy to be called your son.'
> ^{22} But the father said to his servants,
> 'Bring quickly the best robe, and put it on him;
> and put a ring on his hand, and shoes on his feet;
> ^{23} and bring the fatted calf and kill it,
> and let us eat and make merry;
>
> ^{24} for this my son was dead,
> and is alive again;
> he was lost,
> and is found.'
> And they began to make merry.

C'

B'

A'

In the above passage, notice the thematic correspondence (similarity or contrast) between the paired sets of parallel panels, as indicated by the capital letters on the right-hand margin.

A = Separation (~ death!)	**A'** = Fellowship (~ resurrection)
B = Everything lost	**B'** = Everything restored
C = Complete rejection	**C'** = Total acceptance
D = Problem (lost-ness)	**D'** = Solution (found)

» Do you have a literary (oral) genre similar to the "parable" in YL? If so, what are its main stylistic features?

» Where does the peak point(s) occur in this parable and how is it (are they) marked?

» How does the discourse structure serve to call attention to this/these areas of emphasis?

» Are there any other important stylistic features of dramatic narrative that you notice—and what is their apparent rhetorical function?

» How can you duplicate these literary effects in YL?

» Are there any additional vernacular features (e.g., deictic highlighters or dramatic ideophones) that you must use to tell this parable effectively according to its genre in your oral tradition? Give three specific examples.

For reflection, research, and response:

1. Green and Pasquerello (2003:46–47) point out the importance of "history-writing":

> In the Greco-Roman world, history-writing was a powerful means for validating or authorizing beliefs and practices, even peoples. By showing the antiquity of a people, one might establish continuity with the past, give that people a sense of identity, teach that people who they must be and how they must live, and/or legitimate their existence and practices among outsiders.…One scene leads to another, and another, moving from

beginning to middle to end, in the service of a grand *telos* that gains its meaning from the whole of the parts, and projects its meaning back over the parts of the whole.

Apply these notions to the Luke–Acts narrative and suggest any possible implications for the translation of these two books.

2. Critically evaluate the following proposal regarding the patterned discourse structure of Luke (and Acts) and the example given to illustrate this feature (McComiskey 2004:1–2, 122). Does it sound credible in terms of form and function? Give your assessment, whether for or against this interpretation. If you feel that this proposal has sufficient validity and credibility, how would it affect your translation (or annotation) of these books? Should such *intratextual* literary arrangements be distinguished or marked in some way, and if so, how might this be done (for other patterns of this nature, consult McComiskey).

> Luke's arrangement of material and his variety of compositional techniques often reveal his perception of interrelatedness between pericopes. As he considered where to place various accounts in his Gospel, or how to interconnect them through previews and the like, the decisions were greatly affected by similarities (or interrelatedness) he observed between them....By this method, the Evangelist communicates how he has interpreted the linked passages in light of each other....The phenomenon ranges from the subtle use of a brief preview or review to bold structural interconnection between extensive blocks of material. Thus, our study covers correspondences that are *not* structural, but guide the reading process by pointing ahead or behind to material that Luke considered relevant for interpreting the passage at hand. It also covers correspondences that *are* structural. These too guide the reading process in similar fashion, but they additionally reflect the intended organization of material from the level of a section to that of the whole Gospel.... It furthermore develops a detailed parallel structure that organizes all of Luke 4:14-24:53, and therefore, coupled with the generally accepted parallel structure of 1:1-4:13, covers the entire Gospel....

JOHN			JESUS	
1:57	Now the time came for Elizabeth to be delivered and she gave birth to a son.	1.	2:1–7	The time came for Mary to be delivered and she gave birth to her first-born son.
1:58	And her kinsfolk and neighbors rejoiced when they heard what the Lord had done.	2.	2:8–[16]	The shepherds rejoiced, glorifying and praising God for all they had seen and heard.
1:65-66	These verses give a description of the reaction (fear) to the events, a mention of the news and of the laying it up in the hearts of those who heard.	3.	2:17-18	These verses give a description of the reaction (wonder) to the event, a mention of the spreading of the news, and of Mary's keeping all this in her heart.
1:59-64	The child is circumcised on the eighth day and named John as the angel had directed.	4.	2:21	The child is circumcised at the end of eight days and named Jesus as the angel had directed.
1:67-79	A prophetic hymn of God's act and John's function.	5.	2:22-38	A prophetic hymn of God's act and Jesus' function.
1:80a	The child grew and became strong in spirit.	6.	2:39-40	The child grew and became strong.
1:80b	He was in the wilderness until...	7.	2:41-52	He went down to Nazareth until...

Now you make a note of the principal correspondence, lexical and/or conceptual, that you see between the following two sets of passages from Luke 24 and Acts 1. What is the literary-functional significance of these *intertextual* similarities? Is there any compositional significance here, for example, regarding the issue of authorship? Is there a need to call attention to these parallels in your translation? If so, how do you suggest doing this in a way that your readers will benefit from?

LUKE 24:	33–34, 36	36–43	49	47–48	51–52
ACTS 1:	3	3	4	8b	9, 12

3. Outline the miracle story in Acts 3:1–10. Where does the peak of this narrative occur? Why do you say so? Are there any markers in the biblical text that would highlight this climax? (If possible refer to the Greek text.) How does this story relate to the Acts 3:11–26 discourse that follows it?

4. Closely compare Matthew 8:14–17, Mark 1:29–34, and Luke 4:38–41. Each text presents the same healing event. Point out two major differences in these miracle stories. How do these differences reflect their respective authors' strategies in relation to different audiences?

5. Review the basic components of a commissioning story. Now identify them in the account of the "calling" of Mary (Luke 1:26–38, NIV):

> 26 In the sixth month, God sent the angel Gabriel to Nazareth, a town in Galilee, 27 to a virgin pledged to be married to a man named Joseph, a descendant of David. The virgin's name was Mary. 28 The angel went to her and said, "Greetings, you who are highly favored! The Lord is with you." 29 Mary was greatly troubled at his words and wondered what kind of greeting this might be. 30 But the angel said to her, "Do not be afraid, Mary, you have found favor with God. 31 You will be with child and give birth to a son, and you are to give him the name Jesus. 32 He will be great and will be called the Son of the Most High. The Lord God will give him the throne of his father David, 33 and he will reign over the house of Jacob forever; his kingdom will ever end." 34 "How will this be," Mary asked the angel, "since I am a virgin?" 35 The angel answered, "The Holy Spirit will come upon you, and the power of the Most High will overshadow you. So the holy one to be born will be called the Son of God. 36 Even Elizabeth your relative is going to have a child in her old age, and she who was said to be barren is in her sixth month. 37 For nothing is impossible with God." 38 "I am the Lord's servant," Mary answered. "May it be to me as you have said." Then the angel left her.

What variations in the standard pattern do you see here? What might be their purpose?

6. What difference(s) do you see between the Matthew 1:1–17 and Luke 3:38 genealogies? Is there a peak point in either one of these passages? If so, where does it occur and how is it marked (if at all)? How does each of these genealogies relate to the rhetorical purpose of its author? Can you suggest why each genealogy is placed where it is in the larger account?

7. The book of Acts contains several short letters that need to be translated distinctly from their surrounding narrative text. Point out three stylistic features that distinguish Acts 15:23–29 (below, RSV) as being such a letter. Point out any potential translation problems that you see here. Tell how you would deal with them in YL.

> 23 "The brethren, both the apostles and the elders, to the brethren who are of the Gentiles in Antioch and Syria and Cilicia, greeting. 24 Since we have heard that some persons from us have troubled you with words, unsettling your minds, although we gave them no instructions, 25 it has seemed good to us, having come to one accord, to choose men and send them to you with our beloved Barnabas and Paul, 26 men who have risked their lives for the sake of our Lord Jesus Christ. 27 We have therefore sent Judas and Silas, who themselves will tell you the same things by word of mouth. 28 For it has seemed good to the Holy Spirit and to us to lay upon you no greater burden than these necessary things: 29 that you abstain from what has been sacrificed to idols and from blood and from what is strangled and from unchastity. If you keep yourselves from these, you will do well. Farewell."

8. What type of text is the Revelation 7:5–8 passage that follows? How does it differ from narrative discourse? What particular problems of translation and format presentation does it pose?

> ⁵ twelve thousand sealed out of the tribe of Judah, twelve thousand of the tribe of Reuben, twelve thousand of the tribe of Gad, ⁶ twelve thousand of the tribe of Asher, twelve thousand of the tribe of Naphtali, twelve thousand of the tribe of Manasseh, ⁷ twelve thousand of the tribe of Simeon, twelve thousand of the tribe of Levi, twelve thousand of the tribe of Issachar, ⁸ twelve thousand of the tribe of Zebulun, twelve thousand of the tribe of Joseph, twelve thousand sealed out of the tribe of Benjamin.

9. The analysis of many of Christ's longer *parables* can be broken down into three sequential steps:

    a. Identify the *specific audience* that Christ has in mind (and their spiritual need).

    b. Pick out the point of *surprise* or an *unusual* and *unexpected* turn in the story.

    c. Specify what kind of a *response* element (b) was intended to elicit from (a).

    Delineate these three steps then as you analyze the two parables found in Luke 18:2–5 and 10–14.

    Do you have to *mark* stage (b) in some special way when translating the parables so that people do not miss the point? If so, how can you do this? Do you have a special way of signaling the parable *genre* in YL? If so, tell what the typical markers are.

10. Analyze Luke 15:25–32 (below, RSV), which is the second—and climactic—half of the Parable of the Lost Sons. First, see if you can detect any special structural patterning in this section. Then format or outline this arrangement on a separate paper. Suggest where the peak point occurs and how it is marked in the text. Do you observe any other important stylistic features that need to be noted? What is their function in the discourse? Finally, explain how this section of the parable relates to the first part (displayed above) and how Christ's implied teaching is thereby clarified as well as foregrounded in a literary manner.

    > ²⁵ "Now his elder son was in the field; and as he came and drew near to the house, he heard music and dancing. ²⁶ And he called one of the servants and asked what this meant. ²⁷ And he said to him, 'Your brother has come, and your father has killed the fatted calf, because he has received him safe and sound.' ²⁸ But he was angry and refused to go in. His father came out and entreated him, ²⁹ but he answered his father, 'Lo, these many years I have served you, and I never disobeyed your command; yet you never gave me a kid, that I might make merry with my friends. ³⁰ But when this son of yours came, who has devoured your living with harlots, you killed for him the fatted calf!' ³¹ And he said to him, 'Son, you are always with me, and all that is mine is yours. ³² It was fitting to make merry and be glad, for this your brother was dead, and is alive; he was lost, and is found.'"

11. Pick out places in the following passages from Romans that presuppose the narrative account of the Genesis 3 account of the human fall into sin: 3:23; 5:12–21; 7:7–12; 8:19–22; and 8:28–30. What is the significance of these allusions for Paul's developing argument? In other words, how does Paul utilize the Genesis narrative to motivate, frame, and guide his current theological discussion? Is it likely that most members of your primary TL audience will detect and understand these meaningful allusions? If not, how would you fill the crucial information gap? Give one example of your strategy.

12. How would you classify the following passage? What kind of discourse does it represent, and what are the formal signals that indicate this? Where in the Bible do you guess this text is found? Note that it manifests a mixed compositional style since it includes several different literary genres.

    > ¹ And a great portent appeared in heaven, a woman clothed with the sun, with the moon under her feet, and on her head a crown of twelve stars; ² she was with child and she cried out in her pangs of birth, in anguish for delivery. ³ And another portent appeared in heaven;

behold, a great red dragon, with seven heads and ten horns, and seven diadems upon his heads. ⁴ His tail swept down a third of the stars of heaven, and cast them to the earth. And the dragon stood before the woman who was about to bear a child, that he might devour her child when she brought it forth; ⁵ she brought forth a male child, one who is to rule all the nations with a rod of iron, but her child was caught up to God and to his throne, ⁶ and the woman fled into the wilderness, where she has a place prepared by God, in which to be nourished for one thousand two hundred and sixty days. ⁷ Now war arose in heaven, Michael and his angels fighting against the dragon; and the dragon and his angels fought, ⁸ but they were defeated and there was no longer any place for them in heaven. ⁹ And the great dragon was thrown down, that ancient serpent, who is called the Devil and Satan, the deceiver of the whole world—he was thrown down to the earth, and his angels were thrown down with him. ¹⁰ And I heard a loud voice in heaven, saying, "Now the salvation and the power and the kingdom of our God and the authority of his Christ have come, for the accuser of our brethren has been thrown down, who accuses them day and night before our God. ¹¹ And they have conquered him by the blood of the Lamb and by the word of their testimony, for they loved not their lives even unto death. ¹² Rejoice then, O heaven and you that dwell therein! But woe to you, O earth and sea, for the devil has come down to you in great wrath, because he knows that his time is short!" ¹³ And when the dragon saw that he had been thrown down to the earth, he pursued the woman who had borne the male child. ¹⁴ But the woman was given the two wings of the great eagle that she might fly from the serpent into the wilderness, to the place where she is to be nourished for a time, and times, and half a time. ¹⁵ The serpent poured water like a river out of his mouth after the woman, to sweep her away with the flood. ¹⁶ But the earth came to the help of the woman, and the earth opened its mouth and swallowed the river which the dragon had poured from his mouth. ¹⁷ Then the dragon was angry with the woman, and went off to make war on the rest of her offspring, on those who keep the commandments of God and bear testimony to Jesus. And he stood on the sand of the sea. (RSV)

Would you translate the preceding text as a narrative in YL? Why, or why not? Do you need to mark its incorporated subgenres stylistically? If so, which portions? What kind of literary marking would you use? Finally, where would you put the paragraph breaks in this passage and why at these points?

6.3.2 The prose of direct speech (locutionary prose)

Often embedded within NT narrative texts are chunks of direct speech of varied sizes and different speakers. In the Gospels the main speaker is almost always Christ. In the book of Acts, it is one of the apostles, usually Peter or Paul, although there are exceptions such as in Acts 7, where Stephen is the main speaker, and Acts 8:26–40, where Philip is.

John's Gospel is known for some of Christ's longest discourses. With whom is Christ speaking in the following passages?

John 3: _____	John 4: _____
John 5: _____	John 6: _____
John 8: _____	John 10: _____

The expert oratory of Christ is extensively demonstrated throughout all four Gospels. The ancient methods of rhetorical *argumentation* (verbal persuasion) can frequently be discerned in his discourses. These sometimes take the form of a simple wisdom saying, or *aphorism*. Aphorisms are used to teach a lesson, challenge the audience in some way, rebuke them, or illustrate some truth about the kingdom of God. Such incisive, at times hyperbolic or paradoxical, sayings may be stated in three different syntactic modes: declaration, question, and imperative. We also see the Semitic style of parallel expressions (coupled lines) as in the following examples:

1. Declaration

> Do not suppose that I have come to bring peace to the earth.
> I did not come to bring peace, but a sword. (Matt. 10:34)

2. Question

> What good is it for a man to gain the whole world, yet forfeit his soul?
> Or what can a man give in exchange for his soul? (Mark 8:36–37)

3. Imperative

> First let the children eat all they want…
> for it is not right to take the children's bread and toss it to their dogs. (Mark 7:27)

The three basic types of Hebrew poetic parallelism—synonymous, contrastive, and additive (e.g., cause-effect)—can be found in one form or another in the discourses of Christ:

1. Synonymous

> What I tell you in the dark, speak in the daylight;
> what is whispered in your ear, proclaim from the roofs. (Matt. 10:27)

2. Contrastive

> For whoever wants to save his life will lose it,
> but whoever loses his life for me and the gospel will save it.[2] (Mark 8:35)

3. Additive

> No one sews a patch of unshrunk cloth on an old garment,
> for the patch will pull away from the garment, making the tear worse. (Matt. 9:16)

Longer passages and collections of such parallel sayings also occur, as in a "judgment saying," which in its fullest form consists of the following five elements.

1. introduction with a *formula* such as "If anyone" or "whoever"

2. use of the *same verb* in both parts

3. reference to God's *eschatological* judicial action

4. based on the principle of *retributive justice* ("an eye for an eye")

5. a chiastic or terraced arrangement of parallel parts

An example of the fifth element may be seen in the textual arrangement of Luke 12:8–9:

> I tell you—
> <u>whoever</u> *acknowledges* me before men
>   the Son of Man will also *acknowledge* him before the angels of God.
>   <u>But</u> he who *disowns* me before men
>   will be *disowned* before the angels of God.

---

[2] Observe here the chiastic A-B=B'-A' construction that is typical of antithetical texts in the New Testament as well as the Old.

The passage in Matthew 9:16 about sewing a patch on a new piece of clothing also exemplifies Christ's use of a rhetorical argument pattern. This one is known as a *syllogism* (actually, its condensed form, the *enthymeme*, cf. Wendland 2004b:206–208). In it there is a general premise underlying the specific example that leads listeners to a particular conclusion in the verbal context at hand:

Premise-general: No normal person deliberately destroys something useful.

Premise-specific: Putting an unshrunk patch on a new garment would ruin it.

Conclusion: Nobody would sew an unshrunk patch on a new garment

Implication-1: Any such action would be regarded as foolish and wasteful.

Implication-2: Do not act in such a way!

Of course, it is not necessary for translators to analyze every saying of Christ so explicitly. In the case of more difficult passages, however, this method may serve to clarify the meaning and also help to ensure that the intended import and implication is represented in the TL. In cases where ambiguity or misunderstanding results from a literal rendering, translators may wish to restructure the text so that both its sense and also its "salt" (impact and appeal) are preserved.

Another subgenre of argumentative discourse that occasionally appears in Christ's speeches is similar to the *midrashic* (*pesher*) interpretation of the Jewish rabbis. By means of this technique a teacher of the Law would make an authoritative comment on a particular text from the Old Testament, whether an interpretation or a contemporary application. In most instances when Christ referred to the Hebrew Scriptures (or the LXX), he would do so without explicitly stating (as the rabbis did) that this was his own interpretation and not equal to God's Word itself. We see this, for example, in the repeated "but I tell you" sayings of the Sermon on the Mount in Matthew 5 (e.g., in vv. 22, 28, 32, 34, 39, and 44).

A longer more developed variation of this style is found in Matthew 12:3–8, where it is applied to the narrative setting that has just been reported. Christ's "argument" is outlined below on the right-hand margin:

² When the Pharisees saw this, they said to him,
 "Look! Your disciples are doing what is unlawful on the Sabbath." *Case* (issue) at hand
³ He answered,
 "Haven't you read what David did when he and his companions were hungry? *Exception* introduced
⁴ He entered the house of God,
  and he and his companions ate the consecrated bread—
   which was not lawful for them to do, but only for the priests. *Example* from Scripture
⁵ Or haven't you read in the Law
  that on the Sabbath the priests in the temple desecrate the day
   and yet are innocent *Analogy* from Scripture
⁶ I tell you that one greater than the temple is here. *Comparison* (lesser => greater)
⁷ If you had known what these words mean,
  'I desire mercy, not sacrifice,' *Citation* (of the opposite case)
  you would not have condemned the innocent.
   ⁸ For the Son of Man is Lord of the Sabbath *Conclusion* (climactic reason)

In passages like the one above, it is important to perceive the often implicit rhetoric of Christ's argument. Otherwise, his underlying point may be missed. In this instance, there is an analogical relationship between the OT incident reported in 1 Samuel 21:1–6 and the apparent infringement of a Sabbath Day law by Jesus' disciples. On both occasions godly men in extreme circumstances did something that was forbidden. In such situations, however, a higher law applies, that of saving lives, and therefore both David and also the disciples were acting within this larger intention of God's law. Besides, the priests and other holy men of God were clearly allowed on occasion to do what was prohibited to others as a Sabbath norm (see Lev. 24:8–9, Num. 28:9). Above all (where the argument reaches its peak), God's Messiah could overrule any prohibition or command made to human beings.

As far as translating such passages is concerned, it is important to employ explanatory footnotes where necessary along with the pertinent cross-references so that readers can recognize the broader context enough to follow the argument. A judicious use of text formatting may also clarify the line of reasoning.

» What do you think about the print arrangement shown above? Does it help to reveal the intricate dynamics of the discourse?

» Would your primary target readership be able to discern the significance of the indentations and parallel lines?

As part of his rhetorical strategy in the so-called Sermon on the Mount, Christ uses a variety of compositional devices to present his persuasive appeal in support of the divinely established principles of the kingdom of heaven (see Wendland 2004b:418–443). Below is a list of ten broad categories of such stylistic features. Following that is a series of Scripture passages. Choose a letter from the options to identify each passage.

a. Evocative imagery and metaphor
b. Ambiguity, enigma, and paradox
c. Old Testament citations and allusions
d. Condensation and ellipsis
e. Contrast, antithesis, and dissociation[3]
f. Rhythm and sound play (alliteration, punning)
g. Hyperbole, irony, caricature
h. Insertion of direct speech
i. Rhetorical and leading questions
j. Syntactic movement, either front- or back-shift

___"You are the light of the world. A city on a hill cannot be hidden. Neither do people light a lamp and put it under a bushel….In the same way, let your light shine before men.…" (Matt. 5:14–16)

___"When you fast, do not look somber as the hypocrites do, for they disfigure their faces to show men that they are fasting….But when you fast, put oil on your head and wash your face so that it will not be obvious to men that you are fasting.…" (Matt. 6:16–17)

___"And when you pray, do not be like the hypocrites, for they love to pray standing in the synagogues and on the street corners to be seen by men. I tell you the truth, they have received their reward in full." (Matt. 6:5)

___"Now let your word/speech be 'Yes', 'Yes', 'No', 'No'; but the excess of these is from [the] evil [one]." (Matt. 5:37)

___"If you love those who love you, what reward will you get? Are not even the tax collectors doing that? And if you greet only your brothers, what are you doing more than others? Do not even pagans do that?" (Matt. 5:46–47)

___"But when you are doing alms, let not your left know what your right does, so that your alms might be in secret; and your Father, the one seeing in secret, will repay you." (Matt. 6:3–4a)

___"So why do you see the chip, the one in the eye of your brother, but the—in your own eye—beam [front-shift focus] you give no thought to?" (Matt. 7:4)

___original text of Matthew 5:13a–b:
  Ὑμεῖς ἐστε τὸ ἅλας τῆς γῆς·   You are the *salt* of the earth;   (9 syllables)
  ἐὰν δὲ τὸ ἅλας μωρανθῇ,   but if the *salt* loses its saltiness,   (9 syllables)

---

[3]Dissociation, such as we find in Matt. 6:1–4, is a contrastive personal form of argumentation that separates the true reality of a situation from its appearance as popularly believed (or as conceived of and practiced by a particular group, like the Pharisees). Another good example of argumentation by dissociation is in Matt. 5:17–20, a text which confronts believers with a new (or renewed) vision of reality; namely, the true nature of the kingdom of God, as well as the "woe" passages of Matt. 23.

ἐν τίνι ἁλισθήσεται;   how can it be made *salty* again?   (8 syllables)

___"You have heard that it was said, 'Love your neighbor and hate your enemy.' But I tell you: Love your enemies and pray for those who persecute you." (Matt. 5:43–44)

___"Many will say to me on that day, 'Lord, Lord, did we not prophesy in your name...?' Then I will tell them plainly, 'I never knew you....'" (Matt. 7:22–23)

» Which of these NT stylistic devices are common in the narrative tradition of YL?

» Look up each of the passages cited above and determine how the artistic-rhetorical device specified functions within its cotext.

» Would the same function be generated by a literal rendering in YL?

» If not, how do you propose maintaining communicative equivalence in each case?

All of these features operate in varied combinations and proportions throughout Matthew 5–7 to constitute a masterfully arranged instance of religious teaching (acclaimed also by those who were actually on the scene, Matt. 7:28–29).

Another such artfully composed instruction is found in Matthew 6:1–18, which includes a number of these devices in rhetorical interaction. Identify the most obvious literary forms in this passage. Refer to the Greek text if possible. The RSV text of Matthew 6:1–18 has been reformatted here in order to highlight its main poetic parallels:

¹ "Beware of practicing your piety before men in order to be seen by them;
for then you will have no reward from your Father who is in heaven.

² "Thus, when you give alms, sound no trumpet before you,
as the hypocrites do in the synagogues and in the streets,
that they may be praised by men.
   Truly, I say to you, they have received their reward.
      ³ But when you give alms,
      do not let your left hand know what your right hand is doing,
         ⁴ so that your alms may be in secret;
            and your Father who sees in secret will reward you.
⁵ "And when you pray, you must not be like the hypocrites;
for they love to stand and pray in the synagogues and at the street corners,
that they may be seen by men.
   Truly, I say to you, they have received their reward.
      ⁶ But when you pray,
      go into your room and shut the door
      and pray to your Father who is in secret;
            and your Father who sees in secret will reward you.

⁷ "And in praying do not heap up empty phrases as the Gentiles do;
for they think that they will be heard for their many words.
      ⁸ Do not be like them,
      for your Father knows what you need before you ask him.
         ⁹ Pray then like this:
         Our Father who art in heaven,
         Hallowed be thy name.
            ¹⁰ Thy kingdom come,

>   Thy will be done,
>   On earth as it is in heaven.
>   ¹¹ Give us this day our daily bread;
>   ¹² And forgive us our debts,
>   As we also have forgiven our debtors;
>   ¹³ And lead us not into temptation,
>   But deliver us from evil.
>   ¹⁴ For if you forgive men their trespasses,
>   your heavenly Father also will forgive you;
>   ¹⁵ but if you do not forgive men their trespasses,
>   neither will your Father forgive your trespasses.
>
> ¹⁶ "And when you fast, do not look dismal, like the hypocrites,
> for they disfigure their faces that their fasting may be seen by men.
>   Truly, I say to you, they have received their reward.
>   ¹⁷ But when you fast, anoint your head and wash your face,
>   ¹⁸ that your fasting may not be seen by men
>   but by your Father who is in secret;
>   and your Father who sees in secret will reward you.

Observe the intricate pattern of parallels in Matthew 6:1–18.

» There is a brief introduction or title: verse ____.

» The text is then composed of ____ (how many?) parallel panels, each of which corresponds to a poetic paragraph/strophe.

» There is also a larger incorporated strophe that does not quite fit the established pattern exhibited by the rest of the pericope. Which verses are included in this extraordinary segment? verse ____ to verse ____

The indentation of the text shows that each of the parallel texts comprises four utterance units. See if you can list below the corresponding verses that belong to this tripartite structure:

Strophe A – a: ____   **Strophe B** – a: ____   **Strophe C** – a: ____

b: ____   b: ____   b: ____

c: ____   c: ____   c: ____

d: ____   d: ____   d: ____

» Can you suggest a reason why the strophe that spans verses 7–15 is distinct in terms of form, content, and/or function?

» How might this affect your translation strategy for these verses?

The persuasive speech of Christ demands decision and provokes action, yet is able to break through the limits of ordinary discourse to encourage new attitudes and behavior by conveying a new vision of truth and reality. This new perspective is not limited to the expressive potential of human discourse but, more importantly, it serves to stimulate effective and insightful communication within the diverse sociocultural settings and interpersonal situations in which language is used. The rhetoric of Christ is captivating, life-challenging, and life-changing speech. His inductively shaped discourse also features many lifelike examples that are characterized by an occasional humorous touch, down-to-earth realism, and immediate personal relevance.

6.3 Identifying and analyzing New Testament prose genres   325

» Fill in the specific textual instances of this appealing manner of argumentation to fit the general categories that are proposed below for Luke 12:22–31:

EXHORTATION (v. 22): _____

_____

REASON (v. 23): _____

_____

ANALOGY-a (v. 24): _____

_____

EXAMPLE (v. 25): _____

_____

EXHORTATION (v. 26): _____

_____

ANALOGY-b (v. 27a): _____

_____

EPITOME (v. 27b): _____

_____

ANALOGY-c (v. 28): _____

_____

EXHORTATION (v. 29): _____

_____

EXAMPLE (v. 30): _____

_____

EXHORTATION (v. 31): _____

_____

Observe that the various analogies in verses 24 to 28 move from the lesser to the greater, while the repeated exhortations are negative (*prohibitions*). However, the exhortation of verse 31 moves from the _____ to the _____, and is _____ in nature (*prescription*). Notice also that a simple, but profoundly significant logical *enthymeme* underlies Christ's overall argument in this passage:

> **Major premise***:* All living beings are cared for by God.
>
> **Minor premise***:* People are living beings.
>
> **Conclusion***:* Therefore, all people too are cared for by God.

Thus by means of varied forms and expressions of content throughout this pericope, through direct exhortation and figurative implication, the Lord's disciples are encouraged—"Don't worry!" They must not set their hearts on this world, but rather upon the kingdom of God, which is the climactic religious principle that is enunciated at the end.

The Sermon on the Mount, along with all of Christ's other speeches, includes many memorable lines to motivate its hearers to respond in thought and action to the spiritual blessings and the responsibilities of the divine rule that the Messiah was in the very process of inaugurating. Such forthright, presupposition-challenging discourse deserves to be formally expressed in the vernacular in such a way that his words have a similar effect on local audiences today.

The discourses of Christ in John's Gospel tend to be stylistically quite different from those of the Synoptic Gospels. They manifest these principal compositional features:

1. A *question and answer technique* that often leaves the person(s) to whom Jesus is speaking puzzled, confused, and misunderstanding what he means.

2. A dialogue that displays *longer and longer speeches by Jesus* until at last the discourse is pretty much transformed into a monologue in which he teaches some profound theological truth(s), the dialogue at times seeming to merge into a commentary by the evangelist on Jesus' words.

3. *Deep figures of speech* (e.g., metaphors such as the self-disclosing "I AM" statements) and *symbols, ambiguous expressions, aphorisms, words with double meanings, much repetition,* and *subtle irony* (saying one thing but really implying the opposite).

See if you can identify some of these stylistic elements in John 3:1–21, which follows (NIV). While the manner of speaking seems rather simple and straightforward, the meaning of Christ's words is not always easily discerned. His teachings are intended to provoke deep thought about his divine mission on behalf of his Father and the corresponding demands upon those who wish to live in fellowship with God. Pick out three examples of this thematic perspective in the text below, especially where expressed in provocative and figurative terms. Point out any translational problems that you anticipate in these instances. Also consider the NIV footnotes to this passage, and suggest any others that you will have to add in YL.

> [1] Now there was a man of the Pharisees named Nicodemus, a member of the Jewish ruling council. [2] He came to Jesus at night and said, "Rabbi, we know you are a teacher who has come from God. For no one could perform the miraculous signs you are doing if God were not with him."
>
> [3] In reply Jesus declared, "I tell you the truth, no one can see the kingdom of God unless he is born again.[a]"
>
> [4] "How can a man be born when he is old?" Nicodemus asked. "Surely he cannot enter a second time into his mother's womb to be born!"
>
> [5] Jesus answered, "I tell you the truth, no one can enter the kingdom of God unless he is born of water and the Spirit. [6] Flesh gives birth to flesh, but the Spirit [b] gives birth to spirit. [7] You should not be surprised at my saying, 'You[c] must be born again.' [8] The wind blows wherever it pleases. You hear its sound, but you cannot tell where it comes from or where it is going. So it is with everyone born of the Spirit."
>
> [9] "How can this be?" Nicodemus asked.

¹⁰ "You are Israel's teacher," said Jesus, "and do you not understand these things? ¹¹ I tell you the truth, we speak of what we know, and we testify to what we have seen, but still you people do not accept our testimony. ¹² I have spoken to you of earthly things and you do not believe; how then will you believe if I speak of heavenly things? ¹³ No one has ever gone into heaven except the one who came from heaven—the Son of Man.[d] ¹⁴ Just as Moses lifted up the snake in the desert, so the Son of Man must be lifted up, ¹⁵ that everyone who believes in him may have eternal life. [e]

¹⁶ "For God so loved the world that he gave his one and only Son,[f] that whoever believes in him shall not perish but have eternal life. ¹⁷ For God did not send his Son into the world to condemn the world, but to save the world through him. ¹⁸ Whoever believes in him is not condemned, but whoever does not believe stands condemned already because he has not believed in the name of God's one and only Son.[g] ¹⁹ This is the verdict: Light has come into the world, but men loved darkness instead of light because their deeds were evil. ²⁰ Everyone who does evil hates the light, and will not come into the light for fear that his deeds will be exposed. ²¹ But whoever lives by the truth comes into the light, so that it may be seen plainly that what he has done has been done through God."

a. 3:3 Or *born from above;* also in verse 7
b. 3:6 Or *but spirit*
c. 3:7 The Greek is plural.
d. 3:13 Some manuscripts *Man, who is in heaven*
e. 3:15 Or *believes may have eternal life in him*
f. 3:16 Or *his only begotten Son*
g. 3:18 Or *God's only begotten Son*

The book of Acts, like the Gospels, contains much argumentative discourse, especially in the sermons or homilies of Peter and Paul. The major public discourses of the apostles fall into two general categories: the *evangelistic* speeches and the *defense* speeches. The first group, when spoken before a *Jewish* audience, usually contains the following compositional elements, any one of which (except the first) may be repeated:

1. a direct address to the audience

2. mention of some serious misunderstanding or wicked behavior

3. background allusion to the OT Scriptures to establish an authoritative frame of reference

4. witness to Jesus the Christ (including the main thesis or theme)

5. proofs from Scripture, declaration of salvation

6. an appeal for repentance

» Identify these elements in Peter's evangelistic sermon in Acts 3:12–26, which follows. Also indicate where you would place paragraph breaks and why. Finally, make a note of any places where important translational issues arise and describe what these are.

¹²"Men of Israel, why does this surprise you? Why do you stare at us as if by our own power or godliness we had made this man walk? ¹³ The God of Abraham, Isaac and Jacob, the God of our fathers, has glorified his servant Jesus. You handed him over to be killed, and you disowned him before Pilate, though he had decided to let him go. ¹⁴ You disowned the Holy and Righteous One and asked that a murderer be released to you. ¹⁵ You killed the author of life, but God raised him from the dead. We are witnesses of this. ¹⁶ By faith in the name of Jesus, this man whom you see and know was made strong. It is Jesus' name and the faith that comes through him that has given this complete healing to him, as you can all see. ¹⁷ "Now, brothers, I know that you acted in ignorance, as did your leaders. ¹⁸ But this is how God fulfilled what he had foretold through all the prophets, saying that his Christ[a] would suffer. ¹⁹ Repent, then, and turn to God, so that your sins may

be wiped out, that times of refreshing may come from the Lord, [20] and that he may send the Christ, who has been appointed for you—even Jesus. [21] He must remain in heaven until the time comes for God to restore everything, as he promised long ago through his holy prophets. [22] For Moses said, 'The Lord your God will raise up for you a prophet like me from among your own people; you must listen to everything he tells you. [23] Anyone who does not listen to him will be completely cut off from among his people.'[b] [24] "Indeed, all the prophets from Samuel on, as many as have spoken, have foretold these days. [25] And you are heirs of the prophets and of the covenant God made with your fathers. He said to Abraham, 'Through your offspring all peoples on earth will be blessed.'[c] [26] When God raised up his servant, he sent him first to you to bless you by turning each of you from your wicked ways."

- a. 3:18 Or *Messiah*; also in verse 20
- b. Deut. 18:15,18,19
- c. Gen. 22:18; 26:4

Paul, when delivering an evangelistic speech to a *Gentile* audience, replaces allusions to and quotations of Scripture quotations with more general references to God's creative and preserving activity (see, e.g., Acts 14:16–17 and 17:24–27).

As for the *defense* (apologetic) speeches found in the closing chapters of Acts, Paul's discourses of this kind include most of the following compositional elements:

1. terms of address

2. reference to Paul's good character

3. clarification of the legal issues involved

4. refutation of the charges against him (including various proofs)

5. claims of innocence

6. testimony to his righteousness

7. evidence of his apostolic authority

Normally, Paul's defense speeches get interrupted towards the end or are even completely shut down by a hostile audience before being completed.

> » Read Paul's words spoken during his trial before Felix as recorded in Acts 24 and analyze them in terms of the main dialogue constituents listed above.

For reflection, research, and response:

1. Find a good example of each of the three forms of *aphorism* (declaration, question, imperative) in the speeches of Christ and write them out on a separate sheet of paper. How would you render these dynamically in YL?

2. List three important stylistic-rhetorical techniques of Christ that we have discussed and find an example to illustrate each one from a single pericope. (If you do not have a favorite text of your own, you may try Luke 17:26–30.) Then explain how these features function in the passage that you have selected. In other words, how do they increase the impact and appeal of Christ's words at that point and in relation to the discourse as a whole?

3. On the basis of a cognitive-stylistic study of popular literature in English, Gerard Steen (in Semino and Culpeper 2002:205) concludes that "metaphors are often found at turning points in conversations. They often function as summaries and assessments there...." Have you noticed this in the conversations of Christ? A good example is found in John 9. Point out the crucial summarizing metaphor complex there. What are the implications of this for translation? Can you preserve this discourse-marking effect in YL with the same impact and appeal? Explain, with an example.

4. Identify the primary ground(s) of comparison for each of the metaphors involved in the seven distinct "I Am" assertions of Christ in John's Gospel (see John 6:35; 8:12; 10:7, 9; 11:25; 14:6; 15:1). Be sure to determine this with reference to the current cotext and the stated or implied extratextual setting. Can you convey these with the same form and meaning (including sense, impact, beauty, pragmatic implication) in YL? If not, what trade-offs do you have to make in order to prepare an acceptable rendition for the problem cases?

5. Study the quotations below from Robert Tannehill's excellent book, *The Sword of His Mouth* (1975), and suggest how they apply to literary text analysis and translation of the Scriptures.

   > It is my conviction that Biblical scholarship has overlooked the significance of forceful and imaginative language in the synoptic sayings....The purpose of a human utterance is seldom restricted to conveying information. If the scholar is concerned only with informational content, he will often not be able to understand fully the speaker's purpose, nor the significance of his strategy of communication, nor the type of response sought from the hearer. (p. 1)

   > One can properly claim to interpret a text only if he takes account of the intention embodied in the text. The interpreter must allow the text to speak in its own way. He must recognize and respect the particular kind of event which is intended to take place between text and reader and clarify the nature of that event for others. (p. 7)

   > [F]orm is an integral aspect of a text which must be considered if its full significance is to be understood....[A]ll formal features which give special qualities to a text, particularly features which increase its power to challenge the will and awaken the imagination, are relevant.... (pp. 8–9)

   > [W]e should look closely at the form of the synoptic sayings to see how part interacts with part, modifying and enriching meaning, and how tension between parts twists words away from their surface meanings and points to something deeper....[W]e must respect the unity of our texts, regarding each as an equilibrium of forces which is disturbed when any part is examined without attention to the whole. (pp. 16–17)

   > Certain formal features of the [biblical] texts are the public signs that we are dealing with a distinctive mode of language....Formal analysis can protect us against superficial responses to imaginative utterance by examining in detail this [inbuilt] system of controls. (pp. 28–29)

   > Through pattern the [biblical] text gains unity and particularity. Pattern heightens the interaction of the parts, enforcing, contrasting, and enriching. The patterns of these sayings contribute especially to tension, which is strong and pervasive. This tension is the formal reflection of the text's desire to challenge prevailing structures of the personal world and to grant a new vision of some region of existence. (pp. 55–56)

6. The following text is Acts 4:24b–30 (RSV). What genre does it manifest, and what are the stylistic and structural markers that support your classification? Point out three translation problems that you notice (other than the archaic English). Suggest how you would handle these problems in YL. How would you format this passage in terms of line and paragraph breaks?

> ^{24b} "Sovereign Lord, who didst make the heaven and the earth and the sea and everything in them, ²⁵ who by the mouth of our father David, thy servant, didst say by the Holy Spirit, 'Why did the Gentiles rage, and the peoples imagine vain things? ²⁶ The kings of the earth set themselves in array, and the rulers were gathered together, against the Lord and against his Anointed'—²⁷ for truly in this city there were gathered together against thy holy servant Jesus, whom thou didst anoint, both Herod and Pontius Pilate, with the Gentiles and the peoples of Israel, ²⁸ to do whatever thy hand and thy plan had predestined to take place. ²⁹ And now, Lord, look upon their threats, and grant to thy servants to speak thy word with all boldness, ³⁰ while thou stretchest out thy hand to heal, and signs and wonders are performed through the name of thy holy servant Jesus."

7. Many dialogues in the Bible may be classified as "dramatic" in nature, that is, a narrative composed for the most part as a sequence of speeches between two (rarely more) chief characters. Various types of argument are often manifested as the dialogue reaches a climax, with one speaker verbally defeating the other (one speaker may represent a group, such as the Pharisees). Outline the debate that takes place in the dramatic dialogue of Matthew 4:3–10 (below, RSV). Would the respective arguments of Jesus and Satan be clear if rendered literally in YL? If not, what must be done to clarify the point and purpose of either speaker? Finally, how would you format this text with paragraphing to make it look more "dramatic" on the printed page?

   > ³ And the tempter came and said to him [Jesus], "If you are the Son of God, command these stones to become loaves of bread." ⁴ But he answered, "It is written, 'Man shall not live by bread alone, but by every word that proceeds from the mouth of God.'" ⁵ Then the devil took him to the holy city, and set him on the pinnacle of the temple, ⁶ and said to him, "If you are the Son of God, throw yourself down; for it is written, 'He will give his angels charge of you,' and 'On their hands they will bear you up, lest you strike your foot against a stone.'" ⁷ Jesus said to him, "Again it is written, 'You shall not tempt the Lord your God.'"
   > ⁸ Again, the devil took him to a very high mountain, and showed him all the kingdoms of the world and the glory of them; ⁹ and he said to him, "All these I will give you, if you will fall down and worship me." ¹⁰ Then Jesus said to him, "Begone, Satan! for it is written, 'You shall worship the Lord your God and him only shall you serve.'"

8. There is a logical *enthymeme* that underlies Christ's question in Luke 14:28. The main elements of this mini-argument are given below, but in mixed-up order. See if you can fit them into the standard pattern for such types of reasoning (fill out the blanks in the box):

   a. requires serious planning (counting the cost)   b. building a larger tower

   c. a major building project   d. therefore, building a tower

   e. requires serious planning (to avoid failure)   f. is an example of a major building project

   Major premise = ____ + ____
   Minor premise = ____ + ____
   Conclusion = ____ + ____

   Is this sort of reasoning and argumentation apparent to most people of your language-culture? If not, what can be done to clarify such passages in your Bible translation? In the case of Luke 14:28, is the immediate cotext (e.g., v. 29) sufficient to clarify Christ's point? Explain your answer.

9. The following speech by Christ is actually a prayer. Name three major discourse characteristics of a prayer and then analyze the one set out below (John 17, RSV, reformatted). Indicate the larger structural units (paragraphs) and list any important patterns and stylistic devices that you notice.

6.3 Identifying and analyzing New Testament prose genres

What is the rhetorical function of each of these devices? Would they cause you any difficulty when translating this passage into YL? Explain any potential problems that you find.

> ¹ When Jesus had spoken these words,
>   he lifted up his eyes to heaven and said,
>
> Father, the hour has come;
>   glorify thy Son that the Son may glorify thee,
> ² since thou hast given him power over all flesh,
>   to give eternal life to all whom thou hast given him.
> ³ And this is eternal life,
>   that they know thee the only true God,
>   and Jesus Christ whom thou hast sent.
>
> ⁴ I glorified thee on earth,
>   having accomplished the work
>   which thou gavest me to do;
> ⁵ and now, Father, glorify thou me in thy own presence
>   with the glory which I had with thee
>   before the world was made.
>
> ⁶ I have manifested thy name to the men
>   whom thou gavest me out of the world;
> thine they were, and thou gavest them to me,
>   and they have kept thy word.
> ⁷ Now they know that everything
>   that thou hast given me is from thee;
> ⁸ for I have given them the words which thou gavest me,
>   and they have received them
>   and know in truth that I came from thee;
>   and they have believed that thou didst send me.
>
> ⁹ I am praying for them;
> I am not praying for the world
>   but for those whom thou hast given me,
>   for they are thine;
> ¹⁰ all mine are thine, and thine are mine,
>   and I am glorified in them.
>
> ¹¹ And now I am no more in the world,
>   but they are in the world,
>   and I am coming to thee.
> Holy Father, keep them in thy name,
>   which thou hast given me,
>   that they may be one, even as we are one.
>
> ¹² While I was with them,
>   I kept them in thy name,
>   which thou hast given me;
>
> I have guarded them,
>   and none of them is lost but the son of perdition,
>   that the scripture might be fulfilled.

¹³ But now I am coming to thee;
    and these things I speak in the world,
        that they may have my joy fulfilled in themselves.

¹⁴ I have given them thy word;
    and the world has hated them
because they are not of the world,
    even as I am not of the world.
¹⁵ I do not pray that thou shouldst take them out of the world,
    but that thou shouldst keep them from the evil one.
¹⁶ They are not of the world,
    even as I am not of the world.
¹⁷ Sanctify them in the truth;
    thy word is truth.
¹⁸ As thou didst send me into the world,
    so I have sent them into the world.
¹⁹ And for their sake I consecrate myself,
    that they also may be consecrated in truth.
²⁰ "I do not pray for these only,
    but also for those who believe in me through their word,

²¹ that they may all be one;
        even as thou,
        Father, art in me, and I in thee,
    that they also may be in us,
        so that the world may believe that thou hast sent me.

²² The glory which thou hast given me I have given to them,
    that they may be one even as we are one,
²³ I in them and thou in me,
    that they may become perfectly one,
so that the world may know
    that thou hast sent me
    and hast loved them even as thou hast loved me.

²⁴ Father, I desire that they also,
    whom thou hast given me, may be with me where I am,
to behold my glory which thou hast given me
    in thy love for me before the foundation of the world.
²⁵ O righteous Father, the world has not known thee,
    but I have known thee;
    and these know that thou hast sent me.

²⁶ I made known to them thy name,
    and I will make it known,
        that the love with which thou hast loved me may be in them,
            and I in them.

What do you think of the poetic format used above? Does it clarify the thoughts of this prayer? Is the text any easier to read? Explain your answers and suggest any revisions that come to mind. How do you propose translating and formatting this well-known pericope in YL—as prose or as poetry? Explain.

10. Analyze Paul's public speech to the Athenians in Acts 17:22–31 (below, NIV). Indicate where you would put paragraph breaks and why. Outline the main aspects of Paul's argument strategy here. How does he

6.3 Identifying and analyzing New Testament prose genres

try to convince his audience of his main point(s)? Point out three effective rhetorical techniques that he employs in this effort. Would this speech be difficult to translate in YL? Tell why, or why not. Make a list of the important *presuppositions* that Paul makes as he unfolds his argument. How apparent would these be to the people of your culture? Identify any major discrepancies or contradictions.

> [22] …"Men of Athens! I see that in every way you are very religious. [23] For as I walked around and looked carefully at your objects of worship, I even found an altar with this inscription: TO AN UNKNOWN GOD. Now what you worship as something unknown I am going to proclaim to you. [24] "The God who made the world and everything in it is the Lord of heaven and earth and does not live in temples built by hands. [25] And he is not served by human hands, as if he needed anything, because he himself gives all men life and breath and everything else. [26] From one man he made every nation of men, that they should inhabit the whole earth; and he determined the times set for them and the exact places where they should live. [27] God did this so that men would seek him and perhaps reach out for him and find him, though he is not far from each one of us. [28] 'For in him we live and move and have our being.' As some of your own poets have said, 'We are his offspring.' [29] "Therefore since we are God's offspring, we should not think that the divine being is like gold or silver or stone—an image made by man's design and skill. [30] In the past God overlooked such ignorance, but now he commands all people everywhere to repent. [31] For he has set a day when he will judge the world with justice by the man he has appointed. He has given proof of this to all men by raising him from the dead."

11. Direct speech, including direct speech in the Epistles, normally manifests a great deal of idiomatic language. Consider the following Semitic-style religious expressions in their textual context and suggest a nonfigurative meaning that most closely renders the idea in English. Then see if you can find a corresponding figure or idiom in YL to convey any of them (from Nida 2003:119):

> let the dead bury their dead (Luke 9:60)
>
> putting the hand to the plow and looking back (Luke 9:62)
>
> give glory to God (John 9:24)
>
> to be in bitter gall (Acts 8:23)
>
> to pour out blood (Rom. 3:15)
>
> bearing a scar (Gal. 6:17)
>
> strengthen weak knees (Heb. 12:12)
>
> gird up the loins of the mind (1 Pet. 1:13)

Now examine the following set of idioms, all of which involve the "heart" (*kardia*) in Greek (Nida ibid.). What do you think is their primary meaning in the passage specified? Under which generic concept could all these usages be classified? Do you have any "heart" idioms in YL (or perhaps a functionally equivalent figure that features a different body part)? Finally, translate each of these passages idiomatically in your language and with reference to your culture.

> to turn the heart towards (Luke 1:17)
>
> to open the heart (Luke 24:45)
>
> to make hard the heart (John 12:40)
>
> to fill the heart (Acts 5:3)

> to put into the heart (Acts 19:21)
>
> to go up upon the heart (1 Cor. 2:9)
>
> to broaden the heart (2 Cor. 6:11)

6.3.3 Epistolary prose

The discourse types and techniques found in the New Testament letters are somewhat different from those of the Gospels and Acts. On the other hand, since the letters are in effect written sermons delivered at a distance, they are characterized by the style of direct speech, which, as we have seen, is also prominent in the Gospels and Acts, most notably in the speeches of Jesus and the apostles, respectively. There are several other important similarities in terms of general composition, most notably:

1. **Argument strategy**

   Argument strategy normally incorporates a number of *deductive* (cause-effect) and *inductive* (exemplifying) devices that pertain to the current topic. Observe, for example, the various kinds of "proofs" that Paul employs in 1 Corinthians 15 in his argument for belief in a bodily resurrection.

   a. a **reductio ad absurdam**, demonstrating in a sequence of conditional clauses the utter folly of denying the fact, or even the possibility, of a bodily resurrection (vv. 12–19)

   b. a **thesis statement** for the entire argument: since Christ has been raised, believers too will be raised (v. 20)

   c. a **paradigm** from Scripture contrasting Adam (death) and Christ (life) (vv. 21–23)

   d. an **explanatory digression**, revealing the temporal sequence and theological significance of the eschatological order that has been brought about by the soteriological work of Christ, as epitomized by his resurrection (vv. 24–28)

   e. **everyday examples** that illustrate the importance of a belief in the resurrection: baptizing for the dead (29), facing danger, persecution and death (vv. 30–32)

   f. a **secular quotation** from the Greek poet Menander (v. 33)

   g. **analogies** from nature, comparing the resurrection to the "rising to life" of seeds (vv. 36–38) and comparing different types of "bodies" in the universe (vv. 39–41) to the resurrection body (vv. 42–44)

   h. **paradigm** from Scripture, returning to the contrast between Adam and Christ, including a citation of Genesis 2:7 (vv. 45–49)

2. **Syllogisms**

   Syllogisms are often partially implicit in Paul's letters and combined, one being purposefully woven within or alongside another. For example, in 1 Corinthians 15:50–57, which is the passage following the text summarized above, one of his major lines of reasoning may be stated in the following syllogistic terms:

   General premise: Human beings need transformed (or heavenly) bodies to enter the heavenly kingdom of God.

   Specific premise: All believers in Christ will become transformed by God at the resurrection.

Conclusion: Therefore, all believers in Christ will be able to enter into eternal life in heaven.

> » What is the importance of Paul's linking the three crucial concepts of faith in Christ, a bodily resurrection, and eternal life in heaven?
>
> » Is the apostle's logic clearly stated and able to be followed when translated into YL? If not, what is the problem and what can be done about it?

3. Midrash

The apostolic writers, following the example of their Lord, normally based their authoritative arguments about salvation and new life in Christ on the Old Testament Scriptures. Four types of *midrashic* exegesis are especially prominent in the New Testament: running commentary, *pesher* interpretation, typological reading, and allegory:

a. In **running commentary** a particular theme is developed in a sequence of alternating Bible texts and comments (e.g., reasons, proofs, assertions), as in Galatians 3:

3:6	refers to	Genesis 15:6 with a comment in	3:7
3:8		Genesis 12:3	3:9
3:10b		Deuteronomy 27:26	3:10a
3:11b		Habakkuk 2:4	3:11a
3:12b		Leviticus 18:5	3:12a
3:13b		Deuteronomy 21:23	3:13a
3:16		Genesis 12:7 (13:15, 24:7)	3:15, 17–18

b. In *pesher* **interpretation** we have what amounts to a paraphrase of one or more Scripture texts, the interpretation of the original passages being modified to fit the contemporary co-text, as in 1 Corinthians 15:54–55.

> verse 54 => Isaiah 25:8 in a modified form as derived from both a Hebrew text as well as the Septuagint with the addition of "in victory" at the end.
>
> verse 55 => Hosea 13:14, but modified in a similar hybrid manner to focus on the main theme, which is Christ's victory over death in the resurrection.

c. In **typological reading** an important OT person or event is shown to correspond to certain aspects of the Christian faith and life, thus demonstrating the continuity in God's saving plan for his people. A prominent instance of this occurs in Romans 5:12–21, where Adam is presented as a contrastive type to Jesus the Christ. Each forerunner brings into the world a new set of circumstances for humanity, Adam in a negative way (sin => death), Christ in a positive way (justification => life).

d. In **allegory** some well-known OT reference is used symbolically to illustrate a closely related series of NT truths. The conflict between Abraham's two wives, for example, is cited in Galatians 4:21–31, with Sarah and her son Isaac representing the "new Jerusalem" of Christ's kingdom of grace and freedom from religious ceremonialism, and Hagar and Ishmael representing "Mount Sinai" and slavery to the demands of the Mosaic law.

4. Homily

Homily is a basic form of instructive pastoral discourse occasionally found in John's Gospel and frequently in the Epistle to the Hebrews. A homily consists of three basic components:

a. Scripture-based or apostolic examples and proofs;

b. a conclusion that arises from the preceding; and

c. a subsequent exhortation pertaining to the Christian faith and/or life.

An example of such a homily is in John 3, in which a = verses 3–15, b = verses 16–17, and c = verses 18–21.

In Hebrews, an interesting feature of the third hortatory segment (c) is that it often functions simultaneously as a bridge to the next distinct homily in the letter. We see this at the very beginning of Hebrews, after the formal introduction to the homily as a whole (1:1–4).

Observe that the linked series (termed a *catena*) of Scripture passages leading up to the conclusion of Hebrews 1:5–13 is very elaborate. The conclusion that Christ is clearly superior to any of the angels, is, on the other hand, rather low-key and left largely implicit, expressed in the form of a rhetorical question. In some languages it may be necessary to make the crucial theological implication of the climactic verse 14 explicit so that it is not overlooked or undervalued in the vernacular development of the author's argument.

» What works best in a translation into YL?

Point out any other potential translation problems that you notice in the passage below.

A. (Heb. 1:5–13)
⁵ For to which of the angels did God ever say,
   "You are my Son;
      today I have become your Father[a] "[b]?

Or again,
   "I will be his Father,
      and he will be my Son"[c]?

⁶ And again, when God brings his firstborn into the world, he says,
   "Let all God's angels worship him."[d]
⁷ In speaking of the angels he says,
   "He makes his angels winds,
      his servants flames of fire."[e]

⁸ But about the Son he says,
   "Your throne, O God, will last for ever and ever,
      and righteousness will be the scepter of your kingdom.
   ⁹ You have loved righteousness and hated wickedness;
      therefore God, your God, has set you above your companions
      by anointing you with the oil of joy."[f]

¹⁰ He also says,
   "In the beginning, O Lord, you laid the foundations of the earth,
      and the heavens are the work of your hands.
   ¹¹ They will perish, but you remain;
      they will all wear out like a garment.
   ¹² You will roll them up like a robe;
      like a garment they will be changed.

> But you remain the same,
> > and your years will never end."[9]
>
> [13] To which of the angels did God ever say,
> > "Sit at my right hand
> > > until I make your enemies
> > > a footstool for your feet"?

B. (Heb. 1:14)
> [14] Are not all angels ministering spirits sent to serve those who will inherit salvation?

C. (Heb. 2:1–4)
> [1] We must pay more careful attention, therefore, to what we have heard, so that we do not drift away. [2] For if the message spoken by angels was binding, and every violation and disobedience received its just punishment, [3] how shall we escape if we ignore such a great salvation? This salvation, which was first announced by the Lord, was confirmed to us by those who heard him. [4] God also testified to it by signs, wonders and various miracles, and gifts of the Holy Spirit distributed according to his will.

> a. **1:5** Or *have begotten you*
> b. **1:5** Ps. 2.7
> c. **1:5** 2 Sam. 7:14; 1 Chr. 17.13
> d. **1:6** Deut. 32.43 (see Dead Sea Scrolls and Septuagint)
> e. **1:7** Ps. 104.4
> f. **1:9** Ps. 45.6, 7
> g. **1:12** Ps. 102.25–27

5. Apocalypse

Apocalypse in the Epistles tends to be organized in terms of four basic elements, just as in the Synoptic Gospels. These elements are summarized below and exemplified from Mark 13:

a. predictions about persecutions and sufferings for believers before the end time (vv. 6–20)

b. predictions about the coming Messiah (or false messiahs) using standard Ancient Near Eastern eschatological imagery (vv. 21–26)

c. description of the final salvation or judgment scene and related events (v. 27)

d. accompanying paraenetic (hortatory) and didactic passages (vv. 28–37 + 5, 9a, 14–16, 18)

Try to pick out these same elements in the epistolary apocalypse of Paul in 1 Thessalonians 4:16–5:11 (below).

> [4:16] For the Lord himself will come down from heaven, with a loud command, with the voice of the archangel and with the trumpet call of God, and the dead in Christ will rise first. [17] After that, we who are still alive and are left will be caught up together with them in the clouds to meet the Lord in the air. And so we will be with the Lord forever. [18] Therefore encourage each other with these words. [5:1] Now, brothers, about times and dates we do not need to write to you, [2] for you know very well that the day of the Lord will come like a thief in the night. [3] While people are saying, "Peace and safety," destruction will come on them suddenly, as labor pains on a pregnant woman, and they will not escape. [4] But you, brothers, are not in darkness so that this day should surprise you like a thief. [5] You are all

sons of the light and sons of the day. We do not belong to the night or to the darkness. ⁶ So then, let us not be like others, who are asleep, but let us be alert and self-controlled. ⁷ For those who sleep, sleep at night, and those who get drunk, get drunk at night. ⁸ But since we belong to the day, let us be self-controlled, putting on faith and love as a breastplate, and the hope of salvation as a helmet. ⁹ For God did not appoint us to suffer wrath but to receive salvation through our Lord Jesus Christ. ¹⁰ He died for us so that, whether we are awake or asleep, we may live together with him. ¹¹ Therefore encourage one another and build each other up, just as in fact you are doing.

» Note any possible problems for translating this particular passage as well as this type of discourse. What solutions can you suggest? Give three specific examples.

» Which element of the four constituents listed above is missing in 1 Thessalonians 4:16–5:11?

» Can you suggest a reason for this vis-à-vis Paul's argument strategy?

» Suggest where the main paragraph breaks need to be made and why you have picked these places in particular.

It is important to observe how the apocalyptic material fits in relation to the discourse that surrounds it, especially the preceding text.

¹³ Brothers, we do not want you to be ignorant about those who fall asleep, or to grieve like the rest of men, who have no hope. ¹⁴ We believe that Jesus died and rose again and so we believe that God will bring with Jesus those who have fallen asleep in him. ¹⁵ According to the Lord's own word, we tell you that we who are still alive, who are left till the coming of the Lord, will certainly not precede those who have fallen asleep.

» Explain the connection to the preceding text in the Thessalonians passage, that is, what Paul teaches his readers in 4:13–15.

» Do you need to introduce an explicit bridge between these two sections in YL? If so, propose an appropriate wording.

» Pick out the four apocalyptic elements in Christ's letter to Ephesus in Rev. 2:1–7 (note how the second element has been modified).

» Which apocalyptic theme is emphasized in Rev. 4–5? What are the important structural and thematic features of these two chapters in relation to the Apocalypse as a whole (cf. Wendland 2008:chapters 8, 11)?

While there are some similarities, as we have seen, between the prose of the NT Epistles and the prose of the Gospels and Acts, their differences—in terms of genres, devices, and the overall discourse structure—are pronounced. The larger organization of a New Testament letter generally consists of just three principal parts: *introduction*, *body*, and *conclusion*, but each of these may be structured in different ways. The Pastoral Epistles, for example, though composed for a similar purpose, are quite varied in their discourse organization and literary style. In most epistles the structural adaptations that occur are most notable in the large, central "body," depending on the communicative circumstances and the content being conveyed, but considerable diversity is displayed even in the more formulaic "introduction" and "conclusion."

In Galatians, for example, we have the initial specification of who the writer and addressees are (Gal. 1:1–2), followed by a standard *salutation* (i.e., "grace" + "peace" in v. 3) along with an expansive *doxology* (vv. 4–5). However, Paul deliberately excludes both the expected *thanksgiving* in which he normally praises the recipients for certain aspects of their Christian character or behavior and also the accompanying prayer that God would strengthen these demonstrated virtues (as in Eph. 1:15–17). Why does Paul feel that it is necessary to omit such a vital pragmatic as well as theological component? The reason is dramatically and forcefully stated in the very next verses: The Galatians were in danger of deserting the central core of apostolic preaching, the only saving "gospel of Christ" (Gal. 1:6–7). Clearly, Paul's introductions were not stereotyped or perfunctory, certainly not after the opening salutation.

The same is true of his conclusions. Typical letters of that day contained a final greeting and last wish for good health as well as a word of farewell. Paul, too, always ended up with a benediction (e.g., "May the grace of our Lord Jesus Christ be with your spirit" in Gal. 6:18), but an assortment of other epistolary elements could precede this, such as a peace wish (e.g., Phil. 4:9), a doxology (Rom. 16:27), references to the circumstances of writing (Gal. 6:11), a personal commendation (Rom. 16:1–2), a call for the holy kiss of Christian fellowship (1 Cor. 16:20), the names of people to be greeted (Rom. 16:3–15), and the names of those sending greetings (Phlm. 23–24). Also included might be last-minute appeals (2 Cor. 13:11), admonitions (Gal. 6:12–17), as well as final instructions (Col. 4:16–17). All of these distinctions may be considered discourse subcategories of the NT epistolary genre. In each case, then, they need to be identified and clearly demarcated within a given letter so that similar styles of TL writing (or speaking) may be found to match them as closely as possible.

As already mentioned, the "body" of a NT letter normally manifests greater compositional variety than the introduction and conclusion. In addition to the subgenres of argument, syllogism, midrash, homily, and apocalypse (described above), a number of other discourse types are prominent (usually combined with each other to form major sections that relate to a particular theme). They are briefly defined and exemplified below:

1. **Doctrinal exposition**

   Doctrinal exposition, which consists of basic instruction, clarification, and scriptural support with respect to the chief doctrines of the Christian faith, in particular, the "gospel" about Jesus the Christ as this relates to the Mosaic law. Thus all people are sinners in the eyes of a holy and righteous God, as clearly revealed by the law (e.g., Rom. 3:9–20), but Christ has redeemed them (us) all through his sacrificial death, this gift of salvation being received solely by faith (e.g., Rom. 3:21–31).

2. **Paraenetic admonition**

   Paraenetic admonition, in which a number of imperatives are often bunched together in order to specify how or how not to live as a faithful, self-sacrificing Christian in everyday communal circumstances. These lists of loosely related precepts and principles are not meant to be exhaustive in any given instance, but rather are representative of what the believer's behavior ought to be. (e.g., Rom. 12:1–21).

3. ***Topoi* discussion**

   Topoi discussion, which is more tightly organized around a particular ethical subject than the two preceding genres. First Corinthians is quite clearly organized according to this principle; it touches on a variety of subjects that were of concern to Christian congregational life, such as church discipline (chap. 5), lawsuits among believers (6:1–11), issues pertaining to marriage (chap. 7), eating certain foods (chap. 8), apostolic rights to congregational support (9:1–14), women's head covering during worship (11:2–16), proper observance of the Lord's Supper (11:17–34), and practice of charismatic gifts (chaps. 12, 14). Frequently, these pastoral "discussions," or deliberations, include arguments that manifest the following five components (illustrated from Rom. 13:1–7):

   a. **Injunction**. An exhortation concerning the desired ethical action—what to do, or avoid doing. "Everyone must submit himself to the governing authorities…" (Rom. 13:1).

b. **Reason.** The apostolic/biblical rationale for such action. "[F]or there is no authority except that which God has established. The authorities that exist have been established by God" (Rom. 13:1).

c. **Refutation.** A contrary position on the matter (occurs optionally). "Consequently, he who rebels against the authority is rebelling against what God has instituted, and those who do so will bring judgment on themselves" (Rom. 13:2).

d. **Elaboration.** Further explanation and reasoning in favor of the injunction (e.g., a specification of the positive results of obedience or, conversely, the negative consequences of disobedience). "For rulers hold no terror for those who do right, but for those who do wrong. Do you want to be free from fear of the one in authority? Then do what is right and he will commend you. For he is God's servant to do you good. But if you do wrong, be afraid, for he does not bear the sword for nothing. He is God's servant, an agent of wrath to bring punishment on the wrongdoer....This is also why you pay taxes, for the authorities are God's servants, who give their full time to governing. Give everyone what you owe him: If you owe taxes, pay taxes; if revenue, then revenue; if respect, then respect; if honor, then honor" (Rom. 13:3–4, 6–7).

e. **Conclusion.** A statement at or near the end that summarizes the apostolic position regarding the issue under discussion (occurs optionally). "Therefore, it is necessary to submit to the authorities, not only because of possible punishment but also because of conscience" (Rom. 13:5).

4. **Virtue and vice lists**

Virtue and vice lists, which consist of a detailed specification of a number of commendable or condemned attitudes and ethical behaviors. Such a list is given in support of a particular exhortation by the writer. The positive and negative parallels are frequently conjoined in the same cotext for added comparative impact (e.g., Gal. 5:19–23, Eph. 4:31–32, Titus 1:7–10). The listing effectively "slows down" the discourse and helps hearers to focus on the apostle's broader faith-life application. The text may manifest certain other literary features, such as internal euphony, rhythm, topical arrangements, and balance. Galatians 5:22–23 is an example:

> Ὁ δὲ **καρπὸς** τοῦ πνεύματός <u>ἐστιν</u>
>   ἀγάπη, χαρά, εἰρήνη,
>   μακροθυμία, χρηστότης, ἀγαθωσύνη,
>   (Note the longest terms in the middle)
>   πίστις, πραΰτης ἐγκράτεια·
> κατὰ τῶν τοιούτων <u>οὐκ ἔστιν</u> **νόμος**.

> 22 But the **fruit** of the Spirit <u>is</u>
>   love, joy, peace,
>   patience, kindness, goodness,
>   faithfulness, 23 gentleness and self-control.
> Against such things <u>there is no</u> **law**.

» What is the larger issue in Paul's argument that this list heightens?

» Do such lists function as heightening devices in your literary-rhetorical tradition?

» Describe any major correspondences or conflicts in regard to lists that you find in YL and literary tradition.

» Translate the preceding passage in a *LiFE*-like manner in YL.

5. **Household codes**

   Household codes, which present a series of instructions directed at key members of the typical Greco-Roman household, especially as they relate to each other in complementary pairs: husband and wife, father and children, master and slaves. This secular literary form was "Christianized" by the apostles to show how a Christ-centered family produced a strong church and a strong society. It also demonstrated to the pagan authorities that Christianity was no threat to the state. It is important to note the variations in these codes in the different letters and to consider how they might reflect or arise from the specific extratextual setting.

   » Contrast Ephesians 5:21–6:9 and Colossians 3:18–4:1.

   » What difference(s) do you notice between these two texts, and how might you account for them with reference to their respective compositional contexts?

6. **Diatribe**

   Diatribe, a rhetorical technique in which the speaker or writer debates with a hypothetical addressee in order to develop his argument concerning a particular issue. Often diatribe is used to emphasize what has just been taught in the letter or to transition to a new point (e.g., Rom. 6:1–4 in response to 5:20–21 and leading up to 6:5–14). In Romans there are many instances of diatribe, the dramatic features of which are listed and exemplified here from Romans 6:1–3:

   a. **Exclamation** "What shall we say, then?"

   b. **Rhetorical question leading to a negative or a false conclusion** "Shall we go on sinning so that grace may increase?"

   c. **Rejection of the implied answer** "By no means!"

   d. **Reasons for the rejection** (in the form of RQs, examples, sayings, biblical quotations, and references) "We died to sin; how can we live in it any longer? Or don't you know that all of us who were baptized into Christ Jesus were baptized into his death?"

   Note that the "reason" of Romans 6:3 acts also as the transition to the new topic that begins in 6:4 ("We were therefore buried with him through baptism into death in order that, just as Christ was raised from the dead through the glory of the Father, we too may live a new life").

   » What is the main topic and point of this following section (6:5–14)?

   » Does it need to be marked more overtly or strongly as such in YL? If so, explain how this may be done.

7. **Formulaic expressions**

   Formulaic expressions to help listeners orient themselves as they hear the body of a letter being read. Paul regularly inserted certain expressions at key junctures in the text's development, usually relating to the doctrinal or paraenetic purpose at hand and often introducing important themes or sub-themes into the discussion. Some examples are "I want you to know that" (Gal. 1:11); "I appeal to you" (1 Cor. 1:10); "I do not want you to be ignorant" (2 Cor. 1:18); "Now concerning" (1 Cor. 7:1). The Pauline Epistles will occasionally also include short liturgical formulae to highlight what Paul has just said. The liturgical formulae are of two types: blessings and doxologies.

a. **Blessings** are typically tripartite, consisting of a reference to God, a description of God (e.g., "who is blessed forever"), and a concluding "Amen!" Such a blessing is seen in the final noun phrase of Romans 1:25, "…they exchanged the truth about God for a lie and worshiped and served the creature rather than <u>the Creator, who is blessed forever</u>! <u>Amen</u>." In this example, the blessing serves to heighten the contrast between a holy Creator and degenerate humanity (see Rom. 1:18–24).

b. **Doxologies** are also tripartite: first a reference to God in the dative case (including also a personal or relative pronoun), then an ascription of glory to God with or without further modification, and finally a concluding "Amen!" In Ephesians 3:21 we find this important doxology: "…to <u>him</u> be <u>glory</u> in the church and in Christ Jesus to all generations, forever and ever. Amen." It is the conclusion to Paul's prayer on behalf of his readers and also brings the first half of the epistle to an end.

Liturgical formulae, in addition to their structural and topical marking functions, perform a phatic function as well in that they relate the letter writer (pastor) to his addressees (congregation), psychologically and spiritually. The use of these formulae supports the view that the epistles often serve communicatively as "sermons proclaimed at a distance."

» Do you have a genre in your literary tradition that corresponds to these religious praises and wishes?

» If so, describe them in comparison with the Greek forms described above.

» If not, how will you translate the NT blessings and doxologies with a distinctive style?

For reflection, research, and response:

1. Study Paul's argument strategy in 1 Corinthians 9 as he defends his right to receive support from those whom he served with the gospel. Make an outline of the different rhetorical features that he uses and tell how they operate to develop and reinforce his reasoning in this chapter.

2. We have already discussed the importance of identifying the major and minor *theses* of hortatory discourse, which thus form the "backbone" of the text, and of distinguishing these from the various types of *supportive* material that may accompany them (cf. sec. 4.2). For example, in 1 Cor. 1:4–17 we find a hortatory thesis in v. 10 ("Now I appeal to you…") surrounded by supportive material, namely, Paul's "thanksgiving" on behalf of the congregation (vv. 4–9) and Paul's summary of the situation in relation to his prior activity among them (vv. 11–17; Levinsohn 2006a:3). These different types of discourse may be marked in specific languages by various surface features, such as conjunctions, special particles, transitional phrases, shifts in word order, tense/aspect markers, and distinctive verb forms. It is important that sufficient research be done in this regard based on natural oral and written text material in the TL.

   Now make a study of Paul's sequence of exhortations in chapters 5 and 6 of 1 Corinthians. First, decide how many distinct "arguments" are present and what their respective themes and text boundaries are. Then identify the main *hortatory theses* and note their different surface forms in the original (if possible). Distinguish the different types of *supportive material* in each case. Finally, determine how you must express the main theses in YL so that they will be readily apparent to your target audience—a group that is only *hearing* the text being read aloud. Discuss as a group any particular problems that you encounter when doing this exercise.

3. What is the major *enthymeme* (implicit syllogism) that underlies Jude's condemnation of false teachers in verses 8–10 of his epistle?

Major premise: _____

Minor premise: _____

Conclusion: _____

4. Review the different aspects of midrashic interpretation that are described earlier in section 6.3.3 and show how these are manifested in 1 Peter 2:1–10. Then tell how this particular instance of interpretation serves as the foundation for Peter's paraenetic exhortation in the next section of his letter, that is, 2:11–17. Make a note of points where this line of argumentation would not be entirely clear if rendered literally in YL. What must you do to explicate the passage and yet also express it as forcefully as in the original text?

5. Point out the *topoi* discussion structure that is present in James 2:1–13; in other words, specify the injunction, reason, refutation, elaboration, and conclusion in these verses. Would any of these present a problem when rendering them in YL? If so, identify these expressions and tell why they would cause difficulties for translators.

6. Consider the list of virtues in 1 Timothy 3:2–7. How do these particular virtues fit into Paul's instruction at this point in the letter (cf. 3:14–15)? Is it necessary to clarify the point of this passage in YL? Explain why, or why not. How does verse 16 link up with the discussion that precedes it? In other words, what is the immediate relevance of this Christological confession to what Paul has just written?

7. Study the "household code" in 1 Peter 2:18–3:7. Where does the focus of the whole passage lie and how have you determined this? Does this particular emphasis come out clearly in your translation? If not, what might you do in order to stylistically mark this foundational peak?

8. Analyze the diatribe discourse of Romans 3 according to the model given earlier in section 6.3.3. What principle is Paul arguing for? How does he make his point by the diatribe method? Point out any places in the text that might cause some difficulty when translating this passage into YL and tell why. Explain how you would solve these problems.

9. Consider the four typical text elements typically found in apocalyptic discourse. Identify examples of these four in Revelation 4–7. How do these features operate together to heighten the overall impression and impact of this type of writing? The book of Revelation is not normally classified as an epistle, but how does the book's structure suggest that it was meant to be read and interpreted that way? Note all the intertextual references and allusions that are found in Revelation 4–7 and suggest why these are a vital part of its apocalyptic "argument."

10. Identify the "doxology" in Gal. 1:1–5. Specify its main parts. Can this be translated as a single sentence in YL? Explain why or why not and explain how you would handle this passage. What is the distinctive discourse constituent in Paul's introduction to the Romans (1:1–7)? What is the literary function of this insertion, and how will you call attention to this in your translation?

11. Ryken (2002:194–195) claims that "the more literary a text is, the more regularly it employs ambiguity in the sense of multiple meanings, so that it is entirely possible that the phrase "the obedience of faith" (Rom. 1:5) can legitimately embrace some of the suggested interpretations…[in the six different versions listed for comparison]." His point is that a more literal rendering preserves the ambiguity and hence is more "literary" in nature as well as being a more accurate translation. How would you respond to this argument from the perspective of a *LiFE* approach to the communicational issues involved? How do you recommend translating "the obedience of faith" in Romans 1:5? Give some reasons for your choice.

12. Use a study Bible, commentary, or other reference book to explore the symbolism of "Babylon" in 1 Peter 5:13 (see Zech. 2:7; Rev. 18:2, 10). How many levels or aspects of significant denotative and connotative meaning do you discern? Which of these might need to be identified in a footnote in your translation? Analyze the literary and theological import of another highly negative symbol in the epistles plus one equally positive image of special significance.

13. What is distinctive about the style of 1 John 2:12–14 (quoted below from the RSV)? How will your decision about textual form influence how you format this text? Study this portion in its context and suggest what communicative function it performs.

    > [12] I am writing to you, little children, because your sins are forgiven for his sake. [13] I am writing to you, fathers, because you know him who is from the beginning. I am writing to you, young men, because you have overcome the evil one. I write to you, children, because you know the Father. [14] I write to you, fathers, because you know him who is from the beginning. I write to you, young men, because you are strong, and the word of God abides in you, and you have overcome the evil one.

    Now evaluate Peterson's translation of this same passage (quoted below from *The Message*)—his interpretation as well as structure. Would you recommend any corrections or improvements?

    > I remind you my dear children: Your sins are forgiven in Jesus' name. You veterans were in on the ground floor, and know the One who started all this; you newcomers have won a big victory over the Evil One.

    > And a second reminder, dear children: You know the Father from personal experience. You veterans know the One who started it all; and you newcomers—such vitality and strength! God's word is so steady in you. Your fellowship with God enables you to gain a victory over the Evil One.

14. The following diagram (from Wendland 2004b:219) summarizes a method for investigating the rhetorical setting of an epistolary argument. After reading pages 219–223, provide a *definition* of each of the ten elements in this diagram.

    Then apply these elements as you summarize the contextual situation that forms the cognitive background to Paul's letter to the Philippians. Write your summary out on a separate piece of paper and indicate which aspects of this information seem to be most crucial to readers for a proper understanding of this epistle. (Note that the feature "potency" might be better termed "authority," since it includes all explicit and implicit references to the author's perceived or ascribed status, prestige, and power to command, which supports his present appeal or command.)

    Why does such background material need to be carefully studies *before* preparing to translate one of the NT epistles, especially in a *LiFE* manner?

    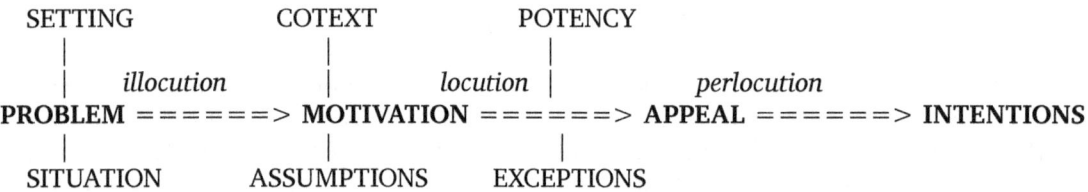

15. **MAJOR ASSIGNMENT:** Review the following steps for analyzing literary discourse in the Scriptures. Then apply these steps to Paul's letter to Philemon. Write out your detailed study so that it may be handed in to the instructor for assessment. Several of the best write-ups will be selected for oral presentation and discussion by the entire class.

6.3 Identifying and analyzing New Testament prose genres 345

    a. Read the entire text aloud (several times) and determine its main genre and subgenres.

    b. Study the complete textual, intertextual, and extratextual context as carefully as possible.

    c. Plot all occurrences of exact and synonymous repetition in the pericope.

    d. Pinpoint all instances of disjunction ("breaks") occasioned by transitional formulae and content shifting (e.g., topic, setting).

    e. Isolate and describe the obvious areas of special stylistic concentration within the text.

    f. Identify the major areas of discourse demarcation and points of projection (peak, climax).

    g. Analyze and display the larger syntactic-semantic structure of the entire pericope.

    h. Prepare a complete thematic study (word/symbol/motif), especially the key concepts and clusters.

    i. Explain any outstanding linguistic and literary features that remain unaccounted for.

    j. Note the major speech functions (speech acts) and their interaction in the discourse.

    k. Make an explicit stylistic and structural comparison for identifying possible form-functional matches between the SL and TL.

    l. Prepare a well-formatted, trial *LiFE* translation and test it comparatively against other versions.

16. [*For students who can refer to the NT Greek text or who can work with an interlinear version:*] Prepare a "structural discourse segmentation chart" for Philemon under the headings below, with special reference to the features of topicalization, focalization, and intensification, as illustrated in section 6.2.4. This will help you to identify the various patterns of repetition in Philemon, the areas of disjunction and content shifting, significant word order variations, and the points of special stylistic concentration. The analysis template is given below, followed by a reformatted (utterance-oriented) version of the Greek text for your reference.

ref.	pre-verb2	pre-verb1	VERB post-	verb	post-verb2	post-verb3

¹ Παῦλος δέσμιος Χριστοῦ Ἰησοῦ καὶ Τιμόθεος ὁ ἀδελφὸς Φιλήμονι τῷ ἀγαπητῷ καὶ συνεργῷ ἡμῶν
² καὶ Ἀπφίᾳ τῇ ἀδελφῇ καὶ Ἀρχίππῳ τῷ συστρατιώτῃ ἡμῶν καὶ τῇ κατ' οἶκόν σου ἐκκλησίᾳ,
³ χάρις ὑμῖν καὶ εἰρήνη ἀπὸ θεοῦ πατρὸς ἡμῶν καὶ κυρίου Ἰησοῦ Χριστοῦ.
⁴ Εὐχαριστῶ τῷ θεῷ μου πάντοτε μνείαν σου ποιούμενος ἐπὶ τῶν προσευχῶν μου,
⁵ ἀκούων σου τὴν ἀγάπην καὶ τὴν πίστιν, ἣν ἔχεις πρὸς τὸν κύριον Ἰησοῦν καὶ εἰς πάντας τοὺς ἁγίους,
⁶ ὅπως ἡ κοινωνία τῆς πίστεώς σου ἐνεργὴς γένηται ἐν ἐπιγνώσει παντὸς ἀγαθοῦ τοῦ ἐν ἡμῖν εἰς Χριστόν.
⁷ χαρὰν γὰρ πολλὴν ἔσχον καὶ παράκλησιν ἐπὶ τῇ ἀγάπῃ σου, ὅτι τὰ σπλάγχνα τῶν ἁγίων ἀναπέπαυται διὰ σοῦ, ἀδελφέ.

⁸ Διό, πολλὴν ἐν Χριστῷ παρρησίαν ἔχων ἐπιτάσσειν σοι τὸ ἀνῆκον
⁹ διὰ τὴν ἀγάπην μᾶλλον παρακαλῶ, τοιοῦτος ὢν ὡς Παῦλος πρεσβύτης νυνὶ δὲ καὶ δέσμιος Χριστοῦ Ἰησοῦ·
¹⁰ παρακαλῶ σε περὶ τοῦ ἐμοῦ τέκνου, ὃν ἐγέννησα ἐν τοῖς δεσμοῖς, Ὀνήσιμον,
¹¹ τόν ποτέ σοι ἄχρηστον νυνὶ δὲ [καὶ] σοὶ καὶ ἐμοὶ εὔχρηστον,
¹² ὃν ἀνέπεμψά σοι, αὐτόν, τοῦτ' ἔστιν τὰ ἐμὰ σπλάγχνα·
¹³ ὃν ἐγὼ ἐβουλόμην πρὸς ἐμαυτὸν κατέχειν, ἵνα ὑπὲρ σοῦ μοι διακονῇ ἐν τοῖς δεσμοῖς τοῦ εὐαγγελίου,
¹⁴ χωρὶς δὲ τῆς σῆς γνώμης οὐδὲν ἠθέλησα ποιῆσαι, ἵνα μὴ ὡς κατὰ ἀνάγκην τὸ ἀγαθόν σου ᾖ ἀλλὰ κατὰ ἑκούσιον.
¹⁵ τάχα γὰρ διὰ τοῦτο ἐχωρίσθη πρὸς ὥραν, ἵνα αἰώνιον αὐτὸν ἀπέχῃς,

¹⁶ οὐκέτι ὡς δοῦλον ἀλλὰ ὑπὲρ δοῦλον, ἀδελφὸν ἀγαπητόν, μάλιστα ἐμοί, πόσῳ δὲ μᾶλλον σοὶ καὶ ἐν σαρκὶ καὶ ἐν κυρίῳ.

¹⁷ Εἰ οὖν με ἔχεις κοινωνόν, προσλαβοῦ αὐτὸν ὡς ἐμέ.
¹⁸ εἰ δέ τι ἠδίκησέν σε ἢ ὀφείλει, τοῦτο ἐμοὶ ἐλλόγα.
¹⁹ ἐγὼ Παῦλος ἔγραψα τῇ ἐμῇ χειρί, ἐγὼ ἀποτίσω· ἵνα μὴ λέγω σοι ὅτι καὶ σεαυτόν μοι προσοφείλεις.

²⁰ ναί, ἀδελφέ, ἐγώ σου ὀναίμην ἐν κυρίῳ· ἀνάπαυσόν μου τὰ σπλάγχνα ἐν Χριστῷ.
²¹ Πεποιθὼς τῇ ὑπακοῇ σου ἔγραψά σοι, εἰδὼς ὅτι καὶ ὑπὲρ ἃ λέγω ποιήσεις.
²² ἅμα δὲ καὶ ἑτοίμαζέ μοι ξενίαν· ἐλπίζω γὰρ ὅτι διὰ τῶν προσευχῶν ὑμῶν χαρισθήσομαι ὑμῖν.

²³ Ἀσπάζεταί σε Ἐπαφρᾶς ὁ συναιχμάλωτός μου ἐν Χριστῷ Ἰησοῦ,
²⁴ Μᾶρκος, Ἀρίσταρχος, Δημᾶς, Λουκᾶς, οἱ συνεργοί μου.
²⁵ Ἡ χάρις τοῦ κυρίου Ἰησοῦ Χριστοῦ μετὰ τοῦ πνεύματος ὑμῶν.

17. As we saw in section 6.3.1, a *narrative* consists of a series of chronologically arranged events (the "story"), which the narrator often rearranges (e.g., as flashbacks or flash-forwards) or otherwise modifies (e.g., through repetition, deletion, and marked intensification) in order to create greater impact and appeal. The resulting restructured, cause-effect-oriented sequence is the "plot," often exhibiting one or more high points of action (the "peak") and/or emotion (the "climax"). Some epistles and other types of argumentative discourse that refer to historical events may also be analyzed with reference to the implied narrative that they incorporate. Similarly, the actual referential sequence of events may be rearranged in plot form as part of the author's rhetorical strategy. Consider the following diagram of a "referential sequence" in comparison with a "plot sequence," either of which may be posited with regard to Paul's letter to Philemon. Note which events have been dislocated in the plot and suggest a reason for this in light of your interpretation of Paul's appeal to Philemon on behalf of Onesimus. Do you need to explain the significance of this rhetorical device for your readers in a marginal comment? If so, propose an appropriate explanation for your intended target group. Does a text analysis of this sort have any important implications for translators? Assuming that it does, mention the most important one that comes to mind.

Referential Sequence	manifested in the text at verse:	**"Plot" Sequence**
1. Philemon incurs a **debt** to Paul.	19b	**7**
2. Paul is imprisoned.	9 (cf. 1, 10, 13, 23)	**2**
3. Onesimus runs away and incurs a **debt**.	15 (cf. 11–13, 18–19a)	**5**
4. Onesimus is converted by Paul in prison.	10	**3**
5. Paul hears of Philemon's love and faith.	4–7	**1**
6. Paul sends Onesimus back to Philemon.	12	**4**
7. Paul sends letter of appeal/repay O's **debt**.	17–19a	**6**
8. (projected) Onesimus arrives with the letter.	12 (implied)	**8**
9. Philemon responds to Paul's appeal (how?).	20–21 (cf. 9)	**9**
10. Paul pays a visit to Philemon.	22	**10**

18. Study the following diagram of a proposed chiastic arrangement for the letter to Philemon. Do the linguistic discourse markers and literary-rhetorical devices in the original text support this arrangement? The center of a chiasmus normally indicates a point of special interest or importance in the text as a whole. Does that hypothesis hold true here in light of what you see below? Does it confirm your interpretation of Paul's argument strategy in this epistle?

A (1–2) *Opening greetings* ("Christ Jesus" + five personal names)
    B (3) *"Grace" blessing* ("Lord Jesus Christ")
        C (4) *"Prayers"*—Paul for Philemon
            D (5–7) *Pre-appeal prayer*—that Philemon would continue to be active in "faith" and "love" to "refresh the hearts of the saints"
                E (8) *Paul's authority*: he could be "bold" and order Philemon (*soi*) to forgive the debt of Onesimus
                    F (9–10) *Paul's appeal (2x) for Onesimus*: focus on Paul's plight—an "old man" in "chains"
                        G (11) *Contrast*: <u>formerly</u> Onesimus was useless, but <u>now</u> useful "to you (Phil.) and to me (Paul)"
                            H (12) *Action*: Paul sends Onesimus back, though his feelings ("my bowels") are deeply affected
                              è **I** (13) **DESIRE**: what Paul would really like to do: **keep Onesimus to serve the gospel in place of Philemon in prison**
                            H' (14) *Non-action*: Paul does not keep Onesimus with him in Rome so as not to adversely affects Phil.'s feelings
                      G' (15-16) *Contrast*: Onesimus is no mere "slave," but a "dear brother"—dear "to me" and "to you"
                  F' (17–19a) *Paul's appeal for Onesimus*: promise of "Paul"; plight of Onesimus, a wrongdoer and a debtor
              E' (19b) *Paul's authority*: Paul reminds Philemon (*soi*) of his spiritual debt to him
            D' (20–22a) *Post-appeal plea*—that Philemon, the "brother," would "refresh [Paul's] heart" through his "obedience" in bringing "benefit" to Paul
        C' (22b) *"Prayers"*—Philemon for Paul
A' (23–24) *Closing greetings* ("Christ Jesus" + five personal names)
    B' (25) *"Grace" blessing* ("Lord Jesus Christ")[4]

Based on the preceding structural perspective, we might conclude that a major aim of Paul's is to make Philemon aware of his desire that Onesimus be released to go back as a free man to serve Paul in his prison ministry, as expressed in segment I. Assuming that hypothesis to be viable, how do you explain the muted manner in which Paul conveys his wish, burying it within a dependent syntactic construction (a purpose clause) that is embedded within yet another subordinate sequence in verses 10–13?

What might you do to make it more manifest in your translation—either within the text or someplace outside? A related question: What is the possible significance of Paul's choosing διακονέω as the word for "helping" in verse 13—as distinct from δοῦλος in verse 16—and how does διακονέω relate to the overall theme of this epistle?

---

[4]Note the twist in the general pattern at the very end, that is, A'–B' perhaps in itself just another unobtrusive way of formally signaling the letter's conclusion.

19. The following is a listing of some specific stylistic devices and rhetorical techniques used within the text of Philemon. Select the three that you consider most important to Paul's overall argument and tell how you would render these with corresponding impact and effectiveness in YL:

   a. the indirect summons of supporting witnesses through the personal references of verses 1–2 and 23–24

   b. the ironic self-abrogation of one's right or authority, such as the power to "command" Philemon what to do (v. 8)

   c. the use of emotive personal terms (e.g., "prisoner" vv. 1, 9; "old man" v. 9; "begotten" v. 10; "in chains" v. 10; "partner" v. 17)

   d. an appeal to divine providence and planning (suggested by the particle "perhaps"), that is, God purposefully working in the "short separation" of Onesimus and Philemon for their "eternal" benefit (v. 15)

   e. "especially to me…how much more to you"—a *qal wehomer* rabbinical rhetorical device that progresses from the lesser to the greater (v. 16)

   f. a vicarious analogy with regard to desired action—to "receive him as me" (v. 17)

   g. the "anticipation" of problems or objections (18)

   h. parenthesis/ellipsis (19a)

   i. "not to mention" what is then immediately mentioned (*paralipsis*) (19b)

   j. concealing one's ultimate objective or primary request and leaving this to the addressee(s) to figure out (21)

   k. committing oneself to the "obedience" of the addressee without actually commanding the person what to do (21a), even what is "above and beyond the call of duty," an instance of calculated understatement (21b)

   l. the further addition of "one thing more" (22), whereby the writer/speaker seemingly adds an afterthought, yet one that is actually tied in with his preceding argument

   m. Paul's "token offer" to repay the financial debt incurred by Onesimus (19—an offer that he was probably not in a position to carry out, though there is some debate on this issue)

6.3.4 Poetic prose

As noted in section 5.3.1, lyric discourse is found in the New Testament over and above the periodic incorporated citations of OT poetry. Such discourse may not be pure "poetry" according to the Greco-Roman literary standards of the day, but it does provide abundant evidence of the stylistic features that characterize artistically composed poetic texts the world over, namely: parallel phrasing, sound effects, figurative language, condensed expression, emphatic devices, and shifting patterns with respect to normal lexical collocations, morphology, and syntax.

We want to take particular notice of devices such as *sustained rhythm, meaningful repetition, lined parallelism, figurative language, rhetorical intensification,* and *syntactic condensation,* most of which are well illustrated in Philippians 2:5–11, which was considered earlier. See how many of these characteristics you can identify in the following text, either the Greek or the English (NIV):

```
⁵ τοῦτο φρονεῖτε ἐν ὑμῖν                                    Introduction
  ὃ καὶ ἐν Χριστῷ Ἰησοῦ,

⁶ ὃς ἐν μορφῇ θεοῦ ὑπάρχων                                  A
  οὐχ ἁρπαγμὸν ἡγήσατο τὸ εἶναι ἴσα θεῷ,
    | ⁷ ἀλλὰ ἑαυτὸν ἐκένωσεν μορφὴν δούλου λαβών,            B
    | ἐν ὁμοιώματι ἀνθρώπων γενόμενος·
    |   | καὶ σχήματι εὑρεθεὶς ὡς ἄνθρωπος                   C
    |   |   | ⁸ ἐταπείνωσεν ἑαυτὸν                           D
    |   |   |   | γενόμενος ὑπήκοος μέχρι θανάτου,           E
    |   |   |   | θανάτου δὲ σταυροῦ.                        E'
    |   |   | ⁹ διὸ καὶ ὁ θεὸς αὐτὸν ὑπερύψωσεν               D'
    |   | καὶ ἐχαρίσατο αὐτῷ τὸ ὄνομα τὸ ὑπὲρ πᾶν ὄνομα,     C'
    | ¹⁰ ἵνα ἐν τῷ ὀνόματι Ἰησοῦ πᾶν γόνυ κάμψῃ              B'
    | ἐπουρανίων καὶ ἐπιγείων καὶ καταχθονίων
¹¹ καὶ πᾶσα γλῶσσα ἐξομολογήσηται                           A'
  ὅτι κύριος Ἰησοῦς Χριστὸς εἰς δόξαν θεοῦ πατρός.
```

⁵ Let this mind be in you,
Which was also in Christ Jesus:

⁶ Who, being in very nature *God*,
did not consider equality with *God* something to be grasped,
  ⁷ but made himself nothing,
  taking the very nature of a servant,
  being made in human likeness.
    ⁸ And being found in appearance as a man,
      he humbled himself
        and became obedient to *death*—
        even *death on a cross!*
      ⁹ Therefore *God* exalted him to the highest place
    and gave him the name that is above every name,
  ¹⁰ that *at the name of Jesus* every knee should bow,
  in heaven and on earth and under the earth,
¹¹ and every tongue confess
that Jesus Christ is Lord, to the glory of *God the Father.*

The following reformatting of the same passage segments the text into its parallel features in a different way (see section 5.3.4). This scheme considers the words in italics to be Pauline additions to an original hymn in Greek. Note that there is no "right" or "wrong" method of formatting such texts; it is just that one may be preferable to another in representing what appears to be the chief aspects of the original discourse structure and purpose.

» Which poetic arrangement of the text do you prefer for use in YL and why?

» Perhaps you have a somewhat different structuring of this passage to suggest. If so, defend your alternative to the class.

Christ Jesus:
  ⁶ Who, being in very nature God,
  did not consider equality with God something to be grasped,

  ⁷ but made himself nothing,
  taking the very nature of a servant,

>   being made in human likeness.
> ⁸ And being found in appearance as a man,
>
> he humbled himself
> and became obedient to death—
>   even death on a cross!
>
> ⁹ Therefore God exalted him to the highest place
> and gave him the name that is above every name,
>
> ¹⁰ that at the name of Jesus every knee should bow,
>   in heaven and on earth and under the earth,
> ¹¹ and every tongue confess that Jesus Christ is Lord,
>   to the glory of God the Father.

There are two closely related poetic genres that we can identify in the NT literature—*hymns* and *creeds*. Hymns, or hymn segments, are scattered throughout the letters of Paul; they are found also in the book of Revelation. The emphasis is on praising God for who he is and what he has done for humanity through his Son, Jesus the Christ. The preceding passage from Philippians exemplifies such a hymn; in it the *affective* (expressive, emotive) and directive functions of communication are foregrounded. The lyrical nature of Philippians 2:6–11 serves to further heighten the divine theme. That is, through the rhythm, power, and beauty of the language the audience is attracted to the subject matter and a greater impression is made upon their perception, understanding, and memory.

Creeds, which are summary confessions of faith, do not manifest quite as many poetic qualities as hymns and they make less use of figurative language. However, they are often composed in parallel-line arrangements that encourage a rhythmic expression when spoken or recited aloud. The creedal statements found in the Pauline letters tend to be marked by four features:

1. a verb of confession (e.g., ὁμολογέω) or transmission (e.g., παραδίδωμι)

2. a conjunction showing that indirect speech follows (e.g., ὅτι 'that')

3. the phrases of testimony uttered in rhythmic sequence

4. some point of special emphasis or an element of major contrast which the confession highlights

This fourth feature can be seen in 1 Corinthians 15:3–8:

>   ³ παρέδωκα γὰρ ὑμῖν ἐν πρώτοις,
>   ὃ καὶ παρέλαβον,
>   ὅτι Χριστὸς ἀπέθανεν ὑπὲρ τῶν ἁμαρτιῶν ἡμῶν
>   κατὰ τὰς γραφάς
>   ⁴ καὶ ὅτι ἐτάφη καὶ ὅτι ἐγήγερται τῇ ἡμέρᾳ τῇ τρίτῃ
> κατὰ τὰς γραφάς
>   ⁵ καὶ ὅτι ὤφθη Κηφᾷ εἶτα τοῖς δώδεκα·
>   ⁶ ἔπειτα ὤφθη ἐπάνω πεντακοσίοις ἀδελφοῖς ἐφάπαξ,
>   ἐξ ὧν οἱ πλείονες μένουσιν ἕως ἄρτι,
>   τινὲς δὲ ἐκοιμήθησαν·
>   ⁷ ἔπειτα ὤφθη Ἰακώβῳ, εἶτα τοῖς ἀποστόλοις πᾶσιν·
>   ⁸ ἔσχατον δὲ πάντων ὡσπερεὶ τῷ ἐκτρώματι ὤφθη **κἀμοί**.
>
>   ³ For what I received I passed on to you
>   as of first importance:

> that Christ died for our sins
>> according to the Scriptures,
> ⁴ that he was buried, that he was raised on the third day
>> according to the Scriptures,
> ⁵ and that he appeared to Peter, and then to the Twelve.
> ⁶ After that, he appeared to more than five hundred of the brothers at the same time,
>> most of whom are still living,
>>> though some have fallen asleep.
> ⁷ Then he appeared to James, then to all the apostles,
> ⁸ and last of all he appeared **to me also**,
>> as to one abnormally born.

» Where does the climax of this confession occur, and how is it marked in the discourse structure? Look at the Greek text, if possible.

» How would you distinguish this passage in YL in order to highlight its important structural and thematic function?

» Do you have a particular genre of literature (orature) that would be most suitable to express a confession of faith such as this? If so, describe its stylistic features.

For reflection, research, and response:

1. Identify all the poetic features that you can see (and hear!) in the "Hymn of Mary" (Luke 1:46–55). Choose three of them and explain how they function to heighten the communication of Mary's words. Tell how you would translate them with equivalent communicative effect in YL.

> "My soul glorifies the Lord
>> ⁴⁷ and my spirit rejoices in God my Savior,
> ⁴⁸ for he has been mindful
>> of the humble state of his servant.
> From now on all generations will call me blessed,
> ⁴⁹ for the Mighty One has done great things for me—
>> holy is his name.
> ⁵⁰ His mercy extends to those who fear him,
>> from generation to generation.
> ⁵¹ He has performed mighty deeds with his arm;
>> he has scattered those who are proud in their inmost thoughts.
> ⁵² He has brought down rulers from their thrones
>> but has lifted up the humble.
> ⁵³ He has filled the hungry with good things
>> but has sent the rich away empty.
> ⁵⁴ He has helped his servant Israel,
>> remembering to be merciful
> ⁵⁵ to Abraham and his descendants forever,
>> even as he said to our fathers."

2. What is the literary genre of 1 Corinthians 11:23–26? (Both the Greek and the NIV rendition are presented below.) Specify three of its prominent poetic style markers and suggest functional equivalents of these in YL. Then propose a suitable poetic or prose format in which to display the structure of this important passage. Finally, prepare a *LiFE* translation of this text and give a literal back-translation into English.

²³ Ἐγὼ γὰρ παρέλαβον ἀπὸ τοῦ κυρίου,
ὃ καὶ παρέδωκα ὑμῖν,
ὅτι ὁ κύριος Ἰησοῦς ἐν τῇ νυκτὶ ᾗ παρεδίδετο ἔλαβεν ἄρτον
²⁴ καὶ εὐχαριστήσας ἔκλασεν καὶ εἶπεν,
Τοῦτό μού ἐστιν τὸ σῶμα τὸ ὑπὲρ ὑμῶν·
τοῦτο ποιεῖτε εἰς τὴν ἐμὴν ἀνάμνησιν.
²⁵ ὡσαύτως καὶ τὸ ποτήριον μετὰ τὸ δειπνῆσαι λέγων,
Τοῦτο τὸ ποτήριον ἡ καινὴ διαθήκη ἐστὶν ἐν τῷ ἐμῷ αἵματι·
τοῦτο ποιεῖτε, ὁσάκις ἐὰν πίνητε, εἰς τὴν ἐμὴν ἀνάμνησιν.
²⁶ ὁσάκις γὰρ ἐὰν ἐσθίητε τὸν ἄρτον τοῦτον καὶ τὸ ποτήριον πίνητε,
τὸν θάνατον τοῦ κυρίου καταγγέλλετε ἄχρις οὗ ἔλθῃ.

²³ For I received from the Lord what I also passed on to you: The Lord Jesus, on the night he was betrayed, took bread, ²⁴ and when he had given thanks, he broke it and said, "This is my body, which is for you; do this in remembrance of me." ²⁵ In the same way, after supper he took the cup, saying, "This cup is the new covenant in my blood; do this, whenever you drink it, in remembrance of me." ²⁶ For whenever you eat this bread and drink this cup, you proclaim the Lord's death until he comes.

3. Both the Greek and the RSV texts of Revelation 19:6b–8 are presented below. Point out the most notable stylistic features of this passage. What is the genre of this text? Why do you say so? Would you be able to render this same passage poetically and purposefully in YL? If so, mention several of the techniques you would use.

Ἁλληλουϊά,
ὅτι ἐβασίλευσεν κύριος
  ὁ θεὸς [ἡμῶν] ὁ παντοκράτωρ.
 ⁷ χαίρωμεν καὶ ἀγαλλιῶμεν
  καὶ δώσωμεν τὴν δόξαν αὐτῷ,
ὅτι ἦλθεν ὁ γάμος τοῦ ἀρνίου
  καὶ ἡ γυνὴ αὐτοῦ ἡτοίμασεν ἑαυτήν
⁸ καὶ ἐδόθη αὐτῇ ἵνα περιβάληται
  βύσσινον λαμπρὸν καθαρόν·
τὸ γὰρ βύσσινον τὰ δικαιώματα τῶν ἁγίων ἐστίν.

"Hallelujah! For the Lord our God the Almighty reigns.
⁷ Let us rejoice and exult and give him the glory,
for the marriage of the Lamb has come,
and his Bride has made herself ready;
⁸ it was granted her to be clothed with fine linen, bright and pure"—
for the fine linen is the righteous deeds of the saints.

What do you make of the final line of the preceding passage? What purpose does it serve?

How would you mark this line in YL so that it does not read (or sound) like part of the hymn?

4. The text below is Colossians 1:15–20. To help you discover the main literary features of this passage prepare a sequential discourse segmentation chart (as you did for Philemon), using the headings for each column on the highlighted line following the English translation below. Write a summary in which you describe the form and function of these different stylistic techniques and tell how they bring out the text's special literary and religious nature. Re-format both the Greek text and the English translation (NIV) in a manner that better represents the genre of this passage; in the case of

6.3 Identifying and analyzing New Testament prose genres

the English, you will have to re-punctuate and re-capitalize it as well.[5] Finally, make a *LiFE* rendering of this passage in YL along with a literal English back-translation.

> [15] ὅς ἐστιν εἰκὼν τοῦ θεοῦ τοῦ ἀοράτου, πρωτότοκος πάσης κτίσεως, [16] ὅτι ἐν αὐτῷ ἐκτίσθη τὰ πάντα ἐν τοῖς οὐρανοῖς καὶ ἐπὶ τῆς γῆς, τὰ ὁρατὰ καὶ τὰ ἀόρατα, εἴτε θρόνοι εἴτε κυριότητες εἴτε ἀρχαὶ εἴτε ἐξουσίαι· τὰ πάντα δι᾽ αὐτοῦ καὶ εἰς αὐτὸν ἔκτισται· [17] καὶ αὐτός ἐστιν πρὸ πάντων καὶ τὰ πάντα ἐν αὐτῷ συνέστηκεν, [18] καὶ αὐτός ἐστιν ἡ κεφαλὴ τοῦ σώματος τῆς ἐκκλησίας· ὅς ἐστιν ἀρχή, πρωτότοκος ἐκ τῶν νεκρῶν, ἵνα γένηται ἐν πᾶσιν αὐτὸς πρωτεύων, [19] ὅτι ἐν αὐτῷ εὐδόκησεν πᾶν τὸ πλήρωμα κατοικῆσαι [20] καὶ δι᾽ αὐτοῦ ἀποκαταλλάξαι τὰ πάντα εἰς αὐτόν, εἰρηνοποιήσας διὰ τοῦ αἵματος τοῦ σταυροῦ αὐτοῦ, [δι᾽ αὐτοῦ] εἴτε τὰ ἐπὶ τῆς γῆς εἴτε τὰ ἐν τοῖς οὐρανοῖς.

> [15] he is the image of the invisible God the firstborn over all creation [16] for by him all things were created things in heaven and on earth visible and invisible whether thrones or powers or rulers or authorities all things were created by him and for him [17] he is before all things and in him all things hold together [18] and he is the head of the body the church he is the beginning and the firstborn from among the dead so that in everything he might have the supremacy [19] for God was pleased to have all his fullness dwell in him [20] and through him to reconcile to himself all things whether things on earth or things in heaven by making peace through his blood shed on the cross.

ref.	pre-verb2	pre-verb1	VERB	post-verb1	post-verb2	post-verb3
15a		ὅς	ἐστιν	εἰκὼν	τοῦ θεοῦ	τοῦ ἀοράτου,
15b			[ἐστιν]	πρωτότοκος	πάσης κτίσεως,...	

5. In all of the preceding examples, we have analyzed poetic NT texts and asked how we might render these poetically in our mother-tongue translation. The following is an interesting illustration of quite a different literary approach. The excerpts below are taken from an article that documents the poetic-theological genius of late President of Tanzania, *Mwalimu* ("Teacher") Julius Nyerere, who translated the *prose* of the four Gospels into a popular *poetic* form of Swahili. Study this example (from Philip Noss and Peter Renju, 2007) and consider its possible relevance and application to your wider translation setting, e.g., as a special portion for youth, for a dramatic stage presentation, or as the basic for a musical rendition of selected familiar texts:

> Up to a third of the Old Testament is written in poetic form. Without attempting to determine why each Biblical author resorted to what may be identified as poetry, there is no doubt that some of the motivation for such literary rendering was emotive, that is, for the creation of impact. Another purpose would have been to serve as an aid to memory. Mwalimu Nyerere, seeking to accomplish similar purposes among his people, recognized that poetry is the most effective means of reaching the people with the best Message of all. He therefore sought to engage his readers and listeners through the well-known and popular sub-genre of *tenzi*. In this form, the message of the Bible can be recited, sung, and retained in memory.

> This was the poetic form that was the most appropriate for President Nyerere's translation of Holy Scripture. It was a familiar form that was suitable for the development of long and serious themes. The

---

[5] "Rhetoric, structure, and pace are all at work in modern English punctuation, whose rules were established by the end of the eighteenth century. Although structure is the strongest rationale today, punctuation remains a largely intuitive art. A writer can often choose among several correct ways to punctuate a passage, each with a slightly different rhythm and meaning" (Lupton 2003:7). *Can the punctuation be used for such a literary-rhetorical purpose in YL? Explain why—or why not. If not, can anything take the place of punctuation in YL, for example, to show where major and minor pauses should occur in your translation when it is read aloud?*

structure was flexible and relatively simple to manipulate. A single line of eight syllables was long enough to express a complete idea, but short enough to allow for the formation of phrases in creating stanzas.

Nevertheless, the poet-translator Nyerere found himself obliged to stretch the limits both of poetic form and of translation accuracy. He maintained the Biblical format of verses and chapters and sections. Therefore, instead of strictly adhering to the four-line stanza of the classical *tenzi*, he allowed himself the freedom to create stanzas of as few as two lines and as many as twelve lines, depending on the content and length of the verses that he was rendering in Kiswahili. He also abandoned the traditional rhyming scheme in favor of rhyming couplets. Although the majority of his stanzas have an even number of lines, some stanzas have an odd number of lines. In these cases, the final syllables of the last three lines in the stanza rhyme with each other. The translator did, however, strictly adhere to the pattern of eight measures per line.

Given the long history of the *tenzi* tradition, a wide variety of devices are available that enable the composer to remain with the prosodic constraints imposed by the poetic form that he has adopted....These devices are present at all levels of language: phonology, morphology, grammar, syntax, and lexicon.

[The following is Mwalimu Nyerere's Swahili version of John 3:16.]

wa maana Bwana Mungu	Because Lord God
Alipenda ulimwengu,	He loved the world,
Akamtoa Mwanawe	He gave Son-his
Wa pekee auawe,	Only that he be killed,
Ili atayemwamini	So that he who him believes (will believe)
Asiangamie sini,	He not perish never,
Bali awe na uzima	But he be with life
Unaodumu daima.	It which remains continually.

[The following are two additional examples from an appendix, as translated and analyzed by Noss.]

Matt. 7:26c

| *Yeye ni kama mjinga,* | He is like a fool, |
| *Mjenga kwenye mchanga:* | A builder where there is sand: |

Analysis:

| *Yeye ni kama mjinga,* | anadiplosis and word play |
| *Mjenga kwenye mchanga:* | apposition |

Matt. 7:27c

| *Na nyumba ikaanguka* | And the house fell |
| *Anguko kubwa hakika.* | [And] the fall [was] great truly. |

Analysis:

| *Na nyumba ikaanguka* | anadiplosis, enjambement |
| *(Na) Anguko (lilikuwa) kubwa hakika.* | asyndeton, ellipsis |

Following the Swahili examples above, try to render these same passages poetically in YL. Describe the poetic devices that make these texts sound "poetic" in YL. Can you think of a local situation of use in which this type of a translation might be very effective? Describe the public (oral) "performance setting" that you have in mind.

Lesson 7
Contextualizing and Testing a *LiFE* Translation

Aim: In this lesson you will learn about several methods of preparing an adequate conceptual context (cognitive framework) so that readers and hearers can better understand and apply your translation of Scripture, whether a portion or an entire book. This will be applied specifically to preparing explanatory and descriptive study notes. You will also learn how to evaluate a translation and its supplementary paratext by carrying out various types of audience research and text testing.

Goals: After working through this lesson you should be able to:

1. Describe the nature of conceptual "contextualization" and its importance to Bible translation, especially with regard to the factor of implicit versus explicit information from a relevance theory perspective.

2. Understand some key aspects of "mental-space theory," a new cognitive approach that has some practical hermeneutical implications for Bible readers, exegetes, and translators.

3. Identify ten key aspects of the biblical text that often need to be contextualized for readers by means of expository notes.

4. Differentiate good study notes from poor ones and compose good ones of your own for selected portions of Luke's Gospel.

5. Assess several alternative methods of providing a suitable conceptual framework to facilitate the interpretation of a biblical text.

6. Investigate some of the crucial factors that determine "acceptability" in relation to Bible translation.

7. Specify the salient criteria that need to be considered when evaluating a translation.

8. Apply these criteria when assessing the quality of a specific *LiFE* translation.

Review:
Section 1.6 about the various situational frames that contextualize any translation.

Lesson 3 about the notion of a literary functional-equivalent method of Bible translation as it may apply in your sociocultural and religious setting.

Read:
Chapter 10 of *Translating the Literature of Scripture* (Wendland 2004b).
Chapter 10 of *Contextual Frames of Reference in Translation* (Wendland 2008).
"Communicating Context in Bible Translation" (Harriet Hill 2003).
"Contextual Adjustment Strategies and Bible Translation" (Ralph Hill 2004).
As much as possible of *Translation Criticism* (Reiss 2000).

7.1 Contextualizing a *LiFE* translation

Recent explorations in translation theory and practice, especially cognitive-based studies, have underscored the importance of context in communication. Without an adequate understanding of the surrounding circumstances that motivate a text, it is very difficult, if not impossible, to understand it as intended by the original author. This is true to a greater or lesser extent even when communicating in the same language, and the difficulties only increase where translation from one language and sociocultural setting to a different one is involved. In short, then, the meaning of a translated text is always contextually conditioned with respect to both its composition and interpretation.

What is the context of a text? It is everything else besides the text itself—any other information that pertains to its interpretation, facilitating its comprehension, whether implicit or assumed, past or present, verbal or nonverbal, personal or impersonal, consciously available or cognitively latent in one's mind. This all goes into creating the "conceptual world" (or "cognitive environment") that a person depends on when seeking to understand and apply any instance of overt communication. In effect, the various linguistic signs of the verbal text act as cues or stimuli that evoke the sociocultural scenes, settings, and situations which provide the conceptual framework for interpreting the entire discourse, not only the whole but also its different parts.

The same applies to a *LiFE*-style Bible translation designed to reach a particular target audience. Unless this audience has an adequate grasp of the historical, social, cultural, environmental, and religious context of the original text, the translation—no matter how expertly, artistically, or rhetorically composed—will not convey an acceptable degree of the intended sense and significance. In fact, without a proper conceptual background, the biblical message may be completely misunderstood in certain critical respects.[1] The version may sound very beautiful or powerful in the vernacular, but if any of the essential meaning is missing, the act of communication has failed and something needs to be done to correct it. This is the first major issue that we will confront in this lesson as we consider how to "contextualize" the text of any type of translation of Scripture.

The literary "context" of a given biblical text, whether an entire book or some pericope within it, includes its documented manuscript history and the evidence that has been accumulated by scholars and textual critics to establish that original Hebrew or Greek text in the first place. "**Textual criticism** of the NT is the study of biblical texts in ancient manuscripts in order to determine as closely as possible the exact text of the original writings (called 'autographs') before copyists made changes and errors as they copied them" (Omanson 2006:11). This is a specialized study that would take us beyond the scope of this workbook (for a good, brief introduction to the subject, see Omanson ibid.:11–33). As far as specifically literary issues and evidence are concerned, these would fall into the category of "intrinsic probabilities [which] depend upon considerations of what the author, not the copyist, was more likely to have written" (ibid.:32). This would include factors such as how one reading 'A' (as distinct from an alternative 'B') fits into the context at hand and how well 'A' jibes with the structure, stylistic usage, and vocabulary of the author throughout the book under investigation as well as harmony with his possible usage elsewhere (in another biblical book). Literary evidence is not often considered in the practice of textual criticism, but it may help to shift one's choice from 'A' to 'B' in doubtful cases—that is, where the existing external and internal textual evidence is not determinative either way. Several examples are given in the exercises that follow.

For reflection, research, and response:

1. How would you define the term "context" in its popular sense? Look it up in a dictionary. How does that differ from the definition given above? How does the extralinguistic setting affect a specific act of communication, for example, a sermon preached for your local congregation? How would the circumstances surrounding a Sunday sermon differ from those of a Bible translation? Which are the most influential aspects that contribute to the wider situational context of Bible translation in your language and human setting?

---

[1] For a case study of this phenomenon in relation to a translation of the Book of Ruth in the Tonga language of Zambia, see chap. 7 in Wendland 1987.

2. How would you assess the level of biblical literacy in the region of the world where you live? Do people generally know a great deal about the various texts of Scriptures and their Ancient Near Eastern setting, or not much at all? What are the main factors that have contributed to the situation as you see it? What are several important implications for the process of Bible translation? If you conclude that the biblical literacy level is unacceptably low, what measures can you propose that might remedy the current situation?

3. Examine the following literary argument that comes into the discussion of a text problem in 1 Corinthians 13:4 (in Omanson 2006:348). How would you evaluate the evidence that has been given? What conclusion do you come to regarding the issue being discussed—that is, whether or not to include a third mention of "[the] love?" Do such discussions ever arise in your translation project? If not, why can such text-contextual not be considered?

> There is good manuscript support for the third occurrence of the words ἡ ἀγάπη. On the other hand, the rhythm and sentence structure (οὐ..., οὐ..., οὐ...) favor understanding ἡ ἀγάπη as a later addition to the text. In order to represent the balance of these considerations, the words are kept in the text but are put in brackets.

> In addition to the textual problem is the difficulty of knowing how Paul structured the words in this verse. According to the punctuation in the text, the second ἀγάπη goes with the verb χρηστεύεται (is kind). But it is possible to take this noun with the following words οὐ ζηλοῖ, as in the following two translations: "Love is patient and kind. Love envies no one, is never boastful, never conceited" (REB) and "Love is always patient and kind; love is never jealous; love is not boastful or conceited" (NJB). Either way, as Thiselton...notes, "nothing other than stylistic rhythm is at stake."

4. What light can a literary analysis shed on matters of *textual criticism*? A good example is found in 1 Jn. 2:20 and concerns the reading πάντες "all [persons]" as opposed to πάντα "all [things]." The UBS4 text selects the former but assigns it a "somewhat doubtful" [B] rating. Metzger comments on this decision (1994:641; cf. Omanson 2006:505–506):

> A majority of the Committee, understanding the passage to be directed against the claims of a few to possess esoteric knowledge, adopted the reading *pantes*, read by....The reading *panta*, which is widely supported by...,was regarded as a correction introduced by copyists who felt the need of an object after *oidamen*.

However, in favor of πάντα is the overall rhetorical structure of the Greek text—in this instance, a rather long *introversion* of parallel lexical and topical elements that stretches from verses 18 through 28 as follows (given only in summary form):

A (18–19): a "manifestation" of the exit (non-"abiding") of the antichrists
[Note the internal chiastic construction of v. 18, centering upon the "antichrists".]

    B (20–21): about an "anointing" from the "Holy One" so that you know **all things**;
        John "writes" about the "truth"
        C (22): the liar = antichrist "denies" (2x) that Jesus is the Christ,
            hence both the Father and the Son
            D (23): no one who denies the "Son" has the "Father";
                whoever confesses the "Son" has the "Father"
                E (24a): as for you, let
                    what *you heard*
                        from the beginning
                          abide
                              in you

        E' (24b):   if *in you*—
                                              it *abides*
                                 what *from the beginning*
                               you heard
        D' (24c): you will abide in both the "Son" and the "Father"
      C' (25): this is the "promise" (2x) which he (= Father/Son) gave us, namely, eternal life
    B' (26–27d): about an "anointing" from him that abides in you
                  and which teaches you "**all things**" concerning what is "true"
A' (27e–28): you must "abide" in him (Christ), for he will be "manifested"

Thus according to this reading, the "all things" (πάντα) of element B would match that of its parallel in B', and the referent would undoubtedly encompass the matter of mutual "abiding," which is stressed in the center of the structure (i.e., E–E', itself a chiastic arrangement). An "internal" argument based on such symmetrical patterns is not conclusive by any means, but it is an additional bit of evidence that needs to be considered in support of one variant ("reading/hearing") or another. How would you evaluate such evidence and argumentation? Is it worth the effort—or have any relevance for the project that you are engaged in? Explain—including any counter-arguments that come to mind regarding this example.

5. In the following quotation, Andy Warren-Rothlin (2008) discusses the wider practical implications of the different types of text and textual traditions that underlie the biblical books that we seek to translate. How would you respond to the challenges that he poses in terms of the project in which you are engaged—if not a regular translation, then perhaps a study Bible project? Is "doing nothing at all" an adequate (or ethical) response? Explain your position on such issues. What do you think of the several text-related, context-building "solutions" that he proposes at the end? Would some of these be helpful in your translation setting? Explain. Do you have other possibilities to suggest?

> What we know as the Bible derives from a wide range of times, places and cultures; I have argued elsewhere that this *historical, geographical* and *social* 'texture' is inadequately reflected in UBS Bible translations, which tend to present the Bible as linguistically homogeneous. Two further aspects of 'texture' in the Bible are *textual* and *canonical*—the plurality of textual traditions in a number of languages, in a range of manuscript families, not only for each testament, but even for individual books, and their plural traditions of combination into sets of special books for distinct Christian communities; these facts, too, tend to be misrepresented by our products.
>
> In the light of the increasing competence of TCs and translators with source languages, and the improved tools available, this paper argues for forms of presentation of Biblical texts which are more *faithful* both to the textual realities and to New Testament doctrines of scripture. It invites consideration of practical ways in which this can be done for African Christian audiences, who may be among those most needing greater awareness of our pluralistic scriptural heritage. In two recent articles, I have argued that the 'smoothed-out', harmonised Bibles that we produce misrepresent the source texts....And these *historical, geographical* and *social* distinctions (or 'texture') are reflected in biblical Hebrew archaisms and neologisms, regional dialects and levels of register respectively. I posed the question: Does not our tradition of presenting the Bible as linguistically homogeneous stem from a quite unbiblical fundamentalist principle which would like to present its theology as consistent? If so, is this not *unethical*?
>
> In the present paper, I turn to a fourth parameter of 'texture' in biblical source texts—the co-existence of multiple *textual* traditions and manuscript families of each tradition—not only for each testament, but even for many individual books. And I ask whether by presenting, without comment, a single canonical version of each book we are not tacitly promoting a set of presuppositions about canon, inerrancy and 'preservation', which though popular in the American church as it confronts post-modern relativism and in the African church as it seeks to keep pace with Islamic positivism,

7.1 Contextualizing a LiFE translation

are not in fact true to New Testament theologies of scripture. In other words, Is it not wrong to present τα βιβλία, 'the books', as if they were one homogeneous (singular!) 'Bible'?...

Various solutions have been employed in popular international-language Bible translations to reflect these facts:

- *Footnotes may indicate textual variants, yet even NRSV refers to DSS [Dead Sea Scrolls] only 78 times!*
- *Some editions of the RSV express 'texture' by means of smaller print for long lists and repeated sections.*
- *Editions of the RSV may give a sense of history by offering possible dates for the events narrated.*
- *The NJB is unusually ready to use omission marks rather than translate conjecturally.*
- *And Chouraqui's literary French translation deliberately alienates the reader by using Hebrew terms and names, and special topography for the name of God.*

Other solutions suitable for use in Africa might include:

- *Clear, factual book introductions describing textual history.*
- *Footnotes where manuscripts do not agree.*
- *Introductory plates of ancient manuscripts, such as those in the TAZI NT.*

6. Ralph Hill (2003:6) brings out an important point:

   Whenever someone retells the same message for a different audience...there is no guarantee that the second audience will be able to access the same set of assumptions the original speaker had in mind. Lack of access to these assumptions is often referred to as contextual mismatches or contextual gaps. Relevance theory suggests that the new audience will always process the message with some set of assumptions; the question is whether they are able to use the right (speaker-intended) set of assumptions. If they are not, they will likely come up with either wrong meaning or zero meaning, or perhaps meaning that is weaker or stronger than the speaker intended. There are obviously implications for reading the Bible. A naïve reader of a text from another time and place will naturally bring his or her own set of assumptions to the reading of the text. Readers may grow in competence, however, if they learn to check their own assumptions to see if they were those intended by the author, and revise them as necessary. Supplemental information can help readers become aware that there are indeed differences, and they learn to value access to such information.

Have you found this true in your own Bible teaching, preaching, and/or translation experience? Give an example of one or more critical "contextual mismatches" that you have observed with respect to certain key Scripture passages. What went wrong in the process of interpretation? Why?

7. Several problems can arise when *too much* contextual information, even though needed for understanding a Bible passage, is introduced within the text of the translation itself. The following example (from Ralph Hill 2004:9) illustrates this point. It is based on Matthew 9:16–17 as rendered in the GNB, but with explanatory material added in italics:

   [16] "No one patches up an old coat with a piece of new cloth, for the new patch will shrink *after it is washed* and make an even bigger hole in the coat. [17] Nor does anyone pour new wine into used wineskins, for the skins will burst *after they become distended by the fermenting wine*, the wine will pour out, and the skins will be ruined. Instead, new wine is poured into fresh wineskins *because the skins will stretch as the wine ferments/expands*, and both will keep in good condition."

First of all, evaluate the added explanatory material in terms of importance. Would it be necessary in your cultural setting? Would different information be more appropriate and helpful? If so, suggest how that might be worded, for example, with regard to the reference to wineskins, and where it should be put. Should it be in the text or in a marginal note? Finally, comment on the "literariness" of the above example. Is the verbal style appealing and compelling? Is it a good example of *LiFE*? Explain your answer.

8. Examine the following passages from Ruth. Would average readers/listeners in YL have difficulty in correctly understanding these texts (including their underlying religious assumptions and implications)? If so, what are some of the problems that you notice? What can you as translator do in order to bridge this crucial comprehension gap? Discuss these various communication-related issues in class.

> 1:1 In the days when the judges ruled there was a famine in the land, and a certain man of Bethlehem in Judah went to sojourn in the country of Moab, he and his wife and his two sons.
> 1:6 Then she started with her daughters-in-law to return from the country of Moab, for she had heard in the country of Moab that the Lord had visited his people and given them food.
> 1:9 The Lord grant that you may find a home, each of you in the house of her husband!" Then she kissed them, and they lifted up their voices and wept.
> 1:16 But Ruth said, "…where you go I will go, and where you lodge I will lodge; your people shall be my people, and your God my God; 17 where you die I will die, and there will I be buried…"
> 1:21 "I went away full, and the Lord has brought me back empty. Why call me Naomi, when the Lord has afflicted me and the Almighty has brought calamity upon me?"
> 2:2 And Ruth the Moabitess said to Naomi, "Let me go to the field, and glean among the ears of grain after him in whose sight I shall find favor."
> 2:4 And behold, Boaz came from Bethlehem; and he said to the reapers, "The Lord be with you!" And they answered, "The Lord bless you."
> 2:12 "The Lord recompense you for what you have done, and a full reward be given you by the Lord, the God of Israel, under whose wings you have come to take refuge!"
> 2:14 And at mealtime Boaz said to her, "Come here, and eat some bread, and dip your morsel in the wine."
> 2:20 And Naomi said to her daughter-in-law, "Blessed be he by the Lord, whose kindness has not forsaken the living or the dead!"
> 3:3 "Wash and perfume yourself, and put on your best clothes. Then go down to the threshing floor, but don't let him know you are there until he has finished eating and drinking. 4 When he lies down, note the place where he is lying. Then go and uncover his feet and lie down. He will tell you what to do."
> 3:7 And when Boaz had eaten and drunk, and his heart was merry, he went to lie down at the end of the heap of grain. Then she came softly, and uncovered his feet, and lay down.
> 3:9 …"I am Ruth, your maidservant; spread your skirt over your maidservant, for you are next of kin." 10 And he said, "May you be blessed by the Lord, my daughter; you have made this last kindness greater than the first, in that you have not gone after young men, whether poor or rich."
> 3:13 "Remain this night, and in the morning, if he will do the part of the next of kin for you, well; let him do it; but if he is not willing to do the part of the next of kin for you, then, as the Lord lives, I will do the part of the next of kin for you. Lie down until the morning."
> 4:3 "Naomi, who has come back from the country of Moab, is selling the parcel of land which belonged to our kinsman Elimelech. 4 So I thought I would tell you of it, and say, Buy it in the presence of those sitting here, and in the presence of the elders of my people…"
> 4:5 Then Boaz said, "The day you buy the field from the hand of Naomi, you are also buying Ruth e the Moabitess, the widow of the dead, in order to restore the name of the dead to his inheritance."
> 4:8 So when the next of kin said to Boaz, "Buy it for yourself," he drew off his sandal.
> 4:11 "May the Lord make the woman, who is coming into your house, like Rachel and Leah, who together built up the house of Israel. May you prosper in Ephrathah and be renowned in Bethlehem; 12 and may your house be like the house of Perez, whom Tamar bore to Judah, because of the children that the Lord will give you by this young woman."
> 4:14 "Blessed be the Lord, who has not left you this day without next of kin; and may his name be renowned in Israel!"

9. Select three of the above passages from the book of Ruth that are conceptually the most difficult for people of your culture to correctly understand. Then compose a brief, contextually relevant explanatory note for each one that would clarify the biblical sociocultural and/or religious setting and specify how that contrasts with your own.

10. Notice how the biblical authors often provide a historical context for the particular text that they happen to be writing, whether prose or poetry. Look up the following references (from Bauckham 2003:41–42) and identify the scope of the historical setting that each one delineates. Then suggest a rhetorical and/or thematic purpose for each inclusion. Finally, discuss any implications of these historical summaries with regard to translating such passages in YL:

    Deuteronomy 6:20–24 _____

    Deuteronomy 26:5–9 _____

    Joshua 24:2–13 _____

    Nehemiah 9:6–37 _____

    Psalm 78 _____

    Psalm 105 _____

    Psalm 106 _____

    Psalm 135:8–12 _____

    Psalm 136 _____

    Acts 7:2–50 _____

    Acts 10:36–43 _____

    Acts 13:17–41 _____

    Acts 22:2–21 _____

11. One important aspect of contextualizing a biblical text, in preparation for translating as well as for interpreting it, is to get a grasp of the "big picture"—the overarching "meta-narrative" that gives both coherence and continuity to all of the individual narratives of a certain corpus. What do you think of the following perspective on the conceptual unity of the Old and New Testament Scriptures (Bauckham 2003:42–43)? What practical advice is here for Bible translators?

    > The narratives [of Scripture] are told from various junctures within the story [i.e., the meta-narrative] and from a variety of perspectives. In the Old Testament, we have something like a master version of the main story up to the exile (Genesis–2 Kings), but we also have diverse readings of it and interactions with it in the Prophets, a significantly different retelling of it in 1–2 Chronicles, tangential narratives that seem to offer corrective angles on it (Ruth, Esther, Jonah), and books that challenge essential features of its theology (Job, Ecclesiastes). In the New Testament, we have fresh and diverse readings of the Old Testament story (e.g., Paul and James on Abraham), while the story of Jesus is told in no less than four different versions in the Gospels, along with comment and interpretation in Paul, Hebrews, 1 Peter, and Revelation.

12. How would you summarize the meta-narrative of the Scriptures as a whole? What are some of the essential stories that make up this macro-history of humanity? How should context-building information of this type be included in the Bible as translated in YL? What else can be done to give your primary target audience a better idea of how the Scriptures as a diverse, but unified whole "hang together" conceptually?

7.1.1 The importance of implicit information

When communicating by means of a written message to an audience of one's own language, it is normal for a relative amount of essential information to be left unexpressed (due to its being presupposed) without serious loss to the intended message. "This 'unwritten part' includes the things an author presumes the audience knows about how the world works, which he or she can leave between the lines of a text, so to speak, yet which are crucial to its understanding" (Malina and Rohrbaugh 1992:9; see section 1.6.2.2).

However, when a *translator* attempts to communicate a written message to an audience of a *different* language and culture, he or she must first consider the historical and cultural background of the original author and his audience in order to estimate what this unexpressed but essential information *was* then—and *is* today. Equally important, the translator must take the worldview of the contemporary target audience into account as well—not only their view of "how the world works" but also their beliefs, presuppositions, values, and felt needs. Also important is how the target audience prefers to package, convey, and receive information, and whether they are a "high-context" (minimal text) or "low-context" (maximal text) society (see section 1.6.1).

Of course, neither an original author nor a translator can explicitly state *everything* of possible significance in the message, for such a mass of detail would undoubtedly leave the text's consumers confused, frustrated, or just plain intimidated by it all—not to mention the expense of publishing it. On the other hand, if too much essential information that was implicit in the original is left unexpressed in the translation, it is likely that targeted readers or hearers will not understand what is being said, whether partly or entirely. They will therefore be tempted to simply give up on the text as being too difficult. The key is *balance*—that is, leaving enough information implicit to challenge the audience and encourage them to participate in the process of conceptualizing the intended message and at the same time expressing a sufficient amount to keep the communication moving along smoothly from point to point, event to event, and scene to scene.

The *manner* in which information, whether explicit or implicit, is presented is vitally important too. The people of some cultures, especially those who have been educated in a print-based culture, tend to prefer a *deductive* (analytical) manner. Oral-aural communicators, on the other hand, benefit much more from an *inductive* (synthetic) manner that features traditional art forms, such as analogies, parables, folktales, proverbs, songs, riddles, personal histories, and anecdotes. In Western logic, which has been the predominant logic of print throughout the ages, one idea tends to follow another sequentially, and what is perceived to be "circular reasoning" (i.e., discourse that is repetitious and not sequentially ordered) is considered unsophisticated and unacceptable. This linear bias makes it very difficult for Westerners to understand people from a pre-literate, oral-aural culture where the spoken word, arranged in iterative patterns from varied, often analogous or analogical, perspectives is still the predominant discourse strategy and communication technique. A society that depends largely on auditory or gestured symbols for the exchange of messages will organize its world in a very different way from the teleological model that is composed and arranged with reference to the silent printed word.

Explicit versus implicit information is a crucial issue in the practice of Bible translation (see Wendland 1985:85–94). The question is how much implicit information in any given SL text can be left unexpressed in a translation. The answer directly affects the process of annotation since whatever *essential* content (or functional intent) is not adequately conveyed in the translated text itself will presumably need to be explained in a marginal note or some other para- or extratextual device. By "essential" is meant content that average members of the target group absolutely require in order to correctly interpret and act upon the text that they

7.1 Contextualizing a LiFE translation

are interacting with. Not everything needs to be said, of course, since to a greater or lesser degree the intended readers/hearers do participate in a common cognitive, and experiential-sensory world and a general framework of language that enables them to "read between the lines" and supply the required background information for a correct interpretation of the message.

One way of describing the conceptualizing process is the "scenario model" of communication:

> We understand a written text as setting forth a succession of implicit and explicit mental pictures consisting of culturally specific scenes or schemes sketched by an author. These in turn evoke corresponding scenes or schemes in the mind of the reader that are drawn from the reader's own experience in the culture. With the scenarios suggested by the author as a starting point, the reader then carries out appropriate alterations to the settings or episodes as directed by clues in the text. In this way an author begins with the familiar and directs the reader to what is new. (Malina and Rohrbaugh 1992:10; cf. Hoyle 2008:ch.1)

This model is rather oversimplified in that it appears to be biased in favor of narrative discourse and ignores other possible compositional strategies, such as the use of certain "pre-logical" or analogical patterns of hortatory text development that vary in accordance with extant genres of accepted oral or written argumentation. Nor does the model explain precisely enough how or why text consumers choose one schema over another (perhaps a closely related or equally likely alternative one) within a given cotext. For example, does the "white stone" of Revelation 2:17 refer to a stone used (a) for admission to a public celebration, (b) for medicinal purposes, (c) as an object of great value, (d) to cast a vote for or against acquittal in a trial, or (e) two or more of the preceding? (Each of these possibilities evokes very different scenarios.) In such cases the hermeneutical principle of relevance is operative:

» Which interpretation would have yielded the greatest cognitive and emotive effects (impact + appeal) in the initial setting of communication and for the original audience?

» Which construal of the white stone seems most "relevant" to you, based on your study of this passage?

» On the other hand, which interpretation would come to mind most naturally in the cultural setting in which you live or work?

Furthermore, as noted in section 1.6.1, we frequently find associated with visual, event-based or action-based "scenarios" various discourse-constituted "scripts" as well as descriptive "sketches." Together, these cognitive-emotive evocations of conventional speeches and familiar images—collectively referred to as "schemas"—serve to outline, summarize, or simply allude to texts that are appropriate to the particular cultural setting and social situation. Examples from one subcategory of religious communication would be a typical "altar call," personal "testimony," or door-to-door evangelistic "invitation." The briefest textual mention or allusion to well-known personages, entities, events, or occasions can conceptually "trigger" most of the details that readers or hearers need to know in order to interpret the sentence at hand. Problems quickly develop, however, when they do not have such a cognitive reservoir of common experience or shared instruction pertaining to events that are characteristic of the culture concerned. This inevitably happens in Bible translation, where the intended message must cross the additional communication barriers of language, time, and place.

The *style* of a literary text also conveys important implicit information that needs to be represented in a translation somehow, if at all possible. One of the most important stylistic devices of the Bible is its various types of *repetition*, whether synonymous or exact, which feature prominently on both the macro- as well as the micro-structure of the text. What can be done to reveal some of these patterns of meaning? Thomas and Thomas offer some suggestions in this regard (2006:57):

> The aim should be, at the minimum, to assist a reader who is preparing to read the [text] orally for a group of hearers. This perspective should also enable comprehension of the macrostructure by silent readers who

are studying the written text. Special attention will be needed for any translation intended to be used by new media producers, who may be less interested in reproducing details of the gross features but who can learn much from the analysis of them....[T]he translator has two simple means for revealing the gross structure:

1. using word repetitions and other related devices found in the original, to the degree this is achievable, as markers by which hearers may sense the structure of the [text], perhaps even subconsciously;

2. laying out the written text in a way that helps visualize the structure, an important step even if a translation is intended only for oral reading by a reciter.

» How would you apply these instructions to Psalm 136? Make a quick discourse analysis of this psalm, summarize its primary structural features, and then tell how you would "display" these in your translation, that is, using the style of the text itself as well as its format on the printed page—to render it in a more "readable" as well as more "hearable" manner (for an application to 1 Peter in a "self-presenting pattern," see Thomas and Thomas 2006:193–200).

For reflection, research, and response:

1. Would you classify most of the people of your culture as those who receive their information primarily through print, face-to-face communication, audiovisual means, or the electronic media? Do certain segments of the society prefer or depend on one of these media more than on the others? Is your society changing is this regard? Illustrate your answers with an example or two. What are the implications for communicating the Scriptures in the next decade or so?

2. Give an example from your experience of a communication failure where some important biblical truth was seriously misunderstood due to the fact that the TL audience (a) did not have a sufficient grasp of the Ancient Near Eastern setting to process the text fully or correctly, (b) accessed one or more crucial facts from their own cultural context that obscured or contradicted those of the original setting, or (c) were unable to extract certain necessary information that was implicit in the text.[2] How would you rectify each of these conceptual-communicative problems?

3. Apply the technique of comparative contextual assessment to Matthew 5:13 (NIV): "You are the salt of the earth. But if the salt loses its saltiness, how can it be made salty again? It is no longer good for anything, except to be thrown out and trampled by men." How would the ordinary members of a specific audience group in your community understand this passage? Assuming that most people do not understand this passage correctly, suggest an explanatory note that would help them understand the significance of Christ's implicit challenge here.

4. In his fascinating application of "scenario theory" to the study of the New Testament and its translation into the Parkari language of Pakistan, Richard Hoyle (2008) includes a great deal of discussion about how to handle different types of *implicit information*. Study the following two selections (from pp. 387–388 and 438–439) and apply the suggested guidelines regarding the problematic terms being considered to the Bible translation in your language. Give your proposed solutions and their rationale

> Since scenarios contain interrelated chunks of information, including probabilities of certain events co-occurring, a mismatch of scenarios between source and target languages causes a mismatch of information communicated and a reduced ability to evaluate what is normal and what is contra-expectation. Since the grammar and lexicon in both Parkari and Greek is influenced by scenarios, a mismatch of scenarios between those languages will affect the grammar and lexicon used in translation.

---

[2]For a handy heuristic methodology for exploring these issues in more detail, see Harriet Hill 2003, and 2006.

The most radical, and obvious, problem of scenario mismatch is when the target language and culture completely lack a scenario found in the source language. This creates classic translation problems such as "How do you translate camel for an Eskimo?" There are several standard approaches for translating unknown items, as listed by Beekman and Callow (1974:191):

- EQUIVALENCE BY MODIFYING A GENERIC WORD
- Modified with features of form / a statement of function /both form and function /a comparison
- EQUIVALENCE BY USING A LOAN WORD
- Modified with a classifier / form or function or both
- EQUIVALENCE BY CULTURAL SUBSTITUTION
- Cultural substitution is "the use of a real world referent from the receptor culture for an unknown referent of the original, both of the referents having the same function" (ibid.).

To these one might add the use of a generic alone, if specific aspects of the source language referent are not focal in the context. For example, if English had no equivalent for ἅρμα 'chariot', in Acts 8:28 and Revelation 9:9, one might translate by using the following:

- A generic word e.g. vehicle

- A modified generic word e.g. horse-drawn vehicle (form), war cart (function)

- horse-drawn war cart (form and function)

- vehicle like a *tonga* (comparison)

- A modified loan word e.g. vehicle called "harma" (generic)

- horse-drawn "harma" (form), war "harma" (function)

- A cultural substitute e.g. carriage, cart

Note that ἅρμα belongs in two different source language scenarios—first class travel and war. Similarly, each word or phrase in the target language evokes its own scenario, which must be compared to the original source language scenario and co-text, to determine its appropriateness. For example, English "chariot" fits both scenarios, but the "cart" scenario does not include "high-class", and the "carriage" scenario does not include "war". Therefore, such translation requires sensitivity to context.

In Acts 8:28, ἅρμα represents a concept unknown in Parkari and is translated $gʰoṛa\ ɠadəi$ 'horse cart' meaning horse-drawn vehicle, whereas ἅρμα 'war-chariot' in Revelation 9:9 is a known concept (through storytelling) and is translated $rətʰ$, which refers either to a war chariot or a ceremonial vehicle for transporting deities. A common Parkari word for a horse-drawn vehicle, ṭõɠo, was avoided in both cases, as its scenario includes "available cheaply for hire" which is clearly inappropriate....

[A]ll scenarios include a variety of discrete elements, and problems occur in translation when these do not match up across cultures. Often the more specific the scenario, the more it contains specific cultural elements, and the more generic the scenario, the more universal its contents. For example, everybody's "food" scenario includes "eat", but the "pig" scenario for some people includes "eat", and for others "do not eat." If the scenario of a specific term contains prototypical elements which are contradictory between source and target language, then whenever those elements are contextually focal, the audience will misunderstand the text, because they will interpret it in the light of their own scenario. In such cases the specific term in the source text may be best translated by a generic term in the target language, to avoid creating false implicatures.

For example, in the parable of the prodigal son (Luke 15:23):
καὶ φέρετε τὸν **μόσχον** τὸν σιτευτόν, θύσατε
RSV: and bring the fatted **calf** and kill it.
Parkari: And the **livestock-animal** which is specially-chosen, slaughter it.

This verse is not about historical fact, i.e. which animals Jews did or did not kill. Here, the contextually focal element of the "calf" scenario is "ideal food for a feast", so this is what must be communicated. The Parkari scenario for "calf", however, due to their Hindu background, includes "killing cattle is sinful". Simply translating "calf" would imply that the father, on his son's return, committed a major sin. By translating with a generic term, which includes both cattle and buffalo, the focus is kept on the element "ideal food for a feast", since Parkaris specially fatten buffalo for just that purpose. The specific term "buffalo", although a good cultural substitute as regards function, was avoided as historically inaccurate.

5. Evaluate the following description of "Strategic Frame Analysis™" (from the website of *FrameWorks*, http://www.frameworksinstitued.org/strategicanalysis/index.shtml, accessed on May 24, 2008; added boldface). Can this approach help us in any way to better conceptualize and analyze the process of Bible translation (cf. Wendland 2008:ch. 4)? Read through the summary below and then answer the questions that follow with reference to the translation project that you are currently engaged in (or know about):

> People use mental shortcuts to make sense of the world. Since most people are looking to process incoming information quickly and efficiently, they rely upon cues within that new information to signal to them how to connect it with their stored images of the world. The[se] "pictures in our heads"…might better be thought of as vividly labeled storage boxes—filled with pictures, images, and stories from our past encounters with the world and labeled youth, marriage, poverty, fairness, etc. The incoming information provides cues about which is the right container for that idea or experience. And the efficient thinker makes the connection, a process called "indexing," and moves on.
>
> Put another way, how an issue is framed is a **trigger** to these shared and durable cultural models that help us make sense of our world. When a **frame** ignites a cultural model, or calls it into play in the interpretation, the whole model is operative. This allows people to reason about an issue, to make inferences, to fill in the blanks for missing information by referring to the robustness of the model, not the sketchy frame….
>
> Recognizing that there is more than one way to tell a story, **strategic frame analysis** taps into decades of research on how people think and communicate. The result is an empirically-driven communications process that makes academic research understandable, interesting, and usable to help people solve social problems….
>
> This interdisciplinary work is made possible by the fact that the concept of **framing** is found in the literatures of numerous academic disciplines across the social, behavioral and cognitive sciences. Put simply, framing refers to the construct of a communication—its language, visuals and messengers—and the way it signals to the listener or observer how to interpret and classify new information. By framing, we mean how messages are encoded with meaning so that they can be efficiently interpreted in relationship to existing beliefs or ideas. **Frames trigger meaning**.
>
> - The questions we ask, in applying the concept of frames to the arena of social policy, are as follows:
>
> - How does the public think about a particular social or political issue?
>
> - What is the public discourse on the issue? And how is this discourse influenced by the way media frames that issue?

- How do these public and private frames affect public choices?

- How can an issue be reframed to evoke a different way of thinking, one that illuminates a broader range of alternative policy choices?

This approach is strategic in that it not only **deconstructs** the dominant frames of reference that drive reasoning on public issues, but it also identifies those **alternative frames** most likely to stimulate public reconsideration and enumerates their elements (reframing). We use the term **reframe** to mean changing "the context of the message exchange" so that different interpretations and probable outcomes become visible to the public....

Instead of "social policy," re-phrase the four questions listed above and apply them to the subject of "translation policy" and the "job commission" (*Brief,* cf. 1.6.4) that has been adopted by the Bible translation program that you are working with: Was such potential-audience research carried out by the organizers of your project? If so, explain how this was done; if not; tell why. Why is such research necessary as an ongoing aspect of every Scripture translation project? Do additional questions need to be asked? Which ones?

Can this procedure of "strategic frame analysis" be adapted for use in determining specific translation issues (in cases where there are several options and/or a difference of opinion) and when testing translation drafts? If so, suggest how. What is a "dominant frame of reference" which you have encountered in Bible translation work that needed to be "deconstructed" and then "reframed"? How was this re-conceptualization process carried out? Was it successful? If not, how could it have been done more effectively?

7.1.2 Sociological knowledge, mental spaces, and conceptual blending

"Mental-space theory" is a recent cognitive linguistic approach to perception, cognition, and text interpretation that may offer translators some assistance as they carry out the essential task of contextualizing a biblical text through paratextual means. This theory helps to explain the integration and manipulation of stereotyped knowledge constellations and conventional cognitive frames in order both to construe and also to communicate new or innovative concepts (and texts) within a particular socio-cultural setting. As in the case of relevance theory and schema theory, this hermeneutical approach views "context" as essentially a matter of the mind.

According to mental-space theory, an initial "conceptual integration network" is formed by a process known as "conceptual blending" from a closely associated set of short-term cognitive representations called "mental spaces." These mental spaces consist of culturally based frames that a speaker or writer constructs from immediate contextual information (including the prior discourse and any topically related texts) as well as pertinent background knowledge that exists in the short-term or long-term memory. These psychological constructs function like different "windows" of access on the computer screen of a hypertext word-processing program. They may be temporal, spatial, eventive, personal, objective, circumstantial, modal, conditional, or hypothetical in nature, whether the reference is to actual or fictional settings and situations. A new window is "activated," or projected, in the mind as a person perceives and then shifts from one cognitive-connotative complex to another (or synthesizes one with another). Fauconnier and Turner (2002:40) provide a good summary:

> Mental spaces are small conceptual packets constructed as we think and talk, for the purposes of local understanding and action....Mental spaces are connected to long-term schematic knowledge called "frames," such as the frame of *walking along a path*, and to long-term specific knowledge, such as a memory of the time you climbed Mount Rainier in 2001....Mental spaces are very partial. They contain [cognitive] elements and are

typically structured by frames. They are interconnected, and can be modified as thought and discourse unfold. Mental spaces can be used generally to model dynamic mappings in thought and language.[3]

Stockwell (2002:97–98) sums up the operation of conceptual blending as follows:

> This involves a [cognitive] mapping between two [mental] spaces, and common general nodes and relationships across the spaces are abstracted into a **generic space**. Specific features which emerge from this mapping then form a new space, the **blend**. Conceptual blends are the mechanism by which we can hold the properties of two spaces together, such as in metaphorical or allegorical thinking, scientific or political analogy, comparisons and imaginary domains involving characters from disparate areas....

The prototypical *network,* then, is composed of four *mental spaces* (roughly schematized by the diagram on the following page). There is one space for each of two "input" domains: The *source* (or *base*) is "given," or already known, information, while the *target* (or *focus*) is the topic currently being referred to in a verbal text, one that "triggers" an accessing of the source domain. A third, *generic* space is all the abstract concepts and components of meaning that are common to both source and target domains and conceptually available, or "accessible," in a particular communicative context. Most important is the *blend*, a "virtual" domain in which the mind selectively "activates," incorporates, and integrates salient information (cognitive elements and relations) from the two initial input spaces.

This hermeneutical process would be guided by the principle of relevance (interpretive effort in relation to ideational enrichment) at various levels of specificity and appropriateness, as determined by the current setting of activity or discourse interaction. The resultant mental representational structure formed in the blend generally differs in one or more respects from that of the input spaces, and this is what allows the language user, as we shall see, to create novel or figurative conceptualizations of persons, actions, events, and situations.

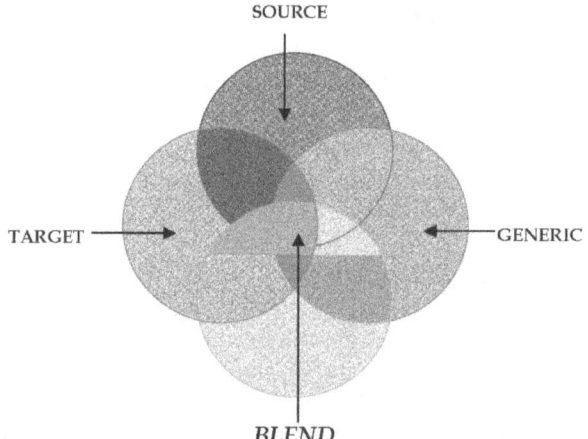

---

[3]The view of Fauconnier and Turner may be compared with the more literary-oriented perspective of S. Coulson (2001:21–25): "Mental space theory...is a theory of referential structure....[M]ental spaces can be thought of as temporary containers for relevant information about a particular domain. A mental space contains a partial representation of the entities and relations of a particular scenario as perceived, imagined, remembered, or otherwise understood by a speaker....Spaces represent such diverse things as hypothetical scenarios, beliefs, quantified domains, thematically defined domains, fictional scenarios, and situations located in time and space. As discourse unfolds, the language user extends existing spaces by adding new elements and relations to the cognitive models already evoked....A new space is also set up when utterances concern objects or events that require different background assumptions from those of the current space....Meaning construction thus consists of mapping cognitive models from space to space while keeping track of the links between spaces and between elements and their counterparts....[M]eaning always emerges from understanding in a particular context." Apparently, missing from this notion of perception, understanding, and meaning construction is a consideration of emotions, attitudes, values, and other connotative elements that characterize most communication events, certainly literary creations.

7.1 *Contextualizing a LiFE translation*   369

The following simple analogy illustrates how mental-space text-processing is believed to operate. The scenario is an impromptu game played with a plastic "football":

> One afternoon a young boy who lives in an urban squatter compound of Lusaka calls out to his friends, "Let's play a game of football [soccer]!" The boys cannot afford to buy a real official-size ball, and so they construct a rough replica by collecting a bunch of used plastic bags that litter their environment, wad them up into a tight roundish artifact, and tie it together on the outside with a long, thin rubber strip formed from an old bicycle tire. They find a small corner of the dusty market next door and pick up a discarded, battered and bottomless garbage can [dustbin] to serve as the goal. Their improvised match can now begin....

Conceptual Network (four progressively interrelated mental spaces):

Target domain: irregular plastic sphere, garbage can, six boys, rough dusty lot, market customers milling all around, no referee

Source domain: "official" soccer ball, goal (metal frame, net, binding), eleven players, rules of the game, marked field of play, referee and linesmen, scorekeeper, timer, spectators

Generic domain: abstract, general semantic components that pertain to balls, goals, games, rules, human competitors, plastic, metal garbage containers, etc.

Blended domain: the "game" occurs in a new mental framework to match the greatly changed physical environment, and the fluid "rules" change accordingly in keeping with the event's new cognitive "domain" (as agreed on the spot by the youthful model makers)

As the preceding example illustrates, the *target* domain presents an actual presently perceived reality that differs in certain crucial respects from the familiar norm; namely, the *source* conceptual space. The latter accesses an idealized reality that is based upon one's current knowledge and local experience of how the world is or ought to be and how it typically operates (the default worldview and way of life). Such background knowledge may be situationally enriched to include a related verbal text (intertextual resonance) or some pertinent cognitively based sociocultural schema. These two "realities" are then cognitively combined in the *generic* space, which draws on elements shared by both input domains. From this, then, some new thought, insight, application, or behavior (or a related set of them) develops in the *blended* output. The more incongruous or fantastic the conceptual relationship that is forged between source and target domains, the more graphic and forceful the consequent blend becomes in speech or behavior. However, in cases where the respective inputs from the source and target space are too diverse, disparate, or foreign to each other, semantic confusion results in the generic space and no meaningful or useful blend emerges. The process of communication then aborts at that point or takes a new tack.

When figurative language is used, the source and target domains normally belong to completely different semantic fields. This is what generates the special cognitive and emotive effects where novel, unusual, or unexpected figures are involved. In the case of a metaphor, for example, we need to redefine the four mental spaces somewhat in order to better reflect this innovative thought process:

1. **Target** (base) space is the verbal or textual starting point for the construction of a conceptual network—the "topic," which is the familiar "real-world"-oriented or literal element of a metaphor, what is being spoken about or referred to.

2. **Source** (image) space is the figurative concept that is used to develop the initial conceptual space by presenting a novel, non-literal perspective—the "image" of a metaphor that is employed to illumine or illustrate the Target.

3. **Generic** (abstract) space is formed from selective "cross-space mapping," as counterparts or correspondences between the two input spaces (Target + Source) initially meet in one's mind; these key cognitive elements that the input spaces have in common are often referred to as a metaphor's "ground of comparison" or "point of similarity."

4. **Blended** (metaphoric) space is the specific features of the generic space that become further activated by the mind's search for relevance within the present discourse context, including the extralinguistic, situational, and circumstantial setting; a virtual "emergent structure" is thus formed in which new relations and aspects of meaning become salient in the setting at hand, often with additional connotative overtones and rhetorical impact.

Take Christ's dramatic reference to King Herod, "Go tell that *fox*" (Luke 13:32), where the following conceptual representation may (hypothetically) have been generated for his audience in the original setting of speech:

Target domain:	Herod (Antipas)—"king of the Jews," actually the Roman-imposed tetrarch of Galilee and Perea, a son of Herod the Great, a politically savvy but ruthless ruler
Source domain:	"fox" (ἀλώπηξ)—a small but stealthy and persistent carnivore, a nocturnal pack animal that roams remote regions and runs with lions, trying to steal their kill
Generic domain:	abstract, general semantic components that pertain to crafty but inferior, or secondary, animal predators and corresponding local political rulers within the land
Blended domain:	Herod may be dangerous but his power is derived and circumscribed. He depends on what his Roman overlords (the "lions") allow him; Herod may be clever, but like the Palestinian fox he must do his dirty work at night, so to speak, so that he is not detected by Caesar's spies and representatives. Christ's reference may thus be sarcastic: He does not fear Herod and will carry on with his divine business; his time for capture and death had not yet come and was not dependent upon Herod's wicked whims.

It may be helpful for translators to conceptualize difficult or complex biblical figures of speech in this way as a handy heuristic strategy aimed at filling out all of the mental spaces involved. The goal is to discover the pertinent components of the blend so that they may be rendered more perceptibly and powerfully in the TL—in a literary translation, for example, through the use of a close cultural equivalent (e.g., Chewa 'jackal' for ἀλώπηξ). Alternatively, if a more literal version is desired, then these essential elements of meaning will have to be specified clearly and succinctly in a marginal note, contextualized to reflect the local cultural, circumstantial, and environmental setting.

Mental-space theory and the related notion of conceptual metaphor have been used with good effect to elucidate the impact and appeal of various types of figurative language in literature (see Stockwell 2002, chaps. 7–8). These cognition-based analytical tools may also be utilized to reveal certain implicit aspects of the interpretation of larger literary forms, such as a "metaphor in story form" or parable (ibid., chap. 9). But in terms of its conceptual representation, a parable differs significantly from a metaphor, and not only because it is longer. In the case of a *parable*, the respective cognitive inputs are reversed and we begin with the *source*, now a *hypothetical* narrative domain—that is, the parable itself. The mind must then evoke by analogy appropriate counterparts in the current real-life human setting, which then constitutes the *target* domain. When what is common to these conceptual inventories is combined in the *generic* space, certain features are highlighted by the principle of relevance, either by the text itself (verbal marking) or by the immediate extratextual, interpersonal situation. In Christ's longer parables, one or more strange, extraordinary, unexpected, or incompatible features generally appear, though this may not be readily apparent to the audience (until subsequently explained). This conceptual

7.1 Contextualizing a LiFE translation

clash is foregrounded and projects a *blended* notion that typically illuminates some vital aspect of the kingdom of God, which is of course the point of the parable.

For example, the following is a possible (partial and condensed) mental-space representation of the parable of the lost sheep (Luke 15:4–7):

Source domain: A shepherd is out in the open country, caring for a large flock of sheep on behalf of the owner; he loses one, searches till he finds it, goes back home, and rejoices greatly with friends and family.

Target domain: Christ is here in this wicked world, caring for many people on behalf of his Father; one of them goes morally astray, and Christ seeks to bring that person to repentance, at which all heaven rejoices.

Generic domain: corresponding components that pertain to difficult occupations, dangerous circumstances, personal responsibility for others, concern over any loss no matter how minor, willingness to expend the effort to achieve a full restoration, communal joy

Blended domain: Who is not rejoicing in the current setting (15:1–2)? More important, *why* not (15:7)? Did those who are unhappy really consider themselves members of God's flock? Did the Pharisees and teachers of the law regard themselves to be among the "safe sheep" or the "lost," whose recovery occasioned the greater heavenly joy?

Christ follows the parable of the lost sheep with two more parables in Luke 15:8–10; 11–32, the second of which hammers his point home with an unmistakable application to his religious opponents as personified by the disgruntled elder brother of the prodigal.

» Which new interpersonal and situational elements are added to the previous communicative mix in the more narratively developed and climactic third parable (vv. 11–32) about a merciful father seeking two lost sons?

» When the more extensive twofold "mental space" evoked by both halves of the third parable is conceptually juxtaposed with the preceding two, what implication emerges about who, in particular, rejoices over the penitent sinner? In other words, could "heaven" be a reference to the heavenly Father (15:7, 10, cf. 32)? Explain your own preferred interpretation of this point.

» Furthermore, how do these three juxtaposed parables reinforce one another to identify who are really "sinners" in the eyes of God?

In some biblical parables, the audience does not immediately recognize the genre, and the result is that they consider the source domain as factual, completely missing the target domain. In other words, they construe it literally with reference to the text's cotext and context. The classic example of this is Nathan's parable of reproof to King David in 2 Samuel 12:1b–4. The irony is that as David angrily completes the conceptual source space of the parable in 5b–6, he at the same time condemns himself with his own words, a fact which Nathan sternly asserts in his blunt condemnation, "*Thou* art the man!" (v. 7a). The prophet thereby reveals the essence of the blended domain along with its awful implication for his king: this is a crime punishable by death.

» How apparent are the implicit conceptual dynamics of this discourse in YL?

> » How might the vernacular text be stylistically sharpened to carry the same sort of cutting edge as the biblical text?

The theory of conceptual network formation further specifies the process of mental representation in terms of the specific domains that appear to be activated at any given moment of communication. As already suggested, the relevant source and target domains, textual and/or extratextual, are not simply added together as units of information; rather, they are selectively mixed in the mind to create a blended cognitive construct that is greater than the sum of the individual domains of knowledge and experience of which it is composed. The more individual domains involved, the more complex the mental representation that results, and the more novel the cognitive elements, including the various figures of speech and rhetorical tropes that are potentially generated.

In the next example, we see how the notion of mental spaces and conceptual blending can be used to enrich our understanding of a familiar biblical scene—in this case, John the Baptist's figurarative designation of Jesus of Nazareth: "Behold, the Lamb of God!" ("Ἴδε ὁ ἀμνὸς τοῦ θεοῦ). In a literary sense, this represents a perspectival "blend," namely, that of the (implied) narrator, John the Evangelist, together with that of the focal character at this point in the account, namely, John the Baptist, who utters the figurative phrase under consideration. The mental space representation of this allusive Christological metaphor is summarized in the following framework:

Target Space (1)	*Source Space (2)*
Jesus of Nazareth is the person being ostensibly referred to by John ("Behold…!"). Jesus has begun his teaching and preaching ministry, perhaps even performing several "mighty works." The Evangelist has already given this "Jesus" an elaborate introduction: He is the Son of God the Father (1:18, i.e., wholly *divine*), who was also fully *human* (1:14), a being who abundantly manifested God's "glory" (1:14) as well as godly love and Covenant faithfulness (i.e., "grace and truth"—1:14, 17; cf. Exo. 33:18–19, 34:5–7) in order to give all people who "received him (by faith) the right to become the children of God" (1:7, 12), that is, to have eternal "life" (1:4). Jesus is the eternal "Word" (1:1), the Creator (1:3, 10), the "Light" (1:5, 7–10; cf. 3:19), the "begotten from the Father" (1:14, 18; 3:16), and "the LORD" (1:23, by implication). John the Evangelist identifies Jesus as being the unique, promised *Messiah* (Savior-Deliverer-Redeemer) of the Hebrew Scriptures through the explicit testimony of John the Baptist (1:6-8, 19-28; 3:17). The messianic intertextual setting of Isaiah would have been evoked by John's reference to his own prophetic ministry on behalf of "the Lord" (Jn. 1:23b—cf. Isa. 40:3	The **lamb** (when fully grown, i.e., a "sheep") was perhaps the most valuable domestic animal in the economic and religious setting of Israel/the Jews in ANE times. Virtually every part of the animal was used, from its horns to its fleshy tail. As in the case of goats, sheep provided for all the necessities of life, both physical (food, clothing) and religious. Thus, sheep and lambs were prescribed "clean" animals in many of the sacrificial rituals stipulated in the Mosaic Law, including the daily burnt offering (e.g., Exo. 29:38–46; Lev. 1:4)—but specifically an "unblemished lamb" in the central "feast" of the *Passover* (Exo. 12:1–13). Although, technically speaking, the Passover lamb was not regarded as a "sacrifice," in popular thought it is very likely that it was viewed as such since, by the first century CE, the Temple priests had taken over the responsibility of killing these lambs selected for the Passover celebration (formerly the responsibility of the heads of households/clans). Thus, by coneceptual association with the sheep sacrificed in the routine Temple rituals, there may well have been strong redemptive symbolism associated with these lambs of life.

Generic Space (3)[a]	*Blended Space (4)*
Note: The underlined semantic features are the ones most likely to be mentally associated according to pragmatic *relevance* in the utterance of John 1:29; they are then cognitively enriched in the "blended space" through *inter-* and *intra*-textual association as well as by the experiences (personal and recounted) of those who heard these words, whether from the "inner" textual perspective of John the Baptist or those who heard this record of the "outer" Gospel perspective of John the Evangelist. **Jesus**: • *human* being—a Jew • *divine* being—the Son of God • sent by his Father *to give "light/life" to all people* • essentially *unique* (cf. Jn. 3:16) **Lamb**: • valuable (*life*-giving) domestic animal (son of a sheep) • source of food (milk, meat) • source of clothes (hide, wool) • source of implements (horn for oil, musical instruments) • source of appropriate *sacrifices* in the daily Temple ritual • central visual symbol of the *Passover* ceremony • *not unique,* so possibley eliciting a search for contextual "relevance" within the OT Scriptures, e.g., the "scape-goat" of Lev. 16 (totally "rejected" by the people—cf. Jn. 1:11 > Lev. 16.21–22 > Isa. 53:2–6.	Jesus is directly identified by John as being associated via *the* (def.) "lamb" figure with "God" (1:29). This creates a crucial *intimation* based on the Generic Space and the narrative context: Jesus is the *supreme sacrifice* supplied God himself to remove the polluting wickedness and damning guilt of sinners. There is also the suggestion that Jesus' role as a sacrificial lamb will actually require and ultimately result in his *death* at some point in the future (cf. Jn. 11:50–51; 12:24, 33; 18:32; cf. 1 Cor. 5:7; 1 Pet. 1:19—Jesus as the "Passover Lamb," "sacrificed" on behalf of sinners). The "Passover connection" appears to be especially strong in this Gospel since John takes pains to point out that Jesus was crucified during the time of the annual Passover celebration (Jn. 18:28; 19:14, 31; cf. I Cor. 5:7) and even fulfilled a (typological) prophecy in that redemptive event, i.e., when he died without a bone of his body being broken (Jn. 19:36; cf. Exo. 12:46; Num. 9:12). The identification of Jesus the Christ with a sacrificial lamb would have naturally been strengthened through the prophetic allusion created by Isaiah 53:6–7, and perhaps even in the minds of some (Jewish rabbis at least) with the earlier "lamb" provided by God in place of Isaac (Gen. 22:8; cf. v. 13).[b] The notion of *redemptive* sacrifice is brought out too by the cotext of the metaphor "lamb of God," which "takes away sin" (cf. 1 Jn. 3:5; Heb. 9:28; 1 Pet. 2:24). Thus, "to bear sin" (*airew*) may involve some form of *expiation* (e.g., Lev. 10:17; 1 Sam. 15:25; 25:28) and/or the *forgiveness* of sin's *guilt* by bearing the penalty attached to it on behalf of others (e.g., Num. 14:33–34; Isa. 53:4–12; Eze. 18:19-20).[c]

[a]During a given text analysis this "generic space" could be readily filled out by the data provided by a good "semantic domain" dictionary, like that of the Semantic domain dictionary of Biblical Hebrew (SDBH) of Reinier de Blois, which is available online at http:www.sdbh.org/vocabula/index.html.

[b]"…early Judaism attached the nuances of sacrifice to the Passover" (Keener 2003:454).

[c]According to some scholars, the apocalyptic "Lamb" identified with Christ in Revelation (ch. 5:6) evokes a different set of intertextual frames via Greek intertestamental literature—namely, that of a great messianic deliverer of God's people, who is depicted as a ram which leads the flock (1 Enoch 90; cf. Testament of Joseph 19:8–11; Testament of Benjamin 3:8) (Green and McKnight 1992:433; Keener 2003:452). Other commentators, however, still view the Passover sacrificial symbolism as being paramount in Revelation 5—"…the lamb whose blood delivers God's people from the coming plagues (7:#)…" (Keener 2003:454). Much more speculative and improbable is this interpretation: "There is but a single lamb in all creation that merits the title 'lamb of God,' and that is the constellation labeled Aries by the Latins. In the book of Revelation, this constellation is directly identified as the 'the Lion of the tribe of Judah, the Root of David' (Rev 5:5), that is, the Messiah of Israel. The same here is true in John's Gospel, where John the prophet identifies Jesus as the Lamb of God (1:29, 36), and his disciples conclude he is Israels Messiah (1:40)….Ancient Israel likewise recognized the prominence of Aries in its original New year Celebration connected with its foundational event, the Exodus (Exod. 12:2…). And the ritual marking the Exodus involved a male lamb, replicating the springtime Aries itself" (Malina and Rohrbaugh 1998:50–51). What a difference a different hermeneutical framework makes!

The visualization process depicted in the chart above depends of course on a common mental perspective: Both "Johns" ostensibly assume that their listeners (the implied audience) share the cognitive spaces that allow this dramatic identificational metaphor to operate, thus stimulating their imagination in the direction of several new areas of thought, being enriched by the textual framework of the Hebrew (or Greek) Scriptures. However, from the point of view of the likely target audience of this Gospel, the much wider perspective of John the Evangelist will be adopted to guide the process of construing the intended sense of the focal figure—the epitome of submissive sacrifice.

The purpose of the preceding exercise is simply to illustrate how the respective "mental spaces" for the metaphor of the "Lamb of God" as applied to Christ in John 1:29 might be inferentially filled out, at least as fully as a translation team's time allows. Certainly the task can be carried out intuitively by competent, well-informed translators; however, the "mental space" methodology illustrated above could act as a helpful heuristic to observe in the case of individual semantically more complex passages, especially where metaphoric language is involved. In any case, if the translators are preparing a meaning-based version, they might come to the conclusion that the notion of "sacrifice" needs to be built into the text, not only to promote the understanding of the primary TL audience (e.g., Chewa: *Mwanawankhosa wodzipereka* wa *Mulungu* "the Lamb of God who offers himself"), but also to prevent possible misunderstanding, e.g., the "child of a sheep" (*mwanaambelele*), which is regarded as an exotic (and rather stupid!) European domestic animal among the cattle-rearing Tonga people of Zambia. Some of the additional information recorded in the four quadrants above could also be used in the composition of a study note on this passage or as part of a glossary entry attached to "Lamb (of God)." Thus, the time and effort expended to work them out would not be wasted.

The preceding example and explanation show how important it is to create the conceptual frames of sociocultural reference necessary to permit an accurate interpretation of a discourse that originates in an entirely different situational setting. An appropriately contextualized cognitive background is in fact required for proper understanding; without it, the desired communicative effect in terms of the quantity and quality of semantic significance (including impact and esthetic appeal) cannot occur. Similarly, in the absence of an adequate grasp of the original biblical setting, today's readers and hearers readily apply a situational context that is most immediate in their current thinking, one that is overly domesticated in terms of their own worldview, value system, social circumstances, and the local physical environment. Consequently, communication is bound to fail to a greater or lesser extent due to information loss, distortion, and/or unwanted addition.

A study Bible provides one means of creating at least some of the necessary sociocultural frames for the biblical text. Its explanatory and descriptive notes can provide essential historical, cultural, religious, intertextual, and other background information to facilitate the intended audience's interpretation of a problematic passage, whether the difficulty is due to textual or extratextual issues. The aim is to ensure that, when the Scripture *source* domain is combined with a typical *target* conceptual domain evoked by the vernacular words of the text, the resultant *blended* domain is an adequate representation of the original source domain and is not unduly skewed in terms of its denotation or connotation. It is this often elusive, composite "cognitive environment" that a given expository note must seek to address in a clear, concise, and relevant manner.

The following framework adapts mental-space theory to the scenario of a translator who is composing an explanatory note in the Chichewa study Bible with reference to Luke 1:69: "[God] has *raised* up a *horn of salvation* for us in the *house* of his *servant* David...." (The vernacular translation is a fairly literal rendition of the English text.)

CONCEPTUAL NETWORK	FEATURES
Target (Chewa) domain:	a non-poetic translation, but one that sounds psalm-like to those familiar with their vernacular Bible; the indigenous concept of "God" has been Christianized for well over a century by a variety of mission organizations; "horn" refers to the horn of an animal, but in the cotext of "lifting up" and "deliverance" would more likely be construed as a manifestation of some act of sorcery ("sorcerer" = *wanyanga* "person of the horn"); the traditional house is simply a place for sleeping at night or being sheltered from inclement weather; a "servant" has a lowly form of employment with long hours and little pay; "David" was Israel's famous king who wrote psalms but also committed adultery and murder
Source (Hebrew) domain:	typical Hebrew hymn/psalm of praise composed in koine Greek, with heavy intertextuality from the book of Psalms; "God" = reference to YHWH, Israel's covenant-making and -keeping deity; "horn" = symbol of power and persistence; "raise ... horn" = demonstration of an overt mighty act; "house" = dynasty/line of descendants; "servant" = someone who acts on behalf of a person of higher status, in this case, God; "David" = the most famous king of Israel and source of its only dynasty; together, the concepts of this passage constitute a figurative reference to YHWH's promised Messiah, who would be born of David's line to become the ultimate deliverer of God's repressed people Israel
Generic domain:	praise poetry and figurative language; concepts of God, salvation/deliverance, house, servant, king and kingship (a central sociopolitical institution common to ancient Israel as well as Africa)
Blended domain:	Not much cognitive commonality exists between the source and target domains; there is also too much difficult figurative language in the SL text for a clear conception of the intended meaning to emerge, especially in the relatively literal Chewa translation. The blended notion represents for most ordinary receptors a veritable paradox: Why is God here apparently involved in some manner of sorcery, delivering David by means of a horn? In what special way is king David engaged or occupied as a servant of God? This verse is very difficult to understand and raises many questions as to its intended meaning at this point in Zechariah's prophecy of praise (1:67).

» What are some of the critical corresponding features of the two disparate referential worlds (SL ⇔ TL) that the translator must comparatively evaluate for both meaning and relevance?

» Try to track this complex process of meaning development (selecting, shaping, specifying, etc.) in terms of your own translation setting.

As a result of this cognitive exercise, the following study Bible note for the Chewa version of Luke 1:69 was proposed with reference to the "horn":

> The horn (nyanga) mentioned here represents great power and has nothing to do with the practice of sorcery as our ancient traditions teach. These words tell us by way of picture language that God's promised "Anointed Person" (Messiah) would come from among King David's descendants in order to deliver God's people in a most powerful way. All this came true in our Savior, Jesus Christ, whom Zechariah is here praising.

Sociocultural frames can be provided by many means other than a study Bible, of course. In recent years, Scripture translation agencies have developed a wide variety of paratextual tools designed to assist readers to mentally situate and particularize the text that they happen to be reading: book and chapter introductions, sectional headings, cross-references, a glossary or mini-dictionary, maps, diagrams, timelines, illustrations, and footnotes or margin notes. Such features help bring to life the different ancient Near Eastern scenarios and scripts that relate to a given Bible passage, enabling people today to understand what the text meant in its original environment. Most of these supplementary helps for readers have become standard features of modern Bibles, including study Bibles with their wealth of explanatory notes. We will focus upon these paratextual tools in the remainder of this lesson since they, along with well-chosen illustrations and diagrams, are so important for contextualizing any translation conceptually.

For reflection, research, and response:

1. Transfer the process of interpretation of Luke 1:69 to your own sociocultural context, given the same scenario as that discussed above. Study this passage further in its biblical setting, using a commentary or two. Make any changes that you feel are necessary in the "generic" and "source" domains. Specify the "target" and "blended" domains as they might apply in your social and religious situation. (Follow the format used in the preceding chart of a conceptual network's four domains: the generic, source, target, and blended cognitive frames.)

2. Now prepare an appropriate contextual note for Luke 1:69 that would establish an adequate cognitive framework to help ordinary readers understand this text in YL.

3. Construct a mental-space diagram for Christ's parable of the great banquet in Luke 14:16–24, referring to the diagrams of section 7.1.2 as a model. The "blended space" will summarize the chief incompatible features that stand out in the original situation. How do these compare with what would be evoked in your sociocultural setting? Identify three potential conceptual incongruities and construct a hypothetical margin note that would clarify them. (If you compose the explanations in YL, please provide a back-translation into English.)

4. Does mental-space theory provide a possible model for the translation process as a whole (e.g., *source* space = Scripture text; *target* space = one possible rendering in the TL; *generic* space = apparent (intended) conceptual correspondence between the SL and TL texts; *blended* space = actual conceptual correspondences between the two texts in the cognitive environment of the TL audience)? Discuss the validity and utility of such a figurative perspective.

5. Robert Koops (2000:12) observes,

    > [T]he text is a minimal set of signals which, when combined with the background knowledge of the readers, whether the original ones or modern ones, will produce a 'meaning.' An important part of our research has been and will continue to be: How does the background knowledge of the original readers differ from the background knowledge of our present readers? Implicit in that question is another question: who are our readers? Only when our audience is defined can we address the issue of what their background knowledge is.

    First, then, ask yourself if you have clearly defined the primary target audience of your translation. If you have done so, how did you do it? What method did you use?

    Second, you need to prepare a comparative analysis of how your TL audience's cognitive framework might differ from that of a biblical audience with respect to a Scripture text such as Galatians 4:21–27, which is Paul's analogy comparing Hagar and Sinai to Sarah and Jerusalem. Do such an analysis now, using a mental-space diagram if you can. If you can't, simply line up the corresponding images and referents of this passage along with their respective grounds of comparison.

Finally, point out any conceptual problem areas that might arise due to conflicting associations generated by your sociocultural setting. Finally, suggest how an appropriately worded note in the margin might resolve these points of hermeneutical tension.

6. Consider the need for providing adequate contextualized background materials to accompany a vernacular Bible translation in light of Harriet Hill's assessment (2003:18–19, italics added):

> Translators need to understand how communication works so that they can not only get a text translated but assure that receptors have access to the contextual information necessary to infer the intended meaning. *Translators must be skilled communication engineers rather than factory workers*. They must be able to analyze communication situations and design products that correspond to receptors' expectations. They must know how to identify the mutual cognitive environment of first and secondary receptors, and how to enlarge the secondary receptors' cognitive environment so that they have the intended contextual assumptions that were available to the first receptors.
>
> Knowledge of linguistics and languages will no longer suffice. *Translators* must also be aware of anthropology and the cultural context of both first and secondary receptors. For this, they *need to know how to do effective cultural research for translation*—neither slipshod research, nor the kind of research appropriate for professional anthropologists who are asking different questions. Translators need not only to know the context of both first and secondary receptors, they must also know how to use this cultural information to improve the receptors' comprehension of Scripture....
>
> *Translators need to be aware of the way their worldview and ethnocentrism color their perceptions of biblical cultures*. This is especially true of translators working in a language other than their own, but even mother tongue translators are not exempt, as education often includes heavy doses of Enlightenment thinking, and students absorb this worldview as they learn. All translators must strive to bring an open mind to their work and learn the facts about the first receptor's context.
>
> *Translators need to take risks using local categories for key terms*, knowing that in the long run this will be advantageous. Even when the local categories are not identical to the biblical ones, the local categories will be transformed over time by being accessed to process the biblical text. Gradually, this leads to worldview conversion. It also incorporates more of the receptors' reality into the mutual cognitive environment they believe they share with the biblical author. This allows more of their reality to be involved in their Christian experience, bringing about an integration of Christian and ethnic identity....

Do you agree with this assessment? Have you implemented Dr. Hill's recommendations in your own translation work? If so, how?

How can a *LiFE* approach to translation help you to function as "a skilled communication engineer" rather than a "factory worker?"

What kind of "effective cultural research for translation" have you carried out to enable you to be a more competent and effective cross-cultural communicator? Give an example.

Can you cite an instance of how your own worldview and ethnocentrism wrongly colored your understanding of a particular passage of Scripture?

Give an example of how you or your translation team have taken "risks using local categories for key [biblical] terms." How has this proven, perhaps over time, to be "advantageous" in terms of better communication of biblical concepts, categories, and/or customs?

Give an example of how you have used your knowledge of the ancient Near Eastern biblical setting to correct a misunderstanding on the part of your primary audience concerning the interpretation of a specific Bible text, one in which the factor of literary genre and its associated stylistic features were also involved.

7. As a follow-up to the preceding exercises, evaluate the following simplified application of the mental-space model to 1 Peter 2:4 (from Koops 2000). Does it help one to understand—or to explain to translators—the imagery involved? Does anything need to be added or adjusted? If so, specify what.

Exploring the text in such added detail helps to bring out the *tragic irony* involved: How could (or why would) "builders" reject such a valuable "stone?" Why is verse 6 (Isa. 28:16) needed to add a necessary frame of reference for interpreting Peter's argument here? Is there any way of doing this in a translation? Explain how.

"Come to him, to that living stone, rejected by men but in God's sight chosen and precious."

The referent of "him" is "the Lord" in the previous verse. The clause "come to him" pictures Peter's readers approaching the Lord. At this point a metaphorical space is created: that **living stone**, which is a blend of two images. The image of stone carries with it qualities of strength and usefulness in building. The image of a human being carries the qualities of being alive (which happens to be made explicit) and human. These come together into one imaginary space.

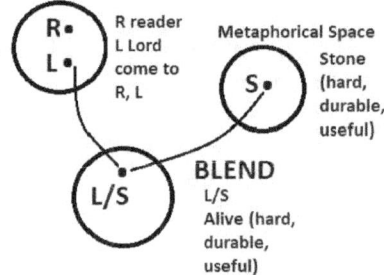

The next clause, "rejected by men," in the immediate environment of "stone," adds information and evokes a BUILDING frame in which there are builders, materials, tools, and a resulting structure. At the same time "rejected" refers to "the Lord." The building frame with its implications "maps" onto the phrase and fills out the scene. The phrase **In God's sight** opens a thought space with a new participant: God. Elements from the blended scene are propagated into this new space, and the description is added: the "stone/Lord" is highly valued.

7.1.3 Ten types of study notes

We will now consider ten specific kinds of supplementary study notes. They deal with the different aspects of implicit information and background knowledge that people need to be made aware of as they are reading a passage of Scripture. It is important to remember that these notes and similar tools such as a glossary can help only *readers* of a text; other devices need to be created to assist listeners. For example, a system of vocally distinct "audio commentary" and appropriate sound effects (e.g., a bell, gong, drum beat) or background "mood music" (joyful, sorrowful, dramatic, meditative, angry, worried, trustful) could accompany the oral presentation of a biblical text. Note too that these paratextual aids need to be extensively complemented by the consistent and comprehensive teaching ministry of the church, parachurch agencies, and fellow Christians (in the manner of the evangelist Philip in Acts 8:26–40).

Two main principles govern the selection and formulation of study notes: *relevance* and *expedience*. Certainly, study notes are highly relevant; the very inclusion of such notes is an overt signal to readers that information is presented that will enrich their cognitive context. However, such notes must not be overly technical or complex or too difficult for the average reader to conceptually process. Furthermore, the material in the notes should be relevant to the audience's theological and ethical perspectives as well as to their lives of faith and moral practice.

The second and closely related principle, *expedience*, pertains to the individual and corporate needs and values of most of the receptor community as determined by credible research. This would reveal that in south-central Africa, for example, it is not necessary to waste precious space on the printed page to defend the existence of God or the fact of Creation. These are already fundamental beliefs in the oral traditions of the ethnic groups who live in this part of the world. On the other hand, biblical teachings concerning the after life—the nature of one's existence after death—are very different from indigenous assumptions. Consequently, they require considerably more elucidation when a given Scripture passage touches on the subject. Even though many of these people do not like to talk or read about death (for them it is a taboo subject), it is, from a biblical perspective, most expedient that they do so.

Ten different types of explanatory note needed to contextualize a translation, including a *LiFE* translation, are summarized and exemplified below with selected notes pertaining to Luke 1–3 from *The NIV Study Bible* (1985). Obviously, there is some overlapping of categories, and there may well be differences of opinion as to how to classify one note or another.

See if you agree as to the broad contours of this approach. Record any comments or corrections you may wish to make as you proceed. As you read through the ten types of notes, consider them from the perspective of your own culture and worldview.

» Would the same general types be needed in YL?

» Would you need to amend any? Or add any? Mention several specific examples.

1. Exegetical

Exegetical notes serve to clarify the presumed referential or implied meaning of the SL text, especially where difficult cultural concepts, technical terms, religious expressions, and proper names are concerned.

> 1:2 **handed down**. A technical term for passing on information as authoritative tradition.
>
> 1:6 **upright…blamelessly**. They were not sinless, but were faithful and sincere in keeping God's ordinances.
>
> 1:19 **Gabriel**. The name can mean "God is my hero" or "mighty man of God."
>
> 2:7 **manger**. The feeding trough of the animals.
>
> 2:33 **child's father**. Luke, aware of the virgin birth of Jesus (1:26–35), is referring to Joseph as Jesus' legal father.
>
> 2:46 **the teachers**. The rabbis, experts in Judaism.

Alternative interpretations should be limited to those that are significant or of special relevance in the receptor setting and which have a relatively high probability of being valid, as is the case in Luke 2:37, "…then [she] was a widow until she was eighty-four," where there is a footnote in the *NIV Study Bible*: "Or *widow for eighty-four years*."

2. Situational

Situational notes supply a broader sort of background information with regard to such matters as ancient Near-Eastern history, politics, religion, culture/customs, geography, flora/fauna, and economy.

> 1:5 **Herod king of Judah**. Herod the Great reigned 37–4 BC, and his kingdom included Samaria, Galilee, much of Perea, and Coele-Syria.…The time referred to here is probably c. 7–6.… *priestly division of Abijah*. From the time of David the priests were organized into 24 divisions, and Abijah was one of the "heads of the priestly families" (Neh. 12:12; see 1 Chr. 24:10).

2:46 **three days.** One day travelling away from Jerusalem, a second travelling back and a third looking for him.

Without a note to call attention to certain significant events or teachings, they could easily be overlooked. This is the case in Luke 1:9 with reference to Zechariah's act of burning incense in the temple, where the *NIV Study Bible* footnote is "...Ordinarily a priest would have this privilege very infrequently, and sometimes never, since duty assignments were determined by lot." A note would also be needed at Luke 2:24 to call attention to Joseph and Mary's relative poverty, like the one in the *Good News Study Bible: TEV* (2000), "The doves or pigeons were offered by people who could not afford to offer a lamb."

3. Thematic

Thematic notes serve to point out major themes, topics, and recurrent motifs within a given corpus, author, book, section, or pericope, including reiterated theological concepts.

1:13 **Do not be afraid.** This word of reassurance is given many times in both OT and NT (see, e.g., Luke 30; 2:10 and note; 5:10; 8:50; 12:7, 32...).

1:14 **joy.** A keynote of these opening chapters (vv. 1:14, 44, 47, 58; 2:10).

2:20 **praising God.** A term often used by Luke (1:64, 2:13...).

3:6 **all mankind.** God's salvation was to be made known to both Jews and Gentiles—a major theme of Luke's Gospel (see note on 2:31).

3:21 **as he was praying.** Only Luke notes Jesus' praying at the time of his baptism. Jesus in prayer is one of the special themes of Luke (see 5:16; 6:12; 9:18, 28–29; 11:1; 22:32, 41; 23:34, 46).[4]

4. Structural

Structural notes serve to clarify the textual organization (i.e., the constituent units and their connections and interrelationships) of a particular verse, section, pericope, or larger portion of a given book. This would include pointing out, where appropriate, the overall development of the discourse (e.g., narrative-plot, letter-argument) and any significant patterns of repetition and literary genres that are evident in the text.

1:1–4 Using language similar to classical Greek, Luke begins with a formal preface, common to historical works of that time, in which he states his purpose for writing and identifies the recipient....

1:46–55 One of the four hymns preserved in Luke 1–2 (see vv. 68–79; 2:14; 2:29–32 and notes)....This song is like a psalm, and should also be compared with the song of Hannah (1 Sam. 2:1–10...).

1:68–79 ...Whereas the Magnificat...is similar to a psalm, the Benedictus is more like a prophecy.

3:20 **locked John up in prison.** This did not occur until sometime after the beginning of Jesus' ministry (see John 3:22–24), but Luke mentions it here in order to conclude his section on John's ministry before beginning his account of Jesus' ministry.

---

[4]Notes that refer readers to Bible passages that are parallel in form or content should be carefully checked to ensure that the cited verses clearly apply. Average readers quickly get discouraged with a system that includes too many cross-references with only a slightly perceptible connection to the passage at hand.

3:23–38 There are several differences between Luke's and Matthew's (1:2–16) genealogy. Matthew begins with Abraham (the father of the Jewish people), while Luke traces the line in the reverse order and goes back to Adam, showing Jesus' relationship to the whole human race.

Notes of this kind must not become too conceptually dense or complex, and they should avoid non-focal information (e.g., "Some scholars suggest that…" and "A more likely explanation, however, is that…").

5. **Stylistic**

Stylistic notes serve to reveal the sense and/or significance of literary features and rhetorical devices such as metaphor, metonymy, irony, hyperbole, punning, and rhetorical questions, whether they are reproduced in the translation or not.

1:51 **his arm.** A figurative description of God's powerful acts. God does not have a body; he is spirit (John 4:24).

1:69 **horn.** Indicates strength…as in the horn of an animal (Deut. 33:17). Jesus, the Messiah from the house of David, has the power to save.

1:78 **the rising sun.** A reference to the coming of the Messiah.…

1:79 **those living in darkness.** The lost, separated from God (Isa. 9:1–2; Matt. 4:16).

2:25 **the consolation of Israel.** The comfort the Messiah would bring to people at his coming.…

2:35 **a sword will pierce your own soul too.** The word "too" indicates that Mary, as well as Jesus, would suffer deep anguish—the first reference in this Gospel to Christ's suffering and death.

6. **Functional**

Functional notes serve to indicate the author's presumed pragmatic purpose or primary communicative aim in using certain expressions, either in a particular verse or within a complete textual unit.

1:3 **carefully investigated.** Luke's account was exact in historical detail, having been checked in every way.…

2:31 **all people.** As a Gentile himself, Luke was careful to emphasize the truth that salvation was offered for the Gentiles (v. 32) as well as for Jews.

2:49 **in my Father's house.** Jesus pointed to his personal duty to his Father in heaven. He contrasted his "my Father" with Mary's "Your father" (v. 48).…

3:23–38…Although tracing a genealogy through the mother's side was unusual, so was the virgin birth. Luke's explanation here that Jesus was the son of Joseph, "so it was thought" (v. 23),… suggests the importance of Mary in Jesus' genealogy.

3:23 **about thirty years old.** Luke, a historian, relates the beginning of Jesus' ministry both to world history (see vv. 1–2) and to the rest of Jesus' life.…

Such functional, or directional, notes also call attention to any noteworthy *illocutionary* features (i.e., what the author presumably wanted his words to *do* as well as to *say*) and *emotive* elements, examples of which include the following:

1:34 **How will this be…?** Mary did not ask in disbelief, as Zechariah did (v. 20). See verse 45.

> 1:54 **remembering to be merciful**. The song ends with an assurance that God will be true to his promises to his people....
>
> 2:10 **Do not be afraid**. Fear was the common reaction to angelic appearances..., and encouragement was needed.

7. Contextual

Contextual notes point out any prominent correspondences or conflicts between the TL situational setting and something mentioned in the SL text. This type of note complements situational notes (no. 2 above).

> 1:80 **lived in the desert**. John's parents, old at his birth, probably died while he was young, and he apparently grew up in the Desert of Judea....

The notion of desert, a dry and barren wasteland, needs to be clarified for many cultures. But the fact of John's living in such an isolated place is no doubt more related to his prophetic calling than his lack of relatives to provide him with a home and take care of him. It may be noted that in an African context, individuals who act in a contra-cultural manner and live off by themselves are often suspected or even accused of being "sorcerers" or "witches."

For Luke 1:25, on the other hand, the *NIV Study Bible* has a note that draws attention to a basic cross-cultural similarity in perspective: "*The Lord...has shown his favor and taken away my disgrace.* Not only did lack of children deprive the parents of personal happiness, but it was generally considered to indicate divine disfavor and often brought social reproach."

Many such "contextual" (culturally related) notes are necessary in order to prevent a wrong understanding of the biblical text as a result of differing beliefs, values, attitudes, presuppositions, and goals in life. Another example is the *NIV Study Bible*'s footnote for "the Holy Spirit was upon him" in Luke 2:25: One may have to point out that such a charismatic event is in no way analogous to a traditional belief in ancestral spirit possession.

8. Translational

Translational notes call attention to terms, concepts, and expressions that cause special difficulty in the rendering or to some familiar or misleading usage from an earlier vernacular Bible version that has been changed in the current one.

The following is a hypothetical example:

> 2:14 **on whom his favor rests**. KJV has "on earth peace, *good will* toward men," and RSV has "on earth peace among men *with whom he is pleased*." But these are less preferred translations (see Omanson 2006:111).

Another example of the need for this type of compositional note is in Luke 3:16, "He will baptize you with the Holy Spirit and with fire." Here it may be necessary to explain the figurative use of "baptism," especially if for various reasons the term must be rendered in transliterated form. It may also be necessary to explain the relationship between the Holy Spirit and fire (fire of judgment, purification, and charismatic enablement).

In Chichewa, the major language of Malawi, a translational problem arose with the title "Christ" in Luke 2:11. Most readers and hearers interpret the literal *Kristu/Khristu* that was used in earlier versions as a proper name referring to Jesus Christ, not as a Messianic designation; therefore, in the Luke portion of the new Chichewa study Bible (see section 7.1.4), a study note is needed here:

Mpulumutsi wolonjezedwa uja "that promised Savior." Another example that requires additional explanation concerns the key term for "grace" in Luke 2:40: The older Chichewa versions used nouns meaning "good fortune" or a "free gift," while the new translation employs a much closer verb-based equivalent: "he kept on blessing him."

9. **Intertextual**

Intertextual notes point out any important Old Testament quotations or allusions in the passage at hand. They may also comment on the original usage, especially where there seems to be either a significant similarity or deviation.

> 2:36 **Anna.** Same name as OT Hannah (1 Sam. 1:2), which means "gracious." Anna praised God for the child Jesus as Hannah had praised God for the child Samuel (1 Sam. 2:1–10).
>
> 2:52 Luke appears to have borrowed the words of 1 Samuel 2:26.
>
> 3:2 **word of God** God's message came to John as it came to the OT prophets (cf. Jer. 1:2; Ezek. 1:3; Hos. 1:1; Joel 1:1).

Major *differences* among the Gospels should be indicated by a note. For example, for Luke 3:21, "as he was praying," the *NIV Study Bible* note says, "Only Luke records Jesus' praying at the time of his baptism. Jesus in prayer is one of the special themes of Luke...." And for Luke 2:39, "they returned to Galilee," the note says, "Luke does not mention the coming of the Magi, the danger from Herod, or the flight to and return from Egypt (cf. Matt. 2:1–23)." On the other hand, major intertextual *correspondences* may also be worth pointing out. For example, the footnote on Luke 1:4 says, "*so that you may know.* Cf. John's purpose for writing (John 20:31)."

10. **Textual**

Textual notes discuss any major variants in the original Greek or Hebrew manuscripts.

There are none present in the *NIV Study Bible* for the first three chapters of Luke, but the following are three typical examples that occur later in the book (the word that appears in the NIV text proper is shown below in brackets following the respective notes):

> 8:43 Many manuscripts *years, and she had spent all she had on doctors* [years]
>
> 10:1 Some manuscripts *seventy*; also in verse 17 [seventy-two]
>
> 11:2 Some manuscripts *Our Father in heaven* [Father]

The committee that prepared the Chichewa study Bible decided to avoid text-critical notes, except where absolutely necessary. In order to conserve space, they have also had to limit "life-application" comments such as the *NIV Study Bible*'s note at Luke 2:14: "...Peace with God is received by faith in Christ...." Alternative readings of the biblical text, especially of the Hebrew or the Septuagint (LXX), may be pointed out if the differences are meaningful or represent different ecclesiastical traditions. But it does no good to offer potentially confusing comments such as "Some manuscripts have..." and "while others have..." and "Hebrew obscure."

7.1.4 Suggested procedures for composing setting-sensitive notes

The following instructions outline a simple, question-driven method of composing expository and descriptive notes for a study Bible. These guidelines were originally prepared for the Chichewa editorial team and are offered here (in adapted form) merely as an illustration of some of the things that need to be kept in mind during the process of contextualizing the text of translated Scripture. The procedures could of course be formulated in much more detail and with greater range and more complexity, but they were intended simply as an introduction to the task of systematically preparing relevant, "indigenized" notes for a particular target audience.

» After reading the following procedures, be prepared to discuss them in light of a major Bible translation program that you know of, whether it is specifically a study Bible project or not. (Pretend that it is!)

» What modifications or additions would you suggest to assist note production editors in the task of relating the translation of Scripture in YL to the cultural setting, social situation, and local environment of the most likely target group of users?

A. Read and Reflect

Carefully read over the entire pericope under consideration and then read the notes on that particular section in the NIV, GNB, and CEV study Bibles. Do these notes contain any information pertaining to the text in question, its larger discourse context, its structural organization, literary genre, or the situational setting that would be of use to your primary target group (e.g., monolingual, rural, lay preachers, or teachers)—that is, to evoke in their minds a more accurate "conceptual scenario" for understanding the text of Scripture? Is there some other type of information that would be helpful to your readers? For example, with regard to Luke 15 as a whole, the *Good News Study Bible* offers the following introductory comment:

> The three PARABLES in chapter 15 illustrate the goodness and mercy of God for all, especially those who are most often neglected or despised. The various details enliven the vividness of each story; they do not teach separate spiritual lessons. The version of the first parable recorded in Mt 18.12–14 teaches a different lesson: namely, that God does not want anyone to be lost.

Do you agree with the general content of this note? Should some or all of the material be included in a note in the study Bible for YL? Are there any other facts about this chapter as a whole that should be included? Would some other type of information be more helpful and relevant to the local setting (e.g., about God's concern for "the lost" in your community)?

B. Analyze

Now to begin the verse-by-verse analysis, read and study a convenient segment (usually one verse or paragraph) in a standard English version as well as in the original Greek text if possible. For example, read Luke 15:1–3 in the NIV:

> Now the tax collectors and "sinners" were all gathering around to hear him. But the Pharisees and the teachers of the law muttered, "This man welcomes sinners and eats with them."
> Then Jesus told them this parable:…

Compare this to the GNB rendering of Luke 15:1–3 below (plus any other versions that you have access to). Does the comparison reveal any significant *differences* in wording or interpretation?

> One day when many tax collectors and other outcasts came to listen to Jesus, the Pharisees and the teachers of the Law started grumbling, "This man welcomes outcasts and even eats with them!" So Jesus told them this parable:…

Do the differences suggest some aspect of meaning that may require a note? For example, what is the difference in meaning between "sinners" and "outcasts" in YL? Which concept comes closest to the biblical concept of people who did not take care to observe the main precepts of the Mosaic law?

(Some of these people—the tax collectors, robbers and thieves, prostitutes, and adulterers—were commonly judged to be living immoral lives.)

At this stage it would also be helpful to consult translation-sensitive commentaries such as the *Translator's Handbook on Luke* (UBS), *Translator's Notes on Luke* (SIL), or *The Translator's Reference Translation* (SIL) to get an idea of the general interpretation of this passage. Pay special attention to any exegetical, cultural, and/or translational problem areas that are discussed in these works. Do any of them indicate that a particular note might be necessary in the study Bible of YL? If so, compose a draft text. (The *Translator's Reference Translation* is helpful in suggesting a number of footnotes that may be needed for a given passage.)

C. Compare

Next re-read the verse as it has been translated in YL. The question to ask is, Has it been rendered both accurately and idiomatically, based on the study carried out during step B? Are there any corrections or improvements to suggest, whether exegetical or stylistic in nature? If so, record them in a special notebook reserved for this purpose. (Proposed revisions may require the approval of a different project committee.) The following is an English back-translation of Luke 15:1–3 in the *Buku Loyera,* a popular-language version in Chichewa:

> All the tax collectors and other Jews who disregard the Laws [of Moses] would come to Jesus to hear his words. So the Pharisees and the teachers of the Laws began to complain [negative implication], saying, "This fellow receives sinners and eats together with them." Then Jesus silenced them with this parable; he said...

Now compare the renderings found in already-published Chichewa versions to see if any sort of translational note is necessary. For example, there may be different key terms or interpretations in the respective versions. Here is Luke 15:1–3 in the *Buku Lopatulika* (the old Protestant Bible):

> But all those tax persons and sinners were coming near to hear him. And the Pharisees and the secretaries complained [positive implication] and said, This one receives sinners and eats with them. But he told them this parable, and said...

What are the main differences between these two versions with respect to sentence structure and vocabulary? Note for example how the newer Chichewa translation renders "sinners" and introduces the distinct parable text. After a comparison like this, ask yourself whether any other background notes suggest themselves (in light of the ten types of study notes suggested in section 7.1.3). If so, compose a possible draft for each note that seems needed.

D. Evaluate

Now examine the study notes for Luke 15:1–3 in the available English study Bibles for their relevance and potential usefulness in the Bible of YL. Is any information presented there that would be helpful for your target audience to know? If so, compose such a note. Here, for example, are the notes in the *NIV Study Bible* for Luke 15:1–3:

> 15:1 **tax collectors and "sinners."** See notes on 3:12; Mk. 2:15.
>
> 15:2 **muttered.** Complained among themselves, but not openly. *eats with them.* More than simple association, eating with a person indicated acceptance and recognition (cf. Acts 11:3; 1 Cor. 5:11; Gal. 2:12).
>
> 15:3 **this parable.** Jesus responded with a story that contrasted the love of God with the exclusiveness of the Pharisees.

The *Good News Study Bible* has the following notes:

1. TAX COLLECTORS...OUTCASTS 5:29–30.

2. **even eats with them.** To sit at table with someone is to link oneself with that person as an equal and a friend. The PHARISEES and TEACHERS OF THE LAW could not accept that these despised people with whom Jesus was eating were their equals in God's sight (15:29–30).

3. PARABLE [the reader is referred to a glossary]

Is any of the information in these notes worth putting into a study Bible for YL? If so, what would be the clearest and most natural way to word it? Is there any important information missing here— some element in the passage that would not be understood correctly by your readers? We assume that the key terms "tax collectors," "sinners," and "parable" would have been explained in an earlier note or in the vernacular translation's glossary (as signaled by the capital letters in the GNSB), but how about "sheep"? Was there an earlier reference to sheep in Luke? If not, what should be said about sheep in a region where they are not familiar?

E. Reconsider

Finally, read the entire Luke 15:1–3 passage again, this time *aloud*. Refer to any other study tools at your disposal (including any translation in a language related to YL, a Bible dictionary, other study Bibles, and/or commentaries). Now imagine yourself in a teaching or preaching situation. What kind of a note would you add to make the text come alive for your audience? Draft any additional notes with this in mind. Then check through all the notes you have composed so far to ensure that they are clear, correct, and easy to read or listen to. Make any revisions that seem needed. As an example, the following is one of the notes on these verses that have been prepared for the Chichewa study Bible (given in English back-translation):

15:2 **they began to complain.** This sort of complaining was manifested through grumbling (see the terms used in the *Buku Lopatulika* and the *Malembo Oyera*). That is to say, those Pharisees were complaining quietly without raising their voices about what Jesus was doing, like eating with sinners. [This technical term is explained in the glossary.] They had the idea that a man of God was holy and would not eat with sinners. Such grumbling caused Jesus to tell the following parables about how God rejoices over the repentance of sinners.

You will have to review all of the notes again when you come to the end of a given section, pericope, or chapter. Put an asterisk (*) by any of those entries that you feel are absolutely essential in case the number of notes must be reduced later.

7.1.5 Contextualized notes for Luke 1–8 in the Chichewa study Bible

A communication gap, or even a complete breakdown of communication, frequently occurs when an indigenous, culturally conditioned perspective is superimposed upon the biblical one as Scripture is read or heard. For example, there may be an *apparent* correspondence between the SL and TL forms and/or functions where there is none at all, or there may seem to be a clash between them that is inexplicable to the reader. The notes of a study Bible are designed to overcome this communication gap and help the reader avoid erroneous inferences.

The examples of notes in this section were chosen to illustrate the nature and degree of linguistic and cultural modification that is required for Chichewa. These examples are mainly of the "contextual" (no. 7) and "translational" (no. 8) type of notes described in section 7.1.3. They give an indication of where problems are likely to occur in the Chichewa text for its readers or hearers. To some extent, then, this is an exercise in hyper-contextualization since it is not likely that any single reader would misconstrue all, or even most, of the cases listed below. On the other hand, it is *highly* likely that without a note at least some readers would stumble at every one of these expressions.

The examples were taken from draft copies of the Luke portion of the Chichewa study Bible, which was not published until 2003. They highlight the general nature of the problems that call for notes—whether cultural/conceptual or semantic/linguistic—and intimate the direction that a note might take in order to resolve a given problem. They also call attention to the potential distorting influence of traditional beliefs and practices upon the average receptor.[5]

It would no doubt help translators interested in preparing a study Bible to know why a particular note in the Chichewa study Bible was generated. To a great extent this is a process based on long personal experience in communicating the message of the Scriptures in the vernacular in varied situations such as preaching, teaching, witnessing, counseling, literature development, and Bible translation. This kind of experience makes a person aware of the passages that are most likely to be misunderstood.[6] When communication fails it is usually occasioned by some linguistic, conceptual, or cultural mismatch resulting from the overall TL situation. Without guidance from a paratextual note, there is a good chance that either the wrong meaning will be conveyed or no meaning at all.

In the Chichewa study Bible both the placement and the wording of the notes have been determined according to the principle of *relevance*—that is, on the assumption that the conceptual effort that needs to be expended in mentally processing a given note will be adequately compensated for by the cognitive gain that will be derived in terms of understanding the content, intent, impact, and/or significance of the text. This principle applies also to the quantity and quality of study notes. If too many notes are supplied, especially those that are not really very informative, the reader's capacity to deal with the material will be diminished. The same outcome may be expected for notes that are too conceptually dense or stylistically difficult to understand. Therefore, the process of critically testing and revising the notes for a given book (by adding, deleting, rewording for clarity, etc.) must be ongoing throughout the editorial process—and even beyond, in preparation for an updated edition within ten years of the original publication.

As you read through the following text cues and associated comments that were prepared for the Chewa setting, consider them in light of your own cultural setting and Bible translation situation.

» Would similar notes be required in YL at each point, or would a different explanation or clarification be needed? If the latter, give a sample wording in YL, with a back-translation into English.

» Pick out at least three passages where there is a much different problem, requiring a completely new note. How would you word this in YL?

---

[5] Any distortion is evaluated as such on the basis of the original text and context of Scripture. A "transculturation" of the biblical message must inevitably be carried out, however, in order to render it meaningful and relevant to the everyday lives of a specific contemporary audience.

[6] I was greatly assisted in this problem-discovery exercise by colleagues in the translation department of the Bible Society of Zambia, by third-year students in the Lutheran Seminary where I teach, and by members of the Chichewa Study Bible Committee, with whom I discussed a number of issues. Bruce Malina and Richard Rohrbaugh's *Social-Science Commentary on the Synoptic Gospels* (1992) also offered valuable background information, confirming and elucidating the nature of certain problem areas likely to be generated by a distinctive and disparate cultural-religious viewpoint.

Ref.	text problem cue	descriptive/explanatory/directive comment
1:7	Elizabeth was barren	How did people know that the lack of children was *her* fault? In the traditional Chewa setting, which is matrilineal and matrilocal, it is the husband who would first be suspected. If a woman is found (by divination) to be barren, it would be attributed either to witchcraft or the anger of ancestral spirits on account of a certain moral violation perpetrated by someone in the two families concerned. In any case, barrenness, as it did in Bible times, puts a severe social strain on any marriage.
1:9	burn incense	What was the purpose of this incense-burning rite? Could the incense-burning ritual of a Chewa medicine man (*sing'anga*) intended to chase evil spirits (*ziwanda*) from a homestead or village suggest to readers that Zechariah was engaged in a magical attempt to cure his wife's barrenness? To some, the immediate appearance of an angel in verse 11 after Zechariah's sacrifice and the corporate prayers of the people (as though to the clan ancestors!) might reinforce this notion. Such a ready answer to petitionary prayer (+/– some mystical appearance such as a large snake/python) occurs regularly in the rain rites carried out at the local shrine. Another problem: from a Christian point of view, the fact that Zechariah's prayer was heard and will result in a child may suggest that God has not reacted favorably to the prayers of people who remain childless.
1:13	give him the name John	In a Bantu cultural context not just anyone can name a child, especially the firstborn son. It is the father's duty to select a name from his ancestral line, and by doing so, he accepts his fatherhood of the child. Did Elizabeth disrespectfully appropriate the father's responsibility in 1:60? The difference between Elizabeth's naming of John and Mary's naming of Jesus (in 1:31) may need to be pointed out.
1:19	I stand in the presence of God	According to Bantu customs of politeness, one does not *stand* in the presence of an elder, let alone a chief. Instead, one sits or kneels to show deference and respect. This angel Gabriel is either greater in authority than God, or else he is manifesting an attitude that is extremely rude or arrogant.
1:24	[she] remained in seclusion	This passage raises the question of why Elizabeth would want to stay in hiding during the period of her wonderful pregnancy. Hiding like this would jibe with traditional fears of being bewitched by a jealous relative or neighbor. Or could it be that she herself (or Zechariah) had practiced magic in order to become pregnant at the expense of the "life-force" of someone else?

1:27	to a virgin pledged to be married	There is no one-word equivalent for "virgin" in Chichewa (rendered here as *namwali wathunthu* "a whole maiden"), and a virginal state is not required for an honorable marriage as in the biblical social setting. On the contrary, in some areas the custom of ritual sexual intercourse is still practiced as part of a young woman's traditional initiation ceremony. The Jewish custom of inviolate engagement (betrothal) is not practiced, although there is the nonequivalent practice of "pledging," whereby a young man promises to marry a girl (*kufunsira mbeta/kutomera*) and seals this with a ceremonial gift to her parents.
1:41	the baby leaped in her womb	Such an event would take place, according to traditional belief, due to the exercise of witchcraft upon the fetus by a malicious, envious person (in this case, by Mary!). The Jewish view that this was the sign of a prophetic call by God may be worth a note. What is more surprising to Chewa readers is the fact that Elizabeth then proceeded to speak about Mary's own pregnancy, which surely was not as yet apparent; from a Bantu point of view this would be socially inappropriate and inauspicious. Elizabeth's subsequent mention of her unborn child's joy (v. 44) further complicates the passage.
1:59	circumcise the child	The Chewa people do not engage in the practice of ritual circumcision and there is no indigenous word to refer to it. In translation the term *kuumbala* was borrowed from the neighboring Yao language. However, Yao circumcision occurs much later in life as an important part of the customary process of youth maturation in this society, among whom are many Muslim adherents. Thus the circumcision of the eight-day-old baby Jesus sounds like a very strange, even cruel practice. An explanation of the socio-religious significance of this rite in an OT setting is essential here.
1:80	he lived in the desert	The Chewa people view it as deviant social behavior if someone goes off to a desert area to live alone. They would attribute John's doing so either to possession by an evil spirit (suggested perhaps by the phrase "became strong in the spirit") or to his desire to practice sorcery in secret.
2:8	shepherds living out in the field… at night	This verse triggers perplexing questions: What kind of herdsmen are these? How can anyone watch over animals in the dark? (Only witches do their business at night.) And why do they live out in the bush, as the Chewa translation says? (This too suggests witchcraft.) Obviously, some background information about Palestinian methods of small animal husbandry is necessary here. But even with that, the popular opinion of these shepherds would be negative.

2:22	time of their purification	A note is needed here to clarify for readers that Mary's "purification" forty days after giving birth (see Lev. 12:2–8) has nothing to do with the Chewa custom of "taking the child" (*kutenga mwana*), which is intended to strengthen and protect the child against sorcery and also sanction the parents' resumption of sexual relations. An understanding of Levitical regulations concerning purity and pollution is important background for understanding the controversies that Christ had with the Pharisees over their legalistic approach to such ritual behavior.
3:2	the word of God came to John	This is not a natural way in any language to refer to the reception of a verbal message. The religious significance of this overtly alien expression is greatly increased due to its intertextual resonance with the OT prophetic formula (e.g., in Jer. 1:2; Ezek. 1:3; Hos. 1:1; Joel 1:1). Such reflected, or associative, meaning is reproduced in the most recent Chewa translation with reference to John, but here it may require reinforcement by means of a footnote because of its theological implication.
3:7	you brood of vipers!	John sounds rudely impolite here, calling the people who have come to hear him "snakes." This metaphor needs to be clarified; it means deceptively clever, not deadly dangerous. It should also be explained that this characterization was only part of John's message; the emphasis was on the people's need for repentance before coming to God for forgiveness and deliverance.
3:17	his winnowing fork	In rural Chewa agriculture, it is the women who do the winnowing (*kupeta*): They winnow pounded maize. It is only women who use the winnowing basket (*lichero*, as dynamically rendered in the new translation). And since the chaff (*gaga* 'husks') is blown away by the wind, why would anyone waste time and energy trying to burn it?
5:10	you will catch men	The wording and context could suggest the aggressive action of witch-finders (*ogwira-mfiti*), whose job it is to magically "catch" (trap) witches or wizards and rid the village of their malevolent activities.
5:19	they went up on the roof	This scenario would be quite extraordinary in central Africa, where village houses have pointed roofs made of grass and town houses have roofs of thin corrugated metal sheets. An explanatory footnote is needed here, and a graphic in the text would be of great assistance (cf. Luke 17:21).

7.1 Contextualizing a LiFE translation

5:30	eat and drink with…sinners	The distinct NT sense of "sinners" in this context is people who do not observe the ceremonial demands of the Mosaic law. Perhaps this needs to be explained in the glossary due to its frequency of occurrence. The implication of drinking with sinners is especially problematic since in Chichewa it suggests imbibing to the point of drunkenness. A note explaining this is called for, and the implications of Christ's words in verse 31 must be brought into the explanation. Jesus' flouting of the customary norms, which drew criticism from many also needs a note. In fact, his behavior laid him open to the charge of being demon-possessed himself according to the widespread practice of pejorative "deviance labeling" (see Malina and Rohrbaugh 1992:353 and also Luke 11:15).
6:18	those troubled by evil spirits	The great difference between the notion of "evil spirits" in the biblical and the Bantu sociocultural settings needs to be carefully explained, perhaps as an expanded glossary entry due to the ubiquity of this conceptual mismatch in the NT. In the NT evil spirits are personal, but nonhuman and Satanic in nature and origin, whereas in a Chewa setting they are essentially human and associated either with sorcery or with aggrieved ancestral spirits that need to be placated. The Chewa medicine man (*sing'anga*) also heals diseases, which is apparently what the disciples were empowered to do (Luke 9:1).
6:24	woe to you who are rich	This seemingly blanket condemnation by Christ of those who are rich fits in well with the Chewa worldview. However, the basis for the Chewa stereotype is quite different from the ancient Jewish perspective. The latter involves the "limited good" principle, making it axiomatic that those who are wealthy have gained their economic standing at the expense of the "poor" by means of deception, extortion, thievery, or some other injustice. In a Bantu setting, however, the rich obtain their wealth through the overt and covert practice of magic (*mankhwala*) and sorcery (*ufiti*).
6:48	foundation on rock	Traditional Chewa houses are never built on rock; rather, they are constructed without a foundation so that the wall poles may be sunk deeply into the ground for support and stability. The kind of house referred to here in the biblical setting therefore needs a note to explain the apparent contradiction in the translation.

7:13 don't cry!	In a Chewa social context Jesus' command here might sound highly inappropriate, even insulting (see also Luke 23:28). Only a witch or a madman would speak like this to people in mourning, especially to a woman who had lost her only son. His words might result in a justified beating. The misunderstanding is compounded when Jesus later "touches the coffin," for no one would ever halt a funeral procession in such a manner. (In the biblical setting, this action would be ritually defiling.) The final straw is when Jesus tells the corpse, "Get up!" Even witches are not so bold as to give such a command in broad daylight; they would say something like this only in the dead of night and accompanied by some nefarious ritual. The evocation of a traditional religious perspective is strengthened by the fact that the young man actually arises and speaks (v. 15)—a resurrection phenomenon (not unheard of) that would be construed as the result of possession by an ancestral spirit (*malombo, mizimu yoipa*). A final noteworthy detail here concerns the social situation of the widow, who is "the stereotypical ancient example of dire vulnerability" and a "symbol of the exploited and oppressed" in a biblical setting (Malina and Rohrbaugh 1992:329, 397). This would certainly not be the case in a typical Chewa matrilineal, matrilocal community.
7:37 an alabaster jar of perfume	The woman's behavior, from a Chewa social viewpoint, is highly improbable or, worse, taboo. It is given an added negative twist by the very language employed in the translation. In particular, the term for jar (*nsupa*), while referentially accurate, carries the unfortunate implication by association of the practice of sorcery (*ufiti*).
8:21 my mother and brothers are	Here Jesus is not denying or repudiating his closest relatives, as suggested by the implied negative of the Chewa text. Such an act would be culturally very strange, if not offensive and worthy of social censure. Rather, it is a matter of "both…and," or even "this and what's more that." This is a rhetorical issue that needs to be explained. Later, in Luke 14:26 (with the problematic "hate") a definite social detachment *is* entailed—from one's biological or familial kinship group to a surrogate relationship based on religious conviction.
8:30 what is your name?	A Chewa medicine man or diviner will cleverly manipulate a spirit of possession to get it to reveal its hidden name. After gaining this vital personal information, he can employ his magic to expel the spirit or determine the magical means whereby the patient can control it. In the ancient Jewish worldview, "the power to use a name is the power to control" (Malina and Rohrbaugh 1992:337).
8:33 [the demons] went into the pigs	The fact that these demons went to "possess" the herd of pigs is not strange from a traditional African perspective. Human spirits can reside in animals and animal spirits can reside in humans. It may be significant to point out, however, that according to Jewish ritual legislation both demon-possessed people and pigs were considered ritually unclean, polluted. So the death of the pigs is hardly a surprise.

8:43 a woman had been…bleeding	This woman would be seen as the victim of a Chewa sorcerer who, either out of spite or on behalf of a jealous client, desired to prevent her from getting married, from having children, or from entering normal society. A note is needed here to explain that hemorrhaging had made her ceremonially unclean, hence an ostracized person during the entire twelve years of her affliction, and that she was considered able to transmit her uncleanness—in this case, to Jesus by touching him (v. 47). In keeping with the practice of a Middle Eastern traditional healer, Christ restores this "daughter" within his spiritual "family" (v. 48) to her biological community. (On the anthropological distinction between disease and illness, see Malina and Rohrbaugh 1992:315–6.)
8:52 she is not dead but asleep	Jesus here seems to add insult to injury (i.e., to his command to "stop wailing"). It sounds as if he is making light of the mourners' grief. But he is not implying that the girl has simply fainted or is not truly dead. A note is needed here to point this out, if it is not already clear in the translation.
8:55 her spirit returned	According to Chewa belief, a miraculous resuscitation can indeed occur when a powerful medicine man is able to reverse a bewitchment in which a person's spirit has been mystically captured by witchcraft and subsequently confined with the intent of "eating" the body after it has been buried.

The preceding comments are very TL oriented. Of course, the various historical, sociocultural, and religious distinctive features of the biblical text and context must not be lost sight of. Otherwise, the translation and/or its paratextual supplements might "over-domesticate" the overall communication process to an unacceptable degree, such that the intended meaning of the original is lost, distorted, or misrepresented in the TL. Take the example of "barrenness" (στεῖρα) with reference to Luke 1:36 which Richard Rohrbaugh offers to illustrate the point "…that English-speaking Westerners are unlikely to conjure up the mental pictures or scenarios needed to complete a text in the same way as would a reader from the ancient Mediterranean world" (2008:20): He provides an excellent "social-scientific" study of this concept and concludes (2008:22):

> [S]tigmatization and ostracism from the community of other women were all too often the childless woman's lot. The worst part of it was the public humiliation, regularly understood as the action of God…. In an honor-shame society such as ancient Israel, the consequences of such humiliation could be a heavy burden, frequently affecting an entire extended family. All would share in the shame visited upon their barren relative.

Rohrbaugh objects to the domesticated translation "infertile" of the *Scholars Version* for στεῖρα because it sounds like a modern medical term that conjures up (at least for Western readers) "pictures of medical counseling, infertility clinics, and the like" and "nothing like that engendered in the minds of ancient women" (2008:22).

» Would you agree with Rohrbaugh's objection regarding "infertile" in English? How about the expression "unable to conceive," which is used in the *New Living Translation?*

» Now re-read the comment on Luke 1:7 in section 7.1.5 from the perspective of your cultural setting and Rohrbaugh's explanation above to see if any additional explanation might be needed in a supplementary note in your language to clarify the biblical point of view.

» Study the other examples from Luke in this section from an Ancient Near Eastern ("Mediterranean") point of view and pick out three particular references that you feel would need to be protected from misrepresentation in your language, even if this means using a more "foreignized" translation. In each case, propose a suggested note that might be able to achieve the necessary clarification in a sufficiently concise manner.

7.1.6 Examples of unhelpful and helpful notes

Not all expository notes are created equal; some are much more helpful than others, depending on the needs and circumstances of a particular TL audience. Some notes may turn out to be relatively useless or even misleading. Below you will see various examples of contextual conditioning in the Chichewa text of Luke, both helpful and unhelpful ones. They are listed in a way that facilitates critical examination and assessment as well as comparison with notes in a different language-culture setting.

As you read sections 7.1.6.1 and 7.1.6.2, evaluate the different kinds of notes and the bracketed comments from the perspective of YL.

» Where and in which respects would conceptual adjustments need to be made?

» How can unhelpful notes be avoided and helpful ones be encouraged?

» What is the best way to organize and operate a coordinated and integrated team approach to the task of composing audience-sensitive notes?

» If time allows prepare a set of study notes in YL for Luke 1–3 (or any other chapters assigned by your instructor).

7.1.6.1 Unhelpful notes

The following notes, which are back-translated from the original Chichewa, are ones that proved to be less than helpful, or even confusing, for readers of the biblical text. They represent various types of information that should *not* have been presented in a note at all or, alternatively, that should have been worded better. They were selected from the notes for Luke in earlier drafts of the study Bible which were later recommended for exclusion or extensive revision. They are grouped here into seven irregular categories (i.e., recognizing the possibility of overlapping and ambiguous classification).

1. **Redundant notes**

   Redundant notes simply repeat or paraphrase much of the verse that they ostensibly comment on. They may confuse readers by seeming to provide some new information when in fact they merely tell what should already be known from the text itself.

   > 9:1 **authority and power.** The disciples of Jesus were given the power to heal diseases, to expel evil spirits, and to preach the word of God. They were also given authority to use this power.
   >
   > [The distinction made here between "authority" and "power" in the Chewa text is not clear; in any case, this comment does not really help the reader very much.]

2. **Deficient notes**

   In notes that are deficient or too brief there is a point that requires explanation, but not enough information is provided to stimulate an adequate understanding of the text in question by most members of the intended audience.

7:34 **A friend of tax collectors.** Pharisees viewed tax collectors as sinners because of the fraud they practiced when collecting taxes....

[Perhaps a more serious problem for the Pharisees was that these tax collectors acted as official agents of the Roman government and worked in close cooperation with the hated, ritually defiling Gentiles. Tax collectors did not even try to live according to the strict laws that the Pharisees had imposed upon themselves over and above those required by the law of Moses.]

3. Erroneous notes

Erroneous notes provide information that is not correct, either entirely or in some specific respect. Alternatively, they may be either misleading in some way or not representative of the most reliable exegetical position on the issue under consideration.

9:41 **And how long am I going to have to put up with you?** That is to say, the Lord does not deal with us in accordance with our perversities....

[This note seems to miss the point of Jesus' words. More than simply perverse behavior was involved here; the disciples' failure stemmed from a basic lack of faith and a deficient perspective on Christ's crucial mission of salvation.]

4. Unapplied notes

Unapplied notes fail to supply a local cultural equivalent or familiar correspondent at a particular juncture, even when it would have been relatively easy to do so in order to contextualize the biblical reference in more understandable, perhaps even visual terms.

7:45 **You did not kiss me.** This was the Jewish custom for giving a greeting when receiving a visitor (2 Sam. 15:5).

[The corresponding traditional Chewa custom is clapping hands or kneeling. The more modern one is shaking right hands. These customs should have been mentioned here by way of comparison or for illustration.]

5. Indeterminate notes

Indeterminate notes discuss issues that biblical scholars cannot really resolve precisely. These notes do not provide answers, they only raise more questions about doubtful and hypothetical matters. Alternatively, they give answers that cannot be substantiated by texts of Scripture.

17:14 **As they were going, they were healed.** Those men were healed at that very moment. This happened because they did what they were told.

[The biblical text does not specify when the ten lepers were healed; all we can say is that this healing took place at some point along their way to show themselves to the priests. The Chewa note is too specific, suggesting as it does that they were healed immediately after Jesus gave his command.]

6. Controversial notes

Notes that comment on a matter of dispute among Christian denominations, especially some fundamental issue that pertains to doctrine or practice, are to be avoided unless all of the major hermeneutical positions can be succinctly given. A variant of this is where the biblical text is not really a problem, but the wording of the note would not be acceptable to one denomination or another.

22:20 **This cup is [the] new agreement**. In the cup was the wine that represents the blood of Jesus....As the Passover was a sign and a reminder of the first agreement between God and the people of Israel as they left Egypt, the supper of the Lord is a sign and reminder of the new agreement between God and all believers....

[This teaching concerning the Sacrament of the Lord's body and blood would not be acceptable to most Catholics and Lutherans, who hold a more "substantial" view of this sacred rite in terms of its nature and significance to partakers.]

7. Technical notes

Technical notes provide too much detail, and as a result the overall meaning or interpretation of a given passage is liable to be obscured or lost. Not even many well-educated readers would be able to profit from all the information supplied by the following note.

23:7 **Herod**. ...After Herod died, the land was divided among his three sons: Archelaus (*Arikeraunsi*) ruled the region of Judea (*Yudea*). Herod Philip ruled the regions of Iturea, Gaulanitis, and Trachonitis (*Iturea, Gawulamtisi, Trakonitisi*). Herod Antipas (*Antipasi*) ruled the regions of Galilee and Perea (*Galileya, Perea*); his capital was the city of Tiberias (*Tiberiasi*) next to the Lake of Galilee....

7.1.6.2 Helpful notes

Contextualizing notes of positive value include those where a serious attempt was made to frame the biblical text within a Chewa linguistic and sociocultural setting. These situation-specific comments pertain either to form or to content and are aimed at creating a cognitive framework that will allow readers to better understand and apply the passage to their lives. There are of course a number of different types of notes that could fit into either category—form or content. The examples that follow are merely suggestive of what might be accomplished in order to encourage local hermeneutical efforts and text applications through the contributions of intelligent and insightful mother-tongue editors and advisers.

1. Form

The examples below illustrate the attention that the new Chewa study Bible gives to natural language *forms*. The notes are not dry theological expositions or overly simplified Sunday-school speech; they are composed in a colloquial, literary style that matches that of the biblical text itself. This special feature should give the target audience a little extra motivation to read the notes. In some cases, a given note may even suggest how a more poetically pleasing or rhetorically powerful rendering of the biblical text might be made.

a. Notes containing idioms

17:32 **Remember the wife of Lot**. Lot's wife was destroyed when she was about to be saved (*opulumukapulumuka* 'saved-saved'). Because her heart was stuck on (*mtima unamamatira*) what was happening at Sodom, she failed to grab her heart (*kuugwira mtima*) until she turned around, finish! (*basi*) and turned into a rock of salt. Her "things" all came to an end at that point (*Zake zinathera pomwepo*)!

b. Notes containing figurative language

9:23 **He must deny himself**. These words speak of a person who is not concerned about his life but is willing to be persecuted and lay his life down on an anthill (*kuika moyo pa chiswe*—i.e., risk his life) because of his faith in Christ....

c. **Notes containing graphically descriptive and/or sensorially evocative verb forms**

   14:28 To count the cost. …Jesus did not beat about the bush (*sanawabisire Chichewa* "he did not hide [his] Chichewa [language] from them" = idiom). He warned them in advance that it's not OK to follow him slackly (*mwachisenjesenje* "to fit loosely" = idiom based on an ideophone). And he told [them] directly (*mwatchutchutchu!* "standing straight up" = ideophone) that everyone who [wants to] follow him must…

d. **Notes containing interactive questions**

   23:16 I will just flog him. Judgment had been given that Jesus was not guilty. Should an innocent man be punished any more? Here Pilate gives innocent Jesus the punishment of a flogging. What sin did Jesus commit that he should receive the punishment of flogging?…

e. **Notes containing novel syntax or morphology**

   23:43 Place of rejoicing ("Paradise"). Jesus said that the very day on which they both would die, they would be together at that place of rejoicing. [a lyric, rhythmic expression: *Yesu anati tsiku lomwelo//limene onse awiri aferewo//adzakhalira limodzi kumalo a chisangalalowo*]

f. **Notes containing a significant sound play**

   17:6 We just did what we ought to have done. …Jesus reveals that the disciples were completely lacking in faith, even without the slightest little bit like the small seed of the mustard plant (*ngakhale kakangonongono komwe konga kambewu kampiru*). Here Jesus says that it is better to have at least a small faith rather than to have none at all. That small faith is able to do (*Kachikhulupiriro kakang'onoko kakhoza kuchita*) great, unexpected things.

g. **Notes containing metalanguage**

   10:21 Uneducated people. In Greek this word means "small children." (See how it has been translated in the Sacred Book and in the Holy Writings [i.e., the old Protestant and Catholic versions]). But he [Jesus] means ordinary people who have not gone far in their education in terms of worldly wisdom.

2. **Content**

This next group of examples illustrate some of the diverse content categories that are to be found in the Chichewa study Bible. Several of the examples are considered the best of the creative work of the study Bible editors. Such a resourceful approach to the handling of content notes is a nice complement to a *LiFE*-like translation.

a. **Notes on theological topics**

   18:12 Righteous before God. That is to say, God forgave her sins. The forgiveness of sins "leans upon" or is "propped up upon" (*chitamira kapena kutsamira*—two similar-sounding verbal idioms) the grace (*kukoma mtima* 'the good-heartedness') of God, not on a person's works, no.

b. **Notes dealing with moral-ethical issues**

   22:31 He will winnow you. As a woman winnows the maize kernels that she has pounded up in order to remove the chaff, so they would do with wheat. In a similar way temptations are like ways of winnowing people because it separates the steadfast and the faltering, the faithful and the unfaithful.

c. **Notes containing local language references**

> 7:2 **Roman soldiers.** At that time the government of Rome ruled the region of Galilee through Herod Antipas. Now when we say "of Rome" it does not mean the Catholic Church, which some call the Roman Church (*mpingo wa Aroma*), not at all....

d. **Notes on the biblical setting**

> 24:1 **The women went to the grave.** In the custom of the Jews it was not a strange thing at all for people to go to a graveyard at any time at all....
>
> [This needs to be stressed because of the opposite beliefs among traditionally minded Chewa folk, who believe that a graveyard is the haunt of evil spirits and witches.]

e. **Notes containing local color**

> 6:18 **Evil spirits.** ...Jesus heals diseases of [= caused by] the spirits to demonstrate that he has authority over all spirits, even the spirits of our ancestors which some people believe sometimes brings sicknesses and cause people to lose their peace of mind.

f. **Notes containing proverbial lore**

> 6:36 **As my Father in heaven.** An example of love is God himself (Matt. 5:48). As you know, in Chichewa there's a hidden saying that "[If] the mother [is] dusty (*mbu!* = ideophone), the child [is] dusty (*mbu!*)," meaning that a child often resembles or imitates its parent. Those who believe in God imitate what God does.

g. **Notes containing devotional thoughts of the Study Bible editors**

> 13:29 **People will come from the south.** ...These will be people who come from different nations like here in Africa, America, Europe, the Asians, and also different tribes of people like the Chewa, Tumbuka, Yao, Sena, Bemba, Lomwe, Tonga, Zulu, and Shona. In other words, in God's kingdom there is no favoritism—all believers in God will be there since they were all created by the same God.

7.1.7 Other types of contextual supplementation

Footnotes are not the only way of supplying a sufficient conceptual background for Scripture passages that cause readers problems due to semantic difficulty or foreignness. Ralph Hill, in his seminal article "Contextual Adjustment Strategies and Bible Translation" (2004),[7] gives some good examples of other ways of doing this, both within the text of a translation and also paratextually ("alongside-the-text") as well as extratextually ("outside-the-text"). The passage he uses to illustrate these other methods is Matthew 22:15–17. First, he identifies the passage's potential problem points from the perspective of the primary target audience in a chart (which follows but with slight modifications of format), introducing the chart with an explanation (ibid.:10–11):

> It is helpful for the translation team to have procedures for identifying some of the key contextual assumptions on which author-intended meaning depends, and then comparing those assumptions with the ability of an average person from the receptor audience to access those assumptions. The following chart illustrates such a procedure applied to Matthew 22:15–22 where Jesus is confronted with a question on paying taxes to Caesar. Contextual assumptions from the biblical setting are noted in the left column, and the likelihood of an Adioukrou reader to access them is evaluated in

---

[7]This article should be read in its entirety, for it provides a theoretical background (based on Relevance Theory) for the various context-management techniques that are illustrated. I am grateful to Ralph Hill for allowing me to cite his helpful examples here.

7.1 Contextualizing a LiFE translation

the right column. One can employ the methodology during exegetical preparation before drafting. On the basis of this assessment, options can be weighed for providing the information the reader needs. Initial assumptions will have to be confirmed by further audience testing.

Background assumptions available to original audience	Matthew 22:15–22 (New Living Translation: chosen for its relative explicitness and naturalness in English)	Likelihood of an average TL reader to access these assumptions: probable, possible, or unlikely
Assumptions from the historical setting • A ruler with the title of Caesar governed the empire of Rome • Rome had conquered Israel and yet allowed them a measure of autonomy in governing their own religious affairs • Through the years, Rome had placed members of the Herod family in positions of authority in Palestine.		• unlikely • unlikely • unlikely
Assumption from the context • Three parables (two sons, tenants of the vineyard and the wedding banquet) angered the Pharisees	15 Then the Pharisees met together to think of a way to trap Jesus into saying something for which they could accuse him	• probable—for someone who has read preceding context.
Other contextual assumptions • Pharisees were nationalists and opposed to Roman rule • Herodians were wealthy and powerful Jews supporting Roman rule. • Their desire was to have Rome establish Herod Antipas as king in Jerusalem. *Contextual implication:* two groups with opposing political agendas are collaborating in order to trap Jesus.	16 They decided to send some of their disciples, along with the supporters of Herod, to ask him this question:	• unlikely • unlikely • unlikely
Explicit set of premises: leading to a— *Contextual implication:* thus you are duty bound to answer one way or another in spite of the consequences.	"Teacher, we know how honest you are. You teach about the way of God regardless of the consequences. You are impartial and don't play favorites."	• possible, derived from text

	17 Now tell us what you think about this: Is it right to pay taxes to the Roman government or not?"	• unlikely
• Jews in Palestine were also under Roman law which specified that a poll tax must be paid annually by each adult male		
Contextual implications:		• unlikely
• a "no" answer would satisfy the Pharisees, but displease the Herodians.		
• A "no" answer could be reported as treasonous and used as grounds to arrest him.		• unlikely
• A "yes" answer would satisfy the Herodians but displease the Pharisees.		• unlikely
• They would take this as disloyalty to the Jewish nation, and surely provide proof for the people that Jesus was not the awaited messianic liberator.		• unlikely

Evaluate the above chart in light of your own exegetical study of this passage:

» Do you agree with all of the author's conclusions regarding the "assumptions" and "implications" that relate to the biblical text?

» Do you have any modifications or additions to suggest?

» How would an average TL reader or hearer in your cultural setting understand this text if translated into YL? In other words, how would you fill in the responses in the boxes that run down the right-hand column?

Hill points out the two main ways of including essential contextual information within the text of a translation: (1) "adaptive retelling" and (2) "bracketing" (ibid.:16–18). Adaptive retelling is an explicit type of paraphrase that aims to present the biblical text in as straightforward, unambiguous, and understandable manner as possible, often sacrificing detail in order to maintain both written and aural clarity in the TL. This may involve a simplification, amplification, and/or condensation of the original. It is well suited for audio productions.

"Bracketing" is the consistent use of some unobtrusive formatting device that indicates added background material, such as italics, parentheses, square brackets, or half brackets, whichever is most suitable for the target readership. The application of such a device must be clearly motivated, managed, and marked. Normally, its use is a "bridging technique" suitable for special groups such as new readers or novice Christians. It should be unmistakably labeled as such (i.e., not as "Scripture") with the advice and approval of the wider church community. The added information must be carefully merged with the biblical text—that is, in a natural style that is not overloaded with details, which would violate the principle of relevance. It must also be tested on the target audience in the same way the biblical text is.

The following examples (ibid.) of adaptive retelling and bracketing based on Matthew 22:15–17 enable us to compare these two ways of incorporating contextual background in the translated text:

1. **Adaptive retelling** (the retelling is in italics; the non-italicized words are from the NLT):

   The Pharisees became angry when they understood that these stories applied to them, so they met together to think of a way to trap Jesus into saying something they could use to accuse him. *They despised the fact that Caesar, the emperor of Rome, ruled over their nation. Along with many Jews, they believed it wrong to pay taxes to Rome. Their allegiance was to God alone, and they did not wish to bring on his judgment. But they also knew there were other wealthy Jews who supported the descendents from the family of Herod, which the emperor of Rome had placed to rule over them. These people thought it was good to pay the tax in order to maintain peace.* So the Pharisees decided to send some of their own followers along with some supporters of Herod Antipas to ask Jesus a trick question. *Any answer would surely displease one group or the other.* They said, "Teacher,…is it right to pay taxes to the Roman government or not?"

2. **Bracketing** (the added background material is in half-brackets):[8]

   ¹⁵ Then the Pharisees met together to think of a way to trap him by tricking him into saying something ⌞which would turn either the Jews or the Roman authorities against him⌟ ¹⁶ They decided to send some of their disciples along with the Herodians, ⌞a political party that supported King Herod⌟, to ask him, … ¹⁷ Is it right to pay taxes to Caesar, ⌞the head of the Roman government⌟ ?"

Evaluate the pros and cons of each of these two contextualizing techniques. Refer, if possible, to Hill's detailed critique on pages 17–18 of his 2004 article.

» Do you see a use for either of these devices in your communication setting? Explain which one would be more helpful and why.

» Mention some of the guidelines that would be needed to enable translators to manage these devices effectively and avoid potential setting-specific pitfalls. For example, would the vernacular term "Rome" or "Roman" in the previous example be confused with a designation for the Roman Catholic Church?

Hill presents several "outside-the-text" supplementary techniques also, which are summarized below. Compare and evaluate them with regard to their potential benefit versus detriment in terms of "relevant" communication. Then suggest how they might be used together in a coordinated and systematically managed program of contextualizing the biblical text.

1. **Section headings**

   A section heading is a title that conveys the main theme and/or communicative purpose of a larger or smaller portion of Scripture. Hill (2004:19) suggests the following section heading for Matthew 22:15–22:

   > Opposing parties plot to trap Jesus through a trick question

2. **Section introductions**

   A clearly demarcated space at the beginning of a section is where an introduction is most helpful. Its function is to orient the reader to the key elements of background information needed to understand the passage as a whole; it often appears together with a section heading. Hill (ibid.) suggests the following introduction for Matthew 22:15–22:

   > As soon as the Pharisees understood these stories applied to them, they set about to catch Jesus with a trick question. Despite the fact that they hated Roman occupation, they allied themselves with their political adversaries who favored Roman rule and the descendents of Herod that Rome

---

[8]The suggested information is from Deibler's *Index of Implicit Information in the Gospels* (1993).

had placed over them. They came up with a question whose answer would either offend Herod's supporters and appear treasonous to Rome, or offend the Pharisees and prove that Jesus could not be the Messiah the people were expecting.

3. Explanatory and descriptive notes

Already described in earlier sections, notes may be used for larger or smaller portions of the biblical text. For larger portions the notes tend to be more expository in nature; for smaller portions they tend to be more succinct. The presence of a note must be patently marked in the text of the translation. The content of the first example below is like a "section introduction"; the rest are typical verse-by-verse progressions (ibid.:20–21):

> **22:15–17** Actually, the Pharisees greatly disdained the Jews who supported the descendents of the Herod family as rulers. The Herodians accepted that Caesar, the emperor who ruled the Roman Empire, had placed Herod the Great (see 2:1) and his son Herod Antipas (see 14:1) to rule over them. They further wanted Antipas to be established as king in Jerusalem. They therefore thought it was good to pay taxes to Caesar, as it would maintain peace. Those Jews who were Pharisees recognized only God as their ruler. They thought that to pay taxes to Caesar was to agree with Roman rule, which would bring punishment from God on the nation of Israel. Thus it would be difficult to give an answer that would not offend one group or the other.
>
> **22:15–22** Although Rome had occupied the nation of Israel at this time, it allowed the Jews to govern their own religious affairs. Thus Jews were under Jewish religious law and Roman civil law.
>
> **22:16 supporters of Herod.** A group of powerful Jews who supported Roman rule and the family of Herod the Great (see 2:1). They wished to see Herod's son Antipas (see 14:1) established as king in Jerusalem. The Pharisees opposed the supporters of Herod on the issue of cooperation with Rome, but both were afraid of Jesus' influence.
>
> **22:17 pay taxes to the Roman government.** Literally, to "Caesar," which is the title of the ruler of the Roman Empire. This involved paying a poll tax for each adult male. Pharisees were opposed to Roman rule and thought that paying taxes contradicted Jewish law and teaching with regard to their allegiance to Yahweh alone. This would bring further punishment on the nation. Supporters of Herod thought that paying the tax was necessary to ensure peace and safety.

4. Marginal notes

Similar to footnotes, *marginal notes* are placed in the margin close to the translated text where they apply, not at the bottom of the page. Such notes tend to be easier to read, though they are more difficult to compose and format because of the alignment requirement. The following example is from R. Hill (2004:22) and covers the entire section of Matthew 22:15–22.

	Paying taxes—to whom do we owe allegiance?
	(Mark 12:13–17, Luke 20:20–26)

22:15–22 Although Rome had occupied the nation of Israel at this time, it allowed the Jews to govern their own religious affairs. Thus Jews were under both Jewish religious law and Roman civil law. **22:16 supporters of Herod:** a group of powerful Jews who supported Roman rule and the family of Herod the Great (see 2:1). They wished to see Herod's son Antipas (see 14:1) established as king in Jerusalem. The Pharisees and supporters of Herod were opposed to each other on the issue of cooperation with Rome, but both were afraid of Jesus' influence. **22:17 pay taxes to the Roman government:** Literally to "Caesar," the title used for the ruler of the Roman Empire. This involved paying a poll tax for each adult male. Pharisees were opposed to Roman rule and thought that paying taxes contradicted Jewish law and teaching with regard to their allegiance to Yahweh alone. This would bring further punishment on the nation. Supporters of Herod thought that paying the tax was necessary to ensure peace and safety. **22:18 evil motives:** In the eyes of the Pharisees someone who was in favor of paying taxes to Caesar could not be the expected Messiah. Yet if Jesus answered negatively, the supporters of Herod could accuse him of treason against Rome. **22:19 the Roman coin:** a silver coin called a denarius with an image of Caesar. On one side was written, "Tiberius Caesar Augustus, Son of the Divine Augustus." The other side referred to Caesar as "Chief Priest." Many Jews considered such a coin with its images to be idolatrous.	15 Then the Pharisees met together to think of a way to trap Jesus into saying something for which they could accuse him
	16 They decided to send some of their disciples, along with the supporters of Herod, to ask him this question:
	  "Teacher, we know how honest you are. You teach about the way of God regardless of the consequences. You are impartial and don't play favorites.
	  17 Now tell us what you think about this: Is it right to pay taxes to the Roman government or not?"
	18 But Jesus knew their evil motives. "You hypocrites!" he said. "Whom are you trying to fool with your trick questions? 19 Here, show me the Roman coin used for the tax."
	When they handed him the coin, 20 he asked, "Whose picture and title are stamped on it?"
	21 "Caesar's," they replied.
	"Well, then," he said, "give to Caesar what belongs to him. But everything that belongs to God must be given to God."
	22 His reply amazed them, and they went away.

» Do you prefer footnotes or marginal notes? Why?

» Should marginal notes be placed on the left or the right side of the biblical text (or on the facing page)? Give reasons for your preference.

» Have you done some systematic audience testing with regard to these issues?

» Why is such research necessary before, during, and after the translation project?

» Who should be tested (which audience groups) and by what method(s)?

» Do literary concerns affect the composition of notes or inside-the-text retelling or bracketed material? If so, where or how? Give an example to illustrate this.

For reflection, research, and response:

1. Which aspects or dimensions of a person's governing conceptual framework (worldview) seem to be the most important for interpreting the message of Scripture? Tell why you think so. How can speakers of your TL be educated to enable them to understand the Scriptures better? How can people, whether young or old, be encouraged to *want* to study the Bible more thoroughly?

2. Mention three important topics of Scripture that are unfamiliar to the people in your setting. These are the subjects that may well need special attention when preparing Bible background notes.

3. Which of the ten proposed types of study notes in section 7.1.3 would be most important to emphasize in your own sociocultural setting? Which type(s) of information can be downplayed? Give reasons for these choices. Also review the procedures given in section 7.1.4 for composing such notes. Is there something you need to correct or add in order to adapt them to your situation or make them more effective?

4. Read chapter 7 ("Provision of Supplementary Information") of Eugene Nida's *Meaning across Cultures* (1981). Write down three important points that you learn there about preparing notes with reference to your own sociocultural and religious setting.

5. Ralph Hill and Harriet Hill have done considerable research in the application of relevance theory to different methods of contextualizing a Bible translation. Their aim is to provide people with an adequate cognitive framework through supplementary materials so that they can better interpret the original text in their own cultural setting. Vernacular context-building materials can be produced in a traditional printed format or by audiovisual means. According to Ralph Hill (2004:10), these include Bible story "retellings" in the following forms:

> Collections of audience-adapted biblical stories or themes that address locally relevant points of contact or worldview issues. These can be designed to reinforce what is similar to biblical worldviews or address what is different or lacking by providing context-generating narrative stories. One example would be the "Lives of the Prophets" series designed for Muslim readers interested in reading about many of the biblical prophets whom they are familiar with by name. (Note: Such collections could be presented either as Scripture translation or as adaptive retellings of Scripture whichever would be more appropriate.)
>
> a. Simplified materials designed for sharing with preschool children or as part of a primary or secondary school-based curriculum.
>
> b. Chronological Bible storying, for example, preparing a "story-teller's Bible" to be used as a source book for those who do not have an adequate narrative framework for understanding the Scriptures as a complete canon, giving priority to translating portions that feature narrative texts.
>
> c. Other nonprint media adaptations of foundational Bible stories, scripted appropriately for audio and/or visual dissemination.

What do you think of these methods of providing extratextual "cognitive conditioning" in a narrative format to assist your readers and hearers to interpret the text of Scripture? Are there any problems that might arise? What are the particular challenges to be faced in this regard? Would this be an effective way of accomplishing the hermeneutical goals of most churches in your translation setting? If so, give reasons why? If not, why not, and what alternatives do you suggest? Outline what *you* have done or are doing to build contextual bridges of cognition for your target audience, and give a concrete example.

6. Richard Brown (2004) presents several strategies for "bridging the contextual gap" that inevitably exists between the SL and TL cultural and cognitive settings. He suggests constructing a new "mental model" for Bible text consumers through paratextual devices and supplementary texts. In particular, he recommends the "abridged Bible" (or "pedagogical Bible") selection method whereby the full Bible is introduced gradually, through a series of portions that progressively build up a cognitive background for interpreting the Scriptures. The easiest and most important Bible texts are prepared first (e.g., OT narrative passages + those that contain key theological themes), accompanied by appropriately contextualized (worldview-sensitive) notes and other supplementary helps. Subsequent publications then incorporate an increasing number of the more challenging non-narrative texts until finally the whole translated Bible is ready for publication in printed or audio form. Have you experimented with a similar selective and gradually progressive introduction of the Scriptures in your translation setting? Discuss the pros and cons of this approach. Would it be possible to use some form of this technique in your translation program? Have you sampled the opinion of various church bodies with regard to this matter? Explain why or why not.

7. Prepare a cursory exegetical analysis of Acts 14:8–20 and a detailed study of verses 11–13. Following the examples given in section 7.1.7, compose a section heading and section introduction for the pericope as a whole; then compose a sample adaptive retelling, bracketing, and explanatory notes for the subsection covering verses 14–18. Do this in English first, and then translate what you have done into YL. Make a note of any important modifications that are necessary as you move from English to YL due to cultural and conceptual differences. Is it possible to prepare these notes in a literary (artistic-rhetorical) manner? If it is not possible, tell why. If it is, give an example.

8. The following comments on the relative value of section headings appeared in a recent blog on English Bible translations (David Ker at www.betterbibles.com on 21/02/2009). Evaluate the author's argument against the conventional use of such headings, that is, when placed within the text of the translation. Would you still prefer the inclusion of these titles—or not? Explain your position and support it with an example or two:

    Why do people get so upset about these helpful titles? I think there are two main reasons:

    1. They tend to interrupt larger units of discourse, introducing discontinuity where there wasn't any.

    2. They tend to misidentify what a passage is really about.

    Here is a sure sign that you have a **"dissection"** problem: If the paragraph after the title begins with a connecting word like, *so, therefore, or then,* you can be certain that this passage is meant to be read with the previous one. Now back in the good old days of English Bibles the verse numbers were in the margins. And the section titles were in the header. Here's a picture of my nice old pocket Bible published in 1861 by the American Bible Society. Each verse begins a new paragraph which is not ideal. But I do like the titles in the header. Also, this Bible has a summary at the beginning of each chapter of the contents. If you're familiar with novels from this era you'll know that this was a common practice at the time. [*Illustration inserted*]

    Notice the summaries under each chapter heading. They even give verse references for the various sections. There is an important difference between the Bible and *Tom Jones* or *Three Men in a Boat*. The authors of these novels chose the chapter divisions in their books and even chose the section titles or summaries. Not so with the Bible….[W]ith the exception of the titles given for Psalms we have few if any examples of section titles in the Bible. This makes me think about the lowly comma. And the period. And even the dreadful semicolon (for those that can't decide). The ancients manuscripts had no punctuation. Sometimes there weren't even spaces between the words. But there existed other means of signaling relations between clauses in a sentence and also in beginning and ending stories or sections of an epistle. *They are there if you know what to look for but they very seldom match up with the section, chapter and verse indications.*

9. Study the nearer and wider context of Eph. 5:21–22 and suggest where a section heading fits best. What heading would you propose? Give reasons for your answer.

10. As the major assignment for this lesson (to be handed in to the instructor on completion), prepare a translation of Paul's letter to Philemon in your mother tongue as well as a corresponding set of contextualizing study notes. Use any available commentaries and study Bibles. Refer to the analysis of Philemon that you prepared as an exercise at the end of section 6.3.3. Make sure that your notes suit the local setting in which most of your people live. Keep the different categories of notes in mind as you do this assignment (see section 7.1.3). In particular, try to compose notes that also exhibit a dynamic, *LiFE*-like style of writing in YL. Select three of your most literarily composed notes and give a back-translation of them into English.

11. (Optional) As part of an "Introduction" to Philemon, try to compose an appropriate overview for your primary target audience based on a narrative approach; in other words, contextualize the epistle's contents in terms of several layered stories. This would include (a) the hypothetical story of the main protagonists—Philemon, Onesimus, and Paul—embedded within (b) the story of the Christian congregation at Colossae (see Colossians), embedded within (c) the life history of Paul the apostle (see, e.g., 1 Cor. 9:27; Gal. 1:10–2 :14; Phil. 2:12–26, 3:1–11), embedded within (d) the great narrative of God and his people, the "Salvation History" centered in Christ (see, e.g., Rom. 1:18–32; 3:1–31; 4:1–25; 5:1–12; chaps. 9–11).

7.2 Testing a *LiFE* translation

As we have seen, the process of contextualizing a biblical text through supplementary aids depends heavily upon target audience participation. The same is true of assessing a translation. During *both* of these processes the translators must continually ask themselves: For whom are we translating and why? And during both processes the project organizers must also continually involve their primary constituency as partners in the task. For this reason the subject of testing a translation, which we will now consider, is treated in the same lesson with the preceding topic of supplementary aids (7.1).

The three essential operations involved in the production of a Bible translation—composition, contextualization, and consultation—are equally important and can be pictured as a mutually interactive triangle (see below). If there is a significant failure with respect to any of these dimensions, then it is highly likely that the translation will not achieve the objectives stated in its overall production plan (*Brief*).

COMPOSITION

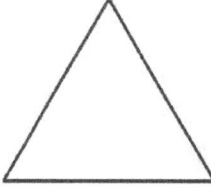

CONTEXTUALIZATION　　　　　　　　**CONSULTATION**

Composition refers to the preparation of the actual translated text of Scripture (see lessons 3–6). *Contextualization* refers to the various methods of providing the target audience with the conceptual background knowledge needed to correctly understand and apply the translated text. (One of the most common means of supplying this cognitive framework, namely, through paratextual expositional notes, was considered in section 7.1.)

In this section, we will be focusing upon the third operation of *consultation*. This refers to a frank "negotiation," a mutual "exchange of views," which in the case of a Bible translation involves the translation staff (a team of translators plus their advisers and reviewers), the administrative committee that is overseeing and facilitating the project, and members of the general public for whom the version at hand is being prepared—the TL audience/readership.

It is vital that the translation team confer with the intended text consumers to get their individual and collective opinions at all times: *before* their work begins, *while* it is being carried out, and then *after* the translation has been published. Audience research and product testing is an integral part of the production procedure. It is how the text producers determine the needs, opinions, attitudes, and wishes of their constituency at large so that they can prepare the kind of translation that will serve them best. They will not always be able to please everyone, but the translators must know *beforehand* what the majority of their readers and hearers are looking for so that they can set their standards and goals accordingly. They also need to monitor their text *while* it is being produced so that they can determine, more or less, how well they are achieving their objectives. Then *after* publication, they need to evaluate how well the translation is meeting the needs of the people and how it is contributing to the spiritual growth and enrichment of the various sponsoring church communities.

An audience that has been kept informed of problems and progress along the way and has been given an adequate forum whereby they can express their opinions and concerns will hopefully feel themselves to be a valued part of the project. As a result, they will be more likely to welcome and use the version as it gradually becomes available to them over the years. Such interactive participation is especially important in the case of a *LiFE* translation, which will most likely be in the form of a portion for a special use and/or a particular audience.

- » To what extent have you and your translation team been engaged in audience research?
- » What methods have you used, and what were the results?
- » By what means did you evaluate these results?
- » To what extent have these results affected your overall production process? Give an example.
- » Have you ever made use of a more "independent" monitoring group to prepare an evaluation of your translation work? If so, give the details as to how this was done.
- » If you have not made use of audience-sampling procedures and feedback techniques, give the reason why not.

7.2.1 Questions, questions, and still more questions

The normal way of conducting research and testing is by means of questions—lots of them, of all kinds and for various purposes. Intensive, but sensitive questioning is needed in order to elicit all the different types of information that would show how well people understand both the translated text and also the background material supplied to contextualize it.

In chapter 10 of *Translating the Literature of Scripture* (Wendland 2004b) there is a detailed case study that illustrates this procedure, including suggestions as to *how* to ask questions of a particular audience in an appropriate manner. This language-specific model could be adapted to assist translators working in another language develop an audience-assessment program.

The following set of sample queries, arranged according to ten major elements of the production process, is likewise intended to emphasize the importance of local engagement[9] and evaluation and to suggest how to develop a suitable strategy for a specific translation project, specifically its *initial* communication setting. Some of these questions overlap; others may need to be asked several times from different perspectives. Of course, they will have to be modified and supplemented in order to adapt them to the particular situation as the project proceeds.

As you work through this section, feel free to modify the framework and its specifics to suit your own setting and the needs that your translation program is facing. That is, try to develop questions that will elicit the information necessary to carry your plans forward on a course that is in tune with the wishes of your target audience.

1. **About producers:** Whom do people perceive as being the primary producers ("owners") of this translation? Are there any potential problems or misconceptions in this respect? Do people think the real producers are "outsiders" in the form of predominant church denominations, expatriate mission agencies, broad ecumenical organizations (perhaps the local Bible Society), or the academicians and theologians on the translation committee? Which denominations of the area are most active in sponsoring the translation project, and what are their main reasons for doing so? Which churches do not wish to participate, and why? Have any church bodies set certain "conditions" that need to be satisfied before they take part in this joint venture? What are these conditions, and to what extent can they be accommodated without alienating other groups that have already signed on? On what basis or according to which criteria are the translators to be selected? What standards and qualifications have been set in this regard?

2. **About consumers:** What does a demographic study reveal about the primary target audience? For example, describe the major dialect proportions, average educational level, economic standard, living conditions, population density and distribution, growth rate, and religious affiliation. What are the commonly spoken languages? Have the main churches participated in any other joint activities before, and what was the outcome? Where is the main call for a new translation coming from—the laity, clergy, others, or all of these? Are they all willing to support the project in a tangible way? Has a written commitment to this effect been made?

3. **About purpose:** Why do people want a translation of the Bible? What do they see as its principal setting of personal or corporate use? Are they being adequately served with the translations currently available, whether in their language or a lingua franca? If not, what are the reasons for this? What kind of version do most respondents want (on the stylistic scale of *formal* versus *functional* correspondence)? Have they been sufficiently educated as to the different options that are available? If so, how has this been done? If not, why has such pre-education been deemed unnecessary? Has any serious difference of opinion arisen, and how possible is a compromise? What do the potential readers feel about the addition of paratextual helps (footnotes, cross references, headings, etc.) to accompany the text? Which of these aids do they consider to be most important? Is there any particular call for a *LiFE* version?

4. **About medium:** Will the translation be prepared only in written form, or will audio Scriptures be produced as well, either simultaneously or some time later? What is the average functional literacy rate of the primary target audience? Do the project organizers even know this crucial figure and its implications for the printed format of a published text (with respect to features such as type size and style, the use of justified right margins, and the amount of white space employed for the sake of greater legibility)? If it is below 70 percent, is a parallel literacy project being

---

[9]The UBS defines "Scripture engagement" along the following lines: It is a process that emphasizes making the Scriptures discoverable, accessible, and relevant, that is, (a) making the Bible recoverable and discoverable as sacred Scripture and (b) making Scripture accessible as the place of life-enhancing and life-transforming encounter. Would you have anything to add to this definition of "engagement" as it concerns the Scriptures? What about the literary beauty and rhetorical power of many (most) biblical texts, where does that fit into the engagement effort?

planned? Would it be helpful to produce graded Scripture portions for new or inexperienced readers to prepare them to read the standard Bible translation(s)?

5. **About text:** Can the translators or reviewers access the original text of Scripture in Hebrew or Greek? If not, how do people view this limitation? How will the team compensate for their inability in this regard, and will that satisfy the primary target audience? What sort of training program has been established both to equip translators to do the work and periodically thereafter to upgrade their skills? If the project involves interchurch cooperation, will any problems arise in connection with the Deuterocanonical books? If so, what can be done to lessen or resolve this? What resources are available to help translators study the biblical text, especially if they cannot do so in the original languages?

6. **About procedures:** What sort of daily working procedures have been established for the translation team? Has an all-inclusive "flow-chart" been prepared? Is it well understood and agreed upon by all participants in the project? How will the work be administered, monitored, and coordinated so that the rate of progress can be maintained at a satisfactory level (or better)? How will the translation team's drafts be reviewed by competent members of the target audience and evaluated by exegetical, vernacular, and communication experts? How will major differences of opinion regarding the translation or the accompanying contextual tools be resolved?

7. **About location:** Where is the project based in terms of its site of production and/or administration? Is this generally regarded as "neutral ground" in terms of church affiliation and language dialect? How easily can support staff (e.g., a translation consultant, computer specialist) who are required to visit on a regular basis reach this place? Where are the main review centers located? Do these locations adequately cover all dialect areas and major population centers of TL speakers?

8. **About time:** Has an adequate period of time for completing the entire translation project been allowed? How has the temporal framework been established in relation to the primary stages and goals of production? Does it allow sufficient time for training translators, for research and testing, and for the preparation of contextualizing materials to accompany the text? How is progress going to be monitored and assessed with regard to both quantity and quality?

9. **About the translation setting:** What is the history and current situation regarding Bible translation in the area under study? What influence on a new translation is there likely to be from other versions, whether in the same language, in related languages, or languages of wider communication in the region? Is it possible that future developments in church or state may change the present circumstances with regard to Scripture usage and needs? What other situational factors need to be considered during the planning, management, and overall support of the translation project? Is the organization of authority in the area (e.g., governmental, ecclesiastical, ethnic, or donor-related) an important consideration?

10. **About testing:** What sort of methodology and strategy of translation assessment has been agreed upon? Who will carry it out? To what extent have the testers been trained to do survey work? How will the results be gathered, categorized, judged, and acted upon? How will the quality of the testing process itself be appraised with a view towards procedural improvement and better audience involvement? How will non-literate, minority, and disadvantaged respondents be included? Has a program been put into place to continue the testing process beyond publication? How will the results of testing be recorded, evaluated, and ultimately used for a future revision of the text and additional contextualizing aids?

For reflection, research, and response:

1. At the end of section 7.1.7 you prepared a translation of Philemon and also contextualized notes for it. Now the assignment is to make a preliminary evaluation of both this translation and also its

accompanying notes. Devise a method for doing this, using the immediate resources at your disposal, including fellow students (translators), nearby church groups, people at the local market place, and so forth. Write up a report summarizing the procedures that you have used, the results that were obtained, and what recommendations you have to offer concerning your Philemon translation and notes. (You may have a week to complete this special research assignment.)

2. How much "contextualization" and audience consultation have been done in the translation program that you are most familiar with? If you feel that not enough has been done in either respect, suggest some ways in which the situation might have been improved.

3. In 2002 the Bible inventory in Chichewa was enriched by the *Chipangano Chatsopano mu Chichewa cha lero* ("New Agreement in Chichewa of Today"). You may get some idea of what type of translation this is by comparing the three following renditions of Ephesians 2:8–9 from *Chipangano Chatsopano* (CC, the 2002 translation), the *Buku Lopatulika* (BL,[10] the 1923 missionary version), and the *Buku Loyera* (BY, the 1997 popular-language edition). Idiomatic features of the BY are in bold so that they can be compared more readily.

> *Pakuti mwapulumutsidwa mwa chisomo, kudzera muchikhulupiriro—ndipo ichi sichochokera mwa inu eni, ndi mphatso ya Mulungu—osati ndi ntchito, kotero kuti wina aliyense asadzitamandire. (CC)*

> Since you have been saved in (through?) good fortune, coming in faith—and so this does not come from you yourselves, it is a gift of God—not by work, so that no one might praise him/herself.

> *Pakuti muli opulumutsidwa ndi cisomo cakucita mwa cikhulupiriro, ndipo ici cosacokera kwa inu: ciri mphatso ya Mulungu; cosacokera kunchito, kuti asadzitamandire munthu ali yense. (BL)*

> Since you are saved ones by good fortune doing with faith, and so this [is] a thing not coming from you: it is a gift of God; it is not coming from work, lest any person might praise himself/herself.

> *Ndi **kukoma mtima kwa Mulungu** kumene kudakupulumutsani pakukhulupirira. **Simudapulumuke** chifukwa cha **zimene inuyo mudaachita ai**, kupulumuka kwanu ndi mphatso ya Mulungu. **Munthu sapulumuka** chifukwa cha ntchito zake, **kuwopa kuti angamanyade**. (BY)*

> It is **the good-heartedness of God** which saved you by believing (i.e., when you believed). **You were not saved** because of **what you yourselves did, no**, your saving is a gift of God. **A person is not saved** because of his works, **fearing that he might act proudly** (or: become proud).

Which version does the CC seem to resemble more, the BL or the BY? You will observe that both the CC and its parent, the BL, are harder to understand than the BY. (The English translations fairly reflect the intelligibility of the respective Chewa originals.) What might be some of the reasons for this relatively close resemblance between the CC and the BL?

Do you have a similar state of affairs in your language setting—that is, where an old, well-loved version has ongoing influence on the current translation scene? If so, explain the pros and cons of such a situation in terms of communicating the Scriptures to a new generation of Bible consumers.

4. One method for checking the relative quality of a translation is to evaluate it *closely* and *comparatively* with several other translations (see Wendland 2000). Ideally, this is done first and foremost with respect to the original Hebrew or Greek text of Scripture, though often it is not possible for translators to do this. In any case, the basic procedure is to note where all significant *differences* of

---

[10]BL refers to Buku Lopatulika ("Sacred Book"), the old Protestant translation of the Bible in Chichewa; BY refers to Buku Loyera ("Holy Book"), the recent popular-language interconfessional version. There is also an older Catholic missionary-produced translation Malembo Oyera ("Holy Writings"). For further background, see *Buku Loyera: An Introduction to the New Chichewa Bible Translation* (Wendland 1998).

form (and possibly also content) occur among the different versions that one has at hand. Then, having identified these (perhaps marking the corresponding places in the respective texts), translators should answer the following questions: What is the precise nature of such-and-such a difference? How important is this difference in terms of correctly understanding this passage? Which text can best serve as a model for translating this passage in the TL?

Practice this comparative procedure by applying it to the four translations of Luke 2:21–22 that follow. (The second pair of texts are back-translations from original Chewa versions.) After noting and assessing all the significant differences, translate Luke 2:21–22 into YL and prepare a relatively literal back-translation into English.

> (RSV) And at the end of eight days, when he was circumcised, he was called Jesus, the name given by the angel before he was conceived in the womb. And when the time came for their purification according to the law of Moses, they brought him up to Jerusalem to present him to the Lord.
>
> (GNB) A week later, when the time came for the baby to be circumcised, he was named Jesus, the name which the angel had given him before he had been conceived. The time came for Joseph and Mary to perform the ceremony of purification, as the Law of Moses commanded. So they took the child to Jerusalem to present him to the Lord.
>
> (Old Chewa) And then when eight days were fulfilled for circumcising Him, they called His name Jesus, which that angel pronounced before He was received in the womb. And then when the days of their preparation were fulfilled, according to the big law of Moses, they climbed up with him going to Jerusalem, to go show him to the Lord.
>
> (Modern Chewa) After eight days, the child was circumcised and they called his name Jesus. This name was the very one which the angel had pronounced, before Mary became pregnant [euphemism: "before she took on her body"]. Later the time arrived for Joseph and Mary to perform the custom of cleansing following the Laws of Moses. So now they brought the child to Jerusalem to go present him to the Lord.

5. In this workbook, we have had much to say about *formatting* a biblical pericope on the printed page so that it will serve as a visual equivalent of the patterned discourse arrangement of the original text. In this respect, then, we can say that FORMAT HAS MEANING; that is, it has a certain conceptual or emotive significance that can either complement or detract from what the original author intended as part of his overall communicative strategy. What happens to the reader's text-processing ability when a format such as the following is used for Isaiah 52:11–53:7? What does the reader miss out on? What is the loss in terms of meaningfulness, let alone literariness?

> [11] Depart, depart, go out thence,
>   touch no unclean thing;
>   go out from the midst of her, purify yourselves,
>   you who bear the vessels of the Lord.
> [12] For you shall not go out in haste,
>   and you shall not go in flight,
>   for the Lord will go before you,
>   and the God of Israel will be your rear guard.
> [13] Behold, my servant shall prosper,
>   he shall be exalted and lifted up,
>   and shall be very high.
> [14] As many were astonished at him—
>   his appearance was so marred, beyond human semblance,
>   and his form beyond that of the sons of men—

¹⁵ so shall he startle many nations;
 kings shall shut their mouths because of him;
 for that which has not been told them they shall see,
 and that which they have not heard they shall understand.

53

¹ Who has believed what we have heard?
 And to whom has the arm of the Lord been revealed?
² For he grew up before him like a young plant,
 and like a root out of dry ground;
 he had no form or comeliness that we should look at him,
 and no beauty that we should desire him.
³ He was despised and rejected by men;
 a man of sorrows, and acquainted with grief;
 and as one from whom men hide their faces
 he was despised, and we esteemed him not.
⁴ Surely he has borne our griefs
 and carried our sorrows;
 yet we esteemed him stricken,
 smitten by God, and afflicted.
⁵ But he was wounded for our transgressions,
 he was bruised for our iniquities;
 upon him was the chastisement that made us whole,
 and with his stripes we are healed.
⁶ All we like sheep have gone astray;
 we have turned every one to his own way;
 and the Lord has laid on him
 the iniquity of us all.
⁷ He was oppressed, and he was afflicted,
 yet he opened not his mouth;
 like a lamb that is led to the slaughter,
 and like a sheep that before its shearers is dumb,
 so he opened not his mouth.

First, prepare a structural analysis of this well-known pericope and then propose a more effective way of formatting it in order to take its manifest literary organization into more serious consideration. Next, find another example of this sort of problem in one of the major language versions that you use, where the printed format is misleading or confusing because of the way the text is arranged on the page (e.g., paragraphing, spacing, indentation), or because of typography (e.g., capital letters, italics, or bold print), or because of the use, or non-use, of appropriate section headings for major divisions within the discourse.

6. Discuss the two opinions that are expressed in the following excerpt from Eco (2003:100):

> Schleiermacher once said: "The translator either disturbs the writer as little as possible and moves the reader in his direction, or disturbs the reader as little as possible and moves the writer in his direction. The two approaches are so absolutely different that no mixture of the two is to be trusted." I [Eco] repeat that a severe criterion perhaps holds for translation from ancient or remote literatures, but that does not hold for modern texts. To choose a target- or source-oriented direction is, once again, a matter of negotiation to be decided at every sentence.

Discuss these opinions in relation to a specifically *LiFE*-approach to translating. To what extent can Scripture translators "negotiate" with the TL constituency—and "at every sentence"?

And there are other aspects of "negotiation" as well: "Translators must negotiate with the ghost of a distant author, with the disturbing presence of a foreign text, with the phantom of the reader they are translating for" (2003:173). What does this statement mean and how does it apply to you?

7. Do you agree with the following assessment of the task of the contemporary Bible translator (from Ryken 2002:114)? Discuss this opinion from the perspective of the original text, a literary rendering of it, and a potential target audience that you know of.

> The farther history moves from Bible times, the more remote the customs, idiomatic expressions, and thought patterns of the original biblical world become for subsequent generations of readers. *In every other way*—the incidence of poetry, of formal style, of unusual or specialized vocabulary, of theological terms—the original audience faced *exactly* what the modern reader encounters when reading the Bible. (italics added)

8. Prepare a relatively *literal* as well as a *literary* translation of 2 Corinthians 5:1–3 in YL. Now test these two versions on three different people (outside of class). How well do they understand either version? Which version do they prefer and why? Write up a summary of your results.

9. Can you suggest any other categories or questions that need to be added to the list in section 7.2.1 (cf. Wilt 2002a:43–58)? In other words, what additions or modifications can you suggest to better fit your situation, if you were to carry out a testing program? Report on any audience testing that you have done in the context of Bible translation in YL.

7.2.2 Aspects of acceptability

Many translators and theorists agree that a Bible translation's general acceptability is the foremost quality they should consider. However, *acceptability* is not an easy notion to define or apply, and the model of principles and procedures outlined here offers only an approximate method for doing so. Testing for the acceptability of a translated passage may be done with reference to six distinct but interrelated criteria (see Wendland 2008b:226–228) which vary with respect to their center of attention in relation to *form* or *meaning*, on the one hand, and *SL focus*) or *TL focus,* on the other. Looking at this process from the translator's perspective, we could say that s/he needs to manifest both *loyalty* to the SL text (i.e., *accuracy + proximity*), as determined by exegetical experts, and also *accountability* in relation to the TL text (i.e., *intelligibility + idiomaticity*), as judged by recognized representatives of the primary target audience. The result would (ideally) be that the translation is seen to manifest *authenticity* with respect to the biblical text and *relevancy* in view of a specific TL audience group.

The following diagram (ibid.:226) illustrates how the six criteria relate to each other within the overall process of assessing a given translation product with regard to its overall level of *acceptability*:

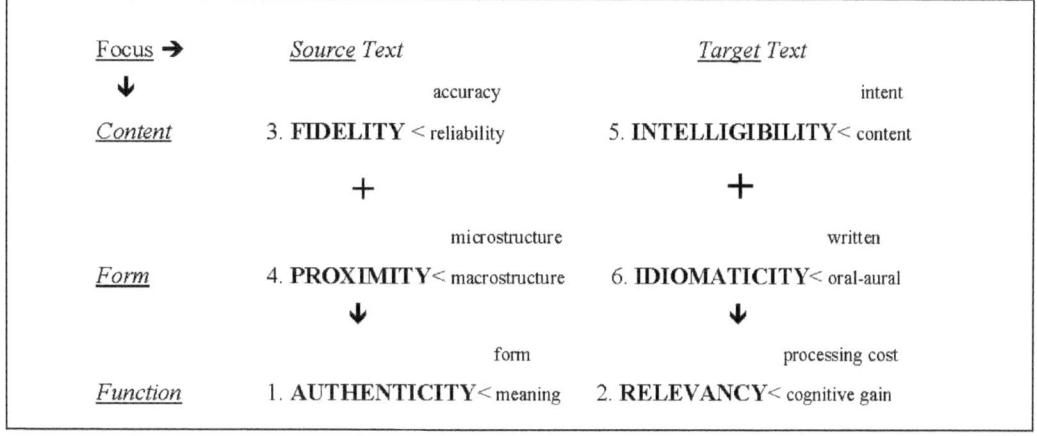

These six features are numbered in order of their *relative* priority (#1 = the highest) in the case of a Bible translation that is intended to be a literary functional-equivalent (*LiFE*) version. Other types of translation would require a reordering or a re-weighting of these characteristics.

"Authenticity" is viewed as being the most important qualitative criterion in a majority of situations (and the most difficult to assess), being the product, as it were, of a positive evaluation with regard to both semantic "fidelity" and formal "proximity" in relation to the biblical text. "Relevancy" is rated number two because it is the sum of conceptual "intelligibility" (including perceived applicability) and stylistic "idiomacity," which are the key factors involved when matters of Scripture use, or engagement, are being considered. These six criteria are perceived and judged *by members of the user community*, with a special focus or emphasis being placed on either the SL text or the TL text as the translation is intended to be utilized in a particular communicative setting (e.g., a liturgical or "pulpit" Bible, common-language translation, youth devotional version, audio-Scriptures, dramatic performance rendition, the basis for a musical composition). When these qualities are thus considered and evaluated together in relation to one another, the result will be a formal or informal (intuitive) determination of relative "acceptability" on the part of the target constituency. Acceptability, then, is the overall cover-term to designate a translation that people are generally happy with and consequently make regular beneficial use of in their everyday lives.

> » Discuss this method of rating acceptability and see if you agree; if you don't, defend the change(s) that you would propose. In any case, how would you rank these six criteria with respect to your Bible translation project?

It is important also to understand the meaning of the paired sub-features under each major criterion.

> » Write a brief definition of each one of them in the blanks below, either in English or your own language (refer to Wendland 2004:337–343, 2008:227–228 if necessary). Feel free to come up with a definition that you feel is most appropriate or applicable in the light of your own experience and the setting of the project in which you are engaged:

1. **AUTHENTICITY**

    Form: _____

    _____

    Meaning: _____

    _____

2. **RELEVANCY**

    Processing cost: _____

    _____

    Cognitive gain: _____

    _____

3. **FIDELITY**

    Accuracy: _____

    _____

Reliability: _____

_____

4. PROXIMITY

Microstructure: _____

_____

Macrostructure: _____

_____

5. INTELLIGIBILITY

Intent:_____

Content:_____

6. IDIOMATICITY

Written: _____

Oral - aural: _____

» Which of the eight sub-features were the hardest for you to define or to distinguish from another? Can you suggest a reason for this?

» In comparison with Wendland 2004b:338–340, the criterion of "authenticity," formerly listed as a quality of "fidelity," is now listed as a separate criterion on its own, in fact, the #1 consideration. Do you agree? Why, or why not?

» How do the criteria listed above for assessing "acceptability" relate to Gutt's principle of relevance (1992:24–25): "A translation is optimally relevant if it provides 'adequate contextual effects' for the intended audience yet 'without requiring unnecessary processing effort.' " In other words, where would the relevance principle operate within the above diagram? How about an additional principle; namely, that of "reliability" (see Wendland 2004b:92, fn. 111)? Is it needed? Explain your answer.

» Is it possible for a single translation to satisfy all of these criteria at once? Can it remain "faithful" to the SL text on the one hand, and "loyal" to the TL audience and project purpose on the other? Who and what must determine where the priority should lie in cases of conflict? How might the questions listed in section 7.2.1 help to resolve any issues of disagreement or ambiguity that arise? Discuss these and related issues as a group in order to compose a joint statement that specifies the goals for a particular translation project, whether actual or hypothetical.

A final comment on the criterion of *proximity* is in order here: The importance of *natural* artistic and rhetorical forms in the TL—that is, *idiomaticity*—has been stressed throughout this workbook, for this is the basis for a *LiFE* translation. But idiomaticity must always be applied in relation to its corollary, *proximity*. In other words, when seeking dynamic literary forms in the translation, translators will first of all try to discover and utilize those forms that are as near as possible to those of the biblical text. The ideal is to find form-functional *matches*. However, where this cannot be fully achieved, the closest forms should be always sought out—perhaps from the same semantic paradigm, field, or domain, provided that there is a basic similarity also in terms of connotation and other emotive associations.

This is true especially where similes and metaphors are concerned, an example being Chichewa *mphande* 'cowrie shell' for the superb 'pearl' (μαργαρίτης) of great price referred to in Christ's parable of Matthew 13:45–46. Translators should not underestimate the ability of their intended audience to learn new biblically based figures of speech. This is a real possibility where a literal rendering also happens to be potentially figurative in the TL, perhaps not with the same sense but with the definite potential to move in that direction, as in the case in Chichewa of opening a "door" (*chitseko*) of opportunity in Col. 4:3. This word is not suitable in John 10:9, however, where Jesus refers to himself as a door, because *chitseko* means "an object for shutting up"; here *khomo* "entrance way" has to be used.

Two further matters need to be considered in relation to translating a *LiFE* version: (1) artistry and (2) "alienness" (i.e., foreignness). Briefly define these two notions (see Wendland 2004b, section 10.5.6):

1. **Artistry:** _____

   _____

   _____

2. **Alienness:** _____

   _____

   _____

The diagram that follows illustrates how artistry and alienness relate to the translating of particularly difficult texts of Scripture. Note that the symbol [+] means relatively *more* artistry, while [–] represents relatively *less* artistry in terms of stylistic form or cultural alienness;[11] the scale of difficulty ranges from 1 (easiest) to 4 (most difficult):

ALIENNESS

```
    +  ←==========================================================→  –
    |        [+ / +]              |        [+ / –]              |
A   |                             |                             |
R   |           4                 |           2                 |
T   |  Exod._____ Mark_____   |  Exod._____ Mark_____   |
I   |─────────────────────────────|─────────────────────────────|
S   |        [– / +]              |        [– / –]              |
T   |                             |                             |
R   |           3                 |           1                 |
Y   |  Exod._____ Mark_____   |  Exod._____ Mark_____   |
    –
```

» In *Translating the Literature of Scripture* (2004b:345), Wendland presents four passages from Genesis that illustrate the four possibilities from *most* difficult passage to translate (+ artistry / + alienness) to least difficult (– artistry / – alienness). Identify four texts from Exodus and Mark that similarly illustrate the range of perceived translational difficulty; write their respective chapter and verse numbers in the blank lines in the above diagram.

---

[11]Overall linguistic disparity between the SL and TL also affects the relative difficulty of translation. That is, it is easier to render Psalm 23 in Arabic than in English. However, this factor is general and does not relate to specific texts.

» Then present your various choices in class to see if others agree or disagree. In cases of disagreement, what are the specific reasons given? Finally, select the most difficult texts that you have chosen from Exodus and Mark respectively and translate these passages using a *LiFE* style in YL.

For reflection, research, and response:

1. Consider the six diagnostic categories suggested in this section for evaluating a *LiFE* translation for "acceptability" in relation to other translations the TL audience is familiar with. Do these categories give you a clear enough idea of the things that need to be researched and tested in YL? If not, suggest some improvements. If necessary, also modify your understanding and use of the subsidiary notions of "artistry" and "alienness."

2. In a study of different translation styles of Psalm 23 among the Una people of Papua, Indonesia, Dick Kroneman (2004:274) says,

   > When native speakers misunderstand a particular aspect of a vernacular translation in their own language, such misunderstandings are often not just anomalies, but they make sense from the perspective of the native speakers' worldview. A lot of these misunderstandings are in fact predictable, once we have a good grasp of the cultural background and the worldview-guided hermeneutics of the informants. A lot of these misunderstandings can be avoided, if we consciously apply a frame approach to translation, and if we constantly keep in mind the cultural background of the users of the translation.

   Do you agree with this conclusion? If you agree, give an example of such contextually conditioned "meaningful misunderstanding" from your translation experience. If you do not agree, tell why not.

3. How does one deal with formal, semantic, and functional mismatches that occur in translation due to cross-cultural skewing? Kroneman (2004:274) has a suggestion:

   > Frame articulation can be done in several ways (ranging from very subtle to very rigorous solutions). It can be done by explicating the frame, by avoiding frame generalization, by choosing lexical terms that are unambiguous, by explicating the purpose of the action, by explicating implicatures, or by reordering elements.

   These are of course overlapping techniques of cognitive contextual conditioning that may be combined in practice, as in Psalm 23:5: "You pour sweet-smelling oil on my head; yes, as an honored guest you welcome me!" (ibid.:479).[12] Give an example from Psalm 23 of how you would solve such a problem in YL, yet without detracting from the literary/oratorical quality of the translation.

4. Landers (2001:160–161) proposes a series of three read-throughs for revising a first-draft literary rendering. Discuss his suggestions, which follow, in relation to your own revision method, whether actual or anticipated.

   a. **First read-through (for mechanics)**—Look for typographical errors, misspellings, inconsistent punctuation, paragraph division, section headings, verse numbering, page formatting, footnoting, glossary entries.

   b. **Second read-through (for content)**—How clearly does the sense of text come through as it is read aloud? How colloquial and appropriate do the dialogue portions sound? One might also fine-tune the choice of words and grammatical constructions during this stage, wherever the text sounds unnatural or difficult to understand.

---

[12]In chapter 13 of his informative dissertation, Kroneman presents a detailed method for checking, evaluating, and correcting various types of translation. His suggested procedures are well worth considering.

c. **Third read-through (for sonority, rhythm, euphony)**—Sound sense is the minimum requirement of a *LiFE* version. Listen to the draft as it is read aloud or else read it aloud yourself.

5. Kenneth Barker (in Scorgie, Strauss, and Voth 2003:61) expressed the aim of the NIV as follows: "we wanted *accuracy*, but not at the expense of *beauty*; we wanted *beauty*, but not at the expense of *clarity*; and we wanted *clarity*, but not at the expense of *dignity*." What do you think of this as a general translation aim? To what extent would this statement apply to the translation that you are preparing in YL (or that already exists in some other language of wider communication)?

6. In her helpful book *Translation Criticism*, Katharina Reiss makes the following recommendations (2000:47–48, italics added):

> Every translation is a compromise and an accommodation to the larger context of life. But it is a compromise that has to be weighed very carefully. Schadewaldt (1964) calls this "the art of the proper sacrifice," which should be dictated for a text by its type. Accordingly it is important to observe the order of priorities which differ for the various types of text….The translation of content-focused texts must give priority to accuracy of the information they convey, *form*-focused (or literary) texts to the structure of their content, *appeal*-focused texts to the function of their appeal, and *audio-medial* texts to the conditioning factors of non-linguistic media.

How do these observations relate to the model of translation evaluation proposed here in section 7.2.2? How do her comments pertain specifically to the various texts of the Scriptures? For example, do you see a special focus arising from her set of three text type priorities that applies to these books: Song of Songs, Leviticus, Psalms, Galatians? If so, how would this affect your translation strategy? Try to give an illustration or two.

7.2.3 Testing methods for printed Scriptures

In an oral-aural, face-to-face society an adaptable question-answer, dialogic technique forms the heart of an effective audience-testing program. (This is different from the methods employed when sampling a highly literate, well-educated constituency.) The process may be based upon, but is certainly not necessarily limited to, a set of standard questions prepared in advance and discussed first with previously trained testers. The aim is not only to elicit answers to these prepared questions, but also to encourage the frank expression of individual preferences or dislikes and the reasons for them from respondents with regard to the various oral text samples.[13] Initial questions about personal background (name, age, sex, home, occupation, education, mother tongue, church affiliation, etc.) are rather clear-cut in nature and easy to obtain, because most people are familiar with these. But "practical assessment" questions are not so straightforward and need to be flexibly applied; thus they can be modified, expanded, or deleted, as the situation may call for. In any case, for the sake of consistency, the text-testers should record all responses themselves, at least in summary form, even if the respondents have the ability to write.

The list of criteria that follows was used for the oral testing of a specially composed Chichewa *LiFE*-style translation upon a largely non-literate audience, although there was one question for readers. The purpose of the test was to compare this artistic-rhetorical version with two standard TL versions—an old "missionary" version and a recent "popular language" edition. During the questioning process (in Chichewa), an attempt was made to assess the *LiFE* translation for *acceptability* in terms of some of these criteria, with particular reference to *intelligibility* and *idiomaticity*. In the list below each criterion is briefly defined and then a key question or two suggested. (These questions will of course have to be modified and supplemented to fit the particular needs of some other project and setting.) The "why" questions, which are intended to elicit

---

[13]One way to encourage a somewhat more objective testing procedure might be to tape the reading of the different text samples by a single competent lector and then play these recordings for each person questioned. On the other hand, a live reading by the testers is probably a more effective method in view of the testees' background as members of an interactive, high-context communal society. An even more rigorous method of standardizing the assessment would be to tape all the audience responses for later analysis. This would provide greater consistency in how a given individual's answers were reported.

7.2 Testing a LiFE translation

a personal preference, are undoubtedly the most difficult for non-specialists to answer. In any case, this is simply a proposal to stimulate discussion on the preparation of effective tests and testing methods.

1. **intelligibility** (clarity of form and content): Which of the sample texts was most difficult for you to understand? Why? Which specific words caused the greatest problems for you? (These words should be recorded, either in a notebook or, to save time, on a recording device.)

2. **readability** (legibility of the print and format): Which of the sample texts is easiest to read? Why do you say so? Which words of each sample were the hardest for you to pronounce? (Is there a problem of orthography here or in how the words have been represented in print?)

3. **sonority** (the aural esthetics): Which sample text or verse sounded the "sweetest" and most "beautiful?" Why do you say this? Give an example of a TL expression from this text which sounded like a song or poem to you. (The sample texts may each have to be read aloud several times in order for people to be able to answer this question, and perhaps most of the other questions as well.)

4. **idiomaticity** (stylistic naturalness and appeal): Which text, as a whole, sounded the most "salty" or "full of pictures" to you? Give a specific example from this text that would illustrate this. (It may be necessary to first give an example of the quality that is being focused upon here. An example may also need to be given with some of the other questions too.)

5. **rhetoricity** (dynamic message impact): Which sample text included words that sound "strong" or which "pulled your heart?" Give an example from the text that was the most powerful in this respect. (Perhaps several expressions may be proposed as the question is being clarified; these can then be examined and evaluated separately once the tester's point is clear.)

6. **authenticity** (accuracy in representing Scripture): Is there an expression in any of the sample texts that seems to be "a little mistaken" or "inappropriate," or perhaps "too youthful" or "too old-fashioned" to use in the Bible? How do such words detract from the authority of the Scriptures or from the respect that is due the Word of God?

7. **memorability** (of both form and content): Which sample text would be the easiest for you to memorize or "enter into your heart?" What quality makes this possible? *(Instead of the abstract designation "quality," some actual text segments that are easy to memorize may be given.)*

These questions usually have to be asked in a certain optimal sequence,[14] which may be determined after some experience has been gained. In addition, the amount of text to be assessed at one time will vary according to the audience. For most groups, it probably works best for each sample text to be considered first as a whole, and after that each of its constituent verses individually. However, the order in which the *LiFE* sample text is presented in comparison with other translations of the same Scripture portion should be varied so that its position in the test line-up does not become predictable.

Of course, the assessment questions suggested here do not fully cover the subject. Moreover, some of the questions may turn out to be too general or elicit answers that fit several different criteria. The testers should be encouraged to consider rewording or supplementing any question that produces an insufficiently specific response or is not properly understood. But testers must seek only to clarify the question, not try to influence the respondent's reply in any way. Where possible, they should write down their added questions or explanations for future reference. Such feedback may indicate the need to revise the questionnaire so that it is less confusing and elicits more pertinent and confident answers.

---

[14]The testers should feel free to rephrase difficult-to-answer questions in order to illuminate their content or intent. But these changes, along with any additional explanation needed for clarification, must be noted along with the apparent reasons, for they may lead to the development of an improved set of evaluative queries.

For reflection, research, and response:

1. Nida and Taber (1969, chap. 8), de Waard and Nida (1986:204–209), and Larson (1984, chap. 37) all give guidelines for the testing of a translation, both before and after publication. Read through one or more of these sets of guidelines and list three of their recommendations that can help you to evaluate a translation draft.

2. Ryken's book *The Word of God in English*, subtitled *Criteria for excellence in Bible translation*, concludes with the following "principles that characterize a good Bible translation in English" (2002:287–293). Discuss these principles in relation to producing a *LiFE*-style translation in YL:

   - Accuracy
   - Fidelity to the words of the original
   - Effective diction
   - Theological orthodoxy
   - Preserving multiple meanings
   - The full exegetical potential of the original text
   - Respect for the principles of poetry
   - Excellence of rhythm
   - Dignity and beauty

3. Ralph Hill (2004:3), writing on the notion of clarity in relation to literary style and naturalness, says,

   > In the literature on Bible translation, one frequently finds that clarity in a message is discussed in terms of whether or not it has been expressed naturally. This is understandable under the code model assumption that the meaning is in the text. But a translation that is perfectly natural or idiomatic in terms of respecting all receptor language norms for style and usage can still encounter problems of clarity if the reader lacks access to those key background assumptions that the original author expected his readers to be able to access.

   Can you give an example of the problem that Hill points out—that is, a biblical text misunderstood in spite of a "clear" translation? In your experience, is this a regular occurrence or is it relatively rare with regard to your primary target audience? Explain your answer.

4. Glen Scorgie (in Scorgie, Strauss, and Voth 2003:25) lists three categories of qualities to keep in mind when assessing Bible translations:

   > Even those of us who are not experts in Bible translation can readily grasp the importance of accuracy (or faithfulness) as a translation ideal. The contributors to this volume readily agree, yet they widen our horizons by explaining that accuracy is not the only criterion by which a good translation should be measured. In different ways, they consistently speak of a second category of qualities that translators should aspire to achieve, namely, those (like clarity, naturalness, and readability) that pertain to audience sensitivity and are so essential to closing the communication loop between sender and receiver. Finally, the authors speak in different ways of a third category of qualities that are of a more esthetic and affective nature. Such ideals as beauty, orality (suitability for public reading), and dignity are also important to a translation's popularity and durability. In short, there is more to a great translation than first meets the eye.

   How many of these ideals have you been able to achieve in your translation (or in a translation that you have chosen here to evaluate)? Have you reached the third category? If so, give an illustration or two.

5. As part of an informal testing process on a draft of 1 Peter in Persian, the following procedures were followed (Thomas and Thomas 2006:127; read the entire "case description" on pp. 127–129).

7.2 Testing a LiFE translation

Evaluate this process: what can you learn from it? Have you ever carried out a similar test? If so, tell what was done and compare notes with other translation teams (if present).

> The selected oral reader for the test was a person who has good oral skills and a strong background in biblical interpretation. He was given the draft translation in a full layout that showed the letter's structure, and he worked in advance with the translator to become familiar with the new translation. The translator pointed out the relationships of the different sections of the letter to each other and the key repetitions throughout the epistle. The reader then read the text orally for the translator, who gave feedback about intonation and emphasis. The objective was for the reader to develop a style growing out of the text of the new translation rather than out of any prior interpretation of the epistle. This preparation process was helpful to the translator, who was able to see how the translation was interpreted and read by the tester. Minor changes in the translation were made at this stage.

6. As has been stressed, Bible translations need to be carefully evaluated and audience-tested for quality and effectiveness. The same thing applies to study Bibles, which include many paratextual helps that must be assessed in relation to the primary target readership. But how does one carry out such an evaluation? Charles Houser, development officer responsible for *The Learning Bible: CEV*, has made a number of recommendations (personal correspondence) which follow. Discuss them in light of a real, proposed, or hypothetical study Bible project that you are familiar with. To what extent does each of these points apply to your situation? What modifications or additions would need to be made to better suit your circumstances?

   a. An initial consultation should be undertaken with key gatekeepers, representatives of your target audience, and educational and publishing professionals to survey the market and establish a vision for your study Bible. Be sure to document and summarize your findings. This documentation should consist of both a wish list ("If funding were bottomless, our study Bible will include…") and a list of very practical do's and don'ts from which you can develop an Editorial Philosophy or Guiding Principles document. Be alert to who the best contributors to the consultation are (whether staff, professional colleague, or denominational volunteer); these people can continue to provide helpful (and hopefully free) guidance and feedback as unexpected challenges arise and prototypes are developed.

   b. If you can afford it, test concepts and prototypes with focus groups at key points in the development phase. ABS tested prototypes of Ruth and, based on feedback, tested a more extensive prototype of Matthew. We queried the focus groups on specific things like the use of icons, the number of icons to be used, the actual design of the icons, the page layout, internal artwork and captions, illustration styles, the use of headings and outlining, the text of book introductions, reflection questions, sidebar notes, and articles. Feedback at this early stage was helpful in (a) confirming what we believed to be strengths and (b) enabling us to revise or adjust things that weren't working for the target audience. While a professional market research firm would have the professional distance to conduct careful, unbiased research, and the skill to document and summarize the results and make meaningful recommendations, I believe it is possible to do a certain amount of testing on one's own at a lesser expense by going directly to church groups.

   c. In addition to focus group testing, it is nice to do "user testing." ABS did this after publishing the full Learning Bible. A certain number of people were given the Learning Bible and allowed a period of time to read it and become familiar with its features. At the end of the "use period" (three or four weeks, I believe), users were telephoned and taken through a questionnaire to find out their impressions. This was done by a professional market research group who had screened the users to make sure they were typical of the intended target group. Again, it might be possible to do user testing without the services of a professional market research firm. Also, it would be advantageous to conduct user testing with a smaller, but substantial, portion of the product (such as a complete Gospel) in advance of publication so that negative features could be corrected before the full Bible is published.

7. Formulate a set of questions in YL that you or your fellow translators might use when testing the draft of a *LiFE* rendition that you have prepared. You may wish to reword some of the questions suggested above, or add others that you used when evaluating your translation and notes for Philemon (see ex. 1, section 7.2.1; cf. Wilt and Wendland 2008:chap. 10). Compose the questions in English first; then go back over them and make a note of the ones that would need to be restructured when expressed in YL. Why would this be necessary culturally, socially, linguistically, or for translational reasons? Explain, with an example or two.

7.2.4 Testing nonprint and nonconventional Scripture products

In our survey of semiotics (section 1.2) and mental-space theory (section 7.1.2), we saw that the total concept that develops during productive thought and purposeful communication, is the collective outcome not only of the occurrence of significant "signs," whether individual or in combination, but also of the "context" that surrounds the human thinker or communicator. The semiotic signs may be represented and transmitted in the form of any sensory medium—graphological, aural, visual, electronic, or musical. Context is not a concrete physical reality, as relevance theorists have correctly pointed out, but a mental one, consisting of memory, the present concrete setting, the current discourse (or ostensible verbal signs), plus any other sensory stimuli that happen to impinge upon one's perception at the moment. To simplify all these possible influences, we might employ the notion of cognitive "frames of reference" (see Wilt 2002a: chap. 2), according to which different kinds of experiences and knowledge are collected, categorized, and organized for use.

Now we will apply our simplified model of conceptual representations to the analysis and evaluation of a musical production, a medium of communication that is of primary significance to many physically and sociologically "remote" audiences today:

> **Scenario**: A musical communication event conveyed by a commercial CD: *WOW Christmas* (Nashville, WORD Entertainment, 2002)—a selection by *tobyMAC* entitled, "This Christmas," now broadcast via a local FM radio station to listeners in Lusaka, Zambia.
>
> The song, which functions like a modern parable, is composed in a "soft" rap style and features a composite musical text, with a lead female voice singing variations on the first stanza of the familiar Christmas carol "Joy to the World." This alternates with the rhythmic narration by *tobyMAC* (the male lead's stage name) of a story line about "Johnnie," a nine-year-old orphan boy, who has just been adopted into a loving family on the day before Christmas. The key theme of the song repeatedly asserts that the God who gives "joy to the world" is also "the Father of the fatherless," who will not forsake "widows and orphans in their distress." The song as a whole makes a general as well as a specific appeal: "You ain't livin' till you choose to give" and "Don't forget children who have no home—who are all alone—at Christmas!"

Conceptual Network	Features
Source (general) domain 1:	Backing up the song's story is an assortment of Scripture passages (especially from the OT) that enjoin help for the helpless of society, epitomized by widows and orphans. In particular, one line of the song paraphrases Psalm 146:9a–b: "The LORD watches over the strangers; he upholds the orphan and the widow." Implicit is the condemnation of all people who fail to help, and instead oppress these unfortunates as in Ezekiel 22:7.

7.2 Testing a LiFE translation

Source (local) domain 2: Familiar Christmas hymns and carols, especially the focal refrain of "Joy to the World." The Christmas holiday season, including its various cross-cultural customs and ritual practices, is as popular (and commercialized) in Zambia as anywhere else in the Christian-influenced world.

There is a metaphorical musical sub-frame within this source domain that superimposes a modern rhythmic style upon the old, well-known Christmas carol, thus contemporizing and to a certain extent also localizing the melody (since the rap sound is popular among Zambian youth today).

Target (general) domain 1: The generally unhappy circumstances of institutionalized orphans all over the world, even in the most affluent of societies. The depressing, often debilitating effects of their situation are presumably worse during those times of the year when family celebrations are enjoyed.

Target (local) domain 2: The plight of orphans is especially pressing in those parts of the world, like Lusaka, where poor social, economic, medical, and health conditions, including the AIDS pandemic, force many of them to live in the vanguard of the vulnerable, as "street kids," without any home or hope at all and battling every day just to stay alive.

Generic (common) domain: Concepts, including many emotions and memories, that are associated with Christmas, Christmas carols, and the Christmas story in contrast to those evoked by widows and orphans and the various hardships and deprivations that they generally face; a less overt reference to the dependence of the needy upon deeds of charity for any amelioration of their miserable situations

Blended domain: The complex combination of biblical allusions to orphans, Christmas imagery and carols, and the pathetic situation of orphans in Zambia creates an especially powerful metaphoric conceptual blend that motivates the imperative message of this song. It is not just about piously reflecting upon the original Christmas event or celebrating the holidays. Rather, the song appeals for an overt charitable response from listeners who are enjoying its rhythms and lyrics: go out and do something about the sad state of orphans in the community. Perhaps the song speaks most insistently to people who live in societies where orphans are not only lonely and neglected, but are in fact suffering terribly and dying daily (cf. the two target domains). The motivation is firmly based on many biblical commands as well as on the "spirit of the season" (cf. the two source domains).

» Consider a similar scenario (real or imagined) in your vernacular setting, for example, a song that has been composed to popularize a particular audio or printed portion of Scripture. Then, following the model above, draw up a "conceptual network" that summarizes the communication process, with special reference to the use of figurative language. Make a note of any actual or hypothetical problems that developed, along with your proposals for avoiding these in a future revised production. If you do not have a musical model like this to draw upon, then try to anticipate the potential problem areas that face the song's producers and suggest what might be done to mitigate their negative effects.

It is important to recognize the communicative power of music and song, for this was obviously very important in the original setting of Scripture composition and transmission (e.g., the Psalms; cf. Col. 3:16). However, musical styles (and their "meanings") are not universal; they are strongly influenced by the sociocultural setting in which the songs are composed. Similarly, the relative appreciation of the same music may be very different as one moves from one cultural context to another. The significance of the code of music for Christian communication has been well stated by Olivia Mather (2003:8):

> Does music have inherent meaning? Do particular words come with ready-made associations? The testimony of music history, even church music history, would seem to say no, that instead it is we who link sonorous material and values. In the past decade or so, many musicologists have come to see musical meaning as something like linguistic meaning. Just as most words have conventional relationships to the things they represent, so do musical details. And just as particular words make sense only in the context of their home language, so musical meaning is contingent upon setting, not a "universal language." For example, a major chord or key can signify an almost endless number of emotions or attitudes: triumph, reason, anger, stability, and instability, to name a few….Therefore, when we evaluate "the music itself," we must remember that its connotations are based on custom and tradition, which can change depending on circumstance.
>
> For some, music's contingency implies that we can never understand music of other times, peoples, or places. Admittedly, we will always lose some things in translation, but we can learn much by assessing music in its social context and inspecting our preexisting perspectives. Remembering that we—as individuals, a local church, or a society—participate in assigning music's values opens the door for meaningful dialogue across musical differences in the church.

As Mather suggests, there are often great differences of opinion among Christians with regard to the sort of music that is deemed "suitable" for the public or even private worship and praise of God. "Christian contemporary music" (CCM) for some believers is considered by some to be eminently unsuitable due to the alleged conceptual "corruption" that occurs when popular secular musical styles and rhythms are combined with Christian, even biblical, lyrics. Nevertheless, you can find CCM nowadays appealing to people who appreciate virtually any modern pop fashion: hard rock, soft rock, country and western, reggae, rap, rhythm and blues, alternative, big band, even new age.

Such is the case not only in Western music; a similar situation prevails in countries and cultures all over the world—throughout Africa, for example. This is not just a matter of personal taste, for some conservative denominations in Africa have seen fit to prohibit, on cited scriptural grounds, all forms of modern music, and often the associated instruments as well (e.g., electric guitars, organs, and drums). There is obviously a generational, an ethnic, and a denominational gap that variously divides African Christians on the issue of music. Unfortunately, this may also be a reflection of earlier cultural differences, harking back to the first missionaries who banned most types of indigenous African music as being implicitly, if not overtly, "pagan." Mather's words above, coupled with a careful study of the biblical text and context, are a good basis for some serious cognitive and emotive "frame adjusting." People must learn to consult and compromise with one another in seeking more tolerant, well-informed attitudes towards the right and the wrong of musical communication in the diverse Christian world community.

Perhaps a different theoretical model or orientation may help us to create the necessary guidelines for the challenging field of new-media Scripture translations: In section 2.1 we briefly touched upon the notion of "conceptual metaphors" that is, those which originate in common human experience and serve to organize the thought and expression of groups of people as well as the themes and motifs of a given literary corpus or work of art. Just as the correct identification of such metaphors is important for Bible translators (since they will want to retain them and the related imagery to the extent possible in their vernacular version), so it is important for producers of nonprint Scripture media. These organizing or dominant images operate on various levels of abstractness in discourse, from the most general (e.g., STATES ARE LOCATIONS, CHANGES

ARE MOVEMENTS, PURPOSES ARE DESTINATIONS, and MEANS ARE PATHS)[15] to the very specific (e.g., THE CHURCH IS A BODY in the Pauline literature, LIFE IS A TRIAL in James, or CHRISTIANS ARE ALIENS in 1 Peter).

> » Do you agree that the general conceptualizations pertaining to these biblical books are valid?
>
> » Do you have any modifications to suggest with respect to either the general examples or the specific ones?
>
> » Name another key conceptual metaphor found in one of Paul's letters and in one of the OT prophets.

Bible media specialist Kenneth J. Thomas (2000:4–5) has suggested four main principles for the identification of basic conceptual (controlling) metaphors in the literature of Scripture:

1. Controlling metaphors are related to language used throughout a particular book. Other figurative terms and metaphors are used that are related to the concepts presented by the controlling metaphors and are understood within their overall scope.

2. Controlling metaphors use terms familiar to the audience. They are taken from traditional language used by the community and are in continuity with past experience and usage.

3. Controlling metaphors are means for understanding the major theme and purpose of the whole writing. They provide a unifying way to understand the various parts and subjects of the book.

4. Controlling metaphors are dynamic in that they enable new aspects of the concepts presented by the authors to be understood.

Correctly identifying these metaphors is essential for visual as well as vocal representations of the text. The goal is to seek out the closest functional equivalents and thus unify the passage *visually* (or *aurally*) for the audience and stimulate their thinking in the direction of the biblical author's intended theme and sub-themes. The functional equivalents will often have to be verbally *contextualized* in terms of a local sociocultural perspective so that they can be more readily understood and applied in real-life settings. In Citonga, for example (a major Bantu language of Zambia), the "body" metaphor must be specified as "human"; a different word is used to designate "animal" (i.e., mammal) bodies.

Thomas (ibid.:9–10, italics added) proposes the following three guidelines for determining appropriate functional equivalents of metaphors as part of preparing for, say, a video production of a biblical pericope:

1. In relation to the biblical metaphor, the functional equivalent image should represent *the same concept as the biblical metaphor*. If possible, it should be one that has some historical continuity with the biblical text, even as particular biblical controlling metaphors regularly have precedents in earlier biblical material.

2. In relation to the audience, the functional equivalent image should be *familiar in contemporary culture* and have associations that are congenial with the biblical concept to be represented. The image should be coherent with the metaphorical values of the recipient culture.

3. The functional equivalent image should be *the primary visual image* that occurs throughout a video. The viewer should understand that this image is a key element for interpretation and understanding. It will be a challenge to find appropriate images that not only unify and provide a key to understanding but also stimulate viewers to ponder their significance. Hopefully, these images can perform a transformative function in the thinking and life of the viewers.

---

[15]Such statements are conventionally symbolized like this: LOCATIONS > STATES, where the wedge (>) indicates the direction of the extension of meaning. A biblical example is TEMPERATURE > EMOTION (general), FIRE > ANGER (specific), e.g., "The LORD's anger [nose] burned" (Num. 32:13).

Thomas then applies these guidelines to "The Neighbor," an American Bible Society video based on Luke 10:25–37 (ibid.:11):

> For the video transmediazation of the Parable of the Good Samaritan in Luke 10:25–37 by the American Bible Society, the research team of biblical scholars identified "journey" as the key metaphor of the passage. Accordingly, a conscious effort was made by the media specialists to provide a functional equivalent for this metaphor in the video. The figure of a train and railroad tracks was chosen to represent this concept in "The Neighbor." Had the biblical scholars begun their work from the perspective of the entire Gospel rather than an isolated passage, a different result of their study would have been likely. It now seems to me, on the basis of a study of the controlling metaphor in the Gospel of Luke and the related key concept of compassion in this parable, that the journey is a literal subject of the parable but not a key concept. The visualization of a journey does not help the viewers to discern that receiving—metaphorically "seeing"—the Kingdom of God is marked by compassion.

» Would you agree that the key metaphoric concept in Luke's Gospel is "the kingdom of God,"—and that "seeing" is the controlling (conceptual) metaphor of this particular parable?[16]

» If so, what are some closely related themes and major metaphors?

» If not, what would you suggest as being Luke's controlling metaphor, or that of the parable?

» Keeping Thomas's criticism in mind, what would you say are some functionally equivalent contemporary images that you could employ to help a general audience visualize the Good Samaritan parable in your socio-religious setting? Briefly explain your thinking.

» In other words, how would you endeavor to visually match the original content and intent of Christ's story with the thought world and experience of your culture and environment?

By their very nature Scripture products that are published in a nonprint medium or a novel kind of format call for a more dynamic manner of expressing the discourse. This is true especially where there is much character dialogue or other form of direct speech, as in a psalm or prophetic oracle.

One appropriate medium for a vivid, even colloquial *LiFE* rendition would be Bible comics or their more extensive upgrade, "graphic novels."[17] A sample of this medium is the page from "Samson and Delilah" that follows.[18] In the white speech bubbles a verbally vigorous but succinct style of speech is the best accompaniment for the striking visual illustrations. Perhaps several sociolects would be needed to properly portray the different backgrounds of the various speakers. For example, the TL constituency might expect Samson to talk quite differently from Delilah because of their disparate ethnic, social, and religious origins (although for some audiences different sociolects may be too sophisticated a technique to apply in a comic book). For an audio or audiovisual production of this pericope, however, a vocal differentiation would certainly be needed.

---

[16] Thomas (2000:7) notes, "The concept of the Kingdom of God in Luke falls into three main sections: chapters 1 to 3 relating the Kingdom of God to Old Testament expectations of the coming of the Messiah; chapters 4 to 19 demonstrating the presence of the Kingdom of God in the life and teaching of Jesus; chapters 20–24 giving the teaching of Jesus about the future consummation of the Kingdom of God." As for the crucial importance of 'sight' in this parable, study Lk. 10:31–33, especially v. 33.

[17] A graphic novel may be defined as "a species of comics which like picture books, are print materials in which pictures and narrative are joined in one interdependent format." Such a novel typically "presents time as unfolding, showing process in static panels that read from upper left to lower right on the page" (Burke and Lebrón-Rivera 2003:2).

[18] A depiction of Judg. 16:6–7 reproduced from Burke and Lebrón-Rivera (2003:14). The actual comic illustration is copyrighted by the American Bible Society and used here by permission.

Samson and Delilah

An idiomatic *LiFE*-style translation would be highly appropriate for use in any sort of *oral-aural* or *visual* presentation of the biblical text, whether an audiocassette, CD, video, or DVD. Due to the sensory nature of the medium, a more vigorous application of functional equivalence would be desirable with regard to the text's *literary* properties, including its specific genre-related attributes. Of course, the text's *auditory* features also need to be taken into consideration—for example, tempo, timbre, tone color, pitch, loudness, and rhythm in relation to the specific characters being depicted in a narrative, or the authorial voice that proclaims the words of a psalmist, prophet, or indeed Yahweh himself. In the case of Samson, for instance, the vocal sound would need to evoke the acoustic impression of some extra large, strong man—perhaps one who is not too bright. Delilah's speaking part would have to be played by a young woman with an enticing, coquettish voice, a caricature typical of the particular TL. These roles must be carefully researched in advance and then cast accordingly. A mismatch could color the text in a negative way, as happened in the Chichewa version of the *Jesus* film, in which the character of Christ speaks in a voice that is much too high and weak, thus detracting noticeably from the impression and impact of his words during his various dialogues.

A nonconventional production is a good opportunity for translators to experiment with a total genre-for-genre *LiFE* translation, using a recognized TL equivalent to represent the biblical text. This might work out especially well for the distinctively poetic texts such as the Proverbs, Psalms, Song of Songs, and Lamentations, where close vernacular correspondents are sought in the area of sapiential, panegyric, amorous, and funerary styles, respectively. The local models may need to be adapted in certain stylistic respects to render them suitable for public Scripture performance, but this should not be too difficult provided that expert verbal artists are available as translators or consultants and enough time is set aside for research and field-testing of experimental editions. For example, selected portions of Proverbs could be composed either in the form of a didactic vernacular song or with an engaging musical background as part of a literary piece that deals with various AIDS-related issues (e.g., Prov. 5–7). An oratorical speech genre might be used to accompany a dynamic poetic rendition of the text of 1 Corinthians 13 aimed at newly married couples. The book of Ruth could be readily transposed into an indigenous narrative style suitable for a public dramatic performance style appropriate for a dramatic "stage" presentation, e.g., at an outdoor Christian "camp meeting." An adaptation of the Song of Songs, this time composed in a lyric pop format, might be very appealing to the young adult members of a choir to add to their repertory.

Of course, in the case of each of these more innovative productions, the aim is not "art for art's sake." Rather, the challenge is to forge a harmonious integration of form (structure, style), content, and function in the service of re-presenting the Scriptures more effectively for particular needs and Aaudience groups. The artistic and rhetorical resources of the TL are thus exploited as a means of rendering certain portions of God's Word in ways that are both meaningful and relevant to the pressing social and spiritual circumstances that listeners find themselves confronting on a daily basis. The goal is not merely to attract people to the translation, but to encourage them through a more vibrant style of discourse to take their Bible study to a deeper level of understanding and personal application.

For reflection, research, and response:

1. Carefully critique some recent Bible Society media product that features a great deal of music, following the model suggested in this section. Are Western musical styles prominent in audio- and videocassette productions meant for local listeners, or is there evidence of domestication of song styles and melodies? Is there a careful synthesis of music or vocal rhythm with the Bible text? Evaluate the product in terms of complementing, competing, or just plain confusing emotive frames that these musical styles and tunes seem to evoke when coupled with the selected Scripture texts which they accompany.

2. In chapter 1 we considered the importance of adopting the correct "frame of reference" (which may be multiple) for interpreting any text, whether religious or secular. What were the four frames of communication that were discussed (section 1.6)?

   Consider the following text of a contemporary song (which of course really needs to be heard as sung and performed).[19] It reads throughout like a typical "Country and Western" lyric—until you reach the very last line. How does this pointed closure change your cognitive perspective on the entire song?

   > Thomas Jefferson Washington—Is only eight years old.
   > He lives with his mother—In an old abandoned car they call home—Since his daddy has been gone.
   > From the windy city skyline—It's easy to look down—On the miracle mile.
   > That might as well be a million miles—From Tommy's side of town.
   >
   > > And there are far-away places—That I would like to think
   > > Keep all the world's suffering—At a safe arm's length.
   > > But I can't keep pretending—When I only have to look as far—As my own backyard!

---

[19] "My Own Backyard" by Geoff Moore, from the CD by the same title © 1999 Fore Front Records.

> Tonight a little girl named Jesse—Will find it hard to sleep
> On a desert reservation—Without the American dream—And without enough to eat.
> Sometimes you will find her—Staring at the sky—Wondering why so many things
> Have to be so hard in her life—And Jesse starts to cry.
>
>> And there are far-away places—That I would like to think
>> Keep all the world's suffering—At a safe arm's length.
>> But I can't keep pretending—When I only have to look as far—As my own backyard!
>
> I will sing of compassion—I will sing of charity.
> I will sing to remember—That in the very least of these—**It is Jesus that we see!**

Thus the singer's parable strikes home with the sympathetic and setting-sensitive hearer. Do you see any implications in this little example for the audio (-visual) Scripture-media products that your Bible society or translation organization is planning? Share any insights that you may have.

Now for a contemporary song text that is much closer to the original, namely, Psalm 51:1-9:[20]

> God be merciful to me; on thy grace I rest my plea.
> Plenteous in compassion thou, blot out my transgressions now.
> Wash me, make me pure within; cleanse, oh cleanse me from my sin.
> My transgression I confess; grief and guilt my soul oppress.
> I have sinned against thy grace, and provoked thee to thy face.
> I confess thy judgment just; speechless, I, thy mercy trust.
> I am evil, born in sin; thou desirest truth within.
> Thou alone my Savior art; teach thy wisdom to my heart.
> Make me pure, thy grace bestow; wash me whiter than the snow.
> Gracious God, my heart renew; make my spirit right and true.
> Thy salvation's joy impart; steadfast make my willing heart.
> Broken, humbled to the dust, by thy wrath and judgment just…
> From my sins, oh hide thy face; blot them out in boundless grace.

What sort of musical style would create a suitable frame of reference for your hearing and reacting favorably to this rendition? Would the modern rock-style of *Jars of Clay* appeal to you? Why or why not? To what extent does the specific setting in which you hear this song as performed make a difference (e.g., whether during public worship or driving along in your car)?

Is your translation agency engaged in transposing the Scriptures to music in this way? Why/why not? If so, what are some of the problems that you have encountered—and promising solutions found?

3. The following are several excerpts from a case study of ethnomusicology in service of Bible translation and Christian communication (Neeley and Hall 1997). As you read through this, reflect on your own translation setting: Have you ever participated in a music-based translation exercise like this, or has one ever been carried out in the history of your project? If so, make is list of the main similarities and differences. If not, does such a project have some potential in your situation? Give reasons why—or why not. If you work among a largely literate society, tell whether you think this type of translation program would (or would not) work and why. Would a more dynamic (*LiFE*-style) translation be appropriate or not? Explain. Would you agree with the conclusion of the last paragraph below? Perhaps that can serve as the basis for a round-table class discussion on the subject of Scripture translation through song.

---

[20] "God be Merciful to Me" by *Jars of Clay* from the CD *Redemption Songs* © 2005 BMG Music.

The Dagomba people (Ghana) number between 600-700,000 and live in over 1000 villages and a few larger towns. A majority of them claim some allegiance to Islam, and most are illiterate. The percentage of Christians is less than 3%. The churches are now seeing the great value in using Scripture songs composed in local music styles to reach the more than half-a-million Dagomba people with the good news of the Gospel. Everyone likes Bamaaya songs, old and young, educated and illiterate; even the Muslims pay attention to the content of the message because they thoroughly enjoy the form of the message.

For this day workshop, we had three experienced local composers lead the 50 participants in making new songs. Each composer chose some Bible verses, then sat under a tree with their composing group. First they decided which part of the verse would be the choral response line; then the lead singer worked on fitting the rest of the verse between the response lines. With some practice, the groups could rough out a song in a few minutes. Then the song was revised and polished for half an hour or so....

The third composer was Peter Denaba, an accomplished musician on the gonje fiddle. This instrument is a single stringed bowed lute. The resonator is a half calabash covered with the skin of a monitor lizard; the string and bowstring are made of horsehair. To accompany that unique sound of horsehair being bowed atop lizard skin came a song made from these words: *"God reconciled everything to himself through Christ. He made peace with everything in heaven and on earth by means of his blood shed on the cross" (Col 1:20).*

Can you imagine the power of these words sung over and over to a Dagomba melody if you were a Dagomba person?...As the composing groups worked under 3 different trees, the Muslim townspeople came out to see the music being made. At least 200 people roamed between the musicians, waiting to see what would happen next. This is an incredible way to get the Scriptures heard: pick a Bible verse, sit under a tree with your instrument and some friends, and 200 people show up to listen to God's Word in song! Our workshop coincided with a local feast day in this village, so it was a great opportunity to have what turned into an indigenous Christian music festival!...

Music has a unique ability to get to the depth of the human heart, and to express those depths in outward form. Every culture in the world has a unique music system, just like it has a unique language and set of customs. Redeeming part of a culture's music system for God can be an important part of redeeming people for God. Let us encourage the nations to "be glad and sing for joy!" (Psalm 67:4)

4. Consider the possibility of composing Zechariah's words in Luke 1:68–79 poetically and musically in a style that would be appropriate for a popular audiocassette or CD for the young people of your culture. What kind of music would be needed to effectively complement the words of this hymn? Discuss the feasibility of such a cross-media project and the difficulty of carrying it out. What problems would be faced? How might these be overcome in your particular sociocultural setting and artistic tradition? Draw up a systematic work plan for such a project.

5. Consider the associations that people in your culture think of when they hear voice qualities that differ in terms of loudness, tempo, pitch, and intonation. Compare them with the voices typically heard in Western dramatizations and readings of Scripture. What differences, if any, come to mind? How can vocal features be effectively researched and evaluated? Suggest a possible method. In the account of Jesus' healing of a blind man in John 9 what sort of voice should Jesus speak with? What about the voice of the healed blind man, or the Pharisees (a representative speaker)? Outline some "production notes" that you would want to direct to a team engaged in preparing a radio-worthy audiocassette of the John 9 account.

6. Study E. R. Hope's "Translating Poetry for Oral Presentation" (in Zogbo and Wendland 2000:179–184). Summarize Hope's main production pointers as they apply to Isaiah 5:1–7. Does this give you enough information to compose a musical rendition of this text in YL? If not, discuss the project in class in order to derive a methodology that you feel confident in using. Then give it a try, working in several teams, making a selection (as assigned by your instructor) from one or more of these texts: 1 Samuel 2:1–10, Psalm 1, Psalm 146, Luke 1:46–55, Luke 1:68–79, 1 Corinthians 13, Philippians 2:6–11, Revelation 4:11,

5:9–10, 5:12, 5:13b. Also consider voice quality as in exercise 3. Evaluate your poetic song compositions in a joint public performance. Who should be the judges and what criteria of assessment should they apply? Be specific in your recommendations.

7. In his detailed study of the process of "transmediazation" during the production of a Scripture video, Kenneth Thomas (2000:11) points out the following:

> It is recognized that the significance of any image cannot be controlled, since images are multivalent. Each person in the audience will be guided by her/his own experience in creating the meaning of images. Thus, rather than expecting the video producer to deliver specific meanings by means of images, it is more realistic to think of using images to establish connections with the viewer as a participant in the construction of meaning. Through the images chosen for biblical videos, producers engage in a dialogue with the audience.

How can such a "dialogue" between Scripture-text producers and consumers be facilitated so that the TL audience will be drawn closer to the conceptual scenario that is supposed to be evoked by a specific Bible pericope? Review Thomas's three guidelines for discovering relevant functional equivalents for metaphoric imagery, and then tell what pictorials you would suggest to illustrate key aspects of the parable of the rich man and Lazarus (Luke 16:19–31). How would these images relate to those that you proposed for Luke's "kingdom of God" metaphor? How would you go about testing such visuals in an objective manner?

What sort of musical background ought to be featured in a video based on Luke 16:19–31? Briefly describe the musical style you would choose. What sort of feelings, attitudes, and overall mood would you seek to evoke? Would the style of music need to change during the course of the parable narrative? How? (Be specific.)

8. In some cultural settings, the best means of contextualizing a biblical text for its primary audience is to present it orally and in a narrative style. This often involves the interspersing of songs or choruses between the different voices that articulate the text. Consider Johnson's (2003:11) conclusion to an experiment that was carried out along these lines for the Kisi people, a largely oral-aural society in Liberia:

> Basic to working with oral societies is to have an understanding of their oral communication traits. Oral communicators prefer passing on information in the form of narratives/stories. They are not as adept at handling information that comes to them by other means….Narrative styles are what oral communicators use to process and carry around information. This factor explains some of the success with the Luke-Song cassette. Our intent while doing it was to provide a narrative/story approach to the entire cassette….
>
> Built into the presentation was the common feature of songs that come out of the story and reinforce it, a common storytelling method among the people. A method they use in their traditional storytelling is carried over into the presentation of Scriptures. This feature follows their cultural methods of presenting information. It uses a method to which they are accustomed.
>
> Because of the love for songs in the culture, the cassette becomes more popular and attracts more listeners. The use of the songs involves the listeners while listening to the tapes. Invariably the listener sings along with the song, participating and simultaneously learning Scripture. This participatory approach helps hold their interest and assists them in remembering the Scriptures presented. The person is not only receiving information/Scripture, but is becoming an active part in the message and becomes open to receive more information.
>
> The narrative approach, reading or telling the Scriptures in a storytelling method, makes the text easy for the non-literate to learn it. It suits their learning style. They memorize the songs, then

follow it up by memorizing the Scriptures related to the song and the material around these verses. Soon they have learned the entire section of Scripture. The songs are the catalyst for listening to the tape and the motivating factor to listen to it again. With each repeated listening to the tape, more Scripture is learned and memorized. As a result their learning follows the way people in oral societies learn.

Would this method work and be appreciated in your culture? Tell why or why not. Would you suggest any modifications? What quality-control measures need to be put into effect? Can you adapt this method to suit a prophetic or epistolary text, for instance, by interspersing Bible narrative and/ or other contextual bridge material as background? Explain your answer and write out a sample "script" for an audiocassette or CD production of the letter of Jude. (The instructor may substitute a different text.)

Is it possible to take a well-done audio Scripture product and transcribe it so that the result is a naturally written Scripture text? What are the obstacles to doing this successfully? In other words, how does an idiomatic oral style often differ from a popular written style? On the other hand, what devices are available to a writer that cannot be used by an oral performer? How might such an oral-to-written adaptation be enhanced by applying a specifically *literary* methodology to the task?

9. A promising new methodology for testing and revising a translation draft or trial publication comes from the discipline of "performance criticism" (Rhoads 2006; the following quotes are from a downloaded version of this article, which should be read in its entirety if possible).

> The overwhelming experience of the earliest Christians was oral/aural in the context of a predominantly oral culture. Virtually all of the Christian traditions were shared in formal and informal contexts of storytelling and letter-sharing, for most people without a direct connection to manuscripts....Even when the traditions were written down, they were put to writing in the service of orality. Letters were dictated as performances and then were used as scripts for performance.

> Evaluate the thesis being supported by the preceding citation—do you agree? Explain your answer. If you agree, what implications do you see here for Bible translating in your setting of communication? Rhoads continues:

> Because the writings were composed to be performed, they yield clues and suggestions for performance...[T]hese may be taken as "stage directions" for the performer to modulate the voice, to act out a gesture, or to express an emotion or to offer "cues" for the audience to respond. Add to this the nuances of speech suggested by sarcasm or irony or rhetorical questions or commands or appeals...Length of sentences and number of clauses serve as directions for the pace and rhythm of performances.

> [D]iscourse analysis gives a thorough scanning of the possible grammatical and semantic patterns of a text and, in so doing, identifies the many stylistic features and configurations of discourse that provide structure to a text.... What, for example, would have been the impact of chiastic patterns or chain sentences or parallelism or transitions upon the temporal, aural experiences of hearers....Only a little has been done with word order...—foregrounding and backgrounding, emphasis, elision, chiasm of sounds, audible parallelisms and transitions, verbal threads, and so on. Other oral/aural features of texts will include clues for performance, such as repetition, parallelism, onomatopoeia, hook words, and mnemonic devices....

> [I]t is now incumbent upon translators to make a further distinction, namely, the distinction between translations for reading and translations for performance (in literate as well as oral cultures). ... The act of translating for oral performance itself is a discipline that leads one to notice aspects of the text often overlooked—repetition, word associations, rhyme and rhythm, historical presents, word order, verbal threads, alliteration, and so on....

Furthermore, might not translations be organized on the page so as to reflect the rhythms, pauses, and pace of a translation?... What about footnotes that offer suggestions for performance? ... If the biblical writings were composed for performance, then we certainly should use performances to interpret these writings. The act of performing helps the interpreter to discern the possible meanings of the texts.... Performance expands the possibilities for interpretation and allows us to act out different exegetical interpretations. Performances can also test interpretations, whether they will "play."

We have been working with a number of these different oral/aural features in this workbook and have suggested that functional equivalents be used in a *LiFE*-style translation (if that is the agreed *Skopos*). Rhoads is here urging translation committees involved in such a project—preparing a version for *oral* presentation, not simply a silent reading to oneself—to test the actual *performance quality* of their text. To do this, one must pay sufficient attention to the nonverbal "subtext" of the text—those meaningful aspects of the discourse that are expressed by intonation, pace or pause, pitch, volume, stress, gestures, facial expressions, posture, body language, and the like. To what extent have you considered such features either when composing or testing and revising your translation? Do you feel that it is important to do this? If so, tell how you might incorporate some of these "performance features" during the various stages of your translation program.

Whether your team is currently in a position to do this or not, try your hand at composing a performance-ready, interpretive version of the well-known pericope of James 2:14-26. The Greek text has been reproduced below along with the NIV translation, plus a number of literary (artistic-rhetorical) "notes" to help guide your analysis. Carry out this extended exercise in stages:

a. Prepare a *LiFE* rendition of this passage, one that is also meant for an oral performance. Incorporate a reader-friendly *format* (lineation, spacing, typography, etc.) to assist the person(s) who will be publicly reading your translation (unless s/he/they prefer to memorize the text so that it can be more realistically "performed").

b. Make a relatively literal English back-translation of your TL version. As you proceed, write up any "compositional notes" (dealing with major translational difficulties) and "directions for performance" (dealing with your proposed *oral interpretation* of this text, including voice qualities, gestures, facial expressions, etc.). Use these notes as the basis for a comparative group discussion when all the versions represented have been completed.

c. Each translation team can dramatize their version in performance (whether an individual voice or several) to which representative members of the public have been invited to give their critical response and feedback. This will provide some concrete results that can serve to stimulate another round-table discussion (or debate) concerning the potential difficulties, challenges, benefits, etc. of a performance-based approach to Bible translation.

JAMES 2:14-26	Analytical comment
¹⁴Τί τὸ ὄφελος, ἀδελφοί μου,	A typical curt (verbless) diatribe aperture; corresponding pair of RQs (expected answer = "No[thing]!")
What good is it, my brothers,	
ἐὰν πίστιν λέγῃ τις ἔχειν	Fronted correlated key thematic terms ("faith vs. works") mark the onset of a hypothetical mini case-study.
if a man claims to have faith	
ἔργα δὲ μὴ ἔχῃ;	Lines 2–3 rhyme and parallel each other contrastively.
but has no deeds?	

μὴ δύναται ἡ πίστις σῶσαι αὐτόν;	σῶσαι imports an implicit eschatological perspective.
Can such faith save him?	
¹⁵ ἐὰν ἀδελφὸς ἢ ἀδελφὴ γυμνοὶ ὑπάρχωσιν	The spotlight suddenly shifts to a hypothetical person; ἢ ἀδελφὴ is a significant alternative—no one is excluded!
Suppose a brother or sister is without clothes	initial extended description—an *"extreme instance"*
καὶ λειπόμενοι τῆς ἐφημέρου τροφῆς	
and daily food.	
¹⁶ εἴπῃ δέ τις αὐτοῖς ἐξ ὑμῶν,	Surprise, immediacy: the initial "someone" becomes "one *of you*—i.e., listeners on the scene!" (backshift focus).
If one of you says to him,	
Ὑπάγετε ἐν εἰρήνῃ,	A wish-prayer, based on the Jewish everyday greeting, here trivializes the predicament of the poor.
"Go, I wish you well;	
θερμαίνεσθε καὶ χορτάζεσθε,	A rhyming couplet heightens the indictment.
keep warm and well fed,"	
μὴ δῶτε δὲ αὐτοῖς τὰ ἐπιτήδεια τοῦ σώματος,	The double δὲ of v. 16 adds a note of consternation.
but does nothing about his physical needs,	
τί τὸ ὄφελος;	The interrogative *apodosis* is placed last for impact (end stress!) and forms an *inclusio* around the hypothetical case; the emphatic implied negative sets up v. 17.
what good is it?	
¹⁷ οὕτως καὶ ἡ πίστις,	This verse applies (οὕτως) the previous example and forcefully makes explicit the implication of v. 14.
In the same way, faith …	
ἐὰν μὴ ἔχῃ ἔργα,	Lines 2-3 rhyme in reverse, closely linking the juxtaposed notions of "death" and a workless "faith"!
if it is not accompanied by action,	
νεκρά ἐστιν καθ' ἑαυτήν.	a vivid closure to first argument-unit ("paragraph"); καθ' ἑαυτήν—the word order imitates the concept referred to, i.e., faith "by itself/on its own"
… by itself, is dead.	
¹⁸ Ἀλλ' ἐρεῖ τις,	Another mini case-study begins—an inductive, deliberative debate regarding the author's thesis.
But someone will say,	
Σὺ πίστιν ἔχεις,	The balanced parallel lines are an *isomorphic equivalent* mimicking the erroneous thesis that "faith" and "works"
"You have faith;	
κἀγὼ ἔργα ἔχω·	can be neatly separated from each other in one's life.
I have deeds."	

δεῖξόν **μοι** τὴν πίστιν σου χωρὶς τῶν ἔργων,	These two chiastically arranged lines suggest a shift in the speaker; they also advance a glaring contradiction:
Show me your faith without deeds,	
κἀγώ **σοι** δείξω ἐκ τῶν ἔργων μου τὴν πίστιν. and I will show you my faith by what I do.	First an *impossibility*, then the *truth* of the matter.
¹⁹ σὺ πιστεύεις ὅτι **εἷς** ἐστιν ὁ θεός,	Any objector ("you") to James' position is ironically set in
You believe that there is one God. Good! καλῶς ποιεῖς· καὶ τὰ δαιμόνια πιστεύουσιν	deliberate syntactic parallel with "demons" in the balanced arrangement of lines 1–3 of v. 19.
Even the demons believe that καὶ φρίσσουσιν.	This concluding "punch line" is foregrounded by sound similarity involving the final verbs of the last 2 lines.
–and shudder.	
²⁰ θέλεις δὲ γνῶναι, ὦ ἄνθρωπε κενέ,	After a diatribe-like initial exclamation, a RQ restates the thesis of this pericope for the proverbial "fool."
You foolish man, do you want evidence	
ὅτι ἡ πίστις χωρὶς τῶν ἔργων ἀργή ἐστιν;	A *wordplay* heightens the nature of faith minus "works."
that faith without deeds is useless? ²¹ **Ἀβραὰμ ὁ πατὴρ** ἡμῶν οὐκ ἐξ ἔργων ἐδικαιώθη	The divine verdict in RQ form is placed ahead of the human work that elicited it. Oral intonation must have
Was not our ancestor Abraham considered righteous for what he did ἀνενέγκας Ἰσαὰκ τὸν υἱὸν αὐτοῦ ἐπὶ τὸ θυσιαστήριον;	marked this lengthy question from its onset; "not by [out of] works" is highlighted by its syntactic position.
when he offered his son Isaac on the altar?	
²² βλέπεις ὅτι ἡ πίστις συνήργει τοῖς ἔργοις αὐτοῦ	A verb discourse-orienter (βλέπεις) underscores the argument. A chiastic construction with punning perhaps serves here to emphasize thematic complementarity.
You see that his faith and his actions were working together,	
καὶ ἐκ τῶν ἔργων ἡ πίστις ἐτελειώθη,	Another N-V / V-N chiasm overlaps 22b with 23a.
and his faith was made complete by what he did. ²³ καὶ ἐπληρώθη ἡ γραφὴ ἡ λέγουσα, And the scripture was fulfilled that says, Ἐπίστευσεν δὲ Ἀβραὰμ τῷ θεῷ,	A midrashic-like citing of biblical "proof texts" supports the case at hand and its crucial implications.
"Abraham believed God, καὶ ἐλογίσθη αὐτῷ εἰς δικαιοσύνην	Some sound similarity plus another chiasmus (V-benefactive / benefactive-V) suggests the close personal relationship the existed between "Abram" and "God"
and it was credited to him as righteousness,"	
καὶ φίλος θεοῦ ἐκλήθη. and he was called God's friend.	(*intertextuality* with 2 Chr. 20:7; Isa. 41:8).

²⁴ ὁρᾶτε ὅτι ἐξ ἔργων δικαιοῦται ἄνθρωπος You see that a person is justified by what he does	Shift of the initial orienter from sg. (22a) to pl. indicates a focus swing away from the hypothetical opponent(s) to James' primary audience in this restatement of v. 22.
καὶ οὐκ ἐκ πίστεως μόνον. and not by faith alone.	The emphasis on ἐξ ἔργων (front-shifted in 24a) is balanced by its corollary, οὐκ ἐκ πίστεως μόνον, at the end of the sentence (24b, with stress on μόνον).
²⁵ ὁμοίως δὲ καὶ **Ραὰβ ἡ πόρνη** <u>οὐκ ἐξ ἔργων ἐδικαιώθη</u> In the same way, was not even Rahab the prostitute considered righteous for what she did	Corresponding line endings (cf. v. 21a) call attention to another biblical example, a *contrastive* personage whose name exhibits *phonological similarity* to the former.
ὑποδεξαμένη τοὺς ἀγγέλους καὶ ἑτέρᾳ ὁδῷ ἐκβαλοῦσα; when she gave lodging to the spies and sent them off in a different direction?	A narrative case study involving a foreign prostitute complements and reinforces the point made in the discursive example of Israel's preeminent patriarch.
²⁶ **ὥσπερ** γὰρ <u>τὸ σῶμα</u> χωρὶς πνεύματος **νεκρόν** ἐστιν, As the body without the spirit is dead,	Phonological likeness and correlative conjunctions (ὥσπερ…οὕτως) foreground the strong *parallelism* of a powerful, proverbial, allusive (Gen. 2:7) Conclusion.
οὕτως καὶ <u>ἡ πίστις</u> χωρὶς ἔργων **νεκρά** ἐστιν. so faith without deeds is dead.	Reiteration, too, highlights the vital contrast between spiritual life and **death** (cf. v.17, which also rounds out a paragraph unit, i.e., structural *epiphora*).

10. Study the following definition of "comics" in relation to Bible publications (Somé 2007):

   "[A] comic Bible is a mixture of pictures, words and various conventional visual symbols designed to express the meaning of the biblical text in a given target language, as faithfully and clearly as possible and in a natural and colloquial style as well. In other words, pictures, words and signs are presented together in sequence to communicate a message about a biblical topic. A comic product is a mixture of these various elements. Among the printed Scriptures, it is convenient for the presentation below to keep in mind the dichotomy between comics on the one hand and non comic Bibles, on the other hand. The non comic materials include all classic Bibles printed without or with more or fewer illustrations as helps to the readers to guide them to a better understanding of the meaning of the biblical message. To be more precise, there are basically four types of Scripture with illustrations:

   a. Standard Bibles with illustrations, few or plenty

   b. Bible Story Book, consisting of re-told stories of the Bible that have a lot of pictures, often one per page. (These often add a lot of detail and commentary and are usually directed toward children), for example: *Ma première Bible à portée de main,* for children by Cécile Olesen (2003); *Ce que dit la Bible,* the collection by Docete and Kees de Kort (1968).

   c. Scripture in the comic medium; that is, the text of the Bible is re-created in words and pictures. These have varying degrees of fidelity to the text. Some add details and commentary; others (like ours, i.e., UBS comics series) stick more strictly to the text, only making explicit what is implicit.

d. Bible in Graphic novel format. These are longer works that employ the comic medium and manipulate elements of plot and perspective more than our comics do. For example: *La Bible*, by Jeff Anderson and Mike Maddox (1999).

How would you define "comics" in your language? (Provide a back translation into English.) Which of the four types of "Scripture with illustrations" listed above are most relevant and/or needed in your cultural setting? List these four in their order of priority (with reasons). Does the comic medium of communication present any particular problems in your situation? If so, specify what these are. How might such difficulties be overcome—what sort of "public relations" strategy would you adopt, if you feel that "Scripture in the comic medium" does have a potential and role to fill.

11. Robert Koops (2003:15) has made a creative attempt to contextualize as well as dramatize 1 Peter as an audio production, a printed excerpt of which is presented below.[21] (The non-italic words represent a rendition of the biblical text; the italicized words are intended to facilitate an oral elocution of the text by creating a dialogue setting; N = narrator's voice; P = Peter's voice.) Koops explains the purpose of this innovative audio production as follows (ibid.:9–10):

> One might speculate that written letters, like the Epistles in the New Testament, would not be suitable as a dramatic presentation. But if you have ever listened to the BBC African Service presenter reading letters from listeners, you will know how to do it....Here the presenter anticipates the words of Peter and expresses them in the form of a question. The listener thus hears the gist of the text two times. This is the kind of redundancy that audio text needs to be effective.

1 Peter 1:1–9: "Hang In There."

N: *Here is a letter from Peter, who describes himself as* an apostle of Jesus Christ. He is writing to refugees *who are followers of Jesus. Peter writes:*

P: ¹Dear refugees scattered all over Pontus, Galatia, Cappadocia, Asia, and Bythinia.

N: *These places, by the way, are all districts in the Roman Empire, and today they are what is now Turkey. The followers of Jesus were scattered because of persecution in Judea. This is how Peter addresses them.*

P: ²You people were chosen by God the Father. He destined you to obey Jesus Christ and to be made holy by his blood. And the Spirit purified you for the same purpose. May grace and peace be to you in abundant measure!

N: *Peter, what do you have to say to these refugee-believers scattered throughout this part of the empire?*

P: ³First, I praise God, the Father of our Lord Jesus Christ, because it is by his great mercy that we have been born anew.

N: *Born anew?*

P: Yes, born with new hope because Jesus Christ rose from the dead.

N: *How does that give you hope?*

P: ⁴We can look forward to an inheritance in heaven. God is holding it there for us, and it will never lose its purity and beauty.

---

[21]Dr. Koops has prepared a number of audio Bible scripts that he is willing to share with interested persons. He may be contacted at rob.koop@gmail.com.

N: *So is this heavenly inheritance for everybody?*

P: ⁵It is for those whom God in his power has been protecting. They have trusted him to reveal his plan of salvation in these last days. And he has!

N: *So how does this work out in practice? What do you say to refugees who are suffering?*

P: ⁶First, you can rejoice, even though now for a little while you may have to suffer through various hardships. ⁷These troubles are a test of your faith. It's like when a goldsmith puts gold in a hot fire to purify it. Your faith is a lot more precious than gold, because it is eternal, not like gold. Gold can endure fire but it won't last forever.

N: *So you're telling us that we will actually be better people because of these troubles?*

P: Yes! And when Jesus comes again your faith will explode in praise and glory and honor.

N: *What if we never actually saw Jesus in person?*

P: ⁸It's true, you never saw him, but you heard about him and love him. And even if you don't see him now, you believe and trust in him. This gives you an enormous amount of joy. I can't begin to describe it.

N: *Peter, does this kind of faith have any practical benefit?*

P: ⁹Quite simply, faith results in salvation. You are saved!

Would this sort of audio Scripture production work out well in YL? Give reasons for your answer. Are there any modifications that you would suggest for your communicative setting and target audience?

Where does a *LiFE* translation approach enter the process during an audio, radio, and/or video production? For example, what sort of speaking style would be most appropriate for dialogue, or does it depend on other factors that must be specified first? What voice quality would be needed in YL for the narrator/presenter (N)? How about the voice of Peter (P) or the voice for a quotation from the Hebrew Scriptures as in 1:24–25? How might the artistic and rhetorical dimension of this type of production be effectively tested? Mention some of the techniques that you would use for this purpose.

12. Suppose you have been assigned to prepare a comic book of Jonah. First study the general guidelines that follow (condensed from Burke and Lebron-Rivera 2003:22).[22] Then consider the first chapter of Jonah and make an effort to illustrate a set of comic book frames for the biblical text. Do the best you can to sketch in each distinct scene on a sheet of paper. For this you may also need to do some research on the extratextual setting of Jonah. Concentrate on the dialogue portions and how you would represent the different speakers in a colloquial *LiFE*-like manner.

    a. The overall guiding principle is to express faithfully and effectively the meaning and intention of the biblical text in a form that exploits the genius of the comic medium.

    b. No attempt is to be made to create scenes or dialogue that are not indicated explicitly or implicitly in the biblical text. All balloons, kinesics and nonverbal communication, pictures, and captions must be faithful to the message of the biblical text.

    c. Narrative and reported speech in the biblical text may be transformed into dialogue, song, or poetry, provided that it does not distort the intent of the biblical text either in the immediate

---

[22]For further details on the theory and practice of composing creative comic texts, see Burke and Lebron-Rivera 2003. The entire article is on the UBS webpage:www.biblesocieties.org

or the wider context. This brings a dimension to the adaptation of the biblical text which may at first be puzzling to the translator. Normally, there is only limited dialogue or conversation in a typical biblical narrative. But the various genres of the comic medium demand continuous speech and/or thoughts in the balloons in each frame. Very few frames do not have someone or something speaking or thinking. This means that in adapting the biblical message to the comic medium, speech is created from what is implicit in the biblical narrative. In the graphic novel genre, context and characterization details will be elaborated from what is implicit in the print text.

d. Transformations of the biblical text should be consistent with known audience attitudes and should be designed to create a response which approximates as closely as possible the response of the original receptors.

e. Transforming biblical text into the comic medium often demands a selection of material out of the biblical text. In cases such as these, the reader should be advised in general terms that a selection has been made, and be referred to the source of the full biblical text. If omission of sections must be made from lengthy stories, it is not necessary to signal every omission from the biblical material in detail, as this will conflict with the expectation of the intended audience.

After completing this assignment, suggest any modifications or additions to these guidelines based on your own experimentation with communicating the Scriptures via this medium. Do you think it is a good way to reach some particular target group in your community? Explain your answer.

Finally, propose some guidelines for assessing the quality of such a production—that is, according to the parameters of fidelity, intelligibility, proximity, and idiomaticity (see section 7.2.2).

13. Harry Harm offers the following thoughts on "checking a translation to be published on video" (1999:36–37). After studying this quotation, respond in group discussion to three points:

Producing a Scripture video is not a simple matter…It involves "exegetical choices" just as [a print] translation does. But in a visual medium there is less room for ambiguities and therefore a video producer is forced to make decisions which a translator seldom has to face. Every scene requires hundreds of decisions. What type of clothes did the characters wear, how tall were they, were they fat or thin, what time of day did the event happen, how many people were involved, how did the animals look? A printed translation may use generic words like man, woman, clothes, and cow and ignore the time of day and the season, but a video must be specific.

When I check a translation knowing that a team plans to publish the translation on one of the shell videos, I now check the translation with the video. I do an exegetical check of the text and then watch to video and compare it with the text. Using a four-head VCR that has a jog and shuttle control on the remote, I can move through the video frame by frame if necessary. After having checked the translation for exegetical accuracy, I am familiar with the choices the translator made and can watch to see which ones are in the video.

Dubbing a shell video with a translation involves many steps, so it is important to plan ahead. The steps include: integration into the overall project plan, script fitting, selecting speakers, recording, postproduction and distribution.

Script fitting refers to the adapting of a translated text to a shell video in respect to timing: the length of the vernacular text has to be adjusted to fit the time slots in the video. To do this, the translator looks at a work print of the video. In the course of doing this, the translator may notice that the vernacular text and the video reflect different exegetical interpretations. Discrepancies between the vernacular text and the video may also show up when the audio track is taped. Both of these circumstances, if they happen after the translation check, may require adjustments to the text without checking with a translation consultant, sometimes under a sever time constraint (e.g., during the taping process). But if the translation consultant checks the video during the regular consultant check of the vernacular text, then hopefully most of the exegetical choices required for the video will have been already made before the dubbing of the video begins.

   a. Can you mention any other exegetical or other problems connected with the production of Scripture video selections?

   b. How does the production team decide whether to favor more or less a "domesticated" as opposed to a "foreignized" approach in this exercise (or vice-versa)?

   c. Do you have any additional suggestions to offer to those involved in such testing for basic exegetical fidelity?

14. Another important "non-print" type of Bible translation is that which is done in "sign language" (SL; see the recent *Bible Translator* issue devoted to this subject, 59:2, April 2008; cf. Wendland 2008:60–62). In this regard, John Harris notes that "the difficult questions faced in SL translations are very similar to the questions faced everywhere every day in Bible translation into spoken languages" (ibid.:101). Harris then discusses seven key issues that SL projects need to give attention to:

   - Clearly identifying the SL audience—who is the Bible translation for?
   - Making the right choice of translators
   - Dealing with potential differences in SL "dialects"
   - Addressing the issue of different church traditions and loyalties
   - Developing new signs—questions of borrowing and inventing
   - Resolving any possible controversy over the use of "finger spelling"
   - Dealing with technology—problems and solutions

   In conclusion, Harris highlights a key guiding principle for all SL projects: "[A]lways maintain the desire to communicate with *this Deaf generation*, [ensuring] that the translations…[produced] will be clear and easy to understand today" (ibid.:111).

   Is your national Bible Society or translation organization involved with any SL translations for the deaf? If not, why not—is some other agency doing the job, or is there no substantial deaf community in your country? If you do know something about SL translation work, how do you assess the various issues of concern identified by Harris above—do you have any additional advice to offer?

   To what extent is the field of *semiotics* (cf. section 1.3) especially relevant to Bible translation in sign languages? Mention some of the special applications of semiotic theory and practice in this regard.

15. Bible media translators would do well to keep the following summary of primary techniques in mind as they carry out their work (adapted from Hodgson 2003:6):

   a. **serialization** (creation of panels, or series, of individual scenes or images)

   b. **condensation** (cooking down a narrative into essentials)

   c. **symbolization** (rendering a story or event into a controlling metaphor—fish, bread, phoenix)

   d. **explication** (implicit information made explicit)

   e. **implication** (explicit information made implicit)

   f. **activation** (from narrative to action, gesticulation, and body language)

g. **lexicalization** (visual elements integrated into description, or narrative into character dialogue)

h. **enculturation** (use of familiar indigenous forms of representation)

i. **spatialization** (use of biblical images and texts in product designs or background scenes)

Pick out several of these techniques and suggest how they might be applied to a *LiFE*-oriented video production of the David and Goliath narrative from 1 Samuel 17—or the account of Peter and Cornelius from Acts 10:1–11:18.

Lesson 8
A Summary and Review of *LiFE* Principles

The following is a summary of seven important concerns and areas of interest that pertain to a *LiFE* translation methodology. As has been the procedure for most of this manual, these issues are expressed mainly in the form of questions for group consideration and class discussion:

1. A *LiFE* approach to Bible translation normally begins with an examination of the larger *compositional structure* that organizes a given passage or pericope of Scripture: What main *genre* or *discourse* type of biblical literature does it manifest? Does this incorporate any subgenres? Does the passage differ from the surrounding cotext? If so, in which respects? How has the content of the pericope been selected, shaped, and systematized? Are there any special patterns of textual arrangement evident (e.g., terrace, chiasmus, inclusio, intercalation)? Where are the text's points of special emphasis, and how are these formally marked—that is, by which specific stylistic features (e.g., patterned repetition, figurative embellishment, phonological foregrounding, direct discourse)?

2. Along with form and content, a *LiFE*-like methodology is concerned with function; namely, the major and minor *communicative goals* of the biblical document under consideration. For what purpose(s) was the pericope composed with respect to its present literary (textual) context and also its most probable "original" situational (extra-textual) setting? In addition to the overall "text act" (genre), what are the chief "speech acts" and associated speaker-based *illocutions* that characterize this discourse. How are these instances of verbal intentionality logically interrelated and formally linked throughout the entire expanse of the text? What are the principal aims of the present translation in relation to other versions that are widely used in the community? In what way(s) can the inductive "cost-versus-gain" principle of *relevance* guide you both in perceiving and also in prioritizing the salient functions of the SL text in relation to the primary goals of the present project?

3. The crucial factor of *textual context (cotext)* is further explored with respect to other portions of Scripture that are clearly conceptually and verbally related to the pericope under study: First, which previously occurring texts or individual passages within the larger document correspond to or contrast with key elements in the discourse at hand (whether in terms of form, content, or function), for example, by exact or partial *intra*textual repetition? Second, which other literary texts, canonical or extrabiblical, may have had an *inter*textual influence on the present document, whether strong or weak (i.e., an actual citation versus a paraphrase, allusion, or implicit echo)? Third, how does a proposed *LiFE* translation relate stylistically to any other version that may be available in the TL?

4. The *extratextual context* of interest to Bible translators includes both the ancient Near Eastern setting and also the contemporary communicative or interpersonal situation in which it will be re-presented today: What influence did the assumed original background most likely have on initial text production? How might the current sociocultural environment (political, religious, literary, educational, ecclesiastical, etc.) affect the present-day understanding and use of the translation being prepared? What about the general cognitive-emotive setting—how may this be evaluated in terms of the principle of *relevance* (text-processing "costs" versus psychological "gains") with respect to any given passage? What is the estimated level of *biblical literacy* among members of the primary TL constituency? Which specific *supplementary helps* may be needed to facilitate the intended audience's overall interpretation and text-contextualization processes (e.g., explanatory notes, section headings, illustrations, cross-references and their aural or video equivalents)? How will these aids be produced and subsequently evaluated for effectiveness?

5. A *LiFE* method of translation, by its very name, places a major emphasis upon the interrelated *artistic* (poetic) and *rhetorical* (purposeful) dimensions of discourse—the former in service of the latter. What are the special points of *appeal* (esthetic attraction) and *impact* (persuasive power) that occur in the biblical document under study and how are these effects achieved—by which formal literary devices (e.g., figures of speech, syntactic modifications, sonic underscoring, dramatic diction, verbal intensifiers)? How do the key stylistic forms of the original text correspond with or differ from those available in the target language to accomplish the same or similar communicative aim? Where no close functional matches appear, what can be done to compensate in the translation for the *LiFE* that would be lost by a relatively literal version? How might the *printed format* be used in a translation to bring out certain key poetic aspects of the original text?

6. A *LiFE*-style exegesis and translation also pays considerable attention to the prominent *oral-aural* characteristics of the biblical message: How is the phonological dimension specifically manifested in the original text? Which equivalent features might be used to reproduce a similar phonic effect in the target language—an appropriate rhythm at the very minimum? What *mode of communication* will be used to re-present the biblical text in the TL; will it be the standard printed format or conveyed through a medium that is audio, visual, electronic, or mixed in nature, or via a traditional live performance of some type (song, dance, drama, recitation)? How might this means of local transmission influence the composition and reception of the translated text in view of the intended audience and primary setting of use? How will the sound-quality of the translation produced be evaluated?

7. A *LiFE* methodology promotes a flexible compositional process, one that is *creative* in relation to TL form, but *constrained* with regard to SL content. It seeks to achieve continual refinement by means of various quality-assessment procedures that follow a sound exegetical and artistic-rhetorical study of the biblical text. What then are the implications of this *functional* approach for planning and implementing an appropriate communication strategy to accomplish it and also to evaluate and improve the results? The entire process of translation needs to be strongly localized—indigenized—in order to achieve a generally "acceptable" outcome, not only exegetically, but also with regard to the style of the text. For example, how would an *indigenous* vernacular artist (e.g., a poet, griot/storyteller, preacher, debater) be inclined to compose the pericope at hand (having carefully examined it) according to its nearest generic equivalent in the TL? Has a sample vocal re-creation actually been prepared, tested, revised, tested, and retested? What modifications will be needed to transform this oral text into print with reference to the envisaged target group and the most likely circumstances of message transmission? <u>Bottom line</u>: How effectively does the translation communicate, all things considered, in comparison with the original text, as nearly as we can tell?

An important reminder: Even a little *LiFE* applied to any translation means a lot in terms of more accurately and acceptably re-presenting the beauty, power, and persuasiveness of the Scriptures. That is, the goal of a *LiFE* version can be accomplished, depending on the circumstances, by utilizing either a measured selection or the full literary (oratorical) complement of the TL resources. A *LiFE* transformation of the biblical text is arguably more faithful to the artistic genius and rhetorical intentions of the original authors, and Author, than any other approach. But before any sort of idiomatic domestication of the vernacular version can be successfully achieved, whether to a greater or lesser extent, translators must clearly understand what *LiFE* is all about—and how to apply the method competently on behalf of and in continual negotiation with a specific target audience, always keeping in mind the particular translation commission and goals that they have been entrusted with.

For reflection, research, and response:

1. Consider the preceding reminder. To what extent can it be applied in your own setting of Bible translation? To what degree must the target audience be educated with respect to what Bible translation involves and what the various options are for carrying out this text-representation process for

the ultimate benefit of a given consumer community? If more *education* is needed, how can such a program be implemented? Give some details to support your suggestions.

2. As we have seen, the literary forms of different languages are used and interpreted in distinct cognitive and emotive frames of reference. Therefore, it helps, when translating, to use a relevance-based, functionally-oriented method of translation, no matter what type of version is being prepared. How do the following comments of Robert Bascom (2003:16) relate to this, especially with reference to "text signs" and the artistic-rhetorical approach recommended in this workbook?

> [T]he idea of frames and framing changes the focus of the task of translation from the text-signs to the frames of reference within which and under whose terms those signs are understood. This is by no means to say that the text-signs are to be disregarded, or that they are somehow less important than before. They are, after all, the only direct clues we have in a written text to what the original frames of communication and understanding were. But without a clear understanding of the various frames of reference, a translator has very little chance of serving…as a proper mediator between the original language and receptor language cultures. Of course the issue becomes even more complicated and thus more crucial when the translation is being done in an indirect way through a third language, as is often the case with Bible translation into minority languages.

Give an example (from YL if possible) of this last sentence about translation's being "even more complicated" when it is "done in an indirect way through a third language."

3. Now that you have reviewed seven important *LiFE* principles (summarized at the beginning of this lesson) and worked through them in this workbook, would you like to propose any changes or additions? If so, list these on a separate piece of paper in preparation for a joint discussion in class. Which of the principles do you feel is the most difficult to carry out? Why do you say so? What can you suggest to lighten the conceptual and procedural load, especially with a view towards communicating them in YL and cultural setting?

4. Translators-in-training are not often introduced to the complexities and challenges of literary translation. Why do you think this is the case? What do you think of the following "effective method" for teaching translation students (Qvale 2003:1):

> …Delisle (1988) explains why he, in common with many other scholars in the field, completely avoids literary texts in his attempt to develop an effective method for teaching translation students. It is, he says, because of the richness of such texts, the subjective feelings and opinions, the suggestive power, the rhetorical and evocative elements of form, the kaleidoscopic wealth of meaning, their beauty and timelessness, and their universal, eternal values and concerns.

How are "literary texts" defined in the preceding quotation, and how does this apply to the Scriptures and your task as a Bible translator? Do you think it is more "effective" to avoid teaching the methods of literary translation or to embrace them as in this workbook? Perhaps it is a case of "artists being born, not made," and consequently, an excellent literary translation can only be composed intuitively, by inspiration? What do you think?

5. The following "basic principles should be considered essential to translator training" (condensed from Nord 1997:78–79). Evaluate these in relation to the training program that you experienced: Which aspects were covered adequately, and which ones were not? Does something else need to be added to this list of "things to do?" Which of these principles do you still need to work on, and how are you going about it? These points may be used as the basis for a class discussion (for example, the appropriateness of the first comparison)—or considered by translation trainers who wish to improve their program.

   a. Translating without clear instructions is like swimming without water. Language is always used in a specific situation; it is always framed by a specific sociocultural context that determines what forms of verbal and nonverbal behavior will be regarded as appropriate by the participants. A functionally adequate translation can only be produced by someone who knows the target situation for which the text is intended and who is familiar with the communicative conventions valid in the target culture.

b. Before piloting a ship, you need some knowledge about tides and shoals and the use of life vests. In order to keep up the motivation of the learners and to save them from unnecessary failures, a certain amount of general theoretical and methodological knowledge about the pragmatic and cultural aspects of translation should prepare them for their first practical training exercises.

c. The most important tool for prospective translators is their own native language. …The deployment of general theoretical knowledge about translation and the development of text-production skills in the native language can be combined in 'intralingual' translation exercises, i.e. rewriting texts for different audiences and purposes.

d. In order to understand the specificity of another culture, you have to know your own culture first….If we want to behave in an adequate way in another culture community, we have to compare the behavior conventions of the foreign culture with those of our own. To do this, we have to replace our intuitive behavior patterns with conscious knowledge of our own culture specificity.

How does point d apply—in reverse—to the practice of communicative Bible translation? What are some other ways of developing compositional naturalness and fluency in one's mother tongue?

6. Explain in your own words the following advice from Qvale (2003:185). How does it apply to your work as a Bible translator, especially if you desire to prepare a literary version?

Literary translators need not—or should not—feel the same duty to paraphrase and explain. It destroys the illusion when translators leave their footprints in footnotes, or park a parenthesis in the middle of the textual flow of traffic; a brief imperceptible detour is better, usually with the help of an apposition that does not cause delay or interrupt the rhythm. Part of the literary translator's skill resides in using that skill to decide which reader the translation is intended for—and that judgement depends very much on which reader the translator believes the author wrote/is writing for.

7. Concerning the artistic qualities of the Scriptures Nida says (2003:81), "The fascination of the Bible for both believers and nonbelievers may be explained to some extent by the remarkable literary character of the texts." Assuming this is true, what does it imply for Bible translators?

8. The Relevance Theory approach to translation uses the analogy of direct and indirect speech to model the translation process, "direct translation" (DT) being analogous to directly quoting the original autographs. This is a notion for class members to discuss, since it raises several questions: First, would DT, where all the "communicative clues" of the original text are preserved, apply only to the manuscript tradition of Scripture, in which the various copies are taken to be exemplars of the original Hebrew or Greek text as established by the discipline of textual criticism? (Textual critics investigate all issues that pertain to establishing among different variants what the *most likely* "direct quote" of a given autograph was.)

Second, would not all other types of translation, from the most literal rendition to the freest paraphrase, then be instances of indirect translation, called "interpretive use" (IU)? Thus there would seem to be a broad continuum of possibility here, depending of course on how much the translator either wishes or is forced to "interpret" the original text in terms of the target language. (Even a "naturalizing" of word order, for example, constitutes an interpretation because there are often two or more options available.) The case of a gross interlinear gloss version might fall somewhere between DT and IU; it is neither fish nor fowl, in that it is neither a copy (direct quote) of the original text nor a translation (indirect quote) of it.

Landers defines "indirect translation" differently (2001:208): "a translation made from other than the source language, as for example, a translation of the Tibetan *Book of the Dead* into Basque via French, bypassing the original language. In the present era the 'middle language' is most often English." This is true also in the field of Bible translation in many parts of the world. Can you give an example?

Evaluate these and related issues in class with respect to how best to conceptualize and model the task of Bible translation in relation to the current approaches that attempt to do this by way of various common analogies.

9. D. A. Carson tells us what the aim of a good translation should be (in Scorgie, Strauss, and Voth 2003:96): "The aim of a good translation is to convey the total content, or as much of it as possible in roughly equivalent compass—informational, emotional, connotational, etc.—of the original message to the reader (or hearer where the translation is publicly read) in the receptor language."

Consider Carson's proposal in light of what has been said about a *LiFE* translation in this workbook. Then state your own proposal for what constitutes "the aim of a good translation." Carson also asks a question (ibid.:95):

> Is it not better, if we are going to define functional equivalence in terms of equivalent response, to understand equivalence in linguistic categories, i.e., in terms of the removal of as many as possible of the false linguistic barriers (along with the associations each linguistic category carries) that actually impede the communication of the content of the text?

Is there a way of asking this in positive terms, that is, with reference to a "restoration" of some significance in addition to the "removal" that is mentioned here? Try it and see what you come up with—as a "*LiFE* principle."

10. Compare Carson's point of view with Ryken's (2002:171):

> What is bad about an unliterary Bible? It distorts the kind of book that the Bible is (mainly an anthology of literary genres). It robs the Bible of the power that literature conveys....[Translators] should make the Bible neither more literary nor less literary than what the original authors gave us. This means, insofar as possible, retaining the concreteness, artistry, indirectness, subtlety, multilayeredness, and language patterns of the original. It is as simple as that.

How does this relate to your conception of the Scriptures and the task of Bible translation?

What do you think of the qualities that are here specified as being especially "literary" in nature? Would you wish to propose a different list? Explain. What kind of a translation can best fulfill the specified goal for such a "literary" version? How can this best be achieved?

11. The following is a suggestion from a professional translator as to how a literary translator works (Qvale 2003:244):

> ...Jamieson advocates completing the first draft very quickly:

> Under this method, the translator works under pressure, at very high speed, to produce the first draft. This often results in a spontaneous breakthrough to a natural sounding equivalent, and also forces the translator to use his/her own 'idiolect', and thus better reflect the flow of the original. The purpose of editing is then to achieve a greater accuracy....

Working uninterruptedly, with the process flowing freely, offers free play to intuition and opens the way to all the impressions of the text (and subtext) have to offer. The flow of the original is reflected in the text the translator produces during 'automatic writing'.

What do you think of this method? Have you ever tried to translate in this manner? What is your preferred method of translating the artful, lyric passages of the Bible?

12. The inevitable compositional constraints placed upon a "faithful" translator can be overcome through the same sort of focused energy that is directed towards composing an original literary text. In other words, even a translator has a measure of freedom and creativity. Consider and discuss this possibility in relation to your own work as a translator of Scripture and in light of the following observations by Boase-Beier and Holman (1999:13):

> [A] translator must take into consideration all the constraints, whether social and contextual, poetic and conventional, or linguistic and formal, which helped to shape the original. In addition, he or she must carry the added burden of constraint imposed by the new target language, culture and audience, and by the need to balance freedom with faithfulness and one's own knowledge, background and beliefs with those of the author. Then, too, there are added constraints caused by cultural, linguistic or pragmatic mismatches between SL and TL....Yet just as constraint moulded and gave rise to the creative impulse in the original, so in translation this added burden of constraint can force a translator into new ways of overcoming it and thus into new creativity.

13. The following four principles pertaining to a literary translation come from the "translator's Ten Commandments" by the German poet Wolf Biermann (cited in Qvale 2003:267, but with a different format). Discuss them in relation to your own attitude and approach to rendering the poetic portions of Scripture. Would you like to add another principle or two that guides your work when dealing with a poetic biblical text?

    a. No translation can be as good as the original. So try to improve the translation at least.

    b. But if you notice that you are not succeeding, strike a blow for art: Drop it! Give up and console yourself with the fact that a better translator will turn up, who will manage better than you.

    c. From the masterpieces you shall learn what distinguishes a master's hand: the totality, the feel. But you shall lay aside any useable elements, keeping them in reserve in the parts department for later use in your own production.

    d. Moreover, while you translate you shall learn, and relearn, the language that will always be the most difficult for you: your own.

14. William A. Smalley (1995:2, 62) presents the "translators' dilemma" as follows:

> For various reasons, most Bible translators start with a predisposition toward literal translation—some out of conviction, others because they do not know what else to do. They use the vernacular but not the idiom of the vernacular....They know that such literalism must be tempered, but they believe that if they "go too far" from a literal rendering, the result will be what they call paraphrase rather than translation. The more sensitive they are to the receptor language and culture, the more they may be torn by the tension between the literalism in which they believe and the need for communication that they perceive. This is a pervasive translators' dilemma.

To what extent can a *LiFE* approach help translators get out of this dilemma? Give an example that comes to mind from your language.

15. Is a single Bible translation—or a single style of translating—sufficient for an active Bible-reading community? Think about the words of Charles Cosgrove below (cited in Scorgie, Strauss, and Voth 2003:170) in view of what you have learned about a literary manner of translating in this workbook and *Translating the Literature of Scripture* (Wendland 2004b). Then suggest what you think can be done about the lack of diverse kinds of Bible translations in most language settings:

    A critical theory of holistic translation reveals that no single translation is sufficient. Seen in this light the democratization of translation is a good thing—if it means informed use of many translations to reformulate Scripture for a particular place and time or to teach Scripture in ways that reveal the dimensions of cognitive and affective content through rhetorical effects of genre and medium.

16. The topic of nonprint media presentations of Scripture would require a separate study on its own. But just consider the words of Charles Cosgrove (in Scroggie, Strauss, and Voth 2003:168–169) in light of a *LiFE* approach to Bible translation. Call attention to any implications or applications that come to mind as you compose your text in the form of the printed word. What more can you say you are preparing a translation for, an audio-cassette or CD medium of communication?

    Moreover, we should not overlook certain similarities between audiovisual communication in an electronic age and the rhetorical enactment of texts in antiquity. The ancient chirograph [handwritten manuscript] was to be read aloud by a skilled reader (not read silently). Skilled readers dramatized with their voices and gestures when they read. This 'theatrical' aspect of ancient reading of Scripture distances ancient oral performance of Scripture from silent reading in a print culture, as well as from the typical grave reading of Scripture from behind the lectern in most churches today. Ancient reading performance has greater affinities with the art of oral interpretation today. Moreover, ancient oral reading also has certain affinities with audiovisual communication, since the ancient reader combined aural and visual effects in rendering the text.

17. If you are now in a position to try a *LiFE*-style Bible translation, outline your vision of this project. Try the following as a review of a literary methodology: (1) Summarize what you have learned in the course of working through this book. (2) Identify areas that you still need to study and practice with reference to preparing an adequate Bible translation in general and a *LiFE*-like version in particular. (3) Write up a tentative action-plan that summarizes what you hope to accomplish, how you aim to do it, and for whom—your target audience.

18. Moisés Silva (1990:134) mentions some important qualifications of Bible translators. Discuss these in relation to your own translation team and the skills still needed to do the job right. How might these essential skills and human resources be obtained in your setting?

    A successful translation requires (1) mastery of the source language—certainly a much more sophisticated knowledge than one can acquire over a period of four or five years; (2) superb interpretation skills and breadth of knowledge so as not to miss nuances of the original; and (3) a very high aptitude for writing in the target language so as to express accurately both the cognitive and the affective [including esthetic] elements of the message.

19. In a formal presentation outlining some of the different aspects of "translation competence," the following "subcompentences" are listed (Albir and Alves 2009:66; boldface added). Evaluate and discuss these in class. From the perspective of preparing a *LiFE*-style translation, which subcompetence does the group consider to be most important? Which least, and why? Does any competence or quality need to be added to this list? If so, describe it.

    - The bilingual subcompetence is made up of pragmatic, socio-linguistic, textual and lexicogrammatical knowledge in each language.

- The extra-linguistic subcompetence is made up of encyclopaedic, thematic and bicultural knowledge.

- The translation knowledge subcompetence is knowledge of the principles that guide translation (processes, methods and procedures, etc.) and knowledge of the professional practice (types of translation briefs, users, etc.).

- The instrumental subcompetence is made up of knowledge related to the use of documentation sources and information and communication technology applied to translation.

- The strategic subcompetence is the most important, solving problems and guaranteeing the efficiency of the process; it intervenes by planning the process in relation to the translation project, evaluating the process and partial results obtained, activating the different subcompetences and compensating for deficiencies, identifying translation problems and applying procedures to solve them.

- The pscho-social components are cognitive and attitudinal components (memory, attention span, perseverance, critical attitude, etc.) and abilities such as creativity, logical reasoning, analysis and synthesis.

20. Comment on the following advice from Davis and Hays (2003:xv–xvi, 2) about reading the Bible. What relevance and implications for Bible translation, especially a *LiFE* version, do you find?

> [R]eading Scripture is an art—a creative discipline that requires engagement and imagination, in contrast to the Enlightenment's ideal of detached objectivity. In our practices of reading the Bible, we are (or should be) something like artists....If reading Scripture is an art, there follows one more conclusion: we learn the practice of an art through apprenticeship to those who have become masters....The Bible must be read "back to front"—that is, understanding the plot of the whole drama in the light of its climax in the death and resurrection of Jesus Christ....Yet the Bible must also be read "front to back"—that is, understanding the climax of the drama, God's revelation in Christ, in the light of the long history of God's self-revelation to Israel.

21. FINAL ASSIGNMENT: *[The instructor may make a choice here.]*

A: Choose a favorite Psalm. Applying the seven principles listed at the beginning of this lesson, do an *analysis, translation,* and *evaluation* of it. Then perform it orally before the class. Try to render the biblical text as poetically as possible so that it can be recited, chanted, or even sung when you present it. Write out your translation along with a word-for-word interlinear translation and a free translation in English. In a separate paper, describe three special artistic devices that you have used in YL to reproduce those found in Hebrew. Indicate the rhetorical functions these forms perform in the discourse. Hand this in to your instructor for assessment once you have completed your individual class performance.

B: Go to your nearest translation library and read a recently published text on the subject of translation, whether biblical or secular. (Alternatively, the class instructor will provide some books from which to choose.) Prepare a book report on the work you have read. Focus in particular on topics related to artistic and rhetorical features, whether of the SL text or of a given TL. Evaluate what the author says in relation to what you have learned and practiced in this *LiFE* workbook. Hand your book report in to your instructor by the due date.

C: This workbook was intended as a tool to assist translators in carrying out their work with more literary sensitivity. How well has it accomplished its purpose? What improvements can you suggest? Make your critique in light of the following advice concerning translator training techniques (Nida 2003:76–77):

> Instead of simply lecturing about principles of correspondence between the source text and the translated text, a far better way to teach translating is to sit with a prospective translator and go over a text as a means of discovering potential problems. In fact, this is one of the most important procedures, because a problem accurately recognized is already half solved....The final process [*of testing a particular text*] involves an oral reading of the translation in order to spot unnatural, awkward, or incorrect renderings.... In fact, one of the best ways to learn how to translate is to pay close attention to how an expert translator explains precisely what he or she is doing in the process of transferring the meaning of a source text into a receptor language.

D: Imagine that you (or your translation team) have been assigned the task of preparing a video, including a new translation of Revelation 5. Discuss the appropriateness of this particular pericope for any stated purposes. Feel free to suggest project purposes *(Skopos)* that may seem warranted in your situation.

Prepare an analysis of the text (given below in the NIV). Consult the Greek text or an interlinear version if you can. Follow the various analytical procedures that have been presented in this workbook. Write out your text study, and then compose a series of "program notes" as you think about how you might apply the results of your analysis to a dramatic presentation of this video production. Try to be as specific as you can.

Reformat the passage to reflect its diverse discourse structure and genre composition. For example, note the paragraph break in the NIV between verses 5 and 6. How does such a division actually misrepresent, or at least blur, the careful organization of the discourse and the special rhetorical effect that occurs at this juncture? Finally, present your project report in class for comparison with the reports of others and for mutual critique.

> [1] Then I saw in the right hand of him who sat on the throne a scroll with writing on both sides and sealed with seven seals. [2] And I saw a mighty angel proclaiming in a loud voice, "Who is worthy to break the seals and open the scroll?" [3] But no one in heaven or on earth or under the earth could open the scroll or even look inside it. [4] I wept and wept because no one was found who was worthy to open the scroll or look inside. [5] Then one of the elders said to me, "Do not weep! See, the Lion of the tribe of Judah, the Root of David, has triumphed. He is able to open the scroll and its seven seals."
>
> [6] Then I saw a Lamb, looking as if it had been slain, standing in the center of the throne, encircled by the four living creatures and the elders. He had seven horns and seven eyes, which are the seven spirits of God sent out into all the earth. [7] He came and took the scroll from the right hand of him who sat on the throne. [8] And when he had taken it, the four living creatures and the twenty-four elders fell down before the Lamb. Each one had a harp and they were holding golden bowls full of incense, which are the prayers of the saints. [9] And they sang a new song:
>
>> "You are worthy to take the scroll
>>> and to open its seals,
>> because you were slain,
>>> and with your blood you purchased men for God
>>> from every tribe and language and people and nation.
>> [10] You have made them to be a kingdom and priests to serve our God,
>>> and they will reign on the earth."
>
> [11] Then I looked and heard the voice of many angels, numbering thousands upon thousands, and ten thousand times ten thousand. They encircled the throne and the living creatures and the elders. [12] In a loud voice they sang:
>
>> "Worthy is the Lamb, who was slain,
>> to receive power and wealth and wisdom and strength
>> and honor and glory and praise!"

¹³ Then I heard every creature in heaven and on earth and under the earth and on the sea, and all that is in them, singing:

> "To him who sits on the throne and to the Lamb
> > be praise and honor and glory and power,
> for ever and ever!"

¹⁴ The four living creatures said, "Amen," and the elders fell down and worshiped.

The translation Brief, or job commission, for this particular project should have included Revelation 4 as well. Study the discourse arrangement of Revelation as a whole and note the important structural function of chapters 4–5 within it, that is, in relation to chapter 1 plus chapters 2–3 on the one side and chapters 6–19 plus chapters 20–22 on the other. After your analysis, suggest some reasons why any textual representation or application of Revelation 5 ought to include chapter 4 as well.

22. GROUP DISCUSSIONS

A: Review some of the main subjects that you have learned as you have worked through this manual. Name the three topics that you feel are most important and tell why you think so. Are there any topics pertaining to a *LiFE* type of analysis or translation that are still not very clear to you or for which you feel more explanation and/or practice are needed? Which ones?

B: Consider the following recommendations (from Dooley 2005:15–16, added italics) regarding the importance of discourse analysis (including also a concern for the *literary* dimension!) as an integral part of "doing translation." Then discuss the implications of such a program as they might relate to your own translation project—or one that is still in the planning stages:

> In conclusion, I mention certain *priorities* for doing discourse analysis as part of the Bible translation task. The most obvious priority, if the translation is to reach a broad spectrum of readers, is for the translator to *know how natural target-language features work on micro-levels*—both single features and multiple structure patterns. (Although in this article I have concentrated on features involving major syntactic restructuring, all kinds of linguistic signals should be included.) A second priority is to *recognize microlevel patterns in the source text,* since they are our best prima-facie evidence as to how the author unpacked his intended mental representation in the process of wording. Third, whether the translator is using source text patterns or target-language patterns on macro-levels, it is important to be aware of *both* of these, for only then can their *differences* be recognized. If imported source-language patterns give problems for readers, they need to be modified in the direction of target-language patterns. If target-language patterns are used, they may need to undergo genre modification because of special characteristics of the source text type. All such modifications will likely have *prototypes in primary texts in the target language.*
>
> A question remains: Do *mother-tongue translators* (MTTs) need to know the discourse features in their language on a conscious level, or can they be expected to get such features right intuitively, as accomplished story-tellers do with primary texts? The complexity of the Bible translation task argues for *conscious knowledge.* Simply judging from the time required to produce the text, Bible translation is more than ten times more complex than storytelling. No translator, MTT or otherwise, can expect to get everything right in a single pass; a translator needs to be able to concentrate on different aspects of the translation at different times, and conscious attention requires conscious knowledge—if not in initial drafting, then certainly in revision, checking and problem solving. Discourse features are often dealt with in later passes (though not exclusively there). So should MTTs study discourse? The following answer was given by Mozambican MTTs at the end of a discourse workshop: "Now I want to go back and revise what I have already translated. *Now I know how to do it.*"

C: Based on what you now understand about a literary-rhetorical approach to the analysis of Scripture, how would you respond to the following severe criticism of this methodology by Berlinerblau (2004:15–16, 25), including its assumptions about the original text of Scripture? Discuss some of the pertinent issues in class, including their implications for Bible interpretation as well as translation:

> The magic trick of "holistic analysis" is to show how a biblical text which seems garbled beyond recognition or thematically chaotic or numbingly repetitive or plain unsightly is actually nothing of the sort. Instead, it is shown to be a masterwork whose hidden meaning or poetics or "purposeful pattern" can be, mirabile dictu, discovered (exclusively) by the exegete performing the analysis.... What is curious about final-editor theories...is the almost preternatural degree of harmonistic literary skill which they ascribe to the conjectured redactor. The cutting, pasting, erasing, interpolating, what have you, of received documents is a process fraught with dangers for those who wish to maintain some semblance of literary coherence....Rather, we must conceptualize countless anonymous contributors living in different times, beholden to different theological, political, and esthetic conceptions and motivations. Their literary specializations varied.

Do you think that the many Scripture passages which you have analyzed in this workbook might possibly be attributed to "countless anonymous contributors?" Compare your answer with others in the class.

D: Evaluate the following remarks by Graeme Goldsworthy on the subject of "What is a good translation?" (shortened from Goldsworthy 2006:294–295). Do you agree or disagree with these points—and why? Perhaps you will find yourself agreeing with some, yet disagreeing with others. This should produce a good group/class debate regarding these issues!

    a. Dynamic equivalence errs in the direction of reader-response hermeneutics.

    b. Dynamic equivalence translations tend to make the original text and its meaning opaque when they remove its form and peculiarities.

    c. Translation should be linguistic, not cultural. It is the role of the teacher to assist people to understand the biblical culture.

    d. Translation should make the language contemporary, but leave the story ancient.

    e. Above all, translation should, as far as possible, preserve the full theological significance and exegetical potential of the original.

    f. There is a difference between translation using the vernacular and the 'vernacularization' of the message. The vernacular is quite capable of telling the story about ancient times in far-away places. To make it sound as if the events take place in the present and in our culture is a gross distortion of the biblical message.

    g. Dynamic equivalence enthusiasts should ask themselves if the role of translation is primarily to bring the text down to the level of the world and culture of the modern, often unbelieving reader. Or is it to help the reader...to enter into and be transformed by the gospel culture and world of the Bible?

Does a *LiFE* approach as presented in this workbook fall into the category of "dynamic equivalence translation"—more or less? Why or why not? Does *LiFE* serve to nuance and refine dynamic equivalence, or not?

E: Author and translation editor Robert Wechsler (1998) provides a number of "quotable quotes" on the why and how of literary translation. He is of course thinking of secular works, but much of what he says applies to Bible translation, especially a *LiFE* version. (My own personal comments and queries follow Wechsler's observations and the page number of their source.)

> The first commandment of literary translation is, "Honor thy original and thy author." (67)

How does a translator "honor" the original text?

> Ezra Pound once wrote, "Tain't what a man sez, but wot he *means* that the traducer has got to bring over." (73)

Can you give an example of this principle?

> [W]hen a work is form-focused, the translator should also be form-focused; and when a work is content-focused, the translator should also be content-focused. (80)

Can you give some examples of Bible texts that are more "form-focused"—and those that are primarily "content-focused"?

> [T]he most ethical stance, I feel, is to make sure the reader is told what he is getting [i.e., in a translation]. (90)

How can one do this in the case of a Bible translation?

> [Translation is] a critical act which cannot and does not replace but rather complements the original, illuminating its strategies. (93, quoting S. J. Levin)

What are meant by "strategies" in this context, or in relation to the literature of the Scriptures?

> Translation is not about betrayal, but rather about the balancing of, the impossible attempt to fulfill, a variety of often contradictory obligations. (113)

List your three most important "obligations" as they pertain to a translation of the Bible.

> Translation is above all a pattern of decisions...and every local decision will commit you to decisions elsewhere. The mark of a bad translation is the completely erratic nature of the decisions. (115, quoting R. Sieburth)

Explain the meaning and implication of this quote. Can you give an example of this sequential and consequential decision-making process from your own experience?

> [G]reat translation moves by touch, finding the matching shape, the corresponding rugosity even before it looks for the counterpart of meaning. (116, quoting B. Belitt)

Look up the word *rugosity* in a dictionary and then explain how it is applied here to a literary translation.

> The success of a translation...is nearly always dependent on the smallest words: prepositions, articles. (118, quoting E. Weinberger)

Is the same thing true in YL? If so, what are those "smallest words" that mean so much?

> [In a literary translation]...what could easily be left out [by a less-gifted practitioner]—rhythm, alliteration, assonance—is often essential to achieving the right effect and even the right meaning. (123)

Try to give an illustration of this principle from your own Bible translation experience.

> The art of literary translation,...and above all the translation of poetry, might almost be defined as the art of balancing different claims. The translator must choose not only what in the original to preserve and what to give up, but also what to add. (139, quoting B. Raffel)

Translators rightly become suspicious, or at least very cautious, when they hear the word "add" in relation to Bible translation. In what sense does addition apply to our work?

> Translators, even more than writers, are never satisfied. Since translators work in the realm of alternatives, there are always other ways it could have been done. (146)

Do you ever experience this feeling of dissatisfaction with your work as a Bible translator? If so, what can you do about it?

> [M]ost literary translators are largely self-taught or have learned informally at the feet of experienced translators or editors who have critiqued their work. (168)

Do you think that this is true? If so, can you think of a way of applying it in the exercise of training and improving Bible translators?

> [T]ranslation is about both reading and writing all at once, and there is no closer reading than a translation. (183)

What is meant by a close reading here, and how does this notion apply in the case of Bible translation?

> In theory, only poets should translate poetry; in practice, poets are rarely good translators.... [P]oetic translation...is a procedure analogous to poetic creation, but it unfolds in the opposite direction. (by Octavio Paz, 199)

Do you agree with the first assertion? Give reasons. Then explain the meaning of the second sentence.

> Knowing a language but not understanding translation can be worse than not knowing anything, because it gives the reviewer the illusion that he is qualified to criticize a translation. (264)

How does this observation apply to the exegetes of a Bible translation team? What are the implications here?

> [R]eviewers look at how well translators write, but not at how well they read [i.e., interpret the original text]. Yet it is this ability to read that differentiates the excellent translator from the merely competent one. (217)

What is the meaning of the first statement? Spell out the implications of the opinion expressed in the second sentence for both Bible translators and their reviewers, with special reference to the literary (artistic-rhetorical) features of the Scriptures.

F: As a final point of discussion, the group might consider the effect and impact of a *LiFE*-style approach to Bible translation upon the translators themselves. Some consultants have noted the excitement, even rejoicing, that is often manifested by translators as they have the opportunity as well as the encouragement to communicate the Word of God using the full literary/oral resources of their mother tongue. Perhaps this cannot be done for every book of the Scriptures, but it can be an encouraging experience for them to have the chance to apply this method for one book at least (e.g., Song of

Songs) or some well-known pericope intended as a special publication (e.g., 1 Cor. 13). Discuss this possibility in the light of the following passages in which there is a special focus on the "rejoicing" that comes from communicating God's Word, whether transmitting or receiving it. To be sure, the main emphasis is on the *content* of the message, but can this not apply also to the *manner* of expressing it? What do you think?

» Sing to him a new song; play skillfully (יטב), and shout for joy (תְּרוּעָה). (Psa. 33:3)

» When your words came, I ate them; they were my joy (שָׂשׂוֹן) and my heart's delight (שִׂמְחָה), for I bear your name, O Lord God Almighty. (Jer. 15:16)

» I bring you good news of great joy (χαρὰν μεγάλην) that will be for all the people....The shepherds returned, glorifying and praising God (δοξάζοντες καὶ αἰνοῦντες τὸν θεὸν) for all the things they had heard and seen, which were just as they had been told. (Lk. 2:10, 20)

» Speak to one another with psalms, hymns and spiritual songs. Sing and make music in your heart to the Lord (ᾄδοντες καὶ ψάλλοντες τῇ καρδίᾳ ὑμῶν τῷ κυρίῳ), always giving thanks to God the Father for everything, in the name of our Lord Jesus Christ! (Eph. 5:19–20)

And when he had taken it, the four living creatures and the twenty-four elders fell down before the Lamb. Each one had a harp (ἔχοντες ἕκαστος κιθάραν) and they were holding golden bowls full of incense, which are the prayers of the saints.
And they sang a new song (καὶ ᾄδουσιν ᾠδὴν καινὴν λέγοντες):
"You are worthy to take the scroll
    and open its seals,
        because you were slain,
and with your blood your purchased men for God
    from every tribe and language and people and nation.
You have made them to be a kingdom and priests to serve our God,
    and they will reign on the earth." (Rev. 5:8–10)

References

Adeyemo, Tokunboh. 2007. Presenting the Scriptures to an African audience. Lecture presented to the opening AFRATCON session, Nairobi, Kenya, May 7, 2007.

Agnes, Michael, ed. 1999. *Webster's new world college dictionary.* New York: Macmillan.

Albir, Amparo Hurtado, and Fabio Alves, 2009. Translation as a cognitive activity. In J. Munday (ed.), 54–73.

Bailey, James L., and vander Broek, Lyle. 1992. *Literary forms in the New Testament: A handbook.* Louisville, Ky.: Westminster/John Knox.

Bandia, Paul F. 2008. *Translation as reparation: Writing and translation in Postcolonial Africa.* Manchester: St. Jerome.

Barker, Kenneth, general editor. 1985. *The NIV Study Bible.* Grand Rapids: Zondervan,

Barker, K. L., and J. Kohlenburger III, eds. 1994. *NIV Bible commentary,* vol. 2. Grand Rapids: Zondervan.

Barnwell, Katharine. 1986. *Bible translation: An introductory course in translation principles,* third edition. Dallas: Summer Institute of Linguistics.

Bartholomew, C., C. Greene, and K. Möller, eds. 2001. *After Pentecost: Language and biblical interpretation,* vol. 2. Grand Rapids: Zondervan.

Bascom, Robert. 2003. Lost in translation: Mental maps and the cultural understanding of scripture. A paper presented at the UBS Triennial Translation Workshop, Foz do Iguaçu, Brazil, June 16–27, 2003.

Bauckham, Richard. 1993. *The climax of prophecy: Studies on the Book of Revelation.* Edinburgh: T. & T. Clark.

Bauckham, Richard. 2003. Reading Scripture as a coherent story. In Davis and Hays, 38–53.

Beekman, John and John Callow. 1974. *Translating the Word of God.* Grand Rapids: Zondervan.

Berlinerblau, Jacques. 2004. The Bible as literature. *Hebrew Studies* 45:9–26.

de Blois, Renier. 2002. *A semantic dictionary of Biblical Hebrew.* In P. Noss, (ed.), *Current Trends in Scripture Translation,* New York: United Bible Societies, 275–295.

de Blois, Renier. 2007. Wine to gladden the heart of man or the art of writing definitions. A paper presented at the AFRATCON Workshop, Nairobi, Kenya, May 7–11, 2007.

Boase-Beier, Jean, and Michael Holman, eds. 1999. *The practice of literary translation: Constraints and creativity.* Manchester: St. Jerome.

Boerger, Brenda. 1997. Extending translation principles for poetry and biblical acrostics. Notes on Translation 11(2):35–56.

Boerger, Brenda Higgie. 2003. *Poetic oracle English translation (POET) of the Psalms.* Trial edition. Self-published.

Brown, Richard. 2004. New dimensions in communicative Bible translation. In International Conference on Bible Translation: Theory and practice. Power-Point presentation on CD. Dallas: SIL International.

Burke, David G., and Lydia Lebrón-Rivera. 2003. Faithful transfer of Scripture text into the format of the graphic novel (or illustrated book). A paper presented at the UBS Triennial Translation Workshop, Foz do Iguaçu, Brazil, June 16–27, 2003.

Callow, Kathleen. 1974. Discourse considerations in translating the Word of God. Grand Rapids: Zondervan.

Cameron, Peter S. 1990. Functional equivalence and the *mot juste. The Bible Translator* 41:1:101–109.

Carlton, Matthew. 2001. *Translator's reference translation: The Gospel of Matthew.* Dallas: SIL International.

Cavanaugh, J. 2003. *Beyond the sacred page.* Grand Rapids: Zondervan.

Chhetri, Chitra B. 2008. "Translating the Hebrew oath formula: A Nepali perspective." *Bible Translator* 58(2):64–75.

Clark, David J., and Howard A. Hatton. 1989. *A translator's handbook on the books of Nahum, Habakkuk, and Zephaniah.* New York: United Bible Societies.

Coulson, S. 2001. *Semantic leaps: Frame-shifting and conceptual blending in meaning construction.* Cambridge: Cambridge University Press.

Crisp, Simon. 2004. Does a literary translation have to be literal? In S. Crisp and M. Jinbachian (eds.), *Text, theology and translation: Essays in honour of Jan de Waard,* 43–51. Reading: United Bible Societies.

Davis, Ellen F., and Richard B. Hays, eds. 2003. *The art of reading Scripture.* Grand Rapids: Eerdmans.

Deibler, Ellis. 1993. *Index of implication in the Gospels.* Dallas: Summer Institute of Linguistics.

Dooley, Robert, and Stephen Levinsohn. 2001. *Analyzing discourse: A manual of basic concepts.* Dallas: SIL International.

Dooley, Robert A. 2005. Source-language versus target-language discourse features in translating the Word of God. *Journal of Translation* 1(2):1–18.

Douglas, Mary. 1993. *In the wilderness: The doctrine of defilement in the book of Numbers.* Sheffield: Sheffield Academic Press.

Douglas, Mary. 1999. *Leviticus as literature.* Oxford: Oxford University Press.

Doyle, Brian. 2003. How do single isotopes meet? "Lord it" (b'l) or "Eat it" (bl'): A rare word play metaphor in Isaiah 25. In Feyaerts, 153–184.

Eco, Umberto. 2003. *Mouse or rat? Translation as negotiation.* London: Weidenfeld & Nicolson.

Fauconnier, Giles, and Mark Turner. 2002. *The way we think: Conceptual blending and the mind's hidden complexities.* New York: Basic Books.

Feyaerts, Kurt, ed. 2003. *The Bible through metaphor and translation: A cognitive and semantic perspective. Religion and discourse,* volume 15. Bern: Peter Lang.

Floor, Sebastian. 2004. From information structure, topic and focus, to theme in Biblical Hebrew narrative. Ph.D dissertation. University of Stellenbosch, South Africa, Dept. of Ancient Studies.

Foster, Stuart. 2005. An experiment in Bible translation as transcultural communication: The translation of *tyrb* 'covenant' into Lomwe with a focus on Leviticus 26. Ph.D. diss., University of Stellenbosch, South Africa, Dept. of Ancient Studies.

Gavins, J., and G. Steen, eds. 2003. *Cognitive poetics in practice.* London/New York: Routledge.

Gibson, J. C. L. 1998. *Language and imagery in the Old Testament.* Peabody, Mass.: Hendrickson.

Goldsworthy, Graeme. 2006. *Gospel-centered hermeneutics: Foundations of evangelical biblical interpretation.* Downers Grove: IVP Academic.

Good News Study Bible: Today's English Version. 2000. New York: American Bible Society.

Green, Joel, and Scot McKnight, eds. 1992. *Dictionary of Jesus and the Gospels.* Downers Grove: InterVarsity Press.

Green, Joel, and Michael Pasquarello, III, eds. 2003. *Narrative reading, narrative preaching: Reuniting New Testament interpretation and proclamation.* Grand Rapids: Baker Academic.

Gutt, Ernst-August. 1992. *Relevance theory: A guide to successful communication in translation.* Dallas: Summer Institute of Linguistics.

Harm, Harry. 1999. Checking a Translation to be Published on Video. *Notes on Translation* 13/14:36–41.

Hart, George, and Helen Hart. 2001. *A semantic and structural analysis of James.* Dallas: SIL International.

van den Heever, Manie. 2007. Translating idioms: Much ado about nothing or a can of worms? A paper presented at the AFRATCON Workshop, Nairobi, Kenya, May 7–11, 2007.

Hill, Harriet. 2003. Communicating context in Bible translation. *manuscript.*

Hill, Harriet. 2006. *The Bible at cultural crossroads: From translation to communication.* Manchester: St. Jerome.

Hill, Ralph. 2003. Adapting to a changing environment. A paper presented at the UBS Triennial Translation Workshop, Foz do Iguaçu, Brazil, June 16–27, 2003.

Hill, Ralph. 2004. Contextual adjustment strategies and Bible translation. *manuscript.*

Hodgson, Robert. 2003. This Bible talks! Reflections on audience expectations and Bible engagement. A paper presented at the UBS Triennial Translation Workshop, Foz do Iguaçu, Brazil, June 16–27, 2003.

Hoyle, Richard A. 2008. *Scenarios, discourse, and translation: The scenario theory of Cognitive Linguistics, its relevance for analysing New Testament Greek and modern Parkari texts, and its implications for translation theory.* SIL e-Books 10 (http://www.sil.org/silepubs/index.asp?series=941). Dallas, SIL International.

Huddleston, Mark. 1988. Equivalent dynamics: For whom do I translate? *The Bible Translator* 39(1):122–125.

Johnson, Larry. 2003. A holistic and systemic presentation of God's Word through a Scripture-song cassette. Paper presented at the UBS Triennial Translation Workshop, Foz do Iguaçu, Brazil, June 16–27 2003.

Johnson, Larry. 2007. A case study in developing literacy work to enhance the use and application of God's Word. A paper presented at the AFRATCON Workshop, Nairobi, Kenya, May 7–11, 2007.

Katan, David. 1999. *Translating cultures: An introduction for translators, interpreters and mediators.* Manchester: St. Jerome.

Keener, Craig. 2003. *The Gospel of John: A commentary,* volume one. Peabody, Mass.: Hendrickson.

Kompaoré, Anne Garber. 2004. Discourse analysis of directive discourse: The case of biblical Hebrew. Master's thesis, Associated Mennonite Biblical Seminary, Elkhart, Indiana.
Kompaoré, Anne Garber. 2005. Discourse analysis of directive texts: The case of biblical law. A paper presented at the UBS AFRETCON workshop, Nairobi, Kenya, April 30, 2005.
Kompaoré, Anne Garber. 2008. Thematic and text type classification strategies: How we can improve on speed and accuracy in our translation projects. A paper presented at the UBS AFRETCON Workshop, Nairobi, Kenya. May 5–9, 2008.
Koops, Robert. 2000. Mental spaces, mapping, and blending in Scripture. A paper presented at the UBS Triennial Translation Workshop in Malaga, Spain, June 19–30, 2000.
Koops, Robert. 2003. Third generation audio Scriptures. A paper presented at the UBS Triennial Translation Workshop, Foz do Iguaçu, Brazil, June 16–27, 2003.
Koudougéret, David. 2000. Poétique et traduction biblique. Doctoral thesis, University of Leiden: Research School of Asian, African, and Amerindian Studies.
Kroneman, Dick. 2004. The LORD is my shepherd: Exploration into the theory and practice of translating biblical metaphor. Ph.D dissertation, Vrije Universiteit, Amsterdam, The Netherlands.
Lahaye, Tito. 2003. Recitative literature or Guaraní orature. *The Bible Translator* 54:401–407.
Landers, Clifford E. 2001. *Literary translation: A practical guide*. Buffalo/Toronto/Sydney: Multilingual Matters.
Larson, Mildred. 1984. *Meaning-based translation: A guide to cross-language equivalence*. Lanham, N.Y.: University Press of America.
Lawrenz, P. J. N. 2008. Avoiding anachronism in OT translation. *The Bible Translator* 59(1):14–17.
The Learning Bible: Contemporary English Version. 2000. New York: American Bible Society.
Levinsohn, Stephen. 2000. *Discourse features of New Testament Greek: A coursebook on the information structure of the New Testament*, second edition. Dallas: SIL International.
Levinsohn, Stephen H. 2006a. Reasoning styles and types of hortatory discourse. *Journal of Translation* 2(2):1–10.
Levinsohn, Stephen H. 2006b. The relevance of Greek discourse studies to exegesis. *Journal of Translation* 2(2):11–21.
Linton, C. 1986. The importance of literary style in Bible translation today. In K. L. Barker (ed.), *The NIV: The making of a contemporary translation*. Grand Rapids, Mich.: Zondervan.
Louwerse, M., and W. van Peer, eds. 2002. *Thematics: Interdisciplinary studies*. Amsterdam/Philadelphia: John Benjamins.
Lunn, Nicholas P. 2006. *Word-order variation in biblical Hebrew poetry: Differentiating pragmatics and poetics*. Bletchley: Paternoster.
Luther, Martin. 1960. *Luther's works*, ed. E. T. Bachmann, vol. 35. Philadelphia: Muhlenberg.
Malina, Bruce, and Richard Rohrbaugh. 1992. *Social-science commentary on the synoptic Gospels*. Minneapolis: Fortress.
Malina, Bruce, and Richard Rohrbaugh. 1998. *Social-science commentary on the Gospel of John*. Minneapolis: Fortress Press.
Martindale, W., and J. Root, eds. 1989. *The quotable Lewis*. Wheaton, Ill.: Tyndale.
Mather, Olivia. 2003. Meaning and 'the music itself.' *Modern Reformation* 12(6):8–11.
Matthews, Victor H. 2008. *More than meets the ear: Discovering hidden contexts of Old Testament conversations*. Grand Rapids, Mich.: Eerdmans.
McComiskey, Douglas S. 2004. *Lukan theology in the light of the Gospel's literary structure*. Bletchley, UK: Paternoster.
Metzger, Bruce. 1994. *A textual commentary on the Greek New Testament*, second edition. New York: American Bible Society.
Miller, Cynthia L. 2005. Translating biblical proverbs in African cultures. *The Bible Translator* 56(3):129–144.
Miller, Cynthia L. 2006. Translating Proverbs by topics. *The Bible Translator* 57(4):170–194.
Möller, Karl. 2001. Words of (in-)evitable certitude? Reflections on the interpretation of prophetic oracles of judgment. In Bartholomew, Greene, and Möller, 352–386.
Morris, William, ed. 1981. *The American heritage dictionary of the English language*. Boston: Houghton Mifflin.
Munday, Jeremy, ed. 2009. *The Routledge Companion to Translation Studies*. London and New York: Routledge.

Naude, J. A., and C. H. J. van der Merwe, eds. 2002. *Contemporary translation. studies and Bible translation: A South African perspective*. Acta Theologica, Supplementum 2. Bloemfontein: University of the Free State.

Neeley, Paul and Sue Hall. "Praising the High King of Heaven." Posted on the website of the Global Council of Ethnodoxologists—Association of Christian Worship (Africa page) May 29, 2007 (http://www.worldofworship.org/ArticlesWorkshops/Africa.htm); based on a longer article, Report on the Dagomba Scripture Use Workshop, *Notes on Sociolinguistics* 2:4, 1997.

Nida, Eugene. 1981. *Meaning across cultures*. Maryknoll, NY: Orbis.

Nida, Eugene. 2003. *Fascinated by languages*. Amsterdam: John Benjamins.

Nida, Eugene, and Charles Taber. 1969. *The theory and practice of translation*. Leiden: E. J. Brill.

Nord, Christiane. 1997. *Translating as a purposeful activity: Functionalist approaches explained*. Manchester: St. Jerome.

Noss, Philip, and Peter Renju. 2007. Mwalimu Nyerere engages his people: Scripture translation in Swahili verse. *Journal of Translation* 3(1):41–53.

Noss, Philip A. ed. 2007. *A history of Bible translation* (Nida Institute for Biblical Scholarship). Roma: Edizioni Di Storia E Letteratura.

Ogden, Graham S. 2003. Literary allusions in Isaiah. *The Bible Translator* 54(3):317–325.

Ogden, Graham S. n.d. Some exegetical issues in Isaiah 1–11. Unpublished.

Omanson, Roger L. 2006. *A textual guide to the Greek New Testament*. Stuttgart: German Bible Society.

Pattemore, Stephen, ed. 2004. *Translator training manual* [Asia-Pacific]. New York: United Bible Societies.

Pattemore, Stephen. 2007. Framing Nida: The relevance of translation theory in the United Bible Societies. In P. A. Noss (ed.), *A history of Bible translation*, 217–163. New York: American Bible Society.

Peterson, Eugene. 2003. *The message: The New Testament in contemporary language*. Colorado Springs: Navpress.

Petruck, Miriam R. L., Charles J. Fillmore, Coflin F. Bakers, Michael Ellsworth, and Josef Ruppenhofer. 2006. Referencing FrameNet data (http://framenet.icsi.berkely.edu/framenet, pp. 1–11).

Qvale, Per. 2003. *From St Jerome to hypertext: Translation in theory and practice*. Tr. N. R. Spencer. Manchester: St. Jerome.

de Regt, Lenart. 1999. *Participants in Old Testament texts and the translator: Reference devices and their rhetorical impact*. Assen: Van Gorcum.

Reid, Daniel G., ed. 2004. *The IVP dictionary of the New Testament*. Downers Grove, Ill.: InterVarsity.

Reis, Pamela Tamarkin. 2002. *Reading the lines: A fresh look at the Hebrew Bible*. Peabody, Mass.: Hendrickson.

Reiss, Katharina. 2000. *Translation criticism*. New York: American Bible Society.

Rhoads, David. 2006. Performance criticism: An emerging methodology in Second Testament studies—Part II. *Biblical Theology Bulletin* 36(4):164–184.

Rohrbaugh, Richard L. 2008. Foreignizing translation. In Neufeld, Dietmar (ed.), *The social sciences and biblical translation* (Symposium Series 41), 11–24. Atlanta: Society of Biblical Literature.

Ryken, Leland. 2002. *The Word of God in English: Criteria for excellence in Bible translation*. Wheaton, Ill.: Crossway.

Ryken, Leland. 2005. *Choosing a Bible: Understanding Bible translation differences*. Wheaton: Crossway Books.

Salisbury, Murray. 2002. *STEPS. Skills for translating and exegeting the primary Scriptures*. Trial CD version. (For information, contact murray_salisbury@sil.org. *STEPS* focuses on the linguistic side of exegesis, while my methodology concentrates more on literary features, but our respective studies overlap and complement each other in many places.)

Sandy, D. B., and Ronald Giese. 1995. *Cracking Old Testament codes: A guide to interpreting the literary genres of the Old Testament*. Nashville: Broadman & Holman.

Schultz, Richard L. 1999. *The search for quotations: Verbal parallels in the Prophets*. Sheffield: Sheffield Academic Press.

Scorgie, Glen, Mark Strauss, and Steven Voth. 2003. *The challenge of Bible translation: Communicating God's Word to the world*. Grand Rapids, Mich.: Zondervan.

Semino, Elena, and Jonathan Culpeper, eds. 2002. *Cognitive stylistics: Language and cognition in text analysis*. Amsterdam and Philadelphia: Benjamins.

Shaw, Daniel. 2004. The impact of a hermeneutical approach on Bible translation. In *International conference on Bible translation: Theory and practice,* 2003. Available on CD. Dallas: SIL International.

Sheads, Stephen L. 2007. Radical frame semantics and biblical Hebrew: Exploring lexical semantics. Ph.D. dissertation, University of Sidney.

Silva, Moisés. 2003. Are translators traitors? Some personal reflections. In Scorgie, Strauss, and Voth (eds.), 37–50.

Smalley, Wm. A. 1995. Language and culture in the development of Bible Society translation theory and practice. *International Bulletin of Missionary Research* 19:2, 61–71.

Smith, Kevin. 2002. Translation as secondary communication: The relevance theory perspective of Ernst-August Gutt. In J. A. Naude and C. H. J. van der Merwe (eds.), *Contemporary translation studies and Bible translation: A South African perspective* (Acta Theologica Supplementum 2), 107–116. Bloemfontein: University of the Free State.

Some, Joachim. 2007. Comics challenge in Africa: Reflection on the present situation of UBS comics, with special reference to Francophone West Africa. A paper presented at the AFRATCON Workshop, Nairobi, Kenya, May 7–11, 2007.

van der Spuy, Roele. 2008. Hebrew alphabetic acrostics—significance and translation. *Old Testament Essays* 21(2):513–532.

Statham, Nigel. 2005. Nida and "functional equivalence." *The Bible Translator* 56(1):29–43.

Stockwell, Peter. 2002. *Cognitive poetics: An introduction.* London: Routledge.

Strauss, Mark L. 2005. Form, function, and the "literal meaning" fallacy in English Bible translation. *The Bible Translator* 56(3):153–168.

Tannehill, Robert. 1975. *The sword of his mouth.* Philadelphia: Fortress.

Thomas, Kenneth K. 2000. Seeing the text: Using biblical metaphors as a basis for visualization of Scripture texts. A paper presented at the UBS Triennial Translation Workshop, Malaga, Spain, June 19–30, 2000.

Thomas, Kenneth J., and Margaret Orr Thomas. 2006. *Structure and orality in 1 Peter: A Guide for translators.* UBS Monograph Series No. 10. New York: United Bible Societies.

Tuggy, David. 2003. The literal-idiomatic Bible translation debate from the perspective of cognitive grammar. In Feyaerts, 239–288.

Unseth, Peter. n.d. Analyzing and using receptor language proverb forms in translation. Unpublished printout.

Unseth, Peter. 2006a. Receptor language proverb forms in translation (Part 1: Analysis). *The Bible Translator* 57(2):79–85.

Unseth, Peter. 2006b. Analyzing and using receptor language proverb forms in translation (Part 2: Application). *The Bible Translator* 57(4):161–170.

Vail, Daniel. 2005. *Solomon's Proverbs poetically paraphrased: An artistic adaptation.* Pittsburgh, Pa.: Dorrance.

Voth. Esteban. 2005. Orality and Writtenness in Ancient Near Eastern Prophecy: Its Effect on Translation as Communication in Latin America. *The Bible Translator* 56(2):91–97.

de Waard, Jan, and Eugene Nida. 1986. *From one language to another: Functional equivalence in Bible translating.* Nashville: Nelson.

Walton, John H. 2006. *Ancient Near Eastern thought and the Old Testament: Introducing the conceptual world of the Hebrew Bible.* Grand Rapids: Baker Academic.

Warren-Rothlin, Andy. 2003. Some linguistic strategies for politeness in Biblical Hebrew and West African languages. Paper presented at the UBS Triennial Translation Workshop, Foz do Iguaçu, Brazil, June 16–27, 2003.

Warren-Rothlin, Andy. 2005. Sub-cultural texture in Bible translation. Paper presented at the UBS AFRETCON workshop meeting, Nairobi, Kenya, April 26, 2005.

Warren-Rothlin, Andy. 2007. Script choice, politics and Bible agencies in West Africa. A paper presented at the UBS AFRATCON Workshop, Nairobi, Kenya, May 7–11, 2007.

Warren-Rothlin, Andy. 2008. The texts of the books. A paper presented at the UBS AFRATCON Workshop, Nairobi, Kenya, May 10–16, 2008.

Webster's New World College Dictionary. Agnes, Michael ed. 1999. N.Y.: Macmillan.

Wechsler, Robert. 1998. *Performing without a stage: The art of literary translation.* North Haven, Conn.: Catbird.

Wendland, Ernst. 1985. *Language, society, and Bible translation.* Bible Society of South Africa.

Wendland, Ernst. 1995. *The discourse analysis of Hebrew prophetic literature: Determining the larger textual units of Hosea and Joel.* Lewiston; Queenston; Lampeter: Mellen Biblical Press.

Wendland, Ernst. 1997. *The cultural factor in Bible translation.* London, NewYork, and Stuttgart: United Bible Societies.

Wendland, Ernst. 1998. *Buku Loyera: An introduction to the new Chichewa Bible translation.* Kachere Monograph, 6. Blantyre: Christian Literature Association in Malawi (CLAIM).

Wendland, Ernst. 2000. A form-functional, text-comparative method of translation/teaching/checking. *Notes on Translation* 14(1):7–27.

Wendland, Ernst. 2002. *Analyzing the Psalms.* Revised edition. Dallas: SIL International.

Wendland, Ernst. 2004a. *Poceza m'madzulo: Some Chinyanja radio plays of Julius Chongo (with English translations).* Lusaka: UNZA Press.

Wendland, Ernst. 2004b. *Translating the literature of Scripture: A literary-rhetorical approach to Bible translation.* Dallas: SIL International.

Wendland, Ernst. 2005. *Sewero! Christian drama and the drama of Christianity in Africa.* Kachere Monograph, 20. Zomba: Kachere Series.

Wendland, Ernst. 2008. *Contextual frames of reference in translation: A coursebook for translators and teachers.* Manchester: St. Jerome.

Wilt, Timothy. 1993. On translating acrostics: Perhaps the form can be represented. *The Bible Translator* 44(2):207–212.

Wilt, Timothy, ed. 2002a. *Bible translation: Frames of reference.* Manchester: St. Jerome.

Wilt, Timothy, transl. 2002b. *Prayer, praise, and protest: The David collection (Psalms 1–72), A liturgy of praise (Psalm 118), The ABC's of grief (Lamentations), Pigeon (Jonah).* Self-published.

Wilt, Timothy. 2003. Translation principles for *LiFE,* inductively derived. Paper presented at the UBS Triennial Translation Workshop, Foz do Iguaçu, Brazil, June 16–27, 2003.

Wilt, Timothy and Ernst Wendland. 2008. *Scripture frames and framing: A workbook for Bible translators.* Stellenbosch: SUN Media Press.

Yu, Suee Yan. 2005. The tower of Babel: Adventures in biblical interpretation. *Journal of Biblical Text Research* 16(4):228–246.

Zogbo, Lynell, and Ernst Wendland. 2000. *Hebrew poetry in the Bible: A guide for understanding and for translating.* New York: United Bible Societies.

Zogbo, Lynell. 2007. Darkness and light: Rendering metaphors of color in an African context. A paper presented at the AFRATCON Workshop, Nairobi, Kenya, May 7–11, 2007.